Object-Oriented Program Development Using Java

A CLASS-CENTERED APPROACH

Gary J. Bronson

Fairleigh Dickinson University

THOMSON

COURSE TECHNOLOGY™

Australia • Canada • Mexico • Singapore •
Spain • United Kingdom • United States

THOMSON

COURSE TECHNOLOGY

Executive Editor: *Mac Mendelsohn*

Product Manager: *Alyssa Pratt*

Associate Product Manager: *Mirella Misiaszek*

Editorial Assistant: *Amanda Piantedosi*

Production Editor: *Summer Hughes*

Senior Manufacturing Coordinator: *Trevor Kallop*

Production Service: *The Book Company/Dustine Friedman*

Copy Editor: *Frank Hubert*

Interior Design: *Lisa Devenish*

Cover Designer: *Joel Sadagursky*

Composition: *Pre-Press Company, Inc.*

Cover Printing, Printing and Binding: *Quebecor World*

Printed in the United States

1 2 3 4 5 6 7 8 9 QWV 09 07 06 05 04

For permission to use material from this text or product, submit a request online at www.thomsonrights.com

Any additional questions about permissions can be submitted by email to thomsonrights@thomson.com

Library of Congress Control Number: 2003111914

ISBN 0-534-38455-2

Course Technology
25 Thomson Place
Boston, Massachusetts 02210
USA

Asia
Thomson Learning
5 Shenton Way #01-01
UIC Building
Singapore 068808

Australia/New Zealand
Thomson Learning
102 Dodds Street
Southbank, Victoria 3006
Australia

Canada
Nelson
1120 Birchmount Road
Toronto, Ontario M1K 5G4
Canada

Europe/Middle East/Africa
Thomson Learning
High Holborn House
50/51 Bedford Row
London WC1R 4LR
United Kingdom

Latin America
Thomson Learning
Seneca, 53
Colonia Polanco
11560 Mexico D.F.
Mexico

Spain/Portugal
Paraninfo
Calle Magallanes, 25
28015 Madrid, Spain

Dedicated to Rochelle, Jeremy, David, Matthew, and Tinker

Brief Contents

Contents

This text represents the solution to a problem that has troubled me for some time; specifically, how does one introduce the Java programming language within a true class-centered approach in a manner that works in a classroom? Texts that present object-oriented theory first generally fail because the code necessary to support a meaningful class structure is not available until all but the most intrepid students have lost interest. Similarly, although introducing code first is more interesting to students, the simplicity of the code tends to highlight a procedural orientation. A noticeable switch, both in thinking and coding, must then be invoked when a class-centered approach is introduced. The motivation for this change is not immediately obvious to students, because they have already established a workable framework for structuring their programs within a procedural paradigm.

The approach taken by this text is to introduce the concept of objects and classes immediately, using not theory but the very accessible and practical recipe analogy presented in Section 1.2. This analogy, which received extremely positive reviews, lays the groundwork and structure upon which the code makes practical and direct sense. It permits construction of data declarations sections to be made immediately in Section 2.2, followed by an introduction to creating class methods in Section 2.3.

This early and practical introduction to Java code, within the context of an understandable class structure, then permits the analysis and coding of typical CS1 programming problems within an object-oriented design solution. For example, the flipping of a coin is analyzed conveniently by emphasizing the coin as an object with two states (an object-orientation) rather than emphasizing random number generation (a procedural orientation). Similarly, the swapping of two values can be approached in object-oriented terms as altering the state of an object's instance variables, rather than in procedural terms as the passing of arguments. Thus, the student gets to think and code basic CS1 programming problems within a self-reinforcing class-centered process. The programming language being used, of course, is Java.

Distinctive Features

Writing Style

I firmly believe that for a textbook to be useful it must provide a clearly defined supporting role to the leading role of the professor. Once the professor sets the stage, however, the textbook must encourage, nurture, and assist the student in acquiring and owning the material presented in class. To do this the text must be written in a manner that makes sense to the student. Thus, first and foremost, I feel that the writing style used to convey the concepts presented is the most important and distinctive aspect of the text.

Flexibility

To be an effective teaching resource, this text provides a flexible tool that each professor can use in a variety of ways, depending on *how many* programming concepts and programming techniques are to be introduced in a single course, and *when* they are to be introduced. The text accomplishes this by partitioning the text into five parts and providing a varied number of Chapter Supplements that contain enrichment and breadth material.

Part One presents the fundamental object-oriented structure and creating Java® programs within this structure. Additionally, both keyboard and dialog-based data entry are presented. This permits an early introduction of the Swing package of visual objects as well as providing a firm grounding in basic Java Development Kit (JDK) techniques.

Part Two completes the introduction by providing the basic sequence, selection, and repetition statements supplied in Java. Additionally, this part contains a basic introduction concepts used in the Unified Modeling Language.

Once Parts One and Two have been completed, the material in Parts Three, Four, and Five are *interchangeable*. For example, in a more traditional introduction to programming course, Part One would be followed by either Arrays (chapter 8) or Files (chapter 12). However, if a requirement is that the course must emphasize class design and development, Part One would be followed by Additional Class Capabilities (chapter 11). In a third instance, if the course is to have a more visual and GUI-based slant, Parts One and Two can just as easily be followed by Part Four (GUIs). In each of these cases, a "pick-and-choose" approach to course structure can be implemented. This flexibility of topic introduction is illustrated by the topic dependency chart.

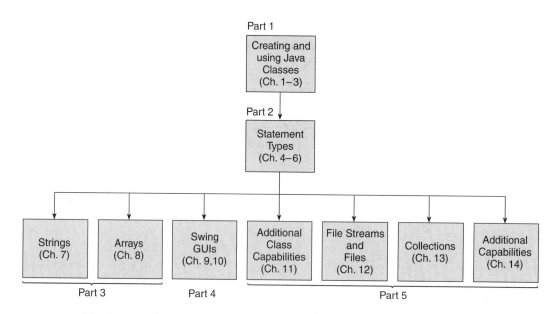

Program Testing

Every single Java program in this text has been successfully entered and executed using Sun® Java 2.0 (Version 1.4). This permits students both to experiment and extend the existing programs and more easily modify them as required by a number of end-of-section exercises.

Pedagogical Features

To facilitate the goal of making Java accessible as a programming language within the context of a theoretically sound object-oriented design and development structure, the following pedagogical features have been incorporated into the text.

Program Design and Development Sections

Although class-centered programming design is interwoven within the text's main language component, these sections are provided to introduce the Unified Modeling Language (UML). They are intended both to introduce and to strengthen the *why* as well as the *how* to design and develop programs using true object-oriented methodologies.

Application Sections

These sections present a number of classical computer science problems (such as coin tossing, swapping values, and simulations), and solve them using the object-oriented design and development techniques.

End of Section Exercises

Almost every section in the book contains numerous and diverse skill-builder and programming exercises. Additionally, solutions to selected odd-numbered exercises are provided on the website (www.course.com).

Common Programming Errors and Chapter Review

Each chapter, except the special topics chapter 14, provides a section on common programming errors. All chapters provide an end-of-chapter section that provides a list of key terms introduced in the chapter and a review of the main chapter topics.

Chapter Supplement Sections

Given the many different emphases that can be applied in teaching Java, a number of basic and enrichment topics have been included. These sections vary among such basic material as understanding bits and bytes, practical material, such as formatting and generating random numbers, and theoretical material, such as insides and outsides. The purpose of these sections is to provide flexibility as to the choice of which topics to present and the timing of when to present them.

Programming Notes

Highlighted text notes that provide alternative and advanced programming techniques. Additionally, they provide brief clarification of commonly used and/or difficult programming concepts, such as abstraction, values versus identities, deques, and stream formatting.

Bit of Background Boxes

To make the study of computer science even more rewarding and to provide breadth material, these boxed notes are carefully placed throughout the book. These notes supplement the technical material with historical, biographical, and other interesting factual asides.

Appendices and Supplements

An expanded set of appendices is provided. This includes appendices on keywords, operator precedence, Unicode codes, packages, and solutions to selected odd-numbered exercises.

CD-ROM

Each copy of this book comes with a CD-ROM containing Sun SDK 1.4.2 as well as jGRASP 1.6.4 for student use. jGRASP is a powerful IDE that provides automatic generation of software visualizations.

Teaching Tools

The following supplemental materials are available for professors when this book is used in a classroom setting. All of the teaching tools available with this book are provided to the instructor via course.com or on a single CD-ROM.

Electronic Instructor's Manual

The Instructor's Manual that accompanies this textbook includes:

- Additional instructional material to assist in class preparation, including suggestions for lecture topics.
- Solutions to all the end-of-chapter materials, including the Programming Exercises.

ExamView®

This textbook is accompanied by ExamView, a powerful testing software package that allows instructors to create and administer printed, computer (LAN-based), and Internet exams. ExamView includes hundreds of questions that correspond to the topics covered in this text, enabling students to generate detailed study guides that include page references for further review. These computer-based and Internet testing components allow students to take exams at their computers, and save the instructor time because each exam is graded automatically.

PowerPoint Presentations

This book comes with Microsoft PowerPoint slides for each chapter. These are included as a teaching aid for classroom presentations, either to make available to students on the network for chapter review, or to be printed for classroom distribution. Instructors can add their own slides for additional topics that they introduce to the class.

Source Code

The source code is available at **www.course.com**, and is also available on the Teaching Tools CD-ROM.

Solution Files

The solution files for all programming exercises, are available at **www.course.com**, and is also available on the Teaching Tools CD-ROM.

Acknowledgments

This text has become a reality due to the encouragement, skills, and efforts supplied by many people. I would like to acknowledge their contributions.

I would like to express my gratitude to the individual reviewers, Gerald Baumgartner of Ohio State University, Peter Capello of the University of California–Santa Barbara, Harry Etlinger of Rochester Institute of Technology, Jose M. Garrido of Kennesaw State University, Jess Irwin of the University of California–Fullerton, Narayan Murthy of Pace University, and Renee Turban of Arizona State University. Each of these individuals supplied extremely detailed and constructive reviews of both the original manuscript and a number of revisions. Their suggestions, attention to detail, and comments were extraordinarily helpful to me as the manuscript evolved and matured through the editorial process.

Once the review process was completed, the task of turning the final manuscript into a textbook depended on many people other than myself. For this I especially want to thank copy editor Frank Hubert, production editor Dusty Friedman of The Book Company, interior designer Lisa Devenish, and Jennifer Harvey, of the Pre-Press Company, Inc. The dedication of this team of people was incredible and very important to me. Almost from the moment the book moved to the production stage this team seemed to take personal ownership of the text and I am very grateful to them.

Special acknowledgment goes to an esteemed colleague who provided material for this text. I am especially grateful to R. Kenneth Walter for his graciously providing the Bit of Background notes. Also I would like to express my thanks to Penny Kelly of Intel Corporation and Jessie Kempter of IBM Corporation. Each of these individuals has been especially helpful in providing industry-specific information that I have used in this text. I am also very grateful to Rudy List for taking time from his busy schedule to provide detailed technical advice. Special mention also goes to Al Branchi, vice-president of DMR Architects for valuable discussions about the object-oriented programming paradigm. These discussions led to the practical introduction of a class as a recipe in Section 1.2. As always, any errors in the text rest solely on my shoulders.

Finally, the direct encouragement and support of Fairleigh Dickinson University is also gratefully acknowledged. Specifically, this includes the constant encouragement, support, and positive academic climate provided by provost Dr. Kenneth Greene, the provost, Dr. David Steele, my dean, and Dr. Paul Yoon, my chairperson. Without their support, this text could not have been written.

Finally, I deeply appreciate the patience, understanding, and love provided by my friend, wife, and partner, Rochelle.

Gary Bronson

Part One

Creating and Using Java Classes

1 Introduction

This chapter provides an introduction to computer science and a brief background on programming languages. It explains the concepts of objects and classes and presents a specific structure that will be used throughout the text for constructing Java classes and programs. Additionally, the chapter presents two specific classes provided in Java for displaying output: one that contains methods for displaying text on a video screen and one for constructing a simple graphical user interface (GUI) using graphical shapes. Both of these class methods are used within the context of a complete program for displaying data on a video screen.

1.1 Computer Science and Programming Languages

Our world is now almost totally dependent and driven by information technology; that is, the application of technology to data and information gathering, processing, and usage. This technology has become a central element in our art, science, literature, business, and engineering endeavors. It pervades our daily communications, transportation, medical care, grocery purchases, and almost every other aspect of our day-to-day activities. In more formal terms, this technology both constitutes and defines what is now called the **Information Age**.

The engines that drive this vast technology-centered culture are computers. These are the machines that are now used for data collection, data storage and retrieval, data processing, and information transmission. The science of computers and computing, in all its varied aspects, is referred to as **computer science**.

Because computer science is a scientific discipline, it has much in common with other natural and physical science areas and can be approached at many different levels. The simplest level is **computer literacy**. People who are computer literate have some knowledge of computers, such as their history and how they can be applied in various ways, such as using a word processor, spreadsheet program, the Internet, or email. Knowing these areas, however, does not make you a computer scientist but merely a computer literate person who knows how to use one or more computer programs.

Rather than being merely a user of computer programs, a computer scientist is a problem solver who develops solutions to computer-related problems, specifically in the areas of

- Algorithm development
- Class development and design
- Programming languages
- Data structures
- Data collection, storage, and retrieval
- Operating systems
- Computer architecture
- Computer applications
- Social, ethical, and professional conduct and considerations

Computer scientists solve problems using the scientific method, which is common to all sciences. The **scientific method** is a method of research in which a problem is identified, relevant data are obtained, a hypothesis is formulated from the data, and the hypothesis is tested in a controlled and repeatable manner. Additionally, computer science requires a foundation in mathematics, model development, implementation experience, human communication, and a knowledge of other disciplines for which solutions are required. These disciplines include biology, medicine, physics, business, law, economics, geology, education, communications, psychology, robotics, image recognition, artificial intelligence, and all areas of engineering interest.

Although this all might sound daunting at first, every journey must start with the first step. It is the intention of this text to start you on your journey into computer science by focusing on fundamental concepts in the following five areas:

A BIT OF BACKGROUND

Augusta Ada Byron, Countess of Lovelace

Augusta Ada Byron, the daughter of Lord Byron, was a colleague of Charles Babbage in his attempt throughout the mid-1800s to build the Analytical Engine. It was Ada's task to develop the algorithms—solutions to problems in the form of step-by-step instructions—that would allow the engine to compute the values of mathematical functions. Babbage's machine was not successfully built in his lifetime, primarily because the technology of the time did not allow mechanical parts to be constructed with necessary tolerances. Nonetheless, Ada is recognized as the first computer programmer. She published a collection of notes that established the basis for computer programming, and the modern Ada programming language is named in her honor.

1. Introduction to computer architecture
2. The Java programming language
3. Class development and design
4. Algorithm development
5. Introduction to data structures

The central element of this text is problem solution and program development using the Java programming language. As we proceed, however, we will need to become familiar with these other very important computer science topics. We begin this journey by considering the evolution of programming languages and the development of Java.

Programming Languages

A computer is a machine made of physical components. In this regard, it is the same as any other machine, such as an automobile or lawn mower. Like these other machines, it must be turned on and then driven, or controlled, to perform its intended task. How this gets done is what distinguishes a computer from other types of machinery.

In an automobile, for example, control is provided by the driver, who sits inside and directs the car. In a computer, the driver is a set of instructions called a program. More formally, a **computer program** is a self-contained set of instructions and data used to operate a computer to produce a specific result. Another term for a program or set of programs is **software**, and we will use both terms interchangeably throughout the text.

The process of developing and writing a program, or software, is called **programming**, and the set of instructions that can be used to construct a program is called a **programming language**. Available programming languages come in a variety of forms and types.

Machine Language

At its most fundamental level, the only programs that can actually operate a computer are **machine language programs**. Such programs, which are also referred to as executable programs, or executables for short, consist of a sequence of binary numbers such as[1]

```
11000000000000000001000000000010
11110000000000000010000000000011
```

At a minimum, each sequence of binary numbers constitutes a machine language instruction that consists of two parts: an instruction part and a data part. The instruction part, which is referred to as the **opcode** (short for operation code) is usually at the beginning of each binary number and tells the computer the operation to be performed, such as add, subtract, multiply, and so on. The remaining part of the number then provides information about the data.

Assembly Language

Although each class of computer, such as IBM personal computers, Apple Macintosh® computers, and Hewlett-Packard computers, has its own particular machine language, it is very tedious and time-consuming to write machine language programs. One of the first advances in programming was the substitution of wordlike symbols, such as ADD, SUB, MUL, for the binary opcodes and both decimal numbers and labels for memory addresses. For example, using these symbols, the following set of instructions could be written to add two numbers, referred to as first and second, multiply the result by a third number known as factor, and store the result as answer.

```
LOAD    first
ADD     second
MUL     factor
STORE   answer
```

Programming languages that use this type of symbolic notation are referred to as **assembly languages**. Since computers can only execute machine language programs, this set of assembly language instructions would still have to be translated into a machine language program before it could be executed on a computer. Translator programs that convert assembly language programs into machine language are known as **assemblers** (Figure 1.1).

FIGURE 1.1   **Assembly language programs must be translated**

---

[1] See Section 1.9 for a review of binary numbers.

Low- and High-Level Languages

Both machine level and assembly languages are classified as **low-level languages**. This is because both of these language types use instructions that are directly tied to one type of computer. Thus, an assembly language program is limited in that it can only be used with the specific computer type for which the program is written. Such programs do, however, permit using special features of a particular computer and generally execute at the fastest level possible.

In contrast to low-level languages are languages that are classified as high-level. A **high-level language** uses instructions that resemble natural languages, such as English, and can be run on a variety of computer types, such as an IBM, Apple, or Hewlett-Packard computers. Pascal, Visual Basic, C, C++, and Java are all high-level languages. Using Java, the previous assembly language instructions used to add two numbers and multiply by a third number can be written as

```
answer = (first + second) * factor;
```

Programs written in a computer language (high or low level) are referred to interchangeably as both **source programs** and **source code**. Once a program is written in a high-level language, it must also, like a low-level assembly program, be translated into the machine language of the computer on which it will be run. This translation can be accomplished in two ways. A unique feature of Java, as you will see, is that it uses both translation techniques, one after another.

When each statement in a high-level source program is translated individually and executed immediately upon translation, the programming language is called an **interpreted language**, and the program doing the translation is called an **interpreter**.

When all the statements in a high-level source program are translated as a complete unit before any one statement is executed, the programming language is called a **compiled language**. In this case, the program doing the translation is called a **compiler**. Both compiled and interpreted versions of a language can exist, although typically one predominates. For example, although interpreted versions of C++ exist, C++ is predominantly a compiled language.

A Java program's translation is a modification of the traditional process that uses *both* a compiler and interpreter. As shown in Figure 1.2, the output of the compilation step is a program in bytecode format. This bytecode is a machine code that *is not* geared to a particular computer's internal processor but rather to a machine referred to as a Java Virtual Machine (JVM). The Java Virtual Machine machine is not a physical machine but rather a software program that can read the bytecode produced by the compiler and execute it.

The computer on which the JVM runs is referred to as the **host computer**. As shown in Figure 1.2, it is within the host computer's JVM that the bytecode is finally translated into a machine language code appropriate to the host computer. Specifically, the JVM is an interpreter that translates each bytecode instruction, as it is encountered, into a computer-specific machine code that is immediately executed by the computer.

This two-phase translation process provides Java with its cross-platform capability that permits each computer, regardless of its internal processor type, to execute the same Java program. It does this by placing the machine-specific details of the final translation step within the host computer's JVM rather than on the computer that compiled the source code.

FIGURE 1.2　**Translating a Java program**

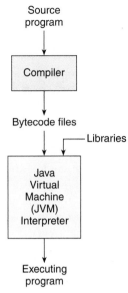

Procedure and Object Orientations

High-level languages are further classified as either procedure oriented or object oriented. In a **procedure-oriented language**, the available instructions are used to create self-contained units referred to as *procedures*. The purpose of a procedure is to accept data as input and transform the data in some manner to produce a specific result as an output. Until the mid-1990s, the majority of high-level languages were procedure oriented.

Currently, a second orientation referred to as object oriented has taken center stage. One of the motivations for **object-oriented languages** was the development of graphical screens and support for graphical user interfaces (GUIs) capable of displaying multiple windows containing both graphical shapes and text. In such an environment, each window on the screen can conveniently be considered an object with associated characteristics, such as color, position, and size. Using an object-oriented approach, a program must first define the objects it will be manipulating, which includes describing both the general characteristics of the objects themselves and specific units to manipulate them, such as changing size and position and transferring data between objects. Java is an object-oriented language.

Application and System Software

Two logical categories of computer programs are application software and system software. **Application software** consists of programs written to perform particular tasks required by the users. Most of the examples in this book would be considered application software.

System software is the collection of programs that must be readily available to any computer system for it to operate at all. In the early computer environments of the 1950s and 1960s, a user initially had to load the system software by hand to prepare the computer to do anything. This was done with rows of switches on a front panel. Those initial hand-entered commands were said to **boot** the computer, an expression derived from "pulling oneself up by the bootstraps." Today, the so-called *bootstrap loader* is internally contained in read-only memory (ROM) and is a permanent, automatically executed component of the computer's system software.

Collectively, the set of system programs used to operate and control a computer is called the *operating system*. Tasks handled by modern operating systems include memory allocation, input and output control, and secondary storage management. Many operating systems handle very large programs, as well as multiple users concurrently, by dividing programs into segments or pages that are moved between the disk and memory as needed. Such operating systems create a *virtual memory*, which appears to be as large as necessary to handle any job, and a *multiuser* environment is produced that gives each user the impression that the computer and peripherals are his or hers alone. Additionally, many operating systems, including most windowed environments, permit each user to run multiple programs. Such operating systems are referred to as both *multiprogrammed* and *multitasking* systems.

The Development of Java

At a very basic level, the purpose of almost all application programs is to process data to produce one or more specific results. In a procedure-oriented language, a program is constructed from sets of instructions, with each set called a procedure. Effectively, each procedure moves the data one step closer to the final desired output along the path shown in Figure 1.3.

It is interesting to note that the programming processes illustrated in Figure 1.3 directly mirror the input, processing, and output hardware units that are used to construct a computer (see Section 1.9). This was not accidental because early programming languages were specifically designed to match and, as optimally as possible, directly control corresponding hardware units.

The first commercially available procedure-oriented language, named Fortran, whose name is derived from *For*mula *tran*slation, was introduced in 1957 and remained popular throughout the 1960s and early 1970s.[2] Fortran had algebralike instructions that concentrated on the processing phase shown in Figure 1.3 and was developed for scientific and engineering applications that required high-precision numerical outputs accurate to many decimal places. For example, calculating the bacterial concentration level in a polluted pond, as illustrated in Figure 1.4, requires evaluating a mathematical equation to a high degree of numerical accuracy and is typical of Fortran-based applications.

The next significant high-level application language was COBOL, which was commercially introduced in the 1960s and remained a major commercial language

FIGURE 1.3   **Basic program operations**

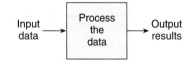

---

[2] ALGOL was another high-level programming language that was developed almost concurrently with Fortran, but it never achieved Fortran's overwhelming acceptance.

FIGURE 1.4   **Fortran was developed for scientific and engineering applications**

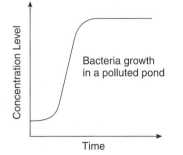

through the 1980s. COBOL is an acronym for COmmon Business-Oriented Language. This language had features geared toward business applications that required simpler mathematical calculations than those needed for scientific applications. One of its main attractions is that it provided extensive output formats that made it quite easy to create reports containing extensive columns of neatly formatted dollar-and-cents numbers and totals (Figure 1.5). It also forced programmers to carefully construct well-defined, structured procedures that followed a more consistent pattern than was required in Fortran.

Contemporary with COBOL was the development of BASIC. BASIC stands for Beginners All-purpose Symbolic Instruction Code and was developed in the 1960s at Dartmouth College. This was essentially a slightly scaled down version of Fortran that was intended as an introductory language for college students. It was a relatively straightforward, easy-to-understand language that did not require detailed knowledge of a specific application. Its main drawback was that it neither required nor enforced a consistent structured approach to creating programs. Frequently, even a programmer could not easily figure out what her or his program did after a short lapse of time.

To remedy this and put programming on a more scientific and rational basis that made understanding and reusing code easier, Pascal was developed. Introduced in 1971, it provided students with a firmer foundation in structured programming design than that provided by early versions of BASIC. Structured programs are constructed using a set of well-defined structures that are organized into individual programming sections, each of which preforms a specific task that can be tested and modified without disturbing other sections of the program. Pascal is not an acronym,

FIGURE 1.5   **COBOL was designed for business applications**

Part No	Description	Quantity	Price
12225	#4 Nails, common	25 boxes	1.09
12226	#6 Nails, common	30 boxes	1.09
12227	#8 Nails, common	65 boxes	1.29
12228	#10 Nails, common	57 boxes	1.35
12229	#12 Nails, common	42 boxes	
12230	#16 Nails, common		

A BIT OF BACKGROUND

Niklaus Wirth

Niklaus Wirth received an M.S. degree from the University of Quebec in 1962 and a Ph.D. from the University of California at Berkeley in 1963. He then returned to his undergraduate alma mater, the Swiss Federal Institute of Technology, to teach. While serving there in 1971, he announced a new language he had designed and named *Pascal*. Pascal became very popular in the 1970s and early 1980s because of its emphasis on structured programming.

---

as are COBOL and BASIC, but is named after the 17th-century mathematician Blaise Pascal. The Pascal language was so rigidly structured, however, that there were no escapes from the structured modules when such escapes would be useful. This was unacceptable for many real-world projects and is one of the reasons Pascal did not become widely accepted in the scientific, engineering, and business fields. Instead, the C language, which is a procedure-oriented language developed in the 1970s at AT&T Bell Laboratories by Ken Thompson, Dennis Ritchie, and Brian Kernighan, became the predominant procedure-oriented language of the 1980s. This language has an extensive set of capabilities that permits it to be written as a high-level language while retaining the ability to directly access the machine-level features of a computer.

In the early 1980s, Bjarne Stroustrup (also at AT&T) used his simulation language background to develop C++. A central feature of simulation languages is that they model real-life situations as objects. This object orientation, which was ideal for graphical screen objects such as rectangles and circles, was combined with existing C features to form a hybrid language that was both procedure oriented and object oriented.

The next step was to create a true object-oriented language. This was accomplished by Java, which is essentially based on the object-oriented features of C++. As has already been stated, one of the prime motivations for object-oriented languages has been the development and extensive use of graphical screens and support for graphical user interfaces (GUIs). Graphical screens are capable of displaying multiple windows that provide data entry and display capabilities that are extremely difficult to program with procedure-oriented techniques.

Java was initially designed at Sun Microsystems in 1991 by James Gosling as a language that could be embedded in consumer electronic items to create intelligent electronic devices. At that time, the language was named Oak. In 1993, when the project for which Oak was being developed was terminated, the Internet was just beginning its phenomenal growth. Sun engineers realized that the Oak language could be easily adapted to the Internet to create dynamic Web pages. Such pages would include an executable program as an integral part of themselves rather than containing only static text and figures. Although this was always theoretically possible using other programming languages, it was not feasible in practice because of the variability of processor types. Because of its design, Oak programs would execute the same on all Web pages, regardless of the computer that displays the page.

To demonstrate the feasibility of this approach, Sun created a Web browser named HotJava™, which was itself programmed using a renamed Oak language called Java.

A BIT OF BACKGROUND

Blaise Pascal

The Pascal language is named after Blaise Pascal, a French mathematician and philosopher who lived from 1623 to 1662. He is credited with having invented the first mechanical calculating machine in 1642 at the age of 19.

"All our dignity consists then in thought. By it we must elevate ourselves, and not by space and time, which we cannot fill. Let us endeavor then to think well; this is the principle of morality."

(Pascal's Penses, *Number 347)*

A **Web browser** is a program that is located and run on a user's computer to display Web pages. Although initially tied to the HotJava browser, it soon became apparent that Java was a very powerful general-purpose object-oriented language in its own right. In this respect, Java's development paralleled the development of C, which was used to program the UNIX® operating system developed in the late 1970s. Just as applications developers had earlier understood that C could be used as a general-purpose procedural language independently of UNIX, a similar type of realization quickly occurred with Java; it could be used independently of the Hot Java browser.

In Java's case, the impetus for its appeal and rapid acceptance as a general-purpose applications programming language resided in its ability to create programs that can execute on any computer, independent of the internal processor on which the computer is based, without the necessity of rewriting or retranslating the program. This capability is referred to as both **cross-platform compatibility** and **write-once-run-anywhere**. As shown in Figure 1.6, there are two main ways in which such a Java program can be created for a user's computer, which is formally referred to as both a local and Web-client computer.[3]

FIGURE 1.6   **The two distinct Java environments**

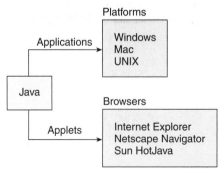

---

[3] A third and more exotic way is as a program that is automatically executed on a Web server computer when a specific Web page is accessed. Such programs are referred to as **servlets**.

1. As a small program embedded within a Web page. This type of program is referred to as an *applet*.

2. As a stand-alone program, similar to a program written in any number of high-level languages, such as C and C++. This type of program is referred to as an *application*.

Although Java was initially used to create applets, this usage is now minimal because applet features are more easily created with a scripting language, such as JavaScript™. Despite the similar name, JavaScript has very little relationship to the Java programming language and is not discussed further in this text.[4] This text is concerned with Java as defined in Sun's Java 2 SDK specification (Versions 1.3 and 1.4), commonly known as Java 2, and using it as a full-featured, general-purpose, object-oriented programming language.

Exercises 1.1

1. Define the following terms:
   a. computer program
   b. programming
   c. programming language
   d. high-level language
   e. low-level language
   f. machine language
   g. assembly language
   h. procedure-oriented language
   i. object-oriented language
   j. source program
   k. compiler
   l. assembler

2a. Describe the difference between high-level and low-level languages.

   b. Describe the difference between procedure-oriented and object-oriented languages.

3. Describe the difference between assemblers, interpreters, and compilers.

4a. Assuming the following operation codes,

```
11000000   means add the 1st operand to the 2nd operand
10100000   means subtract the 1st operand from the 2nd operand
11110000   means multiply the 2nd operand by the 1st operand
11010000   means divide the 2nd operation by the 1st operand
```

---

[4] JavaScript was developed by Netscape Corporation and only the name is a property of Sun Microsystems.

translate the following instructions into English:

```
              address of    address of
   opcode    1st operand    2nd operand
   -------------------------------------
   11000000  000000000001   0000000000010
   11110000  000000000010   0000000000011
   10100000  000000000100   0000000000011
   11010000  000000000101   0000000000011
```

b. Assume the following locations contain the following data and determine the result produced by the instructions listed in Exercise 4a.

```
                      initial value
                       (in decimal)
   address        stored at this address
   -----------------------------------
   00000000001             5
   00000000010             3
   00000000011             6
   00000000100            14
   00000000101             4
```

5. Rewrite the machine-level instructions listed in Exercise 4a using assembly language notation. Use the symbolic names ADD, SUB, MUL, and DIV for addition, subtraction, multiplication, and division operations, respectively. In writing the instructions, use decimal values for the addresses.

6. Assuming that A = 10, B = 20, and C = 0.6, determine the numerical result of the following set of assembly language type statements. For this exercise, assume that the LOAD instruction is equivalent to entering a value into the display of a calculator and that ADD means add and MUL means multiply by.

```
   LOAD   A
   ADD    B
   MUL    C
```

1.2 Objects and Classes

We live in a world full of objects—planes, trains, cars, cell phones, books, computers, and so on. It should not seem surprising then that programming languages themselves would be based on objects, such as the data entry areas, check boxes, and command buttons shown in Figure 1.7.

Objects, such as those in Figure 1.7, are so commonly used that they are provided as part of the Java programming language as component types, which can then be custom tailored by the programmer to provide the specific shape, color, size, and other options required by each program. In addition to graphical objects, Java provides mathematical object types, such as lists and tables, which can also be customized as a particular list, such as a list of names and addresses, or a specific table of numbers and their square roots. And finally, Java provides the ability for

FIGURE 1.7 **Commonly encountered programming objects**

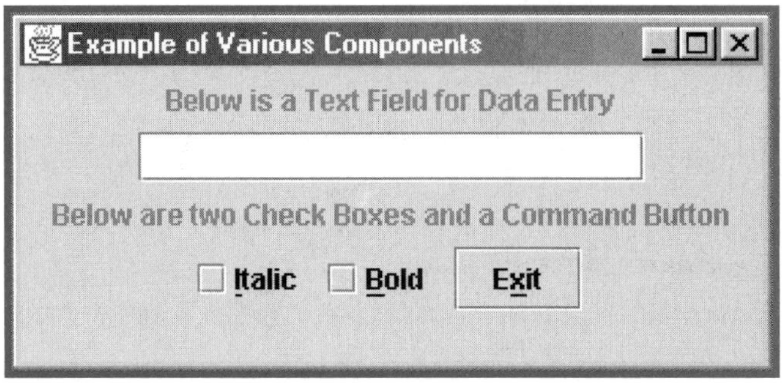

programmers to construct their own object types, out of which specific objects can then be created.

In this text, we will present all three aspects of the Java language: how to use and customize the provided graphical object types, such as those in Figure 1.7; how to adapt and modify the provided mathematical object types, such as lists and tables; and how to construct our own object types. We will do this in reverse order, however. First, we will present the structure on which all objects used in a Java program are constructed, and then we will show how to use and customize Java's preexisting graphical and mathematical object types. As you might expect, these preexisting object types are themselves built using the same structure; thus, once we have constructed our own objects, we will have a much better grasp of how to use many of the preexisting graphical and mathematical objects.

Although the terms *objects* and *object types* that we have been using make sense from an intuitive viewpoint, we need to refine our understanding of these terms for our programming work. To make this clearer, and as an example, consider any automobile that you have recently driven. From an object viewpoint, a specific car is a particular instance, or object, of a more general class of car. Thus, my particular Ford Taurus can be considered as one object, in this case a car object, from the broader class of all possible Ford Tauruses that could have been built. Similarly, your BMW 525 can be considered as one object from the broader class of all possible BMW 525s that could have been built. The plan for building a particular car is held by the respective manufacturers. Only when such a plan is put into action and a car is actually built does a specific object come into existence. This relationship of creating a particular object from a larger defining set, or class, of objects is central to all object-oriented programming languages, such as Java. In programming terminology, a class is simply what we have been referring to as an object type. It is from the object type, or more accurately, from a class, that any one specific object is created.

A Class Is a Plan

Programming in Java requires that the structure, or plan, for a class of objects be created at the start of the programming process. For example, before having a house built, you would require that a detailed set of plans be available. Similarly, before attempting to assemble a bicycle or a backyard basketball hoop, you would want to know that a set of assembly instructions was available. And in preparing a dinner, you might consult a recipe, which provides a list of food ingredients and how they are to be assembled. Although a formal set of assembly instructions might not be explicitly written down, it would be in the mind of a builder, or a recipe in the mind of a chef, and at some level, forms the basis of constructing any object, be it a bicycle, staircase, computer, or dinner.

The same planning is required in constructing a Java program, where the plan *must be* explicitly written down and is formally called a **class**. Once the parts and assembly instructions defining a class are completed, a Java program is developed by using specific objects created according to the assembly instructions contained in the class. For example, we may first design a class for calculating the floor space of a room and then use the class in a program to calculate the total floor space of a house, or we may design a class for shuffling a deck of cards and then use the class in a program that simulates a game of solitaire.

From a programming perspective then, a class is a plan with a complete set of parts and instructions needed to create items that will be used in a program. Again, as an example, a program for simulating a card game might include items such as a deck of cards that can be shuffled, a means of dealing individual cards, individual card displays that can be presented on a screen and moved under mouse control, and so forth. In this regard, a useful analogy is to relate a class to a food recipe, with only one significant modification; a Java class is a plan for assembling data and graphical elements rather than food items. Other than this, the relationship between a Java class and a food recipe is almost one to one and extremely informative.

To make this more concrete, consider a typical food recipe provided in Figure 1.8. It will come as no surprise that all food recipes, of which our example is but a specific case, contain similar types of components. More surprising, however, is that almost

FIGURE 1.8   **The Recipe for Al's Sardine Spread**

Recipe Name: Al's Sardine Spread
Ingredients:

Measure	***Contents***
1 can	Boneless and skinless sardines
2 stalks	Celery
1/4 medium	Red onion
1 tablespoon	Mayonnaise
1/4 cup	Parsley
dash	Olive oil
splash	Red wine vinegar
dash	Salt
dash	Pepper

Method of Preparation:
Finely shred the sardines using two forks
Finely dice the celery and onion and mix well with sardines
Add olive oil and mix well
Add mayonnaise and mix well
Add red wine vinegar and mix well
Finely dice the parsley and mix well
Salt and pepper to taste

the exact same elements are required in constructing a Java class. Let's see what these elements are.

First, notice that the recipe itself is not the spread; it merely provides a plan for creating the spread. The recipe can be used many times, and each time it is used, a particular batch of sardine spread is produced.

Now examine the actual structure of the recipe and notice that it consists of two main sections: The top section provides a list of ingredients, and the bottom section provides a method for using these ingredients. Additionally, the top section of ingredients itself consists of two parts: The left side provides the type of measure, such as can, tablespoon, cup (including less precise measures, such as stalk, dash, and splash), and the right side lists the actual ingredient, such as sardines, celery, oil, vinegar, onion, and so on. This same division will hold true, with some modification, for Java classes. For example, instead of using measures such as a teaspoon or cup, we will be dealing with measures for holding data values, such as integer, real number, string, and other suitable programming types.

Now we can make one addition to the top section of the recipe in Figure 1.8 by giving each ingredient and its measure a specific name so that the ingredient section appears as shown in Figure 1.9. We have placed the name between the *Measure* and *Contents* columns because this is where the name is placed when constructing a Java class. In using our modified recipe, it is useful to read each ingredient using its name (even though the name is provided in the second column) first. Thus, the first ingredient should be read as "sardineIngredient consists of 1 can of boneless and skinless sardines." The names we have provided, such as `sardineIngredient`, and the fact

FIGURE 1.9   **Using Named Ingredients for Al's Sardine Spread**

Ingredients:

Measure	*Name*	*Contents*
1 can	sardineIngredient	Boneless and skinless sardines
2 stalks	celeryIngredient	Celery
1/4 medium	onionIngredient	Red onion
1 tablespoon	mayo	Mayonnaise
1/4 cup	parsley	Parsley
dash	dashOil	Olive oil
splash	splashVinegar	Red wine vinegar
dash	dashSalt	Salt
dash	dashPepper	Pepper

Method of Preparation:

Finely shred the sardineIngredient using two forks

Finely dice the celeryIngredient and onionIngredient, and mix well with the sardineIngredient

Add dashOil and mix well

Add mayo and mix well

Add splashVinegar and mix well

Finely dice the parsley and mix well

Add dashSalt and dashPepper to taste

that we have only capitalized the first letter of the word `Ingredient`, with no spaces contained within the name is purely a matter of choice at this stage. As we will see in the next section, this choice is the convention used in naming Java programming ingredients. Also, once we have provided each ingredient with a name, the method section can also be rewritten to make use of these names, as illustrated in the new method section provided in Figure 1.9.

From Recipe to Class

We can now make the almost direct connection from the recipe in Figure 1.9 to a Java class. As we have stated, a class can be considered as the plan or recipe from which individual programming objects can be created. Like its food recipe counterpart, a class typically contains ingredient and method sections.

Within the ingredient section, instead of measures such as a teaspoon or cup, Java deals with measures for holding integer (whole) numbers, real numbers (numbers that contain fractional parts), strings, and other types of suitable "ingredients." These ingredients, in programming terminology, are referred to as data. Thus, each piece of data used in Java will have a measure, such as *this datum is an integer*. It will also have a specific value, such as *the value of this integer is 5*, and it will be given a name, such as `firstIntegerNumber`. The description of the data used in a Java class will be, like a food recipe, contained in a specific section, which is referred to as the **data declaration section**. This corresponds to the ingredients section of a recipe. At a minimum, the data declaration section will list the type of data needed and a name for each data item. Specific values for the data are typically assigned later.

Following the class data declaration section, a Java class provides a **methods section**, which defines how to combine the data components to produce a desired result. This section is equivalent to the method preparation section in a recipe.

As a specific example, consider that we are required to create a Java program to calculate the average of two numbers. The data elements and methods for doing this are rather simple and can be described with the components shown in Figure 1.10.

Notice that Figure 1.10 contains the same elements as Figure 1.9 with two important modifications. The first modification is that the column labeled *Measure* in Figure 1.9 is relabeled *Type* in Figure 1.10. The second modification is that the third column, labeled *Contents* in Figure 1.9, is missing in Figure 1.10. In the latter figure, the actual values, or contents, of the data are assigned in the methods section. Although values

FIGURE 1.10   **A programming plan for determining an average**

```
Class Name: AverageOfTwoNumbers

    Data (Ingredients)    <--- this starts the data declaration section
      Type                Name
      real number         firstNumber
      real number         secondNumber


    Methods   <--- this starts the methods section
      Assign Values to each firstNumber and secondNumber.
      Calculate and display the average of firstNumber and SecondNumber.
```

FIGURE 1.11 **A programming plan for address labels**

```
Class Name: CreateALabel
      Data (Ingredients)     <--- this starts the data declaration section
        Type                        Name
        String of characters        message


      Methods   <--- this starts the methods section
        Assign text to the message.
        Display message on the screen.
```

can be assigned in the data section, it is more typically the case that actual data values are assigned using a method. This provides the user with the opportunity to assign values interactively while a program is being executed.

As our last example, consider that we need to create a Java class that can be used to display a message on the screen. For this application, the preliminary class structure shown in Figure 1.11 can be constructed.

All of the Java classes that we design will have the same basic structure illustrated in Figures 1.10 and 1.11 but will require a slightly more formal placement of items. This formal placement, which each and every one of our Java classes will follow, has the general format

```
Class  Name
    Class Data Declaration Section
        A list of the types of data to be used with a name provided for each individual item
    Class Method Definition Section
        The methods that can be used by this class
```

Using this basic structure, we now develop a working Java class for displaying a single line of text on a computer screen.

A First Java Class

With an understanding that a Java class is a formal programming plan, we now present a Java class that can be used for displaying a message consisting of a single line of text on your computer screen. Although it is necessary to know how to structure and create our own classes, it should be understood that part of Java's appeal is that a very rich set of classes is provided as part of the language. This means that many programs and classes that you will write can be constructed by using existing classes.

Formally, a class consists of a class header line and a body. The basic class header line, which we will almost exclusively use and which is always the first line of a class, contains three words.

1. The word public
2. The word class
3. The name of the class

The body of a class, which always follows the header line, is enclosed within a set of braces, { and }. This set of braces determines the beginning and end of the class's

FIGURE 1.12   **The structure of a Java class named `ShowFirstMessage`**

```
Class Header Line  ----> public class ShowFirstMessage
                  ------>{
      Class's Body |         class data and methods go in here
                  ------>}
```

body and encloses the data and methods that make up the class. Figure 1.12 illustrates the basic structure of a class that we have named `ShowFirstMessage`.

Within the body of a class (i.e., between the opening and closing braces of the class), there are typically two sections of code. The first section declares the types of data that will be used, and the second section defines procedures that will be used on the data. This is in keeping with our concept that a class can be thought of as a plan, or recipe consisting of a list of ingredients and the methods for combining them.

Now consider the Java class shown in Figure 1.13, which can be used to display the text `I need a cup of Java` on your computer screen. Although it is too early to understand this code, important basic elements can be easily identified. First, because every Java class must contain a class header line and a body, the three initial items to notice in the figure are

1. the class header line
2. the start of the class's body, which is designated by a left-facing brace, {
3. the end of a class's body, which is designated by a right-facing brace, }

Be aware that braces are used elsewhere in the code, so in addition to always defining the beginning and ending of a Java class, braces do have other uses.

Internal to the class in Figure 1.13, notice that two sections are provided. These are the ones previously introduced and consist of a data section and a methods section.

FIGURE 1.13   **A sample Java class**

```
❶ Class Header Line -------->public class ShowFirstMessage
❷ Start of Class's Body --->{
                      // class data declaration section   ❹ Start of Data Section
                      private String message;

                      // class method definition section  ❺ Start of Methods Section
                      ShowFirstMessage()
                      {
                        message = "I need a cup of Java.";
                      }

                      public void displayMessage()
                      {
                        System.out.println(message);
                      }
❸ End of Class's Body   --->}
```

Every Java class will include either one or both of these sections. The purpose of each of these sections is described in detail in the next chapter, and they are used throughout the text. Briefly, however, the data section, which is formally referred to as the **class data declaration section**, describes the type of data that will be used. The methods section, which is formally referred to as the **class method definition section**, defines how the data are to be used. For example, the data section might include two integers, and the method section might provide procedures for computing and displaying the average of the data. For the code in Figure 1.13, the data section declares a single piece of data, which can be used to hold text and is referred to as String data. The method section provides two methods. When the first method is executed, it places the text `I need a cup of Java.` in the String, which is named `message`. The second method, when executed, displays the text on the screen.

To relate the class provided in Figure 1.13 with our concept of a class as a programming recipe, Table 1.1 summarizes the basic components of our example Java class and the correspondence between these components and those found in the more familiar elements of a food recipe.

Table 1.1 **Java Class Components**

Class Component	Corresponds to
Class Name, such as `ShowFirstMessage`	Recipe Name, such as Al's Sardine Spread
Data Declaration Section	Ingredients Section
Data Type, such as a String	Measure, such as a cup
Data Name, such as message	Ingredients Name, such as sardineIngredient
Text , such as "I need a cup of Java"	Contents, such as 1 can of skinless and boneless sardines
Methods Section	Procedures for combining ingredients

One additional point needs to be made here; the code in Figure 1.13 *is not* an executable Java program. Although each and every executable Java program must conform to the class structure shown in the figure, a Java program must additionally contain a special class method having the name `main`. Typically, a Java program will make use of other Java classes, each of which has the basic structure illustrated in Figure 1.13. For now, you should compile the code provided in the figure using the procedures given in Appendix C. When the compilation is successfully completed, you will have a new file named `ShowFirstMessage.class`, which is the compiled version (bytecode format) of the program (see Figure 1.2).

Exercises 1.2

1a. What are the two main sections of a Java class?

b. Within the first section of a Java class, what information must be provided?

c. What is the information provided by the second section of a Java class?

2. Figure 1.14 is a simplified diagram for assembling a birdhouse. For this figure, create a set of instructions for constructing the birdhouse and a parts list. Then, identify the elements that correspond to the major items identified in Figure 1.9.

FIGURE 1.14   **Building a birdhouse**

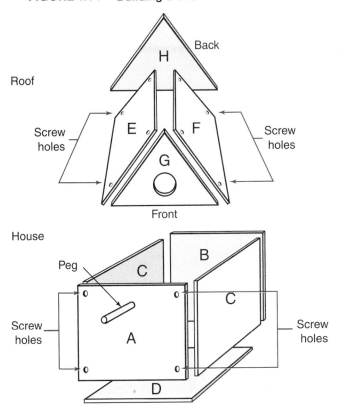

3a.   List the items that you would need to build a staircase having five steps.

b.   Write a set of instructions for assembling the items listed in Exercise 3a.

4a.   List the ingredients that you would need to create 10 Easter eggs.

b.   Write a set of instructions for assembling the items listed in Exercise 4a.

5.   Obtain a set of assembly instructions from a recent item that you have built (e.g., a bicycle or a backyard basketball hoop). Identify the major elements in the assembly instructions that correspond to the sections and items listed in Figure 1.9.

6.   Assume that you are to create a Java class that prints address labels, where an individual label consists of a name, two address lines, a city, state, and zip code. For this plan, list the data item(s) and a set of methods that would be useful for such a program. Select your own class name and data item names.

7.   Assume you are to create a plan for a Java program that simulates the tossing of a single die. For this plan, list the data item(s) and a set of methods that would be useful for such a program. Select your own class name and data item names.

8.   Assume that you are to create a plan for a Java program that simulates the selection of a state lottery that randomly selects four numbers. For this plan, list the data item(s) and a set of methods that would be useful for such a program. Select your own class name and data item names.

9. Assume that you are to create a Java program that calculates the floor space of a rectangular room. For this plan, list the data item(s) and a set of methods that would be useful for such a program. Select your own class name and data item names.

10. Assume that you are to create a Java program that displays a rectangle on the console. List the data item(s) and a set of methods that would be useful for such a program. Select your own class name and data item names.

11. Assume that you are to create a Java program that calculates and displays the volume of a cylinder (volume $= \pi r^2 l$, where r is the radius of the cylinder and l is the length). List the data item(s) and a set of methods that would be useful for such a program. Select your own class name and data item names.

12. Assume that you are to create a Java program the uses dates. List the data item(s) and a set of methods that would be useful for such a program. Select your own class name and data item names.

13. Enter and compile the class provided in Figure 1.13.

14a. Enter and compile the following class on your computer. To compile the program, use the command

```
javac UseShowFirstMessage.java

public class UseShowFirstMessage
{
  public static void main(String[] args)
  {
    ShowFirstMessage messageOne;

    messageOne = new ShowFirstMessage();
    messageOne.displayMessage();
  }
}
```

b. Run the program entered in Exercise 14a. using the command `java UseShowFirst-Message`. Notice that it is necessary for the `ShowFirstMessage` class presented in this section (Figure 1.13) to have been compiled for your program to execute.

c. Remove the file named `ShowFirstMessage.class` from your computer and attempt to run the program entered in Exercise 14a. What error message did you receive?

15. Modify the `ShowFirstMessage` class (Figure 1.13) to display the message `I hate coffee!`

16. For the following class, identify (a) the class name, (b) the names of data items that are used in the class, and (c) the number of methods contained within the method definition section.

```
public class ShowSecondMessage
{
   // class data declaration section
  private String message;

   // class method definition section
  ShowSecondMessage()
```

```
  {
    message = "I really prefer tea!";
  }

  public void changeMessage(String newMessage);
  {
    message = newMessage;
  }

  public void displayMessage()
  {
    System.out.println(message);
  }
}
```

1.3 Constructing a Java Program

A distinct advantage of using classes is that the objects constructed from them can be designed, developed, and tested to provide known quantities that can be used by any program. Because a very rich set of classes is provided as part of the Java language, many programs can be constructed by using these existing classes. Figure 1.15 illustrates how a typical Java program might be constructed. As illustrated, existing classes, which can be either programmer created or Java supplied, can be used to create other classes, all of which are then used by a Java program. Additionally, a Java program is a class itself that has a special method permitting it to be executed.

No matter how many classes are used in creating a Java program, the overwhelming majority of them will have the structure presented in the previous section and repeated in Figure 1.16 for convenience, where the ClassName will be replaced by the actual name of a specific class.

The fundamental difference between a Java class and a Java program is that a Java program, which is considered an executable applications program, is a class that *must contain a method named* main. This class may or may not have a data section or any additional methods in its methods section, and it need not use other existing or

FIGURE 1.15   **A Java program is constructed from one or more classes**

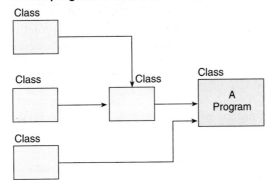

FIGURE 1.16   **The basic structure for a Java class**

```
Class Header Line  ---> public class ClassName
                   ------>{
     Class's Body |          class data and methods go in here
                  ------->}
```

programmer-created classes. As a practical matter, however, the main method, at a minimum, typically will use at least one method from an existing class. In this section, we present the fundamentals of creating a Java program and the basic structure required of a main method.

The main Method

Figure 1.17 illustrates the basic structure for a main method that will be used throughout this book. Notice that this method consists of two parts: a header line and a body. The header line is always the first line of a method. The header line shown in Figure 1.17 is

```
public static void main(String [] args)
```

For all of the main methods presented in the text, we will use this header line without an initial full understanding of what information is being provided (a full understanding of the parts of this header line is provided in Chapter 6). Even though it is really too early in our exploration of Java to fully understand each item in this header line, it is useful to realize that this line provides five distinct pieces of information.[5]

1. A primary scope specification for the method, in this case designated by the word public, which is also referred to as a *visibility modifier*.
2. A secondary scope designation for the method, in this case designated by the word static, which specifies how the method is created and stored in the computer's memory. General-purpose methods, which can be used independently of any specific object, must be declared as static. (Thus, main is a general-purpose method.)
3. The type of data, if any, that is returned from the method. The reserved word void designates that the method will not return any value when it has completed executing.
4. The name of the method, which in this case is main.
5. What type of data, if any, is sent into the method. Information within the parentheses defines the type of data that will be transmitted into the method when it is run. Such data are referred to as **arguments** of the method.

The braces, { and }, in Figure 1.17 define the beginning and end of the method body, and they enclose all statements that make up the method. The statements within the braces determine what the method does. In general, each statement inside the method 's body must end with a semicolon (;).

---

[5] Items 4 and 5, which start from the method's name to the end of the header line, are referred to as a method's signature. The importance and use of the signature are described in Section 3.1.

FIGURE 1.17   **The structure of a `main()` method**

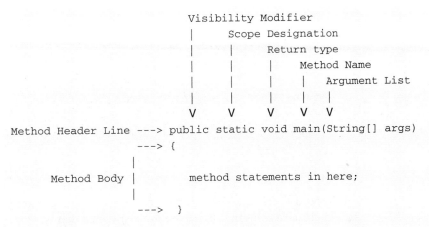

```
                          Visibility Modifier
                          |      Scope Designation
                          |      |      Return type
                          |      |      |   Method Name
                          |      |      |   |   Argument List
                          |      |      |   |   |
                          V      V      V   V   V
Method Header Line ---> public static void main(String[] args)
                  ---> {
                        |
     Method Body   |        method statements in here;
                        |
                  --->   }
```

You will be naming and writing many of your own Java classes and methods. In fact, the rest of this book is primarily about the statements required to construct useful class methods and programs. Each program, however, must have a main method. Until we learn how to pass data into a method and return data from a method, the class and method structures illustrated in Figures 1.16 and 1.17, respectively, will serve us for all the programs we need to write. At this stage, you can regard the first two lines of the `main()` method

```
public static void main(String[] args)
{
```

as stating that "the main method begins here" and regard the last line, consisting of a single brace

```
}
```

as stating that "the method ends here." Since every Java method requires parentheses following its name, we will always include them to clearly indicate that the identifier refers to a method name. Thus, for the rest of this text, we will always refer to the main method as `main()` and follow this practice for all other method names. This will make it easier for you to clearly distinguish that a method is being discussed. So whenever you see a name followed by parentheses, such as `displayMessage()` and `println()`, you should understand that the name is that of a method.

Because each Java program must be a class that contains a `main()` method, the simplest Java program would be a class having only one method named `main()` in its methods section. Thus, the simplest Java program that you can construct would have the format shown in Figure 1.18.

Notice the structure in Figure 1.18 consists of a single class that contains no data section and a methods section consisting of one method named `main()`. This is the simplest structure for a Java program and will be referred to throughout this text as the **QuickTest Program structure**. Additionally, notice that the code listed in the figure consists of both words and special symbols, such as the braces, {}. The words permitted in Java, as in all other programming languages, consist of three types: *reserved words, predefined words,* which are referred to as *standard identifiers,* and *programmer-supplied words,* which are referred to as *identifiers.*

FIGURE 1.18 **The structure of a Java program**

```
public class className
{
  // class method definition section
  public static void main(Sting[] args)
  {
      other Java statements in here;
  }
}
```

Reserved Words

A **reserved word** is a word that is predefined by the programming language for a special purpose and can only be used in a specified manner for its intended purpose. Attempts to use reserved words for any other purpose will generate an error when the code is compiled. In Java, a reserved word is also referred to as a **keyword**.

Table 1.2 lists the reserved words that you initially need to become familiar with, and as you progress in your programming studies, you will learn where, why, and how these words are used.

Standard Identifiers

Standard identifiers are Java-defined words that have a predefined purpose but can be redefined by a programmer. Generally, these are the names of classes and methods provided in Java, a small sample of which is listed in Table 1.3.

As a matter of good programming practice, standard identifiers should only be used for their intended purpose. For example, the standard identifier named random is the name of a Java method defined in a class named Math. This method can be used to create a set of one or more random numbers, which are extremely useful in constructing simulation programs. In certain situations, however, it might be advantageous for a programmer to develop a specialized or more efficient random number generation method and use the name random for this method. This can be done because random is a standard identifier. Although you are always free to reuse a stan-

Table 1.2 **Java Reserved Words**

abstract	default	if	private	this
boolean	do	implements	protected	throw
break	double	import	public	throws
byte	else	instanceof	return	transient
case	extends	int	short	try
catch	final	interface	static	void
char	finally	long	strictfp	volatile
class	float	native	super	while
const	for	new	switch	
continue	goto	package	synchronized	

Table 1.3 **Sub-Set of Java Standard Identifiers**

ActionEvent	Collections	FocusEvent	Paint()	showMessageDialog()
append	Cookie	insertElement	PI	size()
binarySearch()	DataInputStream	isEmpty()	print	swing
BoxLayout	DataOutputStream	javax	println()	Tree
charAt()	draw()	JOptionPane()	PrintStream	Vector
clone	drawImage()	Math	random()	Window
Collection	firstElement()	MessageBox()	setForeground()	WindowClosed

dard identifier name, good programming practice requires that you only use the name for its intended purpose.

Identifiers

Identifiers are programmer-supplied words, such as those you will use to name your classes as well as other elements of the Java language. **Identifiers** can be made up of any combination of letters, digits, underscores (_), or dollar signs ($) selected according to the following rules:

1. The first character of an identifier cannot be a digit.
2. Only letters (both uppercase and lowercase), digits, underscores, and dollar signs may follow the initial character. Blank spaces are not allowed.
3. An identifier cannot be a reserved word (see Table 1.2).
4. The maximum number of characters in an identifier name is unlimited.

As a practical matter and to minimize both typing time and typing errors, a typical identifier should be limited to fewer than 14 characters, with 20 characters as an outside maximum. Additionally, by convention, the first letter of each and every word, starting with the second word in a multiword identifier, is capitalized. Dollar signs are included for historical reasons and should only be used to access preexisting names in code written in versions prior to 2.0. Examples of valid Java identifiers are

CheckItems	DisplayAMessage	randomNumbers	computeSalesTax
addNums	degToRad	multByTwo	bessel

Notice that all of these identifiers have been typed almost exclusively in lowercase letters. The convention in Java (it is not required, but is almost universally used), and one that we will adhere to in this book, is that the first letter of an identifier used for a class name is always capitalized and that nonclass names begin with a lowercase letter. Additionally, capital letters will always be used for distinguishing words in multiword identifiers such as CheckItems, Display-AMessage, computeSalesTax, and addNums. Following the Java naming convention, we can see that the identifiers CheckItems and DisplayAMessage, which begin with a capital letter, are class names, whereas all the other examples of identifiers are not the names of Java classes.

The one exception to the capital letter rules is that you will encounter identifiers consisting of all uppercase letters. These are usually used to indicate a symbolic constant, a topic covered in Chapter 3. To separate individual words in a symbolic constant, an underscore character (_) is sometimes used.

Examples of invalid java identifiers are

```
4ab7     (begins with a number, which violates rule 1)
e*6      (contains a special character, which violates rule 2)
while    (is a reserved word, which violates rule 3)
```

One important requirement for selecting an identifier is that it should convey some idea about what the identifier will be used for. Thus, identifiers such as `DisplayAMessage` or `CalculateSalesTax` are good choices for class names only if the classes they are used for have something to do with displaying a message or calculating a sales tax. Identifiers, such as

```
Easy     duh     JustDoIt     mary     bill     TheForce
```

that provide no indication of their use are examples of extremely bad programming and should be avoided. Identifiers should always be descriptive and indicate their purpose or how they will be used.

Finally, it is important to understand that Java is a **case-sensitive** language. This means that the language distinguishes between uppercase and lowercase letters. Thus, in Java, the identifiers `TOTAL`, `total`, and `TotaL` represent three distinct and different names.

Exercises 1.3

1. State whether the following are valid identifiers. If they are valid, state whether they are descriptive. A mnemonic identifier conveys some idea about its intended purpose. If they are not valid identifiers, state why.

   ```
   1m1234       newBal       abcd         A12345       1A2345
   power        absVal       invoices     do           while
   add5         taxes        netPay       12345        int
   newBalance   a2b3c4d5     salesTax     amount       $taxes
   ```

2a. Assuming a case-insensitive compiler, determine which of these identifiers are equivalent.

   ```
   AVERAGE      average      MODE     BESSEL     Mode
   Total        besseL       TeMp     Density    TEMP
   denSITY      MEAN         total    mean       moDE
   ```

b. Redo Exercise 2a assuming a case-sensitive compiler.

3. Which of the following identifiers could be class names?

   ```
   NewBalance   addValues      CalculateTax
   power        absVal         DisplayAMessage
   invoices     SendMessage    taxes
   netPay       amount         salestax
   CardGame     newBalance     ComputeGPA
   ```

4. Determine appropriate names for methods that do the following (multiple names are possible).

PROGRAMMING NOTE

What Is Syntax?

A programming language's *syntax* is the set of rules for formulating grammatically correct language statements. In practice, this means that a Java statement with correct syntax has the proper form specified for the compiler. Thus, the compiler will accept the statement and not generate an error message.

It should be noted that an individual statement or program can be syntactically correct and still be logically incorrect. Such a statement or program would be correctly structured but produce an incorrect result. This is similar to an English statement that is grammatically correct but makes no sense. For example, although the sentence "The tree is a ragged cat" is grammatically correct, it makes no sense.

a. Find the maximum value in a set of numbers.

b. Find the minimum value in a set of numbers.

c. Convert a lowercase letter to an uppercase letter.

d. Convert an uppercase letter to a lowercase letter.

e. Sort a set of numbers from lowest to highest.

f. Alphabetize a set of names.

5. Just as the reserved word `void` signifies that a method returns no value, the reserved words `int`, `char`, `float`, and `double` signify that a method will return an integer, a character, a floating-point number, and a double-precision number, respectively. Using this information, write header lines for a `main()` method that returns

a. an integer

b. a character

c. a floating-point number

d. a double-precision number

1.4 The `PrintStream` Class's `print()` and `println()` Methods

The success of Java rests on two significant features. The first is that Java is a true object-oriented language that is suited to a windowed environment. The second is that Java provides an extremely extensive and very useful set of predefined and thoroughly tested classes. This latter feature permits many programming applications either to be completed using this existing class code or to create new classes easily by extending these existing classes. In this section, we introduce two methods from the `PrintStream` class that are used in the majority of Java programs for output creating text displays.

The two methods that we are interested in are named `print()` and `println()`. These methods are both defined in the class method definition section of the `PrintStream` class and, as their names suggest, are print methods.

Before seeing how to use either of these two methods, it will be useful to understand how classes are stored and related in Java. Doing so will make it much easier for you to obtain your own information about a desired class or method.

FIGURE 1.19   **The PrintStream class's hierarchy diagram**

```
java.lang.Object
       |
       +--java.io.OutputStream
              |
              +--java.io.FilterOutputStream
                     |
                     +--java.io.PrintStream
```

Figure 1.19 presents a hierarchy diagram for the PrintStream class. This diagram shows how one class is derived from other classes. The class name is always listed as the final name after the last period, with all identifiers before the last period signifying a package name. Formally, a **package** consists of one or more individual classes that are stored in the same directory. Classes that are packaged (i.e., stored) together are usually related in providing similar or complementary objects and methods. Thus, the identification java.io.PrintStream indicates that the PrintStream class is contained in the java.io package of classes. The fact that the PrintStream class is indented under the class named FilterOutputStream tells us that the PrintStream class is derived from FilterOutputStream, which itself is derived from OutputStream, which itself is derived from java.lang.Object.

The information provided by hierarchy diagrams, such as Figure 1.19, is useful for three reasons. First, it tells us the location of the desired class. This information is required for all classes that are not automatically provided by the Javac compiler.[6] Second, it documents how one class is derived from another. Why and how this is important are presented in Chapter 12. In brief, however, many times you will have to follow the classes up the chain to locate documentation for a particular method. And finally, the diagram provides the correct spelling for class and package names. As you will see numerous examples of hierarchy diagrams in your professional work, it is worthwhile getting used to seeing them at this stage of your programming career. As you expand your programming expertise and need to consult these diagrams for the documentation "audit trail" they provide, you will appreciate their usefulness to a much greater extent.

Specifically, the function of both print() and println(), which are provided by the PrintStream class, is to display data given to them on the standard output display device, which for most systems is the video screen. The difference between these methods is that, when the print() method is finished, it leaves the screen cursor positioned immediately after the last character it has sent to the monitor, whereas the println() method positions the cursor down to the start of a new line after it has finished operating. The cursor position determines where the next character sent to the monitor, using a new print() or println() method, is displayed. For now, we concentrate on the print() method, although everything that we say about this method applies identically to the println() method as well.

---

[6] Location information for classes contained in packages that must be explicitly referenced is provided by an import statement, which includes the package information provided by a hierarchy diagram. Import statements are presented in the next section.

PROGRAMMING NOTE

Java Documentation

There are two main sources of documentation on the classes and methods provided in Java. The first is the online site

http//java.sun.com/docs/search.html

This site provides the official documentation for Java Versions 1.2, 1.3, and 1.4. It is extremely useful in providing information on what a class does, the methods each class provides, and the arguments required by each method.

The second source is to use hard copy books. Two that are particularly well written and extremely useful are provided by Sun Microsystems. They are *The Java Class Libraries* by Chan, Lee, and Kramer and the *JFC Swing Tutorial* by Walrath and Campione. The first book provides complete documentation for all classes in the `java.io`, `java.lang`, `java.net`, `java.text`, and `java.util` packages and includes many instructive code examples. The second book provides documentation and a tutorial on constructing GUIs using the `javax.swing` package of classes.

The general syntax of the `print()` method is

```
objectName.print(data);
```

The *objectName* to the left of the required period identifies the object to which the display will be sent, and the name to the right of the period identifies the method, which in this case is `print()`. Any data that are to be displayed by this method must be enclosed in the parentheses following the method's name.

For example, if the data `Hello World!` are passed to `print()`, these data will be displayed by the method. When the data consist of characters, as they do in this example, they are also referred to as a *string*, which is short for string of characters. Sending data to a method is formally referred to as passing data to the method. A string, such as `Hello World!`, is passed to the `print()` method by enclosing the string in double quotation marks and placing it inside the parentheses following the method's name as follows:

```
System.out.print("Hello World!");
```

In this statement, `out` is the name of an object that is automatically created from a Java class named `System` whenever a Java program is executed. Specifically, the `out` object is referred to as the **standard output stream**, which, for most systems, connects your program's output to a video monitor. The combined term `System.out` thus uniquely identifies an object that effectively lets the `print()` method know where to display its data. Because there are a number of areas where the string could be printed, such as the video monitor, a printer, or a file, the `print()` method must be given the name of the object to which we want the output displayed. The additional period between the object's name, `System.out`, and the `print()` method's name is required.

The parentheses after the method's name provide a means by which information can be passed to the method (Figure 1.20). This is true for all methods that we will encounter and is not restricted to the `print()` methods. The items that are passed to

FIGURE 1.20   **Passing a string to `print()`**

```
System.out.print("Hello World!");
```

a method through the parentheses are referred to as **parameters**, **actual arguments**, and **arguments** (the terms are synonymous). Although these terms are used interchangeably, we will generally refer to a piece of data that is passed into a method as an argument. Now we can put all this together into a working Java program that can be run on your computer. Consider QuickTest Program 1.1.

QuickTest Program 1.1

```
// File: DisplayHelloWorld.java
// Description: Displays Hello World!
// Programmer: G. Bronson
// Date: 9/3/03

public class DisplayHelloWorld
{
  public static void main(String[] args)
  {
    System.out.print("Hello World!");
  }    // end of main() method
} // end of class
```

The first four lines of program code, each of which begins with two slash symbols, //, are comments. We will have much more to say about comments in the next section, but for now it is important to understand that each source code program should begin with comments similar to those used here. These initial comment lines, at a minimum, should provide the file name under which the source code is saved, a short program description, the name of the programmer, and the date that the program was last modified. For all of the programs contained in this text, the file name refers to the name of the source code file that is provided with this text. Notice that this name is the same as the class name (line 6, counting the blank line) plus the extension .java, which is a requirement of Java.

Lines 6 (counting the blank) through 12 of the program is the basic QuickTest class structure presented in the previous section. Line 6, by itself, is the header line for the class. Internal to the class is a single method named `main()`, which every executable Java program must have. The `main()` method begins with the header line developed in the previous section, and the body of the method, enclosed in braces, consists of a single statement, which ends with a required semicolon. This statement passes the string `"Hello World!"` to the `print()` method. Because `print()` is a method of the `PrintStream` class, which itself is one class provided by the `java.lang` package, and this package of classes is automatically made available to us in every Java program that we write, we can use it just by activating it correctly, as is done in QuickTest Program 1.1.

In general, a string can consist of any number of letters, numbers, and special characters enclosed in double quotation marks (`"string in here"`). The double quotation marks are used to delimit (mark) the beginning and ending of the string and are not considered part of the string.

PROGRAMMING NOTE

The System *Class*

Java's System class provides a number of methods for examining system-related information, such as the name of the operating system and the Java version number, and for changing system-related information, such as a user's home directory. Additionally, and more important for our immediate purposes, this class also supports basic input and output services. In this regard, it provides a means of sending data from a program to a standard output device, which is usually a video screen. This connection is accomplished by an object named out, which is uniquely identified using the name System.out.

As you might expect, the System class also provides a means of sending data from a standard input device into a program. This standard device is typically a keyboard, and the connection is accomplished by an object named in. The use of the System.in object is presented in Chapter 4.

We can write another program to illustrate print()'s versatility. Read QuickTest Program 1.2 to determine what it does.

QuickTest Program 1.2

```
// File: DisplayTwoLines.java
// Description: Test program
// Programmer: G. Bronson
// Date: 9/3/03

public class DisplayTwoLines
{
  public static void main(String[] args)
  {
    System.out.print("Computers, computers everywhere");
    System.out.print("\n as far as I can see");
  }
}
```

When QuickTest Program 1.2 is run, the following is displayed:

```
Computers, computers everywhere
 as far as I can see
```

You might be wondering why the \n did not appear in the output. The two characters \ and n, when used together, are called a **newline escape sequence**. They tell print() to send instructions to the display device to move to a new line. In Java, the backslash (\) character provides an "escape" from the normal interpretation of the character following it by altering the meaning of the next character. If the backslash was omitted from the second print statement in QuickTest Program 1.2, the n would be printed as the letter n and the program would print

```
Computers, computers everywheren as far as I can see
```

Newline escape sequences can be placed anywhere within the message passed to print. See if you can determine the display produced by QuickTest Program 1.3.

QuickTest Program 1.3

```java
// File: ShowEscapeSequences.java
// Description: Test program
// Programmer: G. Bronson
// Date: 9/3/03

public class ShowEscapeSequences
{
  public static void main(String[] args)
  {
    System.out.print("Computers, computers everywhere\n as far as\n\nI can see");
  }
}
```

The output for QuickTest Program 1.3 is

```
Computers, computers everywhere
 as far as

I can see
```

Very frequently, and especially in introductory and simple programs, you will want to display a single line of text followed by a new line. In these situations, use the printn() method, which automatically appends a newline character to the end of the displayed data. Thus, the statement

```java
System.out.println("This is a test.");
```

produces the same display the statement

```java
System.out.print("This is a test.\n");
```

You might be wondering why, if the printn() method automatically prints a line and places the cursor at the start of the next line, you would ever need the print() method. The reason is that many programming situations will force you to assemble parts of a single line in sections as the data to be displayed become available. It is this fine control over the construction of a line that ultimately makes the print() method so valuable. For simple single-line messages, however, the println() method can be used more conveniently. Finally, it should be noted that you can also include newline characters within a println() method; the only advantage of using println() is that it automatically provides a newline character at the end of its output.

Exercises 1.4

1.   Enter and run QuickTest Program 1.1 on your computer.

2.   Enter and run QuickTest Program 1.2 on your computer.

3a.   Using print(), write a Java program that displays your name on one line, your street address on the second line, and your city, state, and zip code on the third line.

  b. Run the program you have written for Exercise 3a on your computer.

4a. Write a Java program to display the following verse:

```
Computers, computers everywhere
  as far as I can see
I really, really like these things,
  Oh joy, Oh joy for me!
```

b. Run the program you have written for Exercise 4a on your computer.

5a. What is the minimum number of print() methods you would need to display the following?

```
PART NO.   PRICE
T1267      $6.34
T1300      $8.92
T2401      $65.40
T4482      $36.99
```

b. What is the minimum number of println() method calls needed to display the table in Exercise 5a?

c. What is the preferable number of either print() or println() methods you would use to display the table in Exercise 5a?

d. Write a complete Java program to produce the output in Exercise 5a.

e. Run the program you have written for Exercise 5d on your computer.

6. In response to a newline escape sequence, the position of the next displayed character is at the start of a new line. This positioning of the next character represents two distinct cursor positioning operations. What are they?

1.5 Using the javax.swing Package

A Java package, as noted in the previous section, consists of one or more individual classes that are stored in the same directory. As you might expect, classes that are packaged, or stored together, are related in some way.[7] For the **Swing package**, the classes provide a convenient means of specifying a fully functional graphical user interface (GUI) with typical window components such as check boxes, data entry fields, command buttons, and dialogs. The first swing component that we will discuss is a dialog. In GUI terminology, a **dialog** is a box that can present a user with information, but it always requests some type of input or response from the user.

There are two types of dialog boxes. In one type, referred to as a *modal* box, the user must respond to the dialog and close it before the application displaying the dialog can continue. The second type of dialog is a *modeless* box, which means that an application can continue without requiring a user to first close the dialog box.

The Swing class named JOptionPane provides a method for creating dialog boxes named showMessageDialog(). All of the dialog the boxes illustrated in Figure 1.21 were created with the showMessageDialog() method.

The hierarchy diagram for the JOptionPane class is shown in Figure 1.22. As indicated, the JOptionPane class is in the javax.swing package.

---

[7] See Appendix F for a more complete description of packages.

FIGURE 1.21 `showMessageDialog()` dialog boxes

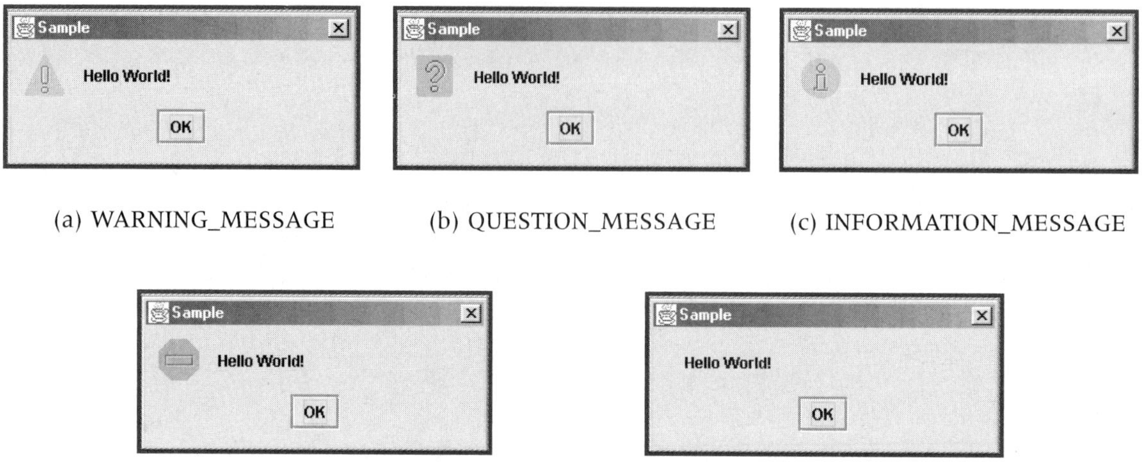

(a) WARNING_MESSAGE (b) QUESTION_MESSAGE (c) INFORMATION_MESSAGE

(d) ERROR_MESSAGE (e) PLAIN_MESSAGE

For our particular needs, the general syntax for a `showMessageDialog()` method call is:

```
JOptionPane.showMessageDialog(null,"message","title",icon-type);
```

Although this method call has the same form as the `messageOne.displayMessage()` statement used in QuickTest Program 1.1, it is actually quite different. Here, as indicated by its initial capital letter, the identifier `JOptionPane` is the name of a Java class and not the name of a specific object. The Programming Note on page 39 explains why a class name rather than an object name is used. For now, however, we can use this syntax to create a dialog.

The `showDialogMessage()` method creates a dialog based on the four arguments it is given when the method is called. The first argument, which we will always specify as null, is a positioning argument that causes the dialog to be centered within the window in which the Java program is being run. The second argument is the message that will be displayed in the dialog, and the third argument is the title that is displayed at the top of the dialog. These two arguments must be strings, which is short for a string of characters. A string, such as `Hello World!`, is passed to the `showMessageDialog()` method by enclosing the string in double quotation marks and placing it inside the parentheses in the correct position within the list of four arguments.

The last argument defines the icon that will be displayed within the dialog. Table 1.4 lists the five icon types that we will be using throughout the text.

FIGURE 1.22 `JOptionPane` class's hierarchy diagram

```
javax.swing.JComponent
     |
     +--javax.swing.JOptionPane
```

Table 1.4   **showMessageDialog()** Icon Types

Type	Icon	Example
WARNING_MESSAGE	An exclamation point within a triangle	Figure 1.21a
QUESTION_MESSAGE	A question mark within a box	Figure 1.21b
INFORMATION_MESSAGE	The letter i within a circle	Figure 1.21c
ERROR_MESSAGE	A hyphen within a stop sign	Figure 1.21d
PLAIN_MESSAGE	No icon	Figure 1.21e

For example, the statement:

```
JOptionPane.ShowMessageDialog(null,"Hello World!", "Sample", JOptionPane.WARNING_MESSAGE);
```

produced the dialog box in Figure 1.21a. Notice that the message Hello World! is included within the dialog box, and the title at the top of the box is Sample. The exclamation icon included within the box is produced by the WARNING_MESSAGE icon-type designation in the statement. (WARNING_MESSAGE is a symbolic constant provided by Java, which is described in detail in Section 3.3.) The icons in Figures 1.21b through 1.21e were produced using the QUESTION_MESSAGE, INFORMATION_MESSAGE, ERROR_MESSAGE, and PLAIN_MESSAGE icon types, respectively. That is, Figure 1.21b was produced by the statement

```
JOptionPane.showMessageDialog(null,"Hello World!", "Sample", JOptionPane.QUESTION_MESSAGE);
```

It should be noted that this statement, as with all Java statements, can spread over multiple lines. The only requirement in doing so is that the method's name and any enclosed strings are not split between lines. Thus, the preceding statement can be written as

```
JOptionPane.showMessageDialog(null,"Hello World!",
            "Sample", JOptionPane.QUESTION_MESSAGE);
```

Because of the length of a statement that uses showMessageDialog(), you will usually see it split across two or more lines.

In the case of the dialog boxes in Figure 1.21, the required input from the user is either clicking the OK button, pressing the Enter or Escape (Esc) key, or clicking the Close button at the top of the dialog. Because all dialogs produced by the showMessageDialog() method are modal, a user must close the dialog before any further program execution can continue.

QuickTest Program 1.4 incorporates the showMessageDialog() that produced Figure 1.21a within the context of the basic program structure provided in Section 1.3 (Figure 1.19). Although the structure of this program should be familiar, there are a number of new items that you should notice.

First, because we are using a class from the Swing package, in this case JOption-Pane, we need to tell the program in which package this class can be found. This information is provided by the import statement (line 6, counting the blank line). When the name JOptionPane is encountered, the compiler will first search a package named java.lang, which is a default package provided to all Java programs without the need for an explicit import statement. Not finding the named class in this package, the search for the class will continue with an explicitly named package provided by an `import` statement, which in this case specifies the `javax.swing` package of classes (be careful to note that the package name begins with `javax` and not `java`). Within this package, the compiler will locate the `showMessageDialog()` method contained within the `JOptionPane` class. The asterisk, `*`, in the `import` statement tells the compiler to search all classes in the package, no matter where the classes are located within the package.

The body of the `main()` method consists of two statements, one of which is a call to the `showMessageDialog()` method to create the dialog box in Figure 1.21a. The second statement is a `System.exit()` method that forces a closure of the program after the dialog box is closed by the user. Without the `System.exit()`, the underlying Java program, even though it is not doing anything, would still be active after the user closed the dialog box. Although the reason for this is presented in Chapter 12, where GUIs are discussed in detail, for now we will always use a `System.exit()` method whenever our application creates a graphical user interface, such as the dialog produced by QuickTest Program 1.4.

QuickTest Program 1.4

```java
// File: DisplayADialog.java
// Description: Construction of a dialog
// Programmer: G. Bronson
// Date: 9/3/03

import javax.swing.*;
public class DisplayADialog
{
  public static void main (String[] args)
  {
    JOptionPane.showMessageDialog(null,"Hello World!",
          "Sample",JOptionPane.WARNING_MESSAGE);

    System.exit(0);
  }
}
```

Both the message and title displayed in a dialog must be strings. Although the title string must reside on a single line, the message string follows the same rules as the strings displayed by the `print()` and `println()` methods. This means that newline escape sequences can be included within the message. For example, consider Quick-Test Program 1.5, which displays the same string as previously displayed by QuickTest Program 1.3, but now the display is contained within a dialog box (Figure 1.21a). The only difference in the displayed string is that the default font used in a dialog is proportionately spaced Times Roman rather than the fixed-spaced Courier font used in character-based output.

```java
// File: MultiLineDialog.java
// Description: Construction of a multi-line dialog
// Programmer: G. Bronson
// Date: 9/3/03

import javax.swing.*;
public class MultiLineDialog
```

PROGRAMMING NOTE

Static and *non-static* Methods

Every method that you use in Java is contained within a class in the same manner as a main() method. However, within a class, there can be two fundamentally different types of methods.

Methods that must be used with objects are referred to as *non-static methods*. Two examples of non-static methods are println() and displayMessage() that were used in Section 1.3. Non-static methods are generally used with the syntax

```
objectName.methodName(arguments);
```

An example of this syntax is messageOne.displayMessage(); that was used in QuickTest Program 1.1. In this example, the object's name is messageOne and the method's name is displayMessage. Because no arguments are used, the parentheses following the method's name are empty. Although non-static methods are restricted to operating on objects, they can be accessed from outside the class they are written in if their header line includes the word public, as is the case with the displayMessage() method.

The second type of method is referred to as a static method. A *static method* is one that *does not* operate on an object but receives all of its data as arguments. As with a non-static method, if a static method's header line includes the word public, the method can be called from outside its own class. In such a case, the method is referred to as a *general-purpose method*. This implies that the method is constructed to perform a general-purpose task that can be useful in a number of places, such as constructing a dialog or computing the square root of a number. An example of such a method is showMessageDialog(), which uses its arguments to position and display a dialog box from within any method that uses it.

In using a general-purpose method outside its class, however, you must indicate where the method is to be found. This is accomplished by listing its class name before the method's name using the syntax

```
ClassName.methodName(arguments);
```

Operationally, the syntax for both non-static and general-purpose methods looks the same in that both precede the method's name with a period and either an object and/or class name. For now, use each method as it is given in the text. In each case, whenever a new method is presented, we will indicate whether it is a static or non-static method, although you can usually figure this out yourself by noticing if the initial letter of the first identifier is capitalized or not.

QuickTest Program 1.5

```
{
  public static void main (String[] args)
  {
    JOptionPane.showMessageDialog(null,
            "Computers, computers everywhere\n  as far as\n\nI can see",
            "Sample", JOptionPane.WARNING_MESSAGE);

    System.exit(0);
  }
}
```

FIGURE 1.23   **The dialog produced by QuickTest Program 1.5**

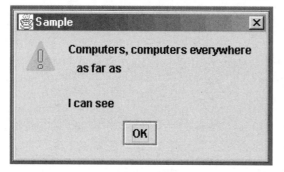

The dialog created by QuickTest Program 1.5 is illustrated in Figure 1.23. As seen in this display, a new line is started for the characters as far as, which is then followed by two new lines (giving the output a double-spaced look) followed by the last line of characters.

Exercises 1.5

1.   Enter and run QuickTest Program 1.4 on your computer.

2a.   Modify QuickTest Program 1.4 to produce the output shown in Figure 1.21c.

b.   Modify QuickTest Program 1.4 to produce the output shown in Figure 1.21e.

3.   Write and run a Java program that displays your name on one line, your street address on a second line, and your city, state, and zip code on the third line within a dialog box that uses an information icon.

4.   Write and run a Java program that displays the following verse in a dialog box that uses a warning icon:

```
Computers, computers everywhere
   as far as I can see
I really, really like these things,
   Oh joy, Oh joy for me!
```

5.   Write and run a Java program that displays the following data in a dialog box that does not display any icon.

```
Part No.        Price
T1267           $6.34
T1300           $8.92
```

6.   Write and run a Java program that displays the following data in a dialog box that does not display any icon.

```
Degrees     Radians
0           0.0000
180         3.1416
360         6.2832
```

1.6 **Programming Style**

Because each executable Java program starts execution at the beginning of a main() method, you must include a main() method in a Java class if you want to run a Java program. As we have seen, all of the statements that make up the main() method are included within the braces { } following the method's name. Although the main() method must be present in every Java program, Java does not require that the word main, the parentheses (), or the braces { } be placed in any particular form. The form used in the last section

```
public static void main(String[] args)
{
    program statements in here;
}
```

was chosen strictly for clarity and ease in reading the program. For example, the following general form of a main() method also works:

```
public static void main
(String[] args
) {first statement;second statement;
          third statement;fourth
statement;
}
```

Notice that more than one statement can be put on a line, or one statement can be written across lines. Except for strings, double quotation marks, identifiers, and reserved words, Java ignores all whitespace (whitespace refers to any combination of one or more blank spaces, tabs, or new lines). For example, changing the whitespace in QuickTest Program 1.1 while making sure not to split the string Hello World! across two lines and omitting all comments results in the following valid program:

```
public class DisplayHelloWorld
{
  public static void main
(String[] args
){System.out.print(
"Hello World!");
}}
```

Although this version of main() will work, it is an example of extremely poor programming style. It is difficult to read and understand. For readability, we will always write the main() method in the following form:

```
public static void main(String[] args)
{
    program statements in here;
}
```

In this form, the method header line starts in column 1 and is placed with the required parentheses on a line by itself. The opening brace of the method body follows on the next line and is placed under the first letter of the line containing the method name. Similarly, the closing method brace is placed by itself in column 1 as the last line of the method. This structure serves to highlight the method as a single unit. This same structure should also be used by the class within which it is located.

Within the method itself, all program statements are indented at least two spaces. Indentation is another sign of good programming practice, especially if the same indentation is used for similar groups of statements. Review QuickTest Programs 1.1 through 1.5 to see that a consistent type of indentation was used for all programs.

As you progress in your understanding and mastery of Java, you will develop your own indentation standards. Just keep in mind that the final form of your programs should be consistent and should always serve as an aid to the reading and understanding of your programs.

Comments

Comments are explanatory remarks made within a program. When used carefully, comments can be very helpful in clarifying what the complete program is about, what a specific group of statements is meant to accomplish, or what one line is intended to do. Java supports two types of comments: line and block.[8] Both types of comments can be placed anywhere within a program and have no effect on program execution. The compiler ignores all comments; they are strictly for the convenience of anyone reading the program.

A line comment begins with two slashes (//) and continues to the end of the line. For example, each of the following is a line comment:

```
// this is a comment
// this program prints out a message
// this program calculates a square root
```

The symbols //, with no whitespace between them, designate the start of the line comment. The end of the line on which the comment is written designates the end of the comment.

A line comment can be written either on a line by itself or at the end of a line containing a program statement. When a comment is too long to fit on one line, two solutions are possible. First, the comment can be separated into two or more line comments, with each separate comment preceded by the double slash symbol. For example, the comment

```
// this comment is invalid because it
   extends over two lines
```

results in a Java error message when compiled. This comment is correct when written as

```
// this comment is used to illustrate a
// comment that extends across two lines
```

Comments that span across two or more lines are, however, more conveniently written as block comments rather than as multiple single-line comments. Block comments begin with the symbols /* and end with the symbols */. For example,

---

[8] A third type of comment, referred to as a document comment, begins with the character sequence /** and ends with the sequence */. These are used to create HTML documents using the javadoc program.

```
/* This is a block comment that
   spans
   across three lines */
```

Frequently, you may see a block comment written as follows:

```
/* This is a block comment that
 * spans
 * across three lines
 */
```

In this style, the extra asterisks, *, are inserted to highlight the comment block. Note, however, that it is only the beginning (/*) and ending (*/) pairs that actually delimit (i.e., mark) the comment. All of the characters within these delimiters constitute part of the comment itself.

In Java, a program's structure is intended to make the program readable and understandable, making the use of extensive comments unnecessary. This is reinforced if method, class, and variable names, which are described in the next chapter, are carefully selected to convey their meaning to anyone reading the program. However, if the purpose of a method, class, or statement is still not clear from its structure, name, or context, include comments where clarification is needed. Obscure code with no comments is a sure sign of bad programming. Excessive comments are also a sign of bad programming because they imply that insufficient thought was given to having the code itself be self-explanatory.

Typically, any program that you write should begin with a set of initial program comments that includes a short program description, your name, and the date that the program was last modified. For space considerations, and because all programs in this text were written by the author, initial comments will only be used for short program descriptions when they are not provided as part of the accompanying text.

Exercises 1.6

1a. Does the following program work?

```
public class TestIt
{
  public static void main(String[] args)
  {System.out.println("Hello World!"); }}
```

 b. Why is the program in Exercise 1a not a good one?

 2. Rewrite the following programs to conform to good programming practice.

 a.
```
public class TestIt
{
 public static void main(String[] args)
 {
   System.out.println(
   "The time has come")
  ; }
}
```

b.
```
public class TestIt
{
 public static void main
(String[] args)
{System.out.println("Newark is a city");System.out.println(
 "in New Jersey"); System.out.println(
 "It is also a city")
; System.out.println("in Delaware")
; }
}
```

c.
```
public class TestIt
{
  public static void main
 (String[] args)
 {System.out.println("Reading a program");System.out.println(
       " is much easier")
        ;System.out.println(" if a standard form for main is used")
        ;System.out.println(" and each statement is written")
     ;System.out.println(" on a line by itself.")
        ; }
}
```

d.
```
public class TestIt
{
  public static void main
 (String[] args) {System.out.println("Every Java application"
);System.out.println
("must have one and only one"
);
System.out.println("main() method."
);
System.out.println(
"The escape sequence of characters"
);System.out.println(
"for a newline can be placed anywhere"
);System.out.println
("within the message passed to System.out.println"
); }
}
```

1.7 Common Programming Errors

Part of learning any programming language is making the elementary mistakes commonly encountered as you begin to work with the language. These mistakes tend to be frustrating because each language has its own set of common programming errors waiting for the unwary. The more common errors made when initially programming in Java are:

1. Rushing to write and run a program before fully understanding what is required, including the classes needed to produce the desired result. A symptom of this haste to get a program entered into the computer is the lack of any documentation or even a program outline.

2. Forgetting to make a backup copy of all classes. Almost all new programmers make this mistake until they lose a class that has taken considerable time to code.

3. Failing to understand that computers respond only to explicitly defined instructions. Telling a computer to add a group of numbers is quite different from telling a friend to add the numbers. The computer must be given the precise instructions for doing the addition in a programming language.

4. Forgetting to save a program with the same file name as the class name used within the program.

5. Forgetting to save a program with a `.java` extension.

6. Omitting the parentheses after `main`.

7. Omitting or incorrectly typing the opening brace { that signifies the start of a class or the start of a method body.

8. Omitting or incorrectly typing the closing brace } that signifies the end of a class or the end of a method body.

9. Misspelling the name of an object or method; for example, typing `pint()` instead of `print()`.

10. Forgetting to type the complete name of the `print()` and `println()` methods as `System.out.print()` and `System.out.println()`, respectively.

11. Forgetting to close a string with a double quotation mark.

12. Forgetting to separate individual data items sent to the `showMessage()`, `print()`, and `println()` methods with the concatenation, +, symbol.

13. Omitting the semicolon at the end of each statement.

14. Forgetting the `\n` to indicate a new line.

15. Misspelling the term `javax.swing` as `java.swing` when importing the Swing package.

16. Not using a `System.exit(0)` to end a program when creating a dialog-based application.

All of these errors, except for errors 14 and 16, result in a compiler error message. Our experience is that errors 4, 13, and 14 tend to be the most common. We suggest that you write a program and specifically introduce each of these errors, one at a time, to see what error messages are produced by your compiler. Then, when these error messages appear due to inadvertent errors, you will have had experience in understanding the messages and correcting the errors.

1.8 Chapter Review

KEY TERMS

application software	coding	escape sequence
assembler	compiler	hardware
assembly language	data declaration section	high-level language
class	dialog box	identifier

interpreter	package	reserved word
low-level language	`print()`	software
machine language	`println()`	software engineering
methods section	procedure-oriented	standard identifier
newline escape sequence	language	Swing package
object	programming	System class
object-oriented language	programming language	system software

SUMMARY

1. Computer science is a discipline that is concerned with the science of computers and computing.

2. The programs used to operate a computer are referred to as software.

3. Programming languages come in a variety of forms and types. Machine language programs, also known as executable programs, contain the binary codes that can be executed by a computer. Assembly languages permit the use of symbolic names for mathematical operations and memory addresses. Programs written in assembly languages must be converted to machine language, using translator programs called assemblers, before the programs can be executed. Assembly and machine languages are referred to as low-level languages.

   Compiled and interpreted languages are referred to as high-level languages. This means that they are written using instructions that resemble a written language, such as English, and can be run on a variety of computer types. Compiled languages require a compiler to translate the program into a binary language form, and interpreted languages require an interpreter to do the translation.

4. Java is unique in that it uses two translator programs. The first translation uses a compiler that produces a generic output that can then be executed using an interpreter. The interpreter is always located on the machine that will ultimately execute the program.

5. In a procedure-oriented language, programs are constructed using self-contained units referred to as procedures. The purpose of a procedure is to accept data as input and transform the data in some manner to produce a specific result as an output.

6. In an object-oriented language, the basic program unit is a class.

7. A class is effectively a plan, consisting of data and instructions, out of which individual programming objects can be created and manipulated. The data items for the class are declared in a class data declaration section while the instructions are contained within class methods.

8. All Java classes use the basic structure consisting of a class header line and a class body as follows:

```
Class header line  ----> public class ShowFirstMessage
                   ------>{
      Class's body |            // data declaration section
                   |              data declarations statements in here
                   |            // method definition section
                   |              method definitions in here
                   ------> }
```

9. A reserved word is a word that is predefined by the programming language for a special purpose and can only be used in a specified manner for its intended purpose. Attempts to use reserved words for any other purpose will generate an error when the code is compiled.

10. Identifiers are programmer-supplied words that can be made up of any combination of letters, digits, underscores (_), or dollar signs ($) selected according to the following rules:

    a. The first character of an identifier cannot be a digit.

    b. Only letters (both uppercase and lowercase), digits, underscores, and dollar signs may follow the initial character. Blank spaces are not allowed.

    c. An identifier cannot be a reserved word.

    d. The maximum number of characters in an identifier name is unlimited.

11. All Java programs must contain at least one class.

12. A Java program must have a `main()` method as one of its class methods. The general syntax of this method is

```
public static main(String[] args)
{
    java statements in here
}
```

13. The `PrintStream` class provides two methods, `print()` and `println()`, that are used to display text and numerical results. The argument to these methods can be a string of characters enclosed in double quotation marks. This string, which may also include escape sequences, such as the newline escape sequence, `\n`, is subsequently displayed within the window in which the Java program is executing. The `println()` method automatically provides a final newline escape sequence. Both `print()` and `println()`, when they are used to send a string to the standard output device connected to your program, which is typically the video screen, operate on the `System.out` object.

14. A Java package consists of one or more individual classes stored in the same directory. This permits classes that are related in some way to be packaged, or stored together. It also provides a way to restrict the compiler's search for classes used in the program using an `import` statement.

15. The Swing package of classes, which can be used to create fully functional graphical user interfaces (GUIs), is named `javax.swing`. To use the classes in the Swing package, place the following statement at the top of your Java program: `import javax.swing.*;`

16. Along with the `javax.swing` package of classes, many other packages are provided with each Java compiler. One such set of classes, which provides language support and basic system services, is defined in the `java.lang` package. Both the `print()` and `println()` methods are part of the `PrintStream` class, which is contained in the `java.io` package of classes. As this package of classes is automatically searched by the compiler, an `import` statement for this package is not explicitly required.

17. Dialog boxes can be created using the `showMessageDialog()` method, which is provided by the `JOptionPane` class. This class is contained in the `javax.swing`

A BIT OF BACKGROUND

Binary ABC

Dr. John V. Atanasoff agonized several years over the design of a computing machine to help his Iowa State University graduate students solve complex equations. He considered building a machine based on binary numbers—the most natural system to use with electromechanical equipment that had one of two easily recognizable states, on and off—but feared people would not use a machine that was not based upon the familiar and comfortable decimal system. Finally, on a cold evening at a roadhouse in Illinois in 1937, he determined that it had to be done the simplest and least expensive way, with binary digits (bits). Over the next two years, he and graduate student Clifford Berry built the first electronic digital computer, called the ABC (for Atanasoff-Berry Computer). Since that time, the vast majority of computers have been binary machines.

package, and thus, a Java program that creates a dialog box must import the `javax.swing` package of classes. The general syntax of a `showMessageDialog()` method call is

```
JOptionPane.showMessageDialog(null,"message","title",icon-type)
```

where `message` is a string that is displayed within the dialog box, `title` is a string that is displayed in the title bar of the dialog box, and `icon-type` is one of the following (see Table 1.4 for a description of each type):

```
JOptionPane.WARNING_MESSAGE
JOptionPane.QUESTION_MESSAGE
JOptionPane.INFORMATION_MESSAGE
JOptionPane.ERROR_MESSAGE
JOptionPane.PLAIN_MESSAGE
```

18. A `main()` method that creates a dialog box should end with a `System.exit(0)` statement.

19. The physical components used in constructing a computer are called its hardware. These components include input, processing, output, memory, and storage units.

1.9 Chapter Supplement: Computer Hardware

This section presents the evolution of the computer, the physical hardware units of modern computers, and the binary number system used internally by this hardware.

History

The first recorded attempt at creating a programmable computing machine was by Charles Babbage, in England, in 1822 (Figure 1.24). The set of instructions to be

FIGURE 1.24   **Charles Babbage's Analytical Engine**

Courtesy Charles Babbage Institute, U. of Minnesota

input to this machine, which Babbage called the Analytical Engine, was developed by Ada Byron, the daughter of poet Lord Byron. Although Babbage's machine was not successfully built in his lifetime, the concept developed by him remained. It was partly realized in 1937 at Iowa State University by Dr. John V. Atanasoff and graduate student Clifford Berry. The machine was known as the ABC, which stood for Atanasoff-Berry Computer. This computer manipulated binary numbers but required external wiring of the machine to perform the desired operations. Thus, the goal of internally storing a replaceable set of instructions had still not been achieved.

Due to the impetus provided by the impending outbreak of World War II, a more concentrated development of the computer began in late 1939. One of the pioneers of this work was Dr. John W. Mauchly of the Moore School of Engineering of the University of Pennsylvania. Dr. Mauchly, who had visited Dr. Atanasoff, began working with J. Presper Eckert in 1939 on a computer called ENIAC (for Electrical Numerical Integrator and Computer) (Figure 1.25). Funding for this project was provided by the U.S. government, and one of the early functions performed by this machine was the calculation of trajectories for ammunition fired from large guns. When completed in 1946, ENIAC contained 18,000 vacuum tubes, weighed approximately 30 tons, and could perform 5,000 additions or 360 multiplications in one second.

While work was progressing on ENIAC using vacuum tubes, work on a computer named the Mark I was under way at Harvard University using mechanical relay switches (Figure 1.26). The Mark I was completed in 1944 but could only perform six multiplications in one second. Both of these machines, however, like the Atanasoff-Berry Computer required external wiring to perform the desired operations.

A BIT OF BACKGROUND

The Turing Machine

In the 1930s and 1940s, Alan Mathison Turing (1912–1954) and others developed the theory of what a computing machine should be able to do. Turing invented a theoretical, pencil-and-paper machine, which is referred to as the Turing machine, that contains the minimum set of operations for solving programming problems. Turing had hoped to prove that all problems could be solved by a set of instructions to such a hypothetical computer.

What he succeeded in proving was that some problems cannot be solved by *any* machine, just as some problems cannot be solved by any person.

Alan Turing's work formed the foundation of computer theory before the first electronic computer was built. His contributions to the team that developed the critical code-breaking computers during World War II led directly to the practical implementation of his theories.

FIGURE 1.25   ENIAC

Courtesy IBM archives

FIGURE 1.26   **The Mark I**

Courtesy IBM archives

The final goal of a stored program computer was achieved at Cambridge University in England with the design of the EDSAC (Electronic Delayed Storage Automatic Computer) computer. In addition to performing calculations, the EDSAC permitted storage of instructions that directed the computer's operation. The means of using the computer's memory to store both instructions and data, and the design to accomplish this so that the computer first retrieved an instruction and then the data needed by the instruction, was developed by John von Neumann. This same design and operating principle are still used by the majority of computers manufactured today. The only things that have significantly changed are the size and speeds of the components used to make a computer and the type of programs that are stored internal to it. Collectively, the components used to make a computer are referred to as **hardware**, and the programs are known as **software**.

Computer Hardware

All computers, from large supercomputers costing millions of dollars to smaller desktop personal computers, must perform a minimum set of functions and provide the capability to

1. Accept input
2. Display output
3. Store information in a logically consistent format (traditionally, binary)
4. Perform arithmetic and logic operations on either the input or stored data
5. Monitor, control, and direct the overall operation and sequencing of the system

FIGURE 1.27   **Basic hardware units of a computer**

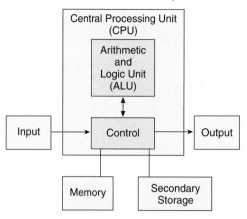

Figure 1.27 illustrates the computer components that support these capabilities. These physical components are collectively referred to as hardware.

Memory Unit

This unit stores information in a logically consistent format. Typically, both instructions and data are stored in memory, usually in separate and distinct areas. Each computer contains memory of two fundamental types: RAM and ROM. *RAM*, which is an acronym for *random access memory*, is usually volatile, which means that whatever is stored there is lost when the computer's power is turned off. Your programs and data are stored in RAM while you are using the computer. The size of a computer's RAM memory is usually specified in terms of how many bytes of RAM are available to the user. Personal computer (PC) memories currently consist of from 32 to 56 million bytes (denoted as megabytes, or MB).

ROM, which is an acronym for *read-only memory*, contains fundamental instructions that cannot be lost or changed by the casual computer user. These instructions include those necessary for loading anything else into the machine when it is first turned on and any other instructions the manufacturer requires to be permanently accessible when the computer is turned on. ROM is nonvolatile; its contents are not lost when the power goes off.

Control Unit

The control unit directs and monitors the overall operation of the computer. It keeps track of where in memory the next instruction resides, issues the signals needed to both read data from and write data to other units in the system, and executes all instructions.

Arithmetic Logic Unit (ALU)

The ALU performs all the arithmetic and logic functions, such as addition, subtraction, comparison, and so forth, provided by the system.

Input/Output (I/O) Unit

This unit provides access to and from the computer. It is the interface to which peripheral devices such as keyboards, cathode ray screens, and printers are attached.

Secondary Storage

Because RAM memory in large quantities is still relatively expensive and volatile, it is not practical as a permanent storage area for programs and data. Secondary or auxiliary storage devices are used for this purpose. Although data have been stored on punched cards, paper tape, and other media in the past, virtually all secondary storage is now done on magnetic tape, magnetic disks, and optical storage media.

The surfaces of magnetic tapes and disks are coated with a material that can be magnetized by a write head, and the stored magnetic field can be detected by a read head. Current tapes are capable of storing thousands of characters per inch of tape, and a single tape may store up to hundreds of megabytes. Tapes, by nature, are sequential storage media, which means that they allow data to be written or read in one sequential stream from beginning to end. Should you desire access to a block of data in the middle of the tape, you must scan all preceding data on the tape to find the block of interest. Because of this, tapes are primarily used for mass backup of the data stored on large-capacity disk drives.

A more convenient method of rapidly accessing stored data is provided by a *direct access storage device (DASD)*, where any one file or program can be written or read independently of its position on the storage medium. The most popular DASD in recent years has been the magnetic disk. A *magnetic hard disk* consists of either a single rigid platter or several platters that spin together on a common spindle. A movable access arm positions the read/write heads over, but not quite touching, the recordable surfaces. Such a configuration is shown in Figure 1.28.

Initially, the most common magnetic disk storage device was the removable **floppy disk**. Currently, the most popular size for these is $3\frac{1}{2}$ inches in diameter, with a capacity of 1.44 megabytes (Figure 1.29). More recent removable disks known as ZIP™ disks have capacities of 250 megabytes, and gigabyte compact discs (CDs) are the current auxilliary storage devices of choice.[9]

A CD is an optical medium on which data are stored by using laser light to change the reflective surface properties of a single removable disc similar or identical to a video compact disc.

FIGURE 1.28   **The internal structure of a hard disk drive**

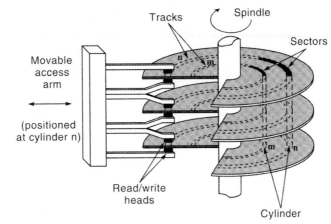

---

[9] One gigabyte equals 1,000 megabytes.

FIGURE 1.29 **Construction of a $3\frac{1}{2}$ Disk**

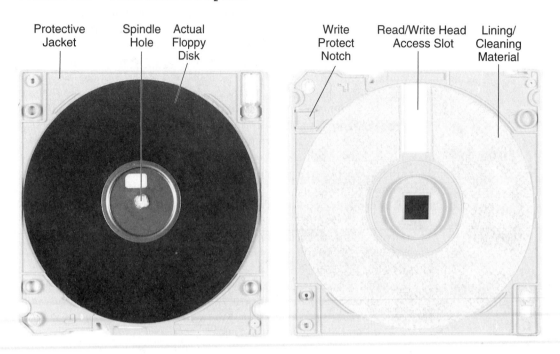

Protective Jacket | Spindle Hole | Actual Floppy Disk | Write Protect Notch | Read/Write Head Access Slot | Lining/ Cleaning Material

Hardware Evolution

In the first commercially available computers of the 1940s and 1950s, all hardware units except the secondary storage, which consisted of punched cards and paper tape, were built using relays and vacuum tubes. The resulting computers were extremely large pieces of equipment, capable of thousands of calculations per second, and costing millions of dollars (Figure 1.30).

With the commercial introduction of transistors in the 1960s, both the size and cost of computer hardware were reduced. The transistor was approximately one-twentieth the size of its vacuum tube counterpart, which allowed manufacturers to combine the arithmetic logic unit with the control unit into a single new unit. This combined unit was called the central processing unit (CPU). The combination of the ALU and control unit into one CPU made sense because a majority of control signals generated by a program are directed to the ALU in response to arithmetic and logic instructions within the program. Combining the ALU with the control unit simplified the interface between these two units and provided improved processing speed.

The mid-1960s saw the introduction of integrated circuits (ICs) that resulted in still another significant reduction in the space required to produce a CPU. Initially, integrated circuits were manufactured with up to 100 transistors on a single 1-cm^2 chip of silicon. Such devices are referred to as small-scale integrated (SSI) circuits. Current versions of these chips contain hundreds of thousands to over a million transistors and are referred to as very-large-scale integrated (VLSI) chips.

VLSI chip technology has provided the means of transforming the giant computers of the 1950s into today's desktop personal computers. Each individual unit

FIGURE 1.30   **An IBM 701 in 1952**

Courtesy IBM archives

required to form a computer (CPU, memory, and I/O) is now manufactured on individual VLSI chips, respectively, and the single-chip CPU is referred to as a *microprocessor*. Figure 1.31 illustrates the size and internal structure of a state-of-the-art VLSI microprocessor chip. The chip itself is in the center of the square on the right, and the cover for the package is on the left. Internally, the chip is connected with wires to the

FIGURE 1.31   **Internal picture of a Pentium® microprocessor chip**

Courtesy Intel

FIGURE 1.32   **VLSI chip connections for a desktop computer**

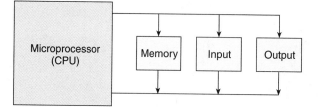

pins on the outside of the package. The insides of these pins appear as a series of silver dots in the square on the right side of the figure.

Figure 1.32 illustrates how the complete set of chips needed for a computer are put on boards and connected internally to create a computer, such as the early IBM personal computers of the 1980s (Figure 1.33) and more current notebook computers (Figure 1.34).

Concurrent with the remarkable reduction in computer hardware size has been an equally dramatic decrease in cost and increase in processing speeds. The equivalent computer hardware that cost over $1 million in 1950 can now be purchased for less than $500. If the same reductions occurred in the automobile industry, for example, a Rolls-Royce could now be purchased for $10! The processing speeds of current computers have also increased by a factor of 1,000 over their 1950s predecessors,

FIGURE 1.33   **An original (1980s) IBM personal computer**

Courtesy IBM Computer

FIGURE 1.34   **A current IBM notebook computer**

AP/Wide World Photos

with the computational speeds of current machines being measured in both millions of instructions per second (MIPS) and billions of instructions per second (BIPS).

Bits and Bytes

If computer hardware could use the same symbols that humans do, the number 126, for example, would be stored using the symbols 1, 2, and 6. Similarly, the letter that we recognize as A would be stored using this same symbol. Unfortunately, a computer's internal components require a different number and letter representation. In this section, we see why computers cannot use our symbols and then see how numbers are represented within the machine.

The smallest and most basic data item in a computer is a *bit*. Physically, a bit is really a switch that can be either open or closed. The convention we will follow is that the open and closed positions of each switch are represented as 0 and 1, respectively.[10]

A single bit that can represent the values 0 and 1, by itself, has limited usefulness. All computers, therefore, group a set number of bits together both for storage and transmission. The grouping of 8 bits to form a larger unit is an almost universal computer standard. Such groups are commonly referred to as bytes. A single byte consisting of 8 bits, where each bit is either 0 or 1, can represent any one of 256 distinct patterns. These consist of the pattern 00000000 (all eight switches open) to the pattern 11111111 (all eight switches closed) and all possible combinations of 0s and 1s in between. Each of these patterns can be used to represent either a letter of the alphabet, other single characters (a dollar sign, comma, etc.), a single digit, or numbers containing more than one digit. The collection of patterns consisting of 0s and 1s used to represent letters, single digits, and other single characters are called *character codes*

---

[10] This convention, unfortunately, is rather arbitrary, and you will frequently encounter the reverse correspondence where the open and closed positions are represented as 1 and 0, respectively.

(two such codes, called the ASCII and Unicode codes, are presented in Section 2.1). The patterns that store numbers are called *number codes*, one of which is presented at the end of this section.

Words and Addresses

One or more bytes may themselves be grouped into larger units, called *words*, which facilitate faster and more extensive data access. For example, retrieving a word consisting of 4 bytes from a computer's memory results in more information than that obtained by retrieving a word consisting of a single byte. Such a retrieval is also considerably faster than four individual byte retrievals. This increase in speed and capacity, however, is achieved by an increase in the computer's cost and complexity.

Early personal computers, such as the Apple IIe® and Commodore® machines, internally stored and transmitted words consisting of single bytes. The first IBM personal computers used word sizes consisting of 2 bytes, whereas more current Pentium-based PCs store and process words consisting of 4 bytes each.

The arrangement of words in a computer's memory can be compared to the arrangement of suites in a large hotel, where each suite is made up of rooms of the same size. Just as each suite has a unique room number so patrons can locate and identify it, each word has a unique numerical address. In computers that allow each byte to be individually accessed, each byte has its own address. Like room numbers, word and byte addresses are always unsigned whole numbers that are used for location and identification purposes. Also, like hotel rooms with connecting doors for forming larger suites, words can be combined to form larger units for the accommodation of different-size data types.

Two's Complement Numbers

The most common number code for storing integer values inside a computer is called the *two's complement* representation. Using this code, the integer equivalent of any bit pattern, such as 10001101, is easy to determine and can be found for either positive or negative integers with no change in the conversion method. For convenience, we will assume byte-size bit patterns consisting of a set of 8 bits each, although the procedure carries directly over to larger size bit patterns.

The easiest way to determine the integer represented by each bit pattern is first to construct a simple device called a value box. Figure 1.35 illustrates such a box for a single byte. Mathematically, each value in the box illustrated in Figure 1.35 represents an increasing power of 2. Since two's complement numbers must be capable of representing both positive and negative integers, the leftmost position, in addition to having the largest absolute magnitude, also has a negative sign.

Conversion of any binary number, for example 10001101, simply requires inserting the bit pattern in the value box and adding the values having 1s under them. Thus, as illustrated in Figure 1.36, the bit pattern 10001101 represents the integer number –115.

The value box can also be used in reverse to convert a base-10 integer number into its equivalent binary bit pattern. Some conversions, in fact, can be made by inspection. For example, the base-10 number –125 is obtained by adding 3 to –128. Thus, the binary representation of –125 is 10000011, which equals –128 + 2 + 1.

FIGURE 1.35   **An 8-bit value box**

```
-128| 64 | 32 | 16 | 8 | 4 | 2 | 1
----|----|----|----|----|----|----|---
    |    |    |    |    |    |    |
```

Similarly, the two's complement representation of the number 40 is 00101000, which is 32 + 8.

Although the value box conversion method is deceptively simple, the method is directly related to the underlying mathematical basis of two's complement binary numbers. The original name of the two's complement code was the weighted-sign code, which correlates directly to the value box. As the name *weighted sign* implies, each bit position has a weight, or value, of 2 raised to a power and a sign. The signs of all bits except the leftmost bit are positive, and the sign of the leftmost bit is negative.

In reviewing the value box, it is evident that any two's complement binary number with a leading 1 represents a negative number, and any bit pattern with a leading 0 represents a positive number. Using the value box, it is easy to determine the most positive and negative values capable of being stored. The most negative value that can be stored in a single byte is the decimal number –128, which has the bit pattern 10000000. Any other nonzero bit will simply add a positive amount to the number. Additionally, it is clear that a positive number must have a 0 as its leftmost bit. From this, you can see that the largest positive 8-bit two's complement number is 01111111, or 127.

FIGURE 1.36   **Converting 10001101 to a base-10 number**

```
-128 | 64 | 32 | 16 | 8 | 4 | 2 | 1
----|----|----|----|----|----|----|---
  1 | 0 | 0 | 0 | 1 | 1 | 0 | 1
-128 + 0 + 0 + 0 + 8 + 4 + 0 + 1 = -115
```

2 Creating Classes

Java programs process different types of data in different ways. For example, calculating the bacteria growth in a polluted pond requires mathematical operations on numerical data, whereas sorting a list of names requires comparison operations using alphabetical data. Java has two fundamental types of data known as primitive and reference types. In this chapter, we introduce Java's primitive data types and the operations that can be performed on them. Additionally, we present the proper use of class and method variables for storing both primitive and reference type data. We then show how to construct a completed class having both a data declaration and method definition section. Assignment operations, which are extremely important in constructing class methods, are introduced. Finally, we begin our introduction into object-oriented design and development by presenting a systematic procedure for identifying objects and constructing object-based models.

2.1 **Data Values and Arithmetic Operations**

Java stores and processes data as one of two general data types referred to as primitive and reference types. The **primitive data types**, which are also referred to as **built-in types**, are shown in Figure 2.1. **Reference types** are associated either with a class, an array, or an interface (Figure 2.2). As a practical observation, the operations provided for primitive types are only provided as arithmetic symbols, such as those for addition, subtraction, multiplication, and so on, whereas for reference types, the overwhelming majority of operations are provided as methods.

In this section, we introduce all eight primitive data types, which consist of the numerical types known as integers and floating-point numbers and the character and Boolean types. In addition, the string reference data type is described. We present the specific types of values, referred to as literals, that are associated with each of these data types. A **literal** is a value that explicitly identifies itself. For example, all numbers, such as 2, 3.6, and −8.2, are referred to in computer terminology as both literals and literal values because they literally display their values. A string such as "Hello World!" is also referred to as a literal string value because the string itself is displayed. You have been using literal values throughout your life and commonly refer to them as numbers and words. Later in this chapter, we will see examples of nonliteral values that do not display themselves but are stored in memory locations accessed by their names.

Integer Literals

An **integer literal**, which is more frequently referred to as either an integer value or simply an integer, is zero or any positive or negative numerical value without a decimal point. Examples of valid integer literals are

```
 0       5      -10     +25     1000     253     -26351     +36
```

FIGURE 2.1   **Primitive data types**

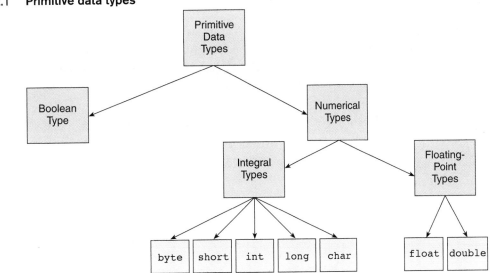

FIGURE 2.2   **Reference types**

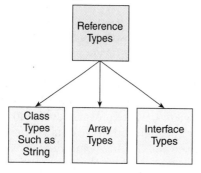

As these examples illustrate, integer literals may be signed (with a leading + or −
sign) or unsigned (with no leading + or − sign). No commas, decimal points, or special symbols, such as the dollar sign, are allowed. Examples of not valid integer literal
values are

```
$255.62    2,523    3.    6,243,892    1,492.89    +6.0
```

The Java language defines an integer data type as any integer value within the
range −2147483648 to +2147483647 that must be stored using 4 bytes (32 bits) in
two's complement form.[1] For cases in which larger integer values are required, Java
also defines a long integer data type. Long integer values, which are stored as 8-byte
two's complement numbers, must reside in the range −9223372036854775808 to
9223372036854775807. Long integer literals are written the same as integer literals,
with an L appended to the end of the value. Thus, the literal values

```
8976929L  2147483649L    62L
```

are all stored as long integers.[2]

Java also supports both byte and short integer data types, which can store integer
values in a restricted range. However, byte and short integers cannot be specified as
literals (i.e., there is no notation for indicating either a short integer value or a byte
integer value). For these two data types, specific values can only be assigned using integer values as part of either an initialization or assignment statement, which are presented in Section 2.3. Table 2.1 lists the storage requirements and range of values for
the various integer types recognized in Java.

Floating-Point Values

A **floating-point literal**, which is also called a **real number**, is any signed or unsigned numerical value having a decimal point. Examples of floating-point literals are

```
+10.625    5.    -6.2    3251.92    0.0    0.33    -6.67    +2.
```

---

[1] It is interesting to note that the absolute value of the negative limit is 1 more than the positive limit. This is because values are stored in the two's complement format described in Section 1.9.

[2] A lowercase l can also be used, but since this letter is often confused with the digit 1, we will
always use an uppercase L to indicate a long integer.

Table 2.1 **Integer Data Types**

Type	Storage	Range of Values	Comments
byte	1 byte	−128 to 127	Values stored by assignment only. There are no byte literal values.
short	2 bytes	−32,768 to 32,767	Values stored by assignment only. There are no short literal values.
int	4 bytes	−2,147,483,648 to 2,147,483,647	The default integer type. Literal values permitted.
long	8 bytes	−9,223,372,036,854,775,808 to 9,223,372,036,854,775,807	Literal values indicated by appending an L to the integer.

Notice that the numbers 5., 0.0, and +2. are classified as floating-point literals, but the same numbers written without a decimal point (5, 0, +2) would be integer values. As with integer literals, special symbols, such as the dollar sign and the comma, are not permitted in real numbers. Examples of invalid real numbers are

       5,326.25   24   6,459 $10.29   7.007.645

Java supports two different types of floating-point data types: double and float. The difference between these types of data is the amount of storage that a Java compiler allocates for each type, which affects both the range (highest to lowest permitted numbers) and the precision (number of decimal places) of the numbers that can be stored. A double floating-point value is required to be stored using 8 bytes.[3] This is the default type assumed for floating-point numbers. The other type of floating-point value is referred to as a float.

A float number is stored using 4 bytes. Because a double number is stored using 8 bytes, or twice the storage used for a float, a double value has approximately twice the precision of a float (for this reason, doubles are sometimes referred to as **double-precision numbers** and floats as **single-precision numbers**). The smallest and largest values that can be stored in each floating-point data type are listed in Table 2.2. To specifically indicate a float literal value, you must append either an F or f to the number. In the absence of these suffixes, a number with a decimal point defaults to a double. For example,

       9.234   indicates a double value
       9.234f   indicates a float value
       9.234F   indicates a float value

Table 2.2 **Floating-Point Data Types**

Type	Storage	Absolute Range of Values (+ or −)	Comments
float	4 bytes	1.40129846432481707e−45 to 3.40282346638528860e+38	Literal values indicated by appending either an f or F to the number.
double	8 bytes	4.94065645841246544e-324 to 1.79769313486231570e+308	The default floating-point type.

---

[3] See Appendix I for a description of floating-point storage.

PROGRAMMING NOTE

What Is Precision?

In numerical theory, the term **precision** typically refers to numerical accuracy. In this context, a statement such as "this computation is accurate, or precise, to the fifth decimal place" is used. This means that the fifth digit after the decimal point has been rounded, and the number is accurate to within ±0.00005.

In computer programming, precision can either refer to the accuracy of a number or the number of significant digits in the number, where significant digits are defined as the number of clearly correct digits plus 1. For example, if the number 12.6874 has been rounded to the fourth decimal place, it is correct to say that this number is precise (i.e., accurate) to the fourth decimal place. This statement means that all of the digits in the number are accurate except the fourth decimal digit, which has been rounded. Similarly, it can be said that this same number has a precision of six digits, which means that the first five digits are correct and the sixth digit has been rounded. Another way of saying this is that the number 12.6874 has six significant digits.

Notice that the significant digits in a number need not have any relation to the number of displayed digits. For example, if the number 687.45678921 has five significant digits, it is only accurate to the value 687.46, where the last digit is assumed to be rounded. In a similar manner, dollar values in many very large financial applications are frequently rounded to the nearest hundred-thousand dollars. In such applications, a displayed dollar value of $12,400,000, for example, is not accurate to the closest dollar. If this value is specified as having three significant digits, it is only accurate to the hundred-thousand digit.

For numbers with more than six significant digits to the right of the decimal point, you should use a double value. Appendix I describes the binary storage format defined by the Institute of Electrical and Electronics Engineers (IEEE—pronounced "eye triple ee") standard 754 and its impact on number precision.

Exponential Notation

Floating-point literals can also be written in exponential notation, which is similar to scientific notation and is commonly used to express both very large and very small values in compact form. The following examples illustrate how numbers with decimals can be expressed in exponential and scientific notation.

Decimal Notation	Exponential Notation	Scientific Notation
1625.	1.625e3	1.625×10^3
63421.	6.3421e4	6.3421×10^4
.00731	7.31e−3	7.31×10^{-3}
.000625	6.25e−4	6.25×10^{-4}

In exponential notation, the letter e stands for exponent. The number following the e represents a power of 10 and indicates the number of places the decimal point should be moved to obtain the standard decimal value. The decimal point is moved to the right if the number after the e is positive or moved to the left if the number after the e is negative. For example, the e3 in 1.625e3 means move the decimal place three places to the right so that the number becomes 1625. The e−3 in 7.31e−3 means move the decimal point three places to the left so that the number becomes .00731.

PROGRAMMING NOTE

Atomic Data

An *atomic data value* is considered a complete entity by itself and is not decomposable into a smaller data type supported by the language. For example, although an integer can be decomposed into individual digits, Java does not have a numerical digit type. Rather, each integer is regarded as a complete value by itself and, thus, is considered atomic data. Similarly, because the integer data type supports only atomic data values, it is said to be an *atomic data type*. As you might expect, all of the primitive data types are atomic data types.

Character Values

The third basic type of data recognized by Java are characters. Characters include the letters of the alphabet (both uppercase and lowercase), the 10 digits 0 through 9, and special symbols such as + $. , - ! . A single character value is any one letter, digit, or special symbol enclosed by single quotation marks. Examples of valid character values are

```
'A'    '$'    'b'    '7'    'y'    '!'    'M'    'q'
```

Character values in Java must be stored as 16-bit unsigned values using Unicode. This code provides an extended set of 65,536 codes, which can be used to handle multilanguage symbols. Currently, more than 35,000 different characters from diverse languages such as Arabic, Greek, and Hebrew have been defined, including the most common pictograph symbols of Chinese and Japanese. Each individual symbol and character from these languages has been assigned to a specific pattern of 0s and 1s. The bit patterns corresponding to the lowercase and uppercase letters of the English language are presented in Table 2.3.[4]

Using Table 2.3, we can determine how the characters 'J', 'E', 'A', 'N', and 'S', for example, are stored by a Java program. In Unicode, this sequence of characters requires 10 bytes of storage (2 bytes for each letter) and would be stored as illustrated in Figure 2.3.

Internally, characters are stored as unsigned integers in the range of 0 to 65,535 inclusive. Because these are integer values, Java formally defines a character as an unsigned integer data type. Although strings are constructed as a sequence of one or more individual characters, strings are not a primitive type in Java. Rather, Java provides a class named `String` for manipulating this type of data. You have already seen how to construct a string value by enclosing individual characters within double quotation marks. The string type is a reference type. As noted at the beginning of this section, this means that the majority of operations available for strings, as reference types, will be provided as methods rather than as arithmetic symbols.

Escape Sequences

When a backslash, \, is placed directly in front of a select group of characters, it tells the compiler to escape from the way these characters would normally be interpreted.

---

[4] The values of the first 128 Unicode characters are identical to the values of the 128 characters in the ASCII code used by most other high-level languages.

Table 2.3   **The English Alphabet Codes**

Letter	Binary Code		Hex. Value	Decimal Value	Letter	Binary Code		Hex. Value	Decimal Value
a	00000000	01100001	0x0061	97	A	00000000	01000001	0x0041	65
b	00000000	01100010	0x0062	98	B	00000000	01000010	0x0042	66
c	00000000	01100011	0x0063	99	C	00000000	01000011	0x0043	67
d	00000000	01100100	0x0064	100	D	00000000	01000100	0x0044	68
e	00000000	01100101	0x0065	101	E	00000000	01000101	0x0045	69
f	00000000	01100110	0x0066	102	F	00000000	01000110	0x0046	70
g	00000000	01100111	0x0067	103	G	00000000	01000111	0x0047	71
h	00000000	01101000	0x0068	104	H	00000000	01001000	0x0048	72
i	00000000	01101001	0x0069	105	I	00000000	01001001	0x0049	73
j	00000000	01101010	0x006A	106	J	00000000	01001010	0x004A	74
k	00000000	01101011	0x006B	107	K	00000000	01001011	0x004B	75
l	00000000	01101100	0x006C	108	L	00000000	01001100	0x004C	76
m	00000000	01101101	0x006D	109	M	00000000	01001101	0x004D	77
n	00000000	01101110	0x006E	110	N	00000000	01001110	0x004E	78
o	00000000	01101111	0x006F	111	O	00000000	01001111	0x004F	79
p	00000000	01110000	0x0070	112	P	00000000	01010000	0x0050	80
q	00000000	01110001	0x0071	113	Q	00000000	01010001	0x0051	81
r	00000000	01110010	0x0072	114	R	00000000	01010010	0x0052	82
s	00000000	01110011	0x0073	115	S	00000000	01010011	0x0053	83
t	00000000	01110100	0x0074	116	T	00000000	01010100	0x0054	84
u	00000000	01110101	0x0075	117	U	00000000	01010101	0x0055	85
v	00000000	01110110	0x0076	118	V	00000000	01010110	0x0056	86
w	00000000	01110111	0x0077	119	W	00000000	01010111	0x0057	87
x	00000000	01111000	0x0078	120	X	00000000	01011000	0x0058	88
y	00000000	01111001	0x0079	121	Y	00000000	01011001	0x0059	89
z	00000000	01111010	0x007A	122	Z	00000000	01011010	0x005A	90

For this reason, the combination of a backslash and these specific characters is called an **escape sequence**. We have already encountered an example of this in the newline escape sequence, \n. Table 2.4 lists Java's most common escape sequences.

Although each escape sequence in Table 2.4 is made up of two distinct characters, the combination of the two characters with no intervening whitespace causes the computer to store one character code. Table 2.5 lists the Unicode byte patterns for the escape sequences in Table 2.4

FIGURE 2.3   **The letters JEANS stored by a Java program**

←——————————— 10 Bytes of Storage ———————————→				
00000000 ┊ 01001010	00000000 ┊ 01000101	00000000 ┊ 01000001	00000000 ┊ 01001110	00000000 ┊ 01010011
J	E	A	N	S

Table 2.4   **Escape Sequences**

Escape Sequence	Meaning
\b	move back one space
\f	move to next page
\n	move to next line
\r	carriage return
\t	move to next tab setting
\\	backslash character
\'	single quotation mark
\"	double quotation mark

Boolean Values

Boolean data are restricted to one of two values: true or false. These data are most useful when examining a specific condition and, as a result of the condition being true or false, taking a prescribed course of action. As the examination of conditions is considered in Chapter 5, we defer further discussion of Boolean data until then.

Arithmetic Operations

Integers and real numbers (either single- or double-precision) may be added, subtracted, multiplied, and divided. Although it is usually better not to mix integers and real numbers when performing arithmetic operations, predictable results are obtained when different data types are used in the same arithmetic expression.

The operators for arithmetic operations are called **arithmetic operators**. They are as follows:

Operation	Operator
Addition	+
Subtraction	−
Multiplication	*
Division	/
Modulus	%

A **simple arithmetic expression** consists of an arithmetic operator connecting two operands of the form

    operand *operator* operand

where the simplest operand is a numerical value.[5] Examples of simple arithmetic expressions are

    3 + 7
    18 − 3
    12.62 + 9.8
    .08 * 12.2
    12.6 / 2.0

---

[5] More formally, an operand can be either a single constant, variable (which is described in Section 2.2), function call, or any valid combination of these elements that yields a single value.

Table 2.5   The Java Escape Sequence Codes

Escape Sequence	Meaning	Unicode Code	
\b	backspace	00000000	00001000
\f	form feed	00000000	00001100
\n	newline	00000000	00001010
\r	carriage return	00000000	00001101
\t	tab	00000000	00010001
\\	backslash	00000000	01011100
\'	single quotation mark	00000000	00100111
\"	double quotation mark	00000000	00100010

The spaces around the arithmetic operators in these examples are inserted strictly for clarity and can be omitted without affecting the value of the expression. Notice that an expression in Java must be entered in a straight-line form. Thus, for example, the Java expression equivalent to 12.6 divided by 2 must be entered as 12.6 / 2 and not as the algebraic expression

$$\frac{12.6}{2}$$

When evaluating simple arithmetic expressions, the data type of the result is determined by the following rules, which are applied in the order listed:

1. If either operand is a double value, the result is a double value, else
2. If either operand is a float value, the result is a float value, else
3. If either operand is a long value, the result is a long value, else
4. The result is an integer value

An expression that contains only integer operands (longs or ints) is an **integer expression**, and the result of the expression is an integer value (rules 3 and 4). Similarly, an expression containing only real-valued operands (doubles or floats) is a **real expression**, and the result of the expression is a floating-point value (rules 1 and 2). An arithmetic expression containing both integer and noninteger operands is a **mixed-mode** expression. The result of a mixed-mode expression is always a floating-point value (rules 1 and 2). For example, in the mixed-mode expression 16.4 + 3, the 3 is converted, internally and only for the computation, to 3.0, and the result of the expression is the floating-point number 19.4.

The value of any arithmetic expression can be displayed as character text using both the print() and println() methods or within a **dialog box** using the showMessage() method. This is done by converting the desired value to a string prior to display. For example, the statement

```
System.out.println((6 + 15));
```

yields the display 21. Strictly speaking, the inner parentheses surrounding the expression 6 + 15 are not required. That is, the statement

```
System.out.println(6 + 15);
```

also displays 21. However, it is always advisable to enclose arithmetic expressions within parentheses because the final argument passed to both `print()` and `println()` is always converted to a string before display. Enclosing the expression in parentheses ensures that the arithmetic operation is completed before any conversion to a string takes place. In a moment, you will see an instance where not enclosing the arithmetic expression results in a string concatenation taking place before the intended arithmetic addition is performed.

In addition to displaying a single numerical value, a string identifying the output can also be displayed by including both the string and a value to the output method. For example, the statement

```
System.out.println("The total of 6 and 15 is " +(6 + 15));
```

concatenates two items into one string, which is then passed to `println()` for display. Here the arithmetic addition is done first, and then the value 21 is concatenated to the string `"The   total   of   6   and   15 is   "`. Since the first operand is a string, the program interprets the first addition sign as a concatenation operation. To perform the concatenation, the numerical value of 21 is internally converted to the string "21", which is then used in the concatenation. Finally, since a single string is obtained, it is passed to the `println()` method for display. The output produced by this statement is

```
The total of 6 and 15 is 21
```

As far as `println()` is concerned, its input is a string of characters that is then displayed. Also notice that the parentheses around the expression 6 + 15 are required here. Without these parentheses, because the first operand encountered is a string, the program would start concatenating all operands from left to right and produce the display

```
The total of 6 and 15 is 615
```

Notice that the space between the word `is` and the displayed number is caused by the space placed within the string passed to the `println()` method. Placing either a space, tab, or newline escape sequence into the string causes this character to be part of the output that is ultimately displayed. For example, the statement

```
System.out.println("The sum of 12.2 and 15.754 is\n" + (12.2 + 15.754));
```

yields the display

```
The sum of 12.2 and 15.754 is
27.954
```

We should mention that the final string sent to the print methods can be continued across multiple lines and contain numerous concatenations. Thus, the prior display is also produced by the statement

```
System.out.println("The sum of 12.2 and 15.754 is\n"
                 + (12.2 + 15.754)
                 );
```

The restrictions in using multiple lines are that a string within double quotation marks cannot be split across lines and the terminating semicolon appears only on the last line. Within a line, multiple concatenation symbols can be used.

As the last display indicates, floating point numbers are displayed with sufficient places to the right of the decimal point to accommodate the fractional part of the number. The specification for the Java language requires that when floating-point or double-precision values are displayed as strings, as many decimal places will be displayed as are necessary to ensure that if the numbers were input, there would be no loss of precision.[6]

QuickTest Program 2.1 illustrates using the `println()` method to display the results of an expression within the statements of a complete program.

QuickTest Program 2.1

```java
public class ShowOperations
{
  public static void main(String[] args)
  {
    System.out.println("15.0 plus 2.0 equals " + (15.0 + 2.0) +'\n'
                     + "15.0 minus 2.0 equals " + (15.0 - 2.0) + '\n'
                     + "15.0 times 2.0 equals " + (15.0 * 2.0) + '\n'
                     + "15.0 divided by 2.0 equals " + (15.0 / 2.0) );
  }
}
```

The output of QuickTest Program 2.1 is:

```
15.0 plus 2.0 equals 17.0
15.0 minus 2.0 equals 13.0
15.0 times 2.0 equals 30.0
15.0 divided by 2.0 equals 7.5
```

In reviewing the display produced by Program 2.1, notice that only one string is ultimately passed as an argument to the `println()` method. This string is constructed by the concatenation of eleven items, four of which are the values computed from arithmetic expressions and three of which are newline escape sequences.

It is worth noting that the arithmetic operations of addition, subtraction, multiplication, and division are implemented differently for integer and floating-point values. Specifically, whether an integer or floating-point arithmetic operation is performed depends on what types of operands (integer or floating-point) are in the arithmetic expression. In this sense, the arithmetic operators are considered overloaded. More formally, an **overloaded operator** is a symbol that represents more than one operation and whose execution depends on the types of operands encountered. Although the overloaded nature of the arithmetic operators is rather simple, we will encounter the concept of overloading many more times in our journey through Java.

Integer Division

The division of two integers can produce rather strange results for the unwary. For example, the integer expression 15/2, which is the division of the integer 15 by the integer 2, yields an integer result (from rule 4). Since integers cannot contain a frac-

---

[6] The Java specification, at the time of this writing, could be obtained at **www.javasoft.com/docs/books/jls/index.html**.

tional part, a result such as 7.5 cannot be obtained. In Java, the fractional part of the result obtained when dividing two integers is dropped (truncated). Thus, the value of 15/2 is 7, the value of 9/4 is 2, and the value of 17/5 is 3.

The Modulus Operator

There are times we would like to retain the remainder of a division. To do this, Java provides an arithmetic operator having the symbol %. This operator, called both the modulus and remainder operator, captures the remainder when either an integer or real-valued number is divided by an integer. For example,

> 9.2 % 4 is 1.2   (the remainder when 9.2 is divided by 4 is 1.2)
> 16.6 % 3 is 1.6   (the remainder when 16.6 is divided by 3 is 1.6)
> 15 % 4 is 3   (the remainder when 15 is divided by 4 is 3)
> 14 % 2 is 0   (the remainder when 14 is divided by 2 is 0)

More precisely, the modulus operator first determines the integer number of times that the dividend, which is the number following the % operator, can be divided into the divisor, which is the number before the % operator, and then returns the remainder. When the dividend is an integer, as is the case for all of the previous examples, the value returned by the modulus operation is a true remainder. This is not the case when the dividend has a nonzero fractional value. For example, 16.6 % 3.2 is 0.6. This result is determined as follows: The maximum number of integer times that 3.2 goes into 16.6 is 5. Thus, 5 times 3.2 is 16, and there is a modulus remainder of 0.6.

Negation

Besides the binary operators for addition, subtraction, multiplication, and division, Java also provides unary operators. A **unary operator** is one that operates on a single operand. One of these unary operators uses the same symbol as binary subtraction $(-)$. The minus sign in front of a single numerical operand negates (reverses the sign of) the number.

Table 2.6 summarizes the six arithmetic operations we have described so far and lists the data type of the result produced by each operator based on the data type of the operands involved.

Operator Precedence and Associativity

Besides such simple expressions as 5 + 12 and .08 * 26.2, we frequently need to create more complex arithmetic expressions. Java, like most other programming languages, requires that certain rules be followed when writing expressions containing more than one arithmetic operator. These rules are

1. Two binary arithmetic operator symbols must never be placed side by side. For example, 5 * %6 is not valid because the two operators * and % are placed next to each other.

2. Parentheses may be used to form groupings, and all expressions enclosed within parentheses are evaluated first. This permits parentheses to alter the evaluation to any desired order. For example, in the expression (6 + 4) / (2 + 3), the 6 + 4 and 2 + 3 are evaluated first to yield 10 / 5. The 10 / 5 is then evaluated to yield 2.

Table 2.6   **Summary of Arithmetic Operators**

Operation	Operator	Type	Operand	Result
Addition	+	Binary	Both are integers.	Integer
			One operand is not an integer.	Floating-point
Subtraction	–	Binary	Both are integers.	Integer
			One operand is not an integer.	Floating-point
Multiplication	*	Binary	Both are integers.	Integer
			One operand is not an integer.	Floating-point
Division	/	Binary	Both are integers.	Integer
			One operand is not an integer.	Floating-point
Modulus	%	Binary	Both are integers.	Integer
			One operand is not an integer.	Floating-point
Negation	–	Unary	Integer	Integer
			Floating-point	Floating-point

3. Sets of parentheses may also be enclosed by other parentheses. For example, the expression (2 * (3 + 7)) / 5 is valid and evaluates to 4. When parentheses are included within parentheses, the expressions in the innermost parentheses are always evaluated first. The evaluation continues from innermost to outermost parentheses until the expressions in all parentheses have been evaluated. The number of closing parentheses,), must always equal the number of opening parentheses, (, so that there are no unpaired sets.

4. Parentheses cannot be used to indicate multiplication. The multiplication operator, *, must be used. For example, the expression (3 + 4) (5 + 1) is not valid. The correct expression is (3 + 4) * (5 + 1).

Parentheses should specify logical groupings of operands and indicate clearly, to both the computer and programmers, the intended order of arithmetic operations. Although expressions with parentheses are always evaluated first, expressions containing multiple operators, both with and without parentheses, are evaluated by the priority, or **precedence**, of the operators, which is as follows:

P1. All negations are done first.

P2. Multiplication, division, and modulus operations are computed first. Expressions containing more than one multiplication, division, or modulus operator are evaluated from left to right as each operator is encountered. For example, in the expression 35 / 7 % 3 * 4, the operations are all of the same priority, so the operations will be performed from left to right as each operator is encountered. Thus, the division is done first, yielding the expression 5 % 3 * 4. The modulus operation is done next, yielding a result of 2. And finally, the value of 2 * 4 is computed to yield 8.

P3. Addition and subtraction are computed last. Expressions containing more than one addition or subtraction are evaluated from left to right as each operator is encountered.

<table>
<tr><td colspan="2" align="center">Table 2.7   **Operator Precedence and Associativity**</td></tr>
</table>

Operator	Associativity
unary $-$	right to left
* / %	left to right
$+$ $-$	left to right

Table 2.7 lists both the precedence and associativity of the operators considered in this section. As we have seen, the precedence of an operator establishes its priority relative to all other operators. Operators at the top of Table 2.7 have a higher priority than operators at the bottom. In expressions with multiple operators of different precedence, the operator with the higher precedence is used before an operator with lower precedence. For example, in the expression 6 + 4 / 2 + 3, since the division operator has a higher precedence than addition (rule P2), the division is done first, yielding an intermediate result of 6 + 2 + 3. The additions are then performed, left to right, to yield a final result of 11. This ordering of computations, in the cases of the operators listed in the last two groups of Table 2.7, from left to right, is referred to as the *associativity* of the operator. Notice that the associativity of the negation operator is from right to left.

Finally, we can use either Table 2.7 or the previous precedence rules to evaluate an expression containing operators of different precedence, such as 8 + 5 * 7 % 2 * 4. Because the multiplication and modulus operators have a higher precedence than the addition operator, these two operations are evaluated first (rule P2), using their left-to-right associativity, before the addition is evaluated (rule P3). Thus, the complete expression is evaluated as

```
8 + 5 * 7 % 2 * 4 =
   8 + 35 % 2 * 4 =
         8 + 1 * 4 =
            8 + 4 = 12
```

String Concatenation

Although there are many available operations for manipulating strings, most of these operations are implemented as methods. The reason is that a string is not a primitive data type in Java but a reference type, which is defined in a class named `String`. One operation, however, that uses the same operator symbol as for numerical addition is the + symbol.

For string data, this symbol joins two or more strings into a single string. Formally, this operation is referred to as **string concatenation**. Although string concatenation is not an arithmetic operation, it is the only operation that directly manipulates string data in a similar fashion as numerical data. For example, the expression

```
"Hot" + " Dog"
```

concatenates the two individual strings `"Hot"` and `" Dog"` into the single string "Hot Dog". The space between the two words was created by the space in front of the word `Dog`.

When used with string and numerical data in the same expression, the + symbol causes the numerical data to be converted to a string before concatenation. For example, the expression `"The result is " + 5` is a concatenation operation that results in the string `"The result is 5"`.

A worthwhile observation is that the concatenation operator has the same precedence as the addition operator, which can sometimes yield initially surprising results. For example, the expression

```
"The result is " + 15.4 * 2
```

yields the string value

```
"The result is 30.8"
```

This occurs because the multiplication operator has a higher precedence than the addition operator, which means the multiplication is done first. Then the resulting value of 30.8 is converted to the string "30.8" and appended to the first string.

Now consider the expression `"The result is " + 15.4 + 2`. Here the addition is performed from left to right, which is dictated by the associativity of the addition operator. Because the addition of a string and a numerical value is a concatenation operation, the intermediate result is `"The result is 15.4" + 2`. Now the 2 is concatenated to the first string yielding `"The result is 15.42"`. To have the two numbers accurately added first, if this was the intention, the correct expression is `"The result is " + (15.4 + 2)`. In this expression, the parentheses are required to change the default order of evaluation and ensure that the numerical values are added before any concatenation is performed.

The general rule to be taken from this discussion is that to prevent any unexpected results, *always use parentheses when performing arithmetic operations in any expression that contains a string*. We will use this rule throughout this text whenever we display the results of numerical calculations using the `print()`, `println()`, and `showMessage()` methods. This is because all of these methods require a string as the item that they display.

Exercises 2.1

1. Determine data types appropriate for the following data:
   a. the average of four speeds
   b. the number of transistors in a circuit
   c. the length of the Golden Gate Bridge
   d. the part numbers in a machine
   e. the distance from Brooklyn, N.Y., to Newark, N.J.
   f. the single-character prefix that specifies circuit components

2. Convert the following numbers into standard decimal form:
   6.34E5   1.95162E2   8.395E1   2.95E−3   4.623E−4

3. Convert the following decimal numbers into exponential notation:
   126.   656.23   3426.95   4893.2   .321   .0123   .006789

4a.   Using Unicode, determine the number of bytes required to store the letters KINGSLEY.

b.   Show how the letters KINGSLEY would be stored inside a computer as a sequence of Unicode codes. That is, draw a figure similar to Figure 2.3 for the letters KINGSLEY.

5a.   Repeat Exercise 4a using the letters of your own last name.

b.   Repeat Exercise 4b using the letters of your own last name.

6.   Following are correct algebraic expressions and incorrect Java expressions corresponding to them. Find the errors and write corrected Java expressions.

Algebra	*Java Expression*
a. $(2)(3) + (4)(5)$	`(2)(3) + (4)(5)`
b. $\dfrac{6 + 18}{2}$	`6 + 18 / 2`
c. $\dfrac{4.5}{12.2 - 3.1}$	`4.5 / 12.2 - 3.1`
d. $4.6(3.0 + 14.9)$	`4.6(3.0 + 14.9)`
e. $(12.1 + 18.9)(15.3 - 3.8)$	`(12.1 + 18.9)(15.3 - 3.8)`

7.   Determine the value of the following integer expressions:

a.   3 + 4 * 6
b.   3 * 4 / 6 + 6
c.   2 * 3 / 12 * 8 / 4
d.   10 * (1 + 7 * 3)
e.   20 − 2 / 6 + 3
f.   20 − 2 / (6 + 3)
g.   (20 − 2) / 6 + 3
h.   (20 − 2) / (6 + 3)
i.   50 % 20
j.   (10 + 3) % 4

8.   Determine the value of the following floating-point expressions:

a.   3.0 + 4.0 * 6.0
b.   3.0 * 4.0 / 6.0 + 6.0
c.   2.0 * 3.0 / 12.0 * 8.0 / 4.0
d.   10.0 * (1.0 + 7.0 * 3.0)
e.   20.0 − 2.0 / 6.0 + 3.0
f.   20.0 − 2.0 / (6.0 + 3.0)
g.   (20.0 − 2.0) / 6.0 + 3.0
h.   (20.0 − 2.0) / (6.0 + 3.0)

9.   Evaluate the following expressions and list the data type of the result. In evaluating the expressions, be aware of the data types of all intermediate calculations.

a.   `10.0 + 15 / 2 + 4.3`
b.   `10.0 + 15.0 / 2 + 4.3`
c.   `3.0 * 4 / 6 + 6`
d.   `3 * 4.0 / 6 + 6`
e.   `20.0 - 2 / 6 + 3`

f. `10 + 17 * 3 + 4`

g. `10 + 17 / 3. + 4`

h. `3.0 * 4 % 6 + 6`

i. `10 + 17 % 3 + 4`

10. Assume that `distance` has the integer value 1, `v` has the integer value 50, `n` has the integer value 10, and `t` has the integer value 5. Evaluate the following expressions:

a. `n / t + 3`

b. `v / t + n - 10 * distance`

c. `v - 3 * n + 4 * distance`

d. `distance / 5`

e. `18 / t`

f. `2t * n`

g. `2v / 20`

h. `(v + n) / (t + distance)`

i. `v + n / t + distance`

11. Repeat Exercise 10 assuming that `distance` has the value 1.0, `v` has the value 50.0, `n` has the value 10.0, and `t` has the value 5.0.

12. Since most computers use different amounts of storage for integer, floating-point, double-precision, and character values, discuss how a program might alert the computer to the amount of storage needed for the various data types in the program.

13. Enter and run QuickTest Program 2.1 on your computer.

14. Determine the output of the following program:

```
public class Test1
{
   // a program illustrating integer truncation
   public static void main(String[] args)
   {
      System.out.println("answer1 is the integer " + (9/4));
      System.out.println("answer2 is the integer " + (17/3));
   }
}
```

15. Determine the output of the following program:

```
public class Test2
{
   // a program illustrating the % operator public static void main(String[] args)
   {
      System.out.println("The remainder of 9 divided by 4 is " + (9 % 4));
      System.out.println("The remainder of 17 divided by 3 is " + (17 % 3));
   }
}
```

16.   Write a Java program that displays the results of the expressions 3.0 * 5.0, 7.1 * 8.3 − 2.2, and 3.2 / (6.1 * 5). Calculate the value of these expressions manually to verify that the displayed values are correct.

17.   Write a Java program that displays the results of the expressions 15 / 4, 15 % 4, and 5 * 3 − (6 * 4). Calculate the value of these expressions manually to verify that the displayed values are correct.

Note: For the following exercise, the reader should have an understanding of basic computer storage concepts. Specifically, if you are unfamiliar with the concept of a byte, refer to Section 1.9 before doing the next exercise.

18.   Although the total number of bytes varies from computer to computer, memory sizes of 65,536 to more than several million bytes are not uncommon. In computer language, the letter K represents the number 1,024, which is 2 raised to the 10th power, and M represents the number 1,048,576, which is 2 raised to the 20th power. Thus, a memory size of 640 K is really 640 times 1,024, or 655,360 bytes, and a memory size of 4 M is really 4 times 1,048,576, which is 4,194,304 bytes. Using this information, calculate the actual number of bytes in

a.   a memory containing 8 M bytes

b.   a memory containing 16 M bytes

c.   a memory containing 32 M bytes

d.   a memory containing 96 M bytes

e.   a memory consisting of 8 M words, where each word consists of 2 bytes

f.   a memory consisting of 16 M words, where each word consists of 4 bytes

g.   a disk that specifies 1.44 M bytes

2.2 Constructing a Data Declaration Section: Variables

All integer, floating-point, and other values in a computer program are stored and retrieved from the computer's memory unit. Conceptually, individual locations in the memory unit are arranged like the rooms in a large hotel. Like hotel rooms, each memory location has a unique address ("room number"). Before high-level languages such as Java existed, memory locations were referenced by their addresses. For example, storing the integer values 45 and 12 in the memory locations 1652 and 2548 (Figure 2.4), respectively, required instructions equivalent to

> ***Put 45 in location 1652***
> ***Put 12 in location 2548***

FIGURE 2.4   **Enough storage for two integers**

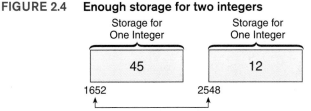

To add the two numbers just stored and save the result in another memory location (e.g., at location 3000) required a statement comparable to

Add the contents of location 1652 to the contents of location 2548 and store the result into location 3000

Clearly, this method of storage and retrieval is cumbersome. In high-level languages such as Java, symbolic names replace actual memory addresses. *For primitive type values, such as integers, real numbers, and individual characters, the symbolic names where the values are stored are called variables.* Thus, a **variable** is a name given by the programmer that refers to computer storage locations that store a primitive data type value. The term *variable* is used because the value stored in the variable can change, or vary. (As we will shortly see, one or more variables can then be combined together into a single object.) For each variable name that the programmer uses, the computer keeps track of the actual memory address corresponding to that name. Naming a variable is equivalent to putting a name on the door of a hotel room and referring to the room by this name, such as the BLUE room, rather than by the actual room number.

In Java, the selection of variable names is left to the programmer as long as the selection follows the rules for identifiers provided in Section 1.3. Thus, the rules for selecting variable names are identical to those for selecting class and method names. As with class and method names, variable names should provide an indication of their use. For example, a good name for a variable used to store the total of a group of values would be sum or total. Variable names that give no indication of the value stored, such as goForIt, linda, bill, and duh, should not be selected. As with method names, variable names are case sensitive.

Now assume that the first memory location illustrated in Figure 2.4, which has address 1652, is given the name num1. Also assume that memory location 2548 is given the variable name num2, and memory location 3000 is given the name total, as illustrated in Figure 2.5.

FIGURE 2.5 **Naming storage locations**

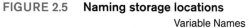
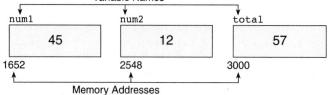

Using these variable names, the operation of storing 45 in location 1652, storing 12 in location 2548, and adding the contents of these two locations is accomplished by the Java statements

```
num1 = 45;
num2 = 12;
total = num1 + num2;
```

Each of these three statements is called an *assignment statement* because it tells the computer to assign (store) a value into a variable. Assignment statements always have an equal, =, sign and one variable name immediately to the left of this sign. The value to the right of the equal sign is determined first, and this value is assigned to the variable to the left of the equal sign. The blank spaces in the assignment statements are inserted for readability. We will have much more to say about assignment statements in Section 2.4, but for now, we can use them to store values in variables.

A variable name is useful because it frees the programmer from concern over where data are physically stored inside the computer. We simply use the variable name and let the compiler worry about where in memory the data are actually stored. Before storing a value into a variable, however, Java requires that we clearly declare the type of data to be stored in it. We must tell the compiler, in advance, the names of the variables that will be used for characters, the names that will be used for integers, and the names that will be used to store other Java data types.

Declaration Statements

Naming a variable and specifying the data type that can be stored in it are accomplished using **declaration statements**. The most commonly used syntax for a class's declaration statement is

    optionalAccessSpecifier   dataType   variableName;

where the *optionalAccessSpecifier* can be either of the reserved words private, public, protected or can be left blank, *dataType* designates a valid Java data type or class name, and *variableName* is a user-selected variable name. Variables that hold integer values are declared using the reserved word int to specify the data type and have the form

    optionalAccessSpecifer int variableName;

Thus, the declaration statement

    private int sum;

declares sum as the name of a variable capable of storing an integer value and uses a private access specification. What this access specification means will be explained shortly, and you need not be concerned with it at this point. In addition to the reserved word int to specify an integer, the reserved word long specifies a long integer. For example, the statement

    private long datenum;

declares datenum as a variable that will store a long integer, again with a private access specification. Additionally, the reserved words short and byte specify the remaining two integer types.

Variables that hold single-precision floating-point values are declared using the reserved word float, whereas variables that hold double-precision values are declared using the reserved word double. For example, the statement

    private float firstNumber;

declares firstNumber as a variable that will store a floating-point number. Similarly, the statement

    private double secondNumber;

declares that the variable secondNumber will store a double-precision number using a private access specification.

In addition to declaring a variable's type, a variable declaration statement can also provide an initial value for the variable (this is not permissible for parameters). For example, the declaration statement

```
private int num1 = 15;
```

both declares the variable `num1` as an integer variable and provides a value of 15. This value, which is referred to as an **initial value**, will be stored in the variable when the variable is first created. When a declaration statement provides an initial value, the variable is said to be **initialized**. Thus, in this example, it is correct to say that the variable `num1` will be initialized to 15 when it is created. Similarly, the declaration statements

```
private double grade1 = 87.0;
private double grade2 = 93.5;
private double total;
```

declare three double-precision variables and provide initial values for two of them.

When providing an initialized value for a single-precision `float` variable, it is important to add either the suffix f or F to the initializing value (recall from Section 2.1 that the Java default for floating-point values is double-precision and that a suffix of either f or F must be used to indicated a `float` value). Failure to add the required suffix results in a compiler error and notification that an incompatible type declaration has been made. The reason is that the compiler is alerting you that numerical precision may be lost in attempting to store a double-precision value in a single-precision variable. Thus, the initialization

```
private float number = 26.3;   // THIS IS AN INVALID INITIALIZATION
```

is not valid, and a correct initialization is

```
private float number = 26.3f;   // Valid, because of the f suffix
```

Literals, expressions using only literals, such as 87.0 + 12 − 2, and expressions using literals and previously initialized variables can all be used as initializers within a declaration statement. Because there is no suffix provided to indicate either a short or a byte literal, these values can only be stored using an assignment statement or by explicitly converting other data types using a cast. Thus, the initialization statement

```
short count = 10;
```

automatically forces the conversion of integer value 10 to a short integer value when it is stored in the variable named `count`. Conversions using casts are described in Section 4.4.

Constructing a Data Declaration Section

There are three classifications of variables, referred to as **instance**, **class**, and **local**, and one additional type that acts like a variable but is formally referred to as a **parameter**. A variable's classification is dependent on its placement within a class and the presence or absence of the reserved word `static`. Table 2.8 lists the determining factors for making this classification. For now, it is only important that you know that declaration statements can be placed in only one of two places: either outside any method or within a method. Any variable declared outside a method automatically

Table 2.8   **Determination of Variable Types**

Type	Placement	Comments
instance	Within a class's body but outside any method. The `static` reserved word (see Section 3.5) *cannot be used* when declaring this type.	These form the majority of all class declaration sections. Every object that is created receives a new variable of this type.
class	Within a class's body but outside any method. The `static` reserved word (see Section 3.5) *must be used* when declaring this type.	Each class variable is created only once per class and is not dependent on the creation of any object.
local	Within a method's body. Neither an access specifier nor the `static` reserved word is permitted.	Used in the creation of objects. Also used to hold intermediate method results.
parameter	Within the parentheses of a method's header line. Neither an access specifier nor the `static` reserved word is permitted.	Used to pass data into a method (see Section 3.1).

becomes part of a class's declaration section, even if the declarations are interspersed between methods.

As indicated in Table 2.8, an **instance variable** is any variable whose declaration statement

1. is placed within a class's body and outside any method.
2. does not contain the `static` reserved word.

As instance variables form the basis for the vast majority of data declaration sections, we are initially only concerned with them. Recall that a basic class structure is

```
    Class Header Line ------> public className
Start of Class Body --------> {
                                // data declaration section
                                // method definition section
End of Class Body ----------> }
```

In constructing a data declaration section, we adhere to the convention of placing all instance declaration statements together at the top of a class's body. This creates an easily identifiable data declaration section for anyone reading the code.

As a specific example of creating a data declaration section, assume that we are required to construct a program for calculating the floor area of a room given its length and width. Thinking in terms of objects, and assuming a rectangular floor, our working object can be a room defined by its length and width. Using these two quantities, we can easily calculate any room's floor area. Providing for lengths and widths that can be floating-point values, a suitable set of declaration statements for a data declaration section is

```
private double length;
private double width;
```

These declaration statements should look familiar. The reserved word `private` at the beginning of each declaration statement is almost universally used for all instance variable declarations.[7] This reserved word restricts access to the declared variable so that only methods defined in the method definition section can retrieve or modify them. Why this is important is discussed in the next section. For now, we will always add this reserved word in front of all variable declaration statements in a data declaration section (this includes both instance and class variables). The variable names `length` and `width` are programmer selected. We have declared these variables to be `doubles` so that we do not have to worry about adding the f suffix every time a value is assigned to them. Clearly, if rooms having only integer-valued lengths and widths were being considered, the reserved word `double` in these declarations would be changed to `int`.

You might be wondering why we did not include a declaration for the area. This is a matter of choice, and including a declaration such as

```
private double area;
```

is acceptable. We did not include this declaration because the area is easily obtained by multiplying the length times the width; thus, whenever we need the area, it can be calculated without providing a specific storage area for it.

To complete our class construction, assume that we name our class `RoomType`. At this stage, the code for this class consists of

```
public class RoomType
{
  // data declarations section
  private double length;   // declare length as a double variable
  private double width;    // declare width as a double variable

  //method definitions section
}
```

Both `length` and `width` are instance variables because of the placement of their declaration statements outside any method and the fact that they do not include the `static` reserved word. As we will see in Section 3.5, the `static` reserved word creates a variable that cannot be included within an object.

Even though our `RoomType` class contains no methods, it is a complete class from which objects can be created. How these objects are created is presented after the next example.

As a second example of constructing a data declaration section, assume that we need to write a program to calculate the average of two integer numbers. Suitable declaration statements for this problem are

```
private int firstNumber;
private int secondNumber;
```

Here the programmer selects the variable names `firstNumber` and `secondNumber`. The reserved word `private` is included as noted previously, and the reserved word `int` is determined by the type of values that will be stored in the variables. Although the average can always be calculated as the total of the two numbers divided by 2, a specific declaration statement for the average can also be included. In this case, however, since

---

[7] Reserved words, in Java, are also referred to as keywords.

the average of two integers can be a floating-point value, the average should be declared as either a `float` or `double`. Assuming we name our class `TwoNumbers` and include a declaration for the average, the class would be

```
public class TwoNumbers
{
  // data declaration section
  private int firstNumber;    // this is an instance variable
  private int secondNumber;   // this is an instance variable
  private double average;     // this is an instance variable

  // method definition section
}
```

In addition to the integer and floating-point declarations we have used, instance variables for character, boolean, and strings can also be made. For example, the declarations

```
private char keyCode;
private boolean inAWord;
private String message;
```

declare instance variables named `keyCode`, `inAWord`, and `message` that can be used to store a character, boolean, and string value, respectively. A complete class that contains this last declaration was presented in Section 1.3 (QuickTest Program 1.1).

Creating Objects

Objects are only created from the instance variables declared in a data declaration section or from other object types. The methods defined in a method definition section are used either to

1. provide operations that can be applied to the created objects or
2. to create general-purpose functions that are independent of any one object

Because the mechanics of creating an object are the same for all classes, we can now see how objects are created using the instance variable declared in our `RoomType` class.

Consider Program 2.2, which creates a single `RoomType` class object.

Program 2.2

```
public class UseRoomType
{
  public static void main(String[] args)
  {
    RoomType roomOne;

    roomOne = new RoomType();
  }
}
```

Program 2.2 produces no output, a defect that will be remedied shortly in the next section when we add methods to our `RoomType` class. The program does, however, create a single object named `roomOne`. Let's see how this object is created.

Program 2.2's `main()` method consists of the two statements

```
RoomType roomOne;
roomOne = new RoomType();
```

The first statement in this method

```
RoomType roomOne;
```

is a declaration statement that declares a variable named `roomOne` to be of type `RoomType`. The format of this declaration statement, with one exception, is the same as an instance variable's declaration statements. Taking the items in reverse order and starting from the semicolon, the name of our variable is `roomOne`, which is a programmer-selected identifier. The data type for this variable is `RoomType`, which is the name of the class from which we want to create an object. For convenience, we repeat this class in Figure 2.6.

FIGURE 2.6   **The** `RoomType` **class**

```
public class RoomType
{
    // data declarations section
    private double length;   // declare length as a double variable
    private double width;    // declare width as a double variable

    //method definitions section
}
```

As can be seen in `main()`'s declaration statement, declaring an object to be of a class type is similar to declaring a variable of a primitive data type, such as `int` or `double`. Although the declaration statement *does not* contain the reserved word `private`, this is not because we are declaring an object. Rather, it is because of the placement of the declaration statement within a method. Referring back to Table 2.8, you will see that declaration statements placed within a method are formally referred to as **local variables**. Local variables, which are variables declared within a method's body, *cannot* include an access specification because these variables cannot be anything but private. Because such variables are private by definition, no explicit `private` designation is either required or permitted.[8] Except for the lack of the `private` reserved word, the syntax for local declarations (i.e., declarations internal to a method) is identical to those for instance variables declared within a class's declaration section. Assuming that the `RoomType` class has been compiled, the result produced by `main()`'s declaration statement is illustrated in Figure 2.7. As shown, a memory storage area has been reserved for a variable named `roomOne`, and the value placed in this variable is an address designated as `null`. This `null` value means that the variable does not currently refer to a valid object.

---

[8] Formally, local variables are private to the method that they are declared in. This means that they can only be used within the method that declares them. Where a variable can be used is referred to as its *scope*, a subject that is presented in detail in Section 3.5.

FIGURE 2.7 **The effect produced by the declaration statement** `RoomType roomOne;`

roomOne

```
null
```

(A reference variable)

The second step is to create an actual object that can be referenced by the `roomOne` variable. In Program 2.2's `main()` method, this is accomplished by the statement

```
roomOne = new RoomType();
```

In Java, an actual object is typically created using the `new` operator.[9] This operator creates an object of the specified type by obtaining sufficient memory to store the required values. In this particular case, enough memory to store two double-precision values is obtained. Because this memory is dynamically allocated while the program is executing, the `new` operator is referred to as the **dynamic memory allocation operator**. Formally, the process of creating a new object using the dynamic memory allocation operator is referred to as both **creating an instance** and **instantiating an object**. Now you can also see why the variables `length` and `width` are known as instance variables; an instance of them only comes into existence when an object is created, and each created object will contain one instance of each instance variable. The information for an object's storage requirements is provided by the class's data declaration section (see Figure 2.7). For Program 2.2, the creation of a `RoomType` object results in the memory storage allocation shown in Figure 2.8.

It is important to understand that the usage of the `roomOne` variable is fundamentally different from that for the primitive data type variables `length` and `width`. The `roomOne` variable, which is declared for an object type, contains a memory address that is either the address of an object or a `null` address if no object has yet been created and referenced. The stored address is used to locate the object. Because this variable only references the location in memory where the actual object's values are located, such variables are referred to as **reference variables**. Thus, a declaration for

FIGURE 2.8 **Instantiating an object**

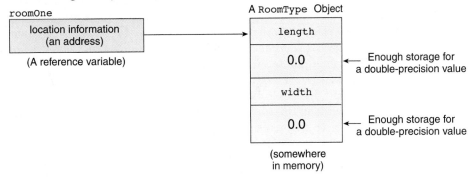

roomOne

location information
(an address)

(A reference variable)

A `RoomType` Object

length

0.0 ← Enough storage for a double-precision value

width

0.0 ← Enough storage for a double-precision value

(somewhere in memory)

---

[9] The two common exceptions that do not require the `new` operator to actually create an object are declaring and initializing String literals (Section 7.1) and the declaration of arrays (Section 8.1).

FIGURE 2.9   **Each object receives its own set of instance variables**

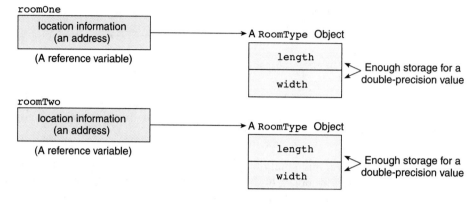

an object is actually a declaration for a reference variable. Once a reference variable is declared, an actual object can then be created using the new operator.

Each object created from a class always receives its own set of the instance variables. For example, in Figure 2.9, each of the two objects, roomOne, and roomTwo, contains its own set of the variables length and width. You might be wondering how we will distinguish between the various length and width variables shown in Figure 2.9. Effectively, this is handled by always providing an object's name. Thus, roomOne.length refers to the length variable in the roomOne object, and roomTwo.length refers to the length variable of the roomTwo object. As you might expect, an object's name will have to be supplied to all methods accessing an object.

Before leaving Figure 2.9, it should be mentioned that instance variables only come into existence when an object containing them is created. Thus, declaring an instance variable does not cause Java to reserve any space for the variable. Rather, the declaration statement simply informs the JVM of the storage requirements that will be needed by any object that contains the variable.

Whenever a primitive data type variable (int, double, float, char, or boolean) is actually created, a value will be stored directly in the variable (Figures 2.8 and 2.9). In computer terminology, this is referred to as storing a value in the variable. In the absence of an explicitly assigned initial value, the default initial value stored in all numerical data types in Java is zero. Notice that this value has been initially placed into the object's length and width variables shown in both figures.

Declaring instance variables as private imposes the restriction that once an object containing these variables is created, the variables internal to the object can only be accessed by methods defined in the class. Thus, to retrieve or modify the length and width variables in the object in Figure 2.9, we need to provide a set of class methods. Rather than being a hindrance, this privacy restriction is a key safety feature provided by object-oriented languages. Specifically, it enforces data security by precisely requiring all access to data members using known class methods, which ensures a reproducible and predictable result. This assures every programmer using the class of the variable's integrity and removes any concern that another programmer has inadvertently altered a value in some undocumented manner. Should a programmer need to add more methods, this is easily be done by extending the class (Section 12.4).

One last point needs to be mentioned before we see how to develop suitable class methods. In practice, the two individual steps of first declaring a reference variable and then instantiating an object as we did with the two statements in Program 2.2

```
RoomType roomOne;
roomOne = new RoomType();
```

are frequently combined into a single statement as follows:

```
RoomType roomOne = new RoomType();
```

In your programming experience, you will find both ways of creating reference variables and objects.

Cleansing Memory

Although a reference variable can only contain location information for a single object, this location information can be changed. That is, the same reference variable can, in the course of a program, be used to locate many objects. For example, as shown in Figure 2.10, the reference variable has been used to locate three different objects. Unfortunately, the only active object in Figure 2.10 is the last one. Because the location information for the first two objects no longer exists, the objects now take up memory space that can no longer be referenced. If too many objects are created and allowed to exist with no means of accessing them or retrieving the wasted storage they take up, the system will run out of memory and come to a halt. Formally, this is called the **memory leak problem**. Its solution is handled rather efficiently in Java and represents a major improvement in using references that was not included in Java's immediate predecessor, C++. In Java, each object automatically and internally keeps track of how many reference variables have its address. Periodically, the Java Virtual Machine (JVM) checks on each object, and if the object's reference count is zero, which it would be for the first two objects in Figure 2.10, the object is removed from computer memory.

FIGURE 2.10   **The location of different objects using the same reference variable**

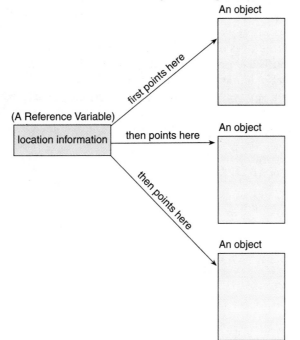

Specifying Storage Allocation[10]

The instance and local declaration statements introduced in this section perform a number of distinct tasks. From a programmer's perspective, both instance and local declaration statements provide a convenient list of variables and their data types. The compiler uses the list to check and control an otherwise common and troublesome error caused by misspelling a variable's name within a program. For example, assume that two local variables named `distance` and `gallons` are declared and initialized using the statements

```
double distance = 260.5;
double gallons = 11.2
```

Now assume that the first variable is inadvertently misspelled in the statement

```
mpg = distnce / gallons;
```

In languages that do not require variable declarations, the program would treat `distnce` as a valid variable and either assign an initial value of zero to this variable or use whatever value happens to be in the variable's storage area. In either case, a value would be calculated and assigned to `mpg`, and finding the error or even knowing that an error occurred could be extremely troublesome. Such errors are impossible in Java because the compiler flags `distnce` as an undeclared variable. The compiler cannot, of course, detect when one declared variable is typed in place of another declared variable.

In addition to these roles, declaration statements also perform a distinct role needed by the JVM. Since each data type has its own storage requirements, the JVM can allocate sufficient storage for a variable only after knowing the variable's data type. Variable declarations provide this information.

In both of these roles, both instance and local declarations perform in the same manner and inform the compiler about the required storage. Local variable declarations, however, serve one additional purpose. When the JVM encounters a local declaration, it automatically creates the variable. Statements that cause variables to be created are referred to as **definition statements**. Because local variables come into existence when the JVM encounters and executes them, local variable declarations statements are also definition statements. This is not the case for instance variables. As we have seen, storage for instance variables is only created when an object containing them comes into existence. Thus, instance variable declarations are not definition statements because they do not cause any new storage to be allocated.

Exercises 2.2

1. State whether the following variable names are valid or not valid. If they are not valid, state the reason.

proda	c1234	abcd	_c3	12345
newbal	while	$total	new bal	a1b2c3d4
9ab6	sum.of	average	grade1	finGrad

---

[10] This topic can be omitted on first reading without loss of subject continuity.

2. State whether the following variable names are valid or not valid. If they are not valid, state the reason. Also indicate which of the valid variable names should not be used because they convey no information about the variable.

salestax	a243	r2d2	firstNum	cca1
harry	sue	c3p0	average	sum
maximum	okay	a	awesome	goforit
3sum	for	tot.a1	c$five	netpay

3a. Write a declaration statement to declare that `count` will be an instance variable used to store an integer value.

b. Write a declaration statement to declare that `grade` will be an instance variable used to store a single-precision number.

c. Write a declaration statement to declare that `yield` will be an instance variable used to store a double-precision number.

d. Write a declaration statement to declare that `initial` will be an instance variable used to store a character.

4. Write declaration statements for the following instance variables:

a. `num1`, `num2`, and `num3` used to store integer numbers

b. `grade1`, `grade2`, `grade3`, and `grade4` used to store single-precision numbers

c. `tempa`, `tempb`, and `tempc` used to store double-precision numbers

d. `ch`, `let1`, `let2`, `let3`, and `let4` used to store character types

5. Write declaration statements for the following instance variables:

a. `firstNumber` and `secondNumber` used to store integers

b. `price`, `yield`, and `coupon` used to store single-precision numbers

c. `maturity` used to store a double-precision number

6. Create a class structure for a class named `Time`. The data declaration section should have instance variables for data consisting of an integer hour, integer minute, and integer second.

7. Create a class structure for a class named `Date`. The data declaration section should have instance variables for data consisting of an integer month, integer day, and integer year.

8. Create a class structure for a class named `LongDate`. The data declaration section should have an instance variable for data consisting of a long integer. For example, assume that a date is stored in the form YearMonthDay so that a date such as 12/15/04 would be stored as 20041512. What might be the advantage of storing dates in this form?

9. Create a class structure for a class named `Circle`. The data declaration section should have an instance variable for data consisting of a single-precision radius.

10. Create a class structure for a class named `MapPoint`. The data declaration section should have instance variables for a map coordinate consisting of a double-precision *x* value and a double-precision *y* value.

11. Compile and run Program 2.2.

12. Modify Program 2.2 to create an additional object named `roomTwo`.

13. Create a QuickTest Program named `UseTwoNumbers` that declares and creates two objects named `firstPair` and `secondPair` from the `TwoNumbers` class presented in this section.

2.3 Completing the Class: Methods

Consider the `RoomType` class, which was developed in the last section and is reproduced in Figure 2.11.

FIGURE 2.11   **The `RoomType` class**

```
public class RoomType
{
    // data declarations section
    private double length;   // declare length as a double variable
    private double width;    // declare width as a double variable

    //method definitions section
}
```

At a minimum, this class's method definitions section should provide methods to initialize the values stored in each instance variable to user-selected values, display the values, and modify them. Such methods are referred to as **constructor methods**, **accessor methods**, and **mutator methods**, respectively, and are generally provided as part of every class's method definitions section. These are described in Table 2.9. Typically, other methods are also included to provide additional operations appropriate for the class.

Like the `main()` method, every class method provided in a class's method definition section consists of two parts: a method header and a method body (Figure 2.12). The purpose of the method header is to specify access privileges, which defines where the method can be used; identify the data type of a value that can be directly returned by the method; provide the method with a name; and specify the number, order, and type of data that can be transmitted into the method. The purpose of the method body is to access an object's variables, use any passed data, operate on the object's variables, and directly return, at most, one value.

FIGURE 2.12   **The general format of a class method**

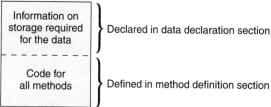

The general syntax for a member method's header line is shown in Figure 2.13. Except for constructors, which must not include a return type, this syntax is used for all other member methods. As shown, the header contains the access reserved word, `public`, a return type, a name, and a set of parentheses that encloses a parameter list.

FIGURE 2.13   **The format of a method header**

```
public returnType methodName(parameter list) <-- Required parentheses
```

Table 2.9 **Class Method Types**

Type of Method	Purpose
Constructor	A method that initializes instance variables when an object is created.
Accessor	A method that reports the value stored in an object's variable.
Mutator	A method that modifies the value stored in an object's variable.

This header line should also look familiar because it is almost identical to the one that we have been using for our `main()` methods. Designating a method as `public` means that the method can be used in other classes besides the class in which it is defined. The `parameter list` in the header line provides the information needed by a method to accept data passed to it when the method is called and is described in detail in Section 3.1. For now, we will use this general header line, with no parameters, to construct a basic set of class methods for our `RoomType` class.

Constructor Methods

A **constructor** method is any method that has the same name as its class. A class can have no user-defined constructors, a single user-defined constructor, or more than one user-defined constructor, as long as each constructor has a unique parameter list.

A constructor method is automatically called each time an object is created. The purpose of the constructor is to initialize each new object's instance variables to a known set of values. If no constructor method is written and no initial values are provided in the instance variable's declaration statement, the compiler supplies a default constructor that initializes each instance variable with the values listed in Table 2.10.

In addition to its primary role of initializing all instance variables, a constructor can also perform other tasks, as we will see in this section.

Figure 2.14 illustrates the most commonly used format for a constructor. As shown, a constructor

- Will be designated as a `public` method
- Must have the same name as the class to which it belongs
- Must have no return type (not even void)

For example, consider the following class that includes a constructor method:

```
public class RoomType
{
  // data declaration section
  private double length;  // declare length as a double variable
  private double width;   // declare width as a double variable

  // method definition section
  public RoomType()  // this is a constructor
  {
    length = 25.0;
    width = 12.0;
  }
}
```

Table 2.10   Default Initial Values for Instance Variables

Declared Data Type	Default Value at Creation
byte	0 as a byte value (8 bits)
short	0 as a short value (16 bits)
int	0 as an integer value (32 bits)
long	0L (64 bits)
float	0.0f (32 bits)
double	0.0d (64 bits)
char	null character, which is '\u0000'
boolean	false
string	null

This class's constructor will initialize each object's length and width variables to 25.0 and 12.0, respectively, when an object of this class type is created. If no user-defined constructor is declared, the compiler creates a default constructor that sets an object's length and width to 0.0, as specified in Table 2.10. Such a default constructor is equivalent to the definition

```
public RoomType()
{
    length = 0.0;
    width = 0.0;
}
```

Although the compiler-provided default constructor may or may not be useful in a particular application, it does provide a known value for each object's data members when no other constructor is declared. In its more general usage, the term *default constructor* refers to any constructor that does not include a parameter list. For example, the constructor that sets the length and width variables to 25.0 and 12.0, respectively, is also a default constructor. It is just a user-defined default constructor as opposed to a compiler-supplied one. Providing a user-defined constructor permits you to initialize an object with specific values other than the default values in Table 2.10.

For our immediate purposes, and to verify that a constructor method is automatically called whenever a new object is created, we will use the following constructor.

```
public RoomType()
{
    length = 25.0;
    width = 12.0;
    System.out.println("Created a new room object using the default constructor\n");
}
```

FIGURE 2.14   The constructor format

```
public className(parameter list)
{
    method body
}
```

PROGRAMMING NOTE

Constructors

A *constructor* is any method that has the same name as its class. A constructor is automatically called whenever an object is created. Its primary purpose is to initialize an object's variables.

A compiler error results when unique identification of a constructor is not possible. If no constructor is provided, the compiler supplies a default constructor that initializes all numerical data members to zero and all string data members to `null`. Instance variables that are declared with an initial value are not affected by the compiler-provided default constructor.

Every constructor method must be declared *with no return type* (not even `void`). Even though they are methods, constructors can only be used in a statement creating an object. Additionally, a class can have multiple constructors provided that each constructor is distinguishable by having a different parameter list.

When an object is now created, in addition to the initialization of the object's `length` and `width` data members, the following output is produced:

```
Created a new room object using the default constructor
```

Although any legitimate Java statement can be used within a constructor method, such as the `println()` method used here, it is best to keep constructors simple and use them for initialization purposes only.

Accessor Methods

The purpose of an **accessor method** is to provide a means for reading the values stored in an object's variables. A true accessor method, which is also referred to as a `get()` method, will return the value stored in one instance variable. Thus, an object containing multiple instance variables would require multiple accessor methods, one for each variable. As a practical matter, a method that either returns a combined value or displays one or more values is also frequently referred to as either an accessor or modified accessor method.

For example, if we were using a `Date` class that used month, day, and year instance variables, a modified accessor might convert the three values into a string such as "12/25/04" and return this string value. An additional modified accessor method might simply display all three values. True accessor methods would return individual year, month, and day values, respectively. Of course, each accessor method would have to be given a different name.

Because we have not yet presented how methods can return values, we will construct a simple modified accessor method for our `RoomType` class that displays the values stored in each object's instance variables. Naming our accessor method `showValues()`, a suitable method definition is

```
public void showValues()    // this is a modified accessor
{
   System.out.println("  length = " + length + "\n  width = " + width);
}
```

PROGRAMMING NOTE

Accessor Methods

An *accessor method*, which is more commonly referred to as an accessor for short, is a member method that accesses a class's private data members for the purpose of returning individual values. Such methods are also known as get() methods. We will designate a method that only displays an object's values as a *modified accessor*. Using this definition, the method showValues() in the RoomType class is a modified accessor method. True accessors (i.e., get() methods) and modified accessor methods are extremely important because they provide a means of retrieving and displaying an object's private data member values.

When you construct a class, make sure to provide a complete set of accessor methods. Each accessor method does not have to return a data member's exact value, but it should return a useful representation of that value. For example, assume that we have created a Date class where a date, such as 12/25/2002, is stored as a long integer in the form 20022512. Although an accessor method could display this value, a more useful representation would typically be either 12/25/02 or December 25, 2002.

Mutator Methods

The purpose of a mutator method is to provide a means for changing one or more of an object's values after the object has been created. This generally means that the user can enter new values and that these values will be passed on to the object using a mutator method. Mutator methods are also known as **set methods**.

Because we do not yet know how to pass data into a method, we will supply our RoomType class with a simple mutator that assigns a RoomType object's length and width variables with fixed values. In the next chapter, we will expand this mutator to permit the values to be passed into the mutator.

Naming our accessor method setNewValues(), a suitable method definition is

```
public void setNewValues()    // this is a mutator
{
  length = 12.5;
  width = 9.0;
}
```

Including our constructor, accessor, and mutator methods into our RoomType class, yields the following class definition:

```
public class RoomType
{
  // data declarations section
  private double length;  // declare length as a double variable
  private double width;   // declare width as a double variable

  // method definitions section
  public RoomType()  // this is a constructor
```

(continued on next page)

PROGRAMMING NOTE

Mutator Methods

A *mutator method*, which is more commonly referred to as a mutator for short, is any nonconstructor class method that changes an object's data values. Mutator methods are used to alter an object's data values after the object has been created and automatically initialized by a constructor method. A class can contain a number of mutators, as long as each mutator has a unique name. For example, in our RoomType class, there could be a mutator that changes an object's length value, a mutator that changes an object's width value, and a third mutator that changes both values.

Constructors, whose primary purpose is to initialize an object's member variables when an object is created, are not considered mutator methods.

(continued)

```
   {
      length = 25.0;
      width = 12.0;
      System.out.println("Created a new room object using the default constructor\n");
   }

   public void showValues()    // this is a modified accessor
   {
      System.out.println("  length = " + length + "\n  width = " + width);
   }

   public void setNewValues()    // this is a mutator
   {
      length = 12.5;
      width = 9.0;
   }
}
```

Constructors, accessors, and mutators provide the basic methods that each class should contain. Additionally, almost all classes provide a set of methods that use an object's values in appropriate ways. For example, the purpose of the RoomType class is to provide a means of calculating a house's total floor area in a room-by-room manner. So before we create objects from this class, we can add a method capable of calculating and displaying a room object's area. The area is obtained by multiplying its length times its width and displaying the result. The following method accomplishes this.

```
   public void calculateArea()    // this performs a calculation
   {
      System.out.println(length * width);
   }
```

Including the calculateArea() method into our RoomType class provides a complete class for calculating and displaying the floor area of a room that is modeled as having a rectangular-shaped floor. The completed class, which can now be used by any other class we choose to write, becomes

```
public class RoomType
{
  // data declarations section
  private double length;  // declare length as a double variable
  private double width;    // declare width as a double variable

  // method definitions section
  public RoomType()  // this is a constructor
  {
    length = 25.0;
    width = 12.0;
    System.out.println("Created a new room object using the default constructor\n");
  }

  public void showValues()    // this is a modified accessor
  {
    System.out.println("  length = " + length + "\n  width = " + width);
  }

  public void setNewValues()    // this is a mutator
  {
    length = 12.5;
    width = 9.0;
  }

  public void calculateArea()  // this performs a calculation
  {
    System.out.println(length * width);
  }
}
```

Every program that uses the RoomType class is restricted to using the methods defined in the method definitions section. This is because only the methods have been declared as public. Access to the two variables, length and width, which are automatically included in each created object, is restricted due to their private designation. Thus, these variables can only be retrieved or modified using the publicly available methods. Let's see how this is accomplished in practice. Consider the class UseRoomType, which creates an object of RoomType and displays the object's internal values.

The first two statements in this class should be familiar. The first statement declares a variable of type RoomType. The second statement then uses the new operator to allocate storage space for an object of this type, creates the object, and initializes its internal variables. The initialization is accomplished by the call to the constructor RoomType(). The next statement uses the println() method to display the message

```
The values for this room are:
```

Program 2.3

```
public class UseRoomType
{
  public static void main(String[] args)
  {
    RoomType roomOne;   // declare a variable of type RoomType

    roomOne = new RoomType();   // create and initialize an object of
                                // type RoomType
    System.out.println("\nThe values for this room are:");
    roomOne.showValues();       // use a class method on this object
    System.out.print("The floor area of this room is: ");
    roomOne.calculateArea();    // use another class method on this object


    roomOne.setNewValues();    // call the mutator

    System.out.println("\nThe values for this room have been changed to:");
    roomOne.showValues();
    System.out.print("The floor area of this room is: ");
    roomOne.calculateArea();
  }
}
```

It is the next statement roomOne.showValues() that is new here. Notice the notation we have used. It consists of an object's reference name and a class method name separated by a period. The standard syntax for using a class method to operate on a specific object is

objectName.classMethodName(arguments);

The *objectName* is the name of a variable that has been declared for a specific object, and the *classMethodName* is the name of a class method. Because our class methods have been declared as public, they can be used outside their defining class to access an object's private data members. In particular, the statement roomOne.showValues() invokes the showValues() method and tells it to operate on the object known as roomOne. Because we are not passing any arguments into the method, the parentheses do not enclose any values.

Similarly, the statement roomOne.calculateArea(); invokes the calculateArea() method and tells it to operate on the same named object. The mutator method is then used to change the length and width values in the roomOne object to 12.5 and 9.0, respectively, and the showValues() and calculateArea() methods are once more invoked on the roomOne object. The output produced by Program 2.3 is

```
Created a new room object using the default constructor

The values for this room are:
   length = 25.0
   width = 12.0
The floor area of this room is: 300.0
```

```
The values for this room have been changed to:
  length = 12.5
  width = 9.0
The floor area of this room is: 112.5
```

There are obvious improvements that should be made to Program 2.3. These include sending data into both the constructor and mutator, which will allow us to initialize objects and change their values with data supplied when the program is executed. Additionally, once we learn how to return a value from a method, we can have our accessor and calculation methods directly return a value rather than only display them. These two modifications are presented in the next chapter. As they stand, however, the two classes RoomType and UseRoomType illustrate the major issues concerned in creating and using classes.

These issues are, first and foremost, consideration of the data and methods that need to be provided. The primary concern of the main() method is then focused on creating objects and invoking the prewritten class methods to manipulate the objects appropriately. Once an object is created, a particular method is activated, or invoked, by effectively saying "run this method on this specific object."

As an example, consider Figure 2.15, which shows two objects of the RoomType type. Notice that each object contains two pieces of data, the first of which is the specific room's length and the second the room's width. In addition, as shown, the three provided operations consist of creating a new room, displaying a room's measurements, and calculating a room's floor area. As indicated, the methods are shared between all of the objects; that is, when a compiled class is loaded for execution into the JVM, only one copy of each method defined in the class's method definition section is stored. Although many objects can be constructed using the variables defined in the class's declaration section, each object, when it uses a class method, gets to use the same single copy of the method that resides in the JVM. Thus, to use a method, we must provide the JVM with both the name of the method and the name of the object that the method is to operate on. This is accomplished by separating the two pieces of information by a period, as was done in Program 2.3.

For example, the message roomOne.calculateArea() is sufficient to cause the calculateArea() method to be executed using the object named roomOne. The parentheses after the method name, as we will see in the next chapter, are used to provide the method with any additional data that might be needed to complete its operation. The object name that precedes the method name when the method is called

FIGURE 2.15 **A set of** RoomType **objects**

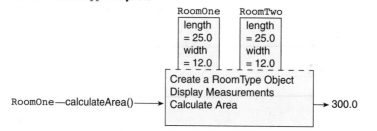

is formally referred to as both the **implied** and **implicit object**. Within the called method, this implied object, which is the object that the method is to operate on, is stored in a reference named this. Although it is usually not necessary to do so, the this reference can be explicitly used in member methods. For example, consider Program 2.4, which is the same as Program 2.2, except that each of its methods specifically uses the this reference.

Program 2.4

```java
public class RoomType
{
   // data declarations section
   private double length;   // declare length as a double variable
   private double width;    // declare width as a double variable

   // method definitions section
   public RoomType()   // this is a constructor
   {
      this.length = 25.0;
      this.width = 12.0;
      System.out.println("Created a new room object using the default constructor\n");
   }

   public void showValues()    // this is an accessor
   {
      System.out.println("  length = " + this.length + "\n  width = " + this.width);
   }

   public void setNewValues()    // this is a mutator
   {
      this.length = 12.5;
      this.width = 9.0;
   }

   public void calculateArea()   // this performs a calculation
   {
      System.out.println(this.length * this.width);
   }
}
```

When a class method is invoked with the name of an object, the this reference within the called method will be provided with the information necessary to locate the implied object, which then tells the method which specific instance variables are to be accessed. For example, if the calculate Area() method where to be called using the statement roomOne.calculateArea(), internally the println() statement effectively becomes

```
System.out.println(roomOne.length * roomOne.width);
```

Because the `this` reference is available to any method that operates on an implicit object (otherwise, the method would have no way of knowing which set of instance variables to access), the reserved word `this` is, by default, used and *need not* be explicitly included within class methods, as is done in Program 2.4. However, there are situations that do require its explicit use. These situations are presented in Section 11.1.

Although we will define our own classes and create objects as we become more fluent in Java, we can use any object and class provided by Java as long as we know the correct ways to activate the appropriate predefined methods. Because Java is based on and provides many prewritten classes, programming in Java requires us to become very familiar with at least a subset of its available classes and their respective methods, such as we did with the `println()` and `showMessageDialog()` methods.

Convenience

Notice that both the `RoomType` and `UseRoomType` classes must be compiled if the `UseRoomType` class is to be subsequently executed. Because there is usually only one public class per file, each of these classes is generally stored separately in its own file. Once a class is fully developed, this is conventionally what is done; the class is stored in a single file, and any program that needs the class is developed separately and stored in a separate file.

When developing a class, however, using two files can become bothersome, forcing the programmer to constantly switch back and forth between the files and forcing two compilations, one for each file. There are two solutions to this problem, both of which use a single file.

In the first method, and the one that we will frequently use in this text, second class's `main()` method is placed within the first class's methods section, making it simply one additional method in the first class's methods section. If this is done for the `RoomType` and `UseRoomType` classes, and renaming the single class as `RoomTypeWM` (which is meant to indicate `RoomType` With Main), the resulting class becomes

Program 2.5

```java
public class RoomType
{
  // data declarations section
  private double length;   // declare length as a double variable
  private double width;    // declare width as a double variable

  // method definitions section
  public RoomType()   // this is a constructor
  {
    length = 25.0;
    width = 12.0;
    System.out.println("Created a new room object using the default constructor\n");
  }

  public void showValues()    // this is a modified accessor
```

(continued on next page)

(continued)

```
   {
      System.out.println("  length = " + length + "\n  width = " + width);
   }


   public void setNewValues()    // this is a mutator
   {
      length = 12.5;
      width = 9.0;
   }


   public void calculateArea()   // this performs a calculation
   {
      System.out.println(length * width);
   }

   public static void main(String[] args)
   {
      RoomType roomOne;  // declare a variable of type RoomType2

      roomOne = new RoomType();  // create and initialize an object of
                                 // type RoomType
      System.out.println("\nThe values for this room are:");
      roomOne.showValues();         // use a class method on this object
      System.out.print("The floor area of this room is: ");
      roomOne.calculateArea();      // use another class method on this object

      roomOne.setNewValues();    // call the mutator

      System.out.println("\nThe values for this room have been changed to:");
      roomOne.showValues();
      System.out.print("The floor area of this room is: ");
      roomOne.calculateArea();
   }
}
```

Notice that the darker shaded region in Program 2.5 highlights the main() method used to test the class. Once a class has been fully tested, the main() method would be removed, and the remaining lighter shaded region would provide the completed class that could then be used by other classes and programs. We will frequently use this shading to clearly differentiate between the class being developed and the main() method used to test the class.

In the second method, both classes are stored in the same file with one modification: The public reserved word must be removed from the class that does not contain a main() method. This is required because there can only be one public class per file. Thus, in saving the single file consisting of two classes, the name given to the file would be the name of the public class that contains the main() method. The placement of the two classes in the file is not important; either class can be placed first, but only the class containing main() should be declared public.

Exercises 2.3

1. Compile Program 2.2.

2. Compile and run Program 2.3. To run this program, you must also first compile Program 2.2.

3. Compile Program 2.4 and run Program 2.3 to use the RoomType class provided in Program 2.4. Verify that the output is the same as that produced in Exercise 2.

4. Modify the constructor in either Program 2.2 or Program 2.5 to initialize th length variable to 15.6 and the width variable to 8.2.

5. Modify the showValues() and calculateArea() methods in either Program 2.3 or Program 2.5 to display all values using a dialog box.

6a. Complete the following class by adding a constructor, accessor, and calculation method. The constructor should initialize all objects with the number pair firstNumber = 10 and secondNumber = 15. The calculation method should calculate and display the average of the two numbers.

```java
public class TwoNumbers
{
  // data declaration section
  private int firstNumber;
  private int secondNumber;
  private double average;

  // method definition section
}
```

b. Construct a second class named UseTwoNumbers that creates a single object and displays the object's values and the average of these values.

7a. Construct a Time class containing integer data members seconds, minutes, and hours. Have the class contain a user-written default constructor that initializes each data member with a default value of 0. The final member method should be an accessor method that displays the value of all data members.

b. Include the class written for Exercise 7a within the context of a complete program.

8a. Construct a class named Student consisting of a long integer student identification number and a double-precision cumulative grade point average. The constructor for this class should initialize the identification number to 111111L and the grade point average to 0.0. Included in the class should be an accessor member method to display all data values.

b. Include the class constructed in Exercise 8a within the context of a complete program. Your program should declare two objects of type Student and display data for the two objects to verify operation of the member methods.

2.4 Assignment Operations

We have already encountered assignment statements in Section 2.2. Assignment statements are the most basic Java statements for initializing variables within constructor methods, assigning new values to variables within mutator methods, and performing computations in other methods. In this section, we focus on this important statement type and consider its capabilities in detail.

The general syntax for an assignment statement is

```
variable = expression;
```

The simplest expression in Java is a single literal value, or literal for short. In each of the following assignment statements, the expression to the right of the equal sign is a literal.

```
length = 25;
width = 17.5;
```

In each of these assignment statements, the value of the constant to the right of the equal sign is assigned to the variable to the left of the equal sign. It is important to note that the equal sign in Java does not have the same meaning as an equal sign in algebra. The equal sign in an assignment statement tells the computer first to determine the value of the operand to the right of the equal sign and then to store (or assign) that value in the locations associated with the variable to the left of the equal sign. In this regard, the Java statement `length = 25;` is read "length is assigned the value 25." The blank spaces in the assignment statement are inserted for readability only.

Before any computation is performed using a variable, the variable should be assigned a value with an assignment statement. This can be done either when the variable is declared, or for instance variables, it is typically accomplished using a constructor method. As we have seen, the first time a value is assigned to a variable, the variable is said to be initialized. After a variable has been initialized, its value can subsequently be changed by another assignment statement. For example, assume that a variable named `total` was initialized to 3.7. A subsequent statement, such as

```
total = 6.28;
```

causes the value of 6.28 to be assigned to `total`. The 3.7 that was in `total` is overwritten with the new value of 6.28. Because a variable can store only one value at a time, it is sometimes useful to think of the variable to the left of the equal sign as a parking spot in a huge parking lot. Just as an individual parking spot can be used only by one car at a time, each individual variable can store only one value at a time. The "parking" of a new value in a variable automatically causes the computer to remove any value previously parked there.

In addition to being a literal value, the operand to the right of the equal sign in an assignment statement can be a variable or any other valid Java expression. An **expression** is any combination of constants and variables that can be evaluated to yield a result. Thus, the expression in an assignment statement can perform calculations using the arithmetic operators introduced in Section 2.1. Examples of assignment statements using expressions containing these operators are

```
sum = 3 + 7;
diff = 15 - 6;
product = 0.05 * 14.6;
tally = count + 1;
newTotal = 18.3 + total;
taxes = 0.06 * amount;
totalWeight = factor * weight;
average = sum / items;
slope = (y2 - y1) / (x2 - x1);
```

As always in an assignment statement, the value of the expression to the right of the equal sign is evaluated first, and then this value is stored in the variable to the left of the equal sign. For example, in the assignment statement `totalWeight = factor * weight;` the arithmetic expression `factor * weight` is first evaluated to yield a result. This result, which is a number, is then stored in the variable `totalWeight`.

In writing assignment expressions, you must be aware of two important considerations. Since the expression to the right of the equal sign is evaluated first, all variables used in the expression must previously have been given valid values if the result is to make sense. For example, the assignment statement `totalWeight = factor * weight;` causes a valid number to be stored in `totalWeight` only if the programmer first takes care to assign valid numbers to `factor` and `weight`. Thus, the sequence of statements

```
factor = 1.06;
weight = 155.0;
totalWeight = factor * weight;
```

ensures that we know the values being used to obtain the result that will be stored in `totalWeight`. Figure 2.16 illustrates the values stored in the variables `factor`, `weight`, and `totalWeight`.

The second consideration to keep in mind is that because the value of an expression is stored in the variable to the left of the equal sign, there must be a variable listed immediately to the left of the equal sign. For example, the assignment statement

```
amount + 1892 = 1000 + 10 * 5;
```

is not valid. The expression on the right side of the equal sign evaluates to the integer 1050, which can be stored only in a variable. Because `amount + 1892` is not a valid variable name, the program does not know where to store the calculated value. QuickTest Program 2.6 illustrates the use of assignment statements in calculating the area of a rectangle.

QuickTest Program 2.6

```
// this program calculates the area of a rectangle
// given its length and width

public class RectangleArea
{
  public static void main(String[] args)
  {
    double length;
    double width;
    double area;
```

(continued on next page)

FIGURE 2.16   **Values stored in the variables**

factor	weight	totalWeight
1.06	155.0	164.3

(continued)

```
    length = 27.3;
    width = 13.4;
    area = length * width;
    System.out.println("The length of the rectangle is " + length);
    System.out.println("The width of the rectangle is " + width);
    System.out.println("The area of the rectangle is " + area);
  }
}
```

When QuickTest Program 2.6 is run, the output is

```
The length of the rectangle is 27.3
The width of the rectangle is 13.4
The area of the rectangle is 365.82
```

Consider the flow of control that the computer uses in executing QuickTest Program 2.6. Execution begins with the first statement in `main()` and continues sequentially, statement by statement, until the closing brace of `main()` is encountered. This flow of control is true for all programs. The computer works on one statement at a time, executing that statement with no knowledge of what the next statement will be. This explains why all operands used in an expression must have values assigned to them before the expression is evaluated.

When the computer executes the statement `area = length * width;` in QuickTest Program 2.6, it uses whatever value is stored in the variables `length` and `width` at the time the assignment is executed. Therefore, to ensure that a correct computation is made, you must assign valid values to these variables. Failure to assign any values to variables declared within a method results in a compiler error message.

It is important to realize that in Java, the equal sign, =, used in assignment statements is itself an operator, *which differs from the way most other high-level languages process this symbol*. In Java (as in C and C++), the = symbol is called the *assignment operator*, and an expression using this operator, such as `interest = principal * rate`, is an assignment expression. Because the assignment operator has a lower precedence than any other arithmetic operator, the value of any expression to the right of the equal sign is evaluated first, prior to assignment.

As always, instead of providing character-based output using the `println()` method, as is done in QuickTest Program 2.6, we can just as easily provide a GUI output. QuickTest Program 2.7 provides the same processing as QuickTest Program 2.6 but displays the results in a dialog box.

In reviewing QuickTest Program 2.7, notice that we have declared a string reference variable named `output` and then have "built up" the string using successive concatenation operations, which include newline escape sequences. The `output` variable is then passed to the `showMessageDialog()` method for display. This method retrieves the value of any variable name passed to it in the same manner as does the `println()` method. Thus, it is the characters stored in `output` that are displayed, resulting in the dialog box in Figure 2.17.

Because the equal sign is an operator in Java, multiple assignments are possible in the same expression or its equivalent statement. For example, in the statement `a = b = c = 25;`, all of the assignment operators have the same precedence. Because the assignment operator has a right-to-left associativity, this statement is equivalent to

```
    a = (b = (c = 25));
```

FIGURE 2.17   **The output displayed by QuickTest Program 2.7**

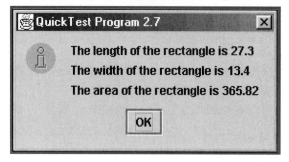

This evaluation has the effect of assigning the number 25 to each of the variables individually in the sequence

```
c = 25;
b = 25;
a = 25;
```

QuickTest Program 2.7

```java
import javax.swing.*;
public class GuiAreaOutput
{
  public static void main(String[] args)
  {
    double length;
    double width;
    double area;
    String output;

    length = 27.3;
    width = 13.4;
    area = length * width;
    output = "The length of the rectangle is " + length
             + "\nThe width of the rectangle is " + width
             + "\nThe area of the rectangle is " + area;

    JOptionPane.showMessageDialog(null, output, "QuickTest Program 2.7",
                              JOptionPane.INFORMATION_MESSAGE);

    System.exit(0);
  }
}
```

Multiple Declarations

Variables with the same data type can always be grouped together and declared using a single declaration statement. Although this is almost never done for a class's instance variables, it is frequently used in declaring a method's internal, or local, variables. For example, the three separate declarations used in QuickTest Program 2.6,

```
double length;
double width;
double area;
```

can be replaced by the single declaration statement

```
double length, width, area;
```

Similarly, the two character declarations,

```
char ch;
char key;
```

can be replaced with the single declaration statement

```
char ch, key;
```

Note that declaring multiple variables in a single declaration requires that the data type of the variables be given only once, that all the variables names be separated by commas, and that only one semicolon be used to terminate the declaration. The space after each comma is inserted for readability and is not required.

Coercion

In restricted cases, data type conversions will take place across assignment operators; that is, the value of the expression on the right side of the assignment operator is converted to the data type of the variable to the left of the assignment operator. This type of forced conversion is referred to as a **coercion**.

A coercion automatically occurs only when a smaller range numerical data type is assigned to a variable of a larger range type. Thus, if an integer is assigned to a variable declared as either a `float` or `double`, the integer will be converted to the variable's declared data type. For example, assigning the integer 14 to a variable defined as a `double` results in the value 14.0 being assigned. However, a compiler error results if an attempt is made in the reverse direction; you cannot assign a larger range numerical value to a numerical data type having a smaller range of values. The reason is that this latter type of conversion can result in a loss of precision. For example, if `temp` is an integer variable, the assignment `temp = 25.89` results in a compiler error because it would cause the loss of the fractional value .89.

A more complete example of data type coercions, which includes both mixed-mode and assignment conversions, is the evaluation of the expression

```
a = b * c
```

where `a` is a double-precision variable, `b` is an integer variable, and `c` is a single-precision (`float`) variable. When the mixed-mode expression `b * c` is evaluated,[11] the value of `b` used in the expression is converted to a `float` for purposes of computation (it is important to note that the value stored in `b` remains an integer number). Finally, data type coercion across the assignment operator comes into play. Because the left side of the assignment operator is a double-precision variable, the value of the

---

[11] Review the rules in Section 2.2 for the evaluation of mixed-mode expressions if necessary.

expression (b * c) is extended to a 64-bit double-precision value and stored in the variable a.

Assignment Variations

Although only one variable is allowed immediately to the left of the equal sign in an assignment expression, the variable to the left of the equal sign can also be used to the right of the equal sign. For example, the assignment expression sum = sum + 10 is valid. Clearly, as an algebra equation, sum could never be equal to itself plus 10. But in Java, the expression sum = sum + 10 is not an equation; it is an expression that is evaluated in two major steps. The first step is to calculate the value of sum + 10. The second step is to store the computed value in sum. See if you can determine the output of QuickTest Program 2.8.

QuickTest Program 2.8

```
public class ReusingAVariable
{
  public static void main(String[] args)
  {
    int sum;

    sum = 25;
    System.out.println("The number stored in sum is " + sum);
    sum = sum + 10;
    System.out.println("The number now stored in sum is " + sum);
  }
}
```

The assignment statement sum = 25; tells the computer to store the number 25 in sum, as shown in Figure 2.18.

FIGURE 2.18 **The integer** 25 **is stored in** sum

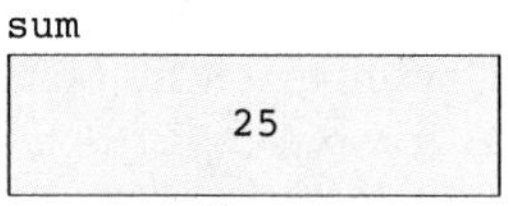

sum

The first println() statement in QuickTest Program 2.8 causes the value stored in sum to be displayed by the message The number stored in sum is 25. The second assignment statement, sum = sum + 10;, causes the program to retrieve the 25 stored in sum and add 10 to this number, yielding the number 35. The number 35 is then stored in the variable to the left of the equal sign, which is the variable sum. The 25 that was in sum is overwritten with the new value of 35, as shown in Figure 2.19.

Assignment expressions like sum = sum + 25, which use the same variable on both sides of the assignment operator, can be written using the following **shortcut assignment operators**:

```
+=   -=      *=      /=      %=
```

For example, the expression sum = sum + 10 can be written as sum += 10. Similarly, the expression price *= rate is equivalent to price = price * rate.

FIGURE 2.19 `sum = sum + 10;` **causes a new value to be stored in** `sum`

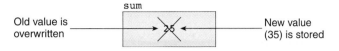

In using these new assignment operators, it is important to note that the variable to the left of the assignment operator is applied to the *complete* expression to the right. For example, the expression `price *= rate + 1` is equivalent to the expression `price = price * (rate + 1)`, not `price = price * rate + 1`.

Accumulating

Assignment expressions like `sum += 10` or its equivalent, `sum = sum + 10`, are very common in programming. These expressions are required in accumulating subtotals when data are entered one number at a time. For example, if we want to add the numbers 96, 70, 85, and 60 in calculator fashion, the following statements could be used:

Statement	Value in sum
`sum = 0;`	0
`sum = sum + 96;`	96
`sum = sum + 70;`	166
`sum = sum + 85;`	251
`sum = sum + 60;`	311

The first statement initializes `sum` to 0. This removes any previous number ("garbage value") stored in `sum` that would invalidate the final total. As each number is added, the value stored in `sum` increases accordingly. After completion of the last statement, `sum` contains the total of all the added numbers.

QuickTest Program 2.9 illustrates the effect of these statements by displaying `sum`'s contents after each addition is made.

QuickTest Program 2.9

```java
public class SubTotals
{
  public static void main(String[] args)
  {
    int sum;

    sum = 0;
    System.out.println("The value of sum is initially set to " + sum);
    sum = sum + 96;
    System.out.println("  sum is now " + sum);
    sum = sum + 70;
    System.out.println("  sum is now " + sum);
    sum = sum + 85;
    System.out.println("  sum is now " + sum);
    sum = sum + 60;
    System.out.println("  The final sum is " + sum);
  }
}
```

The output displayed by QuickTest Program 2.9 is

```
The value of sum is initially set to 0
   sum is now 96
   sum is now 166
   sum is now 251
   The final sum is 311
```

Although QuickTest Program 2.9 is not a practical program (it is easier to add the numbers by hand), it does illustrate the subtotaling effect of repeated use of statements having the form

```
variable = variable + newValue;
```

As we will see when we become more familiar with the repetition statements introduced in Chapter 5, we will find many uses for this type of statement. One immediately useful application, however, is the successive buildup of a single output string. For example, in QuickTest Program 2.7, the string variable named `output` was assigned a value using the statement

```
output = "The length of the rectangle is " + length
        + "\nThe width of the rectangle is " + width
        + "\nThe area of the rectangle is " + area;
```

The final value assigned to `output` can just as easily be assembled as follows:

```
output = "The length of the rectangle is " + length;
output += "\nThe width of the rectangle is " + width;
output += "\nThe area of the rectangle is " + area;
```

The advantage here is that the individual statements can now be separated from one another and placed within a program as you see fit, rather than as a single unit just after the value of `area` is obtained. This permits you to initialize the string with the first assignment statement and then accumulate additional pieces of the final string later in the program (clearly, each statement must be placed after values of the respective variables are assigned). For example, consider QuickTest Program 2.10, which uses these statements in different parts of the program to construct the final displayed string.

QuickTest Program 2.10

```java
import javax.swing.*;
public class BuildAString
{
  public static void main(String[] args)
  {
    double length, width, area;
    String output;

    length = 27.3;
    output = "The length of the rectangle is " + length;
    width = 13.4;
    output += "\nThe width of the rectangle is " + width;
    area = length * width;
```

(continued on next page)

(continued)

```
    output += "\nThe area of the rectangle is " + area;

    JOptionPane.showMessageDialog(null, output, "QuickTest Program 2.10",
                        JOptionPane.INFORMATION_MESSAGE);

    System.exit(0);
  }
}
```

The output displayed by QuickTest Program 2.10 is identical to that of QuickTest Program 2.7; for convenience, it is repeated in Figure 2.20. Although there is no inherent advantage to QuickTest Program 2.10 as opposed to QuickTest Program 2.7, the concept of building-up a single string from individually distinct pieces is used so often that you should be familiar with it. In certain situations, which are presented in Chapter 5, it is in fact the only means of creating the desired string.

FIGURE 2.20   The output displayed by QuickTest Program 2.10

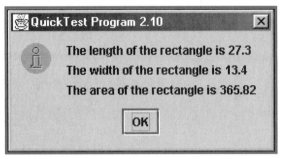

Counting

An assignment statement that is very similar to the accumulating statement is the counting statement. Counting statements have the form

```
    variable = variable + fixedNumber;
```

Examples of counting statements are

```
    i = i + 1;
    n = n + 1;
    count = count + 1;
    j = j + 2;
    m = m + 2;
    kk = kk + 3;
```

In each of these examples, the same variable is used on both sides of the equal sign. After the statement is executed, the value of the respective variable is increased by a fixed amount. In the first three examples, the variables i, n, and count have all been increased by 1. In the next two examples, the variables j and m have been increased by 2, and in the final example, the variable kk has been increased by 3.

For the special case in which a variable is either increased or decreased by 1, Java provides two unary operators. Using the **increment operator**, ++, the expression

variable = variable + 1 can be replaced by either the expression variable++
or ++variable. Examples of the increment operator are

Expression	*Alternative*
i = i + 1	i++ or ++i
n = n + 1	n++ or ++n
count = count + 1	count++ or ++count

QuickTest Program 2.11 illustrates the use of the increment operator.

QuickTest Program 2.11

```java
public class IncrementOperator
{
  public static void main(String[] args)
  {
    int count;

    count = 0;
    System.out.println("The initial value of count is " + count);
    count++;
    System.out.println("   count is now " + count);
    count++;
    System.out.println("   count is now " + count);
    count++;
    System.out.println("   count is now " + count);
    count++;
    System.out.println("   count is now " + count);
  }
}
```

The output displayed by QuickTest Program 2.11 is

```
The initial value of count is 0
   count is now 1
   count is now 2
   count is now 3
   count is now 4
```

When the ++ operator appears before a variable, it is called a **prefix increment
operator**; when it appears after a variable, it is called a **postfix increment operator**. The distinction between a prefix and postfix increment operator is important
when the variable being incremented is used in an assignment expression. For example, the expression k = ++n does two things in one expression. Initially, the value of
n is incremented by 1, and then the new value of n is assigned to the variable k. Thus,
the statement k = ++n; is equivalent to the two statements

```java
n = n + 1;   // increment n first
k = n;       // assign n's value to k
```

The assignment expression k = n++, which uses a postfix increment operator, reverses this procedure. A postfix increment operates after the assignment is completed.

Thus, the statement `k = n++;` first assigns the current value of n to k and then increments the value of n by 1. This is equivalent to the two statements

```
k = n;          // assign n's value to k
n = n + 1;      // and then increment n
```

In addition to the increment operator, Java also provides a **decrement operator**, `- -`. As you might expect, the expressions `variable--` and `--variable` are both equivalent to the expression `variable = variable - 1`. Examples of the decrement operator are

Expression	Alternative
`i = i - 1`	`i--` or `--i`
`n = n - 1`	`n--` or `--n`
`count = count - 1`	`count--` or `--count`

When the `--` operator appears before a variable, it is called a **prefix decrement operator**. When the decrement appears after a variable, it is called a **postfix decrement operator**. For example, both of the expressions `n--` and `--n` reduce the value of n by 1. These expressions are equivalent to the longer expression `n = n - 1`. As with the increment operator, however, the prefix and postfix decrement operators produce different results when used in assignment expressions. For example, the expression `k = --n` first decrements the value of n by 1 before assigning the value of n to k, whereas the expression `k = n--` first assigns the current value of n to k and then reduces the value of n by 1.

Exercises 2.4

1. Determine and correct the errors in the following `main()` methods:

a.
```
public static void main(String[] args)
    {
      width = 15
      area = length * width;
      System.out.println("The area is " + area);
    }
```

b.
```
public static void main(String[] args)
    {
      int length, width, area;
      area = length * width;
      length = 20;
      width = 15;
      System.out.println("The area is " + area);
```

c.
```
public static void main(String[] args)
    {
      int length = 20; width = 15, area;
      length * width = area;
      System.out.println("The area is " , area;
    }
```

2a. Write a QuickTest program to calculate and display the average of the numbers 32.6, 55.2, 67.9, and 48.6.

  b. Run the program written for Exercise 2a on your computer.

3a. Write a QuickTest program to calculate the circumference of a circle. The equation for determining the circumference of a circle is *circumference = 2 * 3.1416 * radius*. Assume that the circle has a radius of 3.3 inches.

  b. Run the program written for Exercise 3a on your computer.

4a. Write a QuickTest program to calculate the area of a circle. The equation for determining the area of a circle is *area = 3.1416 * radius * radius*. Assume that the circle has a radius of 5 inches.

  b. Run the program written for Exercise 4a on your computer.

5a. Write a QuickTest program to calculate the volume of a swimming pool. The equation for determining the volume is *volume = length * width * depth*. Assume that the pool has a length of 25 feet, a width of 10 feet, and a depth of 6 feet.

  b. Run the program written for Exercise 5a on your computer.

6a. Write a QuickTest program to convert temperature in degrees Fahrenheit to degrees Celsius. The equation for this conversion is *Celsius = 5.0 / 9.0 * (Fahrenheit − 32.0)*. Have your program convert and display the Celsius temperature corresponding to 98.6 degrees Fahrenheit.

  b. Run the program written for Exercise 6a on your computer.

7a. Write a QuickTest program to calculate the dollar amount in a piggy bank. The bank currently contains 12 half dollars, 20 quarters, 32 dimes, 45 nickels, and 27 pennies.

  b. Run the program written for Exercise 7a on your computer.

8a. Write a QuickTest program to calculate the distance, in feet, of a trip that is 2.36 miles long. One mile equals 5,280 feet.

  b. Run the program written for Exercise 8a on your computer.

9a. Write a QuickTest program to calculate the elapsed time it took to make a 183.67-mile trip. The equation for computing elapsed time is *elapsed time = total distance / average speed*. Assume that the average speed during the trip was 58 miles per hour.

  b. Run the program written for Exercise 9a on your computer.

10a. Write a QuickTest program to calculate the sum of the numbers from 1 to 100. The formula for calculating this sum is *sum = (n / 2) * (2 * a + (n − 1) * d)*, where *n* = the number of terms to be added, *a* = the first number, and *d* = the difference between each number.

  b. Run the program written for Exercise 10a on your computer.

11. By mistake, a programmer reordered the statements in QuickTest Program 2.9 as follows:

```
public class SubTotals
{
  public static void main(String[] args)
  {
    int sum;
```

(continued on next page)

(continued)

```
    sum = 0;
    sum = sum + 96;
    sum = sum + 70;
    sum = sum + 85;
    sum = sum + 60;
    System.out.println("The value of sum is initially set to " + sum);
    System.out.println("  sum is now " + sum);
    System.out.println("  sum is now " + sum);
    System.out.println("  sum is now " + sum);
    System.out.println("  The final sum is " + sum);
  }
}
```

Determine the output this program produces.

2.5 Program Design and Development: Object Identification

The `RoomType` class developed in this chapter is based on the model of a room as a rectangular object. This is always the first step in constructing an object-based programs—developing an object-based model of the problem. Each class then becomes a description of the model written in Java (Figure 2.21). In this section, we explore this object-based concept in more detail and begin a systematic development of programs using object-based models.

Formally, a **model** is a representation of a problem. The first step in creating an object-based model is to begin "thinking in objects." As a specific example, if we wanted to obtain the result of tossing a coin 100 times, we could do this by tossing a real coin. However, if we could accurately model a coin, we could also obtain the result by writing a program to simulate a coin toss. Here the object being modeled is a coin. Similarly, if we wanted to play a game of solitaire, we could model a deck of cards and simulate the game using a program.

Objects, such as coins, cards, and more complicated graphical objects, are well suited to a programing representation because they can all be specified by two basic characteristics: attributes and behaviors. **Attributes** define the properties of interest, and **behaviors** define how the object reacts to its environment.

To make this more tangible, let us reconsider our coin tossing experiment. For this experiment, the object under consideration is a coin. In terms of attributes, a coin has a denomination, size, weight, color, condition (tarnished, worn, proof), country of origin, and a side (head or tail). If we were purchasing a coin for collectable purposes, we would be interested in all but the last of these attributes. For the purpose of a coin toss, however, the only attribute that is of interest is the side; whether the coin is a

FIGURE 2.21   **A Java class is a programming language description of a model**

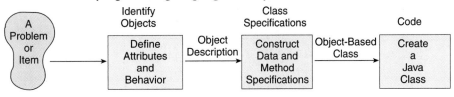

penny or a quarter, copper or silver colored, tarnished or not is of no concern to us. Thus, in terms of modeling a coin for performing a coin toss, the only attribute that we need to consider initially is what side is visible after the coin is tossed. It is important to understand the underlying significance of our choice of attributes because very few models are ever complete. A model typically does not reveal every aspect of the object it represents and should only include those attributes that are of relevance to the problem being considered.

Having determined the attributes to be used in modeling a coin, the next step requires identifying the behavior that this object should exhibit. To model a coin toss, we must have a means of simulating a toss and determining the side that faces up after the toss is completed. Figure 2.22 illustrates an **object diagram** that describes a coin object. For programming purposes, this description will have to be translated into a programming language, be it Java or some other object-oriented language.

Although this is a relatively simple example, it illustrates the initial approach in designing and developing an object-oriented program. This approach consists of the following two steps:

Step 1. Identify the required objects
Step 2. For each object,
  a. Identify the attributes of interest
  b. Identify the behavior (operations) of interest

As the design proceeds, you will frequently have to refine and expand the initial object description. Refinement, which means improving and modifying the model, is generally always required for all but extremely simple situations.

In Chapters 5 and 6, we will present a more structured approach to modeling based on a methodology known as the Unified Modeling Language (UML). This methodology, as with all object-oriented design and development techniques, is based on first identifying the objects needed and then further identifying the objects' attributes and behavior. Once a model is built, however, it still must be translated into Java. How this is accomplished forms the basis of most of this text.

From Objects to Classes

Identifying the objects that will be used in a program is only the first step in the modeling process. The attributes and behavior actually define a category or type of object out of which many individual objects can then be designated. To make this more tangible, consider a geometric object, such as a rectangle that we want to display on a screen. In its simplest representation, a rectangle has a shape and location, which can be described by the object diagram in Figure 2.23.

We can now refine this model to more accurately define what we mean by shape and location. A rectangle's shape is traditionally specified by attributes of length and

FIGURE 2.22 **An initial object description**

```
Object: A coin

Attributes: Side (head or tail)

Behavior: Toss the coin
```

FIGURE 2.23   **An initial object diagram**

Rectangle
shape
location

width, and its location can be specified in a number of ways. One simple way is to list the values of either two adjacent or two opposite corner positions. The behavior we provide a rectangle depends on what we are want our rectangle do. For example, if we intend to display a rectangle on a screen, we might provide it with the ability to move its position and change either its length or width. Figure 2.24 illustrates our refined object description.

FIGURE 2.24   **A refined object diagram**

Rectangle
length
width
top-left corner
opposite corner
move
change length
change width

As we have already seen, in object-based programming, the category of objects defined by a given set of attributes and behavior is called a **class**. For example, the attributes length and width can define a general type of shape called a rectangle. Only when specific values have been assigned to these attributes have we represented a specific and particular rectangle. This distinction carries over into Java: The attributes and behavior we describe in an object diagram are used to define a general class, or type, of object. An object itself only comes into existence when we assign specific values to the attributes. The created object is then said to have a **state**, which describes how the object appears at the moment.

In practice, an object's state is defined by the values that have been assigned to its attributes. For example, if a rectangle has a width of 1 inch, a length of 2 inches, and its upper left corner is positioned at 4 inches from the top of a video screen and 5 inches from the left side of the screen, and its opposite corner is 5 inches from the top of the screen and 7 inches from the left side of the screen, its state is completely specified (Figure 2.25).

FIGURE 2.25   **Defining the state of a rectangle**

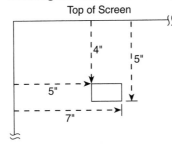

Program 2.12

```
public class RoomType
{
  // data declarations section
  private double length;  // declare length as a double variable
  private double width;   // declare width as a double variable

  // method definitions section
  public RoomType()  // this is a constructor
  {
    length = 25.0;
    width = 12.0;
    System.out.println("Created a new room object using the default constructor\n");
  }

  public void showValues()
  {
    System.out.println("  length = " + length + "\n  width = " + width);
  }

  public void calculateArea()
  {
    System.out.println(length*width);
  }
}
```

```
public class UseRoomType
{
  public static void main(String[] args)
  {
    RoomType roomOne;  // declare a variable of type RoomType

    roomOne = new RoomType();  // create and initialize an object of
                               // type RoomType
    System.out.println("The values for this room are:");
    roomOne.showValues();         // use a class method on this object
    System.out.print("\nThe floor area of this room is: ");
    roomOne.calculateArea();      // use another class method on this object
  }
}
```

Finally, at its creation, each object must be given an **identity**. This means that each object, when created, must be given a name by which it can be uniquely identified within a program. This is similar to giving each automobile a vehicle identification number (VIN) when it is assembled or giving a unique name to each individual in a family. We can identify these basic elements in Program 2.3, which was constructed in Section 2.3 and is reproduced, along with the RoomType class, as Program 2.12[12]

Note that the RoomType class in Program 2.12, which is listed in the lighter shaded region, defines a class from which objects can be constructed. It is important to understand that this class successfully encapsulates the plans for building a Room-Type object. The actual creation of an object from this class and the exercising of its behavior are then provided in a second class, which is the UseRoomType class that is provided in the darker shaded region. This is the essence of object-oriented design. Once a class is constructed and tested, it can be used by any other class to create as many objects as needed and manipulate these objects using the provided methods.

Procedural versus Object Orientations[13]

Consider QuickTest Program 2.13.

QuickTest Program 2.13

```
public class QTRoomType
{
  public static void main(String[] args)
  {
    double length = 25.0;
    double width = 12.0;

    System.out.println("\nThe values for this room are:");
    System.out.println("  length = " + length + "\n  width = " + width);
    System.out.print("The floor area of this room is: ");
    System.out.println(length * width);

    length = 12.5;
    width = 9.0;

    System.out.println("\nThe values for this room have been changed to:");
    System.out.println("  length = " + length + "\n  width = " + width);
    System.out.print("The floor area of this room is: ");
    System.out.println(length * width);
  }
}
```

Although QuickTest Program 2.13 uses a class structure and produces the same result as Program 2.12, the QuickTest program is fundamentally *not* an object-oriented program. Rather, it is a procedure-oriented program that provides a single method for quickly calculating and displaying a room's floor area. No objects are named, created, and initialized in this program. A method by itself is a procedure for creating a result, and programs that only use methods with no object creation are

---

[12] As was noted in the previous section, because there can only be one public class per file, this program would have to be stored in two source files. To see how this program can be stored in a single file, see Program 2.5.

[13] This topic can be omitted on first reading without loss of subject continuity.

fundamentally procedure-oriented programs. So the fact that a program uses a method within a class structure does not make the program object oriented.

The essential difference between Programs 2.12 and 2.13 is the model on which they are based, and as you program, you should be aware of this difference. QuickTest programs are very helpful when learning how to use a specific Java statement or method, such as `println()`. They are also useful for constructing output quickly for extremely simple programming problems. But such programs can become detrimental for serious programmers who eventually will have to address more complex programming situations. So even when you need to create a QuickTest program, which is fundamentally based on a procedural orientation, it is useful to at least contemplate how you might construct a programming solution using objects. In procedure-oriented programming, the emphasis is always on the operations to be performed, such as add, divide, and display, whereas in object-oriented programming, the emphasis is on the attributes and behavior of the objects that will be used.

Exercises 2.5

1. Define the following terms:
   a. attribute
   b. behavior
   c. class
   d. identity
   e. model
   f. object
   g. object diagram
   h. state
   i. value

2a. In place of specifying a rectangle's location by listing the position of two corner points, what other attributes could be used?

   b. What other attributes, besides length and width, might describe a rectangle if the rectangle is to be drawn on a color monitor?

   c. Describe a set of attributes that could be used to define circles that are to be drawn on a black-and-white monitor.

   d. What attributes would you add to those selected in response to Exercise 2c if the circles were to be drawn on a color monitor?

3. Classify each of the following as either classes or objects:
   a. maple trees
   b. Ford automobiles
   c. my collie dog
   d. the oak tree in my yard
   e. Boeing 767 planes
   f. your Ford Taurus

g. kitchen tables

h. student desks

i. the chair you are sitting on

4a. For each of the following, determine what attributes might be of interest to someone considering buying the item.

    i. a book

    ii. a can of soda

    iii. a pen

    iv. a cassette tape

    v. a cassette tape player

    vi. an elevator

    vii. a car

b. Do the attributes you used in Exercise 4a model an object or a class of objects?

5. For each of the following, what behavior might be of interest to someone considering buying the item?

a. a car

b. a cassette tape player

6a. List five attributes of a character that could be used in a video game.

b. List five behaviors that a character in a video game should have.

7a. List as many attributes and behaviors that would be of interest in a program that simulates dealing a hand of playing cards. For this, assume any card game that you are familiar with.

b. What attributes of the cards would not be of interest for purposes of the simulation?

8a. List as many attributes and behaviors that would be of interest in a program intended to simulate an elevator that moves between floors of a building from the 1st to the 15th floor.

b. What attributes of the elevator would not be of interest for purposes of the simulation?

9. The class examples considered in this section have consisted of inanimate objects. Do you think that animate objects such as pets and even human beings could be modeled in terms of attributes and behavior? Why or why not?

10a. Attributes represent how objects appear to the outside world, whereas behaviors represent how an object can respond to an external stimulus. Given this, what do you think is the mechanism by which one object "triggers" the designated behavior in another object?

b. If behavior is constructed by defining an appropriate method, how is a particular behavior activated in Java?

11. Consider the problem of adding two numbers.

a. From a procedural orientation, what mathematical operation would you concentrate on?

b. From an object orientation, what objects are required? What behavior should these objects have?

2.6 **Common Programming Errors**

The most common errors associated with the material presented in this chapter are:

1. Forgetting to declare all the variables used in a class. This error is detected by the compiler, and an error message is generated for all undeclared variables.

2. Forgetting to assign or initialize values for all variables before the variables are used in an expression. Such values can be assigned by assignment statements, initialized within a declaration statement, or assigned interactively by entering values using an Input dialog.

3. Mistyping or misreading the lowercase version of the letter L (l) for the number 1, or vice-versa.

4. Mistyping or misreading the uppercase letter O for the number zero (0), or vice-versa.

5. Attempting to store a higher precision value in a lower precision data type. Thus, integer values will be accepted for both `float` and `double` variables and are automatically converted to the correct data type, but a `double` value cannot be stored in a `float` variable. This error is detected by the compiler, and an error message equivalent to `Incompatible type for declaration` is provided (the exact error message is compiler dependent).

6. Using a variable in an expression before a value has been initially assigned to the variable. This will result in the compiler error message equivalent to `Variable ..... may not have been initialized` (the exact error message is compiler dependent).

7. Dividing integer values incorrectly. This error is usually disguised within a larger expression and can be troublesome to detect. For example, the expression

      3.425 + 2/3 + 7.9

   yields the same result as the expression

      3.425 + 7.9

   because the integer division of 2/3 is 0.

8. Mixing data types in the same expression without clearly understanding the effect produced. Since Java allows mixed-mode expressions, it is important to be clear about the order of evaluation and the data type of all intermediate calculations. When evaluating a numerical expression, the following rules are applied in the order listed:

   a. If either operand is a `double` value, the result is a `double` value, else

   b. If either operand is a `float` value, the result is a `float` value, else

   c. If either operand is a `long` value, the result is a `long` value, else

   d. The result is an `int` value

   As a general rule, it is better not to mix data types in an expression unless a specific effect is desired.

9. Failing to enclose an arithmetic expression within parentheses when the expression is meant to be evaluated and concatenated to a string. Depending on the precedence and associativity of the arithmetic operation, either the evaluation will take place without the parentheses, an inadvertent string concatenation will take place with no numerical evaluation, or an error will occur.

10. Including a return type in a constructor's header line.

11. Failing to include a return type in a nonconstructor member method's header line.

12. Defining more than one default constructor for a class.

13. Applying either the increment or decrement operator to an expression. For example, the expression

```
(count + n)++
```

is incorrect. The increment and decrement operators can only be applied to individual variables.

2.7 **Chapter Review**

KEY TERMS

accessor method	implicit (implied) object	reference data types
attribute	instance variable	simple arithmetic expression
behavior	int	single-precision number
boolean	integer	state
char	integer literal	string concatenation
class	model	this reference
constructor	object	value
dialog box	object diagram	variable
double	operator associativity	
double-precision number	operator precedence	
float	primitive data types	
floating-point literal	real number	
identity		

SUMMARY

1. The primitive types of data recognized by Java are numerical and Boolean types. The numerical types are further classified as integer, floating-point, and character types. Each of these types of data is typically stored in a computer using different amounts of memory. A void data type cannot be instantiated.

2. Primitive type values can be displayed using `print()`, `println()`, and `showMessage()` methods.

3. Every variable in a Java program must be declared as to the type of value it can store. Declarations within a method may be placed anywhere within the method, although a variable can only be used after it is declared. Variables may also be initialized when they are declared. In addition, variables of the same type may be declared using a single declaration statement. Variable declaration statements have the general form

```
dataType variableName1, variableName2, . . . ;
```

4. Declaration statements always perform the task of informing both a programmer reading the program and the compiler translating the program of a method's valid variable names. A variable declaration also tells the compiler to set aside memory locations for the variable.

5. Reference variables are associated either with a class, an array, or an interface.

6. A class is a programmer-defined data type. Objects of a class may be defined and have the same relationship to their class as variables do to Java's built-in data types.

7. A class is defined using a class variable declaration section and a class method definition section. The most common form of a class definition is

```
public className
{
  // class variable declaration section
  variables typically declared as private;

  // class method definition section
  methods typically declared as public
}
```

   The variables are individually referred to as class data members, and the methods are referred to as class member methods. The terms private and public are referred to as both visibility modifiers and access specifiers. The reserved word private specifies that the class members following it are private to the class and can only be accessed by member methods. The reserved word public specifies that the class members following may be accessed from outside the class. Generally, all data members should be specified as private and all member methods as public.

8. Except for constructor methods, all class methods defined in the class definition section typically have the header line syntax

```
public returnType  methodName(parameter list)
```

9. A constructor method is a special method that is automatically called each time an object is declared. It must have the same name as its class and cannot have any return type. Its purpose is to initialize each declared object.

10. If no constructor is declared for a class, the compiler will supply a default constructor. The compiler-provided constructor initializes all numerical data members to zero and all string data members to a null.

11. The term default constructor refers to any constructor that does not require any arguments when it is called.

12. Each class may only have one default constructor. If a user-defined default constructor is provided, the compiler will not create its default constructor.

13. An *accessor* method is a member method that accesses a class' private data members for the purpose of displaying or returning their values.

14. In addition to constructor and accessor methods, each class should provide a number of methods that perform appropriate calculations and operations on objects that will be constructed from the class.

15. Objects are created using either a single- or double-statement declaration. The double-statement style of declaration has the form

```
className objectName;
objectName = new className(optional list of arguments);
```

An example of this style of declaration, including initializers, for a class named RoomType is:

```
RoomType firstRoom; // declare an object of type RoomType
firstRoom = new RoomType(); // instantiate the object
```

Although the variable `a` is commonly referred to as an object, it is actually a reference variable. The `new` operator then creates an actual object in memory that can be accessed using this reference variable. When an object is created using the `new` operator, it is also said to be instantiated.

The single-statement declaration and instantiation, including the optional list of initializers, have the form

```
className objectName = new className(list of initializers);
```

An example of this style of declaration is

```
RoomType firstRoom = new RoomType();
```

16. An expression is a literal, a variable, or a sequence of one or more literals and/or variables separated by operators. A value is associated with an expression.

17. Expressions are evaluated according to the precedence and associativity of the operators used in the expression.

18. The assignment symbol, =, is an operator. Expressions using this operator assign a value to a variable; in addition, the expression itself takes on a value. Since assignment is an operation in Java, multiple uses of the assignment operator are possible in the same expression.

19. The increment operator, ++, adds 1 to a variable, whereas the decrement operator, --, subtracts 1 from a variable. Both of these operators can be used as prefixes or postfixes. In a prefix operation, the variable is incremented (or decremented) before its value is used. In a postfix operation, the variable is incremented (or decremented) after its value is used.

3 Developing Class Methods

To be useful, objects must be capable of interacting with other objects. Specifically, one object may desire another object to perform some task on its behalf. In theoretical terms, this is referred to as one object sending a message to a second object. In response, the second object either sends the message on to another object or directly uses a method to complete the request of the first object. Ultimately, however, it is a method that performs any task or state change performed on an object. In this chapter, we see how methods are constructed to accept information through its parameter list and directly return a value that can then be passed to other methods for further processing or display.

3.1 **Method and Parameter Declarations**

In the last chapter, we created a class containing methods for initializing, modifying, and displaying an object's state. For convenience, this class named `RoomType` is repeated as Program 3.1.

Program 3.1

```
public class RoomType
{
  // data declarations section
  private double length;  // declare length as a double variable
  private double width;    // declare width as a double variable

  // method definitions section
  public RoomType()  // this is a constructor
  {
    length = 25.0;
    width = 12.0;
    System.out.println("Created a new room object using the default constructor\n");
  }

  public void showValues()   // this is a  modified accessor
  {
    System.out.println("  length = " + length + "\n  width = " + width);
  }

  public void setNewValues()    // this is a mutator
  {
    length = 12.5;
    width = 9.0;
  }

  public void calculateArea()   // this performs a calculation
  {
    System.out.println(length * width);
  }
}
```

A severe restriction of the `RoomType` class's constructor method is that it uses the same literal values, 25.0 and 12.0, which are coded within the method, to initialize each newly created room to the same fixed size. This same restriction applies to the mutator method, which resets a room object's `length` and `width` variables to the literal values 12.5 and 9. Figure 3.1 illustrates this restriction. As shown, the only values that we can currently supply to an object are literal values supplied as part of a method.

We will now modify both the mutator and constructor methods to make use of data supplied at the time the method is invoked. What we are aiming at is the situation

---

A BIT OF BACKGROUND

Procedural Abstraction

Assigning a name to a method in such a way that the method is invoked by using the name with appropriate arguments is formally referred to as *procedural abstraction*. Therefore, in writing your own class methods, you are actually creating procedural abstractions.

Notice that procedural abstraction effectively hides the implementation details of how a method performs its task. This hiding of the details is one of the hallmarks and strengths of abstraction. By thinking of tasks on a procedural level, programmers can formulate the solution of a specific task without immediately being concerned with the nitty-gritty details of the actual solution implementation.

---

shown in Figure 3.2, where the method accepts external data that are not part of an object and are not literal data that are hard-coded into the method.

Creating a method that can use externally supplied data that are not part of the object they are operating on requires defining the method to correctly receive, store, and process these data. As we have seen with the `println()` method, passing such data to a method is accomplished by including them within the parentheses following the method's name when the method is invoked. The passed data, as noted previously in relation to the `println()` method, are called **arguments** of the method. If no data are expected by the method, no arguments are permitted to be passed to the method when it is invoked. An example of this situation is the method call `roomOne.setNewValues()`, which is illustrated in Figure 3.1.

Now assume that the mutator method `setNewValues()` in Program 3.1 has been written to accept two double-precision values and that `roomOne` has been created as a `RoomType` object. In this case, the statement

```
roomOne.setNewValues(6.2, 3.5);
```

FIGURE 3.1   **Altering an object's state using a method's literal values**

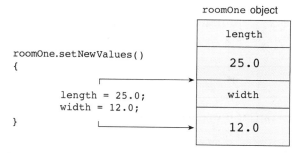

FIGURE 3.2   **A method that accepts external data independent of an object**

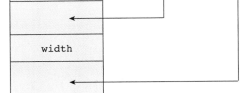

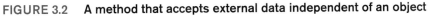

would provide two values that can be used to reset roomOne's values. If the room was later designed to be larger, a statement such as

    roomOne.setNewValues(10.0, 11.5);

could be used. In place of literal data, arguments can also be variable names, in which case the values stored in the variables are passed into the method. In all cases, it is the parentheses that permit us to pass additional data, other than the data contained in a named object, when the method is used. Effectively, as shown in Figure 3.3, the parentheses provide a funnel into the method through which data can be passed.

No matter how a method is constructed, when it is used or summoned into action, it is referred to as the **called method.** The act of invoking the method is referred to as **calling the method,** and the method doing the calling is referred to as the **calling method.** Theses terms comes from standard telephone usage, where one person calls another on the telephone. The person initiating the call is referred to as the calling party, and the person receiving the call is the called party.

FIGURE 3.3   **Passing data to the setNewValues() method**

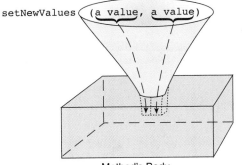

Method's Body

Writing the Method

To successfully pass data into a called method requires that the method be written to accept the data. Only after the called method successfully receives the data can it then

FIGURE 3.4   **The general structure of a method**

```
Method's Header Line  ----> public ... methodName()
                     ------>{
  Method's Body |                Java statements go in here
                     ------>}
```

be used to produce a useful result. Recall that a method consists of two parts, a **method header** and a **method body,** as illustrated in Figure 3.4. The purpose of the method header is to specify access privileges (where the method can be called), identify the data type of the value returned by the method, provide the method with a name, and specify the number, order, and type of arguments expected by the method. The purpose of the method body is to operate on the passed data and directly return, at most, one value back to the calling method. (We will see, in the next section, how a method can be made to return multiple values.)

The structure of a method's header that is capable of receiving arguments is illustrated in Figure 3.5. As shown, the header will typically contain the `public` access reserved word, a mandatory return type, a name, and a set of parentheses.

Except for the `parameter list`, this header line should look familiar. To review, the reserved word `public` means that the method can be used both within and outside the class that includes the method, which is appropriate for a class method. As we will see in Chapter 9, we can restrict access to a class's methods using the reserved words `protected` and `private`. The `parameter list` in the header line provides the data types and names that will be used to hold the values passed to the method when it is called. Among other things, this list, which we will describe in detail shortly, specifies the number, sequence, and data types of the argument values that the called method expects to receive.

Using this generic header line, we can now construct a specific header line for our `setNewValues()` method. Because `setNewValues()` will not formally return any value and is to receive two double-precision values, one to set an object's `length` variable and one to set its `width` variable, the following header line can be used:

```
public void setNewValues(double len, double wid) <---- no semicolon
```

The identifier names within the parentheses in the header are referred to as **formal parameters** of the method. You will also see them referred to as **formal arguments, arguments,** and **parameters.** Thus, the parameter `len` will store the first value passed to `setNewValues()`, and the parameter `wid` will store the second value passed at the time of the method call. All parameters, such as `len` and `wid`, receive values from the calling method, be they primitive or reference data types. The called method does not know where the values come from when the call is made. All values passed to `set-NewValues()` are ultimately stored in the parameters `len` and `wid` (Figure 3.6).

The method name and all parameter names in the header, in this case, `setNew-Values`, `len`, and `wid`, are programmer-selected identifiers. Thus, any names selected

FIGURE 3.5   **The general syntax for a method header**

```
public returnType methodName(parameter list) <--- Required parentheses
```

FIGURE 3.6   **`setNewValues()` Receives actual values**

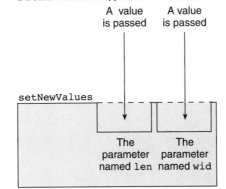

according to the rules for choosing identifier names can be used. All parameters listed in the method header line must be separated by commas and must have their individual data types declared separately.

Notice that as far as the method `setNewValues()` is concerned, the parameters named `len` and `wid` will be dealt with exactly as variables. These parameter declarations are similar to variable declarations and are used to declare the data type of the values expected by the method. The only difference between a method's parameter declarations and its variable declarations is their placement in the method. Parameter declarations are always placed within the parentheses following the method's name, whereas method variable declarations are placed within the method's body. From a programming viewpoint, parameters can be considered as variables whose initialization occurs from outside the method.

When a method is called, the number, order (sequence), and data types of the arguments passed to the method *must agree* in number, order, and data type with the parameters declared in the method's header line. If the values passed to a method do not agree with the data types declared for a parameter and would result in a possible loss of precision (e.g., attempting to send a double-precision argument into an integer parameter), the compiler error message `Incompatible type for method.` `Explicit cast needed to convert ...` or an equivalent is provided. If the number of passed arguments does not agree with the number of declared parameters, a compiler error message equivalent to `Wrong number of arguments in method` is provided.

Now that we have written the method header for `setNewValues()`, we can construct its body. As illustrated in Figure 3.7, a method body begins with an opening brace, {, contains any necessary declarations and other Java statements, and ends with a closing brace, }. Again, this should look familiar.

In the body of the `setNewValues()` method, we use the parameters to set an object's `length` and `width` variables. The new definition for this method is

FIGURE 3.7   **The structure of a method body**

```
{
    variable declarations
    and other Java statements
}
```

```
public void setNewValues(double len, double wid) // this is a mutator
{
  length = len;
  width = wid;
}
```

Program 3.2 includes the setNewValues() method within the context of a complete program.

Program 3.2

```
public class RoomTypeOne
{
  // data declarations section
  private double length;  // declare length as a double variable
  private double width;    // declare width as a double variable

  // method definitions section
  public RoomTypeOne()  // this is a constructor
  {
    length = 25.0;
    width = 12.0;
    System.out.println("Created a new room object using the default constructor\n");
  }

  public void showValues()   // this is a modified accessor
  {
    System.out.println("  length = " + length + "\n  width = " + width);
  }

  public void setNewValues(double len, double wid)    // this is a mutator
  {
    length = len;
    width = wid;
  }

  public void calculateArea()  // this performs a calculation
  {
    System.out.println(length * width);
  }

  public static void main(String[] args)
  {
    RoomTypeOne roomOne;  // declare a variable of type RoomTypeOne

    roomOne = new RoomTypeOne();  // create and initialize an object of
                                  // type RoomTypeOne
    System.out.println("\nThe values for this room are:");
    roomOne.showValues();          // use a class method on this object
```

```
        System.out.print("The floor area of this room is: ");
        roomOne.calculateArea();     // use another class method on this object

        roomOne.setNewValues(6.2, 3.5);    // call the mutator

        System.out.println("\nThe values for this room have been changed to:");
        roomOne.showValues();
        System.out.print("The floor area of this room is: ");
        roomOne.calculateArea();
    }
}
```

Notice that both the `setNewValues()` method and the call to this method have been highlighted with shading. Also, the `main()` method has been directly incorporated within the `RoomTypeOne` class for convenience. The output produced when this program is compiled and executed is

```
Created a new room object using the default constructor

The values for this room are:
   length = 25.0
   width = 12.0
The floor area of this room is: 300.0

The values for this room have been changed to:
   length = 6.2
   width = 3.5
The floor area of this room is: 21.7
```

As is clearly shown in this output, the `setNewValues()` method successfully received and processed the arguments passed to it.

Reusing Method Names (Overloading)

Java provides the capability of using the same method name for more than one method, which is referred to as method **overloading**. The only requirement in creating more than one method with the same name is that the compiler must be able to determine which method to use based on the data types of the parameters (not the data type of the return value, if any). Overloaded methods are particularly useful in writing constructor methods because they allow the programmer to initialize an object in more than one way. For example, consider the following two constructor methods, both named `RoomType()`.

```
public RoomType()  // this is a constructor
{
  length = 25.0;
  width = 12.0;
  System.out.println("Created a new room object using the default constructor\n");
}
public RoomType(double len, double wid)  // this is a constructor
```

(continued)

(continued)
```
    {
      length = len;
      width = wid;
    }
```

Which of the two methods named `RoomType()` is called depends on the argument types supplied at the time of the call. Thus, the method call `RoomType kitchen = new RoomType();` would cause the default constructor to be used (recall that a default constructor is one that requires no arguments), and the call `RoomType hall = new RoomType(6.0, 3.5);` would cause the compiler to use the constructor that expects two double-precision arguments.

Notice that overloading a method's name simply means using the same name for more than one method. Each method that uses the name must still be written and exists as a separate entity. The use of the same method name does not require that the code within the methods be similar, although good programming practice dictates that methods with the same name should perform similar operations.

Clearly, overloading a method requires that the compiler can distinguish which method to select based on the method's name and its parameter list. The part of a header line that contains this information (i.e., name and parameter list) is referred to as the method's **parameter signature**. For a class to compile correctly, each method must have a unique parameter signature. This terminology is derived from everyday usage where it is expected that each individual has a unique signature that can uniquely identify a person. From a compiler's viewpoint, unless each method has a unique parameter signature, the compiler cannot correctly determine which method is being referenced.

Passing a Reference Value

Java passes the value that is stored in both a primitive data type variable and a reference variable in the same manner: A copy of the value in the variable is passed to the called method and stored in one of the method's formal parameters. A consequence is that any change to the parameter's value has no effect on the argument's value. From a programming viewpoint, this means that an argument's value can never be altered from within a called method.

Passing arguments in this manner has distinct advantages. It allows methods to be written as independent entities that can use any variable or parameter name without concern that other methods may also be using the same name. It also alleviates any concern that altering a parameter or variable in one method may inadvertently alter the value of a variable in another method.

Although both primitive and reference variable values are passed in the same way, passing a reference value does have implications that passing a primitive value does not. With respect to primitive values, the best a called method can do is receive values from the calling method, store and manipulate the passed values, and directly return at most a single value. With respect to reference values, however, the called method gets to access the object being referenced. This *does not*, however, permit a nonclass method to alter an object's privately declared instance variables because doing so would clearly destroy the private nature of these variables. As an example, Program 3.3 illustrates passing a `String` object. Notice that the method call and parameter declaration are essentially the same as those used for primitive data types.

Program 3.3

```java
public class PassAReference
{
  public void main(String[] args)
  {
    String message = "Original Message";

    display(message);    // call the method
  }  // end of main() method

  public void display(String msg)
  {
    System.out.println("From within display(): " + msg);
  }
}  // end of class
```

The output produced by Program 3.3 is

```
From within display(): Original Message
```

As you can see by this output, we have successfully passed a reference value as an argument to a called method. The called method, `display()`, has been coded to receive the reference to the `String` object and display the stored text.

In extremely limited cases (one of which is presented in Section 7.3), it is possible to alter the value in the referenced object and pass the new value back to the calling method using the reference argument. When this is the case, the object referenced will have a new value in the calling method. More typically, however, Java will alert you that you are attempting to alter a private instance variable.

In the case of strings, a new text value will not be passed back through the parameter even if a new string value is set in the `display()` method. The reason is that strings created from the `String` class are always immutable objects. This means that once a `String` object is initialized, its contents cannot be changed, and you actually create a new `String` object each time you assign a string constant to a string variable. Thus, for example, if the string referenced by `msg` in Program 3.3 is changed in `display()` by a statement such as `msg = "Have a happy day";`, the change will not be accessible from within `main()`. As shown in Figure 3.8, `display()` receives a copy of `message`, which is stored in the parameter named `msg`. Creating a new string in `display()` destroys the copy of the value stored in `msg` but has no effect on the value located by `message`. The value in `msg` is changed to refer to the new string, and `message` still refers to the original string.

FIGURE 3.8   **String arguments provide copies**

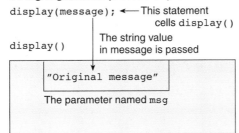

Exercises 3.1

1. For the following method headers, determine the number, type, and order (sequence) of the values that must be passed to the method.

   a. `public void factorial(int n)`

   b. `public void price(int type, double yield, double maturity)`

   c. `public void yield(int type, double price, double maturity)`

   d. `public void interest(char flag, double price, double time)`

   e. `public void total(double amount, double rate)`

   f. `public void roi(int a, int b, char c, char d, double e, double f)`

   g. `public void getVal(int item, int iter, char decflag, char delim)`

2. Enter and run Program 3.2 on your `computer`.

3. Add two mutator methods named `setLength()` and `setWidth()` to Program 3.2's `RoomType` class that can be used to individually set an object's `length` and `width`, respectively.

4. Write a class declaration and definition section for each of the following specifications. In each case, include a constructor and a mutator that use parameters to set all instance variables and an accessor member method named `showData()` that displays an object's values.

   a. A class named `Complex` that has double-precision instance variables named `real` and `imaginary`.

   b. A class named `Circle` that has integer instance variables named `xcenter` and `ycenter` and a floating-point data member named `radius`.

   c. A class named `Computer` that has string instance variables named `computer`, `printer`, and `screen` and double-precision instance variables named `compPrice`, `printPrice`, and `screenPrice`.

5. Modify Program 3.2 to include two constructors. The first constructor should be a default constructor that initializes an object's `length` and `width` variables to 12.0 and 9.9, respectively, while the second constructor should use two parameters, named `initLength` and `initWidth`, that can be used to initialize an object's instance variables when the object is created.

6. Determine whether the following statements are true or false:

   a. A constructor method must have the same name as its class.

   b. A class can have only one constructor method.

   c. A class can have only one default constructor method.

   d. A default constructor can only be supplied by the compiler.

   e. A default constructor can have no parameters.

   f. A constructor must be declared for each class.

   g. A constructor must be declared with a return type.

   h. A constructor is automatically called each time an object is created.

7. Determine the errors in the following class:

```
            public class Employee
            {
              public int empnum;
              public char code;

              private void showemp(int, char)
              {
                    .
                    .
              }
            }
```

8.   Determine the error in the following class:

```
public class RoomType
{
  // data declarations section
  private double length;  // declare length as a double variable
  private double width;   // declare width as a double variable

  // method definitions section
  public RoomType  // this is a constructor
  {
    length = 25.0;
    width = 12.0;
  }

  public void setNewValues(double len, double wid)   // this is a mutator
  {
    length = len;
    width = wid;
  }

  public void setNewValues(double len)    // this is a mutator
  {
    length = len;
  }

  public void setNewValues(double wid)    // this is a mutator
  {
    width = wid;
  }

  public void showValues()    // this is a modified accessor
  {
    System.out.println("  length = " + length + "\n  width = " + width);
  }
}
```

9.   The following program provides the same functionality as Program 3.2 but places each method in its own class. Enter and store each class in a separate file and then compile each class. Run `UseRoomTypeOne` to verify that it produces the same result as Program 3.2.

```java
public class RoomTypeOne
{
  // data declarations section
  private double length;  // declare length as a double variable
  private double width;   // declare width as a double variable

  // method definitions section
  public RoomTypeOne()  // this is a constructor
  {
    length = 25.0;
    width = 12.0;
    System.out.println("Created a new room object using the default constructor\n");
  }

  public void showValues()  // this is a modified accessor
  {
    System.out.println("  length = " + length + "\n  width = " + width);
  }

  public void setNewValues(double len, double wid)  // this is a mutator
  {
    length = len;
    width = wid;
  }

  public void calculateArea()  // this performs a calculation
  {
    System.out.println(length * width);
  }
}

public class UseRoomTypeOne
{
  public static void main(String[] args)
  {
    RoomTypeOne roomOne;  // declare a variable of type RoomTypeOne

    roomOne = new RoomTypeOne();  // create and initialize an object of
                                  // type RoomType
    System.out.println("\nThe values for this room are:");
    roomOne.showValues();         // use a class method on this object
    System.out.print("The floor area of this room is: ");
    roomOne.calculateArea();      // use another class method on this object

    roomOne.setNewValues(6.2, 3.5);   // call the mutator

    System.out.println("\nThe values for this room have been changed to:");
    roomOne.showValues();
    System.out.print("The floor area of this room is: ");
```

```
      roomOne.calculateArea();
  }
}
```

10. Determine the error in the following program. If necessary, compile the program to see the compiler error message generated.

```
public class UseRoomType
{
  public static void main(String[] args)
  {
    RoomType roomOne;  // declare a variable of type RoomTypeWM

    roomOne = new RoomType();  // create and initialize an object of
                               // type RoomTypeWM
    System.out.println("\nThe values for this room are:");
    roomOne.showValues();        // use a class method on this object
    System.out.print("The floor area of this room is: ");
    roomOne.calculateArea();    // use another class method on this object

    roomOne.setNewValues();    // call the mutator

    System.out.println("\nThe values for this room have been changed to:");
    roomOne.showValues();
    System.out.print("The floor area of this room is: ");
    roomOne.calculateArea();

    display(roomOne);
  }

  public static void display(RoomType a)
  {
    System.out.println("Into display()");
    a.calculateArea();
    a.length = 23.2;
  }
}
```

11a. Construct a `Time` class containing integer instance variables named `seconds`, `minutes`, and `hours`. Have the class contain two constructors: The first should be a default constructor that initializes each data member with a default value of zero. The second constructor should accept three integer arguments that will be used to set each instance variable. The class should also include a mutator that accepts three integer arguments for setting the instance variables and an accessor method for displaying the time.

   b. Include the class written for Exercise 11a within the context of a complete program.

12a. Construct a class named `Student` consisting of an integer instance variable for storing a student identification number, an integer instance variable for storing the number of credits completed by the student, and a double-precision value for storing a student's grade point average. The default constructor for this class should initialize all `Student` data members to zero. Additionally, an overloaded constructor should be provided to initialize a new `Student`'s instance variables to programmer-selected values using method arguments (this second constructor would be used for transfer students). Included in the class should be mutator methods to alter a student ID number and alter both the number of credits taken and the new GPA at the same time. Additionally, an accessor method should be provided to display all of a `Student`'s data.

b. Include the class constructed in Exercise 12a within the context of a complete program. Your program should declare two objects of type `Student` and accept and display data for the two objects to verify operation of the member methods.

3.2 Returning a Single Value

Passing arguments into a method as presented in the previous section provides the called method with copies of the values contained in the arguments at the time of the call (review Figure 3.6 if this is unclear). This is true for both built-in and reference arguments. Although this procedure for passing data to a method may seem surprising, it is really a safety procedure for ensuring that a called method cannot inadvertently change any data stored in the variables of the calling method. The called method gets a copy of the data to use. It may change its copy and, of course, change any variables declared inside itself. This procedure, where only values are passed to a called method, is formally referred to as **pass by value** (the term **call by value** is also used).

The method receiving the passed-by-value arguments may process the data sent to it in any fashion desired and directly return at most one, and only one, "legitimate" value to the calling method (Figure 3.9). In this section, we first see how such a value is returned to the calling method when primitive data types are used as arguments. As you might expect, given Java's flexibility, there is a way of returning more than a single value. How to do this is presented at the end of this section after the passing and processing of reference variables are discussed.

As with the calling of a method, directly returning a single value requires that the interface between the called and calling methods be handled correctly. From its side of the return transaction, the called method must provide the following items:

■ the data type of the returned value
■ the actual value being returned

A method returning a value specifies the data type of the value that will be returned in its header line. As a specific example, consider the `calculateArea()`

FIGURE 3.9 **A method directly returns at most one value**

A method can receive many values

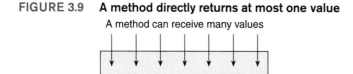

Only one value can
be directly returned

method in our `RoomType` class. This method, which is listed here for convenience, determines and displays the area of a `RoomType` object.

```
public void calculateArea()  // this performs a calculation
{
   System.out.println(length * width);
}
```

As written, the method's header line is

```
public void calculateArea()
```

The reserved word `void` in the header line specifies that the method will return no value. If `calculateArea()` is now to return a value, this reserved word must be changed to indicate the data type of the value being returned. For example, if a double-precision value is to be returned, the proper method header line is

```
public double calculateArea()
```

Observe that this is the same as the original method header line for `calculateArea()` with the substitution of the reserved word `double` for `void`. Similarly, if the method were to return an integer value, the correct method header line is

```
public int calculateArea()
```

and if the method were to return a single-precision value, the header line is

```
public float calculateArea()
```

Because `calculateArea()` will be used to return a double-precision value, which is the area of a room, the appropriate header line is

```
public double calculateArea()
```

Having declared the data type that `calculateArea()` will return, we must now alter the method's body by including a statement that will force the return of the correct value. To return a value from a method requires using a `return` statement, which has the syntax:[1]

```
return expression;
```

When the `return` statement is encountered, the *expression* is evaluated first, and it is this value that is sent back to the calling method. After the value is returned, program control reverts to the calling method. Because the area determined by `calculateArea()` is calculated as the expression `length * width`, it is the value of this expression that should be returned. To return this value, all we need to do is add the statement `return length * width;` before the closing brace of the `calculateArea()` method. The complete method code is

```
public double calculateArea()
{
   return length * width;
}
```

---

[1] Some programmers place the expression within parentheses, yielding the statement return (expression);. The parentheses are not required but can be used.

In this new code for `calculateArea()`, pay particular attention to the fact that the data type of the expression contained in the `return` statement correctly matches the double-precision return data type declared in the method's header line. It is up to the programmer to ensure that this is so for every method returning a value. Failure to match the return value exactly with the method's declared return data type will result in a compiler error if an attempt is made to return a value that has more precision than the return type declared in the header line. For this case, the compiler will alert you with the error message `Incompatible type for return. Explicit cast needed to convert` ... For example, you will receive this error message if you attempt to return a double-precision value when an integer has been declared as the return type. However, attempting to return a value that has less precision than that declared in the header line is permitted. Thus, if you attempt to return an integer value from a method that has been declared as returning a double-precision value, the integer is automatically promoted to a double-precision value and no compiler error occurs.

The value returned by a method can be used wherever an expression is valid. For example, the expression `2 * roomOne.calculateArea()` multiplies the value returned by `calculateArea()` by 2. The statement

```
System.out.println(roomOne.calculateArea());
```

displays the returned value, and the statement

```
area = roomOne.calculateArea();
```

assigns the returned value to the variable named `area`. Because the returned value has been declared a double-precision value in the method's header line, the variable `area` would also have to be declared as a double-precision variable.

Program 3.4 illustrates the new `calculateArea()` method within the context of a complete program.

The output produced by Program 3.4 is

```
Created a new room object using the default constructor

The values for this room are:
  length = 25.0
  width = 12.0
The floor area of this room is: 300.0
```

In reviewing Program 3.4, it is important to note the two items we have introduced in this section concerning the coding of the `calculateArea()` method. The header line for `calculateArea()` declares that the method will return a double-precision value, and the expression in the `return` statement evaluates to a matching data type. Thus, `calculateArea()` is internally consistent in returning a double-precision value whenever the method is called. As demonstrated by this output, the calculated area of 300.0 has been correctly returned and subsequently displayed.

Although `calculateArea()` returns a single value, no data are passed to the method when it is called. This is because this method does not require any arguments to complete its assigned task. More generally, a method can receive arguments, can declare variables, can create objects, and can directly return a single value. Following

Program 3.4

```
public class RoomType
{
   // data declarations section
   private double length;  // declare length as a double variable
   private double width;   // declare width as a double variable

   // method definitions section
   public RoomType()  // this is a constructor
   {
     length = 25.0;
     width = 12.0;
     System.out.println("Created a new room object using the default constructor\n");
   }

   public void showValues()   // this is a modified accessor
   {
     System.out.println("  length = " + length + "\n  width = " + width);
   }

   public void setNewValues()   // this is a mutator
   {
     length = 12.5;
     width = 9.0;
   }

   public double calculateArea()  // this performs a calculation
   {
     return length * width;
   }

   public static void main(String[] args)
   {
     RoomType roomOne;  // declare a variable of type RoomType

     roomOne = new RoomType();  // create and initialize an object of
                                // type RoomType

     System.out.println("\nThe values for this room are:");
     roomOne.showValues();         // use a class method on this object

     System.out.print("The floor area of this room is: ");
     System.out.println(roomOne.calculateArea());   // display the returned value
   }
}
```

on page 144 is the general syntax for defining a method that includes both a return type and parameter declarations.

```
public returnType methodName(parameter declarations)
{
  variable and object declarations

  other Java statements
  return expression;
}
```

As we progress in our understanding of Java, we will create many methods that use all of the elements included in this more general syntax. Specifically, we will be creating methods that use parameters, declare their own internal variables, and return a value.

Returning Multiple Values

There are a number of ways that a method can return multiple values. As a specific case, we can assume that a `RoomType` object must have both its perimeter and area calculated.

One way to do this is to use two methods: one method to calculate and return the room's area and another method to calculate and return the room's perimeter. If one method is desired, the correct procedure would be to return the values directly through a named object. This would mean expanding the class's instance variables to include both an area and perimeter variable, which could automatically be calculated and stored from within each constructor and mutator method.

A third solution is to calculate both the area and perimeter, concatenate these two values into a single string, and then return the string. The following method can be used:

```
public String areaAndPerim()
{
  return ( " " + (length*width) + "    " + (2 * (length + width)) );
}
```

Notice that the expression in the `return` statement starts with a string value. This forces the plus signs to be interpreted as concatenation operations so that the calculated area and perimeter values will be converted to their equivalent string representation. The returned value from this method could then be displayed using a statement such as

```
System.out.println(roomOne.areaAndPerim());
```

or additional string information could be added to clearly document what the returned data represents. The returned string could be also be separated into its constituent parts (referred to as **parsing**) and each part converted into a true numerical value. How this can be accomplished is presented in Chapter 7. You may be thinking that this is a rather cumbersome process for returning multiple values. And it is. But remember, Java does not want you to return more than one value from a method, so any scheme devised to circumvent this is going to be a somewhat cumbersome workaround.

Finally, in Chapter 7, we introduce the `StringBuffer` class. This class provides a bit more flexibility than the `String` class and can also be used to return multiple values. A specific example using the `StringBuffer` class to do this is provided in Program 7.7 (Section 7.3), where the multiple values are passed back to a calling method using the called method's parameters.

Exercises 3.2

1. For the following method headers, determine the number, type, and order (sequence) of values that should be passed to the method when it is called and the data type of the value returned by the method.

   a. `public double getLength()`

   b. `public int getNumber()`

   c. `public void showPrice()`

   d. `public double calculatePrice(int type)`

   e. `public double calculateYield(double price, double maturity)`

   f. `public char interest(char flag, double price, double time)`

   g. `public int total(double amount, double rate)`

   h. `public double roi(int a, int b, char c, char d, double e, double f)`

   i. `public void getVal(int item, int iter, char decflag)`

2. Enter and run Program 3.4 on your computer.

3. Modify the `calculateArea()` method in Program 3.4 so that its header line declares a return of an integer value. Determine the error message generated by the compiler because a double-precision value is provided in the `return` statement.

4. Write method headers for the following:

   a. A class method named `getMonth()` that accepts no parameters and returns an integer value.

   b. A class method named `getDate()` that accepts three integer parameters named month, day, and year and returns a string value.

   c. A class method named `check()` that has three parameters. The first parameter should accept an integer number, the second parameter a floating-point number, and the third parameter a double-precision number. The class method returns no value.

   d. A class method named `findAbs()` that accepts a double-precision number parameter named number and returns a double-precision value.

   e. A class method named `calculateRadius()` that accepts two floating-point numbers named center and perimeter as integer parameters and returns an integer value.

   f. A class method named `getIncrease()` that accepts a double-precision parameter named factor and returns a double-precision value.

5a. Write a Java class named `Fahrenheit` that contains a single double-precision instance variable named `temperature`. The class should include a constructor and mutator method that permits a programmer to set an object's temperature value to a programmer-selected value. Additionally, there should be an accessor method that returns an object's temperature value and a class method named `celsiusValue()` that returns the Celsius temperature corresponding to a Fahrenheit temperature. The Celsius value can be determined using the formula

Celsius = 5.0 / 9.0 (Fahrenheit − 32.0).

b. Include the method written for Exercise 5a in a working Java program. Make sure that all class methods are called from `main()`. Have `main()` display the value returned by `celsiusValue()` and verify the returned value by a hand calculation.

6a. Write a Java class named `Cylinder` that contains two double-precision instance variables named `radius` and `height`. The class should include a constructor and mutator method that permits a programmer to set an object's variables to programmer-selected values. Additionally, there should be two accessor methods that return an object's `radius` and `height`, respectively, and a class method named `volume()` that returns the volume of a `Cylinder` object. The volume of a cylinder is given by its radius squared times its height times π. You can either use the value 3.1416 for π or use the Java-provided value named `Math.PI`.

b. Include the method written for Exercise 6a in a working Java program. Make sure that all class methods are called from `main()`. Have `main()` display the value returned by `volume()` and verify the returned value by a hand calculation.

7a. Write a Java class named `PolyTwo` that contains three double-precision instance variables named `a`, `b`, and `c`, which represent the coefficients of a second-degree polynomial (a second-degree polynomial in x is given by the expression $ax^2 + bx + c$, where a, b, and c are referred to as coefficients; if the coefficient `a` is 0, the expression becomes a first-degree polynomial). The class should include a constructor and mutator method that permits a programmer to set an object's variables to programmer-selected values. Additionally, there should be a single accessor method that displays an object's values and a class method named `polyValue()` that accepts a double-precision value as the parameter named x and returns the value determined by the expression $ax^2 + bx + c$, where a, b, and c are coefficients contained in a `PolyTwo` object.

b. Include the method written for Exercise 7a in a working Java program. Make sure that all class methods are called from `main()`. Have `main()` display the value returned by `polyValue()` for various values of x that are passed into the method when it is called. Verify the returned value by performing a hand calculation.

8a. Write a Java class named `Point` that contains two double-precision instance variables named x and y. The class should include a constructor and mutator method that permits a programmer to set an object's variables to programmer-selected values. Additionally, there should be an accessor method that displays the values and a class method named `distance()` that returns the distance of a `Point` object from the point having coordinates (0,0). The distance, d, between a point (x,y) and (0,0) is given by the formula

$$d = \sqrt{x^2 + y^2}$$

(Tip: You must use the Java-provided method named `Math.sqrt()`. For example, the value of `Math.sqrt(x * x = y * y)` will return the correct value.)

b. Include the method written for Exercise 8a in a working Java program. Make sure that all class methods are called from `main()`. Have `main()` display the value returned by `distance()` and verify the returned value by a hand calculation. For example, the distance returned for a `Point` object having x and y values of 3 and 4, respectively, should be 5.

9a. Write a Java class named `Triangle` that contains three instance variables named `sideOne`, `sideTwo`, and `angle`. The class should include a constructor and mutator method that permits a programmer to set an object's variables to programmer-selected values. Additionally, there should be an accessor method that displays an object's values and a class method named `hypotenuse()` that returns the hypotenuse of a triangle object. (Tip: Use the Pythagorean theorem, $c^2 = a^2 + b^2$, where c is the hypotenuse and a and b are the other two sides of the triangle. To do this, you will have to use the Java-provided method named `Math.sqrt()`. For example, the value of `Math.sqrt(25.0)` is 5.0.)

b. Include the method written for Exercise 9a in a working Java program. Make sure that all class methods are called from `main()`. Have `main()` display the value returned by `hypotenuse()` and verify that the returned value is correct.

3.3 Method Development: Algorithms

Before a method is written, a programmer must clearly understand the data that will be used, the desired result, and the procedure that will produce this result. The procedure to accomplish this is referred to as an algorithm. More precisely, an **algorithm** is a step-by-step set of instructions that describes how data are to be processed to produce the desired result. In essence, an algorithm answers the question: What steps are you going to use to produce the result?

To illustrate an algorithm, consider the following simple problem: Assume you want to calculate the sum of all whole numbers from 1 through 100. Figure 3.10

FIGURE 3.10   **Summing the numbers from 1 through 100**

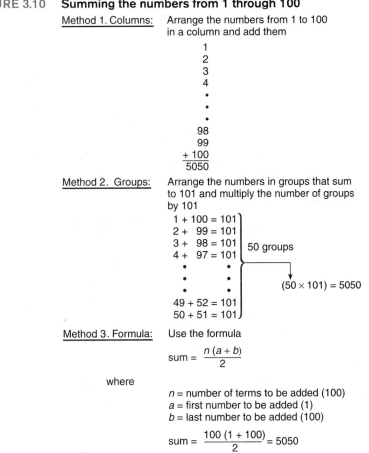

Method 1. Columns: Arrange the numbers from 1 to 100 in a column and add them

```
    1
    2
    3
    4
    •
    •
    •
   98
   99
 + 100
 ─────
 5050
```

Method 2. Groups: Arrange the numbers in groups that sum to 101 and multiply the number of groups by 101

```
 1 + 100 = 101 ⎫
 2 +  99 = 101 ⎪
 3 +  98 = 101 ⎬ 50 groups
 4 +  97 = 101 ⎪
    •       •  ⎪          (50 × 101) = 5050
    •       •  ⎪
    •       •  ⎪
49 + 52 = 101 ⎪
50 + 51 = 101 ⎭
```

Method 3. Formula: Use the formula

$$\text{sum} = \frac{n\,(a + b)}{2}$$

where

n = number of terms to be added (100)
a = first number to be added (1)
b = last number to be added (100)

$$\text{sum} = \frac{100\,(1 + 100)}{2} = 5050$$

A BIT OF BACKGROUND

Al-Khowarizmi

One of the first great mathematicians was Mohammed ibn Musa al-Khowarizmi, who wrote a treatise in about A.D. 825 called *Ilm al-jabr wa'l muqabalah* ("the Science of Reduction and Calculation"). The word *algorism*, or *algorithm*, is derived from al-Khowarizmi's name, and our word *algebra* is derived from the word *al-jabr* in the title of his work.

illustrates three procedures that could be used to find the required sum. Each procedure constitutes an algorithm.

Clearly, most people do not bother to list the possible alternatives in a detailed step-by-step manner, as in Figure 3.10, and then select one of the algorithms to solve the problem. But then, most people do not think algorithmically; they tend to think intuitively. For example, if you had to change a flat tire on your car, you would not think of all the steps required; you would simply change the tire or call someone else to do the job. This is an example of intuitive thinking.

Unfortunately, computers do not respond to intuitive commands. A general statement such as "add the numbers from 1 through 100" means nothing to a computer because the computer can only respond to algorithmic-like commands written in an acceptable language such as Java. To write a method that will perform a task and successfully execute, you must clearly understand this difference between algorithmic and intuitive commands. A computer is an "algorithm-responding" machine; it is not an "intuition-responding" machine. You cannot tell a computer to change a tire or to add the numbers from 1 through 100. Instead, you must give the computer a detailed step-by-step sequence of instructions that, collectively, forms an algorithm. The algorithm must be written in a programming language, which is called **coding the algorithm,** and is typically coded as a method. For example, the sequence of instructions

$$
\begin{aligned}
&\textit{Set n equal to 100}\\
&\textit{Set a} = 1\\
&\textit{Set b equal to 100}\\
&\textit{Calculate sum} = \frac{n \times (a + b)}{2}
\end{aligned}
$$

forms a detailed procedure, or algorithm, for determining the sum of the numbers from 1 through 100. Notice that these instructions are not a Java method. Unlike a method, which must be written in a language the computer can respond to, an algorithm can be written or described in various ways. When English-like phrases are used to describe the algorithm (the processing steps), the description is called **pseudocode.** When mathematical equations are used, the description is called a **formula.** When diagrams that employ the symbols shown in Figure 3.11 are used, the description is referred to as a **flowchart.** Figure 3.12 illustrates the use of these symbols in depicting an algorithm for determining the average of three numbers.

FIGURE 3.11   **Flowchart symbols**

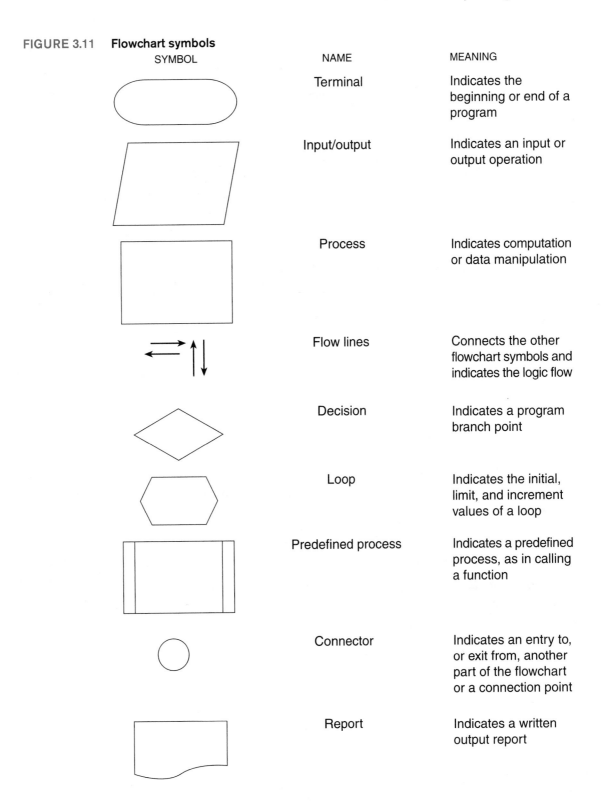

SYMBOL	NAME	MEANING
	Terminal	Indicates the beginning or end of a program
	Input/output	Indicates an input or output operation
	Process	Indicates computation or data manipulation
	Flow lines	Connects the other flowchart symbols and indicates the logic flow
	Decision	Indicates a program branch point
	Loop	Indicates the initial, limit, and increment values of a loop
	Predefined process	Indicates a predefined process, as in calling a function
	Connector	Indicates an entry to, or exit from, another part of the flowchart or a connection point
	Report	Indicates a written output report

Because flowcharts are cumbersome to revise and can easily support unstructured programming practices, they have fallen out of favor among professional programmers, except for visually describing basic programming structures. In their place, pseudocode has gained increasing acceptance. In describing an algorithm using pseudocode, short English phrases are used. For example, acceptable

FIGURE 3.12 **A flowchart for calculating the average of three numbers**

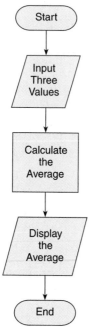

pseudocode for describing the steps needed to compute the average of three numbers is

Input the three numbers into the computer
Calculate the average by adding the numbers and dividing the sum by 3
Display the average

Only after an algorithm has been selected and the programmer understands the steps required can the algorithm be written as a method using computer language statements (Figure 3.13).

FIGURE 3.13   **Coding an algorithm**

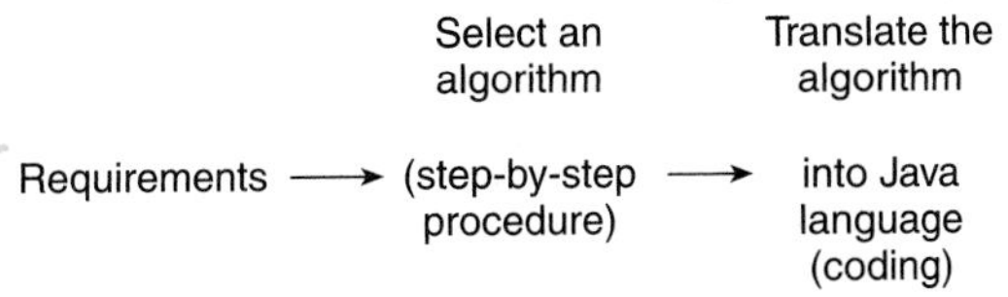

Requirements ⟶ Select an algorithm (step-by-step procedure) ⟶ Translate the algorithm into Java language (coding)

Exercises 3.3

1a.   Determine the six possible step-by-step procedures (list the steps) to paint the flower in Figure 3.14, with the restriction that each color must be completed before a new color can be started. (Tip: One of the algorithms is: Use yellow first, green second, black last.)

b.   Which of the six painting algorithms (series of steps) is best if we are limited to using one paintbrush and there is no way to clean the brush?

2.   Determine a step-by-step procedure (list the steps) to do the following tasks. (*Note:* There is no single correct answer for each of these tasks. The exercise is designed to give you practice in converting intuitive commands into equivalent algorithms and understanding the differences in the thought processes involved in the two types of responses.)

a.   Replace a flat tire with the spare tire.

b.   Make a telephone call.

c.   Go to the store and purchase a loaf of bread.

d.   Roast a turkey.

FIGURE 3.14   **A paint-by-number figure**

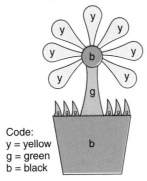

Code:
y = yellow
g = green
b = black

3. Determine and write an algorithm (list the steps) to interchange the contents of two cups of liquid. Assume that a third cup is available to hold the contents of either cup temporarily. Each cup should be rinsed before any new liquid is poured into it.

4. Write a detailed set of instructions, in English, to calculate the dollar amount of money in a piggy bank that contains h half dollars, q quarters, n nickels, d dimes, and p pennies.

5. Write a set of detailed, step-by-step instructions, in English, to find the smallest number in a group of three integer numbers.

6a. Write a set of detailed, step-by-step instructions, in English, to calculate the change remaining from a dollar after a purchase is made. Assume that the cost of the goods purchased is less than a dollar. The change received should consist of the smallest number of coins possible.

b. Repeat Exercise 6a but assume the change is given only in pennies.

7a. Write a set of detailed, step-by-step instructions, in English, to calculate the least number of dollar bills needed to pay a bill of amount `Total`. For example, if `Total` were $98, the bills would consist of one $50 bill, two $20 bills, one $5 bill, and three $1 bills. For this exercise, assume that only $100, $50, $20, $10, $5, and $1 bills are available.

b. Repeat Exercise 7a but assume the bill is paid only in $1 bills.

8a. Write an algorithm to locate the first occurrence of the name Jeans in a list of names arranged in random order.

b. Discuss how you could improve your algorithm for Exercise 8a if the list of names was arranged in alphabetical order.

9. Determine and write an algorithm to sort three numbers in ascending (from lowest to highest) order. How would you solve this problem intuitively?

3.4 Application: Swapping Values

The need to exchange the data that are either stored or referenced by two variables occurs frequently in programming when either lists of numbers or names need to be sorted. In this section, we develop the basic algorithm used in swapping two values and then write this algorithm as a class method.

Swapping the values stored in two variables is almost identical to switching the contents of two glasses. For example, assume that the first glass in Figure 3.15a contains pink lemonade and that the second glass contains yellow lemonade. Because the children who use these glasses only want to drink from their own glass, we want to switch the contents in the glasses to give the correct drink to each child. In practice, this is easily done using a temporary holder glass and following the three-step algorithm:

> *Step 1. Put the contents of the first glass into the temporary holder glass (Figure 3.15b)*
>
> *Step 2. Put the contents of the second glass into the first glass (Figure 3.15c)*
>
> *Step 3. Put the contents of the temporary glass into the second glass (Figure 3.15d)*

A similar three-step algorithm is used in programming to swap the values that are either stored directly or referenced by two variables. Specifically, the swap algorithm becomes

FIGURE 3.15 **Switching the contents of two glasses**

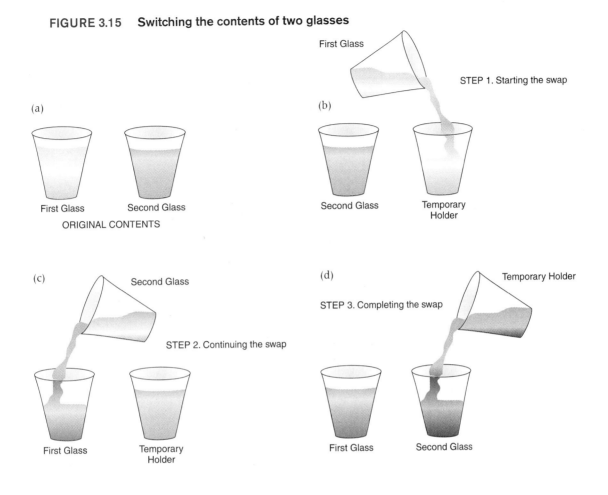

(a)

First Glass   Second Glass
ORIGINAL CONTENTS

(b)

First Glass

STEP 1. Starting the swap

Second Glass   Temporary Holder

(c)

Second Glass

STEP 2. Continuing the swap

First Glass   Temporary Holder

(d)

Temporary Holder

STEP 3. Completing the swap

First Glass   Second Glass

Step 1. Store the first variable's value into a temporary location (Figure 3.16a)
Step 2. Store the second variable's value into the first variable (Figure 3.16b)
Step 3. Store the temporary value into the second variable (Figure 3.16c)

The reason for step 1, which uses the temporary variable to hold the first variable's value, is immediately obvious once you consider what happens if this variable were not used. For example, if the value of the second variable were initially moved into the first variable (step 2) before temporarily saving the first value (step 1), the first value would be lost.

Once the basic swapping algorithm is understood, we can implement it within a Java method. The key question now becomes: How should the two variables be made available to the method that will swap their values? As illustrated in Figure 3.17, a method can receive data either as parameters (shown at the top of the figure) or as data members of a single object (shown on the figure's left side). Passing the two variables directly as parameters won't work because the method will only receive a copy of the values in the variables. Thus, switching values within the method will have no effect on the calling method's variables. The correct approach is to enclose the

FIGURE 3.16A **Save the first value**

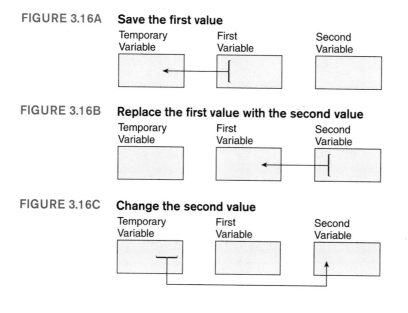

FIGURE 3.16B **Replace the first value with the second value**

FIGURE 3.16C **Change the second value**

variables within an object as instance variables and pass the object as an implicit parameter. Then, when the method is applied to the object, the method can directly alter the values stored in these variables. Algorithmically, the overall procedure we will use becomes

Encapsulate the two variables within a single object
Use a class method to implement the swap algorithm and switch the values in the instance variables

To illustrate this procedure, we will assume that we are dealing with names that must be alphabetically arranged. Once two names are found to be out of order, we will use our overall swapping procedure to switch names. For our immediate application, this translates into creating a class that supports objects having two instance variables, each of which can reference a string value. Initially, we will supply our class

FIGURE 3.17 **A method's interfaces**

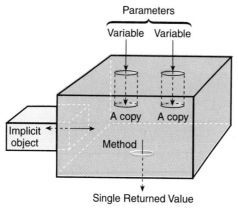

with a constructor that permits us to initialize an object's two variables with the names that must be switched, accessor methods to extract and return individual names, and mutator methods to alter individual names. Once we understand this basic class, we will add a swap() method capable of interchanging the strings referenced by an object. The following class, EncapsulateNames, provides the required two data members and initial class methods.

Program 3.5

```
public class EncapsulateNames
{
  // data declarations section
  private String nameOne;    // first name is referenced by this variable
  private String nameTwo;    // second name is referenced by this variable

  // method definitions section
  public EncapsulateNames(String s1, String s2)    // constructor
  {
    nameOne = s1;
    nameTwo = s2;
  }

    // methods to get and set individual string values
  public String getFirst()
  {
    return nameOne;
  }
  public String getSecond()
  {
    return nameTwo;
  }
  public void setAName(String s1)
  {
    nameOne = s1;
  }
  public void setBName(String s2)
  {
    nameTwo = s2;
  }
}
```

Program 3.5's class methods are relatively straightforward. The constructor permits an object to be initialized when it is created, the accessor methods return an object's nameOne and nameTwo values, and the mutator methods permit altering an object's nameOne and nameTwo values. Before testing this class's individual methods, it is worth noting that in practice you will frequently see methods whose body consists of a single statement written on a single line. For example, Program 3.5's first accessor method would more generally be written as

```
public String getFirst(){return nameOne;}
```

Applying this single line style to all of the accessor and mutator methods yields the class listed in Program 3.6. From an operational viewpoint, both programs are identical.

Program 3.6

```java
public class EncapsulateNames
{
  // data declarations section
  private String nameOne;   // first name is referenced by this variable
  private String nameTwo;   // second name is referenced by this variable

  // method definitions section
  public EncapsulateNames(String s1, String s2)   // constructor
  {
    nameOne = s1;
    nameTwo = s2;
  }


    // methods to get and set individual string values
  public String getFirst(){return nameOne;}
  public String getSecond(){return nameTwo;}
  public void setAName(String s1){nameOne = s1;}
  public void setBName(String s2){nameTwo = s2;}
}
```

Program 3.7 verifies that all of the EncapsulateNames class methods are operating correctly.

Program 3.7

```java
public class UseEncapsulateNames
{
  public static void main(String[] args)
  {
    String firstName = "Billings";
    String secName = "Ajax";
    EncapsulateNames namePair;     // declare an object type

    namePair = new EncapsulateNames(firstName, secName);  // create an object
      // verify the accessors
    System.out.println("The first name is " + namePair.getFirst());
    System.out.println("The second name is " + namePair.getSecond());
      // verify the mutators
    namePair.setAName("Calisto");
    namePair.setBName("Breyer");
    System.out.println("\nThe first name is " + namePair.getFirst());
    System.out.println("The second name is " + namePair.getSecond());
  }
}
```

The output produced by Program 3.7 is executed is

```
The first name is Billings
The second name is Ajax

The first name is Calisto
The second name is Breyer
```

As seen by this output, the created object named namePair is correctly initialized, and each accessor and mutator method correctly accesses and alters the strings referenced by this object's individual internal variables.

Now that we have our basic two-variable class, we can add a swap() method to switch the strings referenced by the two variables. The code for this method, which implements our three-step swap algorithm, is

```
public void swap()
{
  String temp; // declare a third variable for temporarily holding a double

  temp = nameOne;      // Step 1. Store the first variable's value into the temporary location
  nameOne = nameTwo; // Step 2. Store the second variable's value into the first variable
  nameTwo = temp;      // Step 3. Store the temporary value into the second variable
}
```

In reviewing swap(), notice that its three assignment statements directly correspond to the three steps previously listed for the swap algorithm and illustrated in Figure 3.16. Including this method into the EncapsulateNames class results in the completed class listed in Program 3.8.

The EncapsulateNames class permits us to create an object using any string variables. Once the object is created, the swap() method permits us to switch the values referenced by the variables, and the accessor methods permit us to return these values. Thus, we can use the EncapsulateNames class anytime we are sorting string data and find values that are out of alphabetical order. In this situation, a single EncapsulateNames object would be created at the start of the sort, and then the mutator methods would be used to set two names each time a swap is needed. If we were ordering numerical data, we would use a similar class by declaring the instance variables as double-precision types rather than string types and modifying the class methods appropriately to deal with double-precision values.

To see how the EncapsulateNames class can be used, consider the TestSwap class presented in Program 3.9. In practice, Program 3.9's main() would be modified to cycle through a complete list of names, and each time names were found out of order, the two offending values would be encapsulated and swapped using an EncapsulateNames object. To cycle through a list of items, be they names or numbers, requires knowledge of reception, selection, and arrays. So for now, we can put our EncapsulateNames class in our own personal library of useful classes and use it later when we have acquired additional programming skills.

Program 3.8

```
public class EncapsulateNames
{
  // data declarations section
  private String nameOne;    // first name is referenced by this variable
  private String nameTwo;    // second name is referenced by this variable

   // method definitions section
  public EncapsulateNames(String s1, String s2)    // constructor
  {
    nameOne = s1;
    nameTwo = s2;
  }

  // methods to get and set individual string values
  public String getFirst(){return nameOne;}
  public String getSecond(){return nameTwo;}
  public void setAName(String s1){nameOne = s1;}
  public void setBName(String s2){nameTwo = s2;}

   // swap method
  public void swap()
  {
    String temp; // declare a third variable for temporarily holding a double

    temp = nameOne;   // Step 1. Store the first variable's value in the temporary location
    nameOne = nameTwo; // Step 2. Store the second variable's value in the first variable
    nameTwo = temp;    // Step 3. Store the temporary value in the second variable
  }
}
```

The following output was obtained using Program 3.9:

```
Before the call to swap():
  The string stored in firstName is: Billings
  The string stored in secName is: Ajax

After the call to swap():
  The string stored in firstName is now: Ajax
  The string stored in secName is now: Billings
```

   As illustrated in this output, the values stored in main()'s variables have been modified from within swap(), which was made possible by the use of an object of type EncapsulateNames.

Program 3.9

```
public class TestSwap
{
  public static void main(String[] args)
  {
    String firstName = "Billings";  // here is the current first name
    String secName = "Ajax";        // here is the current second name
    EncapsulateNames namePair;

    System.out.println("Before the call to swap():");
    System.out.println("  The string stored in firstName is: " + firstName);
    System.out.println("  The string stored in secName is: " + secName);

     // enclose the two strings within a single object
    namePair = new EncapsulateNames(firstName, secName);
     // swap the string values within the object
    namePair.swap();  // apply the swap() method to the object

     // now extract the two strings
    firstName = namePair.getFirst();
    secName = namePair.getSecond();

    System.out.println("\nAfter the call to swap():");
    System.out.println("  The string stored in firstName is now: " + firstName);
    System.out.println("  The string stored in secName is now: " + secName);

  }
}
```

Exercises 3.4

1. Compile and run Program 3.7. To run Program 3.7, you also have to compile either Program 3.5 or 3.6.

2. Compile and run Program 3.9. To run Program 3.9, you also have to compile Program 3.8.

3. Modify Program 3.8 so that it declares only one string instance variable named `name`. Then rewrite the `swap()` method so that it accepts an `EncapsulateNames` as a parameter and swaps the value referenced by the parameter with the value referenced by the object used when the method is called. For example, the method call `AName.swap(BName)` should switch the values contained in the objects `AName` and `BName`. The method header should be `public void swap(EncapsulateNames secName)`.

4. Rewrite Program 3.8 to include a swap method named `swapOne()` that accepts an `EncapsulateNames` object as a parameter. The `swapOne()` method should then exchange the two values contained within this parameter. The method header should be `public static void swapOne(XYValue namePair)`. (The reason for inclusion of the reserved word `static` is explained in the next section.)

5a. Using the `EncapsulateNames` class as a model, construct a class named `XYValues` that can be used to swap the values stored in two double-precision instance variables.

b. Test the class constructed in Exercise 5a using a class named `TestXYValues`.

6. Modify the program written for Exercise 5a so that it declares only one double-precision instance variable named `x`. Then rewrite the `swap()` method so that it accepts an `XY-Values` object as a parameter and swaps the value in the parameter with the value contained in the object used when the method is called. For example, the method call `firstValue.swap(secondValue)` should switch the values contained in the objects `firstValue` and `secondValue`. The method header should be `public void swap(XYValues secVar)`.

3.5 `static` and `final` Variables

Each object created from a class gets its own block of memory for the instance variables declared within its class's data declaration section. In some cases, however, it is convenient for all objects to share the same memory location for a specific variable. For example, consider a class consisting of employee records, where each employee is subject to the same state tax rate. Clearly, we could declare the tax rate as an instance variable, in which case it would be included with every employees' data. But this solution is wasteful of computer storage and can result in an error if the tax rate changes and the change is not made to all existing employee objects. Additionally, we might want a single variable to keep track of the number of employees. Each time a new employee is hired, we would want to increment the employee count by one. Similarly, each time an employee leaves, we would want to decrement the employee count by one.

This type of situation is handled in Java using `static` variables. A `static` variable is created only once for each class, is shared by all objects created from the class, and exists even if no object is instantiated. `static` variables are declared in the same way as instance variables, with one modification: The reserved word `static` is included in the declaration. For example, consider the `Employee` class Program 3.10.

Program 3.10 declares two `static` methods in the `Employee` class's data declaration section. Like instance variables, `static` variables *must always be* declared outside any class method. The first `static` variable, named `numEmployees`, is declared in Program 3.10 by the statement

```
private static int numEmployees;  // this will be initialized to 0
```

Notice that this declaration statement does not include an explicit initial value, which is optional.[2] In keeping with the default value that Java assigns to all numerical variables, when memory storage is allocated to it, the `static` variable `numEmployees` will be initialized to zero (see Table 2.10). This initialization occurs at the time storage is allocated for the variable (when the `Employee` class is loaded into the JVM).

The second declaration statement includes an explicit initial value for the `taxRate` variable. This is accomplished by the statement

```
private static double taxRate = 0.025;
```

---

[2] Instance variables may also be explicitly initialized when they are declared. The initialization, however, only takes effect when an object is created and no default constructor exists that will automatically overwrite the initialization provided by the declaration statement.

Program 3.10

```java
public class Employee
{
  // data declarations section

  private static int numEmployees;  // this will be initialized to 0
  private static double taxRate = 0.025;
  private int idNum;

  // class method definitions section

  public Employee(int num)  // constructor
  {
    idNum = num;
    numEmployees++;  // add one to the employee count
  }

  public void showValues()
  {
    System.out.println("Employee number " + idNum
            + " has a tax rate of " + taxRate + ".\n");
  }

  public static void main(String[] args)
  {
    System.out.println("The value in numEmployees is " + numEmployees);
    System.out.println("The tax rate for all employees is " + taxRate + '\n');

      // now create two Employee objects
    Employee BSMITH = new Employee(11122);
    System.out.println("The number of employees is now " + numEmployees);
    BSMITH.showValues();

    Employee JJONES = new Employee(11133);
    System.out.println("The number of employees is now " + numEmployees);
    JJONES.showValues();
  }
}
```

which stores a value of 0.025 into `taxRate` when storage for this variable is allocated by the JVM. The storage sharing produced by these two `static` data members and the two objects created in Program 3.10 is illustrated in Figure 3.18. Because `static` variables are shared by all objects created from a class and, unlike instance variables, exist outside any single object, `static` variables are also referred to as **class variables.**

The output produced by Program 3.10 is:

```
The value in numEmployees is 0
The tax rate for all employees is 0.025
```

PROGRAMMING NOTE

The Reserved Word static

In Java, a variable declared as static belongs to a class as a whole. Thus, a static variable is created only once, no matter how many objects of the class are created, and it exists even if no objects are created. Each object shares the same static variable, and a change to the static variable's value by one object effectively changes the value of the static variable for all objects. This is because only one static variable is actually created, and the same variable is shared by all instantiated objects.

Because static variables exist outside any specific object, Java provides a means of accessing such variables independently of any object. This is the purpose of a static method. A very useful side effect of the fact that static methods can be invoked independently of any object is that it also permits such methods to perform any tasks not associated with a specific object. One such task is to start program processing with a main() method before any object has had a chance to be created. Because of this capability, static methods are frequently referred to as general-purpose methods.

From within both static and non-static methods, a static variable can be accessed by simply using the variable's name within the class that declared the variable. When it is accessed as a data member of a specific object, it is prefixed with the object's name and a period. If it were public static variable can also be accessed by prefixing it with its class name and a period when it is used outside its defining class.

```
The number of employees is now 1
Employee number 11122 has a tax rate of 0.025.

The number of employees is now 2
Employee number 11133 has a tax rate of 0.025.
```

Notice that the values of the static variables numEmployees and taxRate are displayed before Program 3.10 declares or creates any objects. This display can be pro-

FIGURE 3.18   **Sharing the static data member taxRate**

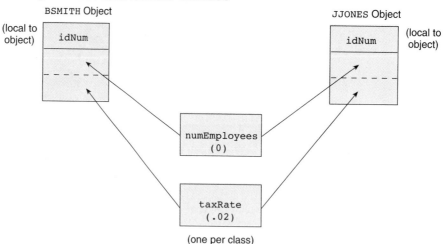

vided precisely because a static variable exists independently and outside any specific object. After each Employee object is created, both the number of employees and their tax rate are displayed. To illustrate that each object has access to its class's static variables, the tax rate has been retrieved as a member of an Employee object using the showValues() accessor.

One last point needs to be mentioned with respect to the numEmployees variable. Incrementing this variable's value within each constructor ensures that the increment takes place whenever an Employee object is created. This can be done using any of the three statements numEmployees++, ++numEmployees, or numEmployees = numEmployees + 1.

static Methods

It is precisely to provide a means of accessing static variables in the absence of, and independently of any specific object, that static methods are provided in Java. Such methods are restricted to using static variables and other static methods, as well as any additional values and objects that are passed as arguments into the method.

As a specific example, consider the following two static methods that can be added to Program 3.10's Employee class.

```
public static double getRate() // an accessor to return a static variable
{
    return taxRate;
}

public static void setRate(double rate) // a mutator to set a static variable
{
    taxRate = rate;
}
```

What makes these methods static is the inclusion of the static reserved word in each method's header line. If these two methods are included within Program 3.10's Employee class, as listed next, they can be called from any outside class either by providing an object or a class name.

Program 3.11   The **Employee** class with **static** methods

```
public class Employee
{
  // data declarations section
private static int numEmployees;  // this will be initialized to 0
private static double taxRate = 0.025;
private int idNum;

  // method definitions section
  public Employee(int num)  // constructor
  {
    idNum = num;
    numEmployees++;  // add one to the employee count
  }
```

(continued)

(continued)

```
public void showValues()
{
   System.out.println("Employee number " + idNum
          + " has a tax rate of " + taxRate);
}

public static double getRate() // an accessor to return a static variable
{
   return taxRate;
}

public static void setRate(double rate) // a mutator to alter the static variable
{
   taxRate = rate;
}
}
```

Program 3.12 uses the Employee class's getRate() and setRate methods from within the class named UseEmployee. As illustrated, these two static methods do not require a specific object reference when they are called but can be called by providing their class name. This name informs the JVM as to where the method is located.

Program 3.12

```
public class UseEmployee
{
   public static void main(String[] args)
   {
      System.out.println("The tax rate is initially " + Employee.getRate());
      Employee BSMITH = new Employee(11122);
      BSMITH.showValues();

      Employee.setRate(.03);
      System.out.println("\nThe tax rate is now " + Employee.getRate());
      BSMITH.showValues();
   }
}
```

The output displayed by Program 3.12 is

```
The tax rate is initially 0.025
Employee number 11122 has a tax rate of 0.025

The tax rate is now 0.03
Employee number 11122 has a tax rate of 0.03
```

As indicated by this output, the value stored in the static variable taxRate is directly accessible using a class's static methods without reference to a specific object. In Program 3.12, taxRate's initial value is first retrieved by getRate(), is subsequently altered by setRate(), and is once again retrieved by the getRate() static accessor method. Additionally, because a static variable is shared by all objects created from the class, the variable can also be accessed using a method, such as showValues(), that acts on a specific object.

A final and frequently useful observation is that static methods, because they can be called without reference to a specific object, can also be used for constructing general-purpose methods. Such methods perform their functions using only data passed to it as arguments at the time of their call. The main() method is an example of this type of method. More generally, however, we can construct other general-purpose methods that perform tasks independently of any object. QuickTest Program 3.13 illustrates one such method, named average(), that returns the average of two values passed to it as arguments when it is called.

QuickTest Program 3.13

```java
public class AverageNumbers
{
  public static void main(String[] args)
  {
    double numOne = 12.5;
    double numTwo = 17.2;
    double avg;

    avg = average(numOne, numTwo);
    System.out.println("The average of " + numOne + " and "
                          +numTwo + " is " + avg);
  }

  public static double average(double numOne, double numTwo)
  {
      return (numOne + numTwo)/2.0;
  }
}
```

In reviewing QuickTest Program 3.13, notice that the average() method satisfies all the requirements for accepting parameters and returning a double-precision number that were presented in Sections 3.1 and 3.2. When average() is called, its double-precision returned value is assigned to a double-precision variable. It could equally have been called directly within the println() method (see Exercise 3). Notice that the call to average() *is not* preceded by an object's name. None is required precisely because average() is a static method. It also does not require a class name because it is called from within the class that defines it. Thus, this method will be loaded by the JVM as part of the AverageNumbers class and will not have to be located as part of some other class.[3]

Specifically, average() expects to receive two double-precision numbers and returns the product of the two argument values passed to it at the time it is called. That

---

[3] Including the class name will not cause any error. Therefore, including it will never cause an error as long as the JVM has access to the named class.

this is successfully accomplished is verified by the output of QuickTest Program 3.13, which is

```
The average of 12.5 and 17.2 is 14.85
```

General-purpose (i.e., `static`) methods are not restricted to being called from a `static` method such as `main()`; they can also be called from non-`static` methods. The only requirement in Java is that one method can never be contained within another method (referred to as **nesting**); each method must be defined outside any other method but within a class.

Scope

The section of a program within which an identifier is valid, or "known," is referred to as its **scope**. On a practical level, the scope of a variable defines the portion of a class where the variable can be used. In Java, two predominant types of scope are defined: **local scope** and **class scope**.

Variables that are declared within a method are formally said to have **local scope**, which starts at the opening left brace, {, that begins the method and stops at the closing right brace, }, that ends the method. In addition, all parameters of a method are considered to have local scope.[4] Internally, within a method, any variables declared inside an inner block defined by a left and right brace pair, {}, have a local scope restricted by the brace pair that defines the inner block. Let's take a moment to see why the name local scope makes sense.

By their very nature, Java methods are constructed to be independent modules. As we have seen, values can be passed to a method using the method's parameter list, and a value can be directly returned from a method using a `return` statement. Seen in this light, a method can be thought of as a closed box with slots at the top to receive values and a single slot at the bottom to return a value (Figure 3.19).

The metaphor of a closed box is useful because it emphasizes the fact that what goes on inside the method, including all variable declarations within the method's body, is hidden from the view of all other methods. Because the variables declared inside a method are available only to the method itself, they are in effect local to the method. Thus, a local variable is one that has had storage locations set aside for it by a declaration statement made within a method's body. Hence, local variables are only meaningful when used in expressions or statements inside the method that declared

FIGURE 3.19 **A method can be considered a closed box**

Values into the method

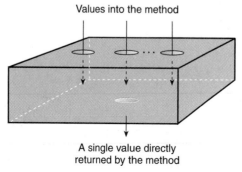

A single value directly
returned by the method

[4] A synonym for local scope is **block scope**.

FIGURE 3.20   **An example of scopes**

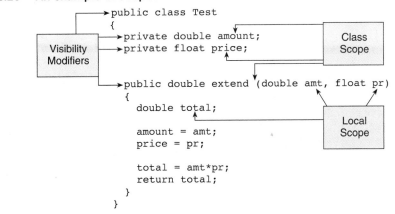

them. This means that the same variable name can be declared and used in more than one method. For each method that declares the variable, a separate and distinct variable is created. The same is true for all parameters declared within a method's header line; method parameters can only be used within the method that declares them. Thus, parameter names are also local to their declaring methods.

   Class scope starts at the opening left brace, {, that begins a class's definition and stops at the closing right brace, }, that ends the class. Thus, class scope includes all instance and static variables declared in the class's variable declaration section and all methods contained within the class's method definition section. Figure 3.20 illustrates the scope of the variables and methods for the listed class.

   In addition to scope, as shown in Figure 3.20, classes and their members have **visibility**, which determines whether the member can be accessed from outside the class in which it is declared. Visibility is set using one or none of the following access modifiers: public, private, or protected. Regardless of these access modifiers, all class variables and methods are accessible everywhere within their class and conform to the following visibility rules.

1. An instance variable can only be accessed outside its class as a member of an object. If the instance variable is private, outside access must be made through a public member method; otherwise, if it is public, it can be accessed directly using an object's name.

2. A static variable declared as private can only be accessed outside its class as a member of an object or using a public and static class method.

3. A static variable declared as public can be accessed outside its class by prefixing the variable's name with its class name and a period.

4. If an instance or static variable has the same name as a method variable, the class variable effectively becomes hidden within the method, and any use of the variable's name will refer to the method variable. In such cases, the class variable can still be accessed within the scope of the method variable having the same name by prefixing the class variable's name with the class's name for static variables and with the object's name or the reserved word this (as demonstrated in Section 12.2) for non-static object variables. In all cases, the prefixed name must be separated from the variable's name with a period.

5. A class method declared as public can be accessed outside its class. In general, such methods present the services that the class provides to the outside world.

> **PROGRAMMING NOTE**
>
> ## *Values and Identities*
>
> Apart from any behavior that an object is supplied with, a characteristic feature that objects share with variables is that they always have a unique **identity**. It is an object's identity that permits distinguishing one object from another. This is not true of a literal value, such as the number 5, because all occurrences of 5 are indistinguishable from one another. Thus, literal values are not considered as objects in object-oriented programming languages such as Java. A value is simply an entity that stands for itself.
>
> Now consider a string such as "Chicago." As a string, this is a literal value. However, since Chicago could also be a specific and identifiable object of type City, the context in which the name is used is important. Notice that if the string "Chicago" were assigned to an object's name attribute, it reverts to being a value.

6. A class method declared as `public` and `static` is a general-purpose method that can perform a task not related to any specific object created from the class.

7. A class method declared as `private` can only be accessed by other methods in the same class that contains the `private` method.

In addition to the visibility of methods and variables defined within a class, the class itself has a visibility. When the reserved word `class` is preceded by the reserved word `public`, the class can be accessed by other classes. If the class is preceded by the reserved word `private`, it can only be accessed by other classes stored in the same source file.

The length of time that storage locations remain reserved for an identifier is referred to as both an identifier's **lifetime** and **duration.** All identifiers with class scope come into being when the class within which they are declared is loaded into the JVM and remain until the program finishes execution. Because `static` variables can have only class scope, these variables always have the same duration as their defining class. Local variables exist only while the block within which they are defined are in scope. Once the block goes out of scope, the storage areas for these variables are released back to the operating system. Should the block come back into scope, new storage areas are reserved and reinitialized as defined by the code within the block.

`final` Variables

Quite frequently, specific values within a program have a more general meaning that is recognized outside the context of the program. Examples of these types of values include 3.1416, which is π accurate to four decimal places; 32.2 ft/sec^2, which is the acceleration due to gravity; and 2.71828, which is Euler's number accurate to five decimal places. The meaning of certain other constants appearing in a program is defined strictly within the context of the application being programmed. For example, in a program to determine bank interest charges, the interest rate typically must be used in a number of different places throughout the program. Similarly, in a program to calculate taxes, the tax rate might appear in many individual instructions. Programmers refer to numbers such as these as **magic numbers**. By themselves, the numbers are ordinary, but in the context of a particular application, they have a special ("magical") meaning.

Frequently, the same magic number appears repeatedly within the same program. This recurrence of the same number throughout a program is a potential source of error should the number have to be changed. For example, if either the interest rate or sales tax rate changes, as rates are prone to do, the programmer has the cumbersome task of changing the value everywhere it appears in the program. Multiple changes, however, are subject to error; if just one rate value is overlooked and not changed, the result obtained when the program is run will be incorrect, and the source of the error will be difficult to locate.

To avoid the problem of having the same number spread throughout a program and to permit clear identification of more universal constants, such as π, Java allows the programmer to give variables an initial value that cannot subsequently be changed. Such variables are formally referred to as **final variables** and informally known as both **named constants** and **symbolic constants** in Java. We shall use these terms interchangeably.

Once a `final` variable has been created, its name is then used throughout a class in place of the literal value it contains. If this value ever has to be changed, the change need only be made once at the point where the `final` variable is initialized.

Creating a `final` variable is accomplished using the `final` reserved word when a variable is declared. Doing so specifies that the variable can only be read after it is initialized; it cannot be changed. Although instance, `static`, and local variables can all be declared as `final`, from a practical standpoint instance variables are almost never made `final`. The reason is that a `final` instance variable would have the same value in all objects containing it, in which case a single `static` variable applicable to all objects is more efficient. Two examples of `static` variables that have been declared as `final` are

```
public final static double PI = 3.1416;
public final static int NUMEMPS = 100;
```

The first declaration statement creates a `final` double-precision variable named `PI` and initializes it to 3.1416. The second declaration statement creates a `final` integer named `NUMEMPS` and initializes it with the value 100. Notice that we have also made the `static` variables `public`. The reason is that the `final` reserved word ensures that the stored value cannot be subsequently altered by any class method, so we lose nothing in making it publicly available for use.

Local variables are also frequently made `final`. For example, a valid local declaration that might be used in a general-purpose method for calculating the weight of steel could be

```
final float DENSITY = 0.238f;
```

This statement creates a `final` variable named `DENSITY` and initializes it with the value 0.238f. Note that the f is required. Without this suffix, we would be attempting to initialize a `float` variable with a double-precision value, which results in a compiler error message. An interesting option with `final` local variables is that their initialization can be deferred. This happens automatically when no initial value is provided within the declaration statement. For example, the following declaration, if it is made inside a method's body (hence, it would be a local declaration)

```
final float DENSITY;
```

creates a `final` variable that is formally referred to as a **blank final**. This permits us to initialize DENSITY at a later time, perhaps with an argument supplied when the method is called. Once initialized, for example with the statement

```
DENSITY = 0.238f;
```

no further assignment to DENSITY is permitted. Thus, once a `final` variable is created and initialized, *the value stored in it cannot be changed.* For all practical purposes, the name of the variable and its value are linked together for the duration of the program. An attempt to assign another value to a `final` variable results in the compiler error message `Can't assign a value to a final variable:`.

Although we have typed the `final` identifiers in uppercase letters, lowercase letters could have been used. It is common in Java, however, to use all uppercase letters for `final` variables to make them easy to identify. Then, whenever a programmer sees uppercase letters in a program, he or she knows the value of the variable cannot be changed within the program.

Once declared, a `final` variable can be used in any Java statement in place of the number it represents. For example, the expressions

```
2 * PI * radius
DENSITY * volume
```

are both valid. These statements must, of course, appear after the declarations for all of their variables. QuickTest Program 3.14 illustrates using a `final` variable within the context of a complete program. In this program, the weight of the steel is calculated as steel's density times the cylinder's volume, which is determined using the expression $\pi * radius^2 * height$. The actual weight calculation is accomplished by a call to the general-purpose method `cylinderWeight()`. This method expects to receive two double-precision arguments and returns no value.

QuickTest Program 3.14

```java
public class ComputeWeight

{
  public static void main (String[] args)
  {
    cylinderWeight(3, 12);  // a call to cylinderWeight
  }


  public static void cylinderWeight(double radius, double height)
  {
    final double PI = 3.1416;     // a final local variable
    final double DENSITY = 0.284;  // a final local variable

    System.out.println("The weight of a steel cylinder with "
                    + "\n  radius = " + radius + " inches"
                    + "\n  height = " + height + " inches"
                    + "\n    is " + DENSITY* (PI * radius * radius * height)
                    + " pounds");
  }
}
```

The output displayed by QuickTest Program 3.14 is

```
The weight of a steel cylinder with
  radius = 3.0 inches
  height = 12.0 inches
is 96.35915519999999 pounds
```

In the next chapter, we will see how to enter data interactively while a program is running. Having this capability in QuickTest Program 3.14 would permit the user to enter any radius and height values needed and not be restricted to the literal values of 3 and 12 coded into the program.

Placement of Statements

At this stage, we have introduced a variety of declaration statement types. The general rule in Java for their placement is that a variable must be declared before it can be used. Although this rule permits declaration statements to be placed throughout a class or method, doing so can result in a very poor program structure. As a general rule, with minor exceptions that will be noted throughout the text, the following statement ordering should be used:

```
public class className
{
   // declaration section
   final static variable declarations
   static variable declarations
   instance variable declarations

   // methods section - example of one method
 method header line(parameter list)
   {
     final variable declarations
     variable declarations
     object declarations

     other Java statements
   }
}
```

Two publicly available `final` variables provided by Java in the `java.lang.Math` class are

```
public static final double PI = 3.14159265358979323846;
public static final double E = 2.7182818284590452354;
```

These variables may be used in any class using the notation `Math.PI` and `Math.E`.

Exercises 3.5

1. Enter and run Program 3.12.

2. Enter and run QuickTest Program 3.13.

3. Does the following program produce the same result as QuickTest Program 3.13?

```
public class AverageNumbers
{
  public static void main(String[] args)
  {
    double numOne = 12.5;
    double numTwo = 17.2;

    System.out.println("The average of " + numOne + " and "
                       +numTwo + " is " + average(numOne, numTwo));
  }

  public static double average(double numOne, double numTwo)
  {
    return (numOne + numTwo)/2.0;
  }
}
```

4. Determine the error in the following program:

```
public class AverageNumbers
{
  public static void main(String[] args)
  {
    float product;

    product = average(12.5, 17.2);
    System.out.println("The answer is " + product);
  }

  public static double average(double numOne, double numTwo)
  {
    return (numOne + numTwo)/2.0;
  }
}
```

5a. For the following section of code, determine the data type and scope of all declared variables. To do this, list the three column headings that follow on a sheet of paper (we have filled in the entries for the first variable).

Identifier	Data Type	Scope
price	integer	class scope

```
public class Test
{
  private static int price;
  private static long years;
  private static double yield;

  public void main(String[] args)
  {
    int bondtype;
    double interest, coupon;

        .

        .

  }
```

```
public double roi(int mat1, int mat2)
{
   int count;
   double effectiveRate;

        .
        .

   return effectiveRate;
}


public int step(double first, double last)
{
   int numofyrs;
   double fracPart;

        .
        .

   return 10*numofyrs;
}
}
```

b. Draw boxes around the appropriate section of the foregoing code to enclose the scope of each variable.

c. Determine the data type of the arguments that the methods `roi()` and `step()` expect and the data type of the value returned by these methods.

6a. For the following section of code, determine the data type and scope of all declared constants and variables. To do this, list the three column headings that follow on a sheet of paper (we have filled in the entries for the first variable).

Identifier	Data Type	Scope
key	char	class scope

```
public class Test
{
   private static char key;
   private static long number;

   public void main(String[] args)
   {
      int a,b,c;
      double x,y;

           .
           .

   }

   public int method1(int num1, int num2)
   {
      int o,p;
      double q;
```

(continued)

(continued)

```
          .
          .
       return p;
     }

     double method2(double first, double last)
     {
       int a,b,c,o,p;
       double r;
       double s,t,x;

          .
          .
       return s * t;
     }
   }
```

b. Draw a box around the appropriate section of the foregoing code to enclose the scope of the variables `key`, `num1`, `y`, and `r`.

c. Determine the data type of the arguments that the methods `method1()` and `method2()` expect and the data type of the value returned by these methods.

7. Besides speaking about the scope of a variable, we can also apply the term to a method's parameters. What is the scope of all method parameters?

8. Remove all references to the `final` variable named `PI` in QuickTest Program 3.13 and, where appropriate, replace them with the Java-provided final variable `Math.PI`.

3.6 Common Programming Errors

1. Attempting to pass incorrect data types is an extremely common programming error related to methods. The values passed to a method must correspond to the data types of the parameters declared for the method. One way to verify that correct values have been received is to display all passed values within a method's body before any calculations are made. Once this verification has taken place, the display can be dispensed with.[5]

2. Declaring the same variable locally within both the calling and called methods and assuming a change in one variable affects the other variable. Even though the variable name is the same, a change to one local variable *does not* alter the value in the other local variable.

3. Terminating a method's header line with a semicolon.

4. Forgetting to include the data type of a method's parameters within the header line.

5. Attempting to alter an object's `private` variables by passing the object into a non-class method as an argument. An object type can be passed as an argument, but Java's privacy rules must still be observed.

---

[5] In practice, a good debugger program should be used.

3.7 **Chapter Review**

KEY TERMS
algorithm	identity	scope
block scope	local scope	state
call by value	magic number	`static` method
class scope	overloading	`static` variable
`final` variable	parameter signature	swap method
formal parameters	pass by value	visibility

SUMMARY

1. A method is called by giving its name and passing any data to it in the parentheses following the name. If a variable is one of the arguments in a method call, the called method receives a copy of the variable's value.

2. The commonly used form of a user-written method is

```
public returnType methodName(parameter list)
{
  declarations and other Java statements;
  return  expression;
}
```

   The first line of the method is called the method header. The opening and closing braces of the method and all statements in between these braces constitute the method's body. The parameter list is a comma-separated list of parameter declarations.

3. A method's return type declares the data type of the value returned by the method. If the method does not return a value, it should be declared as a `void` type.

4. Methods can directly return at most a single value to their calling methods. This value is the value of the expression in the `return` statement.

5. A called method cannot alter either a primitive data type argument's value or a reference variable's value by changing the value of the equivalent parameter.

6. Reference values are passed to a called method in the same manner as primitive data types; the called method receives a copy of the reference value. Passing a reference does not permit a nonclass method to alter an object's privately declared instance variables because doing so would violate the `private` nature of these variables.

7. An algorithm is a step-by-step procedure that must terminate and describes how a single computation or task is to be performed. An algorithm is typically coded as a Java method.

8. The section of a program within which an identifier is valid, or "known," is referred to as its scope. This section of the program is also referred to as where the variable is visible, which means that it can be legitimately accessed and will cause no compiler errors.

9. A method's variables and parameters all have local scope (the term block scope is also used). This scope begins at the point of declaration and ends at the closing brace of the block of code within which they are declared. Variables having local scope are also referred to as local variables.

10. Class scope begins at the left brace, {, that starts a class definition and continues to the closing right brace, }, that ends the class definition. Thus, all methods within a class have class scope, as do all instance and `static` variables.

11. Instance and `static` variables must be declared outside any method.

12. `static` variables can be accessed without being referenced as a data member of a specific object.

3.8 Chapter Supplement: Inside and Outside

In programming terms, an object's attributes are described by data, such as the length and width of a rectangle, and the operations that can be applied to the attributes are described by methods. As a practical example, assume that we will be writing a program that can deal a hand of cards. From an object-oriented approach, one of the objects that we must model is a deck of cards. For our purposes, the attribute of interest for the card deck is that it contains 52 cards consisting of four suits (hearts, diamonds, spades, and clubs), with each suit consisting of 13 pip values (ace to ten, jack, queen, and king).

Now consider the behavior of our deck of cards, which consists of the operations that can be applied to the deck. At a minimum, we will want the ability to shuffle the deck and deal single cards. Let's now see how this simple example illustrates an inside-outside concept that is characteristic of all classes.

A useful visualization of the inside-outside concept is to consider an object as a boiled egg (Figure 3.21). Notice that the egg consists of three parts: a very inside yolk, a less inside white surrounding the yolk, and an outer shell, which is the only part of the egg visible to the outside world.

In terms of our boiled egg model, the attributes and behavior of an object correspond to the yolk and white, respectively, which are inside the eggshell. That is, the innermost protected area of an object, its data attributes, can be compared to the egg yolk.

Surrounding the data attributes, in a similar manner as an egg's white surrounds its yolk, are the operations that we choose to provide for the object. Finally, in this analogy, the interface to the outside world, which is depicted by the shell, represents how a user gets to invoke the class' methods on the object's instance variables.

The egg model, with its eggshell interface separating the inside of the egg from the outside, is useful precisely because it so clearly depicts the separation between what should be contained inside an object and what should be seen from the outside. This separation forms an essential element in object-oriented programming. Let's see why this is so.

From an inside-outside perspective, an object's data attributes and the details of how methods are implemented are always inside issues that are hidden from the

FIGURE 3.21 **The boiled egg object model**

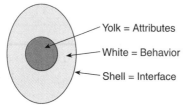

Yolk = Attributes

White = Behavior

Shell = Interface

view of an object user. What remains — how a user or another object can actually activate an inside procedure — is an outside issue.

Now we can apply this concept to our card deck example. First, consider how we might represent cards in the deck. Any of the following attributes (and there are others) could be used to represent a card.

1. Two integers, one representing a suit (a number from 1 to 4) and one representing a value (a number from 1 to 13).

2. One character value and one integer value. The character represents a card's suit, and the integer represents a card's value.

3. One integer variable having a value from 1 to 52, each of which corresponds to a unique card in the deck.

Whichever representation we select, however, is not relevant to the outside. The specific way we choose to represent a card is an inside issue to be decided by the designer of a `Deck` class. From the outside, the only concern is that we have access to a deck consisting of 52 cards having the necessary suit and pip values.

The same is true for the operations we decide to provide as part of our card deck class. Consider just the shuffling for now.

There are a number of algorithms for producing a shuffled deck. For example, we could use Java's random number method, `Math.random()`, described in Section 6.7, or create our own random number generator. Again, the selected procedure is an inside issue to be determined by the designer of the class. The specifics of the selection and how it is applied to the attributes we have chosen for each card in the deck are not relevant from the object's outside. For purposes of illustration, assume that we decide to use Java's `Math.random()` method to produce a randomly shuffled deck.

If we use the first attribute set previously given, each card in a shuffled deck is produced using `Math.random()` at least twice: once to create a random number from 1 to 4 for the suit and then again to create a random number from 1 to 13 for the card's pip value. This sequence must be done to construct 52 different attribute sets with no duplicates allowed.

If, on the other hand, we use the second attribute set previously given, a shuffled deck can be produced in exactly the same fashion just described, with one modification: The first random number (from 1 to 4) must be changed into a character to represent the suit.

Finally, if we use the third representation for a card, we need to use `Math.random()` once for each card to produce 52 random numbers from 1 to 52 with no duplicates allowed.

The important point here is that the selection of how a deck is selected and shuffled is a definition issue described in a class's data and methods section, *and definition issues are always inside issues*. A user of the card deck, who is outside, does not need to know how the shuffling is done. All the user of the deck must know is how to produce a shuffled deck. In practice, this means that the user is supplied with sufficient information to correctly instantiate a deck object and invoke the shuffle method. This corresponds to the interface, or outer shell of the egg.

Abstraction and Encapsulation

The distinction between inside and outside relates directly to the concepts of abstraction and encapsulation. **Abstraction** means concentrating on what an object is and does before making any decisions about how a class will be implemented. Thus, abstractly, we define a deck and the operations we want to provide. (Clearly, if our abstraction is to be useful, it had better capture the attributes and operations of a real-world deck.) Once we have decided on the attributes and operations, we can actually implement them.

Encapsulation means incorporating the definition details of the chosen abstract attributes and behavior inside a class. The external side of an object should provide only the necessary interface to users of the object for activating class methods. Imposing a strict inside-outside discipline when creating classes is really another way of saying that the class successfully encapsulates all definition details. In our deck of cards example, encapsulation means that users need never be concerned with how we have internally modeled the deck or how an operation, such as shuffling, is performed; they only need to know how to activate the given operations.

Code Reuse and Extensibility

A direct advantage of an inside-outside approach is that it encourages both code reuse and extensibility. This is a direct result of having all interactions between objects centered on the outside interface and restricting all definition details within the object's inside.

For example, consider the object in Figure 3.22. Here any of the two class' operations can be activated by correctly stimulating either the circle or square on the outside. In practice, the stimulation is simply a method call. We have used a circle and square to emphasize that two different methods are provided for outside use. In our card deck example, activation of one method might produce a shuffled deck, while activation of another method might result in a card suit and pip value being returned from the object.

Now assume that we want to alter the definition of an existing operation or add more functionality to our class. *As long as the existing outside interface is maintained, the internal definition of any and all operations can be changed without the user ever being aware that a change took place.* This is a direct result of encapsulating the attribute data and operations within a class.

In addition, as long as the interface to existing methods are not changed, new methods can be added as they are needed. Essentially, from the outside world, all that is being added is another method call that accesses the inside attributes and modifies them in a new way.

FIGURE 3.22   Using a class interface

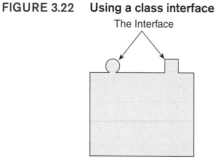

Part Two

Methods and Statements

4 Input and Formatting Class Methods

In this chapter, we present Java-supplied class methods for entering data interactively while a program is running. Additionally, this chapter presents the use of such methods for creating formatting output and provides a set of useful mathematical methods from Java's `Math` class. To illustrate and isolate the methods and statements introduced, we make frequent use of QuickTest programs. Finally, to stress the importance of using existing classes, which include those provided by Java and those you create as your programming proficiency improves, we show how to construct a personal class library.

4.1   **Interactive Keyboard Input**

Except for demonstration programs, almost every Java program requires externally supplied input, which is data provided to the program while it is running. These data can be entered by a user at the keyboard, via a graphical user interface (GUI) from either a restricted set of selections using a mouse or by entering the data into pre-assigned areas, or as data contained in a data file. In this section, we see how to construct programs that accept data entered at the keyboard, which is called character data entry. In the following section, we will see how to accept the same data entered using a GUI.

Data can be entered into a program while it is running using the `System.in` object. Just as the `System.out` object is used to display a string value on the standard output device, the `System.in` object is used to enter data from the standard input device, which is the keyboard (Figure 4.1). Both objects are referred to as **stream objects**, or **streams** for short, because they transmit data as a stream of individual data bytes. In the case of the `System.in` object, the transfer of data is into a program, while the `System.out` object transfers data out of a program.

FIGURE 4.1   `System.in` **is used to enter data;** `System.out` **is used to display data**

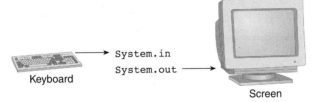

Although a program can accept data entered from the keyboard in a more or less "cookbook" manner, it is useful to understand what data are actually being sent to the program and how the program must react to process the data correctly. Table 4.1 lists the various classes and methods that we will use to accept keyboard input.

By itself, the `read()` method in Table 4.1 is not of much value at this stage because it returns one character at a time as an integer value. One reason for using an integer value is that the Java system must provide a means of indicating when keyboard input is over. This is accomplished with a special end-of-data value, which is formally referred to as an **end-of-file (EOF)** marker. Clearly, this EOF value cannot be one that could be mistaken for any character or other key typed at the keyboard, so it must have a numerical value that cannot be converted into a legitimate character value.

Table 4.1   Keyboard Input Classes and Methods

Class	Method	Description	Example
`InputStream`	`read()`	Returns the key typed at the keyboard as an integer value.	`System.in.read();`
`InputSteamReader`	—	An object of this class is used to convert an integer value to a character value.	-
`BufferedReader`	`readLine()`	Returns the characters typed at the keyboard as a string	`br.readLine();`

FIGURE 4.2　**Generating the EOF value**

From a user's viewpoint, if a Windows-based system is being used, pressing both the Ctrl and Z keys at the same time generates the EOF value, while on a UNIX-based system the Ctrl and D keys produce the same effect. As shown in Figure 4.2, when the appropriate keys are pressed simultaneously, the read() method returns the EOF marker, which in Java has the numerical value of −1.

As a practical matter, requiring users to enter either a Ctrl and Z or Ctrl and D when they have completed entering a value is clearly unacceptable. In addition, using the read() method requires the processing shown in Figure 4.3. This processing consists of accepting each key as it is typed, converting the received integer value into a corresponding character value, and assembling the characters into a string. Once the EOF character is detected, the string is considered complete and can be converted, if necessary, into a primitive data type using the class methods in Table 4.2. These methods are a subset of a larger set of conversion methods that are more fully explained in Section 4.5.

Although the process shown in Figure 4.3 is far too complicated for us to achieve at this time, it can be replaced using the **readLine()** method in Table 4.1. However, to use this method, we have to construct a number of objects from System.in. The first object that must be constructed is an **InputStreamReader** stream object. The benefit of this object is that it automatically converts the integer values of the System.in stream from their integer values to character values. An InputStream-Reader object can be constructed from the System.in object with the statement

```
InputStreamReader isr = new InputStreamReader(System.in);
```

In this statement, the reference variable isr can be changed to any valid programmer-selected Java identifier.

The next and last object that has to be constructed is a **BufferedReader** stream object. The benefit of this object is that it automatically constructs a string from the character values provided by the InputStreamReader object. This string can then be read using a readLine() method. The desired BufferedReader stream object can be constructed using the statement

```
BufferedReader br = new BufferedReader(isr);
```

Table 4.2　**Java Conversion Routines**

Class	Method	Description	Example	Returned Value
Integer	parseInt(string)	Converts a string to a primitive type int.	Integer.parseInt("1234")	1234 (an int value)
Long	parseLong(string)	Converts a string to a primitive type long.	Long.parseLong("128365489")	128365489L (a long)
Float	parseFloat(string)	Converts a string to a primitive type float.	Float.parseFloat("345.89")	345.89f (a float value)
Double	parseDouble(string)	Converts a string to a primitive type double.	Double.parseDouble ("2.3456789")	2.3456789 (a double value)

FIGURE 4.3   **The required processing using** `System.in.read()`

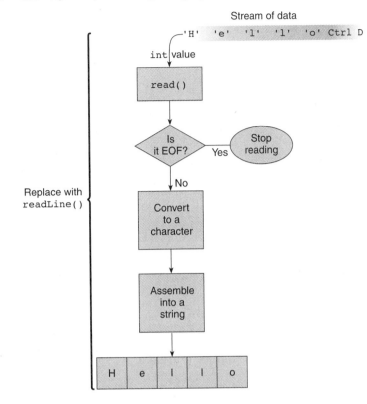

Although the reference variable `br` can be any valid programmer-selected name, the reference variable `isr` must be the same name as used in creating the `InputStreamReader` object. From a strict programming aspect, then, the statements that should be included in your program to use `readLine()` are the following, where the comment lines can be omitted and the variable names changed to any valid programmer-selected name.

```
    // needed for conversion capabilities
InputStreamReader isr = new InputStreamReader(System.in);
    // needed to use readLine()
 BufferedReader br = new BufferedReader(isr);
```

QuickTest Program 4.1 illustrates these declarations within the context of a complete application that accepts user input from the keyboard.

The statements related to keyboard input are boldfaced in QuickTest Program 4.1. The import statement at the top of the program is required to access the `Input-StreamReader` and `BufferedReader` classes in the program. The statement `throws java.io.IOException` is required when using `readLine()` and is explained fully at the end of the next section. For now, include this line if your program will use keyboard input. The next boldfaced lines in QuickTest Program 4.1 contain the input stream declarations that we have already discussed. Now we can analyze what Quick-Test Program 4.1 does.

QuickTest Program 4.1

```java
import java.io.*;    // needed to access input stream classes
public class MultiplyNumbers
{
  public static void main (String[] args)
  throws java.io.IOException
  {
    String s1;
    String s2;
    double num1, num2, product;

    // set up the basic input stream
      // needed for conversion capabilities
    InputStreamReader isr = new InputStreamReader(System.in);
      // needed to use readLine()
    BufferedReader br = new BufferedReader(isr);

    System.out.print("Enter a number: ");
    s1 = br.readLine();
    num1 = Double.parseDouble(s1);

    System.out.print("Great! Now enter another number: ");
    s2 = br.readLine();
    num2 = Double.parseDouble(s2);

    product = num1 * num2;
    System.out.println(num1 + " times " + num2 + " is " + product);
  }
}
```

The statement `System.out.print("Enter a number: ");` displays a string that tells the person at the terminal what should be typed. When an output string is used in this manner, it is called **a prompt.** In this case, the prompt tells the user to type a number. The computer then carries out the next statement, which is a call to `readLine()`. This statement puts the program into a temporary pause (or wait) state for as long as it takes the user to type in data. The user signals that the data entry is finished by pressing the Enter key after the value has been typed. The entered string value is stored in the string referenced by the name `s1`, and the computer is taken out of its paused state. Program execution then proceeds with the next statement, which in QuickTest Program 4.1 is a call to convert the string into a value of type `double`.

The next `println()` method causes the string `Great! Now enter another number:` to be displayed. The second `readLine()` method again puts the program into a temporary wait state while the user types a second value. This second value is initially stored as the string `s2`, which is then converted into a `double` value and stored in the variable `num2`.

The following is a sample run of QuickTest Program 4.1:

```
Enter a number: 300.
Great! Now enter another number: 0.05
300.0 times 0.05 is 15.0
```

Notice that each time `readLine()` is used in QuickTest Program 4.1, it retrieves a string that is then converted into a single numerical value. With the `String-Tokenizer` class, we can actually use `readLine()` to accept a string consisting of multiple values. How to do this is presented next. Before leaving QuickTest Program 4.1, however, it is useful to note that the two declarations for the input streams that we have used can be combined into the single statement

```
BufferedReader br = new BufferedReader(new InputStreamReader(System.in));
```

You will frequently see this latter statement written across two lines as

```
BufferedReader br = new BufferedReader(
                    new InputStreamReader(System.in));
```

For clarity and to explicitly comment what each input stream does, we will initially use the individual comments and declarations found in QuickTest Program 4.1. We will then switch to the single-statement declaration so that you become comfortable with the version that you will most commonly see in practice.

The `StringTokenizer` Class[1]

In addition to accepting a single string value that is converted into one numerical value, `readLine()` can be used to accept a string consisting of multiple items, each of which can be converted into an individual numerical value. To understand how this is done, consider the string in Figure 4.4. This string consists of three items, which are individually referred to as tokens. Formally, a **token** is defined as a string of characters separated by a delimiting character. In Java, the default **delimiting characters,** or **delimiters** for short, consist of the **whitespace characters** (space, tab, newline, and return).

For the string in Figure 4.4, the three tokens consist of the strings "98.5", "12", and "3.25". If these three tokens could be separated from the overall string, each token could then be converted into a primitive data type value. The process of separating individual tokens from a string is formally referred to as **parsing the string** and is easily achieved using methods from the `StringTokenizer` class. The overall process for doing this is shown in Figure 4.5.

As shown in Figure 4.5, the first step in the process of parsing tokens is to create an object of the class `StringTokenizer` from the string. Assuming that the string read from the keyboard is named `inputString`, the statement

```
StringTokenizer st = new StringTokenizer(inputString);
```

FIGURE 4.4   A string consisting of three tokens

---

[1] This topic can be omitted on first reading without loss of subject continuity.

FIGURE 4.5   Parsing tokens from a string

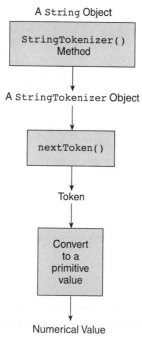

creates the required `StringTokenizer` object. Here the object's name, `st`, can be replaced by any valid programmer-selected identifier, and the single statement can be replaced using the two-step process of first declaring a `StringTokenizer` variable and then creating an actual object using the statements

```
StringTokenizer st;
st = new StringTokenizer(inputString);
```

Once a `StringTokenizer` object has been created, the `nextToken()` method can be used to extract the next token in the string. For example, for the string in Figure 4.4, and assuming that the variables `s1`, `s2`, and `s3` have been declared as string variables, the three statements

```
s1 = st.nextToken();
s2 = st.nextToken();
s3 = st.nextToken();
```

consecutively "strip off" tokens from the object named `st`. Thus, after these statements have been carried out, the string `s1` references the string value "98.5", the string `s2` references the string value "12", and the string `s3` references the string value "3.25". Once these individual string values have been isolated, each one can be converted to a primitive data type value.

The acceptance of the original string from the keyboard and its parsing and conversion into three individual numerical values are presented in QuickTest Program 4.2.

QuickTest Program 4.2

```java
import java.io.*;     // needed to read the keyboard
import java.util.*;   // needed to access the StringTokenizer class
public class MultipleLineInputs
{
  public static void main(String[] args)
  throws java.io.IOException
  {
    String inputString;
    String s1, s2, s3;
    double num1, num3;
    double num2, result;

     // set up the basic input stream
      // needed for conversion capabilities
    InputStreamReader isr = new InputStreamReader(System.in);
      // needed to use readLine()
    BufferedReader br = new BufferedReader(isr);

    System.out.print("Enter three numbers: ");
    inputString = br.readLine();

      // declare and create a StringTokenizer object from the input line
    StringTokenizer st = new StringTokenizer(inputString);

      // strip off individual items
    s1 = st.nextToken();
    s2 = st.nextToken();
    s3 = st.nextToken();

    System.out.println("The strings extracted are: " + s1 + "   " + s2
                                                    + "   " + s3);

    num1 = Double.parseDouble(s1);
    num2 = Double.parseDouble(s2);
    num3 = Double.parseDouble(s3);

    result = (num1 + num2) / num3;
    System.out.println("The value of (" + num1 +" + " + num2 +")/"
                                        + num3 +" is " +result);

  }
}
```

A sample run of QuickTest Program 4.2 produced the following:

```
Enter three numbers: 98.5  12  3.25
The strings extracted are:
98.5
12
```

```
3.25
The value of (98.5 + 12.0)/3.25 is 34.0
```

As shown by this output, the three tokens in the input line have been successfully parsed and converted to numerical values, which are then used within an arithmetic computation. Notice that the statement `import java.util.*;` is needed to access the `StringTokenizer` class.

The technique in QuickTest Program 4.2 to parse the input line requires that we know how many items will be entered. This information, however, is not strictly necessary because the `StringTokenizer` class provides a method named `hasMore-Tokens()` that returns a Boolean `true` value whenever the object contains additional tokens. At this stage, however, this method is not useful to us because in practice it is used with the `while` statement presented in Chapter 5.

A First Look at User-Input Validation[2]

Validating user input and ensuring that a program does not crash due to unexpected input are signs of a well-constructed program. Programs that respond effectively to unexpected user input are formally referred to as robust programs and informally as "bulletproof" programs. One of your jobs as a programmer is to produce such programs. As written, QuickTest Programs 4.1 and 4.2 are not robust programs. Let's see why.

The first problem with both programs becomes evident when a user presses the Enter key accidentally before any value is entered. Should this happen, the entered string read by `readLine()` will contain no characters at all. The returned string is thus the zero length empty string `""`. In QuickTest Program 4.1, an empty string results in an error because it cannot be converted to a legitimate numerical value. It also causes an error in QuickTest Program 4.2 because an empty string has no tokens that can be extracted. This causes the `nextTtoken()` method to issue an error message, which in Java is referred to as an exception. This particular error condition is formally designated as a `NoSuchElementException`. Unless this error condition is correctly handled, both programs will terminate. This type of termination, which occurs while a program is executing due to an error in the program, is called a **crash**.

Another type of error occurs whenever a user types in any other input that cannot be converted to a double-precision value. For example, entering the string `oops` and pressing the Enter key causes the `parseDouble()` method to fail in QuickTest Program 4.1 because it cannot convert the characters `oops` to a valid double-precision number. This error condition is designated as a `NumberFormatException`, which is displayed on the terminal by the program before it stops running.[3] For example, Figure 4.6 shows the error message provided when a `NumberFormatException` occurs.

---

[2] This topic can be omitted on first reading without loss of subject continuity.

[3] Documentation on exceptions can be found using Sun's Java documentation Web site at java.sun.com/docs/search.html, clicking v1.4 items, and then using the provided search engine. An equally good source of documentation is *The Java Class Libraries* (2nd ed., Vol. 1) by Chan, Lee, and Kramer (Reading, MA: Addison-Wesley, 1998). It provides a wealth of well-organized reference material, with many short code examples.

FIGURE 4.6   **A** `NumberFormatException` **notification**

```
C:\jdk>
C:\jdk>
C:\jdk>
C:\jdk>
C:\jdk>
C:\jdk>
C:\jdk>

C:\jdk>java MultiplyNumbers
Exception in thread "main" java.lang.NumberFormatException: oops
        at java.lang.FloatingDecimal.readJavaFormatString(FloatingDecimal.java:
180)
        at java.lang.Double.parseDouble(Double.java:188)
        at MultiplyNumbers.main(MultiplyNumbers.java:11)

C:\jdk>
C:\jdk>
C:\jdk>
C:\jdk>

C:\jdk>

C:\jdk>

C:\jdk>
```

There are separate basic means of handling invalid data input, and both of these error handling techniques can be incorporated into the same program. The first technique that should be applied is referred to as **user-input validation,** which means validating the entered data either during or immediately after the data have been entered and providing the user with a way of reentering any invalid data. User-input validation is an essential part of any commercially viable program, and if done correctly, it will protect a program from attempting to process data types that can cause a program crash. We will see how to provide this type of validation after Java's selection and repetition statements have been presented in Chapters 5 and 6, respectively.[4]

The next line of defense against such errors is to provide error processing code that either corrects the problem or permits the program to terminate gracefully without reporting a run-time crash to the user. The means of providing this in Java is referred to as exception handling and is discussed at the end of the next section.

It should be noted that the expression `throws java.io.IOException` in Programs 4.1 and 4.2 is required because of the `readLine()` method and is not related to any exceptions that might occur either in parsing the string or converting it to a primitive data type. The `readLine()` method requires that the programmer explicitly defines how any input error detected by it should be handled. The easiest way to satisfy this requirement is to tell the compiler to pass any related input error that occurs in `main()` up to the operating system. This is known as "throwing the error up to the operating system" and is designated by the reserved word `throws` in the `throws java.io.IOException` expression. If this expression is not included, the compiler will provide the error message `Exception java.io.IOException`

---

[4] It should be noted that `readLine()` does not permit the programmer to put the screen into "raw mode," where each character can be intercepted before it is sent to the screen. This means that validation using `readLine()` is usually restricted to verification after the complete string value has been entered and not during individual character input. This is true even for the character-based `read()` method. The cause of this is that `System.in` is actually a buffered stream. The positive side is that editing, using the Backspace and Delete keys, is automatically provided.

must be caught, or it must be declared in the throws clause of this method. At the end of the next section, we will see how to explicitly "catch" an exception.

Exercises 4.1

1. Write two statements that could be used after each of the following prompts to perform the following tasks. The first statement should read a string value from the keyboard, assuming that the string is to be accessed by the string variable named `inputString`. The second statement should convert `inputString` into a variable of the correct primitive data type. Assume that an integer value is required for a, a long value for b, a floating-point value for c, and a double-precision value for d.

   a. `System.out.println("Enter a grade: ");`

   b. `System.out.println("Enter an identification number: ");`

   c. `System.out.println("Enter a price: ");`

   d. `System.out.println("Enter an interest rate: ");`

2. Enter and run QuickTest Program 4.1.

3. Enter and run QuickTest Program 4.1 but leave out the line containing the expression `throws java.io.IOException` after the `main()` header line. Record the error message provided by the compiler.

4. Write, compile, and run a QuickTest program that displays the following prompt:

   ```
   Enter the radius of a circle:
   ```

   After accepting a value for the radius, your program should calculate and display the area of the circle. (Tip: *area = 3.1416 * radius².*) For testing purposes, verify your program with a test input radius of 3 inches. After manually determining that the result produced by your program is correct, use your program to complete the following table:

Radius (in.)	Area (sq. in.)
1.0	
1.5	
2.0	
2.5	
3.0	
3.5	

5a. Write a QuickTest program that first displays the following prompt:

   ```
   Enter the temperature in degrees Celsius:
   ```

   Have your program accept a value entered from the keyboard and convert the temperature entered to degrees Fahrenheit, using the formula *Fahrenheit = (9.0 / 5.0) * Celsius + 32.0.* Your program should then display the temperature in degrees Celsius with an appropriate output message.

   b. Compile and run the program written for Exercise 5a. Verify your program by hand calculation and then use your program to determine the Fahrenheit equivalent of the following test data:

Test data set 1: 0 degrees Celsius

Test data set 2: 50 degrees Celsius

Test data set 3: 100 degrees Celsius

When you are sure your program is working correctly, use it to complete the following table:

Celsius	Fahrenheit
45	
50	
55	
60	
65	
70	

6a. Write a QuickTest program that displays the following prompts:

```
Enter the length of the room:
Enter the width of the room:
```

After each prompt is displayed, your program should use a `readLine()` method to accept data from the keyboard for the displayed prompt. After the width of the room is entered, your program should calculate and display the area of the room. The area displayed should be included in an appropriate message and calculated using the equation *area = length * width*.

b. Check the area displayed by the program written for Exercise 6a by calculating the result manually.

7a. Write, compile, and run a QuickTest program that displays the following prompts:

```
Enter the miles driven:
Enter the gallons of gas used:
```

After each prompt is displayed, your program should use a `readLine()` method to accept data from the keyboard for the displayed prompt. After the gallons of gas used number is entered, your program should calculate and display miles per gallon obtained. This value should be included in an appropriate message and calculated using the equation *miles per gallon = miles / gallons used*. Verify your program with the following test data:

Test data set 1: miles = 276, gas = 10 gallons
Test data set 2: miles = 200, gas = 15.5 gallons

When you have completed your verification, use your program to complete the following table:

Miles Driven	Gallons Used	mpg
250	16.00	
275	18.00	
312	19.54	
296	17.39	

b. For the program written for Exercise 7a, determine how many verification runs are required to ensure the program is working correctly and give a reason supporting your answer.

8a. Write a QuickTest program that displays the following prompts:

```
Enter the length of the swimming pool:
Enter the width of the swimming pool:
Enter the average depth of the swimming pool:
```

After each prompt is displayed, your program should use a `readLine()` method to accept data from the keyboard for the displayed prompt. After the depth of the swimming pool is entered, your program should calculate and display the volume of the pool. The volume should be included in an appropriate message and calculated using the equation *volume = length * width * average depth.*

b. Check the volume displayed by the program written for Exercise 8a by calculating the result manually.

9a. Write a QuickTest program that displays the following prompts:

```
Enter a number:
Enter a second number:
Enter a third number:
Enter a fourth number:
```

After each prompt is displayed, your program should use a `readLine()` method to accept a number from the keyboard for the displayed prompt. After the fourth number is entered, your program should calculate and display the average of the numbers. The average should be included in an appropriate message.

b. Check the average displayed for the program written in Exercise 9a by calculating the result manually.

c. Repeat Exercise 9a, making sure that you use the same variable name, `number`, for each number input. Also use the variable `sum` for the sum of the numbers. (Tip: To do this, you must use the statement `sum = sum + number;` after each number is accepted. Review the material on accumulating presented in Section 4.1.)

10. Write a QuickTest program that prompts the user to type in a number. Have your program accept the number, convert it to an integer, and display the integer value. Run your program three times. The first time you run the program, enter a valid integer number, the second time enter a floating-point number, and the third time enter a character. Using the output display, see what number your program actually accepted from the data you entered.

11. Repeat Exercise 10 but have your program convert the entered string to a floating-point value and store the converted value in a floating-point variable. Run the program four times. The first time you run the program, enter an integer, the second time enter a decimal number, the third time enter a decimal number with an f as the last character entered, and the fourth time enter a character. Using the output display, keep track of what number your program actually accepted from the data you entered. What happened, if anything, and why?

12. Repeat Exercise 10 but have your program convert the number to a double-precision value and store the converted value in a double-precision variable.

13a. Why do you think successful application programs contain extensive data input validity checks? (Tip: Review Exercises 10, 11, and 12.)

b. What do you think is the difference between a data type check and a data reasonableness check?

c. Assume that a program requests that a month, day, and year be entered by the user. What are some checks that could be made on the data entered?

14. Enter and run QuickTest Program 4.2 on your computer.

15. Enter and run QuickTest Program 4.2 on your computer but make both of the following changes:

    i. omit the line after the `main()` header line that contains the expression

    ```
    throws java.io.IOException
    ```

    ii. change the statement `inputString = br.readLine();` to `inputString = "98.5 12";`

    Compile and run the program to determine what error message is provided. Discuss what occurred and why.

16. QuickTest Program 4.1 prompts the user to input two numbers, where the first value entered is stored in `num1` and the second value is stored in `num2`. Using this program as a starting point, write a program that swaps the values stored in the two variables.

4.2 Interactive Dialog Input

In addition to keyboard data entry, Java provides a GUI method of entering user data using a method named `showInputDialog()`, which is in the `JOptionPane` class. A call to this method creates a dialog box (recall from Section 1.5 that a dialog is any box that requires the user to supply additional information to complete a task) that permits a user to enter a string at the terminal. The string can then be converted to a primitive data type value, as is done for keyboard input.

The syntax for the `showInputDialog()` method is

```
JOptionPane.showInputDialog(string);
```

where the *string* argument is a prompt displayed within the input dialog box. For example, the statement

```
s = JOptionPane.showInputDialog("Enter a number:");
```

calls the `showInputDialog()` method with the argument `"Enter a number:"`, which is the prompt. When this statement is executed, the input dialog shown in Figure 4.7 is displayed.

Once an input dialog box is displayed, the keyboard is continuously scanned for data. As keys are pressed, the `showInputDialog()` method displays them within the input area of the dialog. When either the Enter key is pressed or the OK command button is clicked, input stops, and the entered text is returned and stored in the string variable on the left side of the assignment statement. Program execution then continues with the next statement immediately placed after the call to `showInputDialog()`.[5]

QuickTest Program 4.3 illustrates a `showInputDialog()` method within the context of a complete application.

---

[5] If the user presses the Cancel button, a null value is returned, which cannot be converted by `parseDouble()`. This results in a program exception, and program execution comes to a halt. We show how to handle this exception correctly at the end of this section, but for now, if this button is pressed, you will have to break out of the program by either pressing the Break or Ctrl and C keys together once or twice.

FIGURE 4.7   **A sample** `showInputDialog()` **dialog**

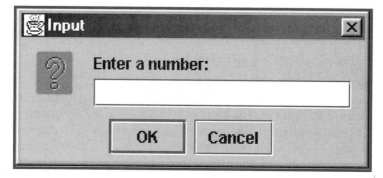

QuickTest Program 4.3

```java
import javax.swing.*;
public class SampleInputDialog
{
  public static void main (String[] args)
  {
    String s1, s2;
    double num1, num2, average;

    s1 = JOptionPane.showInputDialog("Enter a number:");
    s2 = JOptionPane.showInputDialog("Great! Now enter another number:");

    num1 = Double.parseDouble(s1);
    num2 = Double.parseDouble(s2);
    average = (num1 + num2)/2.0;

    JOptionPane.showMessageDialog(null,
            "The average of " + num1 + " and " + num2 + " is " + average,
            "QuickTest Program 4.3",
            JOptionPane.INFORMATION_MESSAGE);

    System.exit(0);
  }
}
```

The first input dialog displayed by QuickTest Program 4.3 is shown in Figure 4.8. The 15 displayed in the input area of the dialog is the value that was entered from the keyboard.

FIGURE 4.8   **The first dialog after data are entered**

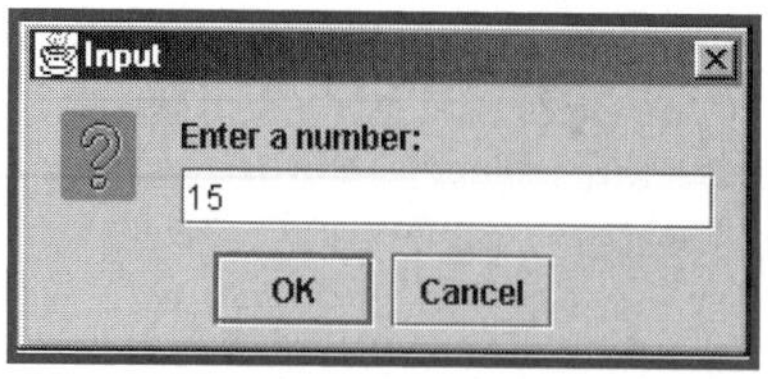

FIGURE 4.9   **The second dialog after data are entered**

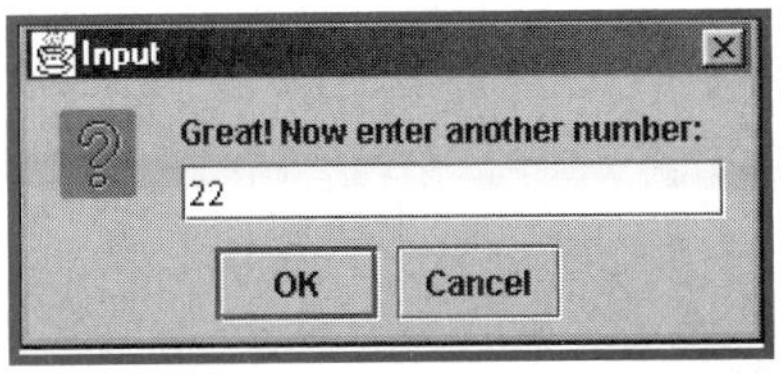

Notice that the dialog's prompt tells the user to enter a number. After this dialog is displayed, the showInputDialog() method puts the application into a temporary pause (or wait) state for as long as it takes the user to type in a value. The user signals the showInputDialog() method that data entry is finished by clicking one of the Command buttons. If the user clicks the OK button (or presses the Enter key), the entered value is stored in the string referenced on the left side of the assignment statement, which in this case is s1, and the application is taken out of its paused state. Program execution then proceeds with the next statement, which in QuickTest Program 4.3 is another call to the showInputDialog() method. This second dialog and the data entered in response to it are shown in Figure 4.9.

While the second dialog is displayed, the application is again put into a temporary wait state as the user types a second value. This second number is stored in the string object named s2. The next two statements convert the string values into double-precision numbers. Based on these converted input values, an average is computed and displayed in a message dialog (Figure 4.10).

Before leaving QuickTest Program 4.3, one last observation is worth making. Notice the parentheses in the statement average = (num1 + num2)/2.0;. The parentheses are required to produce a correct calculation. Without these parentheses, the only number that would be divided by 2 is the value in num2 (because division has a higher precedence than addition).

To ensure that you have a good grasp of how to use the showInputDialog() method to obtain user input, we provide one further example. Consider QuickTest Program 4.4, which is a Fahrenheit to Celsius temperature conversion program. In this program, the user is prompted to enter a Fahrenheit temperature. Once the user enters a temperature, the program converts the entered string into a double-precision value, converts the temperature to its equivalent Celsius value, and displays the computed value.

Figure 4.11 shows the input dialog box created by the program after the user has entered a value of 212. The display produced for this input value appears in

FIGURE 4.10   **A sample output produced by QuickTest Program 4.3**

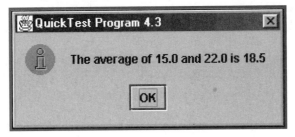

FIGURE 4.11   **The input dialog created by QuickTest Program 4.4**

Figure 4.12. Notice that, within the program, a string reference named `output` is constructed using two assignment statements. The second assignment statement appends additional information to the string, and it is the string reference's name, `output`, that is passed to the `showMessageDialog()` method for final display.

QuickTest Program 4.4

```java
import javax.swing.*;
public class ConvertTemp
{
  public static void main (String[] args)
  {
    String fahr, output;
    double tempfahr, celsius;

    fahr = JOptionPane.showInputDialog("Enter a Fahrenheit Temperature:");

    tempfahr = Double.parseDouble(fahr);
    celsius = 5.0/9.0 * (tempfahr - 32);

    output = "The equivalent Celsius temperature for " + tempfahr
          + " degrees Fahrenheit is " + celsius;
    JOptionPane.showMessageDialog(null, output, "QuickTest Program 4.4",
                          JOptionPane.INFORMATION_MESSAGE);

    System.exit(0);
  }
}
```

FIGURE 4.12   **A sample output produced by QuickTest Program 4.4**

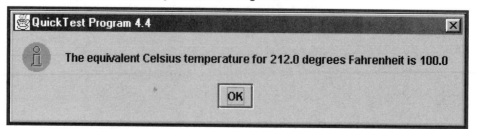

Exception Handling[6]

A feature of Java that is quite different from most high-level languages is the way in which Java handles error conditions. Most other languages have traditionally required that each method, such as `main()`, returns specific values to indicate specific failures by the method. If this approach were followed by Java, the `Double.parse-Double()` method would be required to return a special value to indicate that it could not successfully complete its conversion task.

There are a number of possible problems with this traditional approach. First, it requires that the programmer actually checks the code to detect if an error did in fact occur. Next, the error handling code becomes intermixed with normal processing code, so it sometimes can be very difficult to clearly determine which part of the code is handling errors as opposed to normal program processing. And finally, returning an error condition from a method means that the condition must be of the same data type as a valid returned value; hence, the error code must be a specially identified value that can be identified as an error alert. Thus, the error code is effectively imbedded as one of the possible valid values and is only available at the point where the method returns a value. None of this is insurmountable, but Java rejected it in favor of an error handling methodology that has come to be known as exception handling.

In **exception handling**, when an error occurs while a method is running, the method creates an object, at the point the error occurs, that contains information about the error. This exception object is then immediately passed, again at the point it was generated, to the Java Virtual Machine, which attempts to locate code to handle the exception. The process of generating and passing the exception object at the point the error was detected is referred to as **throwing an exception**. Notice that the exception is thrown from within the method while it is still running. This permits handling the error and returning control back to the method so that it can complete its assigned task correctly.

In particular, there are two fundamental types of errors that can cause Java exceptions: those that result from an inability of the program to obtain a required resource and those that result from flawed code.

Examples of the first error type are attempts to obtain memory for a reference type, such as a string, when insufficient memory is available or an attempt to open a file for input that does not exist. Notice that these errors are the result of external resources over which the programmer has no control. To ensure that such exceptional conditions are provided for should they occur during program execution, Java checks that some mechanism is explicitly in place for receiving and processing the exception object. This check is made at compile time, and because the check is made by the compiler, it is formally referred to as a **checked exception.**

Examples of the second type of error are provided in QuickTest Programs 4.3 and 4.4, where a user can either enter a string that cannot be converted to a numerical value, click the OK button without entering any string, or click the Cancel button. Because this type of error can always be prevented by programming, in this case by providing user-input validation, Java does not check that an exception handling mechanism is in place at compile time. As a result, this second type of exceptions is referred to as an **unchecked exception**. The fact that it is unchecked, however, does

---

[6] This topic can be omitted on first reading without loss of subject continuity.

Table 4.3 **Exception Handling Terminology**

Terminology	Description
Exception	An error that occurs while a program is running.
Throw an exception	Generate an exception object.
Catch or handle an exception	Identify an exception and pass it to a handler.
Catch clause or handler	The section of code that performs the error processing.

not mean that we cannot still apply Java's exception handling techniques to it. Because Java's exception handling techniques are so easy to use, we will show how they can be applied to the user-input errors that we have identified for QuickTest Program 4.4.[7] Before doing so, however, review Table 4.3 to see that you are comfortable with the terminology that is used in relation to the processing of exceptions.

The general syntax of the code required to throw and handle an exception is

```
try
{

  // one or more statements,
  // at least one of which should
  // be capable of throwing an exception;
}
catch(exceptionName argument)
{
  // one or more statements
}
finally
{
  // one or more statements
}
```

This code uses three new reserved words: `try`, `catch`, and `finally`. Let's see what each of these words does.

The reserved word `try` identifies the start of an exception handling block of code. At least one of the statements within the braces defining this block of code should be capable of throwing an exception. For example, the `try` block in the following section of code contains six statements, only two of which may throw an exception that we want to catch. These are the two statements that use the `Double.parseDouble()` method to convert a string into a double-precision number. In particular, we want to handle the `NumberFormatException`, which is thrown when either s1 or s2 contains invalid characters that cannot be converted, and the `NullPointerEx-`

---

[7] Exception processing should generally be restricted to checked exceptions. Errors such as invalid user entered data or attempts to divide by zero can and should be detected and handled using Java's conventional selection and repetition statements. In later sections, we will show how this is done. At this stage, however, QuickTest Programs 4.3 and 4.4 provide a very easy and intuitive introduction to exception processing, and we will use them for this purpose.

PROGRAMMING NOTE

Three Useful Exceptions

Java provides three exceptions that you will find especially useful in your programming career. These are

Exception	Description
`ArithmeticException`	Thrown whenever an attempt is made to perform an illegal arithmetic operation, such as an attempt to divide by zero.
`NumberFormatException`	Thrown whenever an attempt is made to convert a string that does not contain the appropriate characters for the desired number type.
`NullPointerException`	Thrown whenever an attempt is made to access an object that does not exist.

ception, which is thrown when either `s1` or `s2` does not reference any object at all. The first exception will occur whenever the user either clicks the OK button without entering any data or enters nonnumerical characters, and the second exception will occur if the user clicks the Cancel button. Thus, from the standpoint of the `try` block, it is only the conversion statements that are of concern. Essentially, the `try` block says "try all of the statements within me to see if an exception occurs."

```
try
{
  s1 = JOptionPane.showInputDialog("Enter a number:");
  num1 = Double.parseDouble(s1);
  s2 = JOptionPane.showInputDialog("Great! Now enter another number:");

  num2 = Double.parseDouble(s2);

  average = (num1 + num2)/2.0;

  JOptionPane.showMessageDialog(null,
        "The average of " + num1 + " and " + num2 + " is " + average,
        "QuickTest Program 4.5",
        JOptionPane.INFORMATION_MESSAGE);
}
```

A `try` block must be followed by one or more `catch` blocks, which serve as exception handlers for any exceptions thrown by the statements in the `try` block. For our particular case, we want to catch two specific exceptions, which is accomplished by the following section of code:

```
catch(NumberFormatException n)
{
  JOptionPane.showMessageDialog(null,
              "You must enter a number",
              "Input Data Error",
              JOptionPane.ERROR_MESSAGE);
```

(continued)

```
(continued)
   }
   catch(NullPointerException n)
   {
      JOptionPane.showMessageDialog(null,
                    "You Pressed the Cancel Button",
                    "Program Termination",
                    JOptionPane.ERROR_MESSAGE);
   }
```

Here the exception handling provided by each `catch` block is a dialog that identifies the particular exception that has been caught. Notice the parentheses following each `catch` reserved word. Listed within each set of parentheses is the name of the exception being caught and an argument identifier, which we have named n. This identifier, which is a programer-selectable name, is used to hold the exception object generated when the exception occurs ("is thrown").

Although we have provided two `catch` blocks, this is not required. All that is required is that at least one `catch` block be provided for each `try` block. Naturally, the more exceptions that can be caught with the same `try` block, the better. The optional `finally` block provides a catchall, default set of instructions that is always executed whether or not any exception occurred. For our case, we will use the code

```
finally{System.exit(0);}
```

This code ensures that the program gracefully closes down in all cases. QuickTest Program 4.5 incorporates this code within the context of a complete program. Notice that the instructions within the `try` block are essentially all of the processing statements used in QuickTest Program 4.4. The difference in these programs is that the two exceptions that we have identified for QuickTest Program 4.4 are reported to a user when they occur, and the program is terminated gracefully, without reporting a run-time system error message.

QuickTest Program 4.5

```
import javax.swing.*;
public class CatchingExceptions
{
  public static void main (String[] args)
  {
    String s1;
    String s2;
    double num1, num2, average;
    try
    {
      s1 = JOptionPane.showInputDialog("Enter a number:");
      num1 = Double.parseDouble(s1);

      s2 = JOptionPane.showInputDialog("Great! Now enter another number:");
      num2 = Double.parseDouble(s2);
      average = (num1 + num2)/2.0;
```

```
         JOptionPane.showMessageDialog(null,
                  "The average of " + num1 + " and " + num2 + " is " + average,
                  "QuickTest Program 4.5",
                  JOptionPane.INFORMATION_MESSAGE);
      }
      catch(NumberFormatException n)
      {
       JOptionPane.showMessageDialog(null,
                  "You must enter a number",
                  "Input Data Error",
                  JOptionPane.ERROR_MESSAGE);
      }
      catch(NullPointerException n)
      {
       JOptionPane.showMessageDialog(null,
                  "You Pressed the Cancel Button",
              "Program Termination",
                  JOptionPane.ERROR_MESSAGE);
      }
      finally{System.exit(0);}
   }
}
```

Figures 4.13 and 4.14 show the dialog boxes for the two exceptions that are now caught in QuickTest Program 4.5.

FIGURE 4.13   **The result of catching the `NumberFormatException`**

FIGURE 4.14   **The result of catching the `NullPointerException`**

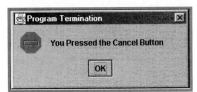

Exercises 4.2

1.   Write assignment statements that store the returned value from an input dialog box in a variable named `test` for the following input prompts:

a.   prompt: `"Enter a grade:"`

b. prompt: `"Enter a temperature:"`

c. prompt: `"Enter an interest rate:"`

d. prompt: `"Enter a name:"`

e. prompt: `"Enter a price:"`

2. Modify QuickTest Program 4.4 so that the computed Celsius temperature value is always displayed with a maximum of two digits after the decimal point.

3. Write a QuickTest program that displays the following prompt in an input dialog box:

    `Enter the amount of the bill:`

   After accepting a value for the amount of the bill, your program should calculate the sales tax, assuming a tax rate of 6 percent, and display the sales tax as a dollar amount in a message dialog. For testing purposes, verify your program using an initial amount of $36.00. After manually checking that the result produced by your program is correct, use your program to complete the following table:

Amount (dollars)	Sales Tax (dollars)
36.00	
40.00	
52.60	
87.95	
125.00	
182.93	

4. Write, compile, and run a QuickTest program that displays the following prompt in an input dialog box:

    `Enter the radius of a circle:`

   After accepting a value for the radius, your program should calculate and display the area of the circle. (Tip: $area = 3.1416 * radius^2$.) For testing purposes, verify your program using a test input radius of 3 inches. After manually determining that the result produced by your program is correct, use your program to complete the following table:

Radius (in.)	Area (sq. in.)
1.0	
1.5	
2.0	
2.5	
3.0	
3.5	

5a. Write a QuickTest program that displays the following prompt in an input dialog box:

    `Enter the temperature in degrees Celsius:`

   Have your program accept a value entered from the keyboard and convert the temperature entered to degrees Fahrenheit using the formula *Fahrenheit = (9.0 / 5.0) * Celsius + 32.0.* Your program should then display the temperature in degrees Celsius with an appropriate output message.

b.   Compile and run the program written for Exercise 5a. Verify your program by hand calculation and then use your program to determine the Fahrenheit equivalent of the following test data:

Test data set 1: `0 degrees Celsius`
Test data set 2: `50 degrees Celsius`
Test data set 3: `100 degrees Celsius`

When you are sure your program is working correctly, use it to complete the following table:

Celsius	Fahrenheit
45	
50	
55	
60	
65	
70	

6.   Write and run a QuickTest program that uses input dialog boxes to display the following prompts:

```
Enter the length of the office:
Enter the width of the office:
```

Your program should use the entered values to calculate and display the area of the office. Verify your procedure with the following test data:

Test data set 1: length = 12.5, width = 10
Test data set 2: length = 12.4, width = 0
Test data set 3: length = 0, width = 10

7a. Write and run a QuickTest program that uses input dialog boxes to display the following prompts:

```
Enter the miles driven:
Enter the gallons of gas used:
```

Your program should use the entered values to calculate and display the miles per gallon. Use the equation *miles per gallon = miles / gallons used*. Verify your procedure with the following test data:

Test data set 1: miles = 276, gas = 10 gallons
Test data set 2: miles = 200, gas = 15.5 gallons

When you have completed your verification, use your procedure to complete the following table:

Miles Driven	Gallons Used	mpg
250	16.00	
275	18.00	
312	19.54	
296	17.39	

b. For the program written in Exercise 7a, determine how many verification runs are required to ensure the procedure is working correctly and give a reason supporting your answer.

8a. Write a QuickTest program that displays the following prompts in three separate input dialog boxes:

```
Enter the length of the swimming pool:
Enter the width of the swimming pool:
Enter the average depth of the swimming pool:
```

After the depth of the swimming pool is entered, your program should calculate and display the volume of the pool. The volume should be included in an appropriate message and calculated using the equation *volume = length * width * average depth*.

b. Check the volume displayed by the program written for Exercise 8a by calculating the result manually.

9a. Write a QuickTest program that displays the following prompts in three separate input dialog boxes:

```
Enter a number:
Enter a second number:
Enter a third number:
```

After the third number is entered, your program should calculate and display the average of the numbers. The average should be included in an appropriate message. Verify your program using the following test data:

Test data set 1: 100, 100, 100
Test data set 2: 100, 50, 0

When you have completed your verification, use your program to complete the following table:

Numbers	Average
92, 98, 79	
86, 84, 75	
63, 85, 74	

b. Repeat Exercise 9a, making sure that you use the same variable name, `number`, for each number input. Also use the variable `sum` for the sum of the numbers. (Tip: To do this, you must use the statement `sum = sum + number;` after each number is accepted. Review the material on accumulating presented in Section 4.1.)

10. QuickTest Program 4.3 prompts the user to input two numbers, where the first value entered is converted and stored in `num1` and the second value is converted and stored in `num2`. Using this procedure as a starting point, rewrite the program so that it swaps the values stored in the two variables.

11. Enter and run QuickTest Program 4.4 on your computer. Record the exception message displayed when you

i. Click the OK button without entering any data

ii. Enter the characters `oops` and click the OK button

iii. Click the Cancel button

12a. Enter and run QuickTest Program 4.5. Determine what happens when you

    i. Click the OK button without entering any data

    ii. Enter the characters `oops` and click the OK button

    iii. Click the Cancel button

  b. Remove the second `catch` block in QuickTest Program 4.5 and see what happens when you click the Cancel button. Determine what part of the code handles the exception that was previously taken care of by the removed `catch` code.

13. Modify QuickTest Program 4.5 so that the `try` block only contains the statements

```
num1 = Double.parseDouble(s1);
num2 = Double.parseDouble(s2);
```

4.3 Creating a Class Library

Until the introduction of personal computers in the early 1980s with their extensive use of integrated circuits and microprocessors, both the speed of computers and their available memory were severely restricted. For example, the most advanced computers of the time had speeds measured in milliseconds (one-thousandth of a second), whereas current computers have speeds measured in nanoseconds (one-billionth of a second) and higher. Similarly, the memory capacity of pre-microprocessor-based computers consisted of 32,000 locations, with each location consisting of 8 bits. Today's computer memories consist of millions of memory locations, each consisting of 32 to 64 bits.

These early hardware restrictions made it imperative that programmers use every possible trick to save memory space and make programs run more efficiently. Almost every program was handcrafted and included what was referred to as "clever code" to minimize run time and maximize the use of memory storage. Unfortunately, this individualized code, over time, became a liability. New programmers had to expend considerable time understanding existing code, and frequently, even the original programmer had trouble figuring out code that was written only months before. This made modifications extremely time-consuming and costly and precluded cost-effective use of existing code for new installations.

The inability to reuse code efficiently combined with expanded hardware capabilities provided the incentive for discovering more efficient ways of programming. Initially, this led to the structured programming concepts incorporated into procedural languages such as Pascal and, currently, to the object-oriented techniques that form the basis of Java. One of the early criticisms of the object-oriented language C++ was that the language itself, although supporting object-oriented programming, did not provide a comprehensive library of classes. This did not happen with Java's introduction.

Starting with Version 1.1, Java provided an extensive set of tested and reliable classes, which only increased with the introduction of each new version. No matter how many useful classes are provided, however, each major type of programming application, such as financial, marketing, engineering, and scientific areas, always has its own specialized requirements. For example, Java provides a rather good date and time class named `GregorianCalendar`. For specialized needs, such as those encountered in the financial industry, however, this class must be expanded. Thus, a more complete date class would have to include class methods for finding the

number of business days between two dates that took into account both weekends and holidays. It would also require methods that implemented prior and next-day algorithms that take into account leap years and the actual days in each month.

What professional programmers do for situations like this is create and share their own libraries of classes with other programmers working on the same or similar projects. Once the classes have been tested, they can be incorporated in any program without further expenditures of coding time.

At this stage in your programming career, you can begin to build your own library of specialized classes that can be used for keyboard input. Because the need for accepting integer and double-precision data is so prevalent, it is much easier to have a pre-written class ready to use, rather than set up the required input streams and validate user input each time you need to implement keyboard user input.

The code for such a class, named `ID`, is presented at the end of this section. You can either enter this class manually, rename the class with any name you wish, or download the class for this text's Web site. Although the code for this class contains a number of statements that we have not yet mentioned, this presents no obstacles to using its `readInt()` and `readDouble()` class methods. Each of these is a general-purpose method that can be used to accept and return either a single integer or double-precision value, respectively, that is entered at the keyboard. Both methods automatically set up the necessary input streams by calling the class method named `readData()`, and both methods are used in essentially the same manner. For example, a statement such as

```
number = ID.readInt();
```

will read data entered at the keyboard. If the data represent a valid integer value, the number is accepted and stored in the variable named `number`. Here `number` can be any programmer-selected variable that has been declared as an integer data type. If the entered data do not correspond to a valid integer value, the method will display an error message and request that the user reenter an integer value. Program 4.6 illustrates all of the `ID` class `read()` methods within the context of a complete program.

Program 4.6

```
public class KeyBoardReadTest
{
  public static void main (String[] args)
  throws java.io.IOException
  {
    int num1;
    double num4;

    System.out.print("Enter an integer value: ");
    num1 = ID.readInt();
    System.out.println("The integer entered is " + num1);

    System.out.print("Enter a double value: ");
    num4 = ID.readDouble();
    System.out.println("The double value entered is " + num4);
  }
}
```

As seen in Program 4.6, the two ID class read() methods are called in the same manner by preceding the desired method with the class name, ID, and a period and assigning the entered value to a variable of the appropriate data type. Also notice in Program 4.6 that no input streams have been declared. The reason is that the required streams are constructed from within the ID class.

All that is required to use the methods in this class is that you place the class into the directory (folder) that you use for your Java programs and compile it using the statement

```
javac ID.java
```

After the class has been compiled, the corresponding class file will be available for use in all of your programs, and the methods can be used as they are shown in Program 4.6. Later, when you acquire more classes that you wish to include in your own personal class library, you can package them together using the techniques presented in Appendix F.

Following is the code for the ID class. For convenience in reading the code, the second method within the class has been highlighted.

Program 4.7 ID Class Code

```java
// This class can be used to enter an integer or double-precision
// values at the keyboard

import java.io.*;    // needed to access input stream classes
public class ID
{

  // This method sets up the basic keyboard input streams
  // and reads a line of characters from the keyboard.
  // It returns all characters entered as a string, with any
  // entered whitespace included.
  public static String readData()
  throws java.io.IOException
  {
      // set up the first input stream, which is
      // needed for conversion capabilities
    InputStreamReader isr = new InputStreamReader(System.in);
      // set up a buffered stream, which is
      // needed to access readLine()
    BufferedReader br = new BufferedReader(isr);

    return br.readLine();  // read and return the entered data
  }
  // This method attempts to convert the characters entered at the
  // keyboard to an integer value. If the conversion cannot
  // be done, an error message is displayed and the read is
  // continued until a valid integer is entered.
  public static int readInt()
  throws java.io.IOException
```

(continued)

(continued)

```
{
   int inValue = 0;   // must initialize the variable
   boolean validNumber = false;
   String inString = null;

   while(!validNumber)
   {
     try
     {
       inString = readData();
       inValue = Integer.parseInt(inString.trim());
       validNumber = true;
     }
     catch(NumberFormatException e)
     {
       System.out.println("  The value you entered is not valid. ");
       System.out.println("  Please enter only numeric digits.");
       System.out.print("Enter an integer value: ");
     }
   }
   return inValue;
}

// This method attempts to convert the characters entered at the
// keyboard to a double value. If the conversion cannot
// be done, an error message is displayed and the read is
// continued until a valid double is entered.
public static double readDouble()
throws java.io.IOException
{
   double inValue = 0;   // must initialize the variable
   boolean validNumber = false;
   String inString = null;

    while(!validNumber)
   {
     try
     {
       inString = readData();
       inValue = Double.parseDouble(inString.trim());
       validNumber = true;
     }
     catch(NumberFormatException e)
     {
       System.out.println("  The value you entered is not valid. ");
       System.out.println("  Please enter only numeric digits");
       System.out.println("  and, at most, a single decimal point.");
```

```
        System.out.print("Enter a double value: ");
      }
    }
    return inValue;
  }
}
```

Exercises 4.3

1. Enter and compile Program 4.7's ID class. (Tip: The class is available with the source code provided on the Brooks/Cole Web site for this text. See Exercise 4 for the downloading procedure.)

2. Enter and run Program 4.6.

3. Rewrite Program 4.1 so that it uses Program 4.7's readDouble() method.

4a. A more complete keyboard input class than that provided in Program 4.7 is listed in Appendix G. To obtain the source code for this class program listed in the text, go to the Web site at www.Brookscole.com and select the Disciplines category. From this category, select Computer Science and then select Java. Locate the text *Object Oriented Program Development Using Java* and click the DownLoad Java Source files.

b. Once you have downloaded and compiled the KBR class for Exercise 4a, write a Java program that tests each class method.

4.4 **Formatted Output**[8]

In addition to displaying correct results, it is important for a program to present its results attractively. In fact, most programs are judged on the perceived ease of data entry and the style and presentation of their output. For example, displaying a monetary result as 1.897000 is not in keeping with accepted reporting conventions. The display should be either $1.90 or $1.89 depending on whether rounding or truncation is used.

The precise display of both integer and floating-point numbers can be controlled by a Java-supplied format() method, which is included within the java.text.DecimalFormat class. Formatted numbers are especially useful in printing columns with numbers in each column aligned correctly. For example, QuickTest Program 4.8 illustrates how a column of integers would align in the absence of any format specification.

The output of QuickTest Program 4.8 is

```
6
18
124
---
148
```

---

[8] This topic can be omitted on first reading without loss of subject continuity.

QuickTest Program 4.8

```
public class NoFormat
{
  public static void main(String[] args)
  {
    System.out.println(6);
    System.out.println(18);
    System.out.println(124);
    System.out.println("---");
    System.out.println((6+18+124));
  }
}
```

Because no explicit format specification is provided, the `println()` function allocates enough space for each number as it is received. To force the numbers to align on the units digit requires a field width large enough for the largest displayed number. For our specific example, a field width of three suffices. QuickTest Program 4.9 illustrates setting the minimum field width to this size.

QuickTest Program 4.9

```
import java.text.*; // this is required to access the DecimalFormat class

public class WithFormats
{
  public static void main(String[] args)
  {
      // this next statement creates the default format
    DecimalFormat num = new DecimalFormat("000");

    System.out.println(num.format(6));
    System.out.println(num.format(18));
    System.out.println(num.format(124));
    System.out.println("---");
    System.out.println(num.format(6+18+124));
  }
}
```

The output of QuickTest Program 4.9 is

```
006
018
124
---
148
```

In reviewing QuickTest Program 4.9 and its output, there are a number of points that need explaining. Although the displayed numbers are now aligned, the most noticeable item is the use of leading zeros within the first two numbers. A simple user-

Table 4.4   **Symbols for User-Defined Format Strings**

Symbol	Description
#	A digit placeholder; zero shows as absent and not as a space
0	A digit placeholder and automatic fill character
.	Decimal placeholder
,	Grouping separator
;	Separate positive and negative format strings
%	Multiply by 100 and add a % sign

defined method is presented in Appendix E that can replace these leading zeros with spaces.[9]

Examining the program itself reveals a number of cookbook items that must be included to create a formatted output. Essentially, these items consist of the following:

1. An `import` statement for the `java.text` package of classes.
2. A statement within the `main()` method that uses the `new` operator to create the desired format string.
3. A `format()` method call that applies the format string to a numerical value.

The first item, the `import` statement, is required because we will be using format capabilities that are provided by the `DecimalFormat` class, which is within the `java.text` package of classes. Including the statement `import java.text.*;` within a program that uses the `DecimalFormat` class's formatting facilities means that you can call the required `format()` method as is done in QuickTest Program 4.9. The second item is provided by the statement

```
DecimalFormat num = new DecimalFormat("000");
```

which is placed at the top of QuickTest Program 4.9's `main()` method. Except for the identifier named `num`, which is a programmer-selectable name and can be chosen by you to be any valid Java identifier, this statement is required before any explicit formatting can be done. In our particular case, this statement creates an object of the `DecimalFormat` class named `num` and creates a format string of "000".[10] Table 4.4 lists the acceptable symbols and what each symbol represents when it is included in a format string. In particular, the format string "000" means that an integer number with three digits should always be produced. If the number has fewer than three digits, leading zeros will be supplied, as they are in the display produced by QuickTest

---

[9] Although the method presented in Appendix E can be used as is, a full understanding of how this method works requires the material presented in both Sections 5.3 (`for` loops) and 12.3 (string methods). The format "##0" does not solve the problem because of the action of the # symbol, as listed in Table 4.4.

[10] Formally, the reserved word `new` in this statement is Java's *dynamic memory allocation operator.* This operator creates space for a reference object and then initializes this object with the string "000". This format string can then be accessed (i.e., referenced) by the identifier named `num`, which is formally referred to as a reference variable. This is explained in detail in Section 2.2.

Program 4.9. If the number has more than three digits, as we will shortly see, the integer specified field width is ignored and the complete number is displayed.

For example, the format string in the statement

```
DecimalFormat num = new DecimalFormat(",###");
```

specifies that an integer number is to be displayed, with no leading zeros, and that each group of three digits is to be separated by a comma. When this format string is applied to the number 12345.648, the string that results is "12,345". To format the fractional part of a number requires two format specifications separated by a decimal point; the symbols before the decimal point represent how the integer part should be formatted, and the symbols after the decimal point represent the format specification for the number's fractional part. For example, the format string in the statement

```
DecimalFormat num = new DecimalFormat(",###.##");
```

specifies that a comma be used between groups of every three integer digits and that a maximum of two digits (rounded) will be placed to the right of the decimal place. Using this format, a value such as 12345.648 will be converted into the string "12,345.65". Notice, however, that if the number 345.60 is formatted with this format string, the result will be the string "345.6". This result is obtained because the # placeholder does not reserve space for either leading or trailing zeros. Thus, if the # placeholder is used, and the number being formatted does not require all the places provided by the #s in the format string, on either side of the decimal point, the extra #s are ignored. If the integer part of the number exceeds the number of #s to the left of the decimal point, however, additional space is allocated to accommodate the number.

The same rules apply to the 0 placeholder with one important difference: If the number does not fill the space designated by the 0s, a 0 will fill the unused spaces, as is shown by the output of QuickTest Program 4.9. For example, using the format string in the following statement

```
DecimalFormat num = new DecimalFormat("0,000.00");
```

the value 12345.648 will be converted to the string value "12,345.65", while the value 345.6 will be converted to the string "0,345.60".

Because leading zeros are typically not required for numerical output, the # format symbol is frequently used to specify the integer part of a number, and the 0 format symbol is used to force a fixed number of decimal digits for the fractional part. For example, using the format string in the following statement

```
DecimalFormat num = new DecimalFormat(",###.00");
```

the value 345.6 will be converted to the string "345.60".

In addition to numerical placeholders, other symbols can be placed both directly before and after the numerical specification, and these symbols will be included in the string returned when a value is formatted. For example, placing a bar symbol, |, within the format string in the statement

```
DecimalFormat barform = DecimalFormat("|,###.00|");
```

will force a bar symbol to be placed before and after each number that is formatted. Notice here that we have used the identifier named `barform` rather than the identi-

Table 4.5   **Examples of Numerical Formats**

Format String	Number	Returned String Value	Comments
`"|##|"`	3	|3|	Only one # position is used.
`"|##|"`	43	|43|	Both # positions are used.
`"|##|"`	143	|143|	# placeholders are ignored.
`"|00|"`	3	|03|	Leading 0 position is used.
`"|00|"`	43	|43|	Both 0 positions are used.
`"|00|"`	143	|143|	0 placeholders are ignored.
`"|00|"`	143.466	|143|	0 placeholders are ignored. Fractional part is truncated.
`"|##.00|"`	2.466	|2.47|	Fractional part is rounded.
`"|##.##|"`	2.466	|2.47|	Fractional part is rounded.
`"|00.00|"`	123.4	|123.40|	Leading placeholders are ignored. Fractional part is forced to two decimal places.
`"|00.##|"`	123.4	|123.4|	Leading placeholders are ignored. Fractional part is not forced to two decimal places.

fier named `num`. Again, the identifier name that you select can be any name that conforms to Java's identifier rules.

Using a bar symbol to clearly mark the beginning and end of the returned string, Table 4.5 illustrates the effect of various user formats.

Notice in the table that the specified integer part of a format string is ignored if the integer format specification is too small; thus, sufficient space is always allocated for the integer part of the number regardless of the format string. The fractional part of a number is only displayed with the number of specified digits if the 0 placeholder is used. In this case, if the fractional part contains fewer digits than specified, the number is padded with trailing zeros. For both 0 and # placeholders, if the fractional part contains more digits than specified in the format, the number is rounded to the indicated number of decimal places.

Once a format string has been defined using the `DecimalFormat` class, it must still be explicitly applied to all numbers that you want formatted. This is done using the `DecimalFormat` class's `format()` method. For example, the actual formatting of numerical values in QuickTest Program 4.9 is done by the expression `num.format()` contained within each `println()` method used to display a numerical value. It is important to note that each of these `format()` method calls is preceded by a period and the identifier name, in this case `num`, which was selected by us when we defined the format string. It is also important to realize that the `format()` function converts each numerical value into a string, and it is the string that is displayed by the various `println()` statements.

In addition to formatting numbers for display by either a `print()` or `println()` method, as is done in QuickTest Program 4.9, the same formatting technique is applicable to a program that creates a dialog box. For example, see if you can identify the three items necessary for creating formatted numbers in QuickTest Program 4.10, which uses a `showMessageDialog()` method to create its output display.

QuickTest Program 4.10

```java
import java.text.*;
import javax.swing.*;
public class GuiFormat
{
 public static void main(String[] args)
 {
  DecimalFormat num = new DecimalFormat("$,###.00");

  JOptionPane.showMessageDialog(null,
    "The result is " + num.format(25625.648),
    "Output Display",
    JOptionPane.INFORMATION_MESSAGE);

  System.exit(0);
 }
}
```

In analyzing QuickTest Program 4.10 for the statements used in creating formatted output numbers, notice that

1. The `import java.text.*;` statement has been included.
2. The statement `DecimalFormat num = new DecimalFormat("$,###.00");` is used to create a format string.
3. The format string is applied to a numerical value using the expression `num.format(25625.648)`. Here the output of this expression, which is the string "$25,625.65", is concatenated to the string `"The result is "`, and the complete string is used as the message part of the `showMessageDialog()` method.

The output produced by QuickTest Program 4.10 is illustrated in Figure 4.15.

FIGURE 4.15   The display produced by QuickTest Program 4.10

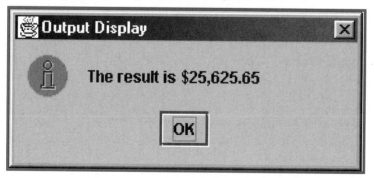

Exercises 4.4

1a. Enter and run QuickTest Program 4.6 on your computer.

b. Determine the output of QuickTest Program 4.6 if the format string "###" is substituted for the format string "000".

2. Enter and run QuickTest Program 4.9 on your computer.

3.   Determine the formatted string that results when

a.   the format string `"##"` is applied to the number 5

b.   the format string `"####"` is applied to the number 5

c.   the format string `"####"` is applied to the number 56829

d.   the format string `"###.##"` is applied to the number 5.26

e.   the format string `"###.##"` is applied to the number 5.267

f.   the format string `"###.##"` is applied to the number 53.264

g.   the format string `"###.##"` is applied to the number 534.264

h.   the format string `"###.##"` is applied to the number 534.0

4.   Determine the formatted string that results when

a.   the format string `"###.##"` is applied to the numbers 126.27, 82.3, and 1.756, and each formatted number is displayed on a line by itself

b.   the format string `"###.##"` is applied to the numbers 26.27, 682.3, 1.968 and the expression (26.27 + 682.3 + 1.968), and each formatted number is displayed on a line by itself

c.   the format string `"###.##"` is applied to the numbers 34.164, 10.003 and the expression (34.164 + 10.003), and each formatted number is displayed on a line by itself

5.   Write a QuickTest program to calculate and display the value of the slope of the line connecting the two points whose coordinates are (3,7) and (8,12). Use the fact that the slope between two points having coordinates $(x1,y1)$ and $(x2,y2)$ is slope = $(y2 - y1) / (x2 - x1)$. The display produced by your program should be: `The value of the slope is xxx.xx`, where `xxx.xx` denotes that the calculated value should be placed in a field wide enough for three places to the left of the decimal point and two places to the right of it.

6.   Write a QuickTest program to calculate and display the coordinates of the midpoint of the line connecting the two points whose coordinates are (3,7) and (8,12). Use the fact that the coordinates of the midpoint between two points having coordinates $(x1,y1)$ and $(x2,y2)$ are $((x1 + x2) / 2, (y1 + y2) / 2)$. The display produced by your program should be

```
The x coordinate of the midpoint is xxx.xx
The y coordinate of the midpoint is xxx.xx
```

where `xxx.xx` denotes that the calculated value should be placed in a field wide enough for three places to the left of the decimal point and two places to the right of it.

4.5   **Mathematical Methods**

As we have seen, assignment statements can be used to perform arithmetic computations. For example, the assignment statement

```
totalPrice = unitPrice * amount;
```

multiplies the value in `unitPrice` by the value in `amount` and assigns the resulting value to `totalPrice`. Although addition, subtraction, multiplication, and division are easily accomplished using Java's arithmetic operators, no such operators exist for raising a number to a power, finding the square root of a number, or determining trigonometric values. To facilitate such calculations, Java provides standard prepro-grammed methods within a class named `Math`. Because these methods are general purpose, they have been written as both `static`, which permits them to be used without an object, and as `public`, which permits them to be used outside the `Math` class.

Before using one of Java's mathematical methods, you need to know

- the name of the desired mathematical method
- what the mathematical method does
- the date type required by the mathematical method
- the data type of the result returned by the mathematical method

To illustrate the use of Java's mathematical methods, consider the mathematical method named `abs()`, which calculates the absolute value of a number. The absolute value of a number is always positive or zero; if the number is not negative, the absolute value is the number itself, and if the number is negative, the absolute value is the number without the negative sign. The absolute value of a number is computed using the expression

```
Math.abs(number)
```

Notice that this expression uses the same syntax as all general-purpose methods in that it provides a class name followed by a period followed by the method's name. Finally, the method name is followed by parentheses that are used to pass data into the method. In this case, the method's name is `abs`, which is a method provided within the `Math` class. The parentheses following the method name effectively provide a funnel through which data are passed to the method (Figure 4.16). The items that are passed to the method through the parentheses, as we have noted previously in relation to the `println()` method, are called *arguments* of the method and constitute its input data. For example, the following expressions are used to compute the absolute value of the arguments 4, -4, -56789L, -17.25f, 1043.29f, and -23456.78:

```
Math.abs(4)
Math.abs(-4)
Math.abs(-56789L)
Math.abs(-17.25f)
Math.abs(1043.29f)
Math.abs(-23456.78)
```

FIGURE 4.16   **Passing data to the** Math **Class's** abs() **method**

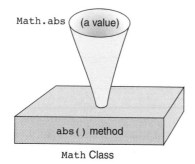

A BIT OF BACKGROUND

Napier's Bones

Scottish mathematician John Napier, born near Edinburgh, Scotland, in 1550, spent most of his life creating methods and devices to make mathematical calculations easier. One of his early inventions was a set of square rods, made of bone, that were used for multiplying whole numbers. Napier is also credited with the discovery that the weight of any object can be found by balancing the object on a scale against weights of relative size 1, 2, 4, 8, ... His most valuable invention, however, was the natural logarithm, which replaced multiplication and division problems with the addition and subtraction of logarithms. For 25 years beginning in 1590, Napier devoted himself almost entirely to generating tables of logarithms.

The contribution of the logarithmic technique to science and technology is immeasurable. Until the advent of electronic calculators and computers, logarithms were *the* approach to lengthy calculations. The logarithmic slide rule, invented by William Oughtred early in the 17th century, was the only reasonably affordable computing tool for engineers, scientists, and students until the mid-1970s.

In most modern high-level languages, including Java, you will find a method for calculating logarithms.

Notice that the argument to the `Math.abs()` method can be either an `int`, `long`, `float`, or `double` real value. This is an example of Java's overloading capabilities. Method overloading permits the same method name to be defined for different argument data types. In this case, there are really four absolute value methods named `abs`—one defined for `int`, `long`, `float`, and `double` arguments, respectively. The correct `abs()` method is called depending on the type of argument given to it. The values returned by the previous expressions are

Expression	Value Returned	Returned Data Type
`Math.abs(4)`	4	integer
`Math.abs(-4)`	4	integer
`Math.abs(-56789L)`	56789	long
`Math.abs(-17.25f)`	17.25	floating-point
`Math.abs(1043.29f)`	1043.29	floating-point
`Math.abs(-23456.78)`	23456.78	double-precision

In addition to the `Math.abs()` method, Table 4.6 lists the mathematical methods provided in Java. Although some of these mathematical methods require more than one argument, all methods by definition can directly return at most one value. Except for the `abs()`, `min()`, `max()`, and `round()` methods, which are overloaded, the other methods convert their arguments into a double-valued number and return a `double`. Table 4.7 illustrates the value returned by selected methods using example arguments.

Table 4.6   **Java's** Math **Class Methods**

Method Name	Description	Returned Value
abs(x)	absolute value	same data type as argument
pow(x1,x2)	x1 raised to the x2 power	double
sqrt(x)	square root of x	double
log(x)	natural logarithm of x	double
exp(x)	e raised to the x power	double
ceil(x)	smallest integer value that is not less than x	double
floor(x)	largest integer value that is not greater than x	double
min(x,y)	smaller of its two arguments	same data type as arguments
max(x,y)	larger of its two arguments	same data type as arguments
rint(x)	closest integer value to the argument (in case of two closest integers, the even integer is returned)	double
round(x)	rounded value	int or long
random	random number between 0.0 inclusive and 1.0 exclusive	double
sin(x)	sine of x (x in radians)	double
cos(x)	cosine of x (x in radians)	double
tan(x)	tangent of x (x in radians)	double
asin(x)	arcsin of x	double
acos(x)	arccos of x	double
atan(x)	arctan of x	double

It is important to remember that each Math class method is called into action by listing the name of the class, a period, the method's name, and passing any data to it within the parentheses following the method's name (Figure 4.17).

The arguments that are passed to a method need not be single constants. An expression can also be an argument provided that the expression can be computed to yield a value of the required data type. For example, the following arguments are valid for the given methods:

```
Math.sqrt(4.0 + 5.3 * 4.0)      Math.abs(2.3 * 4.6)
Math.sqrt(16.0 * 2.0 - 6.7)     Math.abs(theta - phi)
Math.sqrt(x * y - z / 3.2)      Math.sin(2.0 * omega)
```

Table 4.7   **Selected** Math **Class Method Examples**

Example	Returned Value
Math.abs(-7.362)	7.362
Math.abs(-3)	3
Math.pow(2.0,5.0)	32.0
Math.pow(10,3)	1000.0
Math.log(18.697)	2.928363083183137
Math.exp(-3.2)	0.040762203978366204

FIGURE 4.17   **Using and passing data to a math class method**

Math.MethodName (data passed to the method);

This locates   This identifies   This passes data
the method   the called   to the method
               method

The expressions in parentheses are first evaluated to yield a specific value. Thus, values have to be assigned to variables such as theta, phi, x, y, z, and omega before their use in the preceding expressions. After the value of the argument is calculated, it is passed to the method.

Methods may also be included as part of larger expressions. For example,

```
4 * Math.sqrt(4.5 * 10.0 - 9.0) - 2.0 =
          4 * Math.sqrt(36.0) - 2.0 =
                    4 * 6.0 - 2.0 =
                    24.0 - 2.0 = 22.0
```

The step-by-step evaluation of an expression such as

```
3.0 * Math.sqrt(5 * 33 - 13.71) / 5
```

is

Step	*Result*
1. Perform multiplication in argument	`3.0 * Math.sqrt(165 - 13.71) / 5`
2. Complete argument calculation	`3.0 * Math.sqrt(151.29) / 5`
3. Return a method value	`3.0 * 12.3 / 5`
4. Perform the multiplication	`36.9 / 5`
5. Perform the division	`7.38`

QuickTest Program 4.11 illustrates the use of the sqrt() method to determine the time it takes a ball to hit the ground after it has been dropped from an 800-foot tower. The mathematical formula to calculate the time, in seconds, that it takes to fall a given distance, in feet, is

$$time = sqrt(2 * distance / g)$$

where g is the gravitational constant equal to 32.2 ft/sec^2.

The output produced by QuickTest Program 4.11 is

```
It will take 7.05 seconds to fall 800 feet.
```

As used in QuickTest Program 4.11, the value returned by the Math.sqrt() method is assigned to the variable time. In addition to assigning a method's returned value to a variable, or using the returned value within a larger expression, it may also be used as an argument to another method. For example, the expression

```
Math.sqrt( Math.pow( Math.abs(num1),num2 ) )
```

is valid. Since parentheses are present, the computation proceeds from the inner to the outer pairs of parentheses. Thus, the absolute value of num1 is computed first and used as an argument to the Math.pow() method. The value returned by the Math.pow() method is then used as an argument to the Math.sqrt() method.

QuickTest Program 4.11

```java
import java.text.*; // needed for formatting
public class FallTime
{
  public static void main(String[] args)
  {
    int height;
    double time;

    DecimalFormat df = new DecimalFormat("#.00");

    height = 800;
    time = Math.sqrt(2 * height / 32.2);
    System.out.println("It will take " + df.format(time)
            + " seconds to fall " + height + " feet.");
  }
}
```

Casts

We have already seen the conversion of an operand's data type within mixed-mode arithmetic expressions (Section 4.2) and across assignment operators (Section 4.1). In addition to these implicit data type conversions that are automatically made in mixed-mode arithmetic and assignment expressions, Java also provides for explicit user-specified type conversions. The operator that forces the conversion of a value to another type is the **cast** operator. This is a unary operator having the form (*dataType*) *expression*, where *dataType* is the desired data type of the expression following the cast. For example, the expression

```java
(int) (a * b)
```

ensures that the value of the expression a * b is converted to an integer value. It should be noted that casts between Java's built-in numerical data types and its reference types, in either direction, are not permitted. This type of conversion is accomplished using the methods presented next.

Conversion Methods

Java provides a number of extremely useful routines for converting a string to a primitive type and primitive type to a string (Figure 4.18). These methods, among others, are in a set of classes referred to as *wrapper classes* because the classes are con-

FIGURE 4.18   **Conversions using a wrapper class method**

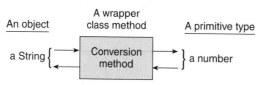

Table 4.8   Wrapper Class Conversion Routines

Wrapper Class	Method	Description	Example	Returned Value
Integer	parseInt(string)	Converts a string to a primitive type int.	Integer.parseInt ("1234")	1234 (an int value)
Integer	toString(x)	Converts the primitive int x value to a String object.	Integer.toString (345)	"345" (a String object)
Long	parseLong(string)	Converts a string to a primitive type long.	Long.parseLong ("128365489")	128365489L (a long value)
Long	toString(x)	Converts the primitive long x value to a String object.	Long.toString (128365489)	"128365489" (a String object)
Float	parseFloat(string)	Converts a string to a primitive type float.	Float.parseFloat ("345.89")	345.89f (a float value)
Float	toString(x)	Converts the primitive float x value to a String object.	Float.toString (345.873)	"345.873" (a String object)
Double	parseDouble(string)	Converts a string to a primitive type double.	Double.parseDouble ("2.3456789")	2.3456789 (a double value)
Double	toString(x)	Converts the primitive double x value to a String object.	Double.toString (345.873)	"345.873"" (a String object)

structed by wrapping a class structure around the built-in integer, long, float, and double numerical data types.[11]

Each primitive data type has a corresponding wrapper class whose name is the same as its equivalent built-in primitive type with the exception that the class names begin with an uppercase letter and Character and Integer are spelled out as complete words. Besides providing the conversions shown in Figure 4.18, these wrapper classes are also useful in converting a primitive type to an equivalent object type for input to any method that requires an object and not a primitive value. For our current purposes, however, these wrapper classes are of interest because of the conversion methods listed in Table 4.8. Notice that a subset of these methods was presented in Table 4.2.

All of the methods in Table 4.8 are public and static, which means that they are general-purpose methods that only operate on their arguments to produce a result. As general-purpose methods, they are used by listing both their class and method names, separated by a period, as illustrated in all of the examples provided in the table. Also notice that all of the conversions from a primitive data type to a string type use the same toString() method. This particular method is overloaded, which means multiple versions of the method exist, and the correct version is determined by the type of argument provided when the method is invoked.

---

[11] There are a total of ten wrapper classes. The additional six classes are named Boolean, Byte, Character, Number, Short, and Void.

In general, we will have much more use for the methods that convert a string value to a numerical type. This is because when values are input to a QuickTest program, as described in Sections 4.1 and 4.2, the input is read in as a string of characters. This string is typically converted to an appropriate numerical type using one of the string to primitive data type conversion methods in Table 4.8. QuickTest Program 4.12 illustrates using two of these methods to convert a string into both an integer and double-precision value.

QuickTest Program 4.12

```
public class SampleConversions
{
 public static void main(String[] args)
 {
   String numstring = "12345";
   int num;
   double dnum;

   // convert to an integer and perform a numerical operation
   num = Integer.parseInt(numstring);
   System.out.println("The string \"" + numstring
           + "\" as an integer number is: " + num);
   System.out.println("This number divided by 3 is: " + (num / 3));

    // convert to a double and perform a numerical operation
   numstring = numstring + ".96";  // concatenate to the original string
   dnum = Double.parseDouble(numstring);
   System.out.println("\nThe string \"" + numstring
           + "\" as a double number is: " + Double.toString(dnum));
   System.out.println("This number divided by 3 is: " + (dnum / 3));
 }
}
```

The output produced by QuickTest Program 4.12 is

```
The string "12345" as an integer number is: 12345
This number divided by 3 is: 4115


The string "12345.96" as a double number is: 12345.96
This number divided by 3 is: 4115.32
```

As this output illustrates, once a string has been converted to either an integer or double-precision value, mathematical operations on the numerical value are valid. These mathematical operations could not have been performed on the original string versions of the numbers.

A number of comments need to be made with respect to the conversion methods in Table 4.8. First, it should be noted that the toString() methods in the table are not nearly as useful as the string to primitive type methods. This is because any numerical type can more simply be converted into a string using the concatenation operator, as in QuickTest Program 4.12. For example, the expression

`Double.toString(123.45)` can always be replaced by the simpler expression `""+ 123.45`, as is typically done in practice.

Second, it is very important to realize that all of the conversion methods require valid argument values. For example, the expression `Integer.parseInt ("123.56")` results in an error because the fractional part of the number cannot be converted into a legitimate integer value. From a programming standpoint, the validity of any string value being converted should always be checked prior to sending the string value into a conversion method. This validity check, which is referred to as **input validation**, is especially important when data are entered by a user interactively as a program is running. This is because we have no control over what characters a user might inadvertently enter, and any characters that cannot be converted will result in a program error. Although we do not, as yet, have the programming tools either to input or validate user-entered data, we will have much more to say about this as we develop our QuickTest programming expertise.

Exercises 4.5

1. Write valid Java statements to determine

   a. The square root of 6.37

   b. The square root of $x - y$

   c The smaller of the values -30.5 and -42.7

   d. The larger of the values 109 and 101

   e. The absolute value of $a^2 - b^2$

   f. The value of e raised to the third power

2. For $a = 10.6$, $b = 13.9$, $c = -3.42$, determine the value of

   a. `(int) a`

   b. `(int) b`

   c. `(int) c`

   d. `(int) (a + b)`

   e. `(int) a + b + c`

   f. `(int) a + b + c`

   g. `(int) (a + b + c)`

   h. `(float) ((int) a) + b`

   i. `(float) ((int) (a + b))`

   j. `Math.abs(a) + Math.abs(b)`

   k. `Math.sqrt(Math.abs(a - b))`

3. Write Java statements for the following:

   a. $c = \sqrt{a^2 + b^2}$

   b. $p = \sqrt{|m - n|}$

   c. $sum = \dfrac{a(r^n - 1)}{r - 1}$

4. Write, compile, and run a QuickTest program that calculates and returns the fourth root of the number 81, which is 3. When you have verified that your program works correctly, use it to determine the fourth root of 728.8964. Your program should make use of the `sqrt()` method.

5. Write, compile, and run a QuickTest program that calculates the distance between two points whose coordinates are (7,12) and (3,9). Use the fact that the distance between two points having coordinates $(x1,y1)$ and $(x2,y2)$ is $distance = sqrt([x1 - x2]^2 + [y1 - y2]^2)$. When you have verified that your program works correctly by calculating the distance between the two points manually, use your program to determine the distance between the points $(-12,-15)$ and $(22,5)$.

6a. A model of worldwide population, in billions of people, after the year 2000 is given by the equation

$$\text{Population} = 6.0 \ e^{.02 \ [\text{Year} - 2000]}$$

Using this formula, write, compile, and run a QuickTest program to estimate the worldwide population in the year 2002. Verify the result displayed by your program by calculating the answer manually. When you have verified that your program is working correctly, use it to estimate the world's population in the year 2012.

b. Modify the program written for Exercise 6a so that the computed population estimate is displayed with a maximum of two digits after the decimal point.

7. Modify QuickTest Program 4.11 so that the displayed time always has a maximum of four digits after the decimal point.

8a. Write a general-purpose method named `findAbs()` that accepts a double-precision number passed to it, computes its absolute value, and displays the absolute value. The absolute value of a number is the number itself if the number is positive and the negative of the number if the number is negative.

b. Include the method written in Exercise 8a in a working program. Make sure your method is called from `main()`. Test the method by passing various data to it.

9a. Write a general-purpose method called `mult()` that accepts two floating-point numbers as parameters, multiplies these two numbers, and displays the result.

b. Include the method written in Exercise 9a in a working program. Make sure your method is called from `main()`. Test the method by passing various data to it.

10a. Write a general-purpose method named `squareIt()` that computes the square of the value passed to it and displays the result. The method should be capable of squaring numbers with decimal points.

b. Include the method written in Exercise 10a in a working program. Make sure your method is called from `main()`. Test the method by passing various data to it.

11a. Write a general-purpose method named `powfun()` that raises a long integer number passed to it to a positive integer power (also passed as an argument) and displays the result. The positive integer should be the second value passed to the method. Additionally, declare the variable used to store the result as a long integer data type to ensure sufficient storage for the result.

b. Include the method written in Exercise 11a in a working program. Make sure your method is called from `main()`. Test the method by passing various data to it.

12. A useful general-purpose method that uses no parameters can be constructed to return a value for π that is accurate to the maximum number of decimal places allowed by your computer. This value is obtained by taking the arcsine of 1.0, which is $\pi / 2$, and multiply-

ing the result by 2. In Java, the required expression is *2.0 * Math.asin(1.0)*, where the `asin()` method is provided by the Java `Math` class. Using this expression, write a Java method named `Pi()` that calculates and displays the value of π.

13. Although we have been concentrating on integer and real arithmetic, Java allows characters to be added or subtracted. This can be done because Java always converts a character to an equivalent integer value whenever a character is used in an arithmetic expression (the decimal value of each character can be found in Appendix B). Thus, characters and integers can be freely mixed in arithmetic expressions. For example, using the Unicode code, the expression `'a' + 1` equals 98, and `'z' - 1` equals 121. These values can be converted back into characters using the cast operator. Thus, `(char) ('a' + 1) = 'b'` and `(char) ('z' - 1) = 'y'`. Similarly, `(char)('A' + 1)` is `'B'`, and `(char)('Z' - 1)` is `'Y'`. With this as background, determine the results of the following expressions (assume that all characters are stored using the Unicode code).

a.	`(char) ('m' - 5)`	e.	`('b' - 'a')`
b.	`(char) ('m' + 5)`	f.	`('g' - 'a' + 1)`
c.	`(char) ('G' + 6)`	g.	`('G' - 'A' + 1)`
d.	`(char) ('G' - 6)`		

14a. The table in Appendix B lists the integer values corresponding to each letter stored using the Unicode code. Using this table, notice that the uppercase letters consist of contiguous codes starting with an integer value of 65 for A and ending with 90 for Z. Similarly, the lowercase letters begin with the integer value of 97 for the letter a and end with 122 for z. With this as background, determine the character value of the expressions `(char) ('A' + 32)` and `(char) ('Z' + 32)`.

b. Using Appendix B, determine the integer value of the expression `'a' - 'A'`.

c. Using the results of Exercises 14a and 14b, determine the character value of the following expression, where *uppercaseLetter* can be any uppercase letter from A to Z.

    `(char) ('uppercaseLetter ' + 'a' - 'A')`

15. Modify QuickTest Program 4.12 so that the following line of code is placed immediately before `main()`'s closing brace

    `Long.parseLong(numstring);`

Attempt to compile and run the modified program and then determine what the error is and when is it reported (at compile time or run time).

16. Complete the following program so that the average of the values represented by the strings `s1` and `s2` is computed and displayed.

```java
public class Average
{
  public static void main(String[] args)
  {
    String s1 = "15";
    String s2 = "14";
```

4.6 Common Programming Errors

In working with the material presented in this chapter, be aware of the following possible errors.

1. Forgetting to precede a mathematical method with the class name `Math` and a period, as in `Math.sqrt(x)`.

2. Not understanding the difference between writing a program for your own personal use and one intended for someone else's use. Programs written for your own use need not have extensive exception checking or exception handling capabilities because you will either not make mistakes that a casual user will or you will know how to recover from such mistakes (such as pressing the Ctrl and C keys to break out of a program). This is not true for programs that will be run by other people. Such programs should have extensive exception handling features.

3. Being unwilling to test a program in depth that is to be used by people other than yourself. After all, because you wrote the program, you assume it is correct or you would have changed it before it was completed. It is extremely difficult to back away and honestly test your own software. As a programmer, you must constantly remind yourself that just because you *think* your program is correct does not make it so. Finding errors in your own program is a sobering experience, but one that will help you become a master programmer.

4.7 Chapter Review

KEY TERMS

BufferedReader	exception handling	streams
cast	formatted output	StringTokenizer class
catch block	input validation	System.in
checked exception	InputStreamReader	System.out
class library	Math class	throwing an exception
crash	readLine()	token
delimiters	showInputDialog()	try block
end-of-file (EOF)	stream objects	unchecked exception

SUMMARY

1. Input from the keyboard can be accomplished using the `readLine()` method, which reads a complete line of input. This method accepts a line of data from the keyboard, which should then be assigned to a string variable. To use this method, a buffered input stream must be created. This is accomplished with the following declarations, where the variable names `isr` and `br` are programmer selectable.

```
InputStreamReader isr = new InputStreamReader(System.in);
BufferedReader br = new BufferedReader(isr);
```

The first statement is required to permit access to the conversion capabilities provided by the `InputStreamReader` class. The second statement is needed to access the `readLine()` method, which is provided by the `BufferedReader` class. Once this set of declarations has been made, a statement such as

```
inputString = br.readLine(isr);
```

can be used to accept a line of keyboard input and store it in the string referenced by the string variable `inputString`.

2. A Java program that uses keyboard input must include the statement `import java.io.*;`. In addition, the method within which `readLine()` is used must include the expression `throws java.io.IOException` after the method's header line.

3. When a `readLine()` method call is encountered, the program temporarily suspends statement execution until the user signals the end of data input by pressing the Enter key.

4. An input dialog box method is used for data input. This dialog accepts a string from the keyboard and assigns the characters entered to a string object. The general syntax of the statement creating an input dialog is

   stringName = JOptionPane.showInputDialog("*prompt*");

   where the *prompt* is a message that is displayed in the input dialog. The characters entered by the user are stored as a string that is referenced by the *stringName*.

5. When an input dialog box is encountered, the computer temporarily suspends further statement execution until either the OK or Cancel button has been clicked.

6. An *exception* is an error condition that occurs when a program is running and notification of which is immediately sent to the Java Virtual Machine for processing. The following terminology is used in Java for processing exceptions:

Terminology	*Description*
Exception	An error that occurs while a program is running.
Throw an exception	Generate an exception object.
Catch or handle an exception	Identify an exception and pass it to a handler.
Catch clause or handler	The section of code that performs the error processing.

7. Exceptions can be caught and processed by a `try` statement. This statement has the syntax

```
try
{

  // one or more statements,
  // at least one of which should
  // be capable of throwing an exception;
}
catch(exceptionName argument)
{
   // one or more statements
}
finally
{
   // one or more statements
}
```

The reserved word `try` identifies the start of the statement. One of the statements within the braces defining this block of code should be capable of throwing an exception.

A `try` block must be followed by at least one `catch` block, which serves as an exception handler for a specific exception thrown by the statements in the `try` block. Additional `catch` blocks are optional. Listed within the parentheses is the name of the exception being caught and a user-selectable argument name. This argument is used to hold the exception object generated when the exception occurs. An optional `finally` block provides a catchall default set of instructions that is always executed, whether or not any exception occurred.

8. Values can be equated to a single constant using the reserved word `final`. This creates a named constant that is read-only after it is initialized within the declaration statement. This declaration has the syntax

   ```
   final dataType constantName = initial value;
   ```

   and permits the constant to be used instead of the initial value anywhere in a method after the declaration. Generally, such declarations are placed before a method's variable declarations.

9. Java provides a `Math` class containing methods for calculating square root, logarithmic, and other mathematical computations. When using a `Math` class method, the method name should be preceded by the class name `Math` and a period.

10. Every `Math` class method operates on its arguments to calculate a single value. To use a `Math` class method effectively, you must know what the method does, the name of the method, the number and data types of the arguments expected by the method, and the data type of the returned value.

11. Each method has its own requirements for the number and data types of the arguments that must be provided. Arguments are passed to a method by including each argument, separated by commas, within the parentheses following the method's name.

12. Methods may be included within larger expressions.

13. The Java `String` class provides a number of methods for converting strings into primitive numerical types. The most commonly used of these methods, with their associated class names are

Method	Description
`Integer.parseInt(string object or value)`	Converts a string to an `int`.
`Long.parseLong(string object or value)`	Converts a string to a `long`.
`Float.parseFloat(string object or value)`	Converts a string to a `float`.
`Double.parseDouble(string object or value)`	Converts a string to a `double`.

4.8 Chapter Supplement: Programming Errors

The ideal in programming is to produce readable, error-free programs that work correctly and can be modified or changed with a minimum of testing required for reverification. In this regard, it is useful to know the different types of errors that can occur, when they are detected, and how to correct them.

Compile-Time and Run-Time Errors

A program error can be detected

1. Before a program is compiled
2. While the program is being compiled
3. While the program is being run
4. After the program has been run and the output is being examined

or it may, oddly enough, not be detected at all. Errors detected by the compiler are formally referred to as **compile-time errors,** and errors that occur while the program is running are formally referred to as **run-time errors.**

By now, you have probably encountered numerous compile-time errors. Although beginning programmers tend to be frustrated by them, experienced programmers understand that the compiler is doing a lot of valuable checking, and it is usually quite easy to correct compiler-detected errors. In addition, because these errors happen to the programmer and not to the user, no one but the programmer generally ever knows they occurred; you fix them and they go away. For example, see if you can detect the error in Program 4.13.

The error in this program, which is not immediately obvious, is that we have not initialized the variable `rate` with any value. This omission is quickly picked up as a compile-time error, and the error message `Variable rate may not have been initialized` is displayed.

Run-time errors are much more troubling because they happen to the user running the program, which in most commercial systems is not the programmer. For example, if a user enters data that result in an attempt to divide a number by zero, a run-time error occurs. Other examples of run-time errors were presented in Section 4.2, where exception processing was introduced. As a programmer, the only way to protect against run-time errors is to sufficiently think out what someone can do to cause errors and submit your program to rigorous testing. Although beginning programmers tend to blame a user for a run-time error caused by entering obviously incorrect data, professionals don't. They understand that a run-time error is a flaw in the final product that can cause damage to the reputation of both program and programmer.

There are known methods for detecting errors both before a program is compiled and after it has been run. The method for detecting errors before a program is compiled is called *desk checking*. Desk checking refers to the procedure of checking a program by hand for syntax and logic errors at a desk or table. The method for detecting errors after a program has been run is called *program testing*.

Syntax and Logic Errors

Computer literature distinguishes between two primary types of errors called syntax and logic errors. A *syntax error* is an error in the structure or spelling of a statement. For example, the statements

```
System.out.printin("There are three syntax errors here")
System.out.println(" Can you find tem?");
```

Program 4.13

```java
import javax.swing.*;
import java.text.*; // needed for formatting
public class FindErrors
{
  public static void main(String[] args)
  {
    String s1, outMessage;
    double capital, amount, rate, nyrs;
    DecimalFormat num = new DecimalFormat(",###.00");

    outMessage = "This program calculates the amount of money\n"
               + "in a bank account for an initial deposit\n"
               + "invested for n years at an interest rate r.";

    JOptionPane.showMessageDialog(null, outMessage,
                        "Program 4.13",
                        JOptionPane.INFORMATION_MESSAGE);
    s1 = JOptionPane.showInputDialog("Enter the initial amount in the account:");
    amount = Double.parseDouble(s1);
    s1 = JOptionPane.showInputDialog("Enter the number of years:");
    nyrs = Double.parseDouble(s1);
    capital = amount * Math.pow((1 + rate/100.0), nyrs);

    outMessage = "The final amount of money is $" +num.format(capital);

    JOptionPane.showMessageDialog(null, outMessage,
                    "Program 4.13",
                    JOptionPane.INFORMATION_MESSAGE);

  System.exit(0);
  }
}
```

contain three syntax errors.

1. The method name `println` is misspelled in the first line.
2. A terminating semicolon is missing in the first line.
3. The string in the second line is not terminated with double quotation marks.

All of these errors will be detected by the compiler when the program is compiled. This is true of all syntax errors because they violate the basic rules of Java; if they are not discovered by desk checking, the compiler detects them and displays an error message.[12] In some cases, the error message is extremely clear and the error is obvious; in other cases, it takes a little detective work to understand the error message

---

[12] They may not, however, all be detected at the same time. Frequently, one syntax error masks another error, and the second error is only detected after the first error is corrected.

displayed by the compiler. Since all syntax errors are detected at compile time, the terms compile-time errors and syntax errors are frequently used interchangeably. Strictly speaking, however, compile-time refers to when the error was detected, and syntax refers to the type of error detected. Note that the misspelling of the word them in the last `println()` method call is not a syntax error. Although this spelling error will result in an undesirable output line being displayed, it is not a violation of Java's syntactical rules. It is a simple case of a typographical error, commonly referred to as a "typo."

Logic errors are characterized by erroneous, unexpected, or unintentional errors that are a direct result of some flaw in the program's logic. These errors, which are never caught by the compiler, may either be detected by desk checking, by program testing, by accident when a user obtains an obviously erroneous output, while the program is running, or not at all. If the error is detected while the program is running, a run-time error occurs that results in an error message being generated and/or abnormal and premature program termination.

Because logic errors are not detected by the compiler and may go undetected at run time, they are always more difficult to detect than syntax errors. If not detected by desk checking, a logic error will reveal itself in one of two predominant ways. In one instance, the program runs to completion but produces incorrect results. Generally, logic errors of this type include

No output: This is caused either by an omission of an output statement or a sequence of statements that inadvertently bypass an output statement.

Unappealing or misaligned output: This is caused by an error in an output statement.

Incorrect numerical results: This is caused either by incorrect values assigned to the variables used in an expression, the use of an incorrect arithmetic expression, an omission of a statement, round-off error, or the use of an improper sequence of statements.

Logic errors can cause run-time errors. Examples of this type of logic error are attempts to divide by zero or to take the square root of a negative number.

Program testing should be well thought out to maximize the possibility of locating errors. An important realization is that *although a single test can reveal the presence of an error, it does not verify the absence of another one*. That is, the fact that one error is revealed by testing does not indicate that another error is not lurking somewhere else in the program; furthermore, *the fact that one test revealed no errors does not indicate that there are no errors.*

Once an error is discovered, however, the programmer must locate where the error occurs and then fix it. In computer jargon, a program error is referred to as a *bug,* and the process of isolating, correcting, and verifying the correction is called *debugging.*[13]

Although there are no hard-and-fast rules for isolating the cause of an error, some useful techniques can be applied. The first of these is a preventive technique. Frequently, many errors are introduced by the programmer in the rush to code and run a program before fully understanding what is required and how the result is to be

---

[13] The derivation of this term is rather interesting. When a program stopped running on the Mark I computer at Harvard University in September 1945, the malfunction was traced to a dead insect that had gotten into the electrical circuits. The programmer, Grace Hopper, recorded the incident in her logbook as "First actual case of bug being found."

achieved. A symptom of this haste to get a program entered into the computer is the lack of an outline of the proposed program (pseudocode or flowcharts) or a handwritten program itself. Many errors can be eliminated by desk checking a copy of the program before it is ever entered or compiled.

A second useful technique is to imitate the computer and execute each statement by hand, as the computer would. This means writing down each variable as it is encountered in the program and listing the value that should be stored in the variable as each input and assignment statement is encountered. Doing this also sharpens your programming skills because it requires that you fully understand what each statement in your program causes to happen. Such a check is called *program tracing*.

A third and very powerful debugging technique is to display the values of selected variables. For example, again consider Program 4.13. If this program produces an incorrect value for `capital`, it is worthwhile displaying the value of all variables used in the computation for `capital` immediately before a value for this variable is calculated. If the displayed values are correct, then the problem is in the assignment statement that calculates a value for `capital`; if the values are incorrect, you must determine where the incorrect values were actually obtained.

In the same manner, another debugging use of output displays is to immediately display the values of all input data. This technique is referred to as *echo printing*, and it is useful in establishing that the program is correctly receiving and interpreting the input data.

The most powerful of all debugging and tracing techniques is to use a program called a **debugger**. A debugger program controls the execution of a Java program, can interrupt the Java program at any point in its execution, and can display the values of all variables at the point of interruption.

Finally, no discussion of debugging is complete without mentioning the primary ingredient needed for successful isolation and correction of errors. This is the attitude and spirit you bring to the task. Since you wrote the program, your natural assumption is that it is correct or you would have changed it before it was compiled. It is extremely difficult to back away and honestly test and find errors in your own software. As a programmer, you must constantly remind yourself that just because you think your program is correct does not make it so. Finding errors in your own programs is a sobering experience, but one that will help you become a master programmer. It can also be exciting and fun if approached as a detection problem with you as the master detective.

5 Selection

Flow of control refers to the order in which a program's statements are carried out. Unless directed otherwise, the normal flow of control for all programs is sequential. This means that each statement is executed in sequence, one after another, in the order in which it is placed within the program.

Both selection and repetition statements allow the programmer to alter the normal sequential flow of control. As their names imply, selection statements provide the ability to select which statement, from a well-defined set, will be carried out next, whereas repetition statements provide the ability to go back and repeat a set of statements. In this chapter, we present Java's selection statements, and Chapter 6 presents repetition statements. Since selection requires choosing between alternatives, we begin this chapter with a description of Java's selection criteria.

5.1 Relational Expressions

Besides providing addition, subtraction, multiplication, and division capabilities, all computers have the ability to compare numbers. Because many seemingly "intelligent" decision-making situations can be reduced to the level of choosing between two values, a computer's comparison capability can be used to create a remarkable intelligence-like facility.

Expressions that compare operands are called **relational expressions.** A **simple relational expression** consists of a relational operator connecting two variable and/or constant operands, as shown in Figure 5.1. The relational operators available in Java are given in Table 5.1. These relational operators may be used with integer, float, double, and character data but must be typed exactly as shown in Table 5.1. Thus, the following examples are all valid:

```
age > 40        length <= 50        temp > 98.6
   3 < 4        flag == done        idNum == 682
day != 5        2.0 < 3.3           hours > 40
```

The following are not valid:

```
length =< 50      // incorrect symbol
2.0 >> 3.3         // invalid relational operator
flag = = done     // spaces between operators are not allowed
```

Relational expressions are sometimes called **conditions**, and we use both terms to refer to these expressions. Like all Java expressions, relational expressions are evaluated to yield a result. For relational expressions, this result is one of the Boolean values, `true` or `false`. For example, the relationship 3 < 4 is always `true` and the relationship 2.0 > 3.3 is always `false`. This can be verified using the statements

```
System.out.println( "The value of 3 < 4 is " + (3 < 4));
System.out.println( "\nThe value of 2.0 > 3.0 is " + (2.0 > 3.3));
```

which result in the displays

```
The value of 3 < 4 is true
The value of 2.0 > 3.0 is false
```

The value of a relational expression such as `hours > 40` depends on the value stored in the variable `hours`. In a Java program, a relational expression such as this is typically used as part of a selection statement. In these statements, which are presented in the next section, the selection of which statement to execute next is then based on the value obtained.

In addition to numerical operands, character data can also be compared using relational operators. For such comparisons, the `char` values are automatically coerced

FIGURE 5.1 **The anatomy of a simple relational expression**

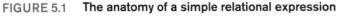
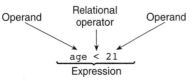

Table 5.1   **Relational Operators for Primitive Data Types**

Relational Operator	Meaning	Example
<	less than	`age < 30`
>	greater than	`height > 6.2`
<=	less than or equal to	`taxable <= 20000`
>=	greater than or equal to	`temp >= 98.6`
==	equal to	`grade == 100`
!=	not equal to	`number != 250`

to `ints` for the comparison. For example, in the Unicode code, the letter 'A' is stored using a code having a lower numerical value than the letter 'B', the code for 'B' is lower in value than the code for 'C', and so on. For character sets coded in this manner, the following conditions are evaluated as listed.

Expression	*Value*
`'A' > 'C'`	`false`
`'D' <= 'Z'`	`true`
`'E' == 'F'`	`false`
`'g' >= 'm'`	`false`
`'b' != 'c'`	`true`
`'a' == 'A'`	`false`
`'B' < 'a'`	`true`
`'b' > 'Z'`	`true`

Comparing letters is essential in alphabetizing names or using characters to select a particular choice in decision-making situations. Strings of characters may also be compared, but not using the relational operators in Table 5.1. Because a string is a reference data type, the `String` class methods presented in Chapter 7 must be used for comparing `String` objects.

Logical Operators

In addition to simple relational expressions as conditions, more complex conditions can be created using the Boolean logical operations AND, OR, and NOT. These operations are represented by the symbols &&, ||, and !, respectively.

When the AND operator, `&&`, is used with two relational expressions, the condition is `true` only if both individual expressions are `true` by themselves. Thus, the logical condition

```
(age > 40) && (term < 10)
```

is `true` only if `age` is greater than 40 and `term` is less than 10. Because relational operators have a higher precedence than logical operators, the parentheses in this logical expression could have been omitted.

The logical OR operator, `||`, is also applied between two expressions. When using the OR operator, the condition is satisfied if either one or both of the two expressions are `true`. Thus, the logical condition

```
(age > 40) || (term < 10)
```

is `true` if either age is greater than 40, `term` is less than 10, or both conditions are true. Again, the parentheses surrounding the relational expressions are included to make the expression easier to read. Because of the higher precedence of relational operators with respect to logical operators, the same evaluation is made even if the parentheses are omitted.

For the declarations

```
int i, j;
float a, b;
boolean complete;
```

the following represent valid conditions:

```
a > b
(a/b > 5) && (i <= 20)
(i == j) || (a < b) || complete
```

Before these conditions can be evaluated, the values of a, b, i, j, and `complete` must be known. Assuming the assignments

```
       a = 12.0;
       b = 2.0;
       i = 15;
       j = 30;
complete = false;
```

the previous expressions yield the following results:

Expression	*Value*
a > b	true
(a / b > 5) && (i <= 20)	true
(i == j) || (a < b) || complete	false

The NOT operation changes an expression to its opposite state; that is, if the expression is `true`, the value of `!expression` is `false`. If an expression is `false` to begin with, `!expression` is `true`. For example, assuming the number 26 is stored in the variable `age`, the expression `(age > 40)` has a Boolean value of `false`, while the expression `!(age > 40)` has a Boolean value of `true`. Since the NOT operation is used with only one operand, it is a unary operation.

The `&&` and `||` operators can only be used with Boolean operands. Such operands can be either Boolean literals, Boolean variables, or Boolean values generated by relational expressions. In addition, both of these operators use a "short-circuited evaluation." This means that the second operand is never evaluated if the evaluation of the first operand is sufficient to determine the final value of the logical operation. For the `&&` operator, this means that if the first condition evaluates to a Boolean `false` value, the second operand is not evaluated. The reason is that if the first operand is `false` and because the AND logical operation can only be `true` if both operands are `true`, the value of the operation must be `false` regardless of the value of the second operand. The same holds for the `||` operator. In this case, if the first operand yields a `true`, the complete OR operation must be `true` regardless of the value of the second operand, and the second operand need not be evaluated.

A BIT OF BACKGROUND

De Morgan's Laws

Augustus De Morgan was born at Madura, India, in 1806 and died in London in 1871. He became a professor of mathematics in London in 1828 and spent many years performing investigations into a variety of mathematical topics. He was a revered teacher and wrote numerous textbooks that contained a wealth of information on mathematics and its history, but which generally were very difficult for his students to understand.

De Morgan's contributions to modern computing include two laws by which AND statements can be converted to OR statements, and vice versa. They are

1. NOT (A AND B) = (NOT A) OR (NOT B)
2. NOT (A OR B) = (NOT A) AND (NOT B)

Thus, from De Morgan's first law, the statement "Either it is not raining or I am not getting wet" says the same thing as "It is not true that it is raining and I am getting wet." Similarly, from the second law "It is not true that politicians always lie or that teachers always know the facts" comes "Politicians do not always lie and teachers do not always know the facts."

In computer usage, De Morgan's laws are typically more useful in the following form:

1. A AND B = NOT ((NOT A) OR (NOT B))
2. A OR B = NOT ((NOT A) AND (NOT B))

The ability to convert from an OR statement to an AND statement and vice versa is extremely useful in many programming situations.

The relational and logical operators have a hierarchy of execution similar to the arithmetic operators. Table 5.2 lists the precedence of these operators in relation to the other operators we have encountered.

The following example illustrates the use of an operator's precedence and associativity to evaluate relational expressions, assuming the following declarations:

```
char key = 'm';
int i = 5, j = 7, k = 12;
double x = 22.5;
```

Expression	*Equivalent Expression*	*Value*
`i + 2 == k - 1`	`(i + 2) == (k - 1)`	`false`
`3 * i - j < 22`	`((3 * i) - j) < 22`	`true`
`i + 2 * j > k`	`(i + (2 * j)) > k`	`true`
`k + 3 <= -j + 3 * i`	`(k + 3) <= ((-j) + (3*i))`	`false`
`'a' + 1 == 'b'`	`('a' + 1) == 'b'`	`true`
`key - 1 > 'p'`	`(key - 1) > 'p'`	`false`

Table 5.2 **Operator Precedence**

Operator	Associativity
++ --	right to left
! unary -	right to left
* / %	left to right
+ -	left to right
< <= > >=	left to right
== !=	left to right
&	left to right
^	left to right
|	left to right
&&	left to right
||	left to right
= += -= *= /=	right to left

```
key + 1 == 'n'          (key + 1) == 'n'          true
25 >= x + 1.0           25 >= (x + 1.0)           true
```

As with all expressions, parentheses can be used to alter the assigned operator priority and improve the readability of relational expressions. By evaluating the expressions within parentheses first, the following compound condition is evaluated as:

```
(6 * 3 == 36 / 2) || (13 < 3 * 3 + 4)  && !(6 - 2 < 5)
      (18 == 18) ||    (13 < 9 + 4)    && !(4 < 5)
            true ||    (13 < 13)        && !true
            true ||     false           && false
            true ||     false
                  true
```

A Numerical Accuracy Problem

A problem that can occur with Java's relational expressions is a subtle numerical accuracy problem relating to floating-point and double-precision numbers. Because of the way computers store these numbers, tests for equality of floating-point and double-precision values and variables using the relational operator == should be avoided.

The reason is that many decimal numbers, such as 0.1, cannot be represented exactly in binary using a finite number of bits. Thus, testing for exact equality for such numbers can fail. When equality of noninteger values is desired, it is better to require that the absolute value of the difference between operands be less than some extremely small value. Thus, for real operands, the general expression

```
operandOne == operandTwo
```

should be replaced by the condition

```
Math.abs(operandOne - operandTwo) < EPSILON
```

where EPSILON is a named constant set to any acceptably small value, such as 0.0000001 (or any other user-selected amount).[1] Thus, if the difference between the two operands is less than the value of EPSILON, the two operands are considered essentially equal. For example, if x and y are floating-point variables, a condition such as

```
x/y == 0.35
```

should be programmed as

```
Math.abs(x/y - 0.35) < EPSILON
```

This latter condition ensures that slight inaccuracies in representing noninteger numbers in binary do not affect evaluation of the tested condition.

Exercises 5.1

1. Determine the value of the following expressions. Assume a = 5, b = 2, c = 4, d = 6, and e = 3, and all variables are ints.

a. `a > b`

b. `a != b`

c. `d % b == c % b`

d. `a * c != d * b`

e. `d * b == c * e`

f. `a * b < a % b *c`

g. `a % b * c > c % b * a`

h. `c % b * a  ==  b % c * a`

i. `b % c * a != a * b`

2. Using parentheses, rewrite the following expressions to indicate their correct order of evaluation. Then evaluate each expression assuming a = 5, b = 2, and c = 4.

a. `a % b * c && c % b * a`

b. `a % b * c || c % b * a`

c. `b % c * a && a % c * b`

d. `b % c * a || a % c * b`

3. Write relational expressions to express the following conditions (use variable names of your own choosing).

a. a person's age is equal to 30

b. a person's temperature is greater than 98.6

c. a person's height is less than 6 feet

---

[1] The comparison to EPSILON as a named constant can also fail when both operands are either extremely large or extremely small. For such cases, EPSILON should be constructed as a function of the two operands.

    d.   the current month is 12 (December)

    e.   the letter input is m

    f.   a person's age is equal to 30 and the person is taller than 6 feet

    g.   the current day is the 15th day of the 1st month

    h.   a person is older than 50 or has been employed at the company for at least 5 years

    i.   a person's identification number is less than 500 and the person is older than 55

    j.   a length is greater than 2 feet and less than 3 feet

4.   Determine the value of the following expressions assuming $a = 5$, $b = 2$, $c = 4$, and $d = 5$.

    a.   `a == 5`

    b.   `b * d == c * c`

    c.   `d % b * c > 5 || c % b * d < 7`

5.2 The `if-else` Statement

The `if-else` statement directs the computer to select a sequence of one or more instructions based on the result of a comparison. For example, if a New Jersey resident's income is less than $20,000, the applicable state tax rate is 2 percent. If the person's income is greater than $20,000, a different rate is applied to the amount over $20,000. The `if-else` statement can be used in this situation to determine the actual tax based on whether the income is less than or equal to $20,000. The general form of the `if-else` statement is

```
if (condition) statement1;
else statement2;
```

The `condition`, which can be either a relational or logical expression, is evaluated first. If the value of the condition is `true`, `statement1` is executed. If the value is `false`, the statement after the reserved word `else` is executed. Thus, one of the two statements (either `statement1` or `statement2`) is always executed depending on the Boolean value of the condition. Notice that the tested relational expression must be put in parentheses, and a semicolon is placed after each statement.

For clarity, the `if-else` statement generally is written on four lines in the form

```
if (condition) <----------------no semicolon here
    statement1;
else   <----------------no semicolon here
    statement2;
```

The form of the `if-else` statement that is selected typically depends on the length of statements 1 and 2. However, when using the second form, do not put a semicolon after the parentheses or the reserved word `else`. The semicolons are placed only at the end of each statement. The flowchart for the `if-else` statement is shown in Figure 5.2.

FIGURE 5.2   **The** `if-else` **flowchart**

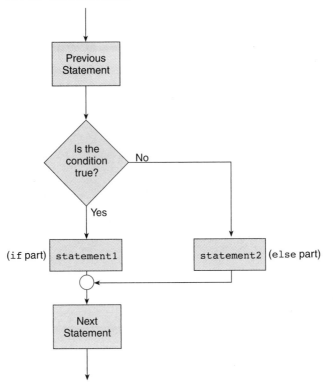

As an example, we can write an income tax computation program containing an `if-else` statement. As previously described, the New Jersey state income tax is assessed at 2 percent of taxable income for incomes less than or equal to $20,000. For taxable income greater than $20,000, state taxes are 2.5 percent of the income that exceeds $20,000 plus a fixed amount of $400. The expression to be tested is whether taxable income is less than or equal to $20,000. An appropriate `if-else` statement for this situation is[2]

```
if (taxable <= 20000.0)
   taxes = 0.02 * taxable;
else
   taxes = 0.025 * (taxable - 20000.0) + 400.0;
```

Here we have used the relational operator <= to represent the relation "less than or equal to." If the value of `taxable` is less than or equal to 20000.0, the condition is `true` and the statement `taxes = 0.02 * taxable;` is executed. If the condition is not `true`, the value of the expression is `false`, and the statement after the reserved word `else` is executed. QuickTest Program 5.1 illustrates the use of this statement in a complete program.

---

[2] Note that in practice the numerical values in this statement would be defined as named constants (see Exercise 2).

QuickTest Program 5.1

```java
import javax.swing.*;
import java.text.*;  // needed for formatting
public class CalculateTaxes
{
  public static void main(String[] args)
  {
    double taxable, taxes;
    String s1;

    DecimalFormat df = new DecimalFormat(",###.00");

    s1 = JOptionPane.showInputDialog("Please type in the taxable income:");
    taxable = Double.parseDouble(s1);

    if (taxable <= 20000.0)
      taxes = 0.02 * taxable;
    else
      taxes = 0.025 * (taxable - 20000.0) + 400.0;

    JOptionPane.showMessageDialog(null, "Taxes are $" + df.format(taxes),
                        "QuickTest Program 5.1",
                        JOptionPane.INFORMATION_MESSAGE);

    System.exit(0);
  }
}
```

A blank line was inserted before and after the `if-else` statement to highlight it in the complete program. We will continue to do this throughout the text to emphasize the statement being presented.

To illustrate selection in action, QuickTest Program 5.1 was run twice with different input data. The results are shown in Figures 5.3 and 5.4.

Observe that the taxable income input in the first run of the program was less than \$20,000, and the tax was correctly calculated as 2 percent of the number entered. In the second run, the taxable income was more than \$20,000, and the `else` part of the `if-else` statement yielded a correct tax computation of

$$0.025 * (\$30,000. - \$20,000.) + \$400. = \$650.$$

Compound Statements

Although only a single statement is permitted in both the `if` and `else` parts of the `if-else` statement, this statement can be a single compound statement. A **compound statement** is any number of single statements contained between braces (Figure 5.5). Although each single statement within the compound statement must end in a semicolon, `;`, a semicolon *is not placed* after the braces that define the compound statement.

The use of braces to enclose a set of individual statements creates a single block of statements, which may be used anywhere in a Java program in place of a single

FIGURE 5.3 **The first sample run of QuickTest Program 5.1**

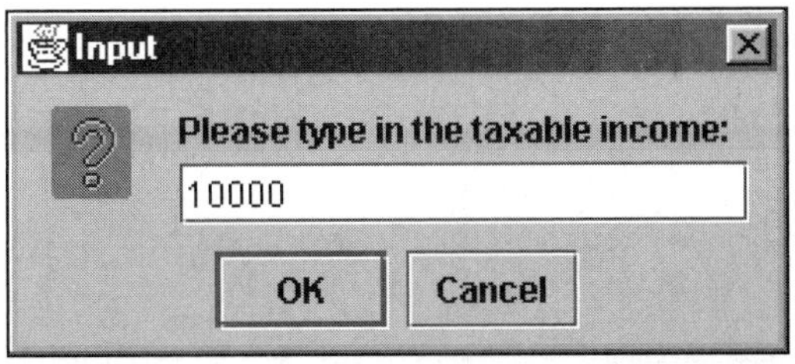

(a) Input

(b) Output

FIGURE 5.4 **The second sample run of QuickTest Program 5.1**

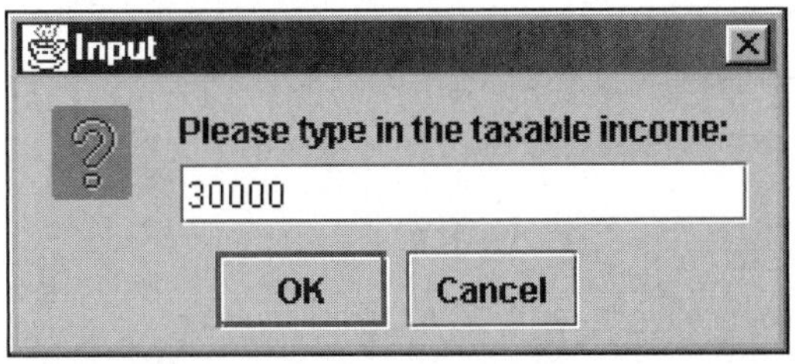

(a) Input

(b) Output

FIGURE 5.5 **A compound statement consists of individual statements enclosed within braces**

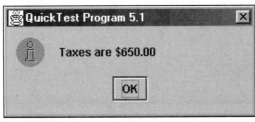

```
{
  statement1;
  statement2;
  statement3;
        .
        .
        .
  last statement;
}
```

statement. The next example illustrates the use of a compound statement within the general form of an `if-else` statement.

```
if (condition)
{
   statement1;    // as many statements as necessary
   statement2;    // can be put within the braces
   statement3;    // each statement must end with a ;
}
else
{
   statement4;
   statement5;
      .

      .

   statementn;
}
```

QuickTest Program 5.2 illustrates the use of a compound statement in an actual program. Notice the statements that have been included to facilitate keyboard input (review Section 3.3, especially Program 3.11, if necessary).

QuickTest Program 5.2

```java
import java.io.*;    // needed for keyboard input
import java.text.*;  // needed for formatting
public class ConvertTemperatures
{
  public static void main(String[] args)
   throws java.io.IOException    // for keyboard input
   {
     int tempType;
     double temp, fahren, celsius;
     String s1;

       // set up format variable
     DecimalFormat num = new DecimalFormat(",###.00");

       // set up the basic input stream for keyboard entry
       // needed for conversion capabilities
     InputStreamReader isr = new InputStreamReader(System.in);
       // needed to use readLine()
     BufferedReader br = new BufferedReader(isr);

     System.out.print("Enter the temperature to be converted: ");
     s1 = br.readLine();
     temp = Double.parseDouble(s1);

     System.out.println("Enter a 1 if the temperature is in Fahrenheit");
     System.out.print(" or a 2 if the temperature is in Celsius: ");
```

(continued on page 246)

PROGRAMMING NOTE

The Boolean Data Type

The tested condition in an if-else statement must always evaluate to a Boolean value. Thus, the value of the condition must be either true and false. Another way of indicating this is that the syntax of the if-else statement is

```
if (Boolean expression is true)
  execute this statement;
else
  execute this statement;
```

Although the boolean data type is generally restricted in its usage as the value of a relational expression, boolean values can be displayed, compared, and assigned. Additionally, the value of !true is false and !false is true. For example, consider the following main() method

```
public static void main(String[] args)
{
  Boolean t1, t2, t3, t4;
  t1 = true;
  t2 = false;

  System.out.println( "The value of t1 is " + t1);
  System.out.println( "The value of t2 is " + t2);

  t3 = !t1;
  t4 = !t2;

  System.out.println( "\nThe value of t3 is " + t3);
  System.out.println( "The value of t4 is " + t4);
}
```

The output displayed by this method is

```
The value of t1 is true
The value of t2 is false

The value of t3 is false
The value of t4 is true
```

In addition, an integer value can be converted into a Boolean value using the expression (x != 0), where x represents an integer value or variable. For example, if x has a value of 3, this expression results in a Boolean value of true. This conversion "trick" follows the C language convention that any nonzero integer is considered true and only a zero value is considered false.

(continued from page 244)

```
      s1 = br.readLine();
      tempType = Integer.parseInt(s1);

      if (tempType == 1)
      {
        celsius = (5.0 / 9.0) * (temp - 32.0);
        System.out.println("\nThe equivalent Celsius temperature is "
                        + num.format(celsius));
      }
      else
      {
        fahren =  (9.0 / 5.0) * temp + 32.0;
        System.out.println("\nThe equivalent Fahrenheit temperature is "
                        + num.format(fahren));
      }
    }
}
```

QuickTest Program 5.2 checks the integer value in `tempType`. If the value is 1, the compound statement corresponding to the `if` part of the `if-else` statement is executed. Any other number results in execution of the compound statement corresponding to the `else` part. A sample run of QuickTest Program 5.2 follows

```
Enter the temperature to be converted: 212
Enter a 1 if the temperature is in Fahrenheit
 or a 2 if the temperature is in Celsius: 1

The equivalent Celsius temperature is 100.00
```

One-Way Selection

A useful modification of the `if-else` statement involves omitting the `else` part of the statement altogether. In this case, the `if` statement takes the shortened and frequently useful form

```
    if (condition)
       statement;
```

The statement following the `if` `(condition)` is only executed if the condition has a `true` value. This modified form of the `if` statement is called a *one-way* if *statement*. It is illustrated in QuickTest Program 5.3, which checks a car's mileage and prints a message if the car has been driven more than 3000.0 miles. Notice that we have defined `value` as the named constant `LIMIT`.

QuickTest Program 5.3

```
import javax.swing.*;
public class CheckLimit
{
  public static void main(String[] args)
  {
    final double LIMIT = 3000.0;
```

PROGRAMMING NOTE

Placement of Braces in a Compound Statement

A common practice for some programmers is to place the opening brace of a compound statement on the same line as the `if` and `else` statements. Using this convention, the `if-else` statement in QuickTest Program 5.2 would appear as follows. This placement is a matter of style only; both styles are used and both are correct.

```
if (tempType == 1){
  celsius = (5.0 / 9.0) * (temp - 32.0);
   message = "The equivalent Celsius temperature is "
            + num.format(celsius);
}
else{
  fahren =  (9.0 / 5.0) * temp + 32.0;
   message = "The equivalent Fahrenheit temperature is "
            + num.format(fahren);
}
```

In practice, you should use whatever style is dictated by your company's policy or your professor's instructions.

```
String s1;
double mileage;

s1 = JOptionPane.showInputDialog("Please enter the mileage driven:");
mileage = Double.parseDouble(s1);

if(mileage > LIMIT)
  JOptionPane.showMessageDialog(null, "For a mileage of " + mileage
                  + "\nThis car is over the mileage limit",
                    "QuickTest Program 5.3",
                    JOptionPane.INFORMATION_MESSAGE);

JOptionPane.showMessageDialog(null, "End of Program",
                    "QuickTest Program 5.3",
                    JOptionPane.INFORMATION_MESSAGE);

System.exit(0);
   }
 }
```

As an illustration of its one-way selection criteria in action, Figure 5.6a shows the display for the case where the input data caused the statement within the `if` to be executed. Figure 5.6b shows the final message acknowledging the end of the program. For the case where the entered data are less than `LIMIT`, the display statement within the `if` statement is not executed and only the final display, shown in Figure 5.6b, would be produced. This final display is especially useful when the input data do not trigger a display of the first type because it lets the user know that the program did finish running (a program that provides no user output is not user-friendly and should be avoided).

FIGURE 5.6 **(a) The display produced by `if` statement**

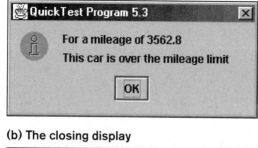

(b) The closing display

Exercises 5.2

1. Write appropriate `if` statements for each of the following conditions:

a. If the variable named `angle` is equal to 90 degrees, print the message `"The angle is a right angle"`; otherwise, print the message `"The angle is not a right angle"`.

b. If the temperature is above 100 degrees, display the message `"above the boiling point of water"`; otherwise, display the message `"below or equal to the boiling point of water"`.

c. If the variable `number` is positive, add `number` to `possum`; otherwise, add `number` to `negsum`.

d. If the variable `slope` is less than .5, set the variable `flag` to zero; otherwise, set `flag` to one.

e. If the difference between the variables `num1` and `num2` is less than .001, set the variable `approx` to zero; otherwise, calculate `approx` as the quantity `(num1 - num2) / 2.0`.

f. If the difference between the variables `temp1` and `temp2` exceeds 2.3 degrees, calculate the variable `error` as `(temp1 - temp2) * factor`.

g. If the variable `x` is greater than the variable `y` and the variable `z` is less than 20, read in a value for the variable `p`.

h. If the variable `distance` is greater than 20 and less than 35, read in a value for the variable `time`.

2. Rewrite QuickTest Program 5.1 using the following statements:

```
final double LOWRATE = 0.02;     // lowest tax rate
final double HIGHRATE = 0.025;   // highest tax rate
final double CUTOFF = 20000.0;   // cut-off for low rate
final double FIXEDAMT = 400.0;   // fixed dollar amount for higher rate
```

(If necessary, review Section 3.4 for the use of named constants.)

3. QuickTest Program 5.1 uses dialog boxes for both input and output. Rewrite QuickTest Program 5.1 to use a `readLine()` method for keyboard input and a `println()` method for display. (Tip: Review Section 3.3.)

4. Run QuickTest Program 5.2 on your computer.

5. QuickTest Program 5.2 uses `readLine()` for keyboard input and `println()` for console display. Rewrite this program to use dialog boxes for both input and output.

6a. If money is left in a particular bank for more than 5 years, the bank's interest rate is 7.5 percent; otherwise, the interest rate is 5.4 percent. Write a Java program that accepts a user-entered number of years into the variable `numYears` and displays the appropriate interest rate depending on the value input into `numYears`.

  b. How many runs should you make for the program written in Exercise 6a to verify that it is operating correctly? What data should you input in each of the program runs?

7a. In a pass-fail course, a student passes if the grade is greater than or equal to 70 and fails if the grade is lower. Write a Java program that accepts a grade and prints the message `A passing grade` or `A failing grade`, as appropriate.

  b. How many runs should you make for the program written in Exercise 7a to verify that it is operating correctly? What data should you input in each of the program runs?

8a. Write a Java program to compute and display a person's weekly salary as determined by the following expressions:

  > *If the hours worked are less than or equal to 40, the person receives $8.00 per hour; otherwise, the person receives $320.00 plus $12.00 for each hour worked over 40 hours.*

  The program should request the hours worked as input and display the salary as output.

  b. How many runs should you make for the program written in Exercise 8a to verify that it is operating correctly? What data should you input in each of the program runs?

9a. A senior salesperson is paid $400 a week and a junior salesperson receives $275 a week. Write a Java program that accepts as input a salesperson's status in the integer variable `status`. If `status` equals 1, the senior person's salary should be displayed; otherwise, the junior person's salary should be output.

  b. How many runs should you make for the program written in Exercise 9a to verify that it is operating correctly? What data should you input in each of the program runs?

10a. Write a Java program that displays either the message `I feel great today!` or `I feel down today #$*!` depending on the input. If the input is the integer 1, entered in the variable `choice`, the first message should be displayed; otherwise, the second message should be displayed.

  b. How many runs should you make for the program written in Exercise 10a to verify that it is operating correctly? What data should you input in each of the program runs?

11a. Write a program to display the following two prompts:

  ```
  Enter a month: (use a 1 for Jan, etc.)
  Enter a day of the month:
  ```

  Have your program accept and store a number in the variable `month` in response to the first prompt and accept and store a number in the variable `day` in response to the second prompt. If the month entered is not between 1 and 12 inclusive, display a message informing the user that an invalid month has been entered. If the day entered is not between 1 and 31, display a message informing the user that an invalid day has been entered.

b. What will your program do if the user types a number with a decimal point for the month? How can you ensure that your `if` statements check for an integer number?

12. Write a Java program that asks the user to input two numbers. After your program accepts the second number, have your program check the numbers. If the first number entered is greater than the second number, display the message `The first number is greater than the second`; otherwise, display the message `The first number is not greater than the second`. Test your program by entering the numbers 5 and 8 and then using the numbers 11 and 2. What will your program display if the two numbers entered are equal?

13. Enter and run QuickTest Program 5.3.

14. Rewrite QuickTest Program 5.3 to use a `readLine()` method for keyboard input and `print()` or `println()` method for console output.

15. The following `main()` method produces the output

```
The value of t1 is true
The value of t2 is false
These values are equal
```

```java
public static void main(String[] args)
{
  Boolean t1, t2;
  t1 = true;
  t2 = false;

  System.out.println( "The value of t1 is " + t1);
  System.out.println( "The value of t2 is " + t2);
  if (t2 = t1)
    System.out.println( "These values are equal");
  else
    System.out.println( "These values are not equal");
}
```

Determine why the output indicates the two Boolean values are equal when they clearly are not and correct the error in the method that produces the erroneous output.

5.3 Nested `if` Statements

As we have seen, an `if-else` statement can contain simple or compound statements. Any valid Java statement can be used, including another `if-else` statement. Thus, one or more `if-else` statements can be included within either part of an `if-else` statement. For example, substituting the one-way `if` statement

```java
if (hours > 6)
  System.out.println("snap");
```

for `statement1` in the following `if` statement

```
if (hours < 9)
   statement1;
else
   System.out.println("pop");
```

results in the nested `if` statement

```
if (hours < 9)
{
   if (hours > 6)
      System.out.println("snap");
}
else
   System.out.println("pop");
```

The braces around the inner one-way `if` are essential because in their absence Java associates an `else` with the closest unpaired `if`. Thus, without the braces, the preceding statement is equivalent to

```
if (hours < 9)
   if (hours > 6)
      System.out.println("snap");
   else
      System.out.println("pop");
```

Here the `else` is paired with the inner `if`, which destroys the meaning of the original `if-else` statement. Notice also that the indentation is irrelevant as far as the compiler is concerned. Whether the indentation exists or not, the statement is compiled by associating the last `else` with the closest unpaired `if`, unless braces alter the default pairing.

The process of nesting `if` statements can be extended indefinitely so that the `println("snap");` statement could itself be replaced by either a complete `if-else` statement or another one-way `if` statement.

The `if-else` Chain

Generally, the case in which the statement in the `if` part of an `if-else` statement is another `if` statement tends to be confusing and is best avoided. However, an extremely useful construction occurs when the `else` part of an `if` statement contains another `if-else` statement. This takes the form

```
if (expression1)
   statement1;
else
   if (expression2)
      statement2;
   else
      statement3;
```

As with all Java programs, the indentation we have used is not required. In fact, the preceding construction is so common that it is typically written in the following arrangement:

```
if (expression1)
   statement1;
else if (expression2)
   statement2;
else
   statement3;
```

This construction is called an **if-else chain** and is used extensively in programming applications. Each condition is evaluated in order, and if any condition is `true`, the corresponding statement is executed and the remainder of the chain is terminated. The final `else` statement is only executed if none of the previous conditions are satisfied. This serves as a default or catchall case that is useful for detecting an impossible or error condition.

The chain can be continued indefinitely by repeatedly making the last statement another `if-else` statement. Thus, the general form of an `if-else` chain is

```
if (expression1)
   statement1;
else if (expression2)
   statement2;
else if (expression3)
   statement3;
             .
             .
             .
else if (expressionn)
   statementn;
else
   laststatement;
```

As with all Java statements, each individual statement can be a compound statement bounded by the braces { and }. To illustrate an `if-else` chain, QuickTest Program 5.4 displays a person's marital status corresponding to a numerical input. The following codes are used:

Marital Status	Input Code
Single	1
Married	2
Divorced	3
Widowed	4

QuickTest Program 5.4

```
import javax.swing.*;
public class MarriedStatus
{
  public static void main(String [] args)
  {
    String s1, inMessage, outMessage;
    int marCode;

    inMessage = "Enter a marriage code:\n"
            + "    1 = Single\n"
            + "    2 = Married\n"
```

```
                  + "      3 = Divorced\n"
                  + "      4 = Widowed";
   s1 = JOptionPane.showInputDialog(inMessage);
   marCode = Integer.parseInt(s1);

   if (marCode == 1)
     outMessage = "Individual is single.";
   else if (marCode == 2)
     outMessage = "Individual is married.";
   else if (marCode == 3)
     outMessage = "Individual is divorced.";
   else if (marCode == 4)
     outMessage = "Individual is widowed.";
   else
     outMessage = "An invalid code was entered.";

   JOptionPane.showMessageDialog(null, outMessage,
                        "QuickTest Program 5.4",
                        JOptionPane.INFORMATION_MESSAGE);

   System.exit(0);

  }
}
```

As a final example illustrating an if-else chain, we can calculate the monthly income of a salesperson using the following commission schedule:

Monthly Sales	Income
greater than or equal to $50,000	$375 plus 16% of sales
less than $50,000 but greater than or equal to $40,000	$350 plus 14% of sales
less than $40,000 but greater than or equal to $30,000	$325 plus 12% of sales
less than $30,000 but greater than or equal to $20,000	$300 plus 9% of sales
less than $20,000 but greater than or equal to $10,000	$250 plus 5% of sales
less than $10,000	$200 plus 3% of sales

The following if-else chain can determine the correct monthly income, where the variable monthlySales stores the salesperson's current monthly sales.

```
if (monthlySales >= 50000.00)
  income = 375.00 + .16 * monthlySales;
else if (monthlySales >= 40000.00)
  income = 350.00 + .14 * monthlySales;
else if (monthlySales >= 30000.00)
  income = 325.00 + .12 * monthlySales;
else if (monthlySales >= 20000.00)
  income = 300.00 + .09 * monthlySales;
```

(continued)

(continued)

```
      else if (monthlySales >= 10000.00)
        income = 250.00 + .05 * monthlySales;
      else
        income = 200.00 + .03 * monthlySales;
```

Notice that this example makes use of the fact that the chain is stopped once a `true` condition is found. This is accomplished by checking for the highest monthly sales first. If the salesperson's monthly sales are less than $50,000, the `if-else` chain continues checking for the next highest sales amount until the correct category is obtained.

QuickTest Program 5.5 uses this `if-else` chain to calculate and display the income corresponding to the value of monthly sales input using an input dialog.

QuickTest Program 5.5

```java
import javax.swing.*;
import java.text.*;  // needed for formatting
public class MonthlyIncome
{
  public static void main(String [] args)
  {
    String s1, outMessage;
    double monthlySales, income;

    DecimalFormat num = new DecimalFormat(",###.00");

    s1 = JOptionPane.showInputDialog("Enter the value of monthly sales:");
    monthlySales = Double.parseDouble(s1);

    if (monthlySales >= 50000.00)
      income = 375.00 + .16 * monthlySales;
    else if (monthlySales >= 40000.00)
      income = 350.00 + .14 * monthlySales;
    else if (monthlySales >= 30000.00)
      income = 325.00 + .12 * monthlySales;
    else if (monthlySales >= 20000.00)
      income = 300.00 + .09 * monthlySales;
    else if (monthlySales >= 10000.00)
      income = 250.00 + .05 * monthlySales;
    else
      income = 200.00 + .03 * monthlySales;

    outMessage = "For monthly sales of $" + num.format(monthlySales)
              + "\nThe income is $" + num.format(income);

    JOptionPane.showMessageDialog(null, outMessage,
                 "QuickTest Program 5.5",
                 JOptionPane.INFORMATION_MESSAGE);

    System.exit(0);
  }
}
```

FIGURE 5.7   **A sample display produced by QuickTest Program 5.5**

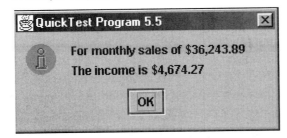

Figure 5.7 illustrates the display produced by QuickTest Program 5.5. As indicated by the display, an income of $4,674.27 was computed for an input value of $36,243.89.

Exercises 5.3

1. A student's letter grade is calculated according to the following schedule:

Numerical Grade	Letter Grade
greater than or equal to 90	A
less than 90 but greater than or equal to 80	B
less than 80 but greater than or equal to 70	C
less than 70 but greater than or equal to 60	D
less than 60	F

    Write a Java program that accepts a student's numerical grade, converts it to an equivalent letter grade, and displays the letter grade.

2. The interest rate on funds deposited in a bank is determined by the amount of time the money is left on deposit. For a particular bank, the following schedule is used:

Time on Deposit	Interest Rate
greater than or equal to 5 years	.0475
less than 5 years but greater than or equal to 4 years	.045
less than 4 years but greater than or equal to 3 years	.040
less than 3 years but greater than or equal to 2 years	.035
less than 2 years but greater than or equal to 1 year	.030
less than 1 year	.025

    Write a Java program that accepts the time that funds are left on deposit and displays the interest rate corresponding to the time entered.

3. Each disk drive in a shipment is stamped with a code from 1 through 4, which indicates a drive manufacturer as follows:

Code	Disk Drive Manufacturer
1	3M Corporation
2	Maxell Corporation
3	Sony Corporation
4	Verbatim Corporation

Write a Java program that accepts the code number as an input and, based on the value entered, displays the correct disk drive manufacturer.

4. Using the commission schedule from QuickTest Program 5.5, the following program calculates monthly income:

```java
import javax.swing.*;
import java.text.*;  // needed for formatting
public class CalculateIncome
{
  public static void main(String[] args)
  {
    String s1, outMessage;
    double monthlySales, income;

    DecimalFormat num = new DecimalFormat(",###.00");

    s1 = JOptionPane.showInputDialog("Enter the value of monthly sales:");
    monthlySales = Double.parseDouble(s1);

    if (monthlySales >= 50000.00)
      income = 375.00 + .16 * monthlySales;
    if (monthlySales >= 40000.00 && monthlySales < 50000.00)
      income = 350.00 + .14 * monthlySales;
    if (monthlySales >= 30000.00 && monthlySales < 40000.00)
      income = 325.00 + .12 * monthlySales;
    if (monthlySales >= 20000.00 && monthlySales < 30000.00)
      income = 300.00 + .09 * monthlySales;
    if (monthlySales >= 10000.00 && monthlySales < 20000.00)
      income = 250.00 + .05 * monthlySales;
    if (monthlySales < 10000.00)
      income = 200.00 + .03 * monthlySales;

    outMessage = "For monthly sales of $" + num.format(monthlySales)
               + "\nThe income is $" + num.format(income);

    JOptionPane.showMessageDialog(null, outMessage,
                "QuickTest Program 5.5a",
                JOptionPane.INFORMATION_MESSAGE);

    System.exit(0);
  }
}
```

a. Does this program produce the same output as QuickTest Program 5.5?

b. Which program is better and why?

5. The following program was written to produce the same result as QuickTest Program 5.5:

```java
import javax.swing.*;
import java.text.*;  // needed for formatting
public class CalculateIncome
{
  public static void main(String[] args)
  {
    String s1, outMessage;
    double monthlySales, income;

    DecimalFormat num = new DecimalFormat(",###.00");

    s1 = JOptionPane.showInputDialog("Enter the value of monthly sales:");
    monthlySales = Double.parseDouble(s1);

    if (monthlySales < 10000.00)
      income = 200.00 + .03 * monthlySales;
    else if (monthlySales >= 10000.00)
      income = 250.00 + .05 * monthlySales;
    else if (monthlySales >= 20000.00)
      income = 300.00 + .09 * monthlySales;
    else if (monthlySales >= 30000.00)
      income = 325.00 + .12 * monthlySales;
    else if (monthlySales >= 40000.00)
      income = 350.00 + .14 * monthlySales;
    else if (monthlySales >= 50000.00)
      income = 375.00 + .16 * monthlySales;

    outMessage = "For monthly sales of $" + num.format(monthlySales)
               + "\nThe income is $" + num.format(income);

    JOptionPane.showMessageDialog(null, outMessage,
               "QuickTest Program 5.5b",
               JOptionPane.INFORMATION_MESSAGE);

    System.exit(0);
  }
}
```

a. Does this program run?

b. What does this program do?

c. For what values of monthly sales does this program calculate the correct income?

5.4 **The switch Statement**

The if-else chain is used in programming applications where one set of instructions must be selected from many possible alternatives. The switch statement provides an alternative to the if-else chain for cases that compare the value of an integer expression to a specific value. The general form of a switch statement is

```
switch (expression)
{                              // start of compound statement
  case value-1:  <----------------------terminated with a colon
      statement1;
      statement2;
            .
            .
            .
      break;
  case value-2:  <----------------------terminated with a colon
      statementm;
      statementn;
            .
            .
            .
      break;
            .
            .


  case value-n:  <----------------------terminated with a colon
      statementw;
      statementx;
            .
            .
            .
      break;
  default:  <----------------------------terminated with a colon
      statementaa;
      statementbb;
}                              // end of switch and compound statement
```

There are four new reserved words in the `switch` statement: `switch`, `case`, `de-fault`, and `break`. Let's see what each of these words does.

The reserved word `switch` identifies the start of the `switch` statement. The expression in parentheses following this word is evaluated, and the result of the expression is compared to various alternative values contained within the compound statement. The expression in the `switch` statement must evaluate to an integer result or a compilation error occurs.

Internal to the `switch` statement, the reserved word `case` is used to identify or label individual values that are compared to the value of the `switch` expression. The `switch` expression's value is compared to each of these `case` values in the order that these values are listed until a match is found. When a match occurs, execution begins with the statement immediately following the match. Thus, as illustrated in Figure 5.8, the value of the expression determines where in the `switch` statement execution actually begins.

Any number of `case` labels may be contained within a `switch` statement in any order. If the value of the expression does not match any of the `case` values, however, no statement is carried out unless the reserved word `default` is encountered. The reserved word `default` is optional and operates the same as the last `else` in an `if-else` chain. If the value of the expression does not match any of the `case` values, program execution begins with the statement following the word `default`.

FIGURE 5.8 **The expression determines an entry point**

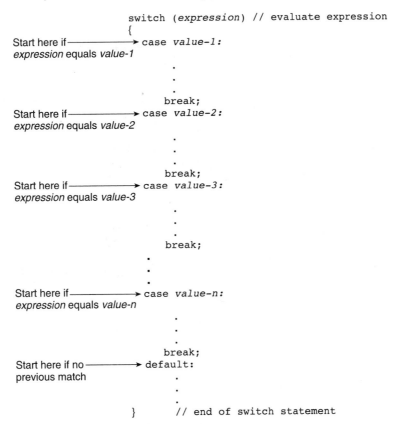

```
                        switch (expression) // evaluate expression
                        {
Start here if————————→ case value-1:
expression equals value-1
                                .
                                .
                                .
                              break;
Start here if————————→ case value-2:
expression equals value-2
                              .
                              .
                              .
                            break;
Start here if————————→ case value-3:
expression equals value-3
                            .
                            .
                            .
                          break;
                    .
                    .
                    .
Start here if————————→ case value-n:
expression equals value-n
                            .
                            .
                            .
                          break;
Start here if no————————→ default:
previous match              .
                            .
                            .
                }       // end of switch statement
```

Once an entry point has been located by the switch statement, all further case evaluations are ignored and execution continues through the end of the compound statement unless a break statement is encountered. This is the reason for the break statement, which identifies the end of a particular case and causes an immediate exit from the switch statement. Thus, just as the word case identifies possible starting points in the compound statement, the break statement determines terminating points. If the break statements are omitted, all cases following the matching case value, including the default case, are carried out.

In writing a switch statement, multiple case values can be used to refer to the same set of statements; the default label is optional. For example, consider the following:

```
switch (number)
{
  case 1:
    outMessage = "Have a Good Morning";
    break;
  case 2:
    outMessage = "Have a Happy Day";
    break;
```

(continued)

(continued)
```
  case 3:
  case 4:
  case 5:
    outMessage = "Have a Nice Evening";
}
```

If the value stored in the variable `number` is 1, the message `Have a Good Morning` is stored in the string referenced by the name `outMessage`. Similarly, if the value of `number` is 2, the message `Have a Happy Day` is assigned. Finally, if the value of `number` is 3 or 4 or 5, the last message is assigned. Because the statement to be executed for these last three cases is the same, the cases for these values can be "stacked together" as is done in the example. Notice that because there is no `default`, no string value is assigned if `number` is not one of the listed `case` values.[3] Although it is good programming practice to list `case` values in increasing order, this is not required by the `switch` statement. A `switch` statement can have any number of `case` values in any order; only the values being tested for need to be listed.

QuickTest Program 5.6 uses a `switch` statement to select a disk drive manufacturer based on a user-entered numerical code as listed in the following table:

Code	Disk Drive Manufacturer
1	3M Corporation
2	Maxell Corporation
3	Sony Corporation
4	Verbatim Corporation

QuickTest Program 5.6
```java
import javax.swing.*;
public class SelectDiskMaker
{
  public static void main(String[] args)
  {
    String s1, outMessage;
    int code;

    s1 = JOptionPane.showInputDialog("Enter a number:");
    code = Integer.parseInt(s1);

    switch (code)
    {
      case 1:
        outMessage = "3M Corporation";
        break;
      case 2:
        outMessage = "Maxell Corporation";
        break;
```

---

[3] This will result in a compiler error if the `outMessage` string is subsequently displayed within a method. Therefore, if you use this code in a program, make sure either to initialize `outMessage` or to add a default case.

```
      case 3:
        outMessage = "Sony Corporation";
        break;
      case 4:
        outMessage = "Verbatim Corporation";
        break;
      default:
        outMessage = "An invalid code was entered";
    }    // end of switch

    JOptionPane.showMessageDialog(null, outMessage,
                        "QuickTest Program 5.6",
                        JOptionPane.INFORMATION_MESSAGE);


    System.exit(0);
  } // end of main()
}   // end of class
```

In reviewing QuickTest Program 5.6, notice that each case statement, except for the default, contains a break statement. This ensures that the switch statement is exited after a matching case is found. Although a break statement can be included in the default case, it serves no purpose there.

Because character data are an integer data type, a switch statement can also be used to "switch" based on the value of a character expression. For example, assuming that choice is a character variable, the following switch statement is valid:

```
switch(choice)
{
 case 'a': case 'e': case 'i': case 'o': case 'u':
    System.out.println("The character in choice is a vowel");
    break;
 default:
    System.out.println("The character in choice is not a vowel");
  }    // end of switch statement
```

Exercises 5.4

1. Rewrite the following if-else chain using a switch statement:

```
if (letterGrade == 'A')
  System.out.println("The numerical grade is between 90 and 100");
else if (letterGrade == 'B')
  System.out.println("The numerical grade is between 80 and 89.9");
else if (letterGrade == 'C')
  System.out.println("The numerical grade is between 70 and 79.9");
else if (letterGrade == 'D');
  System.out.println("How are you going to explain this one?");
else
{
  System.out.println("Of course I had nothing to do with my grade.");
  System.out.println("\nThe professor was really off the wall.");
}
```

2. Rewrite the following `if-else` chain using a `switch` statement:

    ```
    if (bondType == 1)
    {
      inData();
      check();
    }
    else if (bondType == 2)
    {
      dates();
      leapYear();
    }
    else if (bondType == 3)
    {
      yield();
      maturity();
    }
    else if (bondType == 4)
    {
      price();
      roi();
    }
    else if (bondType == 5)
    {
      files();
      save();
    }
    else if (bondType  == 6)
    {
      retrieve();
      screen();
    }
    ```

3. Rewrite QuickTest Program 5.4 in Section 5.3 using a `switch` statement.

4. Determine why the `if-else` chain in QuickTest Program 5.5 cannot be replaced with a `switch` statement.

5. Repeat Exercise 3 in Section 5.3 using a `switch` statement instead of an `if-else` chain.

6. Write a Java program that displays a student's status based on the following codes:

Code	Student Status
1	Freshman
2	Sophomore
3	Junior
4	Senior
5	Masters Program
6	Doctoral Program

    Your program should accept the code number as a user-entered input value and based on this value display the correct student status. If an incorrect code is entered, your program should display the string `"An incorrect code was entered"`.

7. Write a Java method named `daysInMonth()` that returns the number of days is a month. The month should be passed into the method as an integer argument (i.e., January = 1, February = 2, etc.). The header line for the method is

   ```
   public static int daysInMonth(int month)
   ```

   In developing the body of the method, use a `switch` statement to implement the following algorithm:

   > *If the month integer is 1, 3, 5, 7, 8, 10, or 12*
   >   *return 31*
   > *ElseIf the month is 2*
   >   *return 28*
   > *Else*
   >   *return 30*
   > *EndIf*

8. Write a Java method named `nameOfDay()` that returns one of the strings, Sunday, Monday, Tuesday, Wednesday, Thursday, Friday, or Saturday depending on the integer value passed into the method. The correspondence is that if a 1 is passed into the method, the method returns Sunday, a 2 causes the string Monday to be returned, and so on. The header line for this method is

   ```
   public static String nameOfDay(int day)
   ```

5.5 Program Design and Development: Introduction to UML

Except for extremely simple programs, an explicit design should always be undertaken before any coding begins. This is equivalent to designing a house using blueprints and physical models before any construction takes place. Formally, the design of an application is referred to as *program modeling*. In this section, we introduce the **Unified Modeling Language (UML)**, which is a program modeling language with its own set of rules and notations. This particular modeling language has achieved wide acceptance as a primary technique for performing an object-oriented development. UML is not a part of the Java language, but a separate language with its own set of rules and diagrams for performing an object-oriented design. If used correctly, a UML design can significantly help in understanding and clarifying a program's requirements. The output of the design becomes both a set of detailed specifications that can easily be coded in an object-oriented programming language such as Java and documentation for the final program.

UML uses a set of diagrams and techniques that are reasonably easy to understand and that support all of the features required for implementing an object-oriented design. Additionally, UML is currently becoming the predominant object-oriented design procedure used by professional programmers. At its most fundamental level, designing an object-oriented application requires understanding and specifying

- What the objects in the system are
- What can happen to these objects
- When it can happen

In a UML analysis, each of these three items is addressed by a number of individual and separate views and diagrams. This situation is very similar to the design of a house, where there are a number of diagrams, all required for the final construction. For example, there must be blueprints for the physical outlay; electrical, plumbing, and heating and cooling duct diagrams; and landscape and elevation diagrams. Each of these diagrams presents a different view of the completed house, and each presents different information, all of which is required for the finished product. The same is true for the diagrams specified in a UML analysis. Specifically, UML provides nine diagram types known as class, object, state, sequence, activity, use-case, component, deployment, and collaboration diagrams.

Not all of these diagram types are required for every analysis, as some provide specific details that are only needed in more advanced situations. In this text, we present the four basic diagram types that you should be familiar with and the rules needed to create them. Once these rules are understood, it is relatively easy to read almost any UML diagram that you will encounter. The diagrams that we will concentrate on in this text are the class, object, state, and sequence types.

Class and object diagrams are extremely similar in structure, with class diagrams used to model classes and object diagrams used to model objects. Thus, both diagrams include the attributes and operations for classes and objects, respectively, and the relationship between either classes or objects. A sequence diagram describes the interactions between objects. Finally, a state diagram describes when things happen to the objects. Although each of these diagrams may contain information present in the other three diagrams, each diagram type is intended to model and emphasize a different aspect of a system. Hence, each diagram type views the same system from a different angle and highlights a particular characteristic of the system. Of the four diagrams, the most important and initially useful are class and object diagrams. These diagram types are described in this section, and state and sequence diagrams are described in Section 6.7. For many systems, the descriptions provided by class and object diagrams are more than sufficient for design and implementation purposes.

Class and Object Diagrams

Class diagrams are used to describe classes and their relationships, whereas **object diagrams** describe the specific objects and their relationships. As you already know, a class refers to a type of object, out of which many specific objects can be created, and an object always refers to a specific single item created from a class. For example, a class of books might be described as either fiction or nonfiction, of which many specific instances, or objects, exist. This book is a specific object of the class nonfiction. Thus, it is always the class that is the basic plan, or recipe, from which real objects are created. The class describes the properties and operations that each object must have to be a member of the class.

An **attribute,** as was described in Section 2.4, is a characteristic that each object in the class must have. For example, title and author are attributes of `Book` objects, while name, age, sex, weight, and height are attributes of `Person` objects. Once data values are assigned to attributes, a unique object is created. It should be noted that each and every object created from a class must also have an identity so that one object can be distinguished from another object of the same class. This is not true of a

FIGURE 5.9   **A class and object representation**

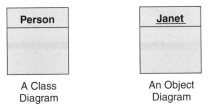

pure data value, such as the number 5, because all occurrences of this number are indistinguishable from one another.

Both classes and objects are represented using a diagram consisting of a box. For class diagrams, the class name is centered at the top of the box and is written in bold-face. For object diagrams, the class name is optional, but when it is included, it is underlined at the top of the diagram. When the class name is provided, an optional object name can precede the class name, with a mandatory colon separating the two names. Alternatively, an object diagram may contain only the object's name, under-lined, with no class name provided. For example, Figure 5.9 illustrates the representation of a `Person` class, along with one `Person` object named Janet.

The basic symbols and notations for constructing class and object diagrams are presented in Figure 5.10.

Once the attributes of a class have been identified, they are listed in a class box below the class name, separated by a line. Specific objects are shown in a similar manner, with data values provided for all attributes. For example, Figure 5.11 shows the attributes and values associated with the class `Country`. As you might expect, the attributes listed in a class diagram will become, in Java, the variables declared in a class's data declaration section.

Attributes have two qualities: *type* and *visibility*. An attribute's **type** is ether a primitive data type, such as integer, real, boolean, or character, or a class type, such as a string. Type is required in a class diagram and is indicated by following an attribute name with a mandatory colon and the data type.

Visibility defines where an attribute can be seen—that is, whether the attribute can be used in other classes or is restricted to the class defining it. If an attribute has a private visibility, it can only be used within its defining class and cannot be directly accessed by other classes. An attribute with public visibility can be used directly in any other class. In UML, public visibility is expressed by placing a plus sign (+) in front of the attribute's name within the class diagram. Similarly, placing a minus sign (−) in front of the attribute's name designates the attribute as private. Protected visibility, means that an attribute can be passed along to a derived class and is indicated by including neither a plus nor minus sign. In a class diagram, an attribute's name and type are required, and all other information is optional. Figure 5.12 illustrates the class diagram for a class named `RoomType` that contains two private attributes named length and width. Notice that we have also included default values that the class is expected to provide to its attributes.

Just as attributes are designated within a class diagram, so are operations. *Operations* are transformations that can be applied to attributes, and it is the operations that are ultimately coded as Java methods. Operation names are listed in a class box be-

FIGURE 5.10   **Basic UML symbols and notation**

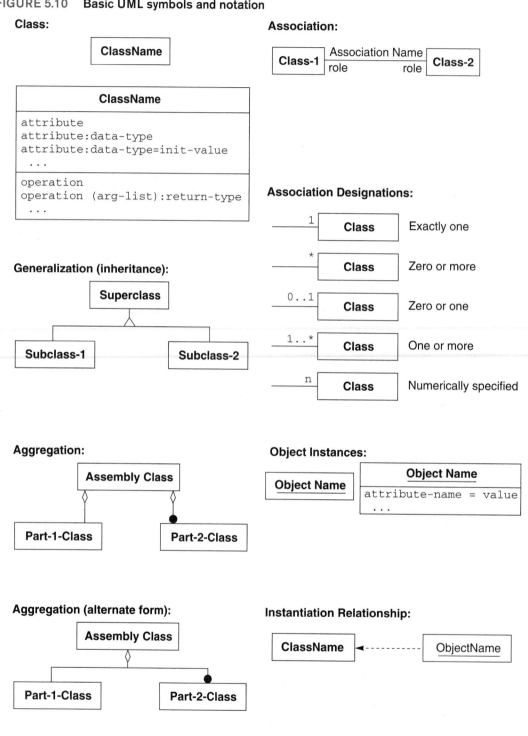

FIGURE 5.11   **Including attributes in UML class and object diagrams**

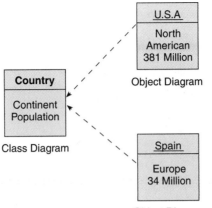

FIGURE 5.12   **A class with attributes**

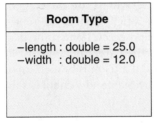

low the attributes and separated from them by a line. Figure 5.13 illustrates two class diagrams that include operations.

Relationships

Besides graphically describing classes and objects, UML class and object diagrams present the relationships existing between classes and objects. The three basic relationships are association, aggregation, and generalization.

Associations between classes are typically signified by phrases such as "is related to," "is associated with," "has a," "is employed by," "works for," and so on. This type of association is indicated by a straight line connecting either two classes or objects, where the type of association is listed above and/or below the line. For example, Figure 5.14 shows an association between a Person and a Company. As indicated, a Person is "employed by" a Company, and a Company "employs" zero or more Persons. The designation of "zero or more," which is referred to as the multiplicity of the relationship, is indicated by the notation 0..1 in the diagram. Table 5.3 lists the symbols used to indicate an association's multiplicity. These symbols can be placed either above or below the line connecting two classes or objects.

An **aggregation** is a particular type of an association where one class or object, referred to as the whole element, "consists of" or, alternatively, "is composed of," other classes or objects, which are referred to as parts. For example, a sentence

FIGURE 5.13   **Including operations in class diagrams**

Person
-name -street address -city -state -zip -age
+setName ( ) +setAddress ( ) +setAge ( ) +changeName ( ) +changeAddress ( ) +changeAge

Gas Pump
-gallonsInTank -costPerGallon
+enablePump ( ) +disablePump ( ) +setPricePerGallon ( )

consists of words, which consists of characters. Thus, characters are parts of words, which are themselves parts of sentences. This type of association is indicated by a diamond symbol. Figures 5.15, 5.16, and 5.17 illustrate three aggregation associations. Reading each of these object diagrams is much easier if you replace the diamond with either the words "consists of" of "is composed of." When the diamond symbol is hollow, as in Figure 5.15, it indicates that the parts can still exist independently of the whole to which they belong. Thus, even if a team is broken up or destroyed, its individual members can still exist. When the diamond symbol is solid, as in Figures 5.16 and 5.17, it indicates that the component parts are intrinsic members of the whole.

FIGURE 5.14   **An association**

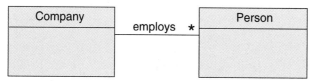

Table 5.3   **UML Association Notation**

Symbol	Relationship
1	One and only one
n	Exactly the specified number (n an integer)
0..1	Zero or one
m..n	From m to n (m and n integers)
*	From zero to any positive integer
0.*	From zero to any positive integer
1.*	From one to any positive integer

FIGURE 5.15 **A single-level aggregation**

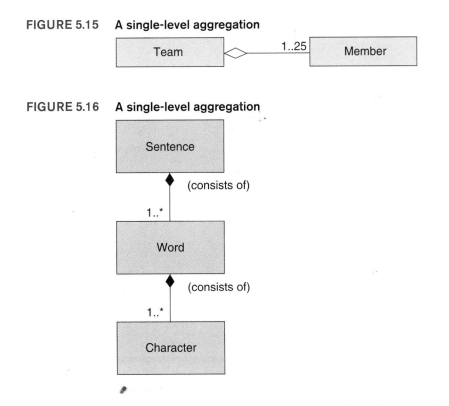

FIGURE 5.16 **A single-level aggregation**

Hence, if the central, or whole, class or object is removed, its aggregated parts will also be destroyed. Therefore, as indicted in Figure 5.16, if a sentence is removed, all of its associated words are removed. Similarly, erasing a word causes the erasure of the characters within the word. As indicated in all three figures, the diamond symbol always attaches to the whole, or central, class or object.

FIGURE 5.17 **A multilevel aggregation**

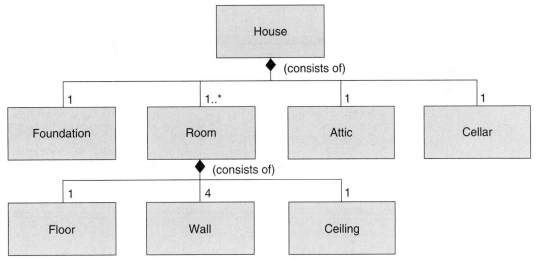

The last type of relationship that we will consider is generalization, which is more commonly referred to as inheritance. **Generalization** is a relationship between a class and a refined version of the class.

For example, a refinement of the object type Vehicle can be either a Land, Space, or Water version. In this case, Vehicle would be the base class, and Land, Space, and Water are the refined classes. Figure 5.18 shows how this generalization relationship is illustrated using an object diagram.

FIGURE 5.18 **A generalization relationship**

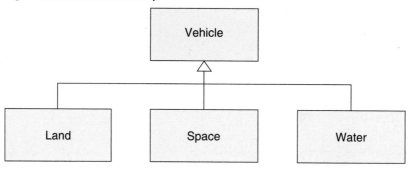

Exercises 5.5

1. Define the following terms:
   a. attribute
   b. aggregation
   c. association
   d. class
   e. class diagram
   f. generalization
   g. multiplicity
   h. program model
   i. object
   j. object diagram
   k. operation

2. Construct a class diagram for a Country class. Each Country has a capital city. The attributes of interest for each country are its population, size, main agricultural product, and main manufactured product.

3a. Construct a class diagram for a single gas tank that is connected to one or more gas pumps. The attributes of interest for the tank are its capacity, current level, and grade of gas. The attributes of interest for a pump are the number of gallons dispensed and the cost per gallon. Additionally, the pump responds to being enabled and disabled.

   b. Modify the class diagram constructed in Exercise 3a to account for the fact that a gas pump may be associated with more than one gas tank.

4. Construct a class diagram for a book consisting of one or more chapters, each of which consists of one or more sections.

5a. Construct a class diagram for a computer that consists of a monitor, keyboard, mouse, printer, and system box.

b. Modify the class diagram constructed in Exercise 5a to account for the fact that one or more monitors and keyboards may be attached to the system box and that the system may have no mouse or may have multiple mouse devices.

c. Extend the class diagram constructed for Exercise 5b to denote that the system box is composed of a CPU chip, a memory board containing zero or more RAM chips, and one case.

6. Construct a class diagram for a class of circles that is the base class to a class of spheres and a class of cylinders.

7. Construct a class diagram for a collection of cards that consists of zero or more individual cards. The collection of cards forms a base class for both a deck of cards and an individual hand of cards.

Working in Teams

8. Have the team as a whole determine a car's major subsystems, such as brakes, steering, and so forth. Then, considering these subsystems as classes, construct a class diagram for a Car class that shows the associations between classes (no attributes or operations). Assign each subsystem to individual team members. Have them determine a set of attributes and operations appropriate to their assigned subsystem. When each member has completed his or her task, modify the original class diagram to include the additional information.

9. Have the team as a whole determine a cellular telephone's major subsystems, such as keypad, antenna, and so forth. Then, considering these subsystems as classes, construct a class diagram for a Cellular class that shows the associations between classes (no attributes or operations). Assign each subsystem to individual team members. Have them determine a set of attributes and operations appropriate to their assigned subsystem. When each member has completed his or her task, modify the original class diagram to include the additional information.

5.6 **Application: A Date Class**

As a specific example of developing a class using UML, consider that we need to develop a date class. This type of class is extremely important in financial programs, where the calculations of settlement dates, accrued interest, and dividend payments all depends on date determinations. Questions such as whether a date falls on a weekend or holiday must be determined. If one day is added to today's date, does this put us into another month or a new year? How many days are between two dates, taking into account the actual number of days in each month? Is this a leap year, where February has 29 days instead of the usual 28? As this is a typical situation faced by most programmers, where the application may not be totally familiar, let us see how we might go about designing and developing it.

FIGURE 5.19   Initial **Date** class diagram

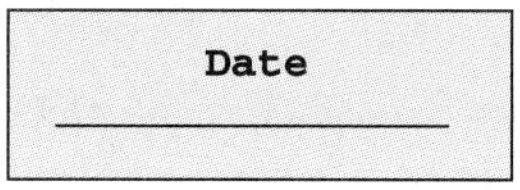

The first stage in any design is to identify the type of objects we will be dealing with. In this situation, the object is clear — it is a date. Assuming that we name our class `Date`, we can now draw the initial class diagram shown in Figure 5.19.

The next step is to decide how we will internally represent each `Date` object that will be constructed from the `Date` class. At a practical level, this means identifying the attributes of a `Date` object. Although there are a number of ways to represent a date (see Exercise 3), we will store a date using three integers: one for the month, day, and year, respectively. We will also store the year as a four-digit number. Thus, for example, we will store the year 1999 as 1999 and not as 99. Making sure to store all years with their correct century designation will eliminate a multitude of problems that can crop up if only the last two digits, such as 99, are stored. For example, the number of years between 2005 and 1999 can be quickly calculated as $2005 - 1999 = $ 6 years, but this same answer is not so easily obtained if only the year values 05 and 99 are used. In addition, we are sure of what the year 2005 refers to, but a two-digit value such as 05 could refer to either 1905 or 2005. So at this stage, our initial class diagram can be refined to that shown in Figure 5.20. Notice that we have also preceded each attribute name with a minus sign (-) to indicate that these attributes are to be private. This is in keeping with the basic convention that, unless there is some overriding reason for making an attribute public, all attributes are private. To ensure that we do not later forget that each year will be stored as a four-digit value, we have included an object diagram with specific values (Figure 5.21).

Notice that, even at this early stage, we can directly translate the `Date` class into Java code as follows:

```
public class Date
{
  // class variable declaration section
  private int month;
  private int day;
  private int year;
}
```

Having identified the class's attributes (and these can be modified or added to as new information becomes available), we now need to identify an initial set of operations. Table 5.4 lists the operations that we initially determine appropriate for our `Date` class.

FIGURE 5.20   First refinement: **Date** class diagram

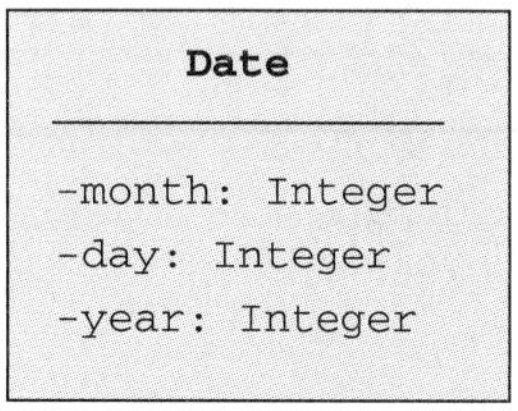

```
        Date
  ─────────────────
  -month: Integer
  -day:  Integer
  -year: Integer
```

FIGURE 5.21   **A Date object diagram**

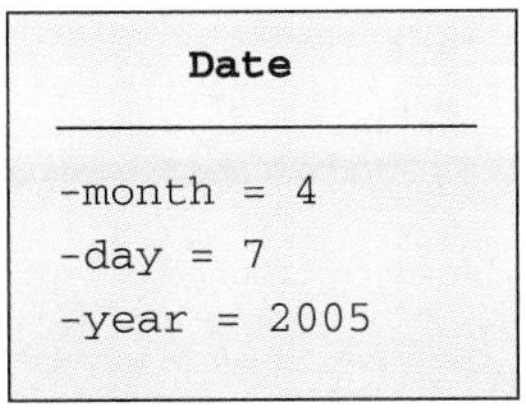

```
         Date
───────────────────────
-month = 4
-day = 7
-year = 2005
```

Table 5.4   **Required Operations for the Date Class**

Operation	Returned Value	Comments
Initialize	None	Constructor
Modify	None	Mutator
Display	None	Accessor
Is the year a leap year	Boolean	Requires a comparison
Is the date a weekday	Boolean	Requires a comparison
Is the day a holiday	Boolean	Requires a comparison and file access of holidays
Are two dates the same	Boolean	Requires a comparison
Is one date before a second date	Boolean	Requires a comparison
Is one date after a second date	Boolean	Requires a comparison
Determine the day of the week	Integer	Requires a comparison
Determine next day's date	Date	Requires a comparison
Determine prior day's date	Date	Requires a comparison
Day difference between two dates	Integer	Requires a comparison

As can be seen in Table 5.4, the majority of the operations require comparisons. Because we have not yet presented the Java statements required for accessing a file (see Chapter 12), we will not be able to code the operation for determining if a date is a holiday or not. Nonetheless, we can include the requirement for this method in our refinement of the Date class diagram (Figure 5.22). In fact, this is one of the useful features provided in a UML analysis; it alerts us to the capabilities we will need to eventually develop a completed class. Notice also that by preceding all method names with a +, we have indicated that these methods will have public visibility.

The first four methods in Figure 5.22 consist of constructor, accessor, and mutator methods. As we have seen, these methods form the basis for almost every class we will develop. Program 5.7 presents a basic Date class that contains these four methods.

Program 5.7

```java
public class Date
{
   // class variable declaration section
   private int month;
   private int day;
   private int year;
```

(continued)

(continued)

```
// class method definition section
public Date()    // this is a constructor method because it has the same
{          // name as the class
  month = 7;
  day = 4;
  year = 2005;
  System.out.println("From the default constructor:"
                + "\n  Created a new Date object with data values"
                + "\n    month = " + month + "  day = " + day
                + "  year = " + year + '\n');
}


public Date(int mm, int dd, int yyyy)  // this is an overloaded constructor
{
  month = mm;
  day = dd;
  year = yyyy;
  System.out.println("From the overloaded constructor:"
                + "\n  Created a new Date object with data values"
                + "\n    month = " + month + "  day = " + day
                + "  year = " + year + '\n');
}


public void setDate(int mm, int dd, int yyyy)
{
  month = mm;
  day = dd;
  year = yyyy;
}


public void showDate()
{
  DecimalFormat df = new DecimalFormat("00");

  System.out.println("The date is " + df.format(month)
          + '/' + df.format(day) + '/'
          + df.format(year % 100)); // extract the last 2 year digits
}
}
```

Explanation of the Basic `Date` Class

Although you should be comfortable understanding the constructor, accessor, and mutator methods provided in Program 5.7's basic `Date` class, we will take a moment to analyze them.

The default constructor, repeated below for convenience, initializes the instance variables named `month`, `day`, and `year` with the values 7, 4, and 2005, respectively. In addition, a `println()` method has been included to display the initialized values.

FIGURE 5.22 **Second refinement: Date class diagram**

```
              Date
    ─────────────────────────
    -month: Integer
    -day: Integer
    -year: Integer
    ─────────────────────────
    +Date()
    =Date(month, day, year)
    +setDate(month, day, year)
    +showDate()
    +isLeapYr()
    +isWeekDay()
    +isHoliday()
    +isEqual()
    +isBefore()
    +isAfter()
    +dayOfWeek()
    +nextDay()
    +priorDay()
    +dayDifference()
```

```
public Date()    // this is a constructor method because it has the same
{          // name as the class
  month = 7;
  day = 4;
  year = 2005;
  System.out.println("From the default constructor:"
                   + "\n  Created a new Date object with data values"
                   + "\n    month = " + month + "  day = " + day
                   + "  year = " + year + '\n');
}
```

Instead of always accepting the values provided by the default constructor, the second constructor provides the capability of initializing a Date object with values selected at the time of an object's creation. This is made possible by first declaring three integer parameters in its header line. The code for this constructor is

```
public Date(int mm, int dd, int yyyy)  // this is an overloaded constructor
{
  month = mm;
  day = dd;
  year = yyyy;
  System.out.println("From the overloaded constructor:"
                   + "\n  Created a new Date object with data values"
                   + "\n    month = " + month + "  day = " + day
                   + "  year = " + year + '\n');
}
```

Here the overloaded constructor is declared as receiving three integer arguments, which are then used to initialize the `month`, `day`, and `year` data members. As with the default constructor, a `println()` method has been included to display the initialized values.

The next method header line

```
public void setDate(int mm, int dd, int yyyy)
```

defines this as the `setDate()` method. This mutator method is almost identical to the overloaded constructor. It expects three integer parameters, `mm`, `dd`, and `yyyy`, and assigns the data members `month`, `day`, and `year` with the values of its parameters, respectively.

Finally, the last method header line in the definition section defines an accessor method named `showDate()`. This method has no parameters and returns no value. The body of this method, however, needs a little more explanation.

Although we have chosen to internally store all years as four-digit values that retain century information, users are accustomed to seeing dates with the year represented as a two-digit value, such as 12/15/99. To display the last two digits of the year value, the expression `year % 100` is initially used. For example, if the year is 1999, the expression `1999 % 100` yields the value 99, and if the year is 2001, the expression `2001 % 100` yields the value 1. Notice that if we had used an assignment such as `year = year % 100;` we would actually be altering the stored value of `year` to correspond to the last one or two digits of the year. Since we want to retain the year as a four-digit number, we must be careful only to manipulate the displayed value using the expression `year % 100`. The formatting ensures that the displayed values correspond to conventionally accepted dates. For example, a date such as December 9, 2002, will appear as `12/09/02` and not as `12/9/2`.

Using the Basic `Date` Class

To see how our basic `Date` class can be used within the context of a complete program, consider Program 5.8. The class in this program is named `UseDate`, which constructs and manipulates objects of the `Date` class.

Program 5.8

```
public class UseDate
{
  public static void main(String [] args)
  {
    Date firstDate;   // declare an object
    Date secondDate;   // declare an object

    firstDate = new Date(); // create a Date object using the default constructor
    secondDate = new Date(5,1,2006); // create another Date object
      // display the Date objects
    firstDate.showDate();
    secondDate.showDate();
      // rest and display one Date
    secondDate.setDate(12,25,2007);
    secondDate.showDate();
  }
}
```

The output displayed by Program 5.8 is

```
From the default constructor:
  Created a new Date object with data values
    month = 7  day = 4  year = 2005

From the overloaded constructor:
  Created a new Date object with data values
    month = 5  day = 1  year = 2006


The date is 7/4/05
The date is 5/1/06
The date is 12/25/07
```

Let us see how this output is produced. Two objects are created in Program 5.8's `main()` method. The first object, which is referenced by the variable named `firstDate`, is initialized using the default constructor. The second object, which is initialized with the arguments 5, 1, and 2006, uses the second, overloaded, constructor. The compiler knows to use this second constructor because three integer arguments are specified, and there is only one constructor that accepts three integer arguments. Notice that a compiler error would occur if the two constructors had the same number and types of parameters because the compiler would not be able to determine which constructor to use.

It is also worth noting that objects have the same relationship to classes as variables do to Java's built-in data types. For example, in a declaration, such as

```
    int FirstNumber;
```

`FirstNumber` is said to be a variable, while in Program 5.8's declaration

```
    Date firstDate;
```

`firstDate` is said to be a reference variable. A variable for a built-in data type contains an actual data value, whereas a reference variable will either store the memory address of an object or a `null` address if no object is referenced.

The first date object, named `firstDate` in Program 5.8, is created by the statement `firstDate = new Date()`. Because we have included a `println()` method in this constructor, the call to it produces the initial output

```
From the default constructor:
  Created a new Date object with data values
    month = 7  day = 4  year = 2005
```

For our purposes, this display verifies that the default constructor was in fact called. The real work done by the default constructor `Date()` is to assign the values 7, 4, and 2005 to the created object's `month`, `day`, and `year` variables, respectively. In a similar manner, when the object named `secondDate` is defined, the overloaded constructor is called (again, although `secondDate` is referred to as an object, it is important to realize that `secondDate` is really a reference to the object and not the object itself), resulting in the initialization of `secondDate`'s data members with `month`, `day`, and `year` values of 5, 1, and 2006, respectively. Because a `println()` method was included in the overloaded constructor, the following output is produced:

```
From the overloaded constructor:
  Created a new Date object with data values
    month = 5  day = 1  year = 2006
```

PROGRAMMING NOTE

User Interfaces, Definitions, and Information Hiding

The terms *user interface* and *definition* are used extensively in the object-oriented programming literature. Each of these terms can be equated to specific parts of a class's declaration and definition sections.

A user interface consists of a class's public member methods' header lines and any supporting comments. Thus, the interface should be all that is required to tell a programmer how to use the class.

The definition consists of both the class's definition section, which consists of both private and public member definitions, and the class's private data members that are contained in a class declaration section.

The definition is the essential means of providing information hiding. In its most general context, *information hiding* refers to the principle that *how* a class is internally constructed is not relevant to any programmer who wishes to use the class. That is, the definition can and should be hidden from all class users precisely to ensure that the class is not altered or compromised in any way. All that a programmer needs to know to use the class correctly should be provided by the interface.

The next two statements in Program 5.8 call the showDate() method to operate on the firstDate and secondDate objects. The first call results in the display of firstDate's data values, and the second call results in the display of secondDate's data values, producing the output

```
The date is 7/4/05
The date is 5/1/06
```

The statement secondDate.setDate(12,25,2007); then calls the setDate() mutator method to operate on the secondDate object, which uses the argument values 12, 25, 2007 to reset secondDate's data members.

Finally, the last statement secondDate.showDate(); causes the values in the secondDate object to once again be displayed. Because these values were reset, the output becomes

```
The date is 12/25/07
```

Notice that a statement such as System.out.println(secondDate); *cannot* be used because the println() method does not know how to handle an object of class Date. Instead, we have supplied our class with an accessor method that can be used to display an object's internal values.

Simplifying the Code

Assuming that you understand what each Date class method accomplishes, the first modification that should be made is to remove the printouts from the constructors and setDate() methods. The next modification is to have the two constructors call the setDate() method to initialize all of the instance variables, rather than repeating each sequence of three assignment statements within these methods. These modifications result in the simpler listing presented as Program 5.7a.

Program 5.7a

```java
import java.text.*;  // needed for formatting
public class Date
{
  // class variable declaration section
  private int month;
  private int day;
  private int year;

  // class method definition section
  public Date()   // this is a constructor method because it has the same
  {         // name as the class
    setDate(7, 4, 2005);
  }

  public Date(int mm, int dd, int yyyy)  // this is an overloaded constructor
  {
    setDate(mm, dd, yyyy);
  }

  public void setDate(int mm, int dd, int yyyy)
  {
    month = mm;
    day = dd;
    year = yyyy;
  }

  public void showDate()
  {
    DecimalFormat df = new DecimalFormat("00");

    System.out.println("The date is " + df.format(month)
            + '/' + df.format(day) + '/'
            + df.format(year % 100)); // extract the last 2 year digits

  }
}
```

Adding Class Methods

Having constructed and tested our basic Date class, we can now begin to add the class methods specified in Figure 5.22. Specifically, we will implement the two methods named isLeapYear() and dayOfWeek() and leave the remaining methods for you to implement in the Exercises. We begin with the isLeapYear() method.

A leap year is any year that is evenly divisible by 4 but not evenly divisible by 100, with the exception that all years evenly divisible by 400 are leap years. For example, the year 1996 was a leap year because it is evenly divisible by 4 and not evenly divisible by 100. The year 2000 was a leap year because it is evenly divisible by 400. Thus, the algorithm for determining a leap year is

Leap Year Algorithm
If the year is divisible by 4 with a remainder of 0 AND the year is divisible by 100
 with a nonzero remainder
OR the year is divisible by 400 with no remainder
 then the year is a leap year
Else
 the year is not a leap year
EndIf

This algorithm can be coded as a Java method as follows:

```java
public boolean isLeapYear()
{
  if ( (year % 4 == 0 && year % 100 != 0) || (year % 400 == 0) )
    return true;   // is a leap year
  else
    return false;  // is not a leap year
}
```

There are two items to notice in this code. First, notice that the AND operation (`&&`) and the OR operation (`||`) correspond to the AND and OR specified in the algorithm. Next, it is not necessary for you to personally develop each algorithm that you code. In this case, the algorithm is provided, and your job as a Java programmer is to understand that you require an algorithm that is capable of determining if a year is a leap year and then to correctly code the algorithm.

Now let us code the `dayOfWeek()` method. To do this, we require an algorithm that can determine the day of the week for any date that is provided. Again, you can either create your own algorithm or find one that appropriately solves the required task. In this case, a commonly used algorithm for determining the day of the week, known as **Zeller's algorithm**, is the following:

Zeller's Algorithm
 If the month is less than 3
  month = month + 12
  year = year − 1
 EndIf
 Set century = int(year / 100)
 Set year = year % 100
 Set T = day + int(26*(month + 1) / 10) + year + int(year / 4) + int(century
  / 4) − 2 * century
 Set dd = T % 7
 If dd is less than 0
  Set dd = dd + 7
 EndIf

Using this algorithm, the variable `dd` will have a value of 0 if the date is a Saturday, 1 if the date is a Sunday, 2 if a Monday, and so on. Java code that implements this algorithm is

```java
/* This method acts on a Date object to determine the Date's day of the week
   Parameters: none
   Return value: an integer representing a day of the week, as follows
```

```
       0 if the date is a Saturday,
       1 if the date is a Sunday,
       2 if a Monday, and so on, with a 6 being a Friday.
*/
public int dayOfWeek()
{
  int T, mm, dd, yy, cc;

  mm = month;
  yy = year;
  if (mm < 3)
  {
    mm = mm + 12;
    yy = yy - 1;
  }
  cc = (int)(yy/100);
  yy = yy % 100;
  T = day + (int)(26 * (mm + 1)/10) + yy;
  T = T + (int)(yy/4) + (int)(cc/4) - 2 * cc;
  dd = T % 7;
  if (dd < 0) dd = dd + 7;;
  return dd;
}
```

We leave it as an Exercise for you to include the `isLeapYear()` and `dayOfWeek()` methods into Program 5.7's `Date` class and then to verify that both methods work correctly.

Exercises 5.6

1. List any additional operations that you think could be included in Figure 5.22 (Tip: Consider additional mutator and accessor operations.)

2. List a set of operations that are appropriate for a complex-number class that consists of two attributes: a real double-precision value and an imaginary double-precision value.

3. Enter and run Program 5.8.

4a. Include the `isLeapYear()`,`dayOfWeek()`, and `isWeekDay()` methods into Program 5.7's `Date` class and then modify Program 5.8 to test these methods. For testing purposes, use the fact that the years 1996 and 2004 are both leap years, that March 12, 2003, was a Wednesday, and March 15, 2003, was a Saturday.

b. Use the updated `Date` class written for Exercise 4a to determine the day of the week you were born and whether this was a weekday or not.

5. Rewrite Program 5.8 to include user-entered input for the day, month, and year. For this program, use the `readInt()` method contained within the `ID` class (Program 4-7, provided in Section 4.4).

6a. Add another member method named `convert()` to the `Date` class used in Program 5.8 that does the following: The method should access the `month`, `year`, and `day` data members and return a long integer that is calculated as `year * 10000 + month *`

100 + day. For example, if the date is 4/1/2002, the returned value is 20020401 (dates in this form are useful when performing sorts because placing the numbers in numerical order automatically places the corresponding dates in chronological order).

b. Include the modified Date class constructed for Exercise 6a in a complete program that tests the convert() method.

7. Add a method named isWeekday() to Program 5.7's Date class that returns a boolean value of true if the date is a weekday; otherwise, it should return a boolean value of false. The method should call dayOfWeek() and then use the returned integer value to determine if the day is a weekday. A weekday is any day between 2 and 6, inclusive, which correspond to the days Monday through Friday. (Tip: Declare the method as static with a single Date object parameter. Use the parameter to call dayOfWeek() and an if-else statement to determine if the returned value corresponds to a weekday.)

8. Add a method named nameOfDay() to Program 5.7's Date class that returns the name of the day of week as a string. Thus, one of the strings Sunday, Monday, Tuesday, Wednesday, Thursday, Friday, or Saturday should be returned by the method. The method should call dayOfWeek() and then use the returned integer value to determine the name of the day of the week. (Tip: Declare the method as static with a single Date object parameter. Use the Date object as an argument to call dayOfWeek() and a switch statement to translate the returned value into a string corresponding to the day's name.)

9. Modify Program 5.7 so that the only instance variable of the class is a long integer named yyyymmdd. Do this by substituting the declaration

    ```
    private long yyyymmdd;
    ```

    for the existing declarations

    ```
    private int month;
    private int day;
    private int year;
    ```

    Once this is done, rewrite each class method to correctly initialize the single class data member.

10. Modify Program 5.7's Date class to include an isLarger() method. This method should compare two Date objects and return a boolean value of true if the first date is larger than the second; otherwise, it should return a value of false. The header for this method should be public int isLarger(Date second) and should be written according to the following algorithm:

    Comparison Method
    Accept one date as the current object being evaluated and a second date as an argument
    Determine the later date using the following procedure:
    Convert each date into a long integer value having the form yyyymmdd. This can be accomplished by using the algorithm described in Exercise 6.
    Compare the corresponding integers for each date.
    If the first date's long integer value is larger than the second date's long integer value, return true; otherwise, return false

11. Modify Program 5.7's Date class to include an isEqual() method. This method should compare two Date objects and return a Boolean value of true if the two dates are equal. The header for this method should be public int isEqual(Date second).

12. Modify Program 5.7's `Date` class to include a `nextDay()` method that increments a date by one day. Test your method to ensure that it correctly increments days into a new month and into a new year.

13. Modify Program 5.7's `Date` class to include a `priorDay()` method that decrements a date by one day. Test your method to ensure that it correctly decrements days into a prior month and into a prior year.

14a. Construct a class named `Rectangle` that has floating-point data members named `length` and `width`. The class should have a member method named `perimeter()` and `area()` to calculate the perimeter and area of a rectangle, a member method named `getData()` to set a rectangle's length and width, and a member method named `showData()` to display a rectangle's length, width, perimeter, and area.

b. Include the `Rectangle` class constructed in Exercise 13a within a working Java program.

15. Construct a class named `Light` that simulates a traffic light. The class should contain a single instance variable having a data type of String. When a new `Light` object is created, its initial color should be red. Additionally, there should be a method that can change the state of a `Light` object and an accessor method that returns the color currently stored in a `Light` object's instance variable.

16a. Construct a class definition that can be used to represent an employee of a company. Each employee is defined by an integer ID number, a floating-point pay rate, and the maximum number of hours the employee should work each week. The services provided by the class should be the ability to enter data for a new employee, the ability to change data for a new employee, and the ability to display the existing data for a new employee.

b. Include the class definition created for Exercise 16a in a working Java program that asks the user to enter data for three employees and displays the entered data.

5.7 Common Programming Errors

The following are programming errors that can be made using Java's selection statements:

1. Assuming the `if-else` statement is selecting an incorrect choice when the problem is really the values being tested. This is a typical debugging problem in which the programmer mistakenly concentrates on the tested condition as the source of the problem rather than the values being tested. For example, assume that the following correct `if-else` statement is part of your program:

```
if (code == 1)
{
  contemp = (5.0/9.0) * (intemp - 32.0);
  System.out.println("Conversion to Celsius was done");
}
else
{
  contemp = (9.0/5.0) * intemp + 32.0;
  System.out.println("Conversion to Fahrenheit was done");
}
```

This statement always displays `Conversion to Celsius was done` when the variable code contains a 1. Therefore, if this message is displayed when you believe the code does not contain 1, an investigation of code's value is called for. As a general rule, whenever a selection statement does not act as you think it should, make sure to test your assumptions about the values assigned to the tested variables by displaying their values. If an unanticipated value is displayed, you have at least isolated the source of the problem to the variables themselves rather than the structure of the `if-else` statement. From there, you will have to determine where and how the incorrect value was obtained.

2. Using nested `if` statements without including braces to clearly indicate the desired structure. Without braces, the compiler defaults to pairing `elses` with the closest unpaired `ifs`, which sometimes destroys the original intent of the selection statement. To avoid this problem and to create code that is readily adaptable to change, it is useful to write all `if-else` statements as compound statements in the form

```
if (expression)
{
    one or more statements in here
}
else
{
    one or more statements in here
}
```

By using this form, no matter how many statements are added later, the original integrity and intent of the `if` statement are maintained.

3. Inadvertently using the assignment operator = in place of the relational operator == when comparing Boolean data. For example, assuming `btrue` and `bfalse` are Boolean variables with the values `true` and `false`, respectively, the statement `if(bfalse = btrue)` is the same as `if(true)`. This is because the assignment statement does not compare the values in the variables but assigns the value of `btrue` to `bfalse`. This particular error tends to be extremely rare in practice because Boolean data are typically only compared in advanced engineering applications. This error cannot be made with non-Boolean data because it results in a non-Boolean value that is caught by the compiler. For example, if a and b are integer variables and you inadvertently use the statement `if(a = b)` instead of `if(a == b)`, the compiler provides the error message `Can't convert int to Boolean`.

4. Forgetting to use a `break` statement to close off a `case` within a `switch` statement. This can be especially troubling when cases are added later. For example, consider the following statement:

```
switch(code)
{
    case 1: price = 2.00;
            break;
    case 2: price = 2.50;
}
```

Here not having a `break` for the last `case` does not immediately cause any problem. It is, however, a potential source of error later if a `case` is subsequently added. With the addition of another `case`, a `break` is necessary to prevent the new `case` 3 from always overriding `case` 2. For example, consider the following code without the `break`:

```
switch(code)
    {
      case 1: price = 2.00;
              break;
      case 2: price = 2.50;
      case 3: price = 3.00;
    }
```

Because there is no `break` between `cases` 2 and 3, whenever `case` 2 is selected the code automatically "falls through" and also executes the `price` assignment for `case` 3. To prevent this error, it is good programming practice to terminate all cases with a `break` (except where the stacking of `cases` is consciously desired).

5.8 Chapter Review

KEY TERMS

aggregation
association
class diagram
compound statement
condition
`false` condition
generalization

`if-else` chain
`if-else` statement
nested `if` statements
object diagram
one-way selection
simple relational
   expression

`switch` statement
`true` condition
type
Unified Modeling
   Language (UML)
visibility

SUMMARY

1. Relational expressions, which are referred to as conditions, are used to compare operands. If a condition is true, the value of the expression is the Boolean value `true`. If the expression is false, it has a Boolean value of `false`. Relational expressions are created by the following relational operators:

Relational Operator	Meaning	Example
<	less than	age < 30
>	greater than	height > 6.2
<=	less than or equal to	taxable <= 20000
>=	greater than or equal to	temp >= 98.6
==	equal to	grade == 100
!=	not equal to	number != 250

2. More complex conditions can be constructed from relational expressions using Java's logical operators, && (AND), || (OR), and ! (NOT).

3. `if-else` statements are used to select between two alternative statements based on the value of a relational or logical expression. The most common form of an `if-else` statement is

```
  if (condition)
      statement1;
    else
      statement2;
```

This is a two-way selection statement. If the *condition* has a Boolean `true` value, `statement1` is executed; otherwise, `statement2` is executed.

4. `if-else` statements can contain other `if-else` statements. In the absence of braces, each `else` is associated with the closest unpaired `if`.

5. The `if-else` chain is a multiway selection statement having the general form

```
if (condition1)
   statement1;
else if (condition2)
   statement2;
else if (condition3)
   statement3;

          .

          .

          .

else if (conditionm)
   statementm;
else
   statementn;
```

Each condition is evaluated in the order it appears in the chain. Once a condition having a Boolean `true` value is detected, only the statement between that condition and the next `else if` or `else` is executed, and no further conditions are tested. The final `else` is optional, and the statement corresponding to the final `else` is only executed if none of the previous conditions were `true`.

6. A compound statement consists of any number of individual statements enclosed within the brace pair `{` and `}`. Compound statements are treated as a single block and can be used anywhere a single statement is called for.

7. The `switch` statement is a multiway selection statement. The general syntax of a `switch` statement is

```
switch (expression)
{                                  // start of compound statement
  case value-1:  <----------  terminated with a colon
    statement1;
    statement2;
        .

        .

    break;
  case value-2:  <----------  terminated with a colon
    statementm;
    statementn;
        .

        .

    break;
        .

        .

  case value-n:  <----------  terminated with a colon
    statementw;
```

```
   statementx;
         .
         .
   break;
 default:  <-------------    terminated with a colon
   statementaa;
   statementbb;
         .
         .
} // end of switch and compound statement
```

For this statement, the value of an integer expression is compared to a number of integer constants, character constants, or expressions containing only constants and operators. Program execution is transferred to the first matching case and continues through the end of the switch statement unless an optional break statement is encountered. The cases in a switch statement can appear in any order, and an optional default case can be included. The default case is executed if none of the other cases is matched.

5.9   Chapter Supplement: Program Testing

In theory, a comprehensive set of test runs would reveal all logic errors and ensure that a program will work correctly for any and all combinations of input and computed data. In practice, this requires checking all possible combinations of statement executions. Due to the time and effort required, this is an impossible goal except for extremely simple programs. To see why, we can consider QuickTest Program 5.9.

QuickTest Program 5.9

```java
import java.io.*;   // needed to access input stream classes
public class CountPaths
{
  public static void main(String[] args)
  throws java.io.IOException
  {
    String s1, outMessage;
    int  num;

      // set up the basic input stream
      // needed for conversion capabilities
    InputStreamReader isr = new InputStreamReader(System.in);
      // needed to use readLine()
    BufferedReader br = new BufferedReader(isr);



    System.out.print("Enter a number: ");
    s1 = br.readLine();
    num = Integer.parseInt(s1);
```

(continued)

(continued)
```
    if (num == 5)
       System.out.println("Bingo!");
    else
       System.out.println("Bongo!");
  }
}
```

QuickTest Program 5.9 has two paths that can be traversed from when the program begins running to when the program reaches its last closing brace. The first path, which is executed when the input number is 5, is in the sequence

```
num = Integer.parseInt(s1);
       System.out.println("Bingo!");
```

The second path, which is executed whenever any number other than 5 is input, includes the sequence of instructions

```
num = Integer.parseInt(s1);
System.out.println("Bongo!");
```

Testing each possible path through QuickTest Program 5.9 requires two runs of the program, with a judicious selection of test input data to ensure that both paths of the `if` statement are exercised. The addition of one more `if` statement in the program increases the number of possible execution paths by a factor of 2 and requires four (2^2) runs of the program for complete testing. Similarly, two additional `if` statements increase the number of paths by a factor of 4 and require eight (2^3) runs for complete testing, and three additional `if` statements would produce a program that requires sixteen (2^4) test runs.

Now consider a modestly sized application program consisting of only 10 methods, with each method containing five `if` statements. Assuming the methods are always called in the same sequence, there are 32 possible paths through each method (2 raised to the fifth power) and more than 1,000,000,000,000,000 (2 raised to the fiftieth power) possible paths through the complete program (all methods executed in sequence). The time needed to create individual test data to exercise each path and the actual computer run time required to check each path make the complete testing of such a program impossible to achieve.

The inability to fully test all combinations of statement execution sequences has led to the programming proverb, "There is no error-free program." It has also led to the realization that any testing that is done should be well thought out to maximize the possibility of locating errors. At a minimum, test data should include appropriate values for input values, invalid input values that the program should reject, and limiting values that are checked by selection statements within the program.

6 Repetition

This chapter presents Java statements that construct repeating sections of code. More commonly, a section of code that is repeated is referred to as a loop because after the last statement in the code is executed the program branches or loops back to the first statement and starts another repetition through the code. Each repetition is also referred to as an iteration or pass through the loop.

Additionally, examples of situations requiring a repetition capability are presented. They include continual checking of user data entries until an acceptable entry, such as a valid password, is entered, counting and accumulating running totals, and accepting input data and recalculating output values that only stop upon entry of a predetermined sentinel value.

6.1 Basic Loop Structures

The real power of a program is realized when the same type of operation must be made over and over. **Repetition statements** provide the capability to type a set of instructions once and then have this same set of instructions repeated continuously until some preset condition is met.

Constructing a repeating section of code requires that four elements be present. The first necessary element is a repetition statement. This repetition statement both defines the boundaries containing the repeating section of code and controls whether the code will be executed or not. In general, there are three different forms of repetition structures, all of which are provided in Java.

1. `while` structure
2. `for` structure
3. `do-while` structure

Each of these structures requires a condition that must be evaluated, which is the second required element for constructing repeating sections of code. Valid conditions are identical to those used in selection statements. If the condition is true, the code is executed; otherwise, it is not.

The third required element is a statement that initially sets the condition. This statement must always be placed before the condition is first evaluated to ensure correct loop execution the first time the condition is evaluated.

Finally, there must be a statement within the repeating section of code that allows the condition to become false. This is necessary to ensure that, at some point, the repetitions stop. The complete section of code that is repeated is commonly referred to as a *loop*.

Pretest and Posttest Loops

The condition being tested can be evaluated at either the beginning or the end of the repeating section of code. Figure 6.1 illustrates the case where the test occurs at the beginning of the loop. This type of loop is referred to as a **pretest loop** because the condition is tested before any statements within the loop are executed. If the condition is true, the executable statements within the loop are executed. If the initial value of the condition is false, the executable statements within the loop are never executed at all and control transfers to the first statement after the loop. To avoid infinite repetitions, the condition must be updated within the loop. Pretest loops are also referred to as **entrance controlled loops.** Both the `while` and `for` loop structures are examples of such loops.

A loop that evaluates a condition at the end of the repeating section of code, as illustrated in Figure 6.2, is referred to as a **posttest loop** or **exit controlled loop.** These loops always execute the loop statements at least once before the condition is tested. Since the executable statements within the loop are continually executed until the condition becomes false, there always must be a statement within the loop that updates the condition and permits it to become false. The `do-while` construct is an example of a posttest loop.

FIGURE 6.1   **A pretest loop**

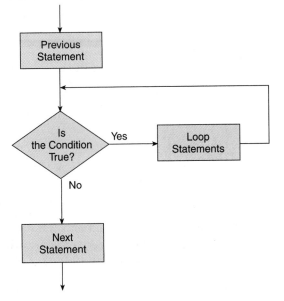

FIGURE 6.2   **A posttest loop**

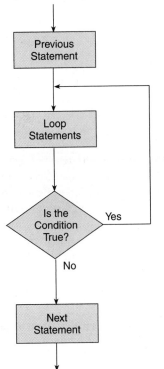

Fixed-Count Versus Variable-Condition Loops

In addition to where the condition is tested (pretest or posttest), repeating sections of code are also classified as to the type of condition being tested. In a **fixed-count loop**, the condition is used to keep track of how many repetitions have occurred. For example, we might want to produce a table of 10 numbers, including their squares and cubes, or a fixed design such as

```
* * * * * * * * * * * * * * * * * * * * * * * *
* * * * * * * * * * * * * * * * * * * * * * * *
* * * * * * * * * * * * * * * * * * * * * * * *
* * * * * * * * * * * * * * * * * * * * * * * *
```

In each of these cases, a fixed number of calculations are performed or a fixed number of lines are printed, at which point the repeating section of code is exited. All of Java's repetition statements can be used to produce fixed count loops.

In many situations, the exact number of repetitions is not known in advance or the items are too numerous to count beforehand. For example, when entering a large amount of market research data, we might not want to take the time to count the number of actual data items to be entered. In cases like this, a variable-condition loop is used. In a **variable-condition loop**, the tested condition does not depend on a count being achieved but rather on a variable that can change interactively with each pass through the loop. When a specified value is encountered, regardless of how many iterations have occurred, repetitions stop. All of Java's repetition statements can be used to create variable-condition loops.[1] In this chapter we will encounter examples of both fixed-count and variable-condition loops.

6.2 The `while` Statement

The `while` statement is a general repetition statement that can be used in a variety of programming situations. The general form of the `while` statement is

```
while (condition)
  statement;
```

The *condition* within the parentheses is evaluated in exactly the same manner as a condition in an `if-else` statement; the difference is how the condition is used. As we have seen, when the condition is true in an `if-else` statement, the statement following the condition is executed once. In a `while` statement, the statement following the condition is executed repeatedly as long as the condition remains true. This naturally means that somewhere in the `while` statement there must be a statement that changes the value of the tested condition to false. As we will see, this is indeed the case. For now, however, considering just the condition and the statement

---

[1] In this, Java differs from most other languages such as BASIC, Fortran, and Pascal. In each of these languages, the `for` structure (which is implemented using a `DO` statement in Fortran) can only be used to produce fixed-count loops. Java's `for` structure, as we will see shortly, is virtually interchangeable with its `while` structure.

A BIT OF BACKGROUND

Comptometer Arithmetic

In the early 1900s, mechanical calculators, called *Comptometers*, performed only addition. Since multiplication is only a quick method of addition (e.g., 5 times 4 is really 5 added 4 times), producing multiplication results presented no problems; it was obtained using repeated additions. Subtraction and division, however, initally did pose a problem. Clever accountants soon discovered that subtraction and division were possible. Subtraction was accomplished by writing the nine's complement on each numeric key. That is, 9 was written on the 0 key, 8 on the 1 key, 7 on the 2 key, and so on. Subtraction was then performed by adding the nine's complement numbers and then adding 1 to the result. For example, consider the subtraction problem

$$637 - 481 = 156$$

The nine's complement of 481 is 518, and

$$637 + 518 + 1 = 1,156$$

which gives the answer (156) to the problem when the leftmost carry digit is ignored.

It did not take the accountants long to solve division problems using repeated subtractions—all on a machine designed to handle only additions.

Early computers, which had only the facilities for doing addition, used similar algorithms for performing subtraction, multiplication, and division. They used, however, two's complement numbers rather than nine's complement. (See Section 1.9 for an introduction to two's complement numbers.)

Although many computers now come with special-purpose hardware, called floating-point processors, to perform multiplication and division directly, they still use two's complement number representation internally and perform subtraction using two's complement addition. And when a floating-point processor is not used, sophisticated software algorithms are employed that perform multiplications and divisions based on repeated additions and subtractions.

following the parentheses, the process used by the computer in evaluating a `while` statement is

1. *Test the condition*
2. *If the condition has a nonzero (true) value*
   a. *execute the statement following the parentheses*
   b. *go back to step 1*
   else
   exit the while statement

Notice that step 2b forces program control to be transferred back to step 1. This transfer of control back to the start of a while statement to reevaluate the condition is what forms the program loop. The while statement literally loops back on itself to recheck the condition until it becomes false. This naturally means that, somewhere in the loop, provision must be made that permits the value of the tested condition to be altered. As we will see, this is indeed the case.

This looping process produced by a while statement is illustrated in Figure 6.3. A diamond shape shows the two entry and two exit points required in the decision part of the while statement.

To make this more tangible, consider the relational condition count <= 10 and the statement System.out.print(count + " ");. Using these, we can write the following valid while statement:

```
while (count <= 10)
    System.out.print(count + "   ");
```

Although this statement is valid, the alert reader will realize that we have created a situation in which the print() method either is called forever (or until we stop the program) or is not called at all. Let us see why this happens.

If count has a value less than or equal to 10 when the condition is first evaluated, a call to print() is made. The while statement then automatically loops back on itself and retests the condition. Since we have not changed the value stored in count, the condition is still true and another call to print() is made. This process continues forever or until the program containing this statement is prematurely stopped by the user. However, if count starts with a value greater than 10, the condition is false to begin with and the call to print() is never made.

FIGURE 6.3   **The anatomy of a while loop**

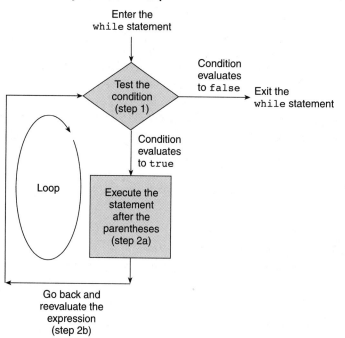

How do we set an initial value in count to control what the while statement does the first time the condition is evaluated? The answer, of course, is to assign values to each variable in the tested condition before the while statement is encountered. For example, the following sequence of instructions is valid:

```
count = 1;
while (count <= 10)
    System.out.print(count + "   ");
```

Using this sequence of instructions, we have ensured that count starts with a value of 1. We could assign any value to count in the assignment statement, but the important thing is to assign *some* value. In practice, the assigned value depends on the application.

We must still change the value of count so that we can finally exit the while statement. This requires a condition such as count = count + 1 to increment the value of count each time the while statement is executed. The fact that a while statement provides for the repetition of a single statement does not prevent us from including an additional statement to change the value of count. All we have to do is replace the single statement with a compound statement. For example,

```
count = 1;               // initialize count
while (count <= 10)
{
   System.out.print(count + "   ");
   count++;              // increment count
}
```

We can now analyze how this complete set of instructions works. The first assignment statement sets count equal to 1. The while statement is then entered, and the condition is evaluated for the first time. Since the value of count is less than or equal to 10, the condition is true and the compound statement is executed. The first statement in the compound statement is a call to the print() method to display the value of count followed by two spaces. The next statement adds 1 to the value currently stored in count, making this value equal to 2. The while statement now loops back to retest the condition. Since count is still less than or equal to 10, the compound statement is again executed. This process continues until the value of count reaches 11. QuickTest Program 6.1 illustrates these statements in an actual program.

The output for QuickTest Program 6.1 is

```
1  2  3  4  5  6  7  8  9  10
```

There is nothing special about the name count used in QuickTest Program 6.1. Any valid integer variable could have been used.

Before we consider other examples of the while statement, two comments concerning QuickTest Program 6.1 are in order. First, the statement count++ can be replaced with any statement that changes the value of count. A statement such as count = count + 2, for example, causes every second integer to be displayed. Second, it is the programmer's responsibility to ensure that count is changed in a way that ultimately leads to a normal exit from the while loop. For example, if we replace the expression count++ with the expression count--, the value of count never exceeds 10 and an infinite loop is created. An **infinite loop** is a loop that never ends. The computer does not reach out, touch you, and say, "Excuse me, you have created an infinite loop." It just keeps displaying numbers until you realize that the program is not working as you expected. For most systems, pressing the Ctrl and C keys at the same time will break program execution.

QuickTest Program 6.1

```java
public class ShowWhile
{
  public static void main(String[] args)
  {
    int count;

    count = 1;                  // initialize count
    while (count <= 10)
    {
      System.out.print(count + "  ");
      count++;                  // increment count
    }


  }
}
```

Now that you have some familiarity with the `while` statement, see if you can read and determine the output of QuickTest Program 6.2.

QuickTest Program 6.2

```java
public class CountDown
{
  public static void main(String[] args)
  {
    int i;

    i = 10;    // initialize i
    while (i >= 1)
    {
      System.out.print(i + "  ");
      i--;    // subtract 1 from i
    }


  }
}
```

The assignment statement in QuickTest Program 6.2 initially sets the `int` variable `i` to 10. The `while` statement then checks to see if the value of `i` is greater than or equal to 1. While the condition is true, the value of `i`, followed by two spaces, is displayed by the `print()` method, and the value of `i` is then decremented by 1. When `i` finally reaches 0, the expression is false and the program exits the `while` statement. Thus, the following display is obtained when QuickTest Program 6.2 is run:

```
10  9  8  7  6  5  4  3  2  1
```

To illustrate the power of the `while` statement, consider the task of printing a table of numbers from 1 to 10 with their squares and cubes. This can be done with a simple `while` statement as illustrated by QuickTest Program 6.3.

QuickTest Program 6.3

```java
import java.text.*;  // needed for formatting
public class CreateTable
{
  public static void main(String[] args)
  {
    int num;

    DecimalFormat df = new DecimalFormat("0000");

    System.out.println("NUMBER    SQUARE    CUBE");
    System.out.println("------    ------    ----");

    num = 1;
    while (num < 11)
    {
      System.out.print(" " + df.format(num));
      System.out.print("      " + df.format(num * num));
      System.out.println("      " + df.format(num * num * num));
      num++;            // increment num
    }
  }
}
```

When QuickTest Program 6.3 is run, the following display is produced:[2]

NUMBER	SQUARE	CUBE
0001	0001	0001
0002	0004	0008
0003	0009	0027
0004	0016	0064
0005	0025	0125
0006	0036	0216
0007	0049	0343
0008	0064	0512
0009	0081	0729
0010	0100	1000

Note that the expression in QuickTest Program 6.3 is num < 11. For the integer variable num, this expression is exactly equivalent to the expression num <= 10. The choice of expression is entirely up to you.

----

[2] See Appendix D for formatting statements that can be used to replace the leading zeros with leading spaces.

If we now want QuickTest Program 6.3 to produce a table of 1000 numbers, all we do is change the expression in the `while` statement from `num < 11` to `num < 1001`. Changing the 11 to 1001 produces a table of 1000 lines—not bad for a simple eight-line `while` loop.

It should be noted that the spaces inserted in the `print()` and `println()` methods are there to line up each column under its appropriate heading. The correct number of spaces can be determined by laying out the display by hand on a piece of paper and counting the required number of spaces or by making trial-and-error adjustments.

All the program examples illustrating the `while` statement have been examples of fixed-count loops because the tested condition is a **counter** that checks for a fixed number of repetitions. A variation on the fixed-count loop can be made where the counter is incremented by some value other than 1 each time through the loop. For example, consider the task of producing a Celsius to Fahrenheit temperature conversion table. Assume that Fahrenheit temperatures corresponding to Celsius temperatures ranging from 5 to 50 degrees are to be displayed in increments of 5 degrees. The desired display can be obtained with the sequence of statements

```
celsius = 5;       // starting Celsius value
while (celsius <= 50)
{
  fahren = (9.0/5.0) * celsius + 32.0;
  System.out.println(celsius + "     " + fahren);
  celsius = celsius + 5;
}
```

As before, the `while` statement consists of everything from the word `while` through the closing brace of the compound statement. Prior to entering the `while` loop, we have made sure to assign a value to the counter being evaluated, and there is a statement to alter the value of the counter within the loop (in increments of 5) to ensure an exit from the `while` loop. QuickTest Program 6.4 illustrates this code in a complete program.

QuickTest Program 6.4

```
import java.text.*;  // needed for formatting
public class ConversionTable
{
  // a method to convert Celsius to Fahrenheit
  public static void main(String[] args)
  {
    final int MAXCELSIUS = 50;
    final int STARTVAL = 5;
    final int STEPSIZE = 5;
    int celsius;
    double fahren;

    DecimalFormat cf = new DecimalFormat("00");  // celsius format
    DecimalFormat ff = new DecimalFormat("000"); // fahrenheit format

    System.out.println("DEGREES    DEGREES\n"
```

```
                          +"CELSIUS   FAHRENHEIT\n"
                          +"-------   ----------");

       celsius = STARTVAL;
       while (celsius <= MAXCELSIUS)
       {
          fahren = (9.0/5.0) * celsius + 32.0;
          System.out.print("  " + cf.format(celsius));
          System.out.println("        " + ff.format(fahren));
          celsius = celsius + STEPSIZE;
       }
    }
}
```

The display obtained by QuickTest Program 6.4 is

```
DEGREES    DEGREES
CELSIUS    FAHRENHEIT
-------    ----------
   05         041
   10         050
   15         059
   20         068
   25         077
   30         086
   35         095
   40         104
   45         113
   50         122
```

As with QuickTest Program 6.3, the spaces in both the `print()` and `println()` methods in QuickTest Program 6.4 were inserted strictly to line up the output values under their appropriate headings. In addition, notice that we have used two differing number formats: one for the Celsius temperatures that consists of two digits and another for the Fahrenheit temperatures that consists of three digits.

Exercises 6.2

1. Rewrite QuickTest Program 6.1 to print the numbers 2 to 10 in increments of 2. The output of your program should be

   ```
    2   4   6   8   10
   ```

2. Rewrite QuickTest Program 6.4 to produce a table that starts at a Celsius value of −10 and ends with a Celsius value of 60 in increments of 10 degrees.

3a. For the following `main()` method, determine the total number of items displayed. Also determine the first and last numbers printed.

   ```
   public static void main(String[] args)
   {
   ```

```
    int num = 0;

    while (num <= 20)
    {
      num++;
      System.out.print(num + "   ");
    }
  }
```

b. Enter and run the program from Exercise 3a on your computer to verify your answers to the exercise.

c. How is the output affected if the two statements within the compound statement were reversed—that is, if the `print()` call were made before the `num++` statement?

4. Write a Java program that converts gallons to liters. The program should display gallons from 10 to 20 in 1-gallon increments and the corresponding liter equivalents. Use the relationship that *1 gallon of liquid contains 3.785 liters.*

5. Write a Java program that converts feet to meters. The program should display feet from 3 to 30 in 3-foot increments and the corresponding meter equivalents. Use the relationship that *3.28 feet equal 1 meter.*

6. A machine purchased for $28,000 is depreciated at a rate of $4,000 a year for 7 years. Write and run a Java program that computes and displays a depreciation table for seven years. The table should have the form

YEAR	DEPRECIATION	END-OF-YEAR VALUE	ACCUMULATED DEPRECIATION
1	4000	24000	4000
2	4000	20000	8000
3	4000	16000	12000
4	4000	12000	16000
5	4000	8000	20000
6	4000	4000	24000
7	4000	0	28000

7. An automobile travels at an average speed of 55 miles per hour for four hours. Write a Java program that displays the distance driven, in miles, that the car has traveled after 0.5, 1.0, 1.5, and so on, hours until the end of the trip.

8. An approximate formula for converting Fahrenheit to Celsius temperatures is

$$Celsius = (Fahrenheit - 30) / 2$$

Using this formula and starting with a Fahrenheit temperature of 0 degrees, write a Java program that determines when the approximate equivalent Celsius temperature differs from the exact equivalent value by more than 4 degrees. (*Tip:* Use a `while` loop that terminates when the difference between the approximate and exact Celsius temperatures exceeds 4 degrees.) The exact conversion formula is $Celsius = 5 / 9(Fahrenheit - 32)$.

9. Using the approximate Celsius conversion formula provided in Exercise 8, write a Java program that produces a table of Fahrenheit temperatures, exact Celsius equivalent tem-

peratures, approximate Celsius equivalent temperatures, and the difference between the exact and approximate Celsius values. The table should begin at 30 degrees Fahrenheit, use 5 degree Fahrenheit increments, and terminate when the difference between exact and approximate values differs by more than 4 degrees.

6.3 **Interactive while Loops**

Combining interactive data entry with the repetition capabilities of the while statement produces very adaptable and powerful programs. To understand the concept involved, consider QuickTest Program 6.5, where a while statement accepts and then displays four user-entered numbers one at a time. Although it uses a very simple idea, the program highlights the flow of control concepts needed to produce more useful programs.

QuickTest Program 6.5

```java
import javax.swing.*;
public class EnterNumbers
{
  public static void main(String[] args)
  {
    String s1, outMessage;

    final int MAXNUMS = 4;
    int count;
    double num;

    outMessage = "This program will ask you to enter "
                + MAXNUMS + " numbers.";
    JOptionPane.showMessageDialog(null, outMessage, "QuickTest Program 6.5",
                        JOptionPane.INFORMATION_MESSAGE);

    count = 1;

    while (count <= MAXNUMS)
    {
      s1 = JOptionPane.showInputDialog("Enter number " + count + ":");
      num = Double.parseDouble(s1);

      JOptionPane.showMessageDialog(null, "The number entered is " + num,
                        "QuickTest Program 6.5",
                        JOptionPane.INFORMATION_MESSAGE);
      count++;
    }

    System.exit(0);
  }
}
```

Figure 6.4 illustrates the initial program message dialog box provided by Quick-Test Program 6.5 and the input and message dialog boxes displayed during the first execution of the loop. As shown in Figure 6.4b, the user entered the number 26.2 in the input dialog.

Let us review the program so we clearly understand how the output was produced. The initial program message dialog (Figure 6.4a) is caused by a call to the `showMessageDialog()`. This call is outside and before the `while` statement, so it is executed once before any statement in the `while` loop.

Once the `while` loop is entered, the statements within the compound statement are executed while the tested condition is true. The first time through the compound statement, the Input dialog containing the message `Enter number 1:` is displayed. The computer remains in a waiting state until a number is entered into this dialog. Once a number is typed and the Enter key is pressed, the entered string value is converted into a double-precision number that is displayed by a call to the `showMessageDialog()` method made within the `while` loop. The variable `count` is then incremented by one. This process continues until four passes through the loop have been made and the value of count is 5. Each pass through the loop causes both an input dialog to be displayed for entering a value and a message dialog to display the value that was entered. Figure 6.5 illustrates this flow of control.

FIGURE 6.4 **(a) The initial program message**

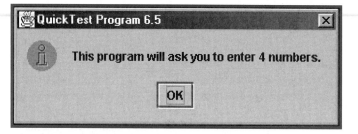

(b) The first input dialog

(c) The first message dialog

FIGURE 6.5   A flow of control diagram for QuickTest Program 6.5

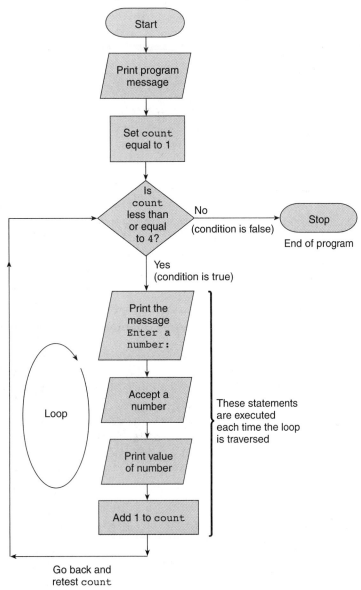

Rather than only displaying the entered numbers, QuickTest Program 6.5 can be modified to use the entered data. For example, we can add the numbers entered and display the total. To do this, we must be very careful about how we add the numbers, since the same variable, num, is used for each number entered. Because of this, the entry of a new number in QuickTest Program 6.5 automatically causes the previous number stored in num to be lost. Thus, each number entered must be added to the total before another number is entered. The required sequence is

Enter a number
Add the number to the total

FIGURE 6.6   **Accepting and adding a number to a total**

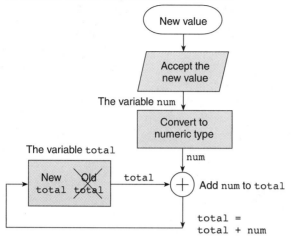

How do we add a single number to a total? A statement such as `total = total + num` does the job perfectly. This is the accumulating statement introduced in Section 3.1. After each number is entered, the accumulating statement adds the number into the total (Figure 6.6). The complete flow of control required for adding the numbers is shown in Figure 6.7.

In reviewing Figure 6.7, observe that we have made a provision for initially setting the total to zero before the `while` loop is entered. If we were to clear the total inside the `while` loop, it would be set to zero each time the loop was executed, and any value previously stored would be erased.

QuickTest Program 6.6 incorporates the necessary modifications to QuickTest Program 6.5 to total the numbers entered. As indicated in the flow diagram (Figure 6.7), the statement `total = total + num;` is placed immediately after a numerical value has been accepted from the user. Putting the accumulating statement at this point in the program ensures that the entered number is immediately "captured" into the total.

QuickTest Program 6.6

```java
import javax.swing.*;
public class AddNumbers
{
  public static void main(String[] args)
  {
    String s1, outMessage;

    final int MAXNUMS = 4;
    int count;
    double num, total;

    outMessage = "This program will ask you to enter "
              + MAXNUMS + " numbers.";
    JOptionPane.showMessageDialog(null, outMessage, "QuickTest Program 6.6",
                    JOptionPane.INFORMATION_MESSAGE);
```

FIGURE 6.7   **Accumulation flow of control**

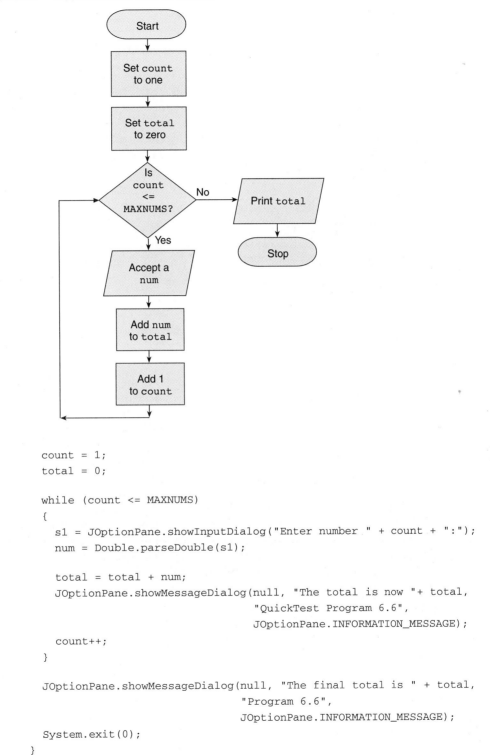

```
count = 1;
total = 0;

while (count <= MAXNUMS)
{
  s1 = JOptionPane.showInputDialog("Enter number " + count + ":");
  num = Double.parseDouble(s1);

  total = total + num;
  JOptionPane.showMessageDialog(null, "The total is now "+ total,
                                "QuickTest Program 6.6",
                                JOptionPane.INFORMATION_MESSAGE);
  count++;
}

JOptionPane.showMessageDialog(null, "The final total is " + total,
                              "Program 6.6",
                              JOptionPane.INFORMATION_MESSAGE);

System.exit(0);
  }
}
```

Let us review QuickTest Program 6.6. The variable `total` was created to store the total of the numbers entered. Prior to entering the `while` statement, the value of `total` is set to zero. This ensures that any previous value present in the storage location(s) assigned to the variable `total` is erased. Within the `while` loop, the statement `total = total + num;` is used to add the value of the entered number to `total`. As each value is entered, it is added to the existing total to create a new total. Thus, `total` becomes a running subtotal of all the values entered. Only when all numbers are entered does `total` contain the final sum of all the numbers. After the `while` loop is finished, the last message dialog, which is made by the call to `showMessage-Dialog()` after the `while` loop has completed running, displays this final sum. Figure 6.8 shows this last message dialog when the following data were input: 26.2, 5.0, 103.456, and 1267.89.

FIGURE 6.8   **A sample output displayed by QuickTest Program 6.6**

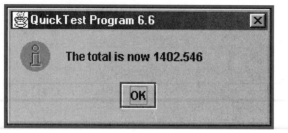

Having used an accumulating assignment statement to add the numbers entered, we can now go further and calculate the average of the numbers. Do we calculate the average within the `while` loop or outside it?

In this case, calculating an average requires that both a final total and the number of items in that total be available. The average is then computed by dividing the final total by the number of items. At this point, we must ask: At what point in the program is the correct total available, and at what point is the number of items available? In reviewing QuickTest Program 6.6, we see that the correct total needed for calculating the average is available after the `while` loop is finished. In fact, the whole purpose of the `while` loop is to ensure that the numbers are entered and added correctly to produce a correct total. We also have the number of items used in the total contained in the named constant `MAXNUMS`. With this as background, see if you can read and understand QuickTest Program 6.7.

QuickTest Program 6.7

```
import javax.swing.*;
public class AverageNumbers
{
  public static void main(String[] args)
  {
    String s1, info, outMessage;

    final int MAXNUMS = 4;
    int count;
    double num, total, average;
```

```
info = "This program will ask you to enter "
        + MAXNUMS + " numbers.";
JOptionPane.showMessageDialog(null, info, "QuickTest Program 6.7",
                              JOptionPane.INFORMATION_MESSAGE);
outMessage = "The average of the numbers:\n";

count = 1;
total = 0;

while (count <= MAXNUMS)
{
  s1 = JOptionPane.showInputDialog("Enter number " + count + ":");
  num = Double.parseDouble(s1);

  total = total + num;
  outMessage = outMessage + num + "   ";
  count++;
}

average = total / MAXNUMS;
JOptionPane.showMessageDialog(null, outMessage + "\nis  " + average,
                              "QuickTest Program 6.7",
                              JOptionPane.INFORMATION_MESSAGE);
System.exit(0);
  }
}
```

QuickTest Program 6.7 is almost identical to QuickTest Program 6.6 except for the calculation of the average. We have also replaced the constant display of the total within and after the `while` loop with a statement that "builds up" the final message that displays the average. The primary purpose of the loop in QuickTest Program 6.7 is to enter and add four numbers. After each entered number is added into the total, the same number is concatenated to the `outMessage` string. Immediately after the loop is exited, the average is computed, appended to the `outMessage` string, and the string is displayed. Figure 6.9 shows the final message dialog produced by QuickTest Program 6.7, which includes both the input values and the final average.

FIGURE 6.9   **A sample output displayed by QuickTest Program 6.7**

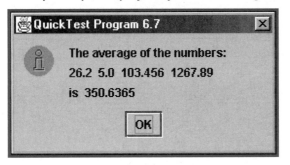

Sentinels

All of the loops we have created thus far have been examples of fixed-count loops, where a counter has been used to control the number of loop iterations. By means of a `while` statement, variable-condition loops may also be constructed. For example, when entering grades, we may not want to count the number of grades that will be entered, but would prefer to enter the grades continuously and, at the end, type in a special data value to signal the end of data input.

In computer programming, data values that signal either the start or end of a data series are called **sentinels**. The sentinel values must, of course, be selected so as not to conflict with legitimate data values. For example, if we were constructing a program to process a student's grades, and assuming that no extra credit is given that could produce a grade higher than 100, we could use any grade higher than 100 as a sentinel value. QuickTest Program 6.8 illustrates this concept. In QuickTest Program 6.8, data are continuously requested and accepted until a number larger than 100 isentered. Entry of a number higher than 100 alerts the program to exit the `while` loop and display the sum of the numbers entered.

QuickTest Program 6.8

```java
import javax.swing.*;
public class Sentinels
{
  public static void main(String[] args)
  {
    final double HIGHGRADE = 100.0;
    String s1, outMessage;
    double grade, total;

    grade = 0;
    total = 0;

    outMessage = "To stop entering grades, type in any number"
              + "\n greater than 100.";
    JOptionPane.showMessageDialog(null, outMessage,
                    "QuickTest Program 6.8", JOptionPane.INFORMATION_MESSAGE);

    s1 = JOptionPane.showInputDialog("Enter a grade:");
    grade = Double.parseDouble(s1);

    while (grade <= HIGHGRADE)
    {
      total = total + grade;
      s1 = JOptionPane.showInputDialog("Enter a grade:");
      grade = Double.parseDouble(s1);
    }

    JOptionPane.showMessageDialog(null, "The total of the grades is " + total,
                    "QuickTest Program 6.8", JOptionPane.INFORMATION_MESSAGE);
    System.exit(0);
  }
}
```

FIGURE 6.10   **A sample display produced by QuickTest Program 6.8**

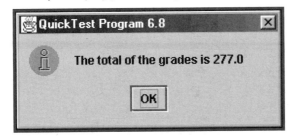

The final message dialog produced by QuickTest Program 6.8 when the numbers 95, 100, 82, and 101 were input is shown in Figure 6.10. As long as values less than or equal to 100 were entered, which is the case for the first three numbers, the program continued to request and accept additional data. For each number that is less than or equal to 100, the program adds the number to the total. When the number 101 is entered, the loop is exited and the sum of the entered values is displayed (Figure 6.10).

The **break** and **continue** Statements

Two useful statements in connection with repetition statements are the break and continue statements. We have encountered the break statement in relation to the switch statement. The syntax of this statement is

```
break;
```

A break statement, as its name implies, forces an immediate break, or exit, from the switch and while statements already presented and the for and do-while statements that are presented in the next sections.

For example, execution of the following while loop is immediately terminated if a number greater than 76 is entered.

```
count = 1;
while(count <= 10)
{
  s1 = JOptionPane.showInputDialog("Enter a number:");
  num = Double.parseDouble(s1);
  if (num > 76)
  {
    JOptionPane.showMessageDialog(null, "You lose!", "Test",
                        JOptionPane.INFORMATION_MESSAGE);
    break;        // break out of the loop
  }
  else
    JOptionPane.showMessageDialog(null, "Keep on trucking!", "Test",
                        JOptionPane.INFORMATION_MESSAGE);
  count++;
}
// break jumps to here
```

The break statement violates pure structured programming principles because it provides a second, nonstandard exit from a loop. Nevertheless, it is extremely useful and valuable for breaking out of loops when an unusual condition is detected. The break statement is also used to exit from a switch statement, but this is because the desired case has been detected and processed.

The continue statement is similar to the break statement but applies only to loops created with while, do-while, and for statements. The general format of a continue statement is:

```
continue;
```

When a continue is encountered in a loop, the next iteration of the loop begins immediately. For while loops, this means that execution is automatically transferred to the top of the loop, and reevaluation of the tested expression is initiated. Although the continue statement has no direct effect on a switch statement, it can be included within a switch statement that itself is contained in a loop. Here the effect of continue is the same: The next loop iteration begins.

As a general rule, the continue statement is less useful than the break statement and is not often used in practice.

The null Statement

All individual statements must be terminated by a semicolon. Oddly enough, a semicolon with nothing preceding it is also a valid statement called the *null statement*. Thus, the statement

```
;
```

is a null statement. This is a do-nothing statement that is used where a statement is syntactically required but no action is called for. null statements typically are used with either while or for statements. An example of a for statement using a null statement is found in QuickTest Program 6.9c in the next section.

Exercises 6.3

1. Rewrite QuickTest Program 6.6 to compute the total of eight numbers.

2. Rewrite QuickTest Program 6.6 to display the prompt

   ```
   Please type in the total number of data values to be added:
   ```

   In response to this prompt, the program should accept a user-entered number and then use this number to control the number of times the while loop is executed. Thus, if the user enters 5 in response to the prompt, the program should request the input of five numbers and display the total after five numbers have been entered.

3a. Write a Java program to convert Celsius degrees to Fahrenheit. The program should request the starting Celsius value, the number of conversions to be made, and the increment between Celsius values. The display should have appropriate headings and list the Celsius value and the corresponding Fahrenheit value. Use the relationship *Fahrenheit =* (9.0 / 5.0) * *Celsius + 32.0.*

b. Run the program written in Exercise 3a on your computer. Verify that your program begins at the correct starting Celsius value and contains the exact number of conversions specified in your input data.

4a. Modify the program written in Exercise 3 to request the starting Celsius value, the ending Celsius value, and the increment. Thus, instead of the condition checking for a fixed count, the condition checks for the ending Celsius value.

b. Run the program written in Exercise 4a on your computer. Verify that your output starts at the correct beginning value and ends at the correct ending value.

5. Rewrite QuickTest Program 6.7 to compute the average of 10 numbers.

6. Rewrite QuickTest Program 6.7 to display the prompt

```
Please type in the total number of data values to be averaged:
```

In response to this prompt, the program should accept a user-entered number and then use this number to control the number of times the while loop is executed. Thus, if the user enters 6 in response to the prompt, the program should request the input of six numbers and display the average of the next six numbers entered.

7. By mistake, a programmer put the statement average = total / count; within the while loop immediately after the statement total = total + num; in QuickTest Program 6.7. Thus, the while loop becomes

```
while (count <= MAXNUMS)
{
    s1 = JOptionPane.showInputDialog("Enter number " + count + ":");
    num = Double.parseDouble(s1);

    total = total + num;
    average = total / count;
    count++;
}
```

Does the program yield the correct result with this while loop? From a programming perspective, which while loop is better? Why?

8a. Modify QuickTest Program 6.8 to compute the average of the grades entered.

b. Run the program written in Exercise 8a on your computer and verify the results.

9a. An arithmetic series is defined by

$$a + (a + d) + (a + 2d) + (a + 3d) + \ldots + (a + (n - 1)d)$$

where a is the first term, d is the "common difference," and n is the number of terms to be added. With this information, write a Java program that uses a while loop both to display each term and to determine the sum of the arithmetic series having $a = 1$, $d = 3$, and $n = 100$. Make sure that your program displays the value it has calculated.

b. Modify the program written for Exercise 9a to permit the user to enter the starting number, ending number, and number of terms to be added.

10a. A geometric series is defined by

$$a + ar + ar^2 + ar^3 + \ldots + ar^{n-1}$$

where *a* is the first term, *r* is the "common ratio," and *n* is the number of terms in the series. With this information, write a Java program that uses a `while` loop both to display each term and to determine the sum of a geometric series having *a* = 1, *r* = .5 , and *n* = 100. Make sure that your program displays the value it has calculated.

b.   Modify the program written for Exercise 10a to permit the user to enter the starting number, common ratio, and number of terms in the series.

6.4 The `for` Statement

The `for` statement performs the same functions as the `while` statement but uses a different form. In many situations, especially those that use a fixed-count condition, the `for` statement format is easier to use than its `while` statement equivalent. The general form of the `for` statement is

```
for (initializer; condition; increment)
  statement;
```

Although the `for` statement looks a little complicated, it is really quite simple if we consider each of its parts separately. Within the parentheses of the `for` statement are three items separated by semicolons. Each of these items is optional, but the semicolons must be present. As we shall see, the items in parentheses correspond to the initialization, condition evaluation, and altering of condition values that we have already used with the `while` statement.

The middle item in the parentheses, the `condition`, is any valid Java expression that yields a Boolean value, and there is no difference in the way `for` and `while` statements use this expression. In both statements, as long as the condition evaluates to a `true` value, the statement following the parentheses is executed. This means that prior to the first check of the expression, initial values for the tested condition's variables must be assigned. It also means that before the condition is reevaluated, there must be one or more statements that alter these values. Recall that the general placement of these statements in a `while` statement follows the pattern

```
initializing statements;
while (condition)
{
  loop statements;
       .
       .
       .
  condition-altering statements;
}
```

The need to initialize variables or make some other evaluations prior to entering a repetition loop is so common that the `for` statement allows one or more initializing expressions to be grouped together as the first set of items within the `for`'s parentheses. These initializations are executed only once, before the condition is evaluated for the first time. Commas must be used to separate multiple initializations, as in i = 1, total = 0.

The for statement also provides a single place for all condition-altering expressions, which is the last item within the for's parentheses. These expressions, which typically increment or decrement a counter, are executed by the for statement at the end of each loop, just before the expression is reevaluated. Again, multiple increment expressions must be separated from each other by commas. Figure 6.11 illustrates the for statement's flow of control diagram.

The following section of code illustrates the correspondence between the for and while statements:

```
count = 1;
while (count <= 10)
{
   System.out.print(count + " ");
   count++;
}
```

FIGURE 6.11   The for statement's flow of control

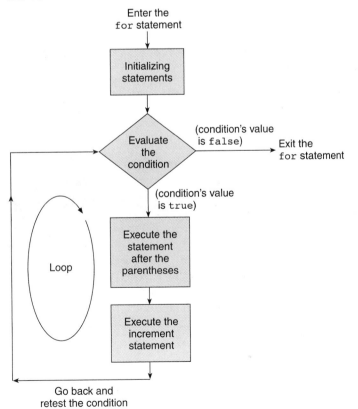

The `for` statement corresponding to this section of code is

```
for (count = 1; count <= 10; count++)
  System.out.print(count + " ");
```

As seen in these examples, the only difference between the `for` statement and the `while` statement is the placement of equivalent expressions. The grouping together of initializer, condition, and increment in the `for` statement is very convenient, especially when they are used to create fixed-count loops. Consider the following `for` statement:

```
for (count = 2; count <= 20; count = count + 2)
  System.out.print(count + " ");
```

In this statement, all the loop control information is contained within the parentheses. The loop starts with a count of 2, stops when the count exceeds 20, and increments the loop counter in steps of 2. QuickTest Program 6.9 illustrates this `for` statement in an actual program. Two blank spaces are placed between each output value for readability.

QuickTest Program 6.9

```
public class SampleFor
{
  public static void main(String[] args)
  {
    int count;

    for (count = 2; count <= 20; count = count + 2)
      System.out.print(count + "  ");
  }
}
```

The output of QuickTest Program 6.9 is

```
2  4  6  8  10  12  14  16  18  20
```

The `for` statement does not require that any of the items in parentheses be present or that they be used for initializing or incrementation purposes. However, the two semicolons must be present within the `for`'s parentheses. For example, the construction `for ( ; count <= 20 ;)` is valid.

If an initializer is missing, the initialization step is omitted when the `for` statement is executed. This means, of course, that the programmer must provide the required initializations before the `for` statement is encountered. Similarly, if the increment is missing, any expressions needed to alter the evaluation of the tested expression must be included directly within the statement part of the loop. The `for` statement only ensures that all initializer expressions within the parentheses are executed once, before evaluation of the tested condition, and that all increment expressions in the parentheses are executed at the end of the loop before the tested condition is rechecked. Thus, QuickTest Program 6.9 can be rewritten in any of the three ways shown in QuickTest Programs 6.9a, 6.9b, and 6.9c.

In QuickTest Program 6.9a, `count` is initialized outside the `for` statement, and the initializer inside the parentheses is left blank. In QuickTest Program 6.9b, both the initializer and the increment are removed from within the parentheses. QuickTest

QuickTest Program 6.9a

```java
public class SampleForA
{
  public static void main(String[] args)
  {
    int count;

    count = 2;    // initializer outside for statement
    for ( ; count <= 20; count = count + 2)
      System.out.print(count + "   ");
  }
}
```

QuickTest Program 6.9b

```java
public class SampleForB
{
  public static void main(String[] args)
  {
    int count;

    count = 2;    // initializer outside for loop
    for( ; count <= 20; )
    {
      System.out.print(count + "   ");
      count = count + 2;    // alteration statement
    }
  }
}
```

QuickTest Program 6.9c

```java
public class SampleForC
{
  public static void main(String[] args)
  {
    int count;

    for (count = 2; count <= 20; System.out.print(count + "   "), count = count + 2)
      ; // null statement
  }
}
```

Program 6.9b also uses a compound statement within the for loop, with an incrementing statement included in the compound statement. In addition, QuickTest Program 6.9c has included all items within the parentheses, so there is no need for any useful statement following the parentheses. Here the null statement satisfies the syntactical requirement of one statement to follow the for's parentheses. Observe also in QuickTest Program 6.9c that the increment part of the statement (the last set of items in parentheses) consists of two items and that a comma separates these items. The use of commas to separate items in both the initializer and increment parts of a for statement, as previously noted, is required if either of these two items contain more than one expression. Finally, note the fact that QuickTest Programs 6.9a, 6.9b, and 6.9c are all inferior to QuickTest Program 6.9. The for statement in QuickTest Program 6.9 is much clearer because all of the expressions pertaining to the tested expression are grouped together within the parentheses.

Although the initializer and increment items can be omitted from a for statement, omitting the tested condition results in an infinite loop, unless a break statement is activated somewhere within the loop. For example, the code

```
for (count = 2;  ; count++)
    System.out.print(count + " ");
```

results in an infinite loop.

As with the while statement, both break and continue statements can be used within a for loop. The break forces an immediate exit from the for loop, as it does in the while loop. The continue, however, forces control to be passed to the altering list in a for statement, after which the tested expression is reevaluated. This differs from the action of a continue in a while statement, where control is passed directly to the reevaluation of the tested expression.

Finally, many programmers use the initializing list of a for statement both to declare and to initialize a counter variable used within the for loop. For example, in the following for statement

```
for(int count = 1; count < 11; count++)
    System.out.print(count + " ");
```

the variable count is both declared and initialized from within the for statement. Being declared this way, however, restricts count's usage within the bounds of the for loop. Attempting to declare a second variable having a different data type within the initialization part of the for loop results in a compiler error. To understand the enormous power of the for statement, consider the task of printing a table of numbers from 1 to 10, including their squares and cubes, using this statement. Such a table was previously produced using a while statement in QuickTest Program 6.3. You may wish to review QuickTest Program 6.3 and compare it to QuickTest Program 6.10 to get a further sense of the equivalence between the for and while statements.

When QuickTest Program 6.10 is run, the display produced is:

NUMBER	SQUARE	CUBE
0001	0001	0001
0002	0004	0008
0003	0009	0027
0004	0016	0064
0005	0025	0125
0006	0036	0216
0007	0049	0343
0008	0064	0512
0009	0081	0729
0010	0100	1000

PROGRAMMING NOTE

Where to Place the Opening Braces

There are two styles of writing for loops that are used by professional Java programmers. These styles only come into play when the for loop contains a compound
statement. The style illustrated and used in the text takes the form

```
for (expression1; expression2; expression3)
{
  compound statement in here
}
```

An equally acceptable style places the initial brace of the compound statement on
the first line. Using this style, a for loop appears as

```
for (expression1; expression2; expression3) {
  compound statement in here
}
```

The advantage of the first style is that the braces line up under one another, making
it easier to locate brace pairs. The advantage of the second style is that it makes the
code more compact and saves a line, permitting more code to be viewed in the same
display area. Both styles are used but are almost never intermixed. As always, the
indentation within a compound statement (two or four spaces or a tab) should also
be consistent throughout your programs. If the choice is yours, select whichever
style appeals to you and be consistent. If the preferred style is dictated by the company or course in which you are programming, find out what the style is and follow
it consistently.

QuickTest Program 6.10

```
import java.text.*;  // needed for formatting
public class ForTable
{
  public static void main(String[] args)
  {
    int num;

    DecimalFormat df = new DecimalFormat("0000");
    System.out.println("NUMBER    SQUARE    CUBE");
    System.out.println("------    ------    ----");

    for (num = 1; num < 11; num++)
    {
      System.out.print(" " + df.format(num));
      System.out.print("        " + df.format(num * num));
      System.out.println("      " + df.format(num * num * num));
    }
  }
}
```

Changing the number 11 to 101 in the for statement of QuickTest Program 6.10 creates a loop that is executed 100 times and produces a table of numbers from 1 to 100. As with the while statement, this small change produces an immense increase in the processing and output provided by the program. Notice also that the expression num++ was used as the incrementing expression in place of the equivalent num = num + 1.

Interactive for Loops

Using a showInputDialog() method inside a for loop produces the same effect as when this method is used within a while loop. For example, in QuickTest Program 6.11, an input dialog is used to input a set of numbers. As each number is input, it is added to a total. When the for loop is exited, the average is calculated and displayed.

QuickTest Program 6.11

```java
import javax.swing.*;
public class AverageFiveNumbers
{
  // This method calculates the average
  // of 5 user-entered numbers

  public static void main(String[] args)
  {
     final int MAXNUMS = 5;

     int count;
     double num, total, average;
     String s1;

     total = 0.0;

     for (count = 0; count < MAXNUMS; count++)
     {
       s1 = JOptionPane.showInputDialog("Enter a number:");
       num = Double.parseDouble(s1);
       total = total + num;
     }

     average = total / MAXNUMS;

     JOptionPane.showMessageDialog(null,
             "The average of the data entered is " + average,
             "QuickTest Program 6.11",
             JOptionPane.INFORMATION_MESSAGE);

     System.exit(0);
  }
}
```

PROGRAMMING NOTE

Do You Use a **for** *or a* **while** *Loop?*

A commonly asked question by beginning programmers is which loop structure should they use: a for or a while loop? This is a good question because each of these loop structures, in Java, can construct both fixed-count and variable-condition loops.

In almost all other computer languages, except C, C++, and Java, the answer is relatively straightforward because the for statement can only be used to construct fixed-count loops. Thus, in these languages (again, excepting C, C++, and Java), for statements are used to construct fixed-count loops and while statements are generally used only when constructing variable-condition loops.

In Java, this easy distinction does not hold because each statement can be used to create each type of loop. The answer for these three languages, then, is really a matter of style. Since a for and while loop are interchangeable in these languages, either loop is appropriate. Some professional programmers always use a for statement and almost never use a while statement; others always use a while statement and rarely use a for statement. Still a third group tends to retain the convention used in early high-level languages—that is, use a for loop to create fixed-count loops and a while loop to create variable-condition loops. In Java, it is all a matter of style, and you will encounter all three styles in your programming career.

The for statement in QuickTest Program 6.11 creates a loop that is executed five times. The user is prompted to enter a number each time through the loop. After each number is entered, it is immediately added to the total. Although total was initialized to zero before the for statement, this initialization could have been included with the initialization of count as follows:

```
for (total = 0.0, count = 0; count < 5; count++)
```

Note, however, that the declarations for both total and count *could not* have been included with their initializations within the for statement because they are different data types. Thus, the statement

```
for (double total = 0.0, int count = 0; count < 5; count++) // INVALID
```

is invalid because the initializing item, by itself, results in an invalid declaration statement. If both total and count were the same data type, however, they could be declared together within the for loop. For example, the statement

```
for (int total = 0, count = 0; count < 5; count++)
```

is valid because the statement int total = 0, count = 0; is a valid declaration statement. In general, and to avoid declaration problems, you should declare and initialize at most a single initializing variable within a for statement.

Nested Loops

In many situations, it is either convenient or necessary to have a loop within another loop. Such loops are called **nested loops**. A simple example of a nested loop is

```
for(i = 1; i <= 5; i++)              // start of outer loop <-----------+
{                                    //                                 |
    System.out.println("\ni is now " + i);  //                         |
                                     //                                 |
    for(j = 1; j <= 4; j++)                  // start of inner loop     |
        System.out.print("  j = " + j);      // end of inner loop       |
}                                    // end of outer loop    <----------+
```

The first loop, controlled by the value of i, is called the *outer loop*. The second loop, controlled by the value of j, is the *inner loop*. Notice that all statements in the inner loop are within the boundaries of the outer loop and that we have used a different variable to control each loop. For each single trip through the outer loop, the inner loop runs through its entire sequence. Thus, each time the i counter increases by 1, the inner for loop executes completely. This situation is illustrated in Figure 6.12.

FIGURE 6.12   **For each i, j loops**

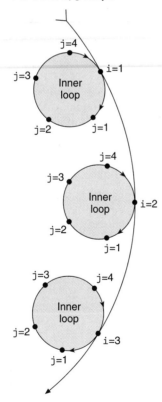

QuickTest Program 6.12 includes the foregoing code in a working program.

QuickTest Program 6.12

```
public class NestedLoop
{
  public static void main(String[] args)
  {
    int i, j;

    for(i = 1; i <= 5; i++)            // start of outer loop <-----------+
    {                                  //                                |
      System.out.println("\ni is now " + i);  //                         |
                                       //                                |
      for(j = 1; j <= 4; j++)                  // start of inner loop    |
        System.out.print("  j = " + j);        // end of inner loop      |
    }                                  // end of outer loop    <-----------+


  }
}
```

Here is the output of a sample run of QuickTest Program 6.12:

```
i is now 1
  j = 1  j = 2  j = 3  j = 4
i is now 2
  j = 1  j = 2  j = 3  j = 4
i is now 3
  j = 1  j = 2  j = 3  j = 4
i is now 4
  j = 1  j = 2  j = 3  j = 4
i is now 5
  j = 1  j = 2  j = 3  j = 4
```

To illustrate the usefulness of a nested loop, we use one to compute the average grade for each student in a class of 20. Assume that each student has taken four exams during the semester. The final grade is calculated as the average of these examination grades.

The outer loop in our program will consist of 20 passes. Each pass through the outer loop is used to compute the average for one student. The inner loop will consist of 4 passes. One examination grade is entered in each inner loop pass. As each grade is entered, it is added to the total for the student, and at the end of the loop, the average is calculated and displayed. QuickTest Program 6.13 uses a nested loop to make the required calculations.

In reviewing QuickTest Program 6.13, pay particular attention to the initialization of `total` within the outer loop before the inner loop is entered. The variable `total` is initialized 20 times, once for each student. Also notice that the average is calculated and displayed immediately after the inner loop is finished. Since the statements that compute and display the average are also within the outer loop, 20 averages are calculated and displayed. The entry and addition of each grade within the inner loop use techniques we have seen before, which should now be familiar.

QuickTest Program 6.13

```java
import javax.swing.*;
public class CalculateGrade
{
  public static void main(String[] args)
  {
    final int NUMGRADES = 4;
    final int NUMSTUDENTS = 20;
    int i,j;
    double grade, total, average;
    String s1;

    for (i = 1; i <= NUMSTUDENTS; i++)     // start of outer loop
    {
      total = 0;                           // clear the total for this student
      for (j = 1; j <= NUMGRADES; j++)   // start of inner loop
      {
        s1 = JOptionPane.showInputDialog(
                      "Enter an examination grade for this student:");
        grade = Double.parseDouble(s1);
        total = total + grade;   // add the grade into the total
      }                                  // end of the inner for loop
      average = total / NUMGRADES;       // calculate the average
      JOptionPane.showMessageDialog(null,
                "The average for student " + i + " is " + average,
                "QuickTest Program 6.13",
                      JOptionPane.INFORMATION_MESSAGE);
    }     // end of the outer for loop

    System.exit(0);
  }
}
```

Exercises 6.4

1. Determine the output of the following methods:

    a.
```java
public static void main(String[] args)
{
  int i;

  for (i = 0; i <= 20; i = i + 4)
    System.out.print(i + " ");
}
```

    b.
```java
public static void main(String[] args)
{
  int i;

  for (i = 1; i < 21; i = i + 3)
```

```
      System.out.print(i + " ");
   }
```

c.
```
   public static void main(String[] args)
   {
      int i;

      for (i = 20; i >= 0; i = i - 4)
         System.out.print(i + " ");
   }
```

2. Modify QuickTest Program 6.10 to produce a table of the numbers 0 through 20 in increments of 2 with their squares and cubes.

3. Modify QuickTest Program 6.10 to produce a table of numbers from 10 to 1 instead of 1 to 10 as it currently does.

4. Write and run a Java program that displays a table of 20 temperature conversions from Fahrenheit to Celsius. The table should start with a Fahrenheit value of 20 degrees and be incremented in values of 4 degrees. Recall that *Celsius = (5.0 / 9.0) * (Fahrenheit − 32.0)*.

5. Modify the program written for Exercise 4 to initially request the number of conversions to be displayed.

6. Write a Java program that converts Fahrenheit to Celsius temperature in increments of 5 degrees. The initial value of Fahrenheit temperature and the total conversions to be made are to be requested as user input during program execution. Recall that *Celsius = (5.0 / 9.0) * (Fahrenheit − 32.0)*.

7. Write and run a Java program that accepts six Fahrenheit temperatures, one at a time, and converts each value entered to its Celsius equivalent before the next value is requested. Use a `for` loop in your program. The conversion required is *Celsius = (5.0 / 9.0) * (Fahrenheit − 32.0)*.

8. Write and run a Java program that accepts 10 individual values of gallons, one at a time, and converts each value entered to its liter equivalent before the next value is requested. Use a `for` loop in your program. There are *3.785 liters in 1 gallon of liquid*.

9. Modify the program written for Exercise 8 to initially request the number of data items that will be entered and converted.

10. Is the following method correct? If it is, determine its output. If it is not, determine and correct the error so the program will run.

```
      public static void main(String[] args)
      {

         for(int i = 1; i < 10; i++)
            System.out.print(i + " ");
         System.out.println();
         for >(int i = 1; i < 5; i++)
            System.out.println(i + " ");

      }
```

11. Write and run a Java program that calculates and displays the amount of money available in a bank account that has an initial deposit of $1000 and earns 8 percent interest a year. Your program should display the amount available at the end of each year for a period of 10 years. Use the relationship that the money available at the end of each year equals the amount of money in the account at the start of the year plus .08 times the amount available at the start of the year.

12a. Modify the program written for Exercise 11 to prompt the user for the amount of money initially deposited in the account.

b. Modify the program written for Exercise 11 to prompt the user for both the amount of money initially deposited and the number of years to be displayed.

c. Modify the program written for Exercise 11 to prompt the user for the amount of money initially deposited, the interest rate to be used, and the number of years to be displayed.

13. A machine purchased for $28,000 is depreciated at a rate of $4000 a year for seven years. Using a `for` loop, write and run a Java program that computes and displays a depreciation table for seven years. The table should have the form

```
              DEPRECIATION SCHEDULE
              ---------------------

                             END-OF-YEAR      ACCUMULATED
  YEAR     DEPRECIATION         VALUE         DEPRECIATION
  ----     ------------      -----------      ------------

   1           4000            24000             4000
   2           4000            20000             8000
   3           4000            16000            12000
   4           4000            12000            16000
   5           4000             8000            20000
   6           4000             4000            24000
   7           4000                0            28000
```

14. A well-regarded manufacturer of widgets has been losing 4 percent of its sales each year. The annual profit for the firm is 10 percent of sales. This year, the firm has had $10 million in sales and a profit of $1 million. Determine the expected sales and profit for the next 10 years. Your program should use a `for` loop to complete and produce a display as follows:

```
              SALES AND PROFIT PROJECTION
              ---------------------------

  YEAR       EXPECTED SALES          PROJECTED PROFIT
  ----       --------------          ----------------
   1          $10000000.00             $1000000.00
   2          $ 9600000.00             $ 960000.00
   3               .                        .
   .               .                        .
   .               .                        .
   .               .                        .
  10               .                        .
  ----------------------------------------------------
  Totals:     $       .                 $       .
```

15. Four experiments are performed, each consisting of six tests, with the following results. Write a Java program using a nested loop to compute and display the average of the test results for each experiment.

Experiment 1 results:	23.2	31.5	16.9	27.5	25.4	28.6
Experiment 2 results:	34.8	45.2	27.9	36.8	33.4	39.4
Experiment 3 results:	19.4	16.8	10.2	20.8	18.9	13.4
Experiment 4 results:	36.9	39.5	49.2	45.1	42.7	50.6

16. Modify the program written for Exercise 15 so that the number of test results for each experiment is entered by the user. Write your program so that a different number of test results can be entered for each experiment.

17a. A bowling team consists of five players. Each player bowls three games. Write a Java program that uses a nested loop to enter each player's individual scores and then computes and displays the average score for each bowler. Assume that each bowler has the following scores:

	Game 1	Game 2	Game 3
Bowler 1:	286	252	265
Bowler 2:	212	186	215
Bowler 3:	252	232	216
Bowler 4:	192	201	235
Bowler 5:	186	236	272

  b. Modify the program written for Exercise 17a to calculate and display the overall team average score. (Tip: Use a second variable to store the total of all the players' scores.)

18. Rewrite the program for Exercise 17a to eliminate the inner loop. To do this, you will have to input three scores for each bowler rather than one at a time. Each score must be stored in its own variable name before the average is calculated.

19. Write a Java program that calculates and displays the yearly amount available if $1,000 is invested in a bank account for 10 years. Your program should display the amounts available for interest rates from 6 percent to 12 percent inclusively, at 1 percent increments. Use a nested loop with the outer loop having a fixed count of 7 and the inner loop having a fixed count of 10. The first iteration of the outer loop should use an interest rate of 6 percent and display the amount of money available at the end of the first 10 years. In each subsequent pass through the outer loop, the interest rate should be increased by 1 percent. Use the relationship that the money available at the end of each year equals the amount of money in the account at the start of the year plus the interest rate times the amount available at the start of the year.

6.5 **The do-while Statement**

Both the while and for statements evaluate an expression at the start of the repetition loop. In some cases, however, it is more convenient to test the expression at the end of the loop. For example, suppose we have constructed the following while loop to add a set of numbers:

```
s1 = JOptionPane.showInputDialog("Enter a value:");
value = Double.parseDouble(s1);
while (value != SENTINEL)
{
  total = total + value;
  s1 = JOptionPane.showInputDialog("Enter a value:");
  value = Double.parseDouble(s1);
}
```

Using this `while` statement requires either duplicating the input dialog and conversion calls before the loop and then within the loop, as we have done, or resorting to some other artifice to force initial execution of the statements within the `while` loop.

The `do-while` statement, as its name implies, allows us to execute statements before an expression is evaluated. In many situations, this can be used to eliminate the duplication illustrated in the previous example. The syntax of the `do-while` statement is

```
do statement;
while(condition);
```

In practice, however, the statement following the reserved word `do` is usually a compound statement, and the `do` statement takes the more generally used form

```
do
{
  any number of statements in here;
}
while(condition); <-------------don't forget the final  ;
```

A flow control diagram illustrating the operation of the `do-while` statement is shown in Figure 6.13. As illustrated in the figure, all statements within the `do-while` statement are executed at least once before the expression is evaluated. Then, if the condition has a true value, the statements are executed again. This process continues until the condition evaluates to false. For example, consider the following `do-while` statement:

```
do
{
  s1 = JOptionPane.showInputDialog("Enter a value:");
  value = Double.parseDouble(s1);
  if ( abs(value - SENTINEL) < 0.0001 ) break;
  total = total + value
}
while(price != SENTINEL);
```

Observe that only one `showInputDialog()` and conversion statement are used here because the tested condition is evaluated at the end of the loop.

As with all repetition statements, the `do-while` statement can always replace or be replaced by an equivalent `while` or `for` statement, although the exact replacement is not always immediately obvious. The choice of statement depends on the application and the style preferred by the programmer. In general, the `while` and `for`

FIGURE 6.13   **The do statement's flow of control**

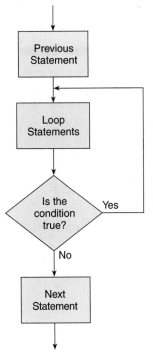

statements are preferred because they clearly let anyone reading the program know what is being tested "right up front" at the top of the program loop.

Validity Checks

The do-while statement is particularly useful in filtering user-entered input and providing **data validity checks**. For example, assume that an operator is required to enter a valid customer identification number between 100 and 1999. Any number outside this range is to be rejected, and a new request for a valid number is made. The following section of code provides the necessary data filter to verify the entry of a valid identification number.

```
do
{
  s1 = JOptionPane.showInputDialog("Enter a value:");
  idNum = Integer.parseInt(s1);
}
while (idNum < 100 || idNum > 1999);
```

Here a request for an identification number is repeated until a valid number is entered. This section of code is "bare bones" in that it neither alerts the operator to the cause of the new request for data nor allows premature exit from the loop if a valid identification number cannot be found. An alternative, removing the first drawback, is

```
do
{
  s1 = JOptionPane.showInputDialog("Enter a value:");
  idNum = Integer.parseInt(s1);
  if (idNum < 100 || idNum > 1999)
  {
    JOptionPane.showMessageDialog(null,
                "Please check the ID number and re-enter",
                "An invalid number was just entered",
                JOptionPane.ERROR_MESSAGE);
  }
  else
    break;    // break if a valid id num was entered
} while(true);  // this expression is always true
```

Here we have used a `break` statement to exit from the loop. Because the expression being evaluated by this `do-while` statement is always `true`, an infinite loop has been created that is only exited when the `break` statement is encountered.

Exercises 6.5

1a. Using a `do-while` statement, write a Java program to accept a grade. The program should request a grade continuously as long as an invalid grade is entered. An invalid grade is any grade less than 0 or greater than 100. After a valid grade has been entered, your program should display the value of that grade.

b. Modify the program written for Exercise 1a so that the user is alerted when an invalid grade has been entered.

c. Modify the program written for Exercise 1b so that it allows the user to exit the program by entering the number 999.

d. Modify the program written for Exercise 1b so that it automatically terminates after five invalid grades are entered.

2a. Write a Java program that continuously requests a grade to be entered. If the grade is less than 0 or greater than 100, your program should display an appropriate message informing the user that an invalid grade has been entered; a valid grade should be added to a total. When a grade of 999 is entered, the program should exit the repetition loop and compute and display the average of the valid grades entered.

b. Run the program written in Exercise 2a on your computer and verify the program using appropriate test data.

3a. Write a Java program to reverse the digits of a positive integer number. For example, if the number 8735 is entered, the number displayed should be 5378. (*Tip:* Use a `do-while` statement and continuously strip off and display the units digit of the number. If the variable num initially contains the number entered, the units digit is obtained as `(num % 10)`. After a units digit is displayed, dividing the number by 10 sets up the number for the next iteration. Thus, `(8735 % 10)` is 5 and `(8735 / 10)` is 873. The `do-while` statement should continue as long as the remaining number is not zero.)

b. Run the program written in Exercise 3a on your computer and verify the program using appropriate test data.

4. Repeat any of the exercises in Section 6.4 using a `do-while` statement rather than a `for` statement.

6.6 **Recursion**[3]

Because Java allocates new memory locations for arguments and local variables each time a method is called, it is possible for a method to call itself. Methods that do so are referred to as *self-referential* or *recursive methods*. When a method invokes itself, the process is called *direct recursion*. Similarly, a method can invoke a second method, which in turn invokes the first method. This type of recursion is referred to as *indirect* or *mutual recursion*.

In 1936, Alan Turing (see A Bit of Background on page 50) showed that, although not every possible problem can be solved by computer, those problems that have recursive solutions also have computer solutions, at least in theory.

Mathematical Recursion

The recursive concept is that the solution to a problem can be stated in terms of "simple" versions of itself. Some problems can be solved using an algebraic formula that shows recursion explicitly. For example, consider finding the factorial of a number n, denoted as $n!$, where n is a positive integer. This is defined as

$$1! = 1$$
$$2! = 2 * 1 = 2 * 1!$$
$$3! = 3 * 2 * 1 = 3 * 2!$$
$$4! = 4 * 3 * 2 * 1 = 4 * 3!$$
and so on

The definition for $n!$ can be summarized by the following statements:

$$1! = 1$$
$$n! = n * (n - 1)! \text{ for } n > 1$$

This definition illustrates the general considerations that must be specified in constructing a recursive algorithm. These are:

1. What is the first case?
2. How is the nth case related to the $(n - 1)$ case?

Although the definition seems to define a factorial in terms of a factorial, the definition is valid because it can always be computed. For example, using the definition, 3! is first computed as

$$3! = 3 * 2!$$

---

[3] This topic can be omitted on first reading without loss of subject continuity.

The value of 3! is determined from the definition as

$$2! = 2 * 1!$$

Substituting this expression for 2! in the determination of 3! yields

$$3! = 3 * 2 * 1!$$

1! is not defined in terms of the recursive formula but is simply defined as being equal to 1. Substituting this value into the expression for 3! gives

$$3! = 3 * 2 * 1 = 6$$

To see how a recursive method is defined in Java, we construct the method factorial. In pseudocode, the processing required of this method is

> **If n = 1**
>   **factorial = n**
> **Else**
>   **factorial = n * factorial(n − 1)**

Notice that this algorithm is simply a restatement of the recursive definition previously given. As a general-purpose Java method, this can be written as

```java
public static long factorial(int n)
{
  if (n == 1)
    return (n);
  else
    return (n * factorial(n-1));
}
```

QuickTest Program 6.14 illustrates this code in a complete program.

QuickTest Program 6.14

```java
public class Recursive
{
  public static void main(String[] args)
  {
    int n = 3;
    long result;

    result = factorial(n);
    System.out.println("The factorial of " + n + " is " + result);
  }

  public static long factorial(int n)
  {
    if (n == 1)
      return (n);
    else
      return (n * factorial(n-1));
  }
}
```

The output produced by QuickTest Program 6.14 is

```
The factorial of 3 is 6
```

How the Computation Is Performed

The sample run of Program 6.14 invoked factorial from `main()` with a value of 3 using the call

```
result = factorial(n);
```

Let's see how the computer performs the computation. The mechanism that makes it possible for a Java method to call itself is Java's allocation of new memory locations for all method arguments and local variables as each method is called. This allocation is made dynamically, as a program is executed, in a memory area referred to as the *stack*.

A memory stack is an area of memory used for rapidly storing and retrieving data. It is conceptually similar to a stack of trays in a cafeteria, where the last tray placed on top of the stack is the first tray removed. This last-in, first-out mechanism provides the means for storing information in order of occurrence. Each method call reserves memory locations on the stack for its arguments, its local variables, a return value, and the address where execution is to resume in the calling program when the method has completed execution. Thus, when the method call `factorial(n)` is made, the stack is initially used to store the address of the instruction being executed (`result = factorial(n);`), the argument value for n, which is 3, and a space for the value to be returned by the factorial method. At this stage, the stack can be envisioned as shown in Figure 6.14. From a program execution standpoint, the method that made the call to factorial, in this case `main()`, is suspended, and the compiled code for the factorial method starts executing.

Within the factorial method itself, another method call is made. That this call is to factorial is irrelevant as far as Java is concerned. The call simply is another request for stack space. In this case, the stack stores the address of the instruction being executed in factorial, the number 2, and a space for the value to be returned by the method. The stack can now be envisioned as shown in Figure 6.15. At this point, a second version of the compiled code for factorial begins execution, while the first version is temporarily suspended.

Once again, the currently executing code, which is the second invocation of factorial, makes a method call. That this call is to itself is irrelevant in Java. The call is once again handled in the same manner as any method call and begins with allocation

FIGURE 6.14   **The stack for the first call to factorial**

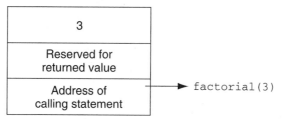

FIGURE 6.15 **The stack for the second call to factorial**

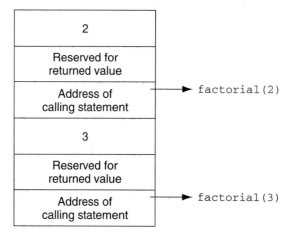

of the stack's memory space. Here the stack stores the address of the instruction being executed in the calling method, which happens to be factorial, the number 1, and a space for the value to be returned by the method. The stack can now be envisioned as shown in Figure 6.16. At this point, the third and final version of the

FIGURE 6.16 **The stack for the third call to factorial**

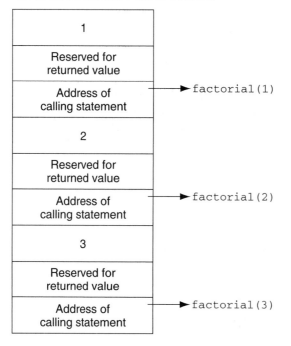

compiled code for factorial begins execution, while the second version is temporarily suspended.

This third call to factorial results in a returned value of 1 being placed on the stack. This completes the set of recursive calls and permits the suspended calling methods to resume execution and be completed in reverse order. The value of 1 is used by the second invocation of factorial to complete its operation and place a return value of 2 on the stack. This value is then used by the first invocation of factorial to complete its operation and place a return value of 6 on the stack, with execution now returning to `main()`. The original calling statement within `main()` stores the return value of its invocation of factorial into the variable result.

Recursion Versus Iteration

The recursive method can be applied to any problem in which the solution is represented in terms of solutions to simpler versions of the same problem. The most difficult tasks in implementing recursion are deciding how to create the process and visualizing what happens at each successive invocation.

Any recursive method can always be written in a nonrecursive manner using an iterative solution. For example, the factorial method can be written using an **iteration** algorithm such as

```
public static long factorial(int n)
{
  int fact;

  for(fact = 1; n > 0; n--)
    fact = fact * n;
  return (fact);
}
```

Since recursion is usually a difficult concept for beginning programmers, under what conditions would you use it in preference to a repetitive solution? The answer is rather simple. If a problem solution can be expressed iteratively or recursively with equal ease, the iterative solution is preferable because it executes faster (there are no additional method calls, which consume processing time) and uses less memory (the stack is not used as it is for the multiple method calls needed in recursion). There are times, however, when recursive solutions are preferable.

First, some problems are easier to visualize using a recursive algorithm than a repetitive one. A second reason for using recursion is that it sometimes provides a much simpler solution. In these situations, obtaining the same result using repetition requires extremely complicated coding that can be avoided by using recursion. An example of this is the quicksort sorting algorithm presented in Section 8.9.

Related to both these reasons is a third. In many advanced applications, recursion is both simpler to visualize and the only practical means of implementing a solution. Examples of these applications are the implementation of a quicksort algorithm (Section 8.9) and in creating dynamically allocated linked list data structures (Chapter 13).

A BIT OF BACKGROUND

The Blockhead

An individual who has had a profound influence on modern science is Leonardo of Pisa (1170–1250). In his youth, he was called Filus Bonacci, which means "son of (Guglielmo) Bonacci," and the name "stuck." Hence, he is commonly known today as Fibonacci. He traveled widely, met with scholars throughout the Mediterranean area, and produced four very significant works on arithmetic and geometry. One of his discoveries is the sequence of numbers that bears his name: 0, 1, 1, 2, 3, 5, 8, 13, ... After the first two values, 0 and 1, each number of the Fibonacci sequence is obtained from the sum of the preceding two numbers.

Fibonacci often referred to himself as Leonardo Bigollo, probably because *bigollo* is Italian for "traveler." However, another meaning of *bigollo* in Italian is "blockhead." Some people suspect he may have adopted this name to show the professors of his time what a blockhead—a person who had not been educated in their schools—could accomplish.

Some blockhead! The Fibonacci sequence alone describes such natural phenomena as the spiraling pattern of nautilus shells, elephant tusks, sheep horns, birds' claws, pineapples, the branching patterns of plants, *and* the proliferation of rabbits. The ratio of successively higher adjacent terms in the sequence also approaches the "golden section," a ratio that describes an aesthetically pleasing proportion used in the visual arts.

Exercises 6.6

1. The Fibonacci sequence is 0, 1, 1, 2, 3, 5, 8, 13, . . . such that the first two terms are 0 and 1, and each term thereafter is defined recursively as the sum of the two preceding terms; that is, $Fib(n) = Fib(n - 1) + Fib(n - 2)$.

   a. Write a recursive method that returns the nth number in a Fibonacci sequence when n is passed to the method as an argument. For example, when $n = 8$, the method returns the eighth number in the sequence, which is 13.

   b. Write a Java program that calculates the nth number in a Fibonacci sequence using a `for` loop, where n is interactively entered into the program by the user. For example, if $n = 6$, the program should display the value 5.

2. The sum of a series of consecutive numbers from 1 to n can be defined recursively as:

   sum(1) = 1;
   sum(n) = n + sum(n − 1)

   Write a recursive Java method that accepts n as an argument and calculates the sum of the numbers from 1 to n.

3a. The value of x^n can be defined recursively as

$$x^0 = 1$$
$$x^n = x * x^{n-1}$$

Write a recursive method that computes and returns the value of x^n.

b.   Rewrite the method written for Exercise 3a so that it uses a repetitive algorithm for calculating the value of x^n.

4a.   Write a method that recursively determines the value of the nth term of a geometric sequence defined by the terms

$$a, ar, ar^2, ar^3, \ldots ar^{n-1}$$

The arguments to the method should be the first term, a, the common ratio, r, and the value of n.

b.   Modify the method written for Exercise 4a so that the sum of the first n terms of the sequence is returned.

5a.   Write a method that recursively determines the value of the nth term of an arithmetic sequence defined by the terms

$$a, a + d, a + 2d, a + 3d, \ldots a + (n - 1)d$$

The arguments to the method should be the first term, a, the common difference, d, and the value of n.

b.   Modify the method written for Exercise 5a so that the sum of the first n terms of the sequence is returned. (*Note:* This is a more general form of Exercise 2.)

6.7   Program Design and Development: UML State Diagrams

The UML object and class diagrams presented in Section 5.5 are considered static models. State diagrams, which present the transition of an object's state over time, are considered dynamic models. Thus, a state diagram shows the different states that an object can have and the events that cause these states to appear. In effect, a state diagram describes how an object's attributes change over time.

The most important part of describing these changes is clearly specifying the events causing the changes. Each event then becomes associated with a behavior that is included in the object model. Figure 6.17 illustrates the relationship between a class and state diagram.

A state diagram consists of events and states. An *event* is defined as an individual signal (stimulus) from one object to another. For example, turning the key in a car's ignition is a signal to the electrical system to turn on or off. Hence, in object terms, turning the key is an event. Similarly, pushing the button in an elevator is considered an event. The press of the button is a signal to the elevator to move to another floor.

In contrast to events are states. An object's *state*, in its simplest form, is defined by the values of an object's attributes. For example, a switch that can be either on or off has two states: on and off. Similarly, if a rectangle is described by three attributes — its length, width, and position — giving values to these attributes defines a single state for a rectangle object.

In a state diagram, each object has a clearly defined set of states. For example, if the system being programmed has three objects, then you will typically have three

FIGURE 6.17　**The state model identifies operations to be included in the class diagram**

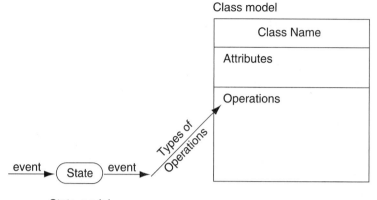

state diagrams, one for each object. Each state diagram is a structured network of events and states. Figure 6.18 illustrates the basic symbols and notation found in a state diagram. The two primary symbols are a flow line, which denotes an event, and a rectangle with rounded corners, which denotes a state. Each event shown in a state diagram can be augmented by a guard, attribute, or action, which are explained later in this section. Similarly, each state can have an optional state name listed in the state rectangle plus activity information.

Notice in Figure 6.18 that events separate states. A state has duration in that it exists over an interval of time and only changes in response to an event, which is assumed to occur in zero time. For example, turning a car's ignition key to start the

FIGURE 6.18　**State diagram notation**

Event causes transition between states:

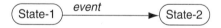

Event with attribute:

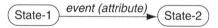

Initial and final states:

Action on a transition:

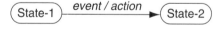

Guarded transition:

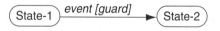

Output event on a transition:

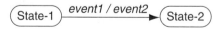

Actions and activity while in a state:

```
State Name
entry / entry-action
do: activity-A
event-1 / action-1
. . .
exit / exit-action
```

Sending an event to another object:

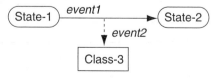

FIGURE 6.19 **A car's ignition system state diagram**

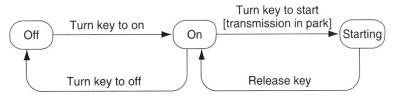

engine is an event. Once the car's engine is started, the state of the engine, which is running, is assumed to continue until an event occurs that turns the engine off. Figure 6.19 illustrates a state diagram for a car's ignition system.

As shown, the ignition system consists of three states: On, Off, and Starting. The events associated with these states are "Turn key to on," "Turn key to start," "Release key," and "Turn key to off. "Notice that the event "Turn key to start" has the precondition "Transmission in Park." Preconditions, which are also referred to as guards, are listed within square brackets after the event's name. A precondition specifies that the event cannot take place unless the precondition is satisfied. In this case, "Turn key to start" will not force a change in state unless the transmission is in Park.

Events are always one-way signals from one object to another. If the signal also provides data values to an object, the data values are listed in parentheses following the event name. As we have seen, these data values are referred to as an event's attributes. Since each event eventually defines an operation, which in Java is coded as a method, an event's attributes become the method's arguments. As one-way signals, however, events never receive a return value from the implemented method. Any reply from the receiving object is considered a separate event to the sending object, which must be realized using another method.

In addition to conditions and attributes, an event may also be associated with some instantaneous action. For example, pressing the right button on a mouse may cause a pop-up menu to appear, while the state of the original menu item becomes highlighted. Such actions are listed after the event and are separated by a slash, /, from the event description (Figure 6.20). These actions form the basis for events that interact with other objects.

Just as events may have actions associated with them, states may have activities. The difference between an action and an activity is the time needed to accomplish them. Actions, as we have noted, are assumed to be accomplished in zero time (instantaneously), while activities take time to complete. Thus, activities are associated with states. The notation *do: activity* within a state rectangle denotes that the activity begins when the state is entered and terminates when the state is left. For example, as illustrated in Figure 6.21, if the state of a house bell-chime system is ringing in response to the event "Push bell button," the action is "ring the chimes."

A state diagram can either represent a continuously operating system or a finite, one-time life cycle. For example, making one phone call or filling a car with gas can be modeled as a finite, one-time activity. The operation of the phone itself or the gas

FIGURE 6.20 **An example of an event activity**

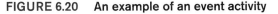

FIGURE 6.21   A state with an activity

pump, however, where the system goes from idle to active, is a continuous operation. One-time activities are typically modeled by a state diagram where the initial state, which represents the creation of an object, is shown by a solid circle. The final state, which represents the end of the cycle and the destruction of an object, is shown by a bull's-eyed circle (Figure 6.22).

Although state diagrams almost always have an initial state, they may have one or more final states or no final state. For example, Figure 6.23 illustrates a state diagram for an elevator. As shown, the elevator initially begins at the first floor, but once in operation, it can be positioned at any other floor. Its activity is restricted to moving either up or down between floors, and it remains at its last destination until a new activity takes place. In the next section, we will create a Java class that implements these activities and states.

FIGURE 6.22   A state diagram of a water sprinkler

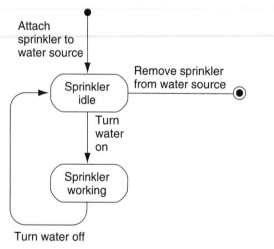

FIGURE 6.23   A state diagram for an elevator

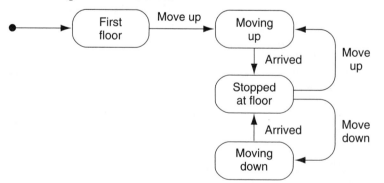

Exercises 6.7

1. Describe the differences between a class and state diagram.

2. Why are state diagrams referred to as dynamic models?

3. Construct a state diagram for a game of checkers.

4. Construct a state diagram for using the brakes on a car.

5. Construct a state diagram for shifting a car's transmission. Assume that there are six gears: Park, Reverse, Neutral, Drive, Drive-1, and Drive-2.

6. The control switch on a thermostat has three positions: Cool, Off, and Heat. Construct a state diagram for the switch.

7. Draw a state diagram for a traffic light that can be in one of three states: green, yellow, or red.

8. List the sequence of events that occur in selecting an item from a soda vending machine. The sequence should start when a customer puts money in the machine and end when the customer removes a can of soda. From this list, complete the sequence diagram in Figure 6.24.

    Each vertical line on the sequence diagram corresponds to an object, and the horizontal lines correspond to events. The arrowhead on the event line corresponds to the event receiver, and the line's tail corresponds to the event sender. Although time is assumed to increase from the top of the diagram to the bottom, the spacing between events is not drawn to time scale. The sequence of events, from first to last, however, is indicated on the diagram starting with the first event shown and ending with the last event. Once you have completed the sequence diagram, use it to create a state diagram for the vending machine.

9. List the sequence of events that occur in using an ATM machine. The sequence should start when the customer inserts the card and end when the card is returned. From this list, complete the sequence diagram in Figure 6.25.

    Each vertical line on the sequence diagram corresponds to an object, and the horizontal lines correspond to events. The arrowhead on the event line corresponds to the event receiver, and the line's tail corresponds to the event sender. Although time is assumed to increase from the top of the diagram to the bottom, the spacing between events is not drawn to time scale. The sequence of events, from first to last, however, is indicated on the diagram starting with the first event shown and ending with the last

FIGURE 6.24

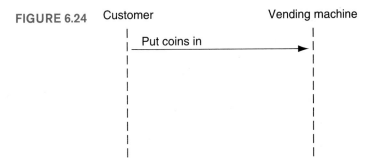

FIGURE 6.25

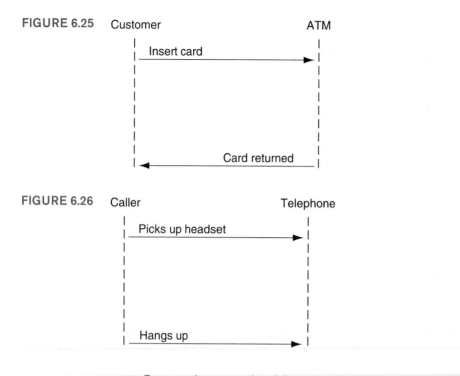

FIGURE 6.26

event. Once you have completed the sequence diagram, use it to create a state diagram for the ATM machine.

10. List the sequence of events that occur in the making of a phone call. The sequence should start when the caller picks up the phone and end when the caller hangs up. From this list, complete the sequence diagram in Figure 6.26.

Each vertical line on the sequence diagram corresponds to an object, and the horizontal lines correspond to events. The arrowhead on the event line corresponds to the event receiver, and the line's tail corresponds to the event sender. Although time is assumed to increase from the top of the diagram to the bottom, the spacing between events is not drawn to time scale. The sequence of events, from first to last, however, is indicated on the diagram starting with the first event shown and ending with the last event. Once you have completed the sequence diagram, use it to create a state diagram for the phone system.

6.8 Applications: Random Numbers and Simulations
Random Numbers

There are many commercial and scientific problems in which probability must be considered or statistical sampling techniques must be used. For example, in simulating automobile traffic flow or telephone usage patterns, statistical models are required. In addition, applications such as simple computer games and more involved gaming scenarios can only be described statistically. All of these statistical models require the generation of **random numbers** — that is, a series of numbers whose order cannot be predicted.

In practice, it is hard to find truly random numbers. Dice are never perfect, cards are never shuffled completely randomly, and digital computers can handle numbers only within a finite range and with limited precision. The best one can do in most cases is generate **pseudorandom numbers**, which are sufficiently random for the task at hand.

Some computer languages contain a library method that produces random numbers; others do not. All Java compilers provide a general-purpose method for creating random numbers named `random()` that is defined in the `Math` class. This method produces a series of double-precision random numbers in the range 0.0 up to, but not including, 1.0.

The general procedure for creating a series of N random numbers in Java is illustrated in QuickTest Program 6.15, which uses the `Math.random()` method to generate a series of 10 random numbers.

QuickTest Program 6.15

```
public class RandomNumbers
{
  public static void main(String[] args)
  {
    double randValue;
    int i;

    for (i = 1; i <= 10; i++)
    {
      randValue = Math.random();
      System.out.println(randValue);
    }

  }
}  // end of class
```

The output produced by one run of Program 6.15 is

```
0.9332932472758279
0.6655689601942523
0.9368189009265464
0.3030248315838068
0.6346712906930385
0.27545891900300157
0.028702213952233935
0.3854898736878013
0.3519811183758321
0.4604059714098424
```

Each time Program 6.15 is run, it creates a different series of 10 random numbers.

Scaling

One modification to the random numbers produced by the `random()` method typically must be made in practice. In most applications, the random numbers are required as integers within a specified range, such as 1 to 100. The method for adjusting the random numbers produced by a random number generator to reside within such ranges is called *scaling*.

Scaling a random number as an integer value between 0 and `N - 1` is accomplished using the expression `(int)(Math.random() * N)`. For example, the expression `int(Math.random() * 100)` produces a random integer between 0 and 99. To produce an integer random number between 1 and `N`, the expression `1 + (int)(Math.random() * N)` can be used. For example, in simulating the roll of a die, the expression `1 + (int)(Math.random() * 6)` produces a random integer between 1 and 6. The more general scaling expression `a + (int)(Math.random() * (b + 1 - a)` can be used to produce a random integer between the numbers `a` and `b`.

Simulations

A common use of random numbers is to simulate events rather than going through the time and expense of constructing a real-life experiment. In this section, we present two examples that illustrate the general concepts and techniques frequently encountered in constructing simulations.

Coin Toss Simulation

Statistical theory tells us that the probability of having a single tossed coin turn up heads is 50 percent. Similarly, there is a 50 percent probability of having a single tossed coin turn up tails. Using these probabilities, we would expect a single coin that is tossed 1000 times to turn up heads 500 times and tails 500 times. In practice, however, this is rarely realized exactly for a single experiment consisting of 1000 tosses. Instead of actually tossing a coin 1000 times, we can use a random number generator to simulate these tosses. In particular, we will use the random number method developed in the previous application.

Figure 6.27 illustrates the class diagram for a coin that can be used in a coin toss simulation. As described by this diagram, each `CoinToss` object will contain a `heads` and `tosses` instance variable. The `tosses` variable will keep track of how many times the coin has been tossed, and the heads variable will keep track of how many times the `head` side came up. We do not need to keep count of the number of tails that appeared because this number can always be calculated as `tosses - heads`.

The `flip()` method will be used to simulate tossing the coin as many times as indicated by the parameter `numTimes`. To determine the number of heads and tails, we will have to simulate random numbers in a manner that permits us to define a result of "heads" or "tails" from each generated number in a statistically correct way. There are a number of ways to do this.

One way is to scale the `random()` method generated numbers to be integers between 1 and 100. Knowing that any single toss has a 50 percent chance of being ei-

FIGURE 6.27 **Class diagram for a** `CoinToss` **class**

CoinToss
-heads: Integer
-tosses: Integer
+flip(numTimes)
+percentages()

ther a head or a tail, we could then designate a head as an even random number and a tail as an odd random number. Another approach would be to use the generated values as is, and simply define a head as any number equal to or greater than 0.5 and any other result as a tail. This is the approach we will adopt.

Having defined how we will create a single toss that has a 50 percent chance of turning up heads or tails, the generation of a sequence of tosses is rather simple: We use a fixed-count loop to generate the desired number of random numbers. For each random number generated, we identify the result as either a head or tail and increment the `heads` variable each time a head is indicated. We will initialize the `heads` and `tosses` variables to zero when a `CoinToss` object is created using the default values supplied by the compiler-provided default constructor. Given this initialization, the flip algorithm becomes

> ### *Flip Algorithm*
> **For numTimes times**
>   *Generate a random number between 0 and 1*
>   *If the random number is equal to or greater than 0.5 increment the heads count*
>   *Increment the tosses count*
> **EndFor**

The implementation of this algorithm into a method named `flip()` is

```java
// this method flips the coin numTimes
// and records the number of tosses and the number of heads
public void flip(int numTimes)
{
  double randValue;
  int i;

  for (i = 1; i <= numTimes; i++)
  {
    randValue = Math.random();
    if (randValue >= 0.5) heads++;
    tosses++;
  }
}
```

The algorithm for the calculating the percentages of heads and tails for the `percentages()` method is

Percentage Algorithm
If the number of tosses equals zero
  Display a message indicating that no tosses were made
Else
  Calculate the number of tails as the number of tosses minus the number of heads
  Display the number of tosses, number of heads, and number of tails
  Calculate the percentage of heads as the number of heads divided by the number of tosses x 100%
  Calculate the percentage of tails as the number of tails divided by the number of tosses x 100%
  Print the percentage of heads and tails
EndIf

Program 6.16 includes the code for this algorithm within the context of a complete class.

Program 6.16

```java
public class CoinToss
{
  // data declaration section
  int heads;
  int tosses;
  // method definition section
    // this method flips the coin numTimes
    // and records the number of tosses and the number of heads
  public void flip(int numTimes)
  {
    double randValue;
    int i;

    for (i = 1; i <= numTimes; i++)
    {
      randValue = Math.random();
      if (randValue >= 0.5) heads++;
      tosses++;
    }
  }

    // this method calculates the percentages of heads
    // and tails, and displays the results
  public void percentages()
  {
    int tails;
    double perheads, pertails;

    if (tosses == 0)
     System.out.println("There were no tosses, so no percentages" +
                        " can be calculated.");
    else
    {
      tails = tosses - heads;
      System.out.println("Number of coin tosses: " + tosses);
      System.out.println("   " + heads + " Heads      " + tails + " Tails");
      perheads = ((double)heads/(double)tosses * 100.0);
      pertails = ((double)(tosses - heads)/(double)tosses * 100.0);

      System.out.println("Heads came up " + perheads +
                        " percent of the time.");
      System.out.println("Tails came up " + pertails +
                        " percent of the time.");

    }
  }
}
```

A BIT OF BACKGROUND

Monte Carlo

Monte Carlo is a community within the principality of Monaco on the Mediterranean coast of France. Monte Carlo's fame as a gambling resort is responsible for its name being adopted for mathematical methods involving random numbers.

Monte Carlo techniques involve creating random numbers within given limits and determining what percentage of those numbers meet certain criteria. They can be used to calculate the area between curves, to estimate the arrival of airplanes at an airport, to predict the percentage of manufactured parts that will be defective, to project the growth and decline of populations with fixed resources, to specify the needed thickness of nuclear-reactor shielding, and so forth.

Monte Carlo calculations were hardly feasible before the development of high-speed computers. In many cases, billions of random numbers must be generated to achieve statistically accurate results. If, on a super-fast computer, one random number selection and test calculation required a microsecond, then a billion calculations would take about 1,000 seconds (roughly 17 minutes). On a typical 486-style personal computer, where the same calculation could take a millisecond, a billion such calculations would require a million seconds (or eleven and a half days).

Clearly, the speed and capacity of a computer are critical for effective application of Monte Carlo techniques. It has not been unusual for a single highly accurate computation of this nature to monopolize a $10-million computer for hours. However, new parallel-processing machines, which can handle many operations concurrently, are reducing the time required for Monte Carlo calculations using large data samples.

Having created a suitable class for a coin toss simulation, we can now perform a simulation by simply creating a coin object, tossing it the desired number of times, and displaying the resulting percentages. This is accomplished by Program 6.17, which simulates the tossing of a coin 1000 times.

Program 6.17

```java
public class DoCoinToss
{
  public static void main(String[] args)
  {
    CoinToss coinOne = new CoinToss();  // create a CoinToss object

    coinOne.flip(1000);  // flip the coin 1000 times
    coinOne.percentages();  // display the results
  }
}
```

Following are two sample runs using Program 6.17.

```
Number of coin tosses: 1000
   509 Heads        491 Tails
Heads came up 50.9 percent of the time
Tails came up 49.1 percent of the time
```

and

```
Number of coin tosses: 1000
   473 Heads        527 Tails
Heads came up 47.3 percent of the time
Tails came up 52.7 percent of the time
```

Writing and running Program 6.16 is certainly easier than manually tossing a coin 1000 times. Notice how simple the simulation program becomes once the `CoinToss` class has been created. This is typical of programs that use objects and is the essence of object-oriented programming; the design process is front-loaded with the requirement that careful consideration of the class—its data declarations and method definitions—be given. Any program that subsequently creates and uses an object does not have to repeat the coding contained in a class's methods. The subsequent program, in this case Program 6.17, need only be concerned with sending messages to its objects to activate them appropriately. How the method is implemented and how the state of the object is retained are not `main()`'s concern because these details are hidden within the class's construction.

Elevator Simulation

In this application, we will simulate the operation of an elevator. The state diagram for an elevator object was provided in Figure 6.23 and is repeated as Figure 6.28 for convenience.

For this application, the only attribute of interest is the location of the elevator. This location, which corresponds to its current floor position, can be represented by an integer instance variable. The value of this variable, which we will name `currentFloor`, effectively represents the current state of the elevator. We will also provide each object with a maximum floor that it can travel to. This will be useful for simulating multiple elevators in larger buildings. For initialization purposes, we will

FIGURE 6.28 **A state diagram for an elevator**

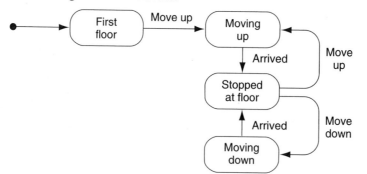

FIGURE 6.29   **A class diagram for an `elevator` class**

```
                    Elevator

-currentFloor: Integer = 1
-maxFloor: Integer = 15

+Elevator()
+setMaxFloor()
+request(newFloor)
```

set this maximum floor to 15. Any value will actually do as long as we explicitly set some value to override the default of zero that would be provided by the compiler. The services that we will provide for changing the state of the elevator will be an initialization method to set the initial floor position when a new elevator is put in service, a method to set the highest floor that the elevator can rise to, and a request method to change the elevator's position (state) to a new floor. Figure 6.29 presents the class diagram for our elevator object.

The actual data declarations for this class and the constructor and mutator methods will be relatively simple. The `request()` method, however, is more complicated and provides the class's primary service. An algorithm that describes this service is

> *If a request is made for either a nonexistent floor or the current floor,*
> > *Do nothing*
> *ElseIf the request is for a floor above the current floor*
> > *Display the current floor number*
> > *While not at the designated floor*
> > > *Increment the floor number*
> > > *Display the new floor number*
> > *EndWhile*
> > *Display the ending floor number*
> *Else   // the request must be for a floor below the current floor*
> > *Display the current floor number*
> > *While not at the designated floor*
> > > *Decrement the floor number*
> > > *Display the new floor number*
> > *EndWhile*
> > *Display the ending floor number*
> *EndIf*

This algorithm consists of an `if-else` statement having three parts: If an incorrect service is requested, no action is taken; if a floor above the current position is selected, the elevator moves up; and if a floor below the current position is selected, the elevator moves down. For movement up or down, a `while` loop can be used to increment or decrement the elevator's position one floor at a time and report the movement using a `println()` method call. This algorithm can be coded as follows:

```
private void request(int newfloor)
{
  if (newfloor < 1 || newfloor > maxFloor || newfloor == currentFloor)
    ;  // do nothing
  else if ( newfloor > currentFloor)  // move elevator up
  {
    System.out.println("\nStarting at floor " + currentFloor);
    while (newfloor > currentFloor)
    {
      currentFloor++;    // add one to current floor
      System.out.println("  Going Up - now at floor " + currentFloor);
    }
    System.out.println("Stopping at floor " + currentFloor);
  }
  else  // move elevator down
  {
    System.out.println("\nStarting at floor " + currentFloor);
    while (newfloor < currentFloor)
    {
      currentFloor--;    // subtract one from current floor
      System.out.println("  Going Down - now at floor " + currentFloor);
    }
    System.out.println("Stopping at floor " + currentFloor);
  }
}
```

Program 6.18 includes this method within the context of a complete class. The remaining methods in this class are straightforward. When an elevator object is created, it can either be initialized to a specified floor by the overloaded constructor, or if no floor is explicitly given, a default value of 1 will be used. In both constructors, a default value of 15 is provided for the highest floor. This value can be explicitly altered by the setMaxFloor() method.

Program 6.18

```
public class Elevator
{
  // class variable declaration section
  private int maxFloor;
  private int currentFloor;

  // class method definition section
  public Elevator()  // this is the default constructor
  {
    currentFloor = 1;
    maxFloor = 15;
  }
  public Elevator(int cfloor)  // an overloaded constructor
  {
    currentFloor = cfloor;
```

```
  maxFloor = 15;
}

public void setMaxFloor(int max)
{
  maxFloor = max;
}

public void request(int newfloor)
{
  if (newfloor < 1 || newfloor > maxFloor || newfloor == currentFloor)
    ;  // do nothing
  else if ( newfloor > currentFloor)  // move elevator up
  {
    System.out.println("\nStarting at floor " + currentFloor);
    while (newfloor > currentFloor)
    {
      currentFloor++;    // add one to current floor
      System.out.println("  Going Up - now at floor " + currentFloor);
    }
    System.out.println("Stopping at floor " + currentFloor);
  }
  else  // move elevator down
  {
    System.out.println("\nStarting at floor " + currentFloor);
    while (newfloor < currentFloor)
    {
      currentFloor--;    // subtract one from current floor
      System.out.println("  Going Down - now at floor " + currentFloor);
    }
    System.out.println("Stopping at floor " + currentFloor);
  }
}
}
```

Using the `Elevator` class requires putting an elevator into service and then requesting various floors and seeing that the elevator responds appropriately. Putting an elevator in service is accomplished by creating an object of type `Elevator`, and requesting a new floor position is equivalent to pushing an elevator button. This is done within Program 6.19.

Program 6.19

```
public class TestElevator
{
  public static void main(String[] args)
  {
    Elevator a = new Elevator();    // declare 1 object of type Elevator
```

(continued)

(continued)

```
    a.request(16);      // try to go above the highest floor
    a.setMaxFloor(6);   // set the highest floor for this elevator
    a.request(7);       // try to go above the new maximum floor

    a.request(6);
    a.request(3);
  }
}
```

The first statement in Program 6.19's `main()` method creates an object of type `Elevator` that can be accessed using the reference variable named a. Since no explicit floor has been given, this elevator will begin at floor 1, which is provided by the default constructor. A request is then made to move the elevator to floor 16. Because this floor number exceeds the highest floor that this elevator can travel to, no elevator movement will be displayed. This sequence of no movement is repeated by setting the maximum floor value to 6 and then requesting that the elevator travel to the 7th floor. The next two statements, however, will cause the elevator to move. This is accomplished by a request to move to the 6th floor, followed by a request to move to the 3rd floor. The output produced by Program 6.19 is

```
Starting at floor 1
    Going Up - now at floor 2
    Going Up - now at floor 3
    Going Up - now at floor 4
    Going Up - now at floor 5
    Going Up - now at floor 6
Stopping at floor 6

Starting at floor 6
    Going Down - now at floor 5
    Going Down - now at floor 4
    Going Down - now at floor 3
Stopping at floor 3
```

One important point should be made concerning Program 6.19, which is the control provided by the `main()` method. Notice that this control is sequential, with subsequent calls made to various class methods using different argument values. This control is perfectly correct for testing purposes. However, by incorporating calls to `request()` within a `while` loop and using the random number method `Math.random()` to generate random floor requests, a continuous simulation of the elevator's operation is possible (see Exercise 5).

Exercises 6.8

1. Enter and run Program 6.17 on your computer.

2. Modify Program 6.17 so that it requests the number of tosses from the user. (*Tip:* Make sure to have the program correctly determine the percentages of heads and tails obtained.)

3. Enter and run Program 6.19 on your computer.

4a. Modify the `main()` method in Program 6.19 to put a second elevator in service starting at the 5th floor. Have this second elevator move to the 1st floor and then move to the 12th floor.

b. Verify that the constructor method is called by adding a message within the constructor that is displayed each time a new object is created. Run your program to ensure its operation.

5. Modify the `main()` method in Program 6.19 to use a `while` loop that calls the `Elevator`'s request method with a random number between 1 and 15. If the random number is the same as the elevator's current floor, generate another request. The `while` loop should terminate after five valid requests have been made and satisfied by movement of the elevator.

6a. Construct a class definition of a `Person` object type. The class is to have no attributes, a single constructor method, and two additional member methods named `arrive()` and `request()`. The constructor method should be an empty, do-nothing method. The `arrive()` method should provide a random number between 1 and 10 as a return value, and the `request()` method should provide a random number between 1 and 15.

b. Test the `Person` class methods written for Exercise 6a in a complete working program.

c. Use the `Person` class method to simulate a random arrival of a person and a random request for a floor to which the elevator should take this person.

7. Construct a class named `Light` that simulates a traffic light. The color attribute of the class should change from green to yellow to red and then back to green by the class's `change()` method. When a new `Light` object is created, its initial color should be red.

8a. Construct a class definition that can be used to represent an employee of a company. Each employee is defined by an integer ID number, a floating-point pay rate, and the maximum number of hours the employee should work each week. The services provided by the class should be the ability to enter data for a new employee, the ability to change data for a new employee, and the ability to display the existing data for a new employee.

b. Include the class definition created for Exercise 8a in a working Java program that asks the user to enter data for three employees and displays the entered data.

6.9 Common Programming Errors

Five errors are commonly made by beginning Java programmers when using repetition statements.

1. Creating a loop that is "off by one," where the loop executes either one too many or one too few times. For example, the loop created by the statement `for(i = 1; i < 11; i++)` executes 10 times, not 11, even though the number 11 is used in the statement. Thus, an equivalent loop can be constructed using the statement `for(i = 1; i <= 10; i++)`. However, if the loop is started with an initial value of `i = 0`, using the statement `for(i = 0; i < 11; i++)`, the loop will be executed 11 times, as will a loop constructed with the statement `for(i = 0; i <= 10; i++)`. Thus, in constructing loops, you must pay particular attention to

both initial and tested conditions that control the loop to ensure that the number of loop repetitions is not off by one too many or one too few executions.

2. As with the `if` statement, repetition statements should not test for equality when testing floating-point (real-values) operands. For example, the condition `fnum == 0.01` should be replaced by a test requiring that the absolute value of `fnum - 0.01` be less than an acceptable amount. One reason is that all numbers are stored in binary form. Using a finite number of bits, decimal numbers such as 0.01 have no exact binary equivalent so that tests requiring equality with such numbers can fail.

3. Placing a semicolon at the end of either the `while` or `for`'s parentheses, which frequently produces a do-nothing loop. For example, consider the statements

```
for(count = 0; count < 10; count++);
  total = total + num;
```

Here the semicolon at the end of the first line of code is a `null` statement. This has the effect of creating a loop that is executed 10 times with nothing done except the incrementing and testing of `count`. This error tends to occur because Java programmers are used to ending most lines with a semicolon.

4. Using commas to separate the items in a `for` statement instead of the required semicolons. An example is the statement

```
for (count = 1, count < 10, count++)
```

Commas are used to separate items within the initializing and altering lists, and semicolons must be used to separate these lists from the tested condition.

5. Omitting the final semicolon from the `do-while` statement. This error is usually made by programmers who have learned to omit the semicolon after the parentheses of a `while` statement and carry over this habit when the reserved word `while` is encountered at the end of a `do-while` statement.

6.10 **Chapter Review**

KEY TERMS

counter	iteration	recursion
data validity check	nested loop	repetition
`do-while` statement	posttest loop	sentinel
fixed-count loop	pretest loop	simulation
`for` statement	pseudorandom numbers	variable-condition loop
infinite loop	random numbers	`while` statement

SUMMARY

1. A section of repeating code is referred to as a loop. The loop is controlled by a repetition statement that tests a condition to determine whether the code will be run. Each pass through the loop is referred to as a repetition or iteration. The tested condition must always be explicitly set prior to its first evaluation by the repetition statement. Within the loop, there must always be a statement that permits altering of the condition so that the loop, once entered, can be exited.

2. There are three basic type of loops:

a. while

b. for

c. do-while

The while and for loops are pretest loops, or entrance controlled loops. In this type of loop, the tested condition is evaluated at the beginning of the loop, which requires that the tested condition be explicitly set prior to loop entry. If the condition is true, loop repetitions begin; otherwise, the loop is not entered. Iterations continue as long as the condition remains true. In Java, while and for loops are constructed using while and for statements, respectively. The do-while loop is a posttest loop, or exit controlled loop, where the tested condition is evaluated at the end of the loop. This type of loop is always executed at least once. A do-while loop continues to execute as long as the tested condition remains true.

3. Loops are also classified as to the type of tested condition. In a fixed-count loop, the condition is used to keep track of how many repetitions have occurred. In a variable-condition loop, the tested condition is based on a variable that can change interactively with each pass through the loop.

4. The while statement checks a condition before any other statement in the loop. This requires that any variables in the tested condition have values assigned before the while is encountered. Within a while loop, there must be a statement that either alters the tested condition's value or forces a break from the loop. The most commonly used form of a loop constructed with a while statement is

```
while(condition)
{
   any number of statements in here;
}
```

5. The for statement is extremely useful in creating loops that must be executed a fixed number of times. Initializing expressions (including declarations), the tested expression, and expressions affecting the tested expression can all be included in parentheses at the top of a for loop. In addition, any other loop statement can be included within the for's parentheses as part of its altering list. A commonly used form of a for statement is

```
for(initializingExpression; condition; incrementExpression)
  {
     any number of statements in here;
  }
```

6. The do-while statement checks its expression at the end of the loop. This ensures that the body of a do-while loop is executed at least once. Within a do-while loop, there must be at least one statement that either alters the tested expression's value or forces a break from the loop. The most commonly used form of a loop constructed with a do-while statement is

```
do
{
   any number of statements in here;
}while(condition);
```

Part Three

Reference and Collection Data Types

7 Strings and Characters

Each computer language has its own method of handling strings of characters. Some languages, such as Java, have an extremely rich set of string manipulation methods and capabilities. Other languages, such as Fortran, which are predominantly used for numerical calculations, added string handling capabilities with later versions of the compiler. Languages such as LISP, which are targeted for list handling applications, provide an exceptional string processing capability. In this chapter, we learn how strings are created and manipulated using Java's object-oriented approach. Thus, this chapter can also be used as an introduction to the general topic of object-oriented programming, which is formally presented in the next chapter, and more precisely to the construction and manipulation of objects using a predefined class.

Specifically, a string in Java is an object that is created from either the String or StringBuffer class. Each class has its own set of methods for both initially creating and manipulating strings. The main difference between these two classes is that a string created from the String class cannot be changed; if a modification is desired, such as adding or changing characters in the original string, a new String object must be created. This is not the case for a string created from the StringBuffer class. Strings created from this class can be altered either by adding, changing, or deleting characters within the string, and the string will dynamically expand or contract as necessary.

In general, the `String` class is more commonly used for constructing strings for input and output purposes, such as for prompts and displayed messages. In addition, because of the provided capabilities, this class is used when strings need to be compared, searched, or individual characters in a string need to be examined or extracted as a substring. The `StringBuffer` class is used in more advanced situations when characters within a string need to be replaced, inserted, or deleted on a relatively regular basis.

7.1 The `String` Class

A **string literal** is any sequence of characters enclosed in double quotation marks. A string literal is also referred to as a string value, a string constant, and more conventionally, simply as a **string**. Examples of strings are `"This is a string"`, "Hello World!" , and `"xyz 123 *!#@&"`. The double quotation marks are used to mark the beginning and ending points of the string and are never stored with the string.

Figure 7.1 shows how the string `Hello` is stored. By convention, the first character in a string is designated as position 0, not 1. This position value is also referred to as both the character's index value and its offset value.

In Java, a string value is always created as an object of either the `String` or `StringBuffer` class. In this and the next section, we describe how strings are stored as objects rather than variables, how they are created, and how they are processed using `String` class methods; this is followed by a similar presentation of the `String-Buffer` class. The main difference between the two classes is that strings created as `String` objects cannot be modified without constructing a new `String` object, whereas `StringBuffer` objects can be modified.

Creating a String

Although a string can be created in a number of different ways, each creation results in taking the same set of steps. For example, in Section 2.4, strings were constructed either using a single declaration and initialization statement of the form

```
String identifier = new String(string-value);
```

or using the equivalent two-statement form

```
String identifier;
identifier = new String(string-value);
```

or using the shorter single-statement form

```
String identifier = string-value;
```

FIGURE 7.1 **The storage of a string as a sequence of characters**

For example, all of the following store the characters H, e, l, l, o into a newly created string.

```
String message = new String("Hello");
```

and

```
String message;
message = new String("Hello");
```

and

```
String message = "Hello";
```

Unlike the declaration of a built-in data type, however, the declared variable, in this case message, *does not* store the value of the declared data type, which in this case is a string. This makes sense because each string can consist of a different number of characters so that a fixed variable length capable of storing all string values cannot realistically be defined. Rather, storage for the string is created in memory when the string is created, and the location of where this string is stored is placed in the variable message. The memory storage allocation that is used is shown in Figure 7.2. Also included in the storage of the string, but not shown in the figure, is the string's length. This value tells Java how many characters to retrieve when the string is accessed.

It is important to understand that although the value in the created string in Figure 7.2 can be displayed with a statement such as System.out.println(message);, the contents of message are not displayed. Rather, the Java system knows that message should be used to locate the actual string and displays the contents of this string. Because the variable message is used to reference where the actual string is stored, it is formally called a **reference variable.** The actual stored data value, which in this case consists of a set of characters that is stored together as a single string entity, as well as other information about the string, such as its length, is formally referred to as an *object.*

Notice that, as a programmer, you did not get the choice of creating message as either a reference or nonreference variable; the choice is automatically made by the Java compiler based on the data type being declared. For the built-in data types presented in Chapter 2, the compiler automatically creates a nonreference variable having the correct size to store a data value of the designated type. For non-built-in data types, a reference variable and an object are automatically created. In Chapters 9 and 10, we will see how to define our own data types, which by definition are not built-in types. Such user-defined data types are always created from classes. In creating strings, however, we are using a class named String that has been provided by the Java compiler. It should be noted that in addition to reference variables created when

FIGURE 7.2 **The storage allocation for both message and the string Hello**

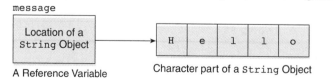

message

A Reference Variable   Character part of a String Object

an object from a class is used, reference variables are also created from array types, which are presented in the next chapter, and from interface types, which are presented in Chapter 12.

To recap, when a data value such as a string is created from a class, such as the String class, the following steps are always taken:

1. A variable, referred to as a reference variable, is declared.
2. An object of the correct data type is created.
3. The location of the object created in step 2 is stored in the reference variable declared in step 1.

Although it is common to refer to a reference variable, such as message, as a string variable with the implication that, as a variable, it contains a string value, it is again important to understand that this is technically incorrect. *A string variable is always a reference variable that provides access to a String object.* The characters making up the string are stored in the memory allocated to the object, not in the memory allocated to the reference variable.

Constructors

The actual storage allocation for a String object and the initialization of this storage with specific characters are created by the new operator. This is true even for the shorter form of a string declaration, which implicitly uses this operator. As was described in Section 2.4, the process of creating a new object is referred to as **instantiating an object.**

The instantiation of a String object always requires the calling of a String method. This call is more clearly seen in a statement such as

```
String message = new String("Have a great day!)";
```

Specifically, in this statement, the expression String("Have a great day!") is a call to a method named String() to which the argument "Have a great day!" is passed. It is no accident that the method name in this call is the same as the data type being declared. In Java, as in most object-oriented languages, the name of the method or methods that can be used to instantiate a new object of a designated class type must be the same name as the class. So in this case, we are declaring a String object and using a method named String() to actually create an object of this type. Methods that have the same name as their class are formally referred to as *constructor methods,* or *constructors* for short, because they are specifically used to construct an object of the declared class.

The String class provides nine different constructors for creating String objects, two of which have been deprecated and should not be used.[1] Table 7.1 provides the syntax of the nondeprecated constructors and an example of each one.

QuickTest Program 7.1 uses each of the examples in Table 7.1 in the context of a complete program.

---

[1] A deprecated method is one that is still supported for consistency with older versions but may be removed in future releases.

Table 7.1   **String Constructors**

Constructor	Description	Example
`String()`	Creates and initializes a `String` object to represent an empty character sequence. The length of the string is 0.	`String str1 = new String();`
`String(string-value)`	Creates and initializes a `String` object to represent the sequence of characters provided as the argument. The argument can be a string constant or string reference variable. The newly created string is a copy of the argument string.	`String str2 = new String("Good Morning");`
`String(char[] charArray)`	Creates and initializes a new `String` object to represent the sequence of characters currently contained in the character array argument.	`char data[]= {'H', 'o', 't', ' ', 'D', 'o', 'g'}; String str3 = new String(data);`
`String(char[] charArray, int offset, int count)`	Creates and initializes a new `String` object to represent a subarray of the characters currently contained in the character array argument.	`char data[]= {'H', 'o', 't', ' ', 'D', 'o', 'g'};String str4 = new String (data, 4 ,3);`
`String(byte[] byteArray)`	Creates and initializes a new `String` object using the bytes currently contained in the byte array argument. Converts bytes to characters using the platform's default character encoding.	`byte bytedata[]= {(byte) 'l', (byte) 'i', (byte) 'n', (byte) 'e', (byte) 'a', (byte) 'r'}; String str5 = new String(bytedata);`
`String(byte[] bytes, int offset, int length)`	Creates and initializes a new `String` object using a subarray of the bytes currently contained in the byte array argument. Converts bytes to characters using the platform's default character encoding.	`byte bytedata[]= {(byte) 'l', (byte) 'i', (byte) 'n', (byte) 'e', (byte) 'a', (byte) 'r'}; String str6 = new String(bytedata, 3, 3);`
`String (StringBuffer buffer)`	Creates and initializes a new `String` object using the characters currently contained in the string buffer argument.	`StringBuffer sb = new StringBuffer("Have a great day!"); String str7 = new String(sb);`

QuickTest Program 7.1

```
public class StringConstructors
{
  public static void main (String[] args)
  {

      String str1 = new String();
      String str2 = new String("Good Morning");
      char data []= {'H', 'o', 't', ' ', 'D', 'o', 'g'};
      String str3 = new String(data);
      String str4 = new String(data, 4 ,3);
      byte bytedata[]= {(byte) 'l', (byte) 'i',
                        (byte) 'n', (byte) 'e',
                        (byte) 'a', (byte) 'r'};
```

```
        String str5 = new String(bytedata);
        String str6 = new String(bytedata, 3, 3);
        StringBuffer sb = new StringBuffer("Have a great day!");
        String str7 = new String(sb);

        System.out.println("str1 is: " + str1);
        System.out.println("str2 is: " + str2);
        System.out.println("str3 is: " + str3);
        System.out.println("str4 is: " + str4);
        System.out.println("str5 is: " + str5);
        System.out.println("str6 is: " + str6);
        System.out.println("str7 is: " + str7);
    }
}
```

The output created by QuickTest Program 7.1 is:

```
str1 is:
str2 is: Good Morning
str3 is: Hot Dog
str4 is: Dog
str5 is: linear
str6 is: ear
str7 is: Have a great day!
```

Although this output is straightforward, two comments are in order. First, notice that str1 is an empty string consisting of no characters. Next, because the first character in a string is designated as position 0, not 1, the character position of the D in the string Hot Dog is located at position 4, which is shown in Figure 7.3.

String objects of the String class are always created as immutable objects. An *immutable object* is one whose stored values cannot be changed or altered in any way. For a string, this means that any characters comprising the string are specified when the string is created, and these characters cannot subsequently be changed.

Because the string concatenation operator introduced in Chapter 2 can make it appear that a String object can be altered, which violates the immutability of the string, we will take a moment to revisit this operator. As we will see, the concatenation operator actually creates a new string and changes the location information stored in the reference variable used to access the string. As an example, consider the following sequence of statements:

```
    // create a string and display its value
String message = "Start";
System.out.println("The string is: " + message);
    // use the concatenation operator and display the new string
message = message + "le";
System.out.println("The string is now: " + message);
```

FIGURE 7.3 **The character positions of the string Hot Dog**

Character Position:	0	1	2	3	4	5	6
	H	o	t		D	o	g

The output produced by this sequence of statements is

```
The string is: Start
The string is now: Startle
```

Although it might look like we have changed the string from `Start` to `Startle`, what is created here is actually two separate `String` objects. After the first statement is executed, the storage allocation shown in Figure 7.4a is created. When the first `println()` call is executed, it displays the string currently referenced by `message`, which is `Start`. The next assignment to `message` creates the storage allocation shown in Figure 7.4b. Notice that the concatenation creates a new `String` object and changes the address in `message` to now reference the second object, which contains the string `Startle`. The last `println()` call then displays this second string, which is located by the reference variable `message`. The reference to the first string is lost, and the storage used by this string will eventually be reclaimed either by Java's automatic memory recovery mechanism or by the operating system when the program containing these statements has finished running. Thus, it appears that the concatenation operator alters an existing string, but this is not the case. `String` objects are always immutable and cannot be changed in any way once they have been created.

String Input and Output

In addition to initializing a string using the constructors in Table 7.1, strings can be input from the keyboard and displayed on the screen. Table 7.2 lists the basic string input and output methods provided in Java.

The `print()` and `println()` methods are extremely useful and have been used throughout the text to display output from Java programs. Essentially, these two methods are interchangeable with the only difference being that the `println()` method automatically positions the cursor at the start of the next line after it has displayed the value of its string argument. This same effect can always be produced using a `print()` method and displaying a newline escape sequence `'\n'` as the last character.

FIGURE 7.4a **The original string and its associated reference variable**

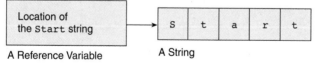

A Reference Variable   A String

FIGURE 7.4b **The new string uses the previous reference variable**

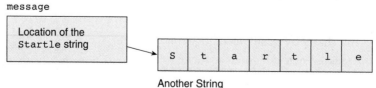

Another String

Table 7.2   **Basic String Input and Output Methods**

Method	Description	Example
print()	General-purpose output, typically to the standard output stream System.out, which is the screen.	System.out.print ("Have a Good Day");
println()	General-purpose screen output that provides an automatic carriage return and new line, typically sent to the standard output stream System.out, which is the screen.	System.out.println ("Have a Good Day");
read()	Restricted-purpose input that reads each character in integer format, typically from the standard input stream System.in, which is the keyboard.	int inchr; inchr = System.in.read()

For input, the read() method is generally not as useful by itself because it reads a character at a time from the keyboard, and each character is input in integer format. In general, it is much easier to use the keyboard and dialog input methods presented in Sections 4.1 and 4.2, respectively, which permit input of strings as a completed unit, than to assemble a string from individual characters input using the read() method.

7.2 String Processing

Strings can be manipulated using either standard **String class** methods or character-at-a-time methods provided by the Character class. Both techniques are presented in this section.

String Class Methods

Because strings are created from a class, except for concatenation using the addition operator, +, and initialization using the equal operator, =, operations on strings are performed using String class methods. This means that assignment and relational operations, as they apply to primitive types, *are not* provided for strings.[2] Extensive collections of String class methods, however, that supply string comparison and other very useful string operations are provided. The more common are listed in Table 7.3.

The most common methods in Table 7.3 are those that are shaded at the beginning of the table. The concatenation method is not included in this group because this operation is almost always implemented using the concatenation operator, +, rather than the concat() method. Exactly like its operator counterpart, however, the concat() method appends one string onto the end of another string. For example, if the contents of a string referenced by string1 is "Hello", then the method call string1.concat(" there World!") results in the string value "Hello there World!"

---

[2] Although the equality operator, ==, can be used, it does not always operate as you might expect, which is explained later in this section.

Table 7.3   **`string` Class Methods**

Method	Description
`int length()`	Returns the length of the string.
`boolean equals(String anotherString)`	Compares two strings for equality.
`boolean equalsIgnoreCase(String anotherString)`	Compares two strings for equality, ignoring whether characters are upper- or lowercase.
`char charAt(int index)`	Returns the character at the specified index.
`int compareTo(String anotherString)`	Compares two strings.
`int compareToIgnoreCase(String anotherString)`	Compares two strings, ignoring case considerations.
`String toLowerCase()`	Returns a new string with all characters in lowercase.
`String toUpperCase()`	Returns a new string with all characters in uppercase.
`String trim()`	Removes whitespace from the beginning and end of the string.
`String concat(String anotherString)`	Concatenates `anotherString` to the end of a string.
`static String copyValueOf(char[] data)`	Returns the string equivalent of the character array.
`static String copyValueOf(char[] data, int offset, int count)`	Returns the string equivalent of a subarray of the character array.
`boolean endsWith(String suffix)`	Tests if the string ends with the specified string.
`void getChars(int srcBegin, int srcEnd, char[] dst, int dstBegin)`	Copies characters from a string into a character array.
`int hashCode()`	Returns an integer number derived from the string.
`int indexOf(int ch)`	Returns the position of the first occurrence of the specified character.
`int indexOf(int ch, int fromPos)`	Returns the position of the first occurrence of the specified character, starting the search at the specified position.
`int indexOf(String str)`	Returns the position of the first occurrence of the specified substring.
`int indexOf(String str, int fromPos)`	Returns the position of the first occurrence of the specified substring, starting at the specified position.
`int lastIndexOf(int ch)`	Returns the position of the last occurrence of the specified character.
`int lastIndexOf(int ch, int fromIndex)`	Returns the position of the last occurrence of the specified character, searching backward starting at the specified position.
`int lastIndexOf(String str)`	Returns the position of the last occurrence of the specified substring.
`int lastIndexOf(String str, int fromPos)`	Returns the position of the last occurrence of the specified substring, searching backward starting from the specified position.
`String replace(char oldChar, char newChar)`	Returns a new string with all occurrences of `oldChar` replaced with `newChar`.
`boolean startsWith(String prefix)`	Tests if the string starts with the specified prefix.
`boolean startsWith(String prefix, int startPos)`	Tests if the string starts with the specified prefix, starting at the specified position.
`String substring(int start)`	Returns a new string that is a substring of the original string. The substring starts at the specified position and extends to the end of the string.
`String substring(int start, int end)`	Returns a new string that is a substring of the original string. The new string starts at the specified position and ends at one character position less than the end argument.

The `length()` method returns the number of characters in the string, which is referred to as the string's length. For example, the value returned by the method call `"Hello World!".length()` is 12. As always, the double quotation marks surrounding a string value are not considered part of the string. Similarly, if the string referenced by `string1` contains the value `"Have a good day."`, the value returned by the call `string1.length()` is 16.

Notice that there is no string copy method that copies one string to another. Because `String` objects cannot be changed, the only way that a string can be copied is to create a new string using the string to be copied as an argument to the constructor. For example, the statement `String s2 = new String(s1);` effectively copies the `String` object referenced by `s1` into a string referenced by the variable `s2`.

Finally, two string expressions may be compared for equality using either the `compareTo()` or `equals()` methods and their variations that ignore case (upper or lower). In Unicode, a blank precedes (is less than) all letters and numbers; the letters of the alphabet are stored in order from A to Z, and the digits are stored in order from 0 to 9. In this sequence, the lowercase letters come before (are less than) the uppercase letters, unless case is ignored, and the letter codes come before (are less than) the digit codes.

When two strings are compared, their individual characters are compared a pair at a time (both first characters, then both second characters, etc.). If no differences are found, the strings are equal; if a difference is found, the string with the first lower character is considered the smaller string. The `equals()` methods simply tell if two strings are equal or not by returning either a Boolean `true` or `false`. The `compareTo()` methods provide additional information indicating the smaller or larger string and the character position that determined the result. If the two strings are equal, the `compareTo()` methods return a 0. When using the `ignoreCase()` versions of these methods, the result of the comparison is independent of a letter's case. Thus, if case is ignored, the letters 'h' and 'H' are considered equal. Following are examples of string comparisons when case is not ignored:

> "Hello" is greater than "Good Bye" because the first 'H' in Hello is greater than the first 'G' in Good Bye.
>
> "hello" is less than "Hello" because the first 'h' in hello is less than the first 'H' in Hello.
>
> "SMITH" is greater than "JONES" because the first 'S' in SMITH is greater than the first 'J' in JONES.
>
> "123" is greater than "1227" because the third character, the '3', in 123 is greater than the third character, the '2', in 1227.
>
> "Behop" is greater than "Beehive" because the third character, the 'h', in Behop is greater than the third character, the 'e', in Beehive.

QuickTest Program 7.2 uses these string methods within the context of a complete program.

QuickTest Program 7.2

```
public class StringMethods
{
  public static void main (String[] args)
  {
```

(continued)

(continued)

```
    String string1 = new String("Hello");
    String string2 = new String("Hello there");
    int n;

    System.out.println("string1 is the string " + string1);
    System.out.println("string2 is the string " + string2);
    System.out.println();   // blank line

    n = string1.compareTo(string2);

    if (n < 0)
       System.out.println(string1 + " is less than " + string2);
    else if (n == 0)
       System.out.println(string1 + " is equal to " + string2);
    else
       System.out.println(string1 + " is greater than " + string2);

    if (string1.equalsIgnoreCase("HELLO"))
       System.out.println("string1 equals (ignoring case) HELLO");
    else
       System.out.println("string1 does not equal (ignoring case) HELLO");

    System.out.println("\nThe number of characters in string1 is " + string1.length());
    System.out.println("The number of characters in string2 is " + string2.length());

    string1 = string1.concat(" there world!");
    System.out.println("\nAfter concatenation, string1 contains the characters " +string1);
    System.out.println("The length of this string is " + string1.length());

    string1 = string1.toLowerCase();
    System.out.println("\nIn lowercase this string is " + string1);

    string1 = string1.toUpperCase();
    System.out.println("In uppercase this string is " + string1);

  }
}
```

Following is a sample output produced by QuickTest Program 7.2:

```
    string1 is the string Hello
    string2 is the string Hello there

    Hello is less than Hello there
    string1 equals (ignoring case) HELLO

    The number of characters in string1 is 5
    The number of characters in string2 is 11

    After concatenation, string1 contains the characters Hello there world!
    The length of this string is 18
```

```
In lowercase this string is hello there world!
In uppercase this string is HELLO THERE WORLD!
```

In reviewing this output, refer to Figure 7.5, which shows how the characters in `string1` and `string2` are stored in memory. Note that the length of each string refers to the total number of characters in the string and that the first character in each string is located at index position 0. Thus, the length of a string is always one more than the index number of the last character's position in the string.

Caution

When comparing two strings for equality, you should never use the equality operator, ==. The reason is that while the `String` class's `compareTo()` and `equals()` methods compare the actual characters in the strings being compared, the == operator compares the values stored in the reference variables used to access the strings. This can lead to seemingly incorrect results. For example, assuming that s1 is declared as `String s1 = "Help";`, the expression (s1 == "Help") is true. However, if the characters H, e, l, p are instantiated in any other way, such as `String s2 = "Helpless".substring(0,4);`, the expression (s1 == s2) is false. The reason is that, although the strings referenced by both s1 and s2 consist of the same characters, the reference variables s1 and s2, as shown in Figure 7.6, reference two different strings. Thus, even though the characters in each string are the same, the reference variables themselves are different.

The important point to bring away from this is that equality of strings should not be tested using the equality operator, ==, that is used for comparing primitive data types. Rather, when testing for string equality, you should use either a `compareTo()` or `equals()` `String` class method.

Other `String` Methods

Although you will predominantly be using the shaded `String` class methods listed in Table 7.3, there are times when you will find the other `String` methods in this table useful. One of the more useful of these is the `charAt()` method, which permits you to retrieve individual characters in a string. QuickTest Program 7.3 uses this method

FIGURE 7.5   The initial strings used in QuickTest Program 7.2

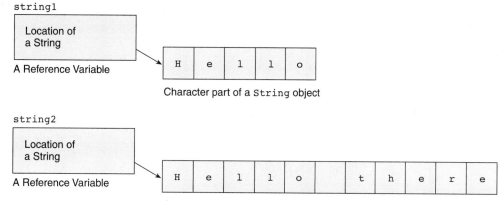

FIGURE 7.6 **Different reference variables can reference equal strings**

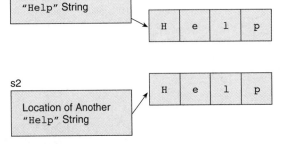

to select one character at a time from the string, starting at string position zero and ending at the position of the last character in the string. This last position is always one less than the number of characters in the string.

QuickTest Program 7.3

```java
public class CountVowels
{
    public static void main (String[] args)
    {

        String str = new String("Counting the number of vowels");
        int i, numChars;
        int vowelCount = 0;

        System.out.println("The string: " + str);

        numChars = str.length();
        for (i = 0; i < numChars; i++)
        {
            switch(str.charAt(i))    // here is where a character is retrieved
            {
                case 'a':
                case 'e':
                case 'i':
                case 'o':
                case 'u':
                    vowelCount++;
            }
        }

        System.out.println("has " + vowelCount + " vowels.");
    }
}
```

The expression `str.charAt(i)` in QuickTest Program 7.3's `switch` statement re-trieves the character at position `i` in the string. This character is then compared to five different character values. The `switch` statement uses the fact that selected cases "drop through" in the absence of `break` statements. Thus, all selected cases result in an increment to `vowelCount`. The output displayed by QuickTest Program 7.3 is

```
The string: Counting the number of vowels
has 9 vowels.
```

In programming practice, the remaining `String` methods in Table 7.3 usually center around locating specific characters in a string and creating substrings. Quick-Test Program 7.4 presents examples of how some of these other methods are used.

QuickTest Program 7.4

```java
public class OtherMethods
{
  public static void main(String[] args)
  {

    String string1 = "LINEAR PROGRAMMING THEORY";
    String s1, s2, s3;
    int j, k, l;

    System.out.println("The original string is " + string1);

    j = string1.indexOf('I');
    System.out.println("  The first position of an 'I' is " + j);

    k = string1.indexOf('I', (j+1));
    System.out.println("  The next position of an 'I' is " + k);

    l = string1.lastIndexOf('I');
    System.out.println("  The last position of an 'I' is " + l);

    j = string1.indexOf("THEORY");
    System.out.println("  The first location of \"THEORY\" is " + j);

    k = string1.lastIndexOf("ING");
    System.out.println("  The last index of \"ING\" is " + k);

    s1 = string1.substring(2,6);
    s2 = string1.substring(18,22);
    s3 = string1.substring(6,14);

    System.out.println(s1.concat(s2).concat(s3));
  }
}
```

The output produced by QuickTest Program 7.4 is

```
The original string is LINEAR PROGRAMMING THEORY
   The first position of an 'I' is 1
   The next position of an 'I' is 15
   The last position of an 'I' is 15
   The first location of "THEORY" is 19
   The last index of "ING" is 15
NEAR THE PROGRAM
```

The main point illustrated by QuickTest Program 7.4 is that both individual characters and sequences of characters can be located in an existing string and extracted from a string. In extracting a substring, however, it is important to realize that the second argument in the substring() method is the position of the character one after the last character that is to be extracted. And as can be clearly seen, the concatenation operator, +, is preferable to the more complicated expression that uses the concat() method in the program's last executable statement.

Character Methods

In addition to the string methods provided by the String class, the Java language provides a number of very useful **Character class** general-purpose methods. A commonly used subset of these methods is listed in Table 7.4.

Because all of the methods in Table 7.4 are public and static, which makes them general-purpose methods that are used independently of any object created from the class, each of these methods is preceded with its class name when it is invoked. Also notice that except for the last three methods, each of the other methods returns a Boolean value of true if the character meets the desired condition and a

Table 7.4 **Character Class General-Purpose Methods**

Method	Description
public static boolean isDigit(char ch)	Returns a true if ch is a digit; otherwise, it returns a false.
public static boolean isLetter(char ch)	Returns a true if ch is a letter; otherwise, it returns a false.
public static boolean isLowerCase(char ch)	Returns a true if ch is a lowercase letter; otherwise, it returns a false.
public static boolean isSpaceChar(char ch)	Returns a true if ch is a space character; otherwise, it returns a false.
public static boolean isUpperCase(char ch)	Returns a true if ch is an uppercase letter; otherwise, it returns a false.
public static boolean isWhitespace(char ch)	Returns a true if ch is a Java-defined whitespace; otherwise, it returns a false.
public static char toLowerCase(char ch)	Returns the lowercase equivalent of ch if the character is lowercase; otherwise, it returns the character unchanged.
public static char toUpperCase(char ch)	Returns the uppercase equivalent of ch if the character is lowercase; otherwise, it returns the character unchanged.
public static char toString(char ch)	Returns the string representation of ch.

value of `false` if the condition is not met. These methods that return a Boolean value are generally used directly within an `if` statement. For example, consider the following code segment, which assumes that `ch` is a character variable.

```
if(Character.isDigit(ch))
  System.out.println("The character is a digit");
else if(Character.isLetter(ch))
  System.out.println("The character is a letter");
```

Here, if the `ch` contains a digit character, the first `println()` method is executed; if the character is a letter, the second `println()` statement is called. In both cases, however, the character to be checked is included as an argument to the appropriate method, which itself is preceded by the class name, `Character`, and a period. Quick-Test Program 7.5 illustrates this type of code within a program that counts the number of letters, digits, and other characters in a string. The individual characters to be checked are obtained using the `String` class's `charAt()` method in the same manner as was previously illustrated in QuickTest Program 7.3. As in QuickTest Program 7.3, this method is used in a `for` loop that cycles through the string from the first to the last.

QuickTest Program 7.5

```
public class CharMethods
{
  public static void main (String[] args)
  {
    String str = new String("This -123/ is 567 A ?<6245> Test!");
    char nextChar;
    int i, numChars;
    int numLetters = 0, numDigits = 0, numOthers = 0;

    System.out.println("The original string is: " + str);

    numChars = str.length();
    System.out.println("This string contains " + numChars + " characters,"
                      + " which consist of");
      // check each character in the string
    for (i = 0; i < numChars; i++)
    {
      nextChar = str.charAt(i);  // get a character
      if (Character.isLetter(nextChar))
        numLetters++;
      else if (Character.isDigit(nextChar))
        numDigits++;
      else
        numOthers++;
    }

    System.out.println("      " + numLetters + " letters");
```

(continued)

(continued)
```
        System.out.println("      " + numDigits + " digits");
        System.out.println("      " + numOthers + " other characters.");


    }
}
```

The output produced by QuickTest Program 7.5 is

```
The original string is: This -123/ is 567 A ?<6245> Test!
This string contains 33 characters, which consist of
        11 letters
        10 digits
        12 other characters.
```

As indicated by this output, each of the 33 characters in the string has correctly been categorized as either a letter, digit, or other character.

Conversion Methods

The last group of string methods, which are listed in Tables 7.5 and 7.6, are used to convert strings to and from primitive numerical data types. The methods in Table 7.5 are both `public` and `static` members of the `String` class, which means they are general purpose and are typically invoked by preceding the method name with the `String` class name and a period. In each case, the value to be converted is provided as a primitive data type argument, and the converted string value is returned from the method. For example, the statement `String str = String.valueOf(42689.65);` causes the string `"42689.65"` to be created from the double-precision number 42689.65 (recall that the default for values with a decimal point is `double`), and this string value can now be referenced by the variable named `str`.

For computational purposes, the conversion methods in Table 7.6, which provide conversions from string types to primitive types are more useful. These methods have been divided into four categories that represent conversions from strings to integers,

Table 7.5 **Primitive Type to String Conversion Methods (All Methods Are Members of the `String` Class)**

Method	Description
`public static String valueOf(Boolean b)`	Returns the string representation of its Boolean argument.
`public static String valueOf(char c)`	Returns the string representation of its `char` argument.
`public static String valueOf(char[] data)`	Returns the string representation of its `char` array argument.
`public static String valueOf(char[] data, int offset, int count)`	Returns the string representation of a specific subarray of its `char` array argument.
`public static String valueOf(double d)`	Returns the string representation of its `double` argument.
`public static String valueOf(float f)`	Returns the string representation of its `float` argument.
`public static String valueOf(int i)`	Returns the string representation of its `int` argument.
`public static String valueOf(long l)`	Returns the string representation of its `long` argument.

Table 7.6   String to Primitive Type Conversion Methods (All Methods Are Members of the `String` Class)

Method	Class	Description
`public static int parseInt(String str)`	Integer	Returns the integer representation of `str`.
`public static valueOf(String str)`	Integer	Returns the Integer value of `str`.
`int inValue()`	Integer	Returns the integer value of an `Integer` object.
`public static long parseLong(String str)`	Long	Returns the long representation of `str`.
`public static LongValueOf(String str)`	Long	Returns the Long value of `str`.
`longValue()`	Long	Returns the long value of a `Long` object.
`public static float parseFloat(String str)`	Float	Returns the float representation of `str`.
`public static FloatvalueOf(String str)`	Float	Returns the Float value of `str`.
`float floatValue()`	Float	Returns the float value of a `Float` object.
`public static double parseDouble(String str)`	Double	Returns the double representation of `str`.
`public static DoublesvalueOf(String str)`	Double	Returns the Double value of `str`.
`double doubleValue()`	Double	Returns the double value of a `Double` object.

longs, floats, and doubles. Within each category of conversion types, there are three methods. In practice, either the first method is used alone to convert from a string to a primitive type, or the last two methods are combined to produce the same conversion. For example, assuming the following declarations

```
String str = "42689.65";
double dvalue;
```

each of the following statements will convert the `str` string to the double-precision number 42689.65.

```
dvalue = Double.parseDouble(str);
```

and

```
dvalue = Double.valueOf(str).doubleValue()
```

Throughout this text, we have consistently used the conversion technique represented by the first statement because it is simpler. Because this conversion uses the general-purpose `parseDouble()` method, it is always invoked by preceding the method's name with the class name `Double` and a period. It is worthwhile examining how the second conversion technique works because you will also see it in your programming work. First, the expression `Double.valueOf(str)` invokes the `Double` class's `static` method `valueOf()` to convert its string argument into an object of type `Double`. Once this object has been created, the `doubleValue()` method, which is a non-`static` method, is applied to it. Thus, a longer equivalent to the second conversion that more clearly shows how the conversion is accomplished is

```
Double tempval = Double.valueOf(str);
dvalue = tempval.doubleValue();
```

Here the first statement uses the general-purpose method `valueOf()` to convert the `str` string to an object of type `Double`, which is then further converted to a `double` value in the second statement by applying a class method to the `Double` object.

Exercises 7.2

1. Enter and run QuickTest Program 7.2 on your computer.

2. Modify QuickTest Program 7.2 to accept a string entered by the user.

3. Determine the value of `text.charAt(0)`, `text.charAt(3)`, and `text.charAt(10)`, assuming that `text` is the following string of characters:

    a. now is the time

    b. rocky raccoon welcomes you

    c. Happy Holidays

    d. The good ship

4. The following program illustrates the problems associated with using the `==` operator when comparing strings. Enter and run this program and then discuss why the second comparison did not indicate that the strings referenced by `s1` and `s3` were equal.

```
public class Caution
{
  public static void main(String[] args)
  {
    String s1 = "Help";
    String s2 = "Helpless";
    String s3;

    System.out.println("The string s1 is: " + s1);
    System.out.println("The string s2 is: " + s2);

    s3 = s2.substring(0,4);
    System.out.println("The string s3 is: " + s3);

    if (s1 == "Help")
     System.out.println("The first comparison returned a true.");
    else
      System.out.println("The first comparison returned a false.");
    if (s1 == s3)
     System.out.println("The second comparison returned a true.");
    else
      System.out.println("The second comparison returned a false.");
  }
}
```

5. Enter and run QuickTest Program 7.3 on your computer.

6.   Modify QuickTest Program 7.3 to count and display the individual numbers of each vowel contained in the string.

7.   Modify QuickTest Program 7.3 to display the number of vowels in a user-entered string.

8.   Using the `charAt()` method, write and run a Java program that reads in a string and prints the string in reverse order. (*Tip:* Once the string has been entered and saved, retrieve and display characters starting from the end of the string.)

9.   Write and run a Java program that retrieves each character in a string, converts the character to uppercase form, and displays the character.

10.   Assuming that the String variable `str` references the string `"1234"`, write two different statements that can be used to convert this string into an integer number that is stored in the integer variable named `intnum`.

11.   Assuming that the String variable `str` references the string `"1234"`, write two different statements that can be used to convert this string into a long number that is stored in the long variable named `longnum`.

12.   Assuming that the String variable `str` references the string `"1234.52"`, write two different statements that can be used to convert this string into a floating-point number that is stored in the floating-point variable named `floatnum`.

13.   Write and run a Java program that counts the number of words in a string. A word occurs whenever a transition from a blank space to a nonblank character is encountered. Assume that the string contains only words separated by blank spaces.

14.   Generate 10 random numbers in the range 0 to 127. If the number represents a printable Unicode character, print the character with an appropriate message that

```
The character is a lowercase letter
The character is an uppercase letter
The character is a digit
The character is a space
```

If the character is none of these, display its value in integer format.

15a. Write a general-purpose method named `countlets()` that returns the number of letters in a string passed as an argument. Digits, spaces, punctuation, tabs, and newline characters should not be included in the returned count.

b.   Include the `countlets()` method written for Exercise 15a in an executable Java program and use the program to test the method.

7.3 **The `StringBuffer` Class**

Although strings created from the `String` class can be manipulated using both `String` and `Character` class methods, the strings are immutable, which means that characters cannot be inserted, replaced, or added to the string once it is created. When this restriction becomes a problem, a better choice for implementing a string is as a `StringBuffer` object. Because `StringBuffer` strings are implemented as a mutable sequence of characters, these strings *can be* modified in a way that alters the total number of characters, replaces existing characters, and inserts or deletes characters within an existing string. The disadvantage is that the `StringBuffer` class does not provide a set of methods for comparing strings or locating characters and substrings within a string. Thus, the `String` class is the preferred class for displaying or comparing strings that tend to remain constant, and for applications that require individual character additions, modifications, and multiple text edits, the `String-Buffer` class should be used. Because `String` and `StringBuffer` conversion methods exist, one object type can always be converted into its other class counterpart when a particular method is required.

Initially, every `StringBuffer` string is created and stored in a buffer having a set character capacity. Because `StringBuffer` objects are stored in expandable buffer areas, and to distinguish them from their `String` counterparts, `StringBuffer` strings are frequently referred to as *string buffers*. In this text, we will use the terms string and string buffer interchangeably whenever it is clear to which class type we are referring.

As long as the number of characters in a string buffer, either because characters were inserted or appended, does not cause the buffer's capacity to be exceeded, the same buffer area is retained. However, if additions exceed the string's capacity, a new string buffer area is automatically allocated. Reducing the number of characters in a string buffer due to deletions does not decrease the capacity of the buffer.

From a user's standpoint, we would expect the `StringBuffer` class to provide methods that permit modifying a string buffer. This is indeed the case. Table 7.7 lists the methods provided by the `StringBuffer` class to create an initial `String` object of this data type, and Table 7.8 lists all of the available class methods.

As is seen in Table 7.8, the majority of the provided methods have to do with appending and inserting characters into an existing string. Both the `append()` and `insert()` methods are overloaded to accommodate a number of different data types. In all cases, the data are first converted to a string and appended or inserted into the existing string. The `StringBuffer` `append()` methods always add characters to the end of the string, and the `insert()` methods insert characters within a string at the designated position.

As an example of some of the more commonly used methods in Table 7.8, assume that we start with a string buffer type string created by the statement

```
StringBuffer str = new StringBuffer("This cannot be");
```

Table 7.7   `StringBuffer` Constructor Methods

Method	Description	Example
`StringBuffer()`	Constructs a string having no characters and an initial capacity of 16 characters.	`StringBuffer str = new StringBuffer();`
`StringBuffer(int length)`	Constructs a string having no characters and an initial capacity specified by length.	`StringBuffer str = new StringBuffer(64);`
`StringBuffer(String str)`	Constructs a string having the same characters as `str` with a capacity of an additional 16 characters. The stored string is a copy of `str`, and the constructor effectively provides a conversion from a `String` to a `StringBuffer` object.	`StringBuffer str1 = new StringBuffer("Hello");`

Table 7.8   **StringBuffer** Class Methods

Method	Description
Append Methods	
`StringBuffer append(Boolean b)`	Appends the string representation of the Boolean value b.
`StringBuffer append(char c)`	Appends the string representation of the char value c.
`StringBuffer append(char[] str)`	Appends the string representation of the char array str.
`StringBuffer append(char[] str, int offset, int len)`	Appends the string representation of the designated subarray.
`StringBuffer append(int i)`	Appends the string representation of the int value i.
`StringBuffer append(long l)`	Appends the string representation of the long value l.
`StringBuffer append(double d)`	Appends the string representation of the double value d.
`StringBuffer append(float f)`	Appends the string representation of the float value f.
`StringBuffer append(String str)`	Appends the string value str.
`StringBuffer append(Object obj)`	Appends the string representation of the Object obj.
Capacity Methods	
`int capacity()`	Returns the current string's capacity.
`void ensureCapacity(int minCap)`	Ensures the capacity of the string is at least equal to minCap. If the current capacity is less than minCap, the capacity is increased; otherwise, the capacity remains the same.
`int length()`	Returns the number of characters currently in the string.
`void setLength(int newLength)`	Increases or decreases the maximum length of the string. If the current length is greater than newLength, characters are discarded from the end of the string. If newLength is greater than the current length, null characters (\0) are added to the string.
Character Manipulation Methods	
`char charAt(int index)`	Returns the character at the specified index.
`void setCharAt(int position, char ch)`	Sets the character at the specified position to the value ch.
`StringBuffer reverse()`	Reverses the characters in the string.
`void getChars(int srcBegin, int srcEnd, char[] dst, int dstBegin)`	Copies the designated characters from the src string into the dst character array.
Replacement Method	
`StringBuffer replace(int start, int end, String str)`	Replaces the characters starting at position start and ending at one less than position end with the characters in the string str. The number of characters in str need not be the same as those being replaced.
Delete Methods	
`StringBuffer delete(int start, int end)`	Removes the specified characters starting at position start and ending at one position less than end. start must be greater than zero and less than the length of the string, or an exception error is generated.
`StringBuffer deleteCharAt(int index)`	Removes the character at the designated position and closes up the string around the deleted characters.
Insert Methods	
`StringBuffer insert(int offset, Boolean b)`	Inserts the string representation of the Boolean value b into the string at the designated position.

(continued)

Table 7.8   *(continued)*

Method	Description
`StringBuffer insert(int offset, char c)`	Inserts the string representation of the `char` value `c` into the string at the designated position.
`StringBuffer insert(int offset, char[] str)`	Inserts the string representation of the `char` array `str` into the string at the designated position.
`StringBuffer insert(int index, char[] str, int offset, int len)`	Inserts the string representation of the designated subarray into the string at the designated position.
`StringBuffer insert(int offset, int i)`	Inserts the string representation of the `int` value `i` into the string at the designated position.
`StringBuffer insert(int offset, long l)`	Inserts the string representation of the `long` value `l` into the string at the designated position.
`StringBuffer insert(int offset, double d)`	Inserts the string representation of the `double` value `d` into the string at the designated position.
`StringBuffer insert(int offset, float f)`	Inserts the string representation of the `float` value `f` into the string at the designated position.
`StringBuffer insert(int offset, String str)`	Inserts the string `str` into the string at the designated position.
`StringBuffer insert(int offset, Object obj)`	Inserts the string representation of the `Object` `obj` into the string.
`String substring(int start)` substring	Returns a new string that is a substring of the original string. The substring starts at the specified position and extends to the end of the string.
`String substring(int start, int end)`	Returns a new string that is a substring of the original string. The substring starts at the specified position and ends at one character position less than the end argument.

Conversion Method

`String toString()`	Converts the `StringBuffer` string into a `String` string.

Figure 7.7 illustrates how this string is stored in the buffer created for it. As indicated in Table 7.7, the initial capacity of the buffer is the length of the string plus 16 characters.

FIGURE 7.7   **The initial storage of a `StringBuffer` object**

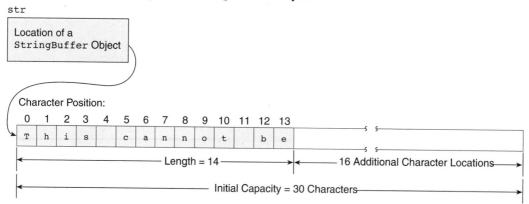

FIGURE 7.8   **The string after the insertion**

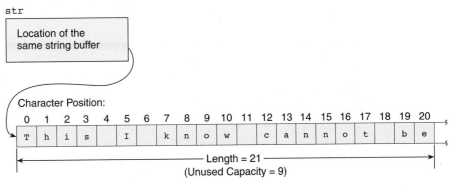

Now assume that the following statement is executed:

```
str.insert(4, " I know");
```

This statement causes the designated seven characters, beginning with a blank, to be inserted starting at index position 4 in the existing string. The resulting string buffer, after the insertion, is as shown in Figure 7.8.

If the statement `str.replace(12, 18, "to");` is now executed, the existing characters in index positions 12 through 17, which is one less than the designated ending index position, will be deleted and the two characters will be inserted starting at index position 12. Thus, the net effect of the replacement is as shown in Figure 7.9. It is worthwhile noting that the number of replacement characters, which in this particular case is two, can be less than, equal to, or greater than the characters that are being replaced, which in this case is six.

Finally, if we append the string "correct" to the string in Figure 7.9 using the statement `str.append(" correct");`, the string illustrated in Figure 7.10 is obtained.

QuickTest Program 7.6 illustrates using the statements we have just examined within the context of a complete program. In addition, after the `append()` method is called, which results in the string shown in Figure 7.10, the program invokes the `reverse()` method to show how this string can be reversed.

FIGURE 7.9   **The string after the replacement**

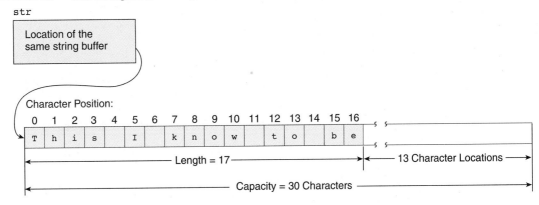

A BIT OF BACKGROUND

Anagrams and Palindromes

Some of the most challenging and fascinating word games are played with anagrams and palindromes.

An *anagram* is a rearrangement of the letters in a word or phrase that makes another word or phrase. Although the letters of the word *door* can be rearranged to spell *orod* and *doro*, it is more exciting to discover the words *odor* and *rood*. A word, phrase, or sentence that reads the same forward and backward, such as *top spot*, is a *palindrome*.

The origins of most known anagrams and palindromes are lost to anonymity. Here are some collected by Richard Manchester in *The Mammoth Book of Fun and Games* (New York: Hart Publishing Co., 1977, pages 229–231).
Apt Anagrams

- The Mona Lisa → No hat, a smile
- The United States of America → Attaineth its cause: freedom!

Interesting Palindromes

- Live not on evil!
- 'Tis Ivan on a visit.
- Yreka Bakery (This is a real business in Yreka, California.)
- Able was I ere I saw Elba. (Might Napoleon have coined this one?)
- Madam, I'm Adam.
- A man, a plan, a canal: Panama!

Computers can be programmed to detect palindromes and find anagrams, but the human brain may be more efficient for doing this.

FIGURE 7.10   The string after the append

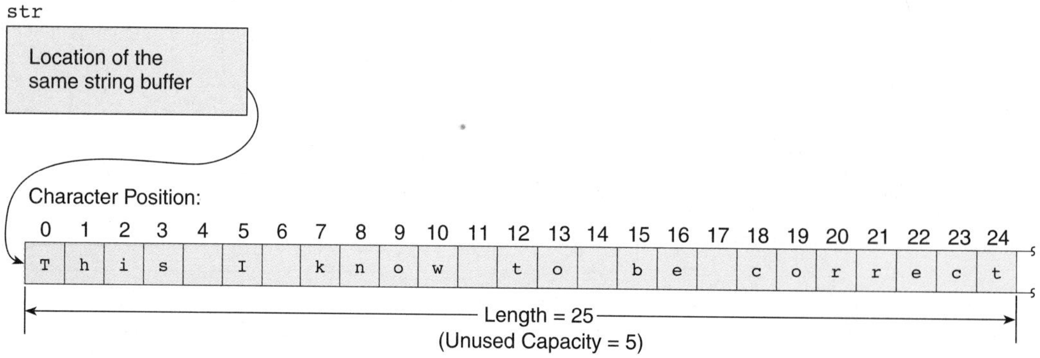

QuickTest Program 7.6

```java
import java.io.*;
public class StringBufferMethods
{
  public static void main (String[] args)
  {
    StringBuffer str = new StringBuffer("This cannot be");
    int i, numChars;

    System.out.println("The original string is: " + str);

    numChars = str.length();
    System.out.println("  This string has " + numChars + " characters.");

      // insert characters
    str.insert(4, " I know");
    System.out.println("The string, after insertion, is now: " + str);
    numChars = str.length();
    System.out.println("  This string has " + numChars + " characters.");

      // replace characters
    str.replace(12, 18, "to");
    System.out.println("The string, after replacement, is: " + str);
    numChars = str.length();
    System.out.println("  This string has " + numChars + " characters.");

      // append characters
    str.append(" correct");
    System.out.println("The string, after appending, is: " + str);
    numChars = str.length();
    System.out.println("  This string has " + numChars + " characters.");

      // reverse the characters
    str.reverse();
    System.out.println("The string, after being reversed, is: " + str);

  }
}
```

The following output is produced by QuickTest Program 7.6. Except for the final reversal of string characters, it matches the individual strings shown in Figures 7.7 to 7.10.

```
The original string is: This cannot be
   This string has 14 characters.
The string, after insertion, is now: This I know cannot be
   This string has 21 characters.
The string, after replacement, is: This I know to be
   This string has 17 characters.
The string, after appending, is: This I know to be correct
   This string has 25 characters.
```

```
The string, after being reversed, is: tcerroc eb ot wonk I sihT
```

It is worthwhile noting that the concatenation operation provided for `String` class strings is actually implemented using the `StringBuffer` class's `append()` method. This is accomplished by first creating a new, initially empty `StringBuffer` object, applying as many `append()` methods as necessary to construct the final string value, and then converting the `StringBuffer` representation to a `String` class value. For example, the statement

```
String message = "Result = " + 2.04 + " feet.";
```

is implemented as

```
String message = new StringBuffer().append("Result = ").append(2.04).append(" feet.").toString();
```

The conversion to a `StringBuffer` value is necessary because `String` class objects are *immutable,* which means they cannot be changed. `StringBuffer` objects permit implementation of a concatenation using an expandable `StringBuffer` object as an intermediary. Thus, if your program is going to require extensive concatenations, you are better off using `StringBuffer` objects directly, which removes the implicitly invoked conversion from `String` to `StringBuffer` at the beginning of each concatenation and the conversion back from `StringBuffer` to `String` at the completion of the concatenation.

Exercises 7.3

1. Enter and run QuickTest Program 7.6 on your computer.

2a. Write a Java method to count the total number of characters, including blanks, contained in a string.

b. Include the method written for Exercise 2a in a complete working program.

3. Write a program that accepts a string of characters from a terminal and displays the hexadecimal equivalent of each character.

4. Write a Java program that accepts a string of characters from a terminal and displays the string one word per line.

5. Write a method that reverses the characters in a string.

6. Write a method named `remove()` that returns nothing and deletes all occurrences of its character argument from a `StringBuffer` value. The method should take two arguments: the `StringBuffer` name and the character to be removed. For example, if the `StringBuffer` object named `message` contains the string `Happy Holidays`, the method call `remove(message, 'H')` should place the string `appy olidays` into message.

7a. Write a general-purpose Java method named `toUpper()` that converts all lowercase letters in a string into uppercase letters. The original string should be passed as an argument to the method, and the uppercase equivalent string should be returned.

b. Add a data input check to the method written in Exercise 7a to verify that a valid lowercase letter is passed to the method. A character in Unicode is lowercase if it is greater than or equal to a and less than or equal to z. If the character is not a valid lowercase letter, have the method `toUpper()` return the passed character unaltered.

8. Write a Java program that accepts a string from a terminal and converts all lowercase letters in the string to uppercase letters. (Tip: See Exercise 7.)

9. Write a Java program that counts the number of words in a `StringBuffer`. A word occurs whenever a transition from a blank space to a nonblank character is encountered. Assume the string contains only words separated by blank spaces.

10. Write a general-purpose method named `trimfrnt()` that deletes all leading blanks from a `StringBuffer` and returns a `String`.

11. Write a general-purpose method named `trimrear()` that deletes all trailing blanks from a `StringBuffer` and returns a `String`.

12. Write a method named `addchars()` that adds n occurrences of a character to a `StringBuffer`. For example, the call `addchars(message, 4, '!')` should add four exclamation marks at the end of `message`.

13. Write a general-purpose method named `extract()` that accepts a string, referenced as `s1`, and two integer numbers, `n1` and `n2`, as arguments. The method should extract `n2` characters from the string referenced by `s1`, starting at position `n1`, and return the extracted characters as a string. For example, if string `s1` contains the characters `05/18/95 D169254 Rotech Systems`, the method call `extract(s1, 18, 6)` should return the string `Rotech` in `s2`.

14. A word or phrase in which the letters spell the same message (with changes in the white-space permitted and punctuation not considered) when written both forward and backward is a palindrome. For example, Yreka Bakery (a palindrome) features menu items such as Not Now Wonton, Yen O'Honey, Le Gab Bagel, and Self-furnace Pecan Ruffles (all palindromes). Write a Java program that accepts a line of text as input and examines the entered text to determine if it is a palindrome. If the entered text is a palindrome, display the message `This is a palindrome`. If a palindrome was not entered, the message `This is not a palindrome` should be displayed.

7.4 Program Design and Development: Program Performance Measures and Object-Oriented Technology (OOT)

Coding a program is always an implementation process, where the word *implement* means "to put into effect according to a definite plan." In practice, the plan being implemented was designed during the design phase. In this sense, programming is the last step the programming process illustrated in Figure 7.11.

Because coding a program produces something tangible, which is a working program that can be run and tested, writing a program is almost always one of the first courses presented in a computer science curriculum. Thus, the sequence of learning all of the tools in the complete programming process is generally that shown in Figure 7.12.

FIGURE 7.11 **The programming process**

```
Requirements Specification --> Analysis --> Design --> Programming
```

FIGURE 7.12   **The programming learning sequence**

```
Programming --> Analysis --> Design --> Requirements Specification
```

The learning sequence in Figure 7.12 is used in learning almost all skills. For example, you learned to read and write English words before you learned how to compose sentences, paragraphs; and structure complete written compositions. Later, some people go on to analyze and design more intricate compositions such as essays and novels. Similarly, you always learn how to use tools, such as a hammer and screwdriver, before building something simple. Later, some people go on to analyze people's requirements and design more complicated structures such as houses. This learning sequence, however, does have its downside, especially in programming.

To enable a student to learn basic programming techniques, simple program requirements are initially used in almost all programming texts, including this one. This permits reducing the analysis and design steps to a minimum. Thus, a new programmer is somewhat like a new carpenter building a house who knows how to build it without necessarily knowing how to design it. The positive side of the traditional learning sequence, however, is that being an implementer does provide a framework for understanding what is actually possible, which is indispensable for a designer. Therefore, before we attempt to understand the design process, we should understand what constitutes a good implementation.

Clearly, at a minimum, a program should be correct. Obviously, any program that works is better than any program that doesn't work. But this criterion provides little help in determining what is a good program. Besides just working, a good program should provide

- Clarity
- Efficiency
- Robustness
- Extensibility
- Reusability
- Programming-in-the-large

Clarity has two meanings. From a programming viewpoint, it means both that another programmer can read and understand your code and that you can read and understand your own code months after you have written it. From a user's viewpoint, it means that the program clearly identifies what inputs are required and what outputs are produced.

Efficiency means that a program or function produces its results in the most time-efficient manner. This includes both computer run time as well as human time spent in preparing to run the program and analyzing and understanding the results of a program or function. Efficiency, although very important, is the least important of all measures and should always be sacrificed in the interest of clarity, robustness, extensibility, and the other measures.

Robustness means that a program or function will not fail even if it receives improper data. For example, if your program is expecting an integer and the user types a letter, the program should not crash. Robust programs are sometimes referred to as bulletproof programs.

Extensibility means that a program can easily be modified and extended to handle cases and situations that the original designers did not expect. Being able to accommodate bigger tasks than originally designed for makes a program industrial strength.

Reusability means that existing code can be reused, both within an existing project and for new projects.

Programming-in-the-large means that large, complex programs can be written using teams of programmers.

Procedure-oriented programming has always had the capability of producing clear, efficient, robust programs that could be programmed in the large. Where procedural techniques have not produced the desired result is in reusability and extensibility. Once written, procedure-oriented programs have generally proven to be very cumbersome and extremely time-consuming and costly to extend or reuse in new applications.

Object-oriented technology (OOT) provides a framework for rectifying this situation by producing both extendable and reusable code. The guidelines for producing object-oriented programs include traditional procedural-programming techniques with the addition of new principles that are unique to the object-oriented methodology.

Moving to OOT

A true object-oriented technology (OOT) is where one works with objects from the problem definition stage through the programming stage. It encompasses all of the following object-oriented methods:

- OOR: object-oriented requirements
- OOA: object-oriented analysis
- OOD: object-oriented design
- OOP: object-oriented programming

Thus, from an OOT viewpoint, the programming process previously shown in Figure 7.11 appears as illustrated in Figure 7.13.

As you might expect, the actual learning of OOT proceeds in the sequence illustrated in Figure 7.14. This, of course, simply implements the standard learning sequence previously shown in Figure 7.12 as it applies to OOT.

FIGURE 7.13   The object-oriented technology (OOT) programming process

```
    Object-Oriented           Object-Oriented   Object-Oriented   Object-Oriented
Requirements Specification   >   Analysis     >    Design      >   Programming
        OOR  ——————————————————> OOA ——————————> OOD ——————————> OOP
```

FIGURE 7.14   The object-oriented technology (OOT) learning sequence

```
 Object-Oriented        Object-Oriented   Object-Oriented        Object-Oriented
   Programming       >    Analysis     >     Design      > Requirements Specification
     OOP ——————————————> OOA ——————————> OOD ——————————————————> OOR
```

FIGURE 7.15   **The introduction of OOT by one development group at AT&T**

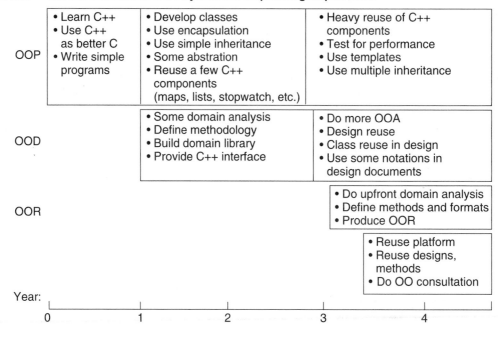

(Source: "Reaping Benefits with Object-Oriented Technology," *AT&T Technical Journal*, Vol. 72, No. 5, pg. 17, 1993. Courtesy of AT&T.)

As a practical application of the learning sequence shown in Figure 7.14, consider Figure 7.15. This figure represents how OOT was introduced by one development group within AT&T over a four-year period. In reviewing Figure 7.15, notice that OOT began with C++ as the implementation language of choice (remember that C++ was developed at AT&T and was the preeminent object-oriented language before Java was developed) and progressed, in an incremental and systematic way, to object-oriented analysis, object-oriented design, and finally to object-oriented requirements specification.

Exercises 7.4

1. Define the terms

    a. clarity

    b. correct

    c. efficiency

    d. robustness

    e. extensibility

    f. reusability

    g. programming-in-the-large

2a. For a demonstration or one-time-use program, which measures of program performance do you think are least important?

b. From a user's viewpoint, which two measures of programming performance do you think are most important in a program written by someone else?

3a. In reviewing how you respond to assignments, have you ever done an assignment just to hand it in on time rather than doing the assignment correctly?

b. In general, do you complete assignments just to turn them in on time or do you do spend the time to do them correctly? What does correctly mean? Do you think your answer to this question is the same answer that an amateur or professional programmer would give when referring to programming projects?

c. Have you ever been so concerned with doing an assignment perfectly that you either fail to start it or fail to complete it? Do you think your answer to this question is the same answer that an amateur or professional programmer would give when referring to programming projects?

4a. Review how you have approached programming assignments made in this and other programming courses you have taken. Have you tended to approach these assignments as an amateur or as a professional? Has your approach been reasonable based on the time pressures of other commitments?

b. Based on your responses to Exercise 4a, what sacrifices or adjustments do you think professionals made in their lives, regardless of their chosen fields, to become professionals?

7.5 Common Programming Errors

1. Breaking a string across two or more lines. For example, the statement

```
System.out.println("The result of the computation
        is: ");
```

results in a compiler error. The correct way to separate a string across multiple lines is to concatenate two or more strings. Thus, the previous statement can be written as

```
System.out.println("The result of the computation"
        + " is: ");
```

2. Not remembering that the first character in a string is located at position 0, not 1.

3. Not remembering that the number returned by the length() method is one more than the position number of the string's last character. For example, the length of the string "Hello" is 5, but the position of the last character is 4. The length of a string is simply the number of characters in the string.

4. Using the == operator to compare two strings rather than the compareTo() or equals() methods. Because the comparison methods compare strings on a character-by-character basis, but the == operator does not, you should not use the == operator when comparing strings.

5. Not specifying one position beyond the desired character to be extracted using the substring() method. For example, to extract the characters near from the string "Linear" requires the statement "Linear".substring(2,6);.

7.6 **Chapter Review**

KEY TERMS

Character class
clarity
conversion methods
efficiency
extensibility
instantiating an object

object-oriented technol-
   ogy (OOT)
performance measures
programming-in-the-large
reference variable
reusability

robustness
string
String class
string constructors
string literal
StringBuffer class

SUMMARY

1. A string literal is any sequence of characters enclosed in double quotation marks. A string literal is also referred to as a string value, a string constant, and more conventionally, simply as a string.

2. String literals can be constructed from either the String or StringBuffer class.

3. Strings constructed from the String class are immutable. This means that characters cannot be inserted, replaced, or added to an existing string without creating a new string.

4. The String class is more commonly used for constructing strings for input and output purposes, such as for prompts and displayed messages. Additionally, because of the provided capabilities, this class is also used when strings need to be compared, searched, or individual characters in a string need to be examined or extracted as a substring.

5. The StringBuffer class is used in more advanced situations when characters within a string need to be replaced, inserted, or deleted on a relatively regular basis.

6. Strings are accessed using reference variables.

7. Because a string is constructed as an object from either the String or String-Buffer class, it must first be created by allocating space for the object. The methods used to initially allocate memory space for a new object, be it a string or some other type of object, are referred to as constructors.

8. Strings can be manipulated using either the methods of the class they are objects of or by using general-purpose string and character methods.

8 Collections: Arrays

The primitive data type variables that we have used so far all have one common characteristic: Each variable can only be used to store a single value at a time. For example, although the variables `key`, `count`, and `grade` declared in the statements

```
char key;
int count;
double grade;
```

are of different data types, each variable can only store one value of the declared built-in data type. These types of variables are called scalar variables. A *scalar variable* is a variable whose value is a single built-in data type value, such as a single integer, character, or double-precision number.

Frequently, we may have a set of values, all of the same data type, that forms a logical group. For example, Figure 8.1 illustrates three groups of *items*. The first group is a list of five integer grades, the second is a list of four character codes, and the last is a list of six floating-point prices.

FIGURE 8.1 **Three lists of items**

Grades	Codes	Prices
98	x	10.96
87	a	6.43
92	m	2.58
79	n	.86
85		12.27
		6.39

In Java, lists are created and processed using a group of classes referred to as `Collection` classes. This name is derived from the fact that the data consist of a number of times that can be processed collectively, as a group.

One such collection is an array type, which is created from the `Array` class. Unlike other collection classes that are described in this chapter, an **array** is the only collection class that can directly hold Java primitive types and is built into the Java language.

A simple list containing individual items of the same data type is called a one-dimensional array. In this chapter, we describe how one-dimensional arrays are declared, initialized, stored, and used. We also explore the use of one-dimensional arrays with example programs and present the procedures for declaring and using multidimensional arrays. Additionally, we will use the `Arrays` class (note the addition of the s) to provide a number of useful methods for sorting and searching arrays. Finally, because arrays are reference data types, we will see that they are also declared differently from the built-in data types that we have predominantly been using.

8.1 One-Dimensional Arrays

A **one-dimensional array**, which is also referred to as a **single-dimensional array,** is a list of related values with the same data type that is stored using a single group name.[1] In Java, as in other computer languages, the group name is referred to as the array name. For example, consider the list of prices illustrated in Figure 8.2.

All the prices in the list are double-precision numbers and must be declared as such. However, the individual items in the list do not have to be declared separately. The items in the list can be declared as a single unit and stored under a common reference variable name called the array name. For convenience, we will choose `prices`

---

[1] Lists can be implemented in a variety of ways. An array is one implementation of a list in which all of the list elements are of the same type and each element is stored consecutively in a set of contiguous memory locations.

FIGURE 8.2   **A list of prices**

Prices
___

10.96

6.43

2.58

.86

12.27

6.39
___

as the name for the list in Figure 8.2. The specification that `prices` is to store six individual double-precision values can be accomplished using the two statements[2]

```
double prices[];
prices = new double[6];
```

The first statement is a declaration statement that declares the data type of the items that will be stored in the array and the array name. As shown in Figure 8.3, this statement causes a reference variable to be created and initialized with a `null` address. The second statement, which uses the `new` operator, forces the program to create an array object consisting of six double-precision storage locations and to store the location of this array object into the reference variable named `prices`. The resulting allocation provided by this statement is shown in Figure 8.4.

When the `new` operator is used to allocate actual storage space for an array, the individual array elements are automatically initialized to zero for numerical built-in types, to `false` for Boolean built-in types, and to `null` for reference types (an example of an array of reference types is provided at the end of this section).

As always with reference types, the declaration and allocation statements can be combined into a single statement. Thus, the previous declaration and allocation of the `prices` array can also be accomplished using the single statement

```
double prices[] = new double[6];
```

FIGURE 8.3   **The results of the declaration `double prices[];` (declaring an array creates a reference variable)**

prices

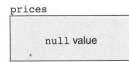

A Reference Variable

___

[2] An alternative and less commonly used declaration syntax, except for `main()`'s argument, is to place the array's name after the brackets rather than before them. Thus, the declarations `double prices[];` and `double []prices;` are equivalent.

FIGURE 8.4   **The results of the allocation `prices = new double[6];`**

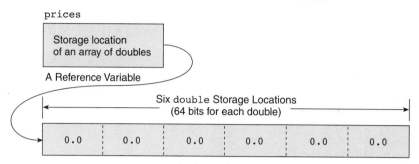

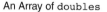

An Array of `doubles`

Although `prices` is truly a reference variable distinct from the array it is used to locate, common usage refers to the array by its reference variable name. Thus, although not technically correct, conventional usage would refer to the newly created array as the `prices` array. We will frequently adhere to this common usage.

A common programming practice is to define the number of array items as a symbolic constant before allocating the array. Using this convention, the declaration and allocation of the `prices` array would appear as either

```
final int NUMELS = 6;    // define a constant for the number of items
double prices[];         // declare the array
prices = new double[NUMELS];   // allocate the array
```

or

```
final int NUMELS = 6;      // define a constant for the number of items
double prices[] = new double[NUMELS]  // declare and allocate the array
```

Further examples of array declarations using symbolic constants are

```
final int ARRAYSIZE = 4; // this creates the symbolic constant
char code[] = new char[ARRAYSIZE];   // declare and allocate the array

final int NUMELS = 5;
int grade[] = new int[NUMELS];

final int SIZE = 100;
double amount[] = new double[SIZE];
```

In these examples, the variable named `code` has been declared and referenced to an array capable of holding four characters, the array referenced by the variable `grade` has storage reserved for five integer numbers, and the array referenced by the variable `amount` has storage reserved for 100 double-precision numbers. The symbolic constants `ARRAYSIZE`, `NUMELS`, and `SIZE` are programmer-selected names. Figure 8.5 illustrates the storage reserved for the arrays referenced by `grade` and `code`.

Each item in an array is called an *element* or *component* of the array. The individual elements stored in the arrays illustrated in Figure 8.5 are stored sequentially, with the first array element stored in the first reserved location, the second element

FIGURE 8.5 **The arrays referenced by `grade` and `code`**

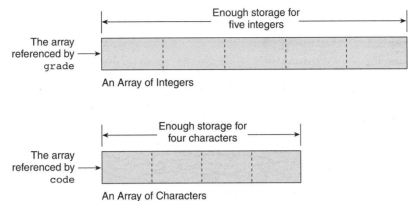

The array referenced by → `grade`

Enough storage for five integers

An Array of Integers

The array referenced by → `code`

Enough storage for four characters

An Array of Characters

stored in the second reserved location, and so on until the last element is stored in the last reserved location. This contiguous storage allocation for the list is a key feature of arrays because it provides a simple mechanism for locating any single element in the list.

Since elements in the array are stored sequentially, any individual element can be accessed by giving the name of the array and the element's position. This position is called the element's **index** or **subscript** value (the terms are synonymous). For a one-dimensional array, the first element has an index of 0, the second element has an index of 1, and so on. In Java, the array name and index of the desired element are combined by listing the index in brackets after the array name. For example, for the `grade` array illustrated in Figure 8.5,

`grade[0]`	refers to the first value stored in the `grade` array
`grade[1]`	refers to the second value stored in the `grade` array
`grade[2]`	refers to the third value stored in the `grade` array
`grade[3]`	refers to the fourth value stored in the `grade` array
`grade[4]`	refers to the fifth value stored in the `grade` array

Figure 8.6 illustrates the `grade` array in memory with the correct designation for each array element. Each individual element is referred to as an **indexed variable** or a **subscripted variable** because both a variable name and an index or subscript value must reference the element. Remember that the index or subscript value gives *the position* of the element in the array.

The subscripted variable `grade[0]` is read as "grade sub zero." This is a shortened way of saying "the grade array subscripted by zero" and distinguishes the first element in an array from a scalar variable that could be declared as `grade0`.

FIGURE 8.6 **Identifying individual array elements**

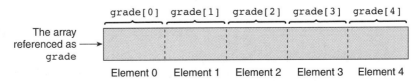

`grade[0]` `grade[1]` `grade[2]` `grade[3]` `grade[4]`

The array referenced as → `grade`

Element 0   Element 1   Element 2   Element 3   Element 4

FIGURE 8.7 **Accessing an individual array element: Element 3**

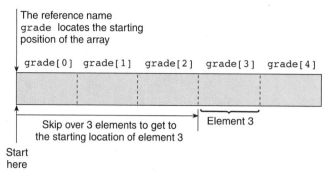

Similarly, grade[1] is read as "grade sub one," grade[2] as "grade sub two," and so on.

Although it may seem unusual to designate the first element with an index of 0, doing so increases the computer's speed when it accesses array elements. Internally, unseen by the programmer, the program uses the index as an offset from the array's starting position. As illustrated in Figure 8.7, the index tells the computer how many elements to skip, starting from the beginning of the array, to reach the desired element. The location of the beginning of the array, as has been noted, is the value stored in the reference variable created when the array is created.

Subscripted variables can be used anywhere that scalar variables are valid. Examples using the elements of the grade array are

```
grade[0] = 95.75;
grade[1] = grade[0] - 11.0;
grade[2] = 5.0 * grade[0];
grade[3] = 79.0;
grade[4] = (grade[1] + grade[2] - 3.1) / 2.2;
sum = grade[0] + grade[1] + grade[2] + grade[3] + grade[4];
```

The subscript contained within brackets need not be an integer constant; any expression that evaluates to an integer may be used as a subscript. In each case, of course, the value of the expression must be within the valid subscript range defined when the array is declared. For example, assuming that i and j are int variables, the following subscripted variables are valid:

```
grade[i]
grade[2 * i]
grade[j - i]
```

One extremely important advantage of using integer expressions as subscripts is that it allows sequencing through an array by using a loop. This makes statements such as

```
sum = grade[0] + grade[1] + grade[2] + grade[3] + grade[4];
```

unnecessary. The subscript values in this statement can be replaced by a for loop counter to access each element in the array sequentially. For example, the code

A BIT OF BACKGROUND

Handling Lists with LISP

Methods for handling lists have been especially important in the development of computer science and applications. In fact, in 1958, John McCarthy developed a language at the Massachusetts Institute of Technology specifically for manipulating lists. This language was named *LISP*, the acronym for *LISt Processing*. It has proved valuable for handling problems based on mathematical logic and is used extensively in artificial intelligence and pattern recognition projects.

One simple language related to LISP is named *Logo*, which has been made particularly user-friendly. It incorporates a technique called "turtle graphics," by which a pointer is moved around the screen to plot geometric figures. Logo has been used widely to teach programming fundamentals to children.

LISP was one of the, if not the, first OOP languages. Java, as one of the newest languages used on the Internet, contains elements of LISP.

```
sum = 0;                       // initialize the sum to zero
for (i = 0; i < NUMELS; i++)
  sum = sum + grade[i];    // add in a grade
```

sequentially retrieves each array element and adds the element to `sum`. Here the variable `i` is used both as the counter in the `for` loop and as a subscript. As `i` increases by one each time through the loop, the next element in the array is referenced. The symbolic constant `NUMELS`, which in this case is 5, is the same symbolic constant used when the array was allocated. This procedure for adding the array elements within the `for` loop is similar to the accumulation procedure we have used many times before.

The advantage of using a `for` loop to sequence through an array becomes apparent when working with larger arrays. For example, if the `grade` array contained 100 values rather than just 5, setting the constant `NUMELS` to 100 is sufficient to both create the larger array and to have the `for` statement sequence through the 100 elements and add each grade to the sum.

A very useful consequence of array storage in Java is that the size of the array is automatically stored in a variable named `length`. Thus, the exact size of any array can be obtained by prefixing this variable with the name of the desired array. For example, if `grade` is an array containing five elements, the identifier `grade.length` will have the value 5 stored in it. Using this variable, the previous loop used to sum all of the values of the `grade` array can be written as

```
sum = 0;                       // initialize the sum to zero
for (i = 0; i < grade.length; i++)
  sum = sum + grade[i];    // add in a grade
```

As another example of using a `for` loop to sequence through an array, assume that we want to locate the maximum value in an array of 1000 elements named `prices`. The procedure we will use to locate the maximum value is to assume initially that the first element in the array is the largest number. Then, as we sequence through the array, the maximum is compared to each element. When an element with a higher value is located, that element becomes the new maximum. The following code does the job:

```
maximum = prices[0];              // set the maximum to element zero
for (int i = 1; i < prices.length; i++)  // cycle through the rest of the array
  if (prices[i] > maximum)        // compare each element to the maximum
    maximum = prices[i];     // capture the new high value
```

In this code, the `for` statement consists of one `if` statement. The search for a new maximum value starts with the element 1 of the array and continues through the last element. Assuming that `prices` is a 1000-element array, the variable `prices.length` will have the value 1000. This is the length of the array whose first element is designated as `prices[0]` and last element as `prices[999]`. In this code, each element is compared to the current maximum, and when a higher value is encountered, it becomes the new maximum.

Input and Output of Array Values

Individual array elements can be assigned values interactively in the same manner as scalar variables, using either a keyboard `readLine()` or `showInputDialog()` method. For example, the statements

```
s1 = JOptionPane.showInputDialog("Enter a grade");
grade[0] = Integer.parseInt(s1);
```

cause a single value to be read and stored in the variable named `grade[0]`.

Alternatively, a `for` loop can be used to cycle through the array for interactive data input. For example, the code

```
for (int i = 0; i < grade.length; i++)
{
  JOptionPane.showInputDialog("Enter a grade: ");
  grade[i] = Integer.parseInt(s1);
}
```

prompts the user for five grades.[3] The first grade entered is stored in `grade[0]`, the second grade entered in `grade[1]`, and so on until five grades have been input.

It should be noted that when accessing an array element, Java does check the value of the index being used at run time (called a *bounds check*). Thus, if an array has been declared as consisting of five elements, for example, and you use an index of 6, which is outside the bounds of the array, Java will notify you of an `ArrayIndexOutOfBounds` exception when the offending index is used to access the nonexistent element at run time.

During output, individual array elements can be displayed using the `print()` and `println()` methods, or complete sections of the array can be displayed by these

---

[3] An equivalent statement is `for (int i = 0; i <= grade.length - 1; i++)`. Which statement you use is a matter of choice.

PROGRAMMING NOTE

Aggregate Data Types

An array object is considered an aggregate data type. This type, which is also referred to as both a *structured type* and a *data structure*, is any type whose individual elements are other data types and whose elements are related by some defined structure. In addition, operations must be available for retrieving and updating individual values in the data structure.

In a one-dimensional array, such as an array of integers, the array is composed of individual integer values where integers are related by their position in the list. Indexed variables provide the means for accessing and modifying values in the array.

---

methods within a `for` loop. Examples using a `println()` method to display subscripted variables are

```
System.out.println(prices[5]);
```

and

```
System.out.println("The value of element " + i + " is " + grade[i]);
```

and

```
for (int k = 5; k < 21; k++)
  System.out.println("index = " + k + "   value = " + amount[k]);
```

The first `println()` call displays the value of the subscripted variable `prices[5]`. The second `println()` call displays the value of the subscript i and the value of `grade[i]`. Before this statement can be carried out, i needs to have an assigned value. The final example includes a `println()` call within a `for` loop. Both the value of the index and the value of the elements from 5 to 20 are displayed.

QuickTest Program 8.1 illustrates these input and output techniques using an array named `grade` that is defined to store five integer numbers. Included in the program are two `for` loops. The first `for` loop cycles through each array element and allows the user to input individual array values. After five values have been entered, the second `for` loop displays the stored values.

QuickTest Program 8.1

```
import javax.swing.*;
public class ElementInputAndDisplay
{
  public static void main(String[] args)
  {
    final int NUMELS = 5;

    String s1;
    int i;
    int grade[];            // declare the array
    grade = new int[NUMELS]; // allocate the array
```

(continued)

(continued)

```java
    for (i = 0; i < NUMELS; i++)     // enter the grades
    {
      s1 = JOptionPane.showInputDialog("Enter a grade: ");
      grade[i] = Integer.parseInt(s1);
    }

    for (i = 0; i < NUMELS; i++)     // print the grades
      System.out.println("grade[" +i +"] is " + grade[i]);
    System.exit(0);
  }
}
```

Assuming that the grades 85, 90, 78, 75, and 92 are entered when QuickTest Program 8.1 is run, the following output is produced:

```
grade[0] is 85
grade[1] is 90
grade[2] is 78
grade[3] is 75
grade[4] is 92
```

In reviewing the output produced by QuickTest Program 8.1, pay particular attention to the difference between the subscript value displayed and the numerical value stored in the corresponding array element. The subscript value refers to the location of the element in the array, whereas the subscripted variable refers to the numerical value stored in the designated location.

In addition to displaying the values stored in each array element, the elements can also be processed by appropriately referencing the desired element. For example, in QuickTest Program 8.2, the value of each element is accumulated in a total, which is displayed on completion of the individual display of each array element.

QuickTest Program 8.2

```java
import javax.swing.*;
public class AccumulateElements
{
  public static void main(String[] args)
  {
    final int NUMELS = 5;

    String s1;
    int i;
    int total = 0;
      // declare and allocate the array
    int grade[] = new int[NUMELS]; // allocate the array

    for (i = 0; i < NUMELS; i++)     // Enter the grades
    {
      s1 = JOptionPane.showInputDialog("Enter a grade: ");
      grade[i] = Integer.parseInt(s1);
```

```
    }

    System.out.print("The total of the grades");

    for (i = 0; i < NUMELS; i++)      // Display and total the grades
    {
        System.out.print("  " + grade[i]);
        total =  total + grade[i];
    }

    System.out.print(" is " + total);

    System.exit(0);
  }
}
```

Again, assuming the grades 85, 90, 78, 75, and 92 are entered, the following output is displayed when QuickTest Program 8.2 is run:

```
The total of the grades   85   90   78   75   92   is   420
```

Notice that in QuickTest Program 8.2, unlike QuickTest Program 8.1, only the values stored in each array element are displayed. Although the second `for` loop was used to accumulate the total of each element, the accumulation could also have been accomplished in the first loop by placing the statement `total  =  total  + grade[i];` after the call to `showInputDialog()` is used to enter a value. Also notice that the `System.out.print()` call used to display the total is made outside the second `for` loop so that the total is displayed only once, after all values have been added to the total. If this `System.out.print()` call is placed inside the `for` loop, five totals would be displayed, with only the last displayed total containing the sum of all the array values.

String Arrays[4]

In addition to arrays of primitive data types, such as arrays of `ints` and `doubles`, arrays of reference data types may be constructed. For example, the declaration and allocation of an array of four strings named `names` can be constructed using either the declaration and allocation statements

```
String names[];
names = new String[4];
```

or the single statement

```
String names[] = new String[4];
```

Once the array has been allocated, individual elements can be assigned values by specifying the element name and supplying it with a string value. For example, the statements

```
names[0] = "Joe";
```

---

[4] This topic can be omitted on first reading without loss of subject continuity.

```
names[1] = "Harriet";
names[2] = "Allyn";
names[3] = "Roberta";
```

would assign the string values "Joe", "Harriet", "Allyn", and "Roberta" to the respective names' elements. The declaration and allocation of a string array and the use of the previous four assignment statements to initialize values into the array elements are illustrated in QuickTest Program 8.3.

QuickTest Program 8.3

```java
public class StringArray
{
  public static void main(String[] args)
  {
    int i;
    String names[];          // declare the array
    names = new String[4]; // allocate the array

       // assign values to each array element
    names[0] = "Joe";
    names[1] = "Harriet";
    names[2] = "Allyn";
    names[3] = "Roberta";

       // display the names
    for (i = 0; i < names.length; i++)
      System.out.println("names[" + i + "] is " + names[i]);
  }
}
```

The output displayed by QuickTest Program 8.3 is

```
names[0] is Joe
names[1] is Harriet
names[2] is Allyn
names[3] is Roberta
```

It should be noted that arrays of reference types, such as strings, are stored differently from arrays of built-in data types. For example, Figures 8.8a through 8.8c illustrate how the array of four strings created in QuickTest Program 8.3 is stored in memory. As shown, the declaration statement String names[]; defines a reference variable named names that will be used to store the address of an array. This first step is identical to that performed for an array of a built-in data type. The actual allocation of the array, which is performed by the statement names = new String[4];, is where the process for reference types differs from that for built-in types. As shown in Figure 8.8b, an array is created that is capable of storing four references, each of which initially contains a null address. Only when we assign an actual string value, as shown in Figure 8.8c, is the storage for the string created and the address of the string stored in the array. If the array were an array of built-in data types, the actual values would be stored directly in the array, rather than a reference to the value, as in Figure 8.8c.

FIGURE 8.8a **The declaration String `names[];` creates a single reference variable**

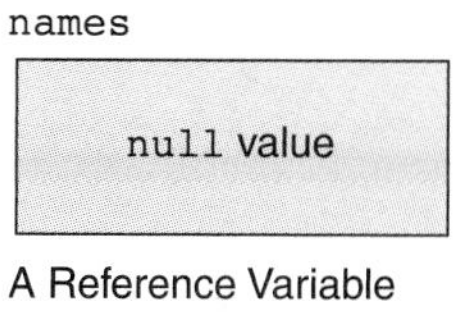

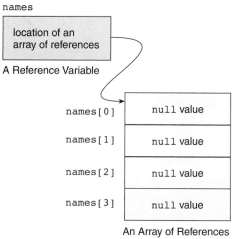

FIGURE 8.8b **The allocation `names = new String[4]` creates an array of references**

FIGURE 8.8c **The assignment of values creates actual array objects**

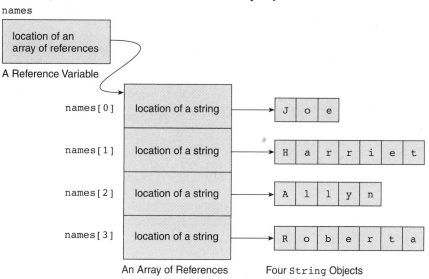

FIGURE 8.9   **A programming view of the `names` Array**

Reference   Object

names[0] | J | o | e |

names[1] | H | a | r | r | i | e | t |

names[2] | A | l | l | y | n |

names[3] | R | o | b | e | r | t | a |

Although each value referenced in the string array in Figure 8.8c is accessed in an identical manner as a built-in data type by giving the array name and index value, as in names[2], it is worthwhile being aware that the actual allocation of storage is different. The reason for this storage is that each element can have a different length, which can only be determined when a string value is actually assigned.

Once a string value has been assigned to an array element, a subsequent assignment can be used to replace the existing string with a new string. For example, assuming the four string assignments have been made in QuickTest Program 8.3, resulting in the storage allocation shown in Figure 8.8c, the assignment

```
names[2] = "Louisa"
```

creates a new string and replaces the reference value in names[2] to correctly reference this new string value. Also notice that, strictly from a programming standpoint, a reference type is accessed in an identical manner as a built-in data type — using the array's name and an index value, as illustrated in Figure 8.9. Thus, the additional level of internal storage required when using arrays of references is in effect hidden from a programming perspective and does not affect the way individual elements are accessed.

Run-Time Dimensioning

In addition to specifying the size of an array at compile time, as has been done in all of the QuickTest programs presented so far, the size of the array can also be entered interactively at run time. The entered value can then be used to allocate space for the array using the new operator. Because the size of an array is referred to as its dimension, sizing an array at run time is also referred to as run-time dimensioning.

As a specific example of run-time dimensioning, consider the sequence of instructions

```
s1 = JOptionPane.showInputDialog("Enter the number of grades to be processed: ");
numgrades = Integer.parseInt(s1);
int grade[] = new int[numgrades]; // declare and allocate the array
```

In this sequence of instructions, the actual dimension of the allocated grade array depends on the value input by the user. QuickTest Program 8.4 illustrates this sequence of code in the context of a complete program.

QuickTest Program 8.4

```
import javax.swing.*;
public class RunTimeDimension
```

A BIT OF BACKGROUND

Statistics

The sum, sum of squares, and average of a list of numbers are commonly used quantities in statistics.

By all means, take a course in statistics! Some of the most important applications of mathematics and computing to the real world are in the area of statistics. Whether you are in business, engineering, politics, government, weather forecasting, sports, education, or virtually any other field you can name, being able to handle statistics will give you a decided advantage. It has been claimed that "statistics don't lie, but some statisticians do," and this is true. Statistical methods and data are sometimes misused by people to convince others – people who do not understand statistics – of something the statistics really do not support.

```
{
  public static void main(String[] args)
  {
    inti, numgrades;
    String s1;

    s1 = JOptionPane.showInputDialog("Enter the number of grades to be processed: ");
    numgrades = Integer.parseInt(s1);

    int grade[] = new int[numgrades]; // allocate the array

    System.out.println("An array was created for " + numgrades + " integers.");
    System.out.println(" The values stored in the array have been initialized to:");
    for (i = 0; i < numgrades; i++)
      System.out.println("grade[" + i +"] is " + grade[i]);

    System.exit(0);
  }
}
```

Following is a sample display produced by QuickTest Program 8.4 in response to a user input of 10 when the program was run:

```
An array was created for 10 integers.
 The values stored in the array have been initialized to:
grade[0] is 0
grade[1] is 0
grade[2] is 0
grade[3] is 0
grade[4] is 0
```

```
grade[5] is 0
grade[6] is 0
grade[7] is 0
grade[8] is 0
grade[9] is 0
```

Exercises 8.1

1. Write array declarations and allocation statements for the following:

   a. a list of 100 integer grades

   b. a list of 50 floating-point temperatures

   c. a list of 30 characters, each representing a code

   d. a list of 100 integer years

   e. a list of 32 floating-point velocities

   f. a list of 1000 floating-point distances

   g. a list of 6 integer code numbers

2. Write appropriate notation for the first, third, and seventh elements of the following arrays:

   a. `int grades[20]`

   b. `double prices[10]`

   c. `double amps[16]`

   d. `int dist[15]`

   e. `double velocity[25]`

   f. `double time[100]`

3a. Using a `showInputDialog()` method and suitable parse method, write statements that can be used to enter values into the first, third, and seventh elements of each of the arrays declared in Exercises 2a through 2f.

   b. Write a `for` loop that can be used to enter values for the complete array declared in Exercise 2a.

4a. Write individual statements that can be used to display the values from the first, third, and seventh elements of each of the arrays declared in Exercises 2a through 2f.

   b. Write a `for` loop that can be used to display values for the complete array declared in Exercise 2a.

5. List the elements that will be displayed by the following sections of code:

   a.
```
for (m = 1; m <= 5; m++)
    System.out.print(a[m] + " ");
```

   b.
```
for (k = 1; k <= 5; k = k + 2)
    System.out.print(a[k] + " ");
```

   c.
```
for (j = 3; j <= 10; j++)
    System.out.print(b[j] + " ");
```

d. ```
    for (k = 3; k <= 12; k = k + 3)
        System.out.print(b[k] + " ");
    ```

e.  ```
    for (i = 2; i < 11; i = i + 2)
        System.out.print(c[i] + " ");
    ```

6a. Write a Java program to input the following values into an array named `prices`: 10.95, 16.32, 12.15, 8.22, 15.98, 26.22, 13.54, 6.45, 17.59. After the data are entered, have your program output the values.

b. Repeat Exercise 6a, but after the data are entered, have your program display them in the following form:

```
10.95       16.32       12.15
 8.22       15.98       26.22
13.54        6.45       17.59
```

7. Write a Java program to input eight integer numbers into an array named `grade`. As each number is input, add the number to a total. After all numbers are input, display the numbers and their average.

8a. Write a Java program to input 10 integer numbers into an array named `fmax` and determine the maximum value entered. Your program should contain only one loop, and the maximum should be determined as array element values are being input. (Tip: Set the maximum equal to the first array element, which should be input before the loop used to input the remaining array values.)

b. Repeat Exercise 8a, keeping track of both the maximum element in the array and the index number for the maximum. After displaying the numbers, display these two messages.

```
The maximum value is: ____
This is element number ____ in the list of numbers
```

Have your program display the correct values in place of the underlines in the messages.

c. Repeat Exercise 8b, but have your program locate the minimum value of the data entered.

9a. Write a Java program to input the following integer numbers into an array named `grades`: 89, 95, 72, 83, 99, 54, 86, 75, 92, 73, 79, 75, 82, 73. As each number is input, add the numbers to a total. After all numbers are input and the total is obtained, calculate the average of the numbers and use the average to determine the deviation of each value from the average. Store each deviation in an array named `deviation`. Each deviation is obtained as the element value less the average of all the data. Have your program display each deviation alongside its corresponding element from the `grades` array.

b. Calculate the variance of the data used in Exercise 9a. The variance is obtained by squaring each individual deviation and dividing the sum of the squared deviations by the number of deviations.

10. Write a Java program that specifies three one-dimensional arrays named `price`, `amount`, and `total`. Each array should be capable of holding 10 elements. Using a `for` loop, input values for the `price` and `amount` arrays. The entries in the `total` array should be the product of the corresponding values in the `price` and `amount` arrays (thus,

`total[i] = price[i] * amount[i]`). After all the data have been entered, display the following output:

```
total          price          amount
-----          -----          ------
```

Under each column heading, display the appropriate values.

11a. Write a program that inputs 10 double-precision numbers into an array named `raw`. After 10 user-input numbers are entered into the array, your program should cycle through `raw` 10 times. During each pass through the array, your program should select the lowest value in `raw` and place the selected value in the next available slot in an array named `sorted`. Thus, when your program is complete, the `sorted` array should contain the numbers in `raw` in sorted order from lowest to highest. (Tip: Make sure to reset the lowest value selected during each pass to a very high number so that it is not selected again. You will need a second `for` loop within the first `for` loop to locate the minimum value for each pass.)

b. The method in Exercise 11a to sort the values in the array is very inefficient. Can you determine why? What might be a better method of sorting the numbers in an array?

12a. Write declaration statements to store the string `"Input the Following Data"` in an array named `message1`, the string `"------------------------"` (24 dashes) in an array named `message2`, the string `"Enter the Date: "` in an array named `message3`, and the string `"Enter the Account Number: "` in an array named `message4`.

b. Include the arrays constructed in Exercise 12a in a program that uses `println()` methods to display the messages. For example, the statement `System.out.println (message1);` causes the string stored in the `message1` array to be displayed. Your program will require four such statements to display the four individual messages.

13. QuickTest Program 8.4 uses a single statement both to declare and allocate space for the `grade` array. Many programmers prefer to place all declarations at the top of a method to make them immediately visible to anyone reading the program. To accomplish this, modify QuickTest Program 8.4 by placing the declaration statement `int grade[];` with the other declarations at the top of the program and change the statement `int grade[] = new int[numgrades];` so that it only allocates space for the `grade` array. Compile and run your program to ensure that it operates correctly.

14. Modify QuickTest Program 8.4 to enable a user to enter values into each element of the `grade` array after the array has been created.

8.2 Array Initialization

Array elements can be initialized within their declaration statements in the same manner as scalar variables, but the initializing elements must be included in braces and the size of the array *must not* be specified. When an initializing list of values is supplied, the array's size is automatically determined by the number of values in the initializing list. Examples of such initializations are

```
int grade[] = {98, 87, 92, 79, 85};
char code[] = {'s', 'a', 'm', 'p', 'l', 'e'};
double width[] = {10.96, 6.43, 2.58, .86, 5.89, 7.56, 8.22};
```

As shown, an initializing list consists of a set of comma-separated values that are enclosed in braces. Values within the braces are applied in the order they are written, with the first value used to initialize element 0, the second value used to initialize element 1, and so on, until all values have been used. Thus, in the declaration

```
int grade[] = {98, 87, 92, 79, 85};
```

`grade[0]` is initialized to 98, `grade[1]` is initialized to 87, `grade[2]` is initialized to 92, `grade[3]` is initialized to 79, and `grade[4]` is initialized to 85. Notice that declarations that include an initializing list do not require explicit allocation using the `new` operator in the same way a string is initialized when it is declared.

Since whitespace is ignored in Java, initializations may be continued across multiple lines. For example, in the declaration

```
int gallons[] = {19, 16, 14, 19, 20, 18,   // initializing values
                 12, 10, 22, 15, 18, 17,   // may extend across
                 16, 14, 23, 19, 15, 18,   // multiple lines
                 21, 5};
```

four lines are used to initialize all of the array elements.

Unfortunately, there is no method of either indicating repetition of an initialization value or initializing later array elements without first specifying values for earlier elements. Thus, when supplying an initializing list, all elements must be supplied with a specific value, and the final size of the array is determined by the number of values in the list. Also, as noted previously, the size of the array must not be included within the brackets []; if a specific size is included, the compiler will provide the error message `Can't specify array dimension in a declaration`.

An array of characters cannot be initialized with a string. Thus, the valid Java declaration

```
char code[] = {'s', 'a', 'm', 'p', 'l', 'e'};
```

cannot be replaced by the declaration

```
char code[] = "sample";   // THIS IS INVALID
```

Attempting to initialize a character array with a string results in the compiler error message `Can't convert java.lang.String to char[]`. An array of strings, however, is valid, and such arrays can be initialized by string values when they are declared. For example, the declaration

```
String names[] ={"Joe", "Harriet", "Allyn", "Roberta"};
```

creates an array of four strings and initializes the four string elements with the string values `Joe`, `Harriet`, `Allyn`, and `Roberta`, respectively. QuickTest Program 8.5 uses this declaration statement within the context of a complete program. Except for the initialization, QuickTest Programs 8.5 and 8.3 are identical.

The output produced by QuickTest Program 8.5 is

```
names[0] is Joe
names[1] is Harriet
names[2] is Allyn
names[3] is Roberta
```

QuickTest Program 8.5

```
public class InitializeNames
{
   public static void main(String[] args)
   {
    int i;
    String names[] = {"Joe", "Harriet", "Allyn", "Roberta"};

      // display the names
    for (i = 0; i < names.length; i++)
      System.out.println("names[" + i + "] is " + names[i]);
   }
}
```

Once values have been assigned to array elements, either through initialization within the declaration statement, assignment, or using interactive input, the array elements can be processed as described in the previous section. For example, QuickTest Program 8.6 illustrates element initialization within the declaration of the array and then uses a for loop to locate the maximum value stored in the array.

QuickTest Program 8.6

```
public class FindMaxValue
{
  public static void main(String[] args)
  {

    int i, max;
    int nums[] = {2, 18, 1, 27, 16};

    max = nums[0];

    for (i = 1; i < nums.length; i++)
      if (max < nums[i])
        max = nums[i];

    System.out.println("The maximum value is " + max);
  }
}
```

The output produced by QuickTest Program 8.6 is

```
The maximum value is 27
```

Deep and Shallow Copies[5]

In addition to allocating and initializing arrays using the various methods presented, an array can be allocated and initialized using the System.arraycopy() method.

---

[5] This topic can be omitted on first reading without loss of subject continuity.

This method copies a user-specified number of elements from one array, referred to as the *source array*, to a second array, referred to as the *target array*. The method requires five arguments and has the syntax

```
System.arraycopy(source array name, starting source element index,
                 target array name, starting target element index,
                 number of elements to be copied);
```

For example, the statement

```
System.arraycopy(nums, 1, newnums, 2, 3);
```

causes three elements (this is the last argument) to be copied from an array named nums (the source array name, which is the first argument) into the newnums array (the target array, which is the third argument). The copy will begin at nums[1], which will be copied to newnums[2], and proceed sequentially until three elements have been copied. Similarly, the statement

```
System.arraycopy(nums, 0, newnums, 0, nums.length);
```

will cause all elements in nums to be copied and stored into the array named newnums. The only restriction in using the System.arraycopy() method is that the target array must be allocated as sufficiently large to accommodate the copied elements. Failure to do so will result in a run-time ArrayIndexOutOfBoundsException error message. QuickTest Program 8.7 illustrates an arraycopy() method within the context of a complete program.

QuickTest Program 8.7

```java
public class DeepCopy
{
  public static void main(String[] args)
  {

    int i, max;
    int nums[] = {2, 18, 1, 27, 16};
    int newnums[] = new int[nums.length];

    // copy all elements from nums to newnums
    System.arraycopy(nums, 0, newnums, 0, nums.length);

    // display newnums
    for (i = 0; i < newnums.length; i++)
      System.out.println("newnums[" + i + "] is " + newnums[i]);

    newnums[2] = 50;   // this only affects newnums
    System.out.println();

    // display nums
    for (i = 0; i < nums.length; i++)
      System.out.println("nums[" + i + "] is " + nums[i]);
  }
}
```

FIGURE 8.10 The initial allocation for the arrays declared in QuickTest Program 8.7

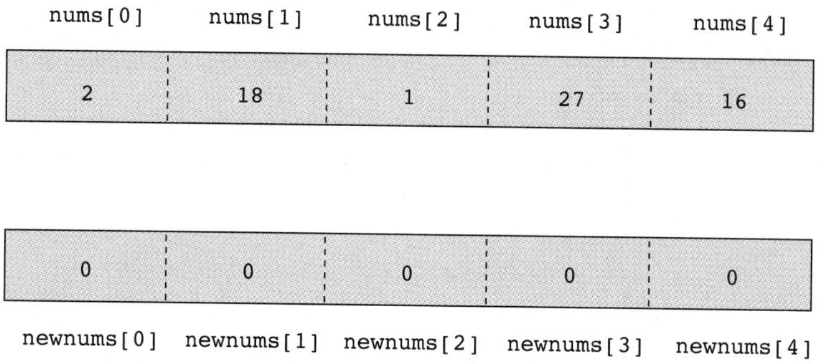

nums[0]	nums[1]	nums[2]	nums[3]	nums[4]
2	18	1	27	16

0	0	0	0	0

newnums[0] newnums[1] newnums[2] newnums[3] newnums[4]

In analyzing QuickTest Program 8.7, first notice that the declaration statement for newnums uses the new operator to allocate the same number of elements as exist in nums. Figure 8.10 illustrates the storage allocation provided by the declaration statements for both nums and newnums. As shown in this figure, two distinct arrays have been constructed, with all of the elements in newnums initialized to zero.

Immediately after the call to arraycopy(), the storage allocation for the two arrays is as shown in Figure 8.11. In this figure, notice that each individual array value in nums has been copied to newnums. This type of complete, element-by-element copy is referred to as a *deep copy*.

The display produced by QuickTest Program 8.7 is

```
newnums[0] is 2
newnums[1] is 18
newnums[2] is 1
newnums[3] is 27
newnums[4] is 16

nums[0] is 2
nums[1] is 18
nums[2] is 1
nums[3] is 27
nums[4] is 16
```

FIGURE 8.11 After the call to `System.arraycopy()`

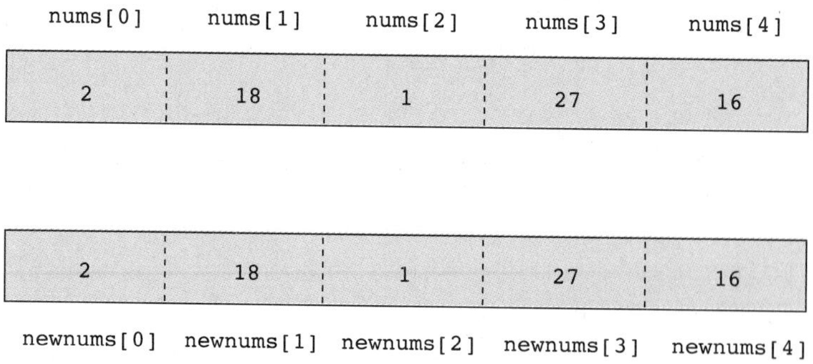

nums[0]	nums[1]	nums[2]	nums[3]	nums[4]
2	18	1	27	16

2	18	1	27	16

newnums[0] newnums[1] newnums[2] newnums[3] newnums[4]

In reviewing this output, notice that the assignment to newnums[2], which is made after the copy, has no effect on the values in nums. This is what we would expect because the deep copy provided by the arraycopy() method preserves the distinct nature of the two arrays created within the program.

In contrast to a deep copy, a *shallow copy* is produced when an array assignment is executed. As an example of a shallow copy, consider QuickTest Program 8.8.

QuickTest Program 8.8

```
public class ShallowCopy
{
  public static void main(String[] args)
  {

    int i;
    int nums[] = {2, 18, 1, 27, 16};
    int newnums[] = new int[nums.length];

    // this produces a shallow copy
    newnums = nums;   // this only copies the address

    // display newnums
    for (i = 0; i < newnums.length; i++)
      System.out.println("newnums[" + i + "] is " + newnums[i]);

    newnums[2] = 50;   // this affects both newnums and nums, because
                       // they are the same array
    System.out.println();

    // display nums and note the change
    for (i = 0; i < nums.length; i++)
      System.out.println("nums[" + i + "] is " + nums[i]);
  }
}
```

In analyzing QuickTest Program 8.8, pay attention to the assignment statement newnums = nums;. All that this statement accomplishes is to copy the address that is stored in nums into the reference variable newnums. Once this statement is executed, the storage allocation for the two arrays will be that shown in Figure 8.12.

As seen in Figure 8.12, both reference variables, nums and newnums, now refer to the same array. In effect, all that we have accomplished by this statement is to force newnums to be an alias for nums, and we now have two array names for the same array. The output produced by QuickTest Program 8.8 is

```
newnums[0] is 2
newnums[1] is 18
newnums[2] is 1
newnums[3] is 27
newnums[4] is 16
```

FIGURE 8.12   **The result of the shallow copy provided by QuickTest Program 8.8**

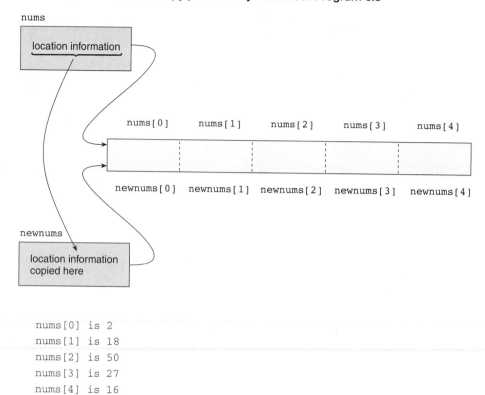

```
nums[0] is 2
nums[1] is 18
nums[2] is 50
nums[3] is 27
nums[4] is 16
```

The equivalence between the two array names illustrated in Figure 8.12 is verified by this output that shows the new value assigned to newnums[2] is displayed when the value of nums[2] is displayed. The storage area initially allocated for the array object referenced by newnums, now that this area no longer has any reference variables pointing to it, will be automatically erased, either when Java's automatic memory cleansing program is run or when QuickTest Program 8.8 is finished running, whichever occurs first. As an aside, since QuickTest Program 8.8 never uses the storage allocated to the array initially located by newnums and simply assigns the address in nums to the reference variable newnums, the declaration statement for newnums did not need to use the new operator to allocate space for the array. In this program, the declaration int newnums[];, which creates the newnum reference variable, is sufficient for the program to compile and run.

Although shallow, as opposed to deep, array copies are not frequently used in programming practice, there is one programming situation that does make good use of such a copy. Where this situation can occur is explored in Exercise 10.

Exercises 8.2

1.   Write array declarations, including initializers, for the following:

a.   a list of the ten integer grades: 89, 75, 82, 93, 78, 95, 81, 88, 77, 82

b.   a list of the five double-precision amounts: 10.62, 13.98, 18.45, 12.68, 14.76

c. a list of the six double-precision interest rates: 6.29, 6.95, 7.25, 7.35, 7.40, 7.42

d. a list of the ten floating-point temperatures: 78.2, 69.6, 68.5, 83.9, 55.4, 67.0, 49.8, 58.3, 62.5, 71.6

e. a list of the seven character codes: f, j, m, q, t, w, z

2. Write an array declaration statement that stores the following values in an array named `amounts`: 16.24, 18.98, 23.75, 16.29, 19.54, 14.22, 11.13, 15.39. Include these statements in a program that displays the values in the array.

3. Write a program that uses an array declaration statement to initialize the following numbers in an array named `slopes`: 17.24, 25.63, 5.94, 33.92, 3.71, 32.84, 35.93, 18.24, 6.92. Your program should locate and display both the maximum and minimum values in the array.

4. Write a program that stores the following numbers in an array named `prices`: 9.92, 6.32, 12.63, 5.95, 10.29. Your program should also create two arrays named `units` and `amounts`, each capable of storing five double-precision numbers. Use a `for` loop and have your program accept five user-input numbers into the `units` array when the program is run. Your program should store the product of the corresponding values in the `prices` and `units` arrays in the `amounts` array (e.g., `amounts[1]` = `prices[1]` * `units[1]`) and display the following output (fill in the table appropriately):

```
Price       Units       Amount
-----       -----       ------
 9.92         .            .
 6.32         .            .
12.63         .            .
 5.95         .            .
10.29         .            .
                        ------
Total:                     .
```

5. Enter and run QuickTest Program 8.6 on your computer.

6. The characters `Good Morning` are to be stored in a character array named `stringChars`. Write the declaration, allocation, and initialization of this array using both one and two statements.

7. Enter and run QuickTest Program 8.7 on your computer.

8. Enter and run QuickTest Program 8.8 on your computer.

9. Change the declaration statement for `newnums` in both QuickTest Programs 8.7 and 8.8 to `int newnums[];`. Explain why this modification results in a run-time error for QuickTest Program 8.7 but does not affect the execution of QuickTest Program 8.8.

10. Java does not provide an explicit redimensioning statement that can be used to change an array's dimension at run time. When such an array redimensioning does become necessary, it can be accomplished by the following steps:

   a. Allocating an array of the desired new size

   b. Performing a deep copy of array elements from the original array to the new array

   c. Performing a shallow copy of the new array's name to the original array's name

This last step makes the reference variable name for the original array reference the newly dimensioned array. Construct a Java program that initially creates and stores the integer values 10, 20, 30, and 40 into an array named `original`. Then permit a user to enter a value greater than four. Once a value has been entered, use the foregoing steps to dynamically allocate a new array named `bigarray`, copy the values from `original` to `bigarray`, and change `new`'s value to point to the new array. Finally, display the values in the expanded `original` array.

8.3 The `Arrays` Class: Searching and Sorting

Java provides a class named `Arrays`, which should not be confused with the `Array` class that we have been using in the previous two sections. The `Arrays` class is referred to as a helper class because it provides a number of extremely useful methods that can be a great help in processing arrays. Specifically, the `Arrays` class contains a number of methods for both sorting an array and then searching the sorted array for a particular item. In general, although it is not necessary to sort an array before searching it, as we shall see in Section 8.9, much faster searches are possible if the list is in sorted order. In this section, we present the fundamentals of both sorting and searching arrays using the Java `Arrays` class's `sort()` and `search()` methods. Use of Java's `search()` method does require that the array elements be in sorted order.

The `sort()` and `binarySearch()` Methods

A common requirement of many programs is to search a list for a given element. For example, in a list of names and telephone numbers, we might search for a specific name so that the corresponding telephone number can be printed, or we might wish to search the list simply to determine if a name is there.

To facilitate searching and sorting arrays, Java provides a class named `Arrays` that contains a number of overloaded methods named `sort()` and `binarySearch()`. The `sort()` method, which uses a modified quicksort algorithm (described in Section 8.9), arranges the elements of an array into ascending (increasing) order, while the `binarySearch()` method searches an array for a specified value. Because `binarySearch()` uses a binary search algorithm (also described in Section 8.9), it requires a sorted array. Thus, in practice, the `sort()` method is typically called immediately before the `binarySearch()` method is invoked. Unless fully qualified names are used, programs that use these methods require either the `import` statement `import java.util.*;` or the statement `java.util.Arrays;`.

In this application, we show how these methods can be used within the context of a complete program. As a specific example, consider QuickTest Program 8.9, which permits keyboard entry of a user-specified number of integer values. Immedi-

FIGURE 8.13 The `Arrays` class hierarchy diagram

```
java.lang.Object
    |
   +--java.util.Arrays
```

ately after the values are entered, the program calls the `Arrays.sort()` method to rearrange the elements into ascending order. Once the sort has been completed, the program requests the entry of a value that is subsequently used as an argument to the `Arrays.binarySearch()` method. If this value is found in the array, `Arrays.binarySearch()` returns its position in the array; otherwise, it returns a negative number. Because the search algorithm does not necessarily locate the first occurrence of a value that has multiple occurrences, a returned positive index number can be that of any of the duplicate values. The statements in QuickTest Program 8.9 that use the `sort()` and `binarySearch()` methods have been boldfaced for easy identification.

QuickTest Program 8.9

```java
import java.io.*;   // needed to access input stream classes
import java.util.Arrays;   // needed for sort() and binarySearch()
public class SearchSort
{
  public static void main (String[] args)
  throws java.io.IOException
  {
    String s1;
    int i, numels;
    int variousNums[];
    int item, location;

    // set up the basic input stream
    BufferedReader br = new BufferedReader(
                       new InputStreamReader(System.in));

    System.out.print("Enter the number of array values: ");
    s1 = br.readLine();
    numels = Integer.parseInt(s1);

    // allocate the array
    variousNums = new int[numels];
    // read the array values
    for (i = 0; i < numels; i++)
    {
      System.out.print("Enter element " + (i+1) + ": ");
      s1 = br.readLine();
      variousNums[i] = Integer.parseInt(s1);
    }

    // sort the array
    Arrays.sort(variousNums);

    // display the sorted array
    System.out.print("The values in sorted order are:");
    for (i = 0; i < numels; i++)
      System.out.print("  " + variousNums[i]);
```

(continued)

(continued)

```
        // now locate a desired element
        System.out.print("\n\nEnter the item you are searching for: ");
        s1 = br.readLine();
        item = Integer.parseInt(s1);

        location = Arrays.binarySearch(variousNums, item);

        if (location > 0)
          System.out.println("This item is at location "
                             + (location + 1) + " in the sorted array.");
        else
          System.out.println("This item is not in the list.");
      }
    }
```

Following is a sample run using QuickTest Program 8.9, where the user enters five values into the array and then requests that the sorted array values be searched for a value of 80.

```
Enter the number of array values: 5
Enter element 1: 101
Enter element 2: 50
Enter element 3: 70
Enter element 4: 2
Enter element 5: 80
The values in sorted order are:   2   50   70   80   101

Enter the item you are searching for: 80
This item is at location 4 in the sorted array.
```

In reviewing QuickTest Program 8.9, the following items should be considered. First, the sort() method arranges array elements into increasing numerical order for primitive data types only. When applied to arrays whose elements are strings, this will result in the strings being arranged in alphabetical order. For other types of objects, the sort is done by a comparison of object reference values, which effectively results in a random ordering of objects.

When the binarySearch() method is used to locate a specified value, the method returns the index of the located element, with 0 referring to the first array position. This is in keeping with the Java indexing convention. If the element is not found, binarySearch() returns a negative number. The magnitude of the negative number is obtained as the position that the value would be inserted into the array, less one. Also notice that both sort and search methods use the array's name as an argument, while the search method requires an addition argument, which is the searched for value. Additionally, both method names are preceded by the class name, Arrays, and a period.

Exercises 8.3

1. Enter and run QuickTest Program 8.9 on your computer.

2. Modify QuickTest Program 8.9 to enter and sort an array of character values.

3. Modify QuickTest Program 8.9 to enter and sort an array of last names.

4. Using the Internet, obtain documentation on the `Arrays` class and list the number of `sort()` methods provided by this class. (Tip: Use the URL java.sun.com/docs/search.html.)

8.4 **Arrays as Arguments**

Individual array elements are passed to a called method in the same manner as individual scalar variables; they are simply included as subscripted variables when the method call is made. For example, the method call `findMaximum(grade[2], grade[6]);` passes the values of the elements `grade[2]` and `grade[6]` to the method `findMaximum()`. When individual array elements are passed to a method, they are always passed by value. This means that the called method receives a copy of the stored value, can use the value in any way it needs to, but cannot directly change the value in the original array.

Passing a complete array of values to a method is in many respects an easier operation than passing individual elements. When a complete array is passed, it is passed by reference. This means the called method receives access to the actual array rather than a copy of the values in the array. The called method can thus not only use the values stored in the array but also modify any array value. First, however, let's see how to pass an array to a called method.

An array is passed to a method by including the array's name as an argument to the called method. For example, if `grade` is a reference to an array, the call statement `findMaximum(grade);` makes the complete `grade` array available to the `findMaximum()` method. Assuming the following array declarations,

```
int nums[] = new int[5];          // an array of five integers
char keys[] = new char[256];      // an array of 256 characters
double units[] = new units[500];  // an array of 500 doubles
```

examples of method calls using these array names are

```
findMaximum(nums);
findCharacter(keys);
calcTotal(nums, units);
```

On the receiving side, the called method must be alerted that an array is being made available. For example, suitable method header lines for the previous methods are

```
int findMaximum(int vals[])
char findCharacter(char inKeys[])
void calcTotal(int array1[], double array2[])
```

In each of these method header lines, the names in the parameter list are chosen by the programmer. However, the parameter names used by the methods still refer to the original array created outside the method. This is made clear in QuickTest Program 8.10.

First, it is important to understand that only one array is created in QuickTest Program 8.10. In `main()`, this array is referenced by the `nums` variable, and in `findMaximum()`, the array is referenced by the `vals` parameter. Because the `vals` parameter contains a location value, it is referred to as a *reference parameter*. As illustrated in Figure 8.14, both nums and vals locate the same array. Thus, in Figure 8.14, vals[3] is the same element as nums[3].

QuickTest Program 8.10

```java
public class ArrayArgument
{
  public static void main(String[] args)
  {
    int nums[ ] = {2, 18, 1, 27, 16};

    // the call is made here
    System.out.println("The maximum value is " + findMaximum(nums));
  }

  // this is the called method
  // it is used to find the maximum value
  // stored in the array
  public static int findMaximum(int vals[])
  {
    int i, max = vals[0];

    for (i = 1; i < vals.length; i++)
      if (max < vals[i]) max = vals[i];

    return max;
  }
}
```

FIGURE 8.14   Only one array is created

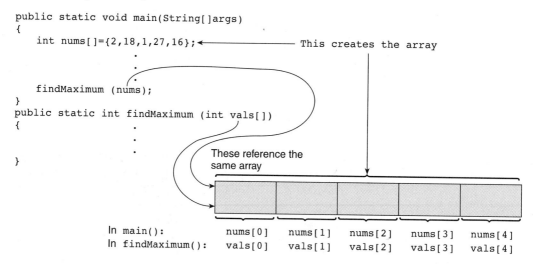

```java
public static void main(String[]args)
{
    int nums[]={2,18,1,27,16};          This creates the array
        .
        .
        .
    findMaximum (nums);
}
public static int findMaximum (int vals[])
{
        .
        .
        .
}
```

These reference the same array

In main():	nums[0]	nums[1]	nums[2]	nums[3]	nums[4]
In findMaximum():	vals[0]	vals[1]	vals[2]	vals[3]	vals[4]

FIGURE 8.15 **The location of the array is passed**

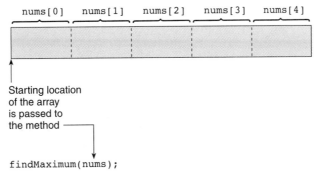

All that findMaximum() must specify in its header line is that the parameter vals refers to an array of integers. Since the actual array has been created in another method, in this case main(), and no additional storage space is needed in findMaximum(), the declaration for vals omits the size of the array. This header line makes sense when you realize that only one item is actually passed to findMaximum() when the method is called, which is the location information (i.e., the memory address) of the array. This is illustrated in Figure 8.15.

Since only an array location is passed to findMaximum(), the number of elements in the array is not included in the declaration for vals and in fact must be omitted. In Java, the array referenced by nums is an object, which contains certain attributes. One of these attributes, as we have already seen, is the size of the array, which is stored in the object's length variable. Within the findMaximum() method, the array must be accessed by its parameter name, which in this case is vals.

As is seen in the program, the header line for findMaximum() declares that the method returns an integer value. Using the length attribute variable as a boundary for its search, the method's for loop causes each array element to be examined in sequential order to locate the maximum value. The following output is displayed when QuickTest Program 8.10 is run:

```
The maximum value is 27
```

As we have already noted, an important consequence of the way arrays are passed is that the method has direct access to each array element. For arrays, this avoids making duplicate copies of the array for each method call and permits a method to make multiple element changes. As an example, consider QuickTest Program 8.11, which uses the changeValues() method to replace each element by 10 times itself.

QuickTest Program 8.11

```java
public class MultiplyElements
{
  public static void main(String[] args)
  {
    int i;
    int nums[ ] = {2, 18, 1, 27, 16};
    changeValues(nums);  // call the method
```

(continued)

(continued)

```
    // display the values
    System.out.print("The values in the nums array are");
    for (i = 0; i < nums.length; i++)
      System.out.print("   " + nums[i]);
  }


  // multiply each element by 10
  public static void changeValues(int vals[])
  {
    int i;

    for (i = 0; i < vals.length; i++)
      vals[i] = 10*vals[i];
  }
}
```

In reviewing QuickTest Program 8.11, notice that the array is referenced as `nums` in `main()` and is referenced as `vals` in `changeValues()`. Because both references refer to the same array, any changes made from within `changeValues()` using the `vals` parameter will be reflected in the array referenced as `nums` in `main()`. This is verified by the program's output, which is

```
The values in the nums array are 20 180   10   270   160
```

As is seen in this output, the values stored in the `nums` array have all been multiplied by 10 after the call to `changeValues()` has been made.

Exercises 8.4

1. The following declarations were used to create an array referenced by the variable `grades`:

    ```
    final int NUMGRADES = 500;
    double grades[] = new double[NUMGRADES];
    ```

    Write a method header line for a method named `sortArray()` that accepts `grades` as a parameter named `inArray` and returns no value.

2. The following declarations were used to create an array referenced by the variable `keys`:

    ```
    final int NUMKEYS = 256;
    char keys[] = new char[NUMKEYS];
    ```

    Write a method header line for a method named `findKey()` that accepts `keys` as a parameter named `select` and returns a `character`.

3. The following declaration was used to create an array referenced by the variable `rates`:

    ```
    final int NUMRATES = 256;
    double rates[] = new double[NUMRATES];
    ```

    Write a method header line for a method named `prime()` that accepts `rates` as a parameter named `rates` and returns a floating-point number.

4a. Rename the `findMaximum()` method in QuickTest Program 8.10 to `findMinimum()` and modify it to locate the minimum value of the passed array.

 b. Include the method written in Exercise 4a in a complete program and run the program on your computer.

5. Write a program that has a declaration in `main()` to store the following numbers into an array referenced by a variable named `rates`: 6.5, 7.2, 7.5, 8.3, 8.6, 9.4, 9.6, 9.8, 10.0. There should be a call to `show()`. The `show()` method should accept `rates` as a parameter named `rates` and then display the numbers in the array.

6. Write a program that declares three one-dimensional arrays referenced by the variables named `price`, `quantity`, and `amount`. Each array should be declared in `main()` and should be capable of holding 10 double-precision numbers. The numbers that should be stored in `price` are 10.62, 14.89, 13.21, 16.55, 18.62, 9.47, 6.58, 18.32, 12.15, 3.98. The numbers that should be stored in `quantity` are 4, 8.5, 6, 7.35, 9, 15.3, 3, 5.4, 2.9, 4.8. Your program should pass references to these three arrays to a method named `extend()`, which should calculate the elements in the `amount` array as the product of the corresponding elements in the `price` and `quantity` arrays (e.g., `amount[1]` = `price[1] * quantity[1]`). After `extend()` has put values into the `amount` array, the values in the array should be displayed from within `main()`.

7. Write a program that includes two methods named `calcAverage()` and `variance()`. The `calcAverage()` method should calculate and return the average of the values stored in an array named `testvals`. The array should be declared in `main()` and include the values 89, 95, 72, 83, 99, 54, 86, 75, 92, 73, 79, 75, 82, 73. The `variance()` method should calculate and return the variance of the data. The variance is obtained by subtracting the average from each value in `testvals`, squaring the differences obtained, adding their squares, and dividing by the number of elements in `testvals`. The values returned from `calcAverage()` and `variance()` should be displayed from within `main()`.

8.5   The Collections Framework: `ArrayLists`

Arrays are the data structure of choice for fixed-length collections of data that are related. Many programming applications, however, require variable-length lists that must constantly be expanded and contracted as items are added to and removed from the list. Although expanding and contracting an array can be accomplished by creating, copying, and deleting arrays, this solution tends to be costly in terms of initial programming, maintenance, and testing time. To meet the need of providing a completely tested and generic set of data structures that can be easily modified, expanded, and contracted, Java provides a set of classes referred to as the collections framework.

The collections framework, which is frequently referred to as the framework, is a set of classes that currently provides seven different types of generic data structures, each of which is referred to as a **container**. The terms *list* and *collection* are frequently used as synonyms for a container; each of these terms refers to a set of data items that form a natural unit or group. Using this definition, an array is also a container; however, it is a container that is provided as a built-in type as contrasted to the containers created with framework classes. Figure 8.16 illustrates the container types provided by the framework and the classes from which each type is created.

FIGURE 8.16 **The collections framework container types**

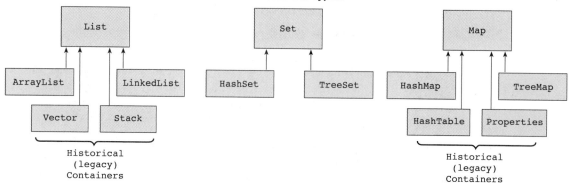

In addition to the container classes, the framework provides a helper class, named Collections, for searching, sorting, random shuffling, and reverse-ordering a list as a whole. The **Collections class** supports the container classes in a similar, but more comprehensive, manner as the support provided by the Arrays class to arrays. Finally, a number of additional classes named Iterator, Comparator, and Comparable are part of the collections framework. The Iterator class has a method for determining if a container has additional elements and a method for returning the next element in the saved list, if such an element exists. The Comparator and Comparable classes provide methods for ordering elements and are used in sorting a list. Table 8.1 summarizes the basic collections framework classes.

As seen in Table 8.1, seven different types of containers are provided by the collections framework classes List, Set, and Map. The eighth container type supported

Table 8.1 **Collections Framework Classes**

Class	Container Types and Support Functions	Comments
List	ArrayList (e.g., a list of temperatures)	List classes permit duplicates.
	LinkedList (e.g., a list of names in alphabetical order)	
	Stack (this is a holdover from Java 1.2)	
	Vector (this is an earlier version of the ArrayList container)	
Set	TreeSet (e.g., a list of individual card hands)	Set classes do not allow duplicates.
	HashSet	
Map	HashMap (e.g., names to social security numbers)	Names must correspond to a unique value.
Collections	Works on a list as a whole to search, sort, fill, shuffle, replace, reverse elements, etc.	
Iterator	Determines if more elements exist in the list and returns the next element.	
Comparator	Places a default order to elements for sorting purposes.	
Comparable	Places a programmer-supplied ordering sequence to elements for sorting purposes.	

by Java, arrays, is provided by the **Array class,** which is separate from the collections framework classes.

For selecting which container type to use, the main differences between framework and the array container types are the following:

- Framework containers are most useful for lists that must be expanded and contracted.
- An array container is most useful for fixed-length lists.
- Framework containers cannot store primitive data types directly.

The implication of this last item is that if you use a framework class to store a list of primitive data types, each primitive value must be converted into its equivalent wrapper class, such as Integer, Double, and so forth, when storing the value and converted back to its primitive type after the wrapper value has been retrieved. An example of this procedure is provided in Program 8.18 at the end of this section.

In its most general usage, a framework class is first used to construct the desired container type. Once a framework container has been created, Collections, Iterator, and Comparator or Comparable class methods can be applied to elements stored in the container. To make this more tangible, we will illustrate this procedure using an ArrayList container. Our initial example instantiates an ArrayList consisting of string values. This example is then expanded to incorporate programmer-defined objects and Collections class methods.

The ArrayList Class

An **ArrayList** is similar to an array in that it stores elements that can be accessed using an integer index that starts at 0. It is dissimilar in that an ArrayList will automatically expand as needed and can be easily contracted to fit the number of elements that are actually referenced. Figure 8.17 illustrates the underlying construction of a list of objects maintained as an ArrayList.

In reviewing Figure 8.17, notice that there are three essential components to the ArrayList structure. The first is a reference variable that is used to locate an array.

FIGURE 8.17　**An ArrayList structure**

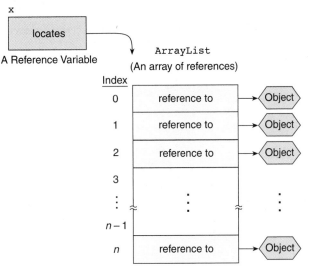

PROGRAMMING NOTE

When to Use an Array or ArrayList *Container*

If you have a list of primitive data types or objects that does not have to be expanded or contracted, the container of choice is an array.

If you have a list of objects that can be grouped as an array but must be expanded or contracted, the container of choice is an ArrayList.

If you have a list of primitive data types that must be expanded or contracted, you will either have to convert the primitive type to its wrapper class equivalent (Integer, Float, etc.) and use an ArrayList or use an array and recurring deep copies between arrays to create expanded and contracted array types.

This reference variable, named x in the figure, can be declared in a number of ways, one of which is by the declaration statement ArrayList x;.

The actual ArrayList array in the figure can be constructed using any one of the three constructors provided by the ArrayList class. For example, the statement x = new ArrayList(); can be used. Similarly, the declaration and creation of both the reference variable and array can, as usual, be accomplished using the single statement

```
ArrayList x = new ArrayList();
```

The array itself begins with a total of 10 elements. Each time the array must be expanded to store additional objects, its capacity is increased using the formula

```
New Capacity = (3 * Old Capacity) / 2 + 1
```

Essentially, this increases the capacity by approximately 50 percent each time the array is automatically expanded. As we will see shortly, there is a trimToSize() method to shrink the array to exactly the number of objects in the final list.

To illustrate how the three components in Figure 8.17 are used in practice, we will initially instantiate an ArrayList with four string values and then use a number of ArrayList methods to determine the number of objects in the list as we add and replace list objects. Following this, we will create a list of programmer-defined records.

First, consider Table 8.2, which lists the complete set of ArrayList class methods, with highlighting used to identify the methods that we will use in our initial demonstration program. The hierarchy diagram for the ArrayList class is provided in Figure 8.18.

Now consider QuickTest Program 8.12, which is intended as a first venture into using an ArrayList. Because the program uses String objects, it permits us to side-step the initial issue of creating our own object types and the final issue of converting

FIGURE 8.18　The **ArrayList** class hierarchy diagram

```
java.lang.Object
   |
   +--java.util.AbstractCollection
           |
           +--java.util.AbstractList
                 |
                 +--java.util.ArrayList
```

Table 8.2   **Summary of `ArrayList` Class Methods**

Method	Return Value	Use
Constructors		
`ArrayList()`	N/A	Creates an empty `ArrayList`.
`ArrayList(Collection c)`	N/A	Creates an `ArrayList` containing the elements of `c`
`ArrayList(int capacity)`	N/A	Creates an empty `ArrayList` with the specified capacity.
Additional Class Methods		
`add(int index, Object element)`	`void`	Inserts the specified element at the specified index position.
`add(Object element)`	`boolean`	Appends the specified element to the end of the `ArrayList`.
`addAll(Collection c)`	`boolean`	Appends all of the elements in the `c` to the end of the `ArrayList`.
`addAll(int index, Collection c)`	`boolean`	Inserts all of the elements in `c` into the `ArrayList` starting at the specified index position.
`clear()`	`void`	Removes all of the `ArrayList`'s elements.
`clone()`	`ArrayList`	Returns a shallow copy of the `ArrayList`.
`contains(Object elem)`	`boolean`	Determines if the element exists.
`ensureCapacity(int minCapacity)`	`void`	Increases the `ArrayList`'s capacity, if needed, to ensure it can hold at least the number of components specified by `minCapacity`.
`equals(Object o)`	`boolean`	Compares the specified `Obj` with the `ArrayList` for equality.
`get(int index)`	`Object`	Returns the element at the specified index position.
`indexOf(Object element)`	`int`	Returns the index value for the first occurrence of element in the `ArrayList`, using the equals method.
`isEmpty()`	`boolean`	Determines if the `ArrayList` has no elements.
`lastIndexOf(Object element)`	`int`	Returns the index of the last occurrence of `element`.
`remove(int index)`	`Object`	Removes the element at the specified index position.
`removeRange(int fromInd, int toInd)`	`void`	Removes all elements starting at the `fromInd` index to one element prior to the `toInd` index.
`set(int index, Object element)`	`Object`	Replaces the element at the specified index position with the specified element.
`size()`	`int`	Returns the number of elements in the `ArrayList`.
`toArray()`	`Array`	Returns an array containing all of the elements in the `ArrayList` with the type of the array specified by the array argument.
`trimToSize()`	`void`	Trims the size of the array to the list's current size.

a retrieved object from the list into a usable form. In subsequent programs, we will increase the complexity of the record type being stored and retrieved, but for now, the use of `String` objects permits us to concentrate on creating and accessing the list. The boldfaced statements highlight the `ArrayList` methods taken from Table 8.2.

QuickTest Program 8.12

```
import java.util.*;  // needed for the collections framework classes
public class ShowArrayList
{
  public static void main(String[] args)
  {
    String names[] = {"Donavan", "Michaels", "Smith", "Jones"};
    int i;

    // instantiate an ArrayList of Strings using a
    // constructor that initializes the Vector with values
    ArrayList x = new ArrayList(Arrays.asList(names));

    System.out.println("\nThe ArrayList x initially has a size of "
                    + x.size() + "," + "\n and contains the elements: ");
    System.out.println(x);

    // modify an element in the ArrayList
    x.set(2, "Farmer");    //set element at position 3 to Farmer
    System.out.println("\nAfter replacing the third name,"
                    + "\n  the ArrayList has a size of " + x.size() + ","
                    + " and contains the elements: ");
    System.out.println(x);

    // insert an element into the ArrayList
    x.add(1, "Williams"); // insert an element at position 2
    System.out.println("\nAfter inserting a name into the second position,"
                    + "\n  the ArrayList has a size of " + x.size() + ","
                    + " and contains the elements: ");
    System.out.println(x);

    // add elements to the end of the ArrayList
    x.add("Adams");  // append Adams at the end of the list
    System.out.println("\nAfter adding a name to the end of the list,"
                    + "\n  the ArrayList has a size of " + x.size() + ","
                    + " and contains the elements: ");
    System.out.println(x);
  }
}
```

The first statement in QuickTest Program 8.12 that uses an `ArrayList` method is

```
ArrayList x = new ArrayList(Arrays.asList(names));
```

This statement both declares the identifier named x as an `ArrayList` reference variable and instantiates and initializes the referenced `ArrayList` with elements from the `names` array. Notice that the array is first converted to a `List` type using an `asList()` method. This method is part of the `Arrays` class, which is a helper class for array types that was presented in Section 8.3. Specifically, the `asList()` method converts an array into a collections framework container type. After this initialization, the `ArrayList` contains four String elements, which are then displayed using a `println()` method. Included in this display is the list's size, which is simply the number of elements stored in the list.

The next statement that contains an `ArrayList` method is

```
x.set(2, "Farmer");
```

This statement changes the third element (remember that the first element has an index value of 0) from its existing value, which is `Smith`, to the name `Farmer`. Similarly, the statement

```
x.add(1, "Williams");
```

is used to insert the name `Williams` at the second position in the list, which increases the list's size to five elements. Finally, the statement

```
x.add("Adams");
```

appends the name `Adams` to the end of the list. The action of all of these statements is verified by the following program output:

```
The ArrayList x initially has a size of 4,
 and contains the elements:
[Donavan, Michaels, Smith, Jones]

After replacing the third name,
   the ArrayList has a size of 4, and contains the elements:
[Donavan, Michaels, Farmer, Jones]

After inserting a name into the second position,
   the ArrayList has a size of 5, and contains the elements:
[Donavan, Williams, Michaels, Farmer, Jones]

After adding a name to the end of the list,
   the ArrayList has a size of 6, and contains the elements:
[Donavan, Williams, Michaels, Farmer, Jones, Adams]
```

The `Collections` Helper Class

Just as the `Arrays` class provides a useful set of methods for operating on arrays, the `Collections` class does the same for Java's additional container data types. Table 8.3 provides a short summary of commonly used `Collections` class methods.

QuickTest Program 8.13 illustrates a number of the methods in Table 8.3 applied to an `ArrayList` that initially consists of four string elements.

QuickTest Program 8.13

```
import java.util.*;  // needed for the collections framework classes
public class UseArrayList
{
```

(continued)

Table 8.3   **Summary of Commonly Used `Collections` Class Methods**

Method	Return Value	Use
`binarySearch(List list, Object elem)`	`int`	Returns the index value of the first occurrence of the specified element in the specified index position using a binary search.
`copy(List listOne, List listTwo)`	`void`	Copies all of the elements of listOne to the listTwo.
`fill(List list, Object element)`	`void`	Replaces all of the list's elements with the specified element.
`max(Collection list)`	`Object`	Returns the maximum element in the list using a natural ordering.
`min(Collection list)`	`Object`	Returns the minimum element in the list using a natural ordering.
`reverse(List list)`	`void`	Reverses the order of elements in the list.
`shuffle(List list)`	`void`	Shuffles the order of elements in the list.
`sort(List list)`	`void`	Sorts the list into ascending order using a natural ordering.

(continued)

```java
public static void main(String[] args)
{
    String names[] = {"Donavan", "Michaels", "Smith", "Jones"};
    int i;

    // instantiate an ArrayList of Strings using a
    // constructor that initializes the ArrayList with values
    ArrayList x = new ArrayList(Arrays.asList(names));

    System.out.println("\nThe ArrayList initially contains the elements: ");
    System.out.println(x);

    //shuffle the ArrayList
    Collections.shuffle(x);
    System.out.println("\nAfter shuffling, the ArrayList's elements are: ");
    System.out.println(x);

    //sort the ArrayList
    Collections.sort(x);
    System.out.println("\nAfter sorting, the ArrayList's elements are: ");
    System.out.println(x);

    //reverse elements in the ArrayList
    Collections.reverse(x);
    System.out.println("\nIn reverse order, the ArrayList's elements are: ");
    System.out.println(x);
}
}
```

The list initially created in Program 8.13 is the same list that was in Program 8.12. This list is initially displayed, and then it is randomly shuffled, sorted, and reversed using the highlighted `Collections` class methods. The following output produced by QuickTest Program 8.13 verifies the operation of these methods.

```
The ArrayList initially contains the elements:
[Donavan, Michaels, Smith, Jones]

After shuffling, the ArrayList's elements are:
[Jones, Michaels, Donavan, Smith]

After sorting, the ArrayList's elements are:
[Donavan, Jones, Michaels, Smith]

In reverse order, the ArrayList's elements are:
[Smith, Michaels, Jones, Donavan]
```

QuickTest Programs 8.12 and 8.13 are useful in illustrating the construction and maintenance of an `ArrayList`. From a practical standpoint, however, one important element is missing from both programs, which is the inclusion of a programmer-designed record type. For example, assume a list of employee records must be maintained where each record consists of an employee's name and pay rate (Figure 8.19).

For this UML description, a class must first be created from which individual programmer-defined objects can be constructed and added into the list. Once the desired class has been constructed and compiled, an `ArrayList` for records constructed from this class can be created, as was done for the `String` objects in QuickTest Programs 8.12 and 8.13.

FIGURE 8.19   **A `NameRate` class UML diagram**

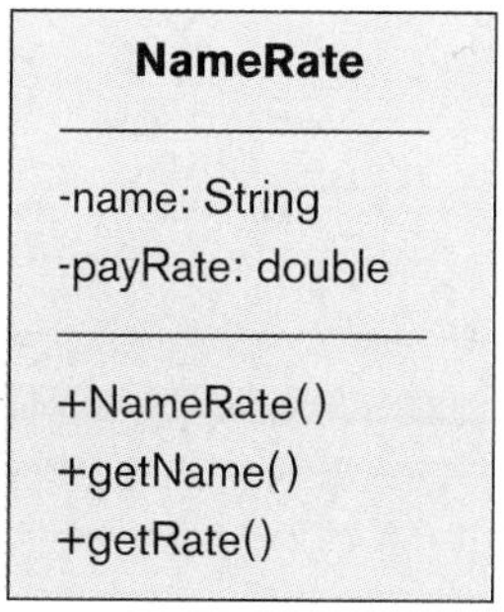

Program 8.14 provides the code for Figure 8.19's class diagram.

Program 8.14

```java
public class NameRate
{
  // data declaration section
  private String name;
  private double payRate;
```

(continued)

(continued)

```
   // method definition section
     // constructor method
   public NameRate(String nn, double rate)
   {
     name = nn;
     payRate = rate;
   }
     // accessor methods
   public String getName(){return name;}
   public double getRate(){return payRate;}

}
```

Having developed a class for our employee records, we can now construct an `ArrayList` for storing objects created from this class. This, of course, requires two distinct operations: instantiating actual records and then storing each record within the list.

Program 8.15 shows how this can be accomplished. Initially, three records of the `NameRate` type are created. Although, for convenience, we have created these records as elements of an array named `nt`, they could just as easily have been created individually and added into the list using an `add()` method.

Program 8.15

```
import java.util.*;
class EmpRecords
{
  public static void main(String args[])
  {
     // for convenience, create an array of records
    NameRate[] nt = {
                     new NameRate("Acme, Sam", 26.58),
                     new NameRate("Mening, Stephen", 15.85),
                     new NameRate("Zeman, Harold", 17.92)
                   };

     // instantiate a list and initialize the list
     // using the records in the array
    ArrayList a = new ArrayList(Arrays.asList(nt));

     // add an individual record into the list
    a.add(1,new NameRate("Bender, Jim", 18.55));
    System.out.println("The size of the list is " + a.size());
    System.out.println("\n     Name            Pay Rate");
    System.out.println("--------------        ----------");

     // retrieve all list objects and cast each one to a NameRate record type
     // use accessor methods to extract the name and pay rate
```

```
    for(int j = 0; j < a.size(); j++)
    {
       System.out.print( ((NameRate)(a.get(j))).getName() );
       System.out.println("\t        " + ((NameRate)(a.get(j))).getRate() );
    }
  }
}
```

In reviewing Program 8.15, note that the statement

```
ArrayList a = new ArrayList(Arrays.asList(nt));
```

both creates an `ArrayList` and adds the records referenced by the `nt` array into the list. Once added into the list, each record is of an `Object` type, which is the generic data type maintained by all collections framework lists. After the list has been created, the program inserts one additional name, Jim Bender, into the list. This is one of the distinguishing advantages of `ArrayLists` over arrays: elements can be inserted and removed internal to the list without the programmer having to explicitly write the code underlying all of these operations, as is required by arrays.

Now review the `for` loop coded at the end of Program 8.15. Specifically, notice that each element is retrieved by the `ArrayList`'s `get()` method. This method returns an object of type `Object`, which is what is stored in the `ArrayList`. The first item of business is to convert this `Object` type into its original record type. This is accomplished by a cast. Thus, the expression `(NameRate)(a.get(j))` converts the `j`th `Object` in the `ArrayList` named a into a record of type `NameRate`. This conversion is an important step that must always be done before any meaningful processing of the record can begin. Once converted, the data fields in the record can be accessed using `NameRate`'s accessor and mutator methods. In Program 8.15, this is restricted to accessing the name and pay rate data using the `getName()` and `getRate()` accessors. That this is successfully accomplished is verified by the following output produced by the programs:

```
The size of the list is 4
        Name              Pay Rate
    ---------------       ----------
    Acme, Sam                26.58
    Bender, Jim              18.55
    Mening, Stephen          15.85
    Zeman, Harold            17.92
```

The `Iterator` Class

A `Collections` class's iterator is similar to an array's index. That is, an iterator can be considered as a generalized index that keeps track of an object's position within a container. For vector containers, which can use an index value to access individual elements, an iterator is not essential. For other container classes, however, the iterator provides the primary means of accessing individual elements and navigating through the container.

Table 8.4 **The Iterator Class Methods**

Method	Return Value	Use
hasNext()	boolean	Returns true if the container has more elements.
next()	boolean	Returns the next element and advances the iterator.
remove()	void	Removes the element at this current iterator position.

Obtaining an iterator is extremely simple. For example, if x is the name of a vector, then a statement such as

```
Iterator iter = x.iterator();
```

can be used.[6] This statement both declares a variable of Iterator type (the identifier iter is a programmer-selected identifier) and initializes the iterator to point to the first element in the container named x. The usefulness of an iterator resides in the fact that it can then be used with the Iterator class methods listed in Table 8.4, which can be very helpful in navigating through a container's elements.

QuickTest Program 8.16 illustrates obtaining and using an iterator for traversing though a vector consisting of Integer objects. Specifically, the declaration of the iterator, its instantiation, and the use of the hasNext() and next() methods for looping through and extracting all container elements have been highlighted. Additionally, the program illustrates the conversion of a primitive int data type into an Integer object data type for storage in a collections container and then reconversion to a primitive type upon retrieval for use in a numerical calculation.

QuickTest Program 8.16

```
import java.util.*;  // needed for the collections framework classes
public class ShowIterator
{
  public static void main(String[] args)
  {
    int intValue;
    double sum = 0.0;
    double average;

    // create an array of Integer objects
    Integer nums[] = {new Integer(1), new Integer(2),
                new Integer(3), new Integer(4),
                new Integer(5)};

    // instantiate an ArrayList of Integer objects using a
    // constructor that initializes the Vector with values
    ArrayList x = new ArrayList(Arrays.asList(nums));

    System.out.println("\nThe ArrayList x initially has a size of "
```

---

[6] The iterator() method is found in the Collection interface class (not Collections).

```
                        + x.size() + "," + "\n  and contains the elements: ");
    System.out.println(x);


    Iterator iter = x.iterator();
    while (iter.hasNext())
    {
      intValue = ((Integer)iter.next()).intValue();
      sum = sum + intValue;
    }
    average = sum / x.size();
    System.out.println("The average of these numbers is: " + average);
  }
}
```

The output produced by QuickTest Program 8.16 is

```
The ArrayList x initially has a size of 5,
  and contains the elements:
[1, 2, 3, 4, 5]
The average of these numbers is: 3.0
```

Parallel Arrays as Records

Consider the data provided in Table 8.5. Clearly, it is possible to store this information using three individual arrays, where one array is used for storing the integer employee numbers, one for the string names, and one for the double-precision pay rates (Figure 8.20). Such arrays, where corresponding data in a record resides in the same position in more than one array, are referred to as **parallel arrays**. The separation of an individual record into parallel arrays was required in earlier programming languages that only supported array data structures. Unfortunately, it sometimes also becomes the first choice of beginning programmers who are familiar with arrays and how to program them.

Table 8.5   Employee Data

Employee Number	Employee Name	Employee Pay Rate
12479	Adams, C	15.72
13623	Brenner, D.	17.54
14145	Dunson, P.	16.56
15987	Franklin, S.	18.43
16203	Jamason, T.	15.72
16417	Kline, H.	19.64
17634	Opper, G.	17.29
18321	Smith, S.	18.67
19435	Voelmer, L.	15.50
19567	Wilson, R.	17.35

FIGURE 8.20   **Records represented using three parallel arrays**

Employee Number	Employee Name	Employee Pay Rate
12479	ADAMS, C.	15.72
13623	BRENNER, D.	17.54
14145	DUNSON, P.	16.56
15987	FRANKLIN, S.	18.43
16203	JAMASON, T.	15.72
16417	KLINE, H.	19.64
17634	OPPER, G.	17.29
18321	SMITH, S.	18.67
19435	VOELMER, L.	15.50
19567	WILSON, R.	17.35

If you find yourself thinking in terms of parallel arrays, use it as a design aid to help you structure the data as an object. For example, using an object approach, each record that is divided across the three arrays in Figure 8.21 can be combined into an object, which accurately encapsulates each employee's data as a single record. Once you have correctly captured a record's structure, the usefulness of the parallel array as a design aid is completed. Except for very simple or specialized applications, you should rarely ever code a set of parallel arrays.

FIGURE 8.21   **Employee records represented as objects**

	Employee Number	Employee Name	Employee Pay Rate
1st Object →	12479	ADAMS, C.	15.72
2nd Object →	13623	BRENNER, D.	17.54
3rd Object →	14145	DUNSON, P.	16.56
4th Object →	15987	FRANKLIN, S.	18.43
5th Object →	16203	JAMASON, T.	15.72
6th Object →	16417	KLINE, H.	19.64
7th Object →	17634	OPPER, G.	17.29
8th Object →	18321	SMITH, S.	18.67
9th Object →	19435	VOELMER, L.	15.50
10th Object →	19567	WILSON, R.	17.35

Exercises 8.5

1. Define the terms container and collections framework.

2. What container types can be created from the `List` class?

3. What container types can be created from the `Set` class?

4. What is the `import` statement that must be included with programs that use the collections framework?

5. Enter and run QuickTest Program 8.12.

6. Modify QuickTest Program 8.12 so that the initial set of names is input by the user when the program runs. Either have the program first request the number of initial names that will be entered or terminate name entry with a sentinel value.

7. Enter and run QuickTest Program 8.13.

8. Modify QuickTest Program 8.13 to use the `binarysearch()`, `fill()`, `max()`, and `min()` methods. Have your program request the name that is to be searched for and the name that is to be used with the `fill()` method.

9. Enter and run Program 8.15. To do this successfully, you will also have to compile Program 8.14.

10. Modify Program 8.15 by removing the cast to `NameRate`. Compile and run the program to determine the displayed error message.

11. Enter and run QuickTest Program 8.16.

12. Modify QuickTest Program 8.13 to use an iterator and a `while` loop similar to that used in QuickTest Program 8.16 to display the `ArrayList`'s elements. Each element should be displayed on a line by itself.

13. For the following class

    ```
    public class Inventory
    {
      private String description;
      private int prodnum;
      private int quantity;
      private float price;
    };
    ```

    write the following:

    a. A declaration for an `ArrayList` of `Inventory` object.

    b. A statement that reads and displays the price of the 15th `Inventory` object.

14. Define an `ArrayList` of objects for factory employees, in which each object contains the name, age, social security number, hourly wage, and number of years that an employee has been with the company. Write the following:

    a. Statements that display the name and number of years with the company for the 25th employee in the array.

    b. A loop that, for every employee, adds 1 to the number of years with the company and that adds 50 cents to the hourly wage.

8.6 Two-Dimensional Arrays

A **two-dimensional array**, which is sometimes referred to as a *table*, consists of both rows and columns of elements. For example, the array of numbers

```
    8      16      9      52
    3      15     27       6
   14      25      2      10
```

is called a two-dimensional array of integers. This array consists of three rows and four columns. To reserve storage for this array, both the number of rows and the number of columns must be included when the array is created. As with a one-dimensional array, however, a reference variable to the array must first be declared. For example, the following statement declares a reference variable named `val` that can subsequently be used in the creation of a two-dimensional array.

```
int val[][];
```

Similarly, the declarations

```
double prices[][];
char code[][];
```

declare that the reference variables named `prices` and `code` are available to reference two-dimensional arrays of double-precision and character values, respectively.

Once a reference variable has been declared, the actual two-dimensional array object can be allocated space using the `new` operator. For example, the allocation statement `val = new int[3][4];` allocates sufficient memory space for a two-dimensional array having three rows and four columns. This allocation statement may be combined with the declaration statement as the single statement `int val[][] = new int[3][4];`. Although `val` is truly a reference variable, it is common to refer to the array using its associated reference variable name, as is the case for one-dimensional arrays.

To locate each element in a two-dimensional array, an element is identified by its position in the array. As illustrated in Figure 8.22, the term `val[1][3]` uniquely identifies the element in row 1, column 3. As with one-dimensional array variables, two-dimensional array variables can be used anywhere scalar variables are valid. Examples using elements of the `val` array are

```
price = val[2][3];
val[0][0] = 62;
```

FIGURE 8.22   Each array element is identified by its row and column position

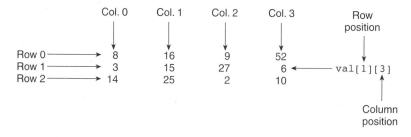

```
newnum = 4 * (val[1][0] - 5);
sumRow = val[0][0] + val[0][1] + val[0][2] + val[0][3];
```

The last statement causes the values of the four elements in row 0 to be added and the sum to be stored in the scalar variable sumRow.

As with one-dimensional arrays, two-dimensional arrays can be initialized from within their declaration statements. This is done by listing the initial values for each row within braces and separating them with commas. For example, the declaration

```
int val[][] = {{8,16,9,52}, {3,15,27,6}, {7,25,2,10}};
```

creates an array of integers with three rows and four columns, with the initial values given in the declaration. The first set of internal braces contains the values for row 0 of the array, the second set of braces contains the values for row 1, and the third set contains the values for row 2. Because whitespace is ignored in Java, this declaration can also be made across three lines as

```
int val[][] = {{8,16,9,52},
               {3,15,27,6},
               {7,25,2,10}};
```

The commas in the initialization braces are always required, and the inner braces cannot be omitted because doing so would not provide the compiler with sufficient information for allocation of the values into rows and columns. Note that because the left side of this statement is a declaration, the statement must omit any array dimensions, which are only specified if the new operator is used to allocate space for the array without an initializing list. An interesting feature of two-dimensional arrays is that the number of columns need not be the same for each row. This feature, which is not used much in practice, is presented at the end of this section.

As with one-dimensional arrays, two-dimensional arrays may be displayed by individual element notation or by using loops. This is illustrated by QuickTest Program 8.17, which displays all the elements of a three-by-four two-dimensional array using two different techniques. Notice in QuickTest Program 8.17 that the variable val.length provides the number of rows in the array referenced by val, and the variable val[i].length provides the number of columns in the ith row. For almost all of the programs you will encounter, the number of columns in each row will be the same, but because Java does provide for arrays in which each row can have a different number of columns, it also provides for a distinct length attribute for each row. Thus, val[1].length provides the number of columns in row 1, which is 4, val[2].length provides the number of columns in row 2, which is also 4, and so on.

QuickTest Program 8.17

```
public class TableDisplay
{
  public static void main(String[] args)
  {
    int i, j;
    int val[][] = {{8,16,9,52}, {3,15,27,6}, {7,25,2,10}};

    System.out.print("\nDisplay of val array by explicit element"
                +'\n' + val[0][0] + "   " + val[0][1] + "   "
                     + val[0][2] + "   " + val[0][3]
```

(continued)

(continued)

```
                        +'\n' + val[1][0] + "   " + val[1][1] + "    "
                            + val[1][2] + "   " + val[1][3]
                        +'\n' + val[2][0] + "   " + val[2][1] + "    "
                            + val[2][2] + "   " + val[2][3]);

    System.out.print("\n\nDisplay of val array using a nested for loop");

    for (i = 0; i < val.length; i++)
    {
      System.out.print('\n');       // print() a new line for each row
      for (j = 0; j < val[i].length; j++)
        System.out.print(val[i][j] + "   ");
    }

    System.out.println();
  }
}
```

Following is the display produced by QuickTest Program 8.17:

```
Display of val array by explicit element
8   16   9   52
3   15   27   6
7   25   2   10

Display of val array using a nested for loop
8   16   9   52
3   15   27   6
7   25   2   10
```

The first display of the array produced by QuickTest Program 8.17 is constructed by explicitly designating each array element. The second display of array element values, which is identical to the first, is produced using a nested for loop. Nested loops are especially useful when dealing with two-dimensional arrays because they allow the programmer to easily designate each element. In QuickTest Program 8.17, the variable i controls the outer loop and the variable j controls the inner loop. Each pass through the outer loop corresponds to a single row, with the inner loop supplying the appropriate column elements. After a complete row is printed, a new line is started for the next row. The effect is a display of the array in a row-by-row fashion.

Once two-dimensional array elements have been assigned values, array processing can begin. Typically, for loops are used to process two-dimensional arrays because they allow the programmer to easily cycle through each array element. For example, the nested for loop in QuickTest Program 8.18 is used to multiply each element in the val array by the scalar number 10 and display the resulting value.

The output produced by QuickTest Program 8.18 is

```
Display of multiplied elements
80   160   90   520
30   150   270   60
70   250   20   100
```

QuickTest Program 8.18

```java
public class MultiplyByTen
{
    public static void main(String[] args)
    {
        int i, j;
        int val[][] = {{8,16,9,52}, {3,15,27,6}, {7,25,2,10}};

            // multiply each element by 10 and display it
        System.out.print("\nDisplay of multiplied elements");
        for (i = 0; i < val.length; i++)
        {
            System.out.println();    // start each row on a new line
            for (j = 0; j < val[i].length; j++)
            {
                val[i][j] = val[i][j] * 10;
                System.out.print(val[i][j] + "  ");
            }  // end of inner loop
        }  // end of outer loop

        System.out.println();
    }
}
```

Passing a two-dimensional array into a method is a process identical to passing a one-dimensional array. Because a reference is passed, the called method receives access to the entire array. For example, assuming that val references a two-dimensional array, the method call display(val); makes the referenced array available to the method named display(). Thus, any changes made by display() are made directly to the val array. As further examples, assume that the following two-dimensional arrays are referenced by the names test, code, and stocks, which are declared as

```java
int test[] = new int[7][9];
char code[] = new char[26][10];
double stocks[] = new double[256][52];
```

Then the following method calls are valid:

```java
findMaximum(test);
obtain(code);
price(stocks);
```

On the receiving side, the called method must be alerted that a reference to a two-dimensional array is being made available. For example, assuming that each of the previous methods returns an integer, character, and double-precision value, respectively, suitable method header lines for these methods are

```java
public static int findMaximum(int nums[][])
public static char obtain(char key[][])
public static double price(double names[][])
```

In each of these method header lines, no values are included for either row or column dimensions. This information will be supplied by the array object that is passed at the time of the call. Although the parameter names are local to each method, the names used by the method still refer to the original array that is created outside the method and passed to it. QuickTest Program 8.19 illustrates passing a two-dimensional array into a method that displays the array's values.

QuickTest Program 8.19

```java
public class PassTwoDimensional
{
    public static void main(String[] args)
    {
      int val[][] = {{8,16,9,52},
                     {3,15,27,6},
                     {7,25,2,10}};

      display(val);
    }

    public static void display(int nums[][])
    {
     int i, j;

     for (i = 0; i < nums.length; i++)
     {
       for(j = 0; j < nums[i].length; j++)
         System.out.print(nums[i][j] + "   ");
       System.out.println();
     }
    }
}
```

Only one array is created in QuickTest Program 8.19. This array is referenced as val in main() and as nums in display(). Thus, val[0][2] refers to the same element as nums[0][2]. As in QuickTest Programs 8.11 and 8.12, a nested for loop is used in QuickTest Program 8.19 for cycling through each array element. The effect is a display of the array in a row-by-row fashion.

```
8   16   9   52
3   15   27  6
7   25   2   10
```

The parameter declaration for nums in display() does not (and must not) contain information about the array's size. This is because each array object "knows" its own size. If any array dimension is inadvertently included in a method's header line, the compiler error Can't specify array dimension in a declaration will be issued.

Advanced Dimensioning Capabilities[7]

Java provides the capability to create two-dimensional arrays in which each row can have a different number of columns. There are two procedures for creating these

---

[7] This topic can be omitted on first reading without loss of subject continuity.

arrays. In one procedure, the differing numbers of columns are created by an initializing list that explicitly lists values for each row when a reference variable is declared for the array. For example, the declaration

```
int nums[][] = {{12, 14, 16}, {20, 40}, {6, 7, 8, 9}};
```

will create a two-dimensional array that has three rows, where row 0 contains three elements, row 1 has two elements, and row 2 has four elements. Alternatively, this same array can be created dynamically using the new operator and then placing values into the newly created array.

The following statements can be used to create the nums array dynamically:

```
int nums[][]; // declare the array
nums = new int[3][];  // allocate three rows
nums[0] = new int[3]; // allocate three columns for row 0
nums[1] = new int[2]; // allocate two columns for row 1
nums[2] = new int[4]; // allocate four columns for row 2
```

As is suggested by this allocation, each row element is actually a reference variable that contains location information for an array of values that constitutes the column elements for that row. These allocations will automatically initialize all values to zero. Once allocated, however, each element can be accessed using its appropriate row and column index value. For row 0, the three valid column indexes are 0, 1, and 2. For row 1, the valid column indexes are 0 and 1. Row 2 can use the four index values 0, 1, 2, and 3.

Larger Dimensional Arrays[8]

Although arrays with more than two dimensions are not commonly used, Java does allow any number of dimensions to be created. This is done in a manner similar to creating and allocating two-dimensional arrays. For example, the declaration statement

```
int val[][][];   // declare a three-dimensional array
```

declares val to be a three-dimensional array, and the statement

```
val = new int[3][2][2];  // allocate the array
```

actually causes storage for a three-by-two-by-two array to be created. As with one- and two-dimensional arrays, the declaration and allocation statements for a three-dimensional array can be combined into a single statement. Thus, the previous two statements can be replaced by the single statement

```
int val[][][] = new int[3][2][2];
```

The first element in the array created by this statement is accessed as val[0][0][0], and the last element as val[3][2][2].

In addition, a three-dimensional array can be created using an initializing list. For example, the statement

```
int val[][][] = {{{1,2},{3,4}}, {{5,6},{7,8}}, {{9,10},{11,12}}};
```

---

[8] This topic can be omitted on first reading without loss of subject continuity.

declares a reference variable, creates a three-dimensional array, and initializes all of its elements. Notice in this statement that the outer braces contain three sets of inner braces, each of which contains two sets of additional brace pairs. The first set of inner braces {{1,2},{3,4}} corresponds to all the elements in row 0. Within these braces, the next set of braces consists of the elements corresponding to column 0, and the second set of braces contains the elements corresponding to column 1. To see this connection more clearly, a declaration containing this initializing list is included within QuickTest Program 8.20.

QuickTest Program 8.20

```
public class MultiDimensional
{
   public static void main(String[] args)
   {
      int i, j, k;
      int val[][][] = {{{1,2},{3,4}}, {{5,6},{7,8}}, {{9,10},{11,12}}};

      for (i = 0; i < 3; i++)
      {
        for (j = 0; j < 2; j++)
        {
          for (k = 0; k < 2; k++)
            System.out.println("val[" + i + "][" + j + "][" + k + "] = " + val[i][j][k]);
        }
      }

      System.out.println();
   }
}
```

When QuickTest Program 8.20 is run, the following output is produced, which shows the assignment of values in the initializing list to their respective index values.

```
val[0][0][0] = 1
val[0][0][1] = 2
val[0][1][0] = 3
val[0][1][1] = 4
val[1][0][0] = 5
val[1][0][1] = 6
val[1][1][0] = 7
val[1][1][1] = 8
val[2][0][0] = 9
val[2][0][1] = 10
val[2][1][0] = 11
val[2][1][1] = 12
```

Conceptually, as illustrated in Figure 8.23, a three-dimensional array can be viewed as a book of data tables. Using this visualization, the first index value can be thought of as the location of the desired row in a table, the second index value as the desired column, and the third index value, which is often called the *rank*, as the

FIGURE 8.23   **The representation of a three-dimensional array**

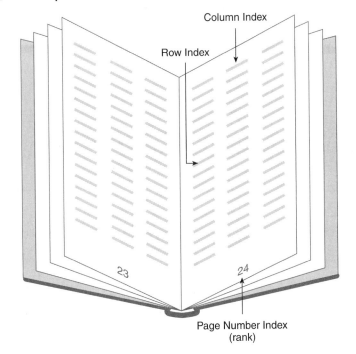

page number of the selected table. Similarly, arrays of any dimension can be declared. Conceptually, a four-dimensional array can be represented as a shelf of books, where the first dimension is used to declare a desired book on the shelf, and a five-dimensional array can be viewed as a bookcase filled with books, where the first dimension refers to a selected shelf in the bookcase. Using the same analogy, a six-dimensional array can be considered as a single row of bookcases, where the first dimension refers to the desired bookcase in the row, a seven-dimensional array can be considered as multiple rows of bookcases, where the first dimension refers to the desired row, and so on. Alternatively, arrays of three, four, five, six, and more dimensions can be viewed as mathematical *n*-tuples of order three, four, five, six, and so forth, respectively.

Exercises 8.6

1.   Write a single declaration and allocation statement for
   a.   an array of integers with 6 rows and 10 columns
   b.   an array of integers with 2 rows and 5 columns
   c.   an array of characters with 7 rows and 12 columns
   d.   an array of characters with 15 rows and 7 columns
   e.   an array of double-precision numbers with 10 rows and 25 columns
   f.   an array of double-precision numbers with 16 rows and 8 columns

2. Determine the output produced by the following method:

```java
public static void main(String[] args)
{
    int i, j, val[][] = {{8,16,9,52},{3,15,27,6},{7,25,2,10}};

    for (i = 0; i < val.length; i++)
        for (j = 0; j < val[i].length; j++)
            System.out.print(val[i][j]+"   ");
}
```

3a. Write a Java program that adds the values of all elements in the `val` array used in Exercise 2 and displays the total.

b. Modify the program written for Exercise 3a to display the total of each row separately.

4. Write a Java program that adds equivalent elements of the two-dimensional arrays named `first` and `second`. Both arrays should have two rows and three columns. For example, element [1][2] of the resulting array should be the sum of `first[1][2]` and `second[1][2]`. The `first` and `second` arrays should be initialized as follows:

First				Second		
16	18	23		24	52	77
54	91	11		16	19	59

5a. Write a Java program that finds and displays the maximum value in a two-dimensional array of integers. The array should be declared as a four-by-five array of integers and initialized with these data: 16, 22, 99, 4, 18, −258, 4, 101, 5, 98, 105, 6, 15, 2, 45, 33, 88, 72, 16, 3.

b. Modify the program written in Exercise 5a so that it also displays the maximum value's row and column subscript values.

6. Write a Java program to select the values in a four-by-five array of integers in increasing order and store the selected values in the one-dimensional array referenced by the name `sort`. Use the data in Exercise 5a to initialize the two-dimensional array.

7a. A professor has constructed a two-dimensional array of double-precision numbers having three rows and five columns. This array currently contains the test grades of the students in the professor's advanced compiler design class. Write a Java program that reads 15 array values and then determine the total number of grades in the ranges less than 60, greater than or equal to 60 and less than 70, greater than or equal to 70 and less than 80, greater than or equal to 80 and less than 90, and greater than or equal to 90.

b. It is cumbersome to enter 15 grades each time the program written for Exercise 7a is run. What method is appropriate for initializing the array during the testing phase?

c. How might the program you wrote for Exercise 7a be modified to include the case of no grade being present? That is, what grade could be used to indicate an invalid grade and how does your program have to be modified to exclude counting such a grade?

8a. Write a method named `findMaximum()` that finds and displays the maximum value in a two-dimensional array of integers. The array should be declared as a 10-row-by-20-column array of integers in `main()`.

b. Modify the method written in Exercise 8a so that it also displays the row and column number of the element with the maximum value.

9. Write a method that can be used to sort the elements of a 10-by-20 two-dimensional array of integers. (Tip: You need to develop a method to exchange two array elements.)

8.7 **Common Programming Errors**

Four common errors associated with declaring, creating, and using arrays are

1. Forgetting the empty bracket pairs when declaring an array's name. Without the brackets, the array name will simply be considered as a scalar variable.

2. Declaring an array reference variable using explicit dimension sizes. A Java array declaration must only specify the type of elements that will be stored by the array being referenced, the array reference name, and one set of empty brackets, `[]`, for each dimension. Thus, a one-dimensional array will be declared by one empty set of bracket pairs, a two-dimensional array by two empty sets of bracket pairs, and so on for larger dimensional arrays. Attempting to include a dimension size results in a compiler error message equivalent to `Can't specify array dimension in a type expression`.

3. Using a subscript that references a nonexistent array element; for example, declaring the array to be of size 20 and using a subscript value of 25. This results in a run-time `ArrayIndexOutOfBoundsException` error.

4. Not using a large enough counter value in a `for` loop counter to cycle through all the array elements. This error usually occurs when an array is initially specified to be of size n and there is a `for` loop within the program of the form `for (int i = 0; i < n; i++)`. The array size is then expanded, but the programmer forgets to change the interior `for` loop parameters. In practice, this error is eliminated by using the same named constant for both the array size and loop parameter.

8.8 **Chapter Review**

KEY TERMS
array
Array class
ArrayList
Arrays class
Collection
Collections class
container
index
indexed variable
one-dimensional array
parallel arrays
single-dimensional array
subscript
subscripted variable
two-dimensional array

SUMMARY
1. A one-dimensional array is a data structure that can be used to store a list of values of the same data type. Such arrays must be declared by giving the data type of the values that will be stored in the array, a reference variable name, and a set of empty brackets. For example, the declaration

```
int num[];
```

declares that the reference variable named `num` will be used to reference a one-dimensional array consisting of integer values. In practice, the reference variable is commonly referred to as the array's name.

2. Once a reference variable has been declared for it, a one-dimensional array must be allocated memory space. This can be done using the `new` operator in an allocation statement. For example, the statement

```
num = new int[25];
```

will cause an integer array of 25 elements to be created with the location of the array stored in the previously declared reference variable (the array name) named `num`. All array elements are set to zero for numerical data type elements and to `null` for arrays of references. Alternatively, a declaration and allocation statement can be combined into a single statement. For example, the statement `int num[] = new int[25];` both declares an array referenced by the name `num` and allocates space for 25 integer values.

3. Array elements are stored in contiguous locations in memory and referenced using the array name and a subscript such as `num[22]`. Any nonnegative integer value expression can be used as a subscript, and the subscript 0 always refers to the first element in an array.

4. A two-dimensional array is declared by providing a data type, a reference variable name, and two sets of empty bracket pairs after the array's name. For example, the declaration

```
int matrix[][];
```

creates a reference variable that can be used to access a two-dimensional array. The reference variable is commonly referred to as the name of a two-dimensional array.

5. The number of rows and columns in a two-dimensional array can be specified when the array is allocated memory space using the `new` operator. For example, assuming that `matrix` has been declared as a reference to a two-dimensional array, the allocation statement `matrix = new int[3][4];` creates a three-by-four integer array in memory, initializes each array value to zero, and stores the array's location into the reference variable named `matrix`.

6. Arrays may be initialized when they are declared. For one-dimensional arrays, this is accomplished by including all array values within braces, starting from element 0. For example, the declaration

```
int num[] = {10, 20, 30, 40, 50};
```

declares, creates, and initializes a one-dimensional array of five elements. For two-dimensional arrays, this type of initialization is accomplished by listing the initial values in a row-by-row manner within brace pairs separated with commas. For example, the declaration

```
int vals[][] = {{1, 2}, {3, 4}, {5, 6}};
```

produces the following three-row-by-two-column array:

```
1   2
3   4
5   6
```

In no case can these inner braces be omitted. Arrays that are initialized when they are declared are automatically created and must not be allocated further space using an allocation statement.

7. Arrays are reference data types that provide an attribute named `length`. This attribute, preceded by the array's name and a period, provides the number of array elements. For example, if an array is referenced by the variable named `vals` and is created with 10 elements, the number 10 will automatically be stored in the variable `vals.length`. In addition, for two-dimensional arrays, the syntax `arrayName[i].length` provides the number of columns in the `ith` array row.

8. Arrays are passed to a method by passing the reference variable name of the array as an argument. The value actually passed is the location of the array as it is stored in memory. Thus, the called method receives direct access to the array and not a copy of the array's elements.

9. The number of columns in a multidimensional array need not be the same for each row.

10. The collections framework, which is frequently referred to as the framework, is set of classes that currently provides seven different types of generic data structures, each of which is referred to as a container.

11. The advantage of collections framework generated containers is that they are automatically expanded as elements are added to the list and contracted as elements are removed from the list.

12. The `Collections` class provides methods for searching, sorting, random shuffling, and reverse ordering lists created using a collections framework class.

8.9 Chapter Supplement: Search and Sort Algorithms

Most programmers encounter the need both to sort and search a list of data items at some time in their programming careers. For example, experimental results may have to be arranged in either increasing (ascending) or decreasing (descending) order for statistical analysis, lists of names may have to be sorted in alphabetical order, or a list of dates may have to be rearranged in ascending date order. Similarly, a list of names may have to be searched to find a particular name in the list, or a list of dates may have to be searched to locate a particular date.

Although the `Arrays` class's `sort()` and `binarySearch()` methods, which were introduced in Section 7.3, work very well for many applications, you may encounter applications where you will want to write your own methods. Also, an understanding of search and sort algorithms is considered part and parcel of a programmer's basic knowledge. In this section, we present these fundamentals.

Search Algorithms

A common requirement of many programs is to search a list for a given element. The two most common methods of performing such searches are the linear and binary search algorithms.

Linear Search

In a *linear search*, which is also known as a *sequential search*, each item in the list is examined in the order in which it occurs in the list until the desired item is found or the end of the list is reached. This is analogous to looking at every name in the phone directory, beginning with the first name, which might be Aardvark, Aaron, until you find the one you want or until you reach the last name, such as Zzxgy, Zora. Obviously, this is not the most efficient way to search a long alphabetized list. However, a linear search has these advantages

1. The algorithm is simple.
2. The list need not be in any particular order.

In a linear search, the search begins at the first item in the list and continues sequentially, item by item, through the list. The pseudocode for a method performing a linear search is

> **For all the items in the list**
> > **Compare the item with the desired item**
> > **If the item was found**
> > > **Return the index value of the current item**
> > **EndIf**
> **EndFor**
> **Return −1 because the item was not found**

Notice that the method's return value indicates whether the item was found or not. If the returned value is −1, the item was not in the list; otherwise, the returned value provides the index of where the item is located within the list.

The method `linearSearch()` illustrates this procedure as a Java method.

```java
// this method returns the location of key in the list
// a -1 is returned if the value is not found
public static int linearSearch(int list[], int key)
{
  int i;
  int size;

  size = list.length;
  for (i = 0; i < size; i++)
  {
    if (list[i] == key)
      return i;
  }

  return -1;
}
```

In reviewing `linearSearch()`, notice that the `for` loop is used to access each element in the list, from first element to last, until a match is found with the desired item. If the desired item is located, the index value of the current item is returned, which causes the loop to terminate; otherwise, the search continues until the end of the list is encountered.

To test this method, we have written a `main()` method to call `linearSearch()` and display the returned result. The complete test program is illustrated in QuickTest Program 8.21.

QuickTest Program 8.21

```java
import java.io.*;   // needed to access input stream classes
public class LinearSearch
```

```java
{
  public static void main (String[] args)
  throws java.io.IOException
  {
    String s1;
    int nums[] = {5,10,22,32,45,67,73,98,99,101};
    int item, location;

    // set up the basic input stream
      // needed for conversion capabilities
    InputStreamReader isr = new InputStreamReader(System.in);
      // needed to use readLine()
    BufferedReader br = new BufferedReader(isr);

    System.out.print("Enter the item you are searching for: ");
    s1 = br.readLine();
    item = Integer.parseInt(s1);

    location = linearSearch(nums, item);

    if (location > -1)
    System.out.println("The item was found at index location "
                       + location);
    else
      System.out.println("The item was not found in the list");
  }

  // this method returns the location of key in the list
  // a -1 is returned if the value is not found
  public static int linearSearch(int list[], int key)
  {
    int i;
    int size;

    size = list.length;
    for (i = 0; i < size; i++)
    {
      if (list[i] == key)
        return i;
    }

    return -1;
  }
}
```

Here are two sample runs of QuickTest Program 8.21.

```
Enter the item you are searching for: 101
The item was found at index location 9
```

and

```
Enter the item you are searching for: 65
The item was not found in the list
```

As has been pointed out, an advantage of a linear search is that the list does not have to be in sorted order to perform the search. Another advantage is that if the desired item is toward the front of the list, only a small number of comparisons will be done. The worst case occurs when the desired item is at the end of the list. On average, however, and assuming that the desired item is equally likely to be anywhere within the list, the number of required comparisons will be $N / 2$, where N is the list's size. Thus, for a 10-element list, the average number of comparisons needed for a linear search is 5, and for a 10,000 element list, the average number of comparisons is 5,000. As we show next, this number can be significantly reduced using a binary search algorithm.

Binary Search

In a *binary search*, the list *must be* in sorted order. Starting with an ordered list, the desired item is first compared to the element in the middle of the list (for lists with an even number of elements, either of the two middle elements can be used). Three possibilities present themselves once the comparison is made: The desired item may be equal to the middle element, it may be greater than the middle element, or it may be less than the middle element.

In the first case, the search has been successful, and no further searches are required. In the second case, since the desired item is greater than the middle element, if it is found at all, it must be in the second half of the list. This means that the first half of the list consisting of all elements from the first to the midpoint element can be discarded from any further search. In the third case, since the desired item is less than the middle element, if it is found at all, it must be in the first half of the list. For this case, the second half of the list containing all elements from the midpoint element to the last element can be discarded from any further search.

The algorithm for implementing this search strategy is illustrated in Figure 8.24 and defined by the following pseudocode:

Set the lower index to 0
Set the upper index to one less than the size of the list
Begin with the first item in the list
While the lower index is less than or equal to the upper index
  Set the midpoint index to the integer average of the lower and upper index values
  Compare the desired item to the midpoint element
    If the desired element equals the midpoint element
      Return the index value of the current item
    Else If the desired element is greater than the midpoint element
      Set the lower index value to the midpoint value plus 1
    Else If the desired element is less than the midpoint element
      Set the upper index value to the midpoint value less 1
    EndIf
EndWhile
Return −1 because the item was not found

As illustrated by both the pseudocode and the flowchart of Figure 8.24, a `while` loop is used to control the search. The initial list is defined by setting the lower index value to 0 and the upper index value to one less than the number of elements in the

FIGURE 8.24   **The binary search algorithm**

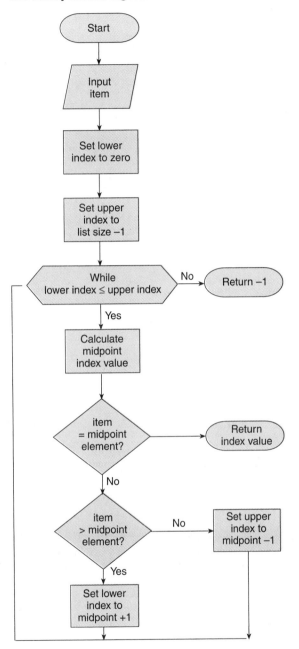

list. The midpoint element is then taken as the integerized average of the lower and upper values. Once the comparison to the midpoint element is made, the search is subsequently restricted by moving either the lower index to one integer value above the midpoint or by moving the upper index one integer value below the midpoint. This process continues until the desired element is found or the lower and upper index values become equal. The method `binarySearch()` presents the Java version of this algorithm.

```
// this method returns the location of key in the list
// a -1 is returned if the value is not found
public static int binarySearch(int list[], int key)
{
  int left, right, midpt, size;

  size = list.length;
  left = 0;
  right = size - 1;

  while (left <= right)
  {
    midpt = (int) ((left + right) / 2);
    if (key == list[midpt])
    {
      return midpt;
    }
    else if (key > list[midpt])
      left = midpt + 1;
    else
      right = midpt - 1;
  }

  return -1;
}
```

We use QuickTest Program 8.22 to test this method.

QuickTest Program 8.22

```
import java.io.*;   // needed to access input stream classes
public class BinarySearch
{
  public static void main (String[] args)
  throws java.io.IOException
  {
    String s1;
    int nums[] = {5,10,22,32,45,67,73,98,99,101};
    int item, location;

    // set up the basic input stream
      // needed for conversion capabilities
    InputStreamReader isr = new InputStreamReader(System.in);
      // needed to use readLine()
    BufferedReader br = new BufferedReader(isr);

    System.out.print("Enter the item you are searching for: ");
    s1 = br.readLine();
    item = Integer.parseInt(s1);

    location = binarySearch(nums, item);
```

```
      if (location > -1)
      System.out.println("The item was found at index location "
                          + location);

      else
        System.out.println("The item was not found in the list");
  }


  // this method returns the location of key in the list
  // a -1 is returned if the value is not found
  public static int binarySearch(int list[], int key)
  {
    int left, right, midpt, size;

    size = list.length;
    left = 0;
    right = size - 1;

    while (left <= right)
    {
      midpt = (int) ((left + right) / 2);
      if (key == list[midpt])
      {
        return midpt;
      }
      else if (key > list[midpt])
        left = midpt + 1;
      else
        right = midpt - 1;
    }

    return -1;
  }
}
```

A sample run of QuickTest Program 8.22 yielded the following:

```
Enter the item you are searching for: 99
The item was found at index location 8
```

The value of using a binary search algorithm is that the number of elements that must be considered is cut in half each time through the `while` loop. Thus, the first time through the loop, N elements must be searched; the second time through the loop, $N / 2$ of the elements have been eliminated and only $N / 2$ remain. The third time through the loop another half of the remaining elements have been eliminated and so on.

In general, after p passes through the loop, the number of values remaining to be searched is $N / (2^p)$. In the worst case, the search can continue until there is less than or equal to 1 element remaining to be searched. Mathematically, this can be expressed as $N / (2^p) \leq 1$. Alternatively, this may be rephrased as p is the smallest integer such that $2^p \geq N$. For example, for a 1,000-element array, N is 1,000, and the maximum number of passes, p, required for a binary search is 10. Table 8.6 compares

Table 8.6 **A Comparison of `while` Loop Passes for Linear and Binary Searches**

Array Size:	10	50	500	5,000	50,000	500,000	5,000,000	50,000,000
Average Linear Search Passes	5	25	250	2,500	25,000	250,000	2,500,000	25,000,000
Maximum Linear Search Passes	10	50	500	5,000	50,000	500,000	5,000,000	50,000,000
Maximum Binary Search Passes	4	6	9	13	16	19	23	26

the number of loop passes needed for a linear and binary search for lists of various sizes.

As illustrated, the maximum number of loop passes for a 50-item list is almost 9 times more for a linear search than for binary search, and even more spectacular for larger lists. As a rule of thumb, 50 elements are usually taken as the switchover point: For lists smaller than 50 elements, linear searches are acceptable; for larger lists, a binary search algorithm should be used.

Big-O Notation

On average, over a large number of linear searches with N items in a list, we would expect to examine half ($N / 2$) of the items before locating the desired item. In a binary search, the maximum number of passes, p, occurs when $N / 2^p = 1$. This relationship can be algebraically manipulated to $2^p = N$, which yields $p = \log_2 N$, which approximately equals $3.33 \log_{10} N$.

For example, finding a particular name in an alphabetical directory with $N = 1,000$ names would require an average of 500 (i.e., $N / 2$) comparisons using a linear search. With a binary search, only about 10 (which is $\approx 3.33 * \log_{10} 1,000$) comparisons would be required.

A common way to express the number of comparisons required in any search algorithm using a list of N items is to give the order of magnitude of the number of comparisons required, on average, to locate a desired item. Thus, the linear search is said to be of order N and the binary search of order $\log_2 N$. Notationally, this is expressed in big-O notation as $O(N)$ and $O(\log_2 N)$, where the O is read as "the order of."

Sort Algorithms

For sorting data, two major categories of sorting techniques exist called internal and external sorts, respectively. *Internal sorts* are used when the data list is not too large, and the complete list can be stored within the computer's memory, usually in an array. *External sorts* are used for much larger data sets that are stored in large external disk or tape files and cannot be accommodated within computer memory as a complete unit. Here we present three internal sort algorithms. For sorting lists with less than approximately 50 elements, either of the first two algorithms can be used. For larger lists, a more sophisticated sorting algorithm, such as the quicksort, which is the third algorithm presented, is typically employed.

Selection Sort

One of the simplest sorting techniques is the selection sort. In a *selection sort*, the smallest value is initially selected from the complete list of data and exchanged with the first element in the list. After this first selection and exchange, the next smallest element in the revised list is selected and exchanged with the second element in the list. Since the smallest element is already in the first position in the list, this second pass need only consider the second through last elements. For a list consisting of N elements, this process is repeated $N - 1$ times, with each pass through the list requiring one less comparison than the previous pass.

For example, consider the list of numbers in Figure 8.25. The first pass through the initial list results in the number 32 being selected and exchanged with the first element in the list. The second pass, made on the reordered list, results in the number 155 being selected from the second through fifth elements. This value is then exchanged with the second element in the list. The third pass selects the number 307 from the third through fifth elements in the list and exchanges this value with the third element. Finally, the fourth and last pass through the list selects the remaining minimum value and exchanges it with the fourth list element. Although each pass in this example resulted in an exchange, no exchange would have been made in a pass if the smallest value were already in the correct location.

In pseudocode, the selection sort is described as

Set interchange count to zero (not required, but done just to keep track of the interchanges)
For each element in the list from first to next-to-last
   Find the smallest element from the current element being referenced to the last element by:
  Setting the minimum value equal to the current element
  Saving (storing) the index of the current element
  For each element in the list from the current element + 1 to the last element in the list
   If element[inner loop index] < minimum value
    Set the minimum value = element[inner loop index]
    Save the index the new found minimum value
   EndIf
  EndFor
  Swap the current value with the new minimum value
  Increment the interchange count
EndFor
Return the interchange count

FIGURE 8.25   **A sample selection sort**

Initial List	Pass 1	Pass 2	Pass 3	Pass 4
----	---	---	---	---
690 -->	32	32	32	32
307 |	307 -->	155	144	144
32 --	690 |	690 -->	307	307
155	155 --	307--	690 -->	426
426	426	426	426 --	690

The method `selectionSort()` incorporates this procedure into a Java method.

```java
public static int selectionSort(int num[])
{
   int i, j, size;
   int min, minidx, temp, moves = 0;

   size = num.length;
   for ( i = 0; i < (size - 1); i++)
   {
     min = num[i];      // assume minimum is the first array element
     minidx = i;        // index of minimum element
     for(j = i + 1; j < size; j++)
     {
       if (num[j] < min)    // if we've located a lower value
       {                    // capture it
          min = num[j];
          minidx = j;
       }
     }
     if (min < num[i])   // check if we have a new minimum
     {                       // and if we do, swap values
       temp = num[i];
       num[i] = min;
       num[minidx] = temp;
       moves++;
     }
   }

   return moves;
}
```

The `selectionSort()` method expects one argument: the list to be sorted. As specified by the pseudocode, a nested set of `for` loops performs the sort. The outer `for` loop causes one less pass through the list than the total number of data items in the list. For each pass, the variable `min` is initially assigned the value `num[i]`, where `i` is the outer `for` loop's counter variable. Because `i` begins at 0 and ends at one less than the number of elements in the array, each element in the list, except the last, is successively designated as the current element.

The method's inner loop cycles through the elements below the current element to select the next smallest value. Thus, this loop begins at the index value `i + 1` and continues through the end of the list. When a new minimum is found, its value and position in the list are stored in the variables named `min` and `minidx`, respectively. Upon completion of the inner loop, an exchange is made only if a value less than that in the current position was found.

For purposes of testing `selectionSort()`, QuickTest Program 8.23 was constructed. This program implements a selection sort for the same list of 10 numbers that was previously used to test our search algorithms. For later comparison to the other sorting algorithms that will be presented, the number of actual moves made by the program to place the data into sorted order is counted and displayed.

QuickTest Program 8.23

```java
public class SelectionSort
{
  public static void main(String[] args)
  throws java.io.IOException
  {
    int nums[] = {22,5,67,98,45,32,101,99,73,10};
    int i, moves, size;

    moves = selectionSort(nums);

    System.out.println("The sorted list, in ascending order, is:");
    size = nums.length;
    for (i = 0; i < size; i++)
      System.out.print("  " + nums[i]);
    System.out.println("\n" + moves + " moves were made to sort this list");
  }

  public static int selectionSort(int num[])
  {
    int i, j, size;
    int min, minidx, temp, moves = 0;

    size = num.length;
    for ( i = 0; i < (size - 1); i++)
    {
      min = num[i];    // assume minimum is the first array element
      minidx = i;      // index of minimum element
      for(j = i + 1; j < size; j++)
      {
        if (num[j] < min)   // if we've located a lower value
        {                   // capture it
        min = num[j];
        minidx = j;
        }
      }
      if (min < num[i])  // check if we have a new minimum
      {                  // and if we do, swap values
        temp = num[i];
        num[i] = min;
        num[minidx] = temp;
        moves++;
      }
    }

    return moves;
  }
}
```

The output produced by QuickTest Program 8.23 is

```
The sorted list, in ascending order, is:
   5   10   22   32   45   67   73   98   99   101
8 moves were made to sort this list
```

Clearly, the number of moves displayed depends on the initial order of the values in the list. An advantage of the selection sort is that the maximum number of moves that must be made is $N - 1$, where N is the number of items in the list. Further, each move is a final move that results in an element residing in its final location in the sorted list.

A disadvantage of the selection sort is that $N(N - 1) / 2$ comparisons are always required, regardless of the initial arrangement of the data. This number of comparisons is obtained as follows: The last pass always requires one comparison, the next-to-last pass requires two comparisons, and so on, to the first pass, which requires $N - 1$ comparisons. Thus, the total number of comparisons is

$$1 + 2 + 3 + \ldots + N - 1 = N(N - 1) / 2 = N^2 / 2 - N / 2$$

For large values of N, the N^2 dominates, and the order of the selection sort is $O(N^2)$.

Exchange (Bubble) Sort

In an *exchange sort*, contiguous elements of the list are exchanged with one another in such a manner that the list becomes sorted. One example of such a sequence of exchanges is provided by the *bubble sort*, where successive values in the list are compared beginning with the first two elements. If the list is to be sorted in ascending (from smallest to largest) order, the smaller value of the two being compared is always placed before the larger value. For lists sorted in descending (from largest to smallest) order, the smaller of the two values being compared is always placed after the larger value.

For example, assuming that a list of values is to be sorted in ascending order, if the first element in the list is larger than the second, the two elements are interchanged. Then the second and third elements are compared. Again, if the second element is larger than the third, these two elements are interchanged. This process continues until the last two elements have been compared and exchanged, if necessary. If no exchanges were made during this initial pass through the data, the data are in the correct order and the process is finished; otherwise, a second pass is made through the data starting from the first element and stopping at the next-to-last element. The reason for stopping at the next-to-last element on the second pass is that the first pass always results in the most positive value "sinking" to the bottom of the list.

As a specific example of this process, consider the list of numbers in Figure 8.26. The first comparison results in the interchange of the first two element values, 690 and 307. The next comparison, between elements two and three in the revised list, results in the interchange of values between the second and third elements, 690 and 32. This comparison and possible switching of adjacent values are continued until the last two elements have been compared and possibly switched. This process completes the first pass through the data and results in the largest number moving to the bottom of the list. As the largest value sinks to its resting place at the bottom of the list,

FIGURE 8.26   **The first pass of an exchange sort**

```
690 <--    307        307        307        307

  |

307 <--    690 <--    32         32         32

             |

  32         32 <--    690 <--    155        155

                         |

 155        155        155 <--    690 <--    426

                                    |

 426        426        426    ·    426 <--    690
```

the smaller elements slowly rise, or "bubble," to the top of the list. This bubbling effect of the smaller elements is what gave rise to the name "bubble sort" for this sorting algorithm.

Because the first pass through the list ensures that the largest value always moves to the bottom of the list, the second pass stops at the next-to-last element. This process continues with each pass stopping at one higher element than the previous pass, until either $N - 1$ passes through the list have been completed or no exchanges are necessary in any single pass. In both cases, the resulting list is in sorted order. The pseudocode describing this sort is

Set interchange count to zero (not required, but done just to keep track of the interchanges)
For the first element in the list to one less than the last element (i index)
  For the second element in the list to the last element (j index)
    If num[j] < num[j − 1]
      Swap num[j] with num[j − 1]
      Increment interchange count
    EndIf
  EndFor
EndFor
Return interchange count

This sort algorithm is coded in Java as the method `bubbleSort()`, which is included within QuickTest Program 8.24 for testing purposes. This program tests `bubbleSort()` with the same list of 10 numbers used in QuickTest Program 8.23 to test `selectionSort()`. For comparison to the earlier selection sort, the number of adjacent moves (exchanges) made by `bubbleSort()` is also counted and displayed.

QuickTest Program 8.24

```
public class BubbleSort
{
  public static void main(String[] args)
  throws java.io.IOException
  {
```

(continued)

(continued)
```java
    int nums[] = {22,5,67,98,45,32,101,99,73,10};
    int i, moves, size;

    moves = bubbleSort(nums);
    System.out.println("The sorted list, in ascending order, is:");
    size = nums.length;
    for (i = 0; i < size; i++)
      System.out.print("   " + nums[i]);

    System.out.println("\n" + moves + " moves were made to sort this list");
  }

  public static int bubbleSort(int num[])
  {
    int i, j, size;
    int temp, moves = 0;

    size = num.length;
    for (i = 0; i < (size - 1); i++)
    {
      for(j = 1; j < size; j++)
      {
        if (num[j] < num[j-1])
        {
        temp = num[j];
        num[j] = num[j-1];
        num[j-1] = temp;
        moves++;
        }
      }
    }

    return moves;
  }
}
```

Here is the output produced by QuickTest Program 8.24

```
The sorted list, in ascending order, is:
   5   10   22   32   45   67   73   98   99   101
18 moves were made to sort this list
```

As with the selection sort, the number of comparisons using a bubble sort is $O(N^2)$, and the number of required moves depends on the initial order of the values in the list. In the worst case, when the data are in reverse sorted order, the selection sort performs better than the bubble sort. Here both sorts require $N(N - 1) / 2$ comparisons, but the selection sort needs only $N - 1$ moves, whereas the bubble sort needs $N(N - 1) / 2$ moves. The additional moves required by the bubble sort result from the intermediate exchanges between adjacent elements to "settle" each element into its final position. In this regard, the selection sort is superior because no intermediate moves are necessary. For random data, such as those used in QuickTest Programs 8.23 and 8.24, the selection sort generally performs equal to or better than the bubble sort. A modification to the bubble sort that causes the sort to terminate as soon as the list is in order, regardless of the number of passes made, can make the bubble sort operate as an O(N) sort in specialized cases.

Quicksort

The selection and exchange sorts both require O(N^2) comparisons, which make them very slow for long lists. The *quicksort* algorithm, which is also called a *partition sort*, divides a list into two smaller sublists and sorts each sublist by partitioning into smaller sublists and so on.[9] The order of a quicksort is $N\log_2 N$. Thus, for a 1,000-item list, the total number of comparisons for a quicksort is on the order of $1,000(3.3 \log_{10} 1,000) = 1,000(10) = 10,000$ compared to $1,000(1,000) = 1,000,000$ for a selection or exchange sort.

The quicksort puts a list into sorted order by a partitioning process. At each stage, the list is partitioned into sublists so that a selected element, called the pivot, is placed in its correct position in the final sorted list. To understand the process, consider the list in Figure 8.27.

The original list consists of seven numbers. Designating the first element in the list, 98, as the pivot element, the list is rearranged as shown in the first partition. Notice that this partition results in all values less than 98 residing to its left and all values greater than 98 to its right. For now, disregard the exact order of the elements to the left and right of the 98 (in a moment, we will see how the arrangement of the numbers came about).

The numbers to the left of the pivot constitute one sublist and the numbers to the right form another sublist, which individually must be reordered by a partitioning process. The pivot for the first sublist is 67 and the pivot for the second sublist is 101. Figure 8.28 shows how each of these sublists is partitioned using their respective pivot elements. The partitioning process stops when a sublist has only one element.

FIGURE 8.27   **A first quicksort partition**

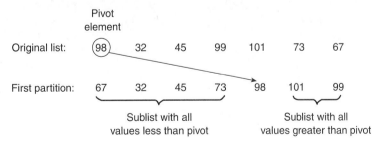

[9] This algorithm was developed by C. A. R. Hoare and first described by him in an article entitled "Quicksort" in *Computer Journal* (vol. 5, pp. 10–15) in 1962. This sorting algorithm was so much faster than previous algorithms that it became known as *the* quicksort.

FIGURE 8.28   **Completing the quicksort**

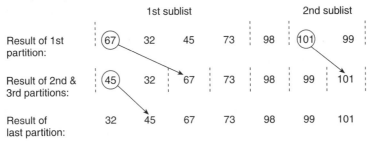

In the case illustrated in Figure 8.28, a fourth partition is required for the sublist containing the values 45 and 32, since all other sublists have only one element. Once this last sublist is partitioned, the quicksort is completed and the original list is in sorted order.

As we have illustrated, the key to the quicksort is its partitioning process. An essential part of this process is that each sublist is rearranged in place; that is, elements are rearranged within the existing list. This rearrangement is facilitated by first saving the value of the pivot, which frees its slot to be used by another element. The list is then examined from the right, starting with the last element in the list, for a value less than the pivot; when one is found, it is copied to the pivot slot. This copy frees a slot at the right of the list for use by another element. The list is now examined from the left for any value greater than the pivot; when one is found, it is copied to the last freed slot. This right-to-left and left-to-right scan is continued until the right and left index values meet. The saved pivot element is then copied into this slot. At that point, all values to the left of the index are smaller than the pivot value and all values to the right are greater. For an understanding of how a quicksort is accomplished in practice, we will show all of the steps required to complete one partition using our previous list of numbers.

Consider Figure 8.29, which shows our original list of Figure 8.27 and the positions of the initial left and right indexes. As shown in the figure, the pivot value has been saved into a variable named pivot; the right index points to the last list element and is the active index. Using this index the scan for elements less than the pivot value of 98 begins.

Since 67 is less than the pivot value of 98, the 67 is moved into the pivot slot (the pivot value is not lost because it has been assigned to the variable pivot), and the left index is incremented. This results in the arrangement shown in Figure 8.30.

FIGURE 8.29   **The start of the scanning process**

FIGURE 8.30 **The list after the first copy**

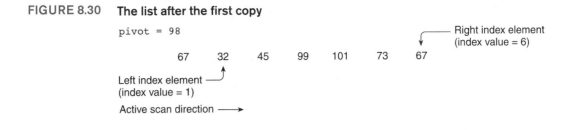

Notice in Figure 8.30 that the element pointed to by the right index is now available for the next copy because its value, 67, has been reproduced as the first element. (This will always be the case; when a scan stops, its index will indicate the position available for the next move.)

FIGURE 8.31 **The start of the second right-side scan**

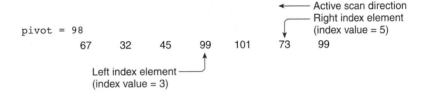

Scanning of the list in Figure 8.30 continues from the left for a search of all values greater than 98. This occurs when 99 is reached. Since 99 is greater than the pivot value of 98, the scan stops and 99 is copied into the position indicated by the right index. The right index is then decremented, which produces the situation illustrated in Figure 8.31.

Scanning of the list in Figure 8.31 now continues from the right in a search for values less than the pivot. Since 73 qualifies, the right scan stops, 73 is moved into the position indicated by the left index, and the left index is incremented. This results in the list shown in Figure 8.32.

Scanning of the list in Figure 8.32 now resumes from the left in a search for values greater than 98. Since 101 qualifies, this scan stops, 101 is moved into the slot indicated by the right index, and the right index is incremented. This results in the list illustrated in Figure 8.33.

FIGURE 8.32 **The start of the second left-side scan**

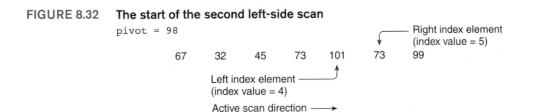

FIGURE 8.33   **The position of list elements after 101 is moved**

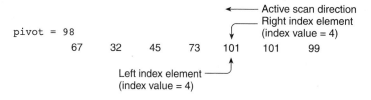

Notice in this figure that left and right indexes are equal. This is the condition that stops all scanning and indicates the position where the pivot should be placed. Doing so results in completion of this partition with the list in the order

67   32   45   73   98   101   99

Compare this list with the one previously shown for the first partition in Figure 8.27. As is seen, they are the same. Here the pivot has been placed so that all elements less than it are to its left and all values greater than it are to its right.

The quicksort algorithm uses the returned pivot value to recursively determine whether additional partitions are required for each sublist defined by the list segments to the left and right of the pivot index. The code implemented by the `Arrays` class's `sort()` method is a modified version of the quicksort algorithm.

Part Four

Creating Swing-Based GUIs

9

Visual Programming Basics

This chapter describes the fundamentals of event-based programming required in using a graphical user interface (GUI). This is followed by a very simple GUI using the Java-provided Swing package of classes. Initially, we construct a simple window with no internal components from a single GUI class. We then expand this GUI class to include a window closing event, which forms the model structure for all subsequent component event handlers. Finally, we provide the GUI with an internal Command button component and an associated event handler that responds to the button being clicked.

9.1 **Event-Based Programming**

In all of the programs that we have examined so far, the sequence of events—that is, what happens when—is determined solely by the program. When such a program is run, the user may be requested to enter input or select between choices, but *when* the requests are made is predetermined by the program's code. This does not mean that a **graphical user interface (GUI)** cannot be provided, but at best, the GUI is a dialog intended either to present information or to request specific input items as dictated by program code. When and where the dialog appears are entirely determined by the program.

A different programming model is based on events. **Event-based programs** provide a fully functioning GUI from which the user has a number of graphical components from which to choose. Although the program no longer controls which graphical component will be selected by the user, it is responsible for correctly reacting to whatever component is selected, if any, in the order that selections are made.

The selection and activation of a specific graphical component by the user, such as clicking an on-screen button, are said to initiate an *event*. It is the responsibility of the program to correctly assess which specific event has occurred and then provide appropriate code to perform an action based on the identified event.

As an example of how an event-based program would be constructed in practice, consider the GUI shown in Figure 9.1. Here the user can click any of the internal buttons in any sequence. Additionally, the user can click any of the buttons on the top line of the window itself. For the moment, we can concern ourselves only with the three internal buttons labeled Message, Clear, and Exit. The selection of any one of these buttons constitutes an event. As a practical matter, such an event can be triggered in one of the following three ways:

1. Placing the mouse pointer over a button and clicking the left mouse button (clicking means pushing and releasing the left mouse button)

2. Using the TAB key until the desired button is highlighted with a dotted line and then pushing the Enter key. The component that is highlighted with the dotted line is said "to have the focus" (Figure 9.1, the Message button has the focus)

3. Pressing an accelerator key. An **accelerator key**, which is also referred to both as a **shortcut key** and **mnemonic key**, is any action that activates a GUI component through the keyboard

Once an event is triggered by a user, which in this case is done by selecting and activating one of the three button components in the window shown in Figure 9.1, program instructions take over. As illustrated in Figure 9.2, an event, such as clicking the mouse on a button, sets in motion a sequence of occurrences. If an

FIGURE 9.1   **A sample GUI**

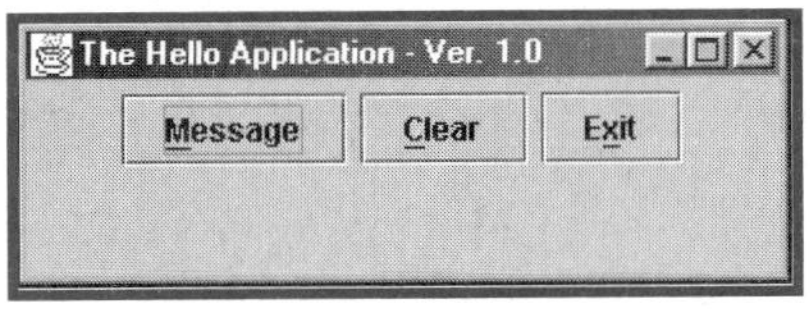

FIGURE 9.2   **An event "triggers" the initiation of an event object**

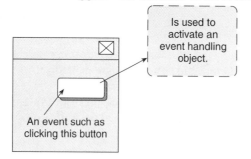

event-handling object has been created and properly connected to an activating component, which is referred to as registering the event object, the event produces a specific result; otherwise, the event is ignored. This is, of course, the essence of a graphical user interface: The selection of which event object is executed depends on what event occurred, which ultimately depends on what the user does. The code from which the event-handling object is created, however, must still be written by the programmer. For the program shown in Figure 9.1, there are three events for which we will provide event code. If the user clicks the Message button, the message Hello There World! will be displayed in the text field. Clicking the Clear button will result in the text field being cleared, and clicking the Exit button will result in termination of the program in the same manner as clicking the window's Close button.

Notice that the sequence of events—that is, which action is to be taken—is controlled by the user. The user can click any one of three buttons, in any order, or even run a different Windows program while the Java program that displays the GUI is running. This user determination of which event will take place next, as the program is running, is quite a different approach from that used in the first three parts of this text. In the programs presented in these earlier parts, the decisions as to which actions are taken and in what order are determined by the program.

An event-based graphical user interface such as that illustrated in Figure 9.1 requires that the programmer provide the code both to create the GUI and then appropriately process the events triggered by activating the displayed GUI components.

The aspect of Java that makes programming a GUI so easy is that Java provides an extensive set of objects that can be placed on a GUI in a very simple manner. Prior to Version 2.0, these objects, which are formally referred to as *components* in Java and informally as *controls*, were available from a package called java.awt, where awt stands for Abstract Window Toolkit. With Version 2.0, a package of components that were much simpler to use was available in the javax.swing package. Because the Swing package is based on the older AWT package, the basic components in both packages are almost identical, but the names of the components were changed for the Swing package. Table 9.1 lists the three generic types of objects used in creating a GUI, and Table 9.2 lists specific component types and their respective names under both AWT and Swing. As can be seen in Table 9.2, the only difference between AWT and Swing object names is that the equivalent Swing name is the same AWT component name prefixed by the letter J.

Table 9.1 **Generic GUI Objects**

Component Type	Description
Top-Level Container	A basic window structure that includes such things as borders and resizing capabilities and can be used to hold both intermediate containers and atomic components. Each GUI must have one of these components that ties the GUI into the operating system.
Intermediate Container	A graphical object displayed in a top-level container that itself can hold other intermediate containers and atomic components. Used to simplify placement and exact positioning of atomic components.
Atomic Components	Graphical objects used to accept and/or display individual items of information. Must be placed into a container using an `add()` method.

In this text, we will only create GUIs using the Swing package of classes. Except for the JMenu component, each of the atomic components in Table 9.2 is presented in detail and used in GUIs that are based on a top-level JFrame container. Using the Swing package of classes and components means that we will not have to be concerned with writing the code for either producing the graphical objects listed in Tables 9.1 and 9.2 or for recognizing when certain events, such as "mouse was clicked," actually occur. Once the desired components are selected and coded into the program, Java takes care of creating the component and recognizing appropriate component events, such as clicking a **button**. What we will have to be concerned about is writing and including code to correctly process events that can be triggered by a user's interaction with the GUI's components when a program is run.

Table 9.2 **AWT and Swing Components**

Component Type	AWT Name	Swing Name
Top-Level Container	Frame	JFrame
Top-Level Container	Applet	JApplet
Top-Level Container	Dialog	JDialog
Top-Level Container	Window	JWindow
Intermediate Container	Panel	JPanel
Intermediate Container	InternalFrame	JInternalFrame
Intermediate Container	LayeredPane	JLayeredPane
Intermediate Container	RootPane	JRootPane
Atomic	Button	JButton
Atomic	Menu	JMenu
Atomic	Label	JLabel
Atomic	CheckBox	JCheckBox
Atomic	RadioButton	JRadioButton
Atomic	TextField	JTextField
Atomic	TextArea	JTextArea

The Event-Based Model

To gain a better understanding of how event-based programs are constructed, it is worthwhile comparing their structure to the procedure-driven programs that we have used until now. As we shall see, the structures of these two types of programs are quite different.

A procedure-driven program is a carryover from earlier times when the predominant operating system was DOS (disk operating system). DOS was a single-tasking operating system, where only a single program would run at one time. Once DOS gave control to a program, the program took control of the computer. This situation is illustrated in Figure 9.3. Notice in this figure that DOS effectively relinquishes control over the computer's operation to the program that is running. Specifically, if a Java program was being run, control would be transferred to the start of the Java program, which is designated by the reserved word main(). Any operating system resources that the Java program needs, such as accessing data from a file, are initiated from within the Java program itself. Only after the Java program has finished running would control pass from the program back to the operating system.

The situation is quite different under a multitasking operating system such as Windows or UNIX. Since multiple programs can be running, it is essential that the operating system retain primary control at all times, in the management of the computer's resources. This control prevents any one program from effectively taking control and inhibiting other programs from running. It also is necessary to ensure that information destined for one application does not become lost or inadvertently accepted by another application. To see why, consider the following case.

Assume that two different programs are running and have open windows on the screen. In this situation, a user could click controls in either application. If one of the applications were in total control of the computer, it would be responsible for determining on what object and in which program the user clicked the mouse. Clearly, the programmer who developed one of the executing programs would not be concerned or even be expected to know how to intercept and correctly route an event used by any of the other myriad of programs that the operating system was also running. So if a mouse click in another program occurred, it would most likely be lost while any one of the other programs had control of the computer's resources.

The solution to this problem is to allow only the operating system, be it Windows, UNIX, or Linux®, to have total control of the computer and never relinquish this control to any executing programs. Under this scheme, most executing programs spend the majority of their time in a sleep type of mode. When the operating system, which is always running, detects an event such as a mouse click, it first determines what the event was and in which application window the event occurred. This type of operation is shown in Figure 9.4.

FIGURE 9.3 **Program control under DOS**

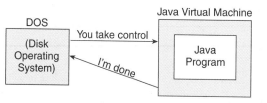

FIGURE 9.4   **Program control under a multitasking operating system**

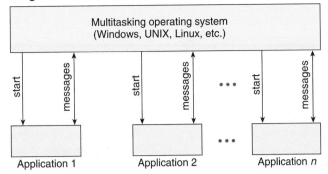

For the type of operation shown in Figure 9.4, it is the operating system's responsibility to first make a determination when the user does something as to what event actually occurred and in which application it took place. Once this is done, the operating system passes this event information, in the form of a specific message, to the appropriate application and only then permits the application to take action. The action, however, may be interrupted at any time if the operating system detects another event taking place.

The process in Figure 9.4 effectively standardizes the user interface provided by the operating system because the operating system determines how events are recognized and passed into an application. In this arrangement, an application only needs to know how to accept and then act on the information received from the operating system. Clearly, how the information is delivered depends on the operating system. Thus, every program being run on a computer must have a standard interface to the specific operating system running the computer. We will now see how this interface is specifically handled in Java using the Swing package of components and their associated methods.

Containment Hierarchy

Every GUI component created in Java has a placement level, with atomic components and containers logically placed within other appropriate containers. This hierarchy of component placement is referred to as a **containment hierarchy**. Each such hierarchy consists of one and only one top-level container and then any number of other intermediate containers and/or atomic components that are placed into it. The top-level container, which for a stand-alone Swing-based GUI is almost always a JFrame, forms the starting point for the hierarchy.[1] Because one of the primary functions of a top-level container is to interface with the operating system directly, earlier versions of Java referred to such containers as **heavyweight components**. This name derived from the fact that only top-level containers were effectively "weighed down" with the additional functionality required for interfacing with the operating system.

---

[1] Although from its name you might think a JWindow would be used, this is actually a very restrictive container. It is rarely used in practice because it does not provide any controls or title bar and is always placed on top of all other windows.

The next important level in a containment hierarchy is a *content pane*. This is an internal component provided by each top-level container into which all of the visible components displayed by a GUI must be placed. Optionally, a menu bar can also be added to a top-level container. When a menu bar is added to a GUI, it is positioned within the top-level container but is placed outside the container's content pane. Figure 9.5 illustrates the most commonly used Swing-based containment hierarchy, which is the one that we will follow in constructing all of our Swing-based GUIs. As shown in the figure, the hierarchy starts with a JFrame. The JFrame automatically provides a root pane, which in turn contains the content pane. Because it is the content pane to which intermediate containers and atomic components are added, you generally will not need to be concerned with the root pane.[2] Notice in the figure that although all visible components must go through the JFrame's content pane, a menu bar is not attached to the content pane.

Each top-level and intermediate container has an associated default **layout manager** that defines how components are positioned and sized within the container's content pane. This default placement can always be changed by explicitly specifying another layout manager. Table 9.3 lists the six layout managers currently available and how they are typically categorized for ease of use. Table 9.4 lists the default layout manager associated with each top-level container type. Detailed use of layout managers is presented in the next chapter.

Finally, the lower levels of a containment hierarchy consist of intermediate containers and atomic components such as buttons, labels, and text areas. These intermediate containers and atomic components are frequently referred to as *lightweight components*. The implication of the term *lightweight* is that because these components are not directly anchored to the underlying operating system, they do not need the heavyweight functionality provided by Java for interfacing with the operating

FIGURE 9.5   **A typical swing-based containment hierarchy**

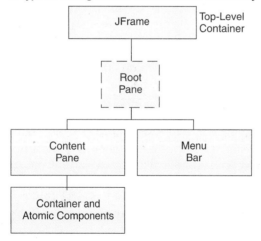

---

[2] The root pane and its internal components must explicitly be dealt with only in more advanced applications where, for example, mouse clicks must be intercepted or multiple components must be painted over.

Table 9.3 **Layout Managers**

Manager	Description	Use Type
FlowLayout	Components are added to the container from left to right and top to bottom, in a row-by-row manner, starting from the top left corner of the container.	Simple
GridLayout	All components are created equal in size and displayed in the requested number of rows and columns. Blank areas fill in unused columns.	Simple
BorderLayout	Up to five components can be placed in the container. The components are placed in positions denoted as north, south, west, east, and center. These positions correspond to the top, bottom, left side, right side, and center positions of the container.	Special Purpose
CardLayout	This layout permits implementation of an area that can contain different components at different times.	Special Purpose
BoxLayout	Components are placed into either a single row or column. Column components can be center, left-edge, or right-edge aligned.	Flexible
GridBagLayout	Components are placed in a spreadsheet type grid of cells, with components permitted to span across and down multiple cells.	Flexible

system. Table 9.5 lists the lightweight atomic components that we will introduce and use in this text.

Exercises 9.1

1. What is the purpose of a GUI and what elements does a user see in a GUI?

2. What gets executed when an event occurs?

3. List the three ways that an event can be triggered by a user.

4. List the three component types that can be used to create a GUI in Java.

5. What top-level container type is used, almost exclusively, to create stand-alone Java application GUIs?

6. What is a containment hierarchy and how it is used to create a GUI?

7. What is the internal component provided by each top-level container to which all visible GUI components must be added?

8a. What is the purpose of a layout manager?

b. What is the default layout manager for a JFrame container?

Table 9.4 **Top-Level Container Default Layout Mangers**

Container	Default Layout Manager
JFrame	BorderLayout
JDialog	BorderLayout
JPanel	BorderLayout
JWindow	FlowLayout

Table 9.5　**Lightweight Atomic Components**

Component	Description
JButton	A component that triggers an event when clicked.
JLabel	A displayed text or icon.
JTextField	A single line where text may be entered and displayed.
JTextArea	An area that can span multiple lines where text can be entered and displayed.
JPasswordField	Same as a JTextField, but entered characters are displayed as asterisks (*).
JCheckBox	A component that may be either checked or unchecked.
JRadioButton	A component consisting of one or more items, only one of which may be selected.

9.2　Creating a Swing-Based Window

It is now time to construct our first functioning GUI window using the Swing package of classes. Although there are numerous ways to create a GUI, most of the various techniques you will encounter are implemented within the context of the following two predominant approaches:

1. Construct the GUI as a separate class using Swing components. Then use a `main()` method to instantiate (i.e., create) an object of the class. When a specific GUI object is instantiated, the GUI will appear on the screen.

2. Construct a GUI object using Swing components from within a `main()` method without first creating a separate GUI class.

In general, the first approach is preferred because it adheres more closely to accepted object-oriented practice. Using this approach, all of the details of the GUI are encapsulated into a separate class, and then when a GUI is required, an object of the class is created. The second approach is sometimes used to introduce Swing components and to create extremely simple GUIs. This is how we will use both of these approaches in this text. Here our first example uses the second approach to introduce an extremely simple GUI using a Swing JFrame container. Consider Program 9.1.

Program 9.1

```
import javax.swing.*;
public class FirstGui
{
  public static void main(String[] args)
  {
    JFrame mainFrame; // declare a JFrame reference variable
    mainFrame = new JFrame("First GUI Window"); //instantiate a JFrame object

    mainFrame.setSize(300,150);
    mainFrame.show();
  }
}
```

The first statement in Program 9.1's `main()` method declares a variable named `mainFrame` to be of type `JFrame`. The next statement uses the `new` operator to create a `JFrame` object that will be referenced by the `mainFrame` variable. This statement also sets the title bar text for the JFrame, which in this case is the string `First GUI Window`. When this program is run, the `JFrame` object becomes a window that is displayed on the screen with the designated title. Although we have used two statements to instantiate a `JFrame` object, the same effect can be achieved by the single statement

```
JFrame mainFrame = new JFrame("First GUI Window");
```

The next statement in `main()`,

```
mainFrame.setSize(300,150);
```

uses a `setSize()` method to set the size of the frame in pixels.[3] The general syntax of the `setSize()` method is

```
objectReferenceName.setSize(width, height)
```

The *objectReferenceName* to the left of the required period identifies a specific object, and the name to the right of the period identifies the method. As we have seen previously, this is the standard object-oriented notation for applying a class method to a specific object.

The fourth line uses the `show()` method to make the `JFrame` object appear on the screen. An entirely equivalent method is `setVisible(true)`; you can, therefore, use these methods interchangeably. When Program 9.1 is compiled and run, the JFrame creates the window in Figure 9.6. Because this window is controlled by the operating system, it can be manipulated using standard window techniques. Thus, we can click the Maximize or Minimize buttons, move or resize the window, and close the window by clicking the Close button (X). Unfortunately, closing the window in Windows *does not* close the Java application. Thus, if you click the Close button, the underlying Java application, which in this case is Program 9.1, is still running. To close the Java program, you must press the Control (Ctrl) and C keys at the same time. This is the "break" sequence recognized by most operating systems that causes the current program to stop running.

An event handling method that will accept the close event from the operating system and correctly close the underlying Java program is presented in the next section. Before considering this event handler, however, we first modify Program 9.1 to encapsulate all of the functionality of the GUI into a basic GUI class. To see how this is done, consider Program 9.2.

FIGURE 9.6   **The window displayed by Program 9.1**

---

[3] A pixel refers to a single position on a computer screen. For example, a screen area of 800 × 600 refers to a width of 800 pixels by a length of 600 pixels.

Program 9.2

```java
import javax.swing.*;
public class FirstWindow extends JFrame
{
  private JFrame mainFrame;

  public FirstWindow() // a constructor
  {
    mainFrame = new JFrame("First GUI Window");

    mainFrame.setSize(300,150);
    mainFrame.show();
  }

  public static void main(String[] args)
  {
    new FirstWindow();
  }
} // end of class
```

Notice that the class provided in Program 9.2 has been named FirstWindow, which has been defined as extending the class JFrame. This means that our First-Window class has access to all of the public and protected methods that are available to the JFrame class, such as setSize() and show(). Within our class, we have defined a single class variable named mainFrame to be of type JFrame. We have also defined a single constructor method. The three statements within this constructor are almost identical to those that we previously used within Program 9.1's main() method. The only difference is the first statement, where we do not have to declare mainFrame as being of type JFrame, precisely because of its declaration as a class variable. Now look at the main() method. Here all that is required to produce the GUI is that a new instance of the class FirstWindow be created. This is accomplished by the statement new FirstWindow(). When this statement is carried out, the constructor for the FirstWindow class is automatically called. This constructor performs the same task previously performed by Program 9.1's main() method and produces the same GUI created by Program 9.1, as shown in Figure 9.6. Because Program 9.2 would be stored on disk as FirstWindow.java, which is derived from its class name, it must be compiled and run using the statements

```
javac FirstWindow.java
java FirstWindow
```

If you are not familiar with the construction of classes presented in Part Two, Program 9.2 will appear more complicated than Program 9.1. Nevertheless, Program 9.2 has very distinct advantages over Program 9.1. The main advantage is that all of the GUI components are encapsulated within a single well-defined class that isolates the GUI code from the application that uses it. This means that the same application can use different GUIs and that different parts of the overall system can be altered without affecting other parts, which is precisely the advantage provided by object-oriented languages. Thus, as more and more functionality is added to Program 9.2's

GUI, its basic structure allows us to focus on the additional components and their relationship to the GUI as a whole and lets us consolidate these design elements into a single self-contained class. The `main()` method can then be used operationally for either independent testing of the GUI or inclusion of it within a larger context that uses the GUI for both user input and display. In practice, a more extensive `main()` method would be included in its own class, as was discussed in Part Two of this text. For our immediate purposes, however, Program 9.2's `FirstWindow` class will be the basic model upon which we will design all of our subsequent Swing-based GUIs.

Look and Feel

A GUI's *look and feel* refers to how the GUI appears on the screen and how a user interacts with it. Although we will always use the default look and feel named Java, the Swing package actually supports the four look and feel types listed in Table 9.6, three of which are illustrated in Figure 9.7. As can be seen from these examples, the differences in the displays are determined by the line thickness, shading, and the two- or three-dimensional look provided.

Also listed in Table 9.6 are the Java statements for explicitly selecting each look and feel type. In the absence of either an explicit look and feel selection or an invalid choice, the default Java look and feel is used. To implement a specific look and feel, the code in Table 9.6 must be included in a `try` and `catch` block similar to the following, which sets a Windows look and feel:

```
try
{
  UIManager.setLookAndFeel("com.sun.java.Swing.plaf.windows.WindowsLookAndFeel");
  SwingUtilities.updateComponentTreeUI(mainFrame);
  mainFrame.pack();
}catch (Exception e){}
```

In this code, the identifier `mainFrame` is the name that has been consistently declared in all of our GUI-based programs as being of type JFrame. The `pack()` method will force the change to the selected look and feel even after the GUI has been displayed. Thus, this section of code can be placed either before or after a `show()` method has been invoked to display a GUI.

Table 9.6 Look and Feel GUI Types

Type	Code	Comment
Java	`setLookAndFeel("javax.swing.plaf.metal.MetalLookAndFeel");`	Can be used on all systems.
Mac	`setLookAndFeel("javax.swing.plaf.mac.MacLookAndFeel");`	Can only be used on Mac systems.
Windows	`setLookAndFeel("com.sun.java.swing.plaf.windows.WindowsLookAndFeel");`	Can only be used on Windows systems.
UNIX	`setLookAndFeel("com.sun.java.swing.plaf.motif.MotifLookAndFeel");`	Can be used on all systems.

FIGURE 9.7   **Look and feel examples**

(a) Java default

(b) Windows

(c) UNIX

Exercises 9.2

1. Describe the two main approaches to constructing GUIs using Swing-based components.

2a. Enter and run Program 9.1 on your computer.

  b. What is a major problem with Program 9.1?

  c. After closing the window constructed by Program 9.1, how can the underlying Java program be halted and return provided to the operating system?

  d. How would Program 9.1 be named and stored on your computer?

3a. Enter and run Program 9.2 on your computer.

  b. What is a major problem with Program 9.2?

  c. After closing the window constructed by Program 9.2, how can the underlying Java program be halted and return provided to the operating system?

  d. How would Program 9.2 be named and stored on your computer?

4. Replace the statement `mainFrame.show()` in Program 9.2 with the statement `main-Frame.setVisible(true)` and run the program to verify that it produces the same effect.

5. Modify Program 9.2 so that the size of the displayed GUI is 400 pixels wide × 200 pixels high.

6. Write a Java program that constructs a window having the title `The Hello Application - Ver. 1.0`.

7. Modify Program 9.2 so that the `main()` method is contained within a class named `TestFirstWindow`. The program should be stored under the name `TestFirstWindow.java`.

8. What is meant by a GUI's look and feel?

9. List the four look and feel types provided by Java's Swing package.

10. Modify Program 9.2 so that it is displayed with a UNIX look and feel.

A BIT OF BACKGROUND

Admiral Grace Hopper, USN

Grace Hopper received a Ph.D. from Yale University and joined the Naval Reserve in 1943. In her assignment to the Bureau of Ordinance Computation Project at Harvard University, she programmed the Mark I, the first large-scale, electromechanical digital computer. Later, she applied her outstanding talents in mathematics as senior programmer of the UNIVAC I.

Commodore Hopper became a pioneer in the development of computer languages and served on the Conference of Data Systems Languages (CODA-SYL) committee. She helped develop COBOL and is credited with producing the first practical program in that language. In 1959, she developed a COBOL compiler, which allowed programs written in a standardized language to be transported between different computers for the first time.

An interesting sidelight to her career was that her entry into her log book, dated September 19, 1945, at 15:45 hours, recorded "First actual case of bug being found." It was an actual insect that had shorted a relay in the Mark I.

Admiral Hopper remained a colorful figure in the computing community after her retirement from active duty in the U.S. Navy in August 1986 at the age of 79.

9.3 Adding a Window Closing Event Handler

When creating a functioning GUI in Java, we will always use the following two-phase process:

Phase 1: Construct the component so that it appears visually
Phase 2: Provide an event handler for the component

We will adhere to this process no matter how many components we add into the GUI. For now, however, our GUI consists of a single JFrame component. Because we have completed phase 1 for this component, when Program 9.2 is run, the component appears visually and a blank window is displayed. If you click the window's Close (X) button, the window will close, but the underlying Java application is still running and must be stopped by pressing the Ctrl and C keys at the same time. In this section, we complete phase 2 for this graphical user interface by providing it with an event handler that closes the underlying Java application when the window's Close button is clicked. Formally, an **event handler** is an object that responds appropriately when an event occurs, such as clicking a window's Close button.

In creating a window closing event handler, we first provide a generic description of Java's event handling methodology. This is followed by an in-depth presentation of the three predominant ways in which event handlers are constructed in practice. Thus, this section is a basic primer on creating event handlers in general, although we will apply each technique to a window closing event. When you have completed this section, you will have all the tools needed to easily understand and construct event handlers for the atomic components presented in the next chapter.

The Event Delegation Model

Although creating a Java event handler is a rather "cookbook" affair once the underlying process is understood, it does require a number of predefined steps. This is because Java implements event handling by what is known as an **event delegation model**. This model requires two basic elements: a component, such as a window or button, that can generate an event, and an event handler, which is a separate object that is formally referred to as a **listener object**. The component delegates responsibility to the listener object for doing something when an event is generated. The glue that attaches an event to a specific event handler (the listener object) is a *registration statement*. Only event handlers that have been correctly registered actually receive the news when a specific event has taken place. Thus, the complete set of steps for phase 2 of our GUI design procedure is

> *Phase 2: Provide an event handler for the component*
> > *Step 1: Write the code for an event handler class, which is known as the listener class*
> > *Step 2: Create an instance of the event handler class (this means instantiating an object of the class using the new operator); the created object is known as a listener object*
> > *Step 3: Register the listener object created in step 2*

Each of these three steps for collectively constructing and activating an event handler are found in Program 9.3, which implements a complete event handler for closing the GUI when the window's Close (X) button is clicked. We have named the GUI class in Program 9.3 `SecondWindow` and delegated the event handling method to a separate class named `WinHandler`, which is the listener class. Notice that we have also added the statement `import java.awt.event.*;` at the top of the program. It is the `java.awt.event` package that provides the underlying methods needed by a listener class.

We can now examine how each of the three event delegation elements, which have been boldfaced for easy recognition, are provided by Program 9.3.

Program 9.3

```java
import javax.swing.*;
import java.awt.event.*;   // this is needed for the event handlers
public class SecondWindow extends JFrame
{
  private JFrame mainFrame;

  public SecondWindow() // a constructor
  {
    mainFrame = new JFrame("Second GUI Window");

    mainFrame.setSize(300,150);
    mainFrame.show();

    WinHandler handler = new WinHandler();     // Phase 2 - Step 2: create an event handler
    mainFrame.addWindowListener(handler);      // Phase 2 - Step 3: register (activate) the handler
  }
```

```
  public static void main(String[] args)
  {
    new SecondWindow();
  }
} // end of GUI class


  // Phase 2 - Step 1: define a listener class to handle window events
class WinHandler implements WindowListener
{
  public void windowClosing(WindowEvent e) {System.exit(0);}
  public void windowClosed(WindowEvent e) {}
  public void windowOpened(WindowEvent e) {}
  public void windowIconified(WindowEvent e) {}
  public void windowDeiconified(WindowEvent e) {}
  public void windowActivated(WindowEvent e) {}
  public void windowDeactivated(WindowEvent e) {}
} // end of listener class
```

In Program 9.3, the event handling (listener) class has been coded as a separate nonnested class. Doing so at this point permits us to concentrate specifically on all of the elements needed by an event handling class. Later in this section, we will provide two useful techniques for significantly reducing the size of the event handling code, but we will do this in stages. The reason is that you will encounter each version in your programming work. Thus, the discussion forms the basis for understanding all of the event handling methods you will see in practice and will use for the atomic components that are added into our basic GUI in the next chapter. For now, however, consider Program 9.3's listener class by itself, which is reproduced for convenience.

```
  // Step 1 - define a listener class to handle window events
  class WinHandler implements WindowListener
  {
  public void windowClosing(WindowEvent e) {System.exit(0);}
  public void windowClosed(WindowEvent e) {}
  public void windowOpened(WindowEvent e) {}
  public void windowIconified(WindowEvent e) {}
  public void windowDeiconified(WindowEvent e) {}
  public void windowActivated(WindowEvent e) {}
  public void windowDeactivated(WindowEvent e) {}
  } // end of listener class
```

First, notice the class's header line specifies that the `WinHandler` class implements a `WindowListener` interface. Except for the name that we have chosen for our class, `WinHandler`, which is a programmer-selectable identifier, the rest of this header is standard for creating a class that will perform as a `WindowListener`. Specifically, a `WindowListener` is implemented because this interface is required by Java for handling window events. Table 9.7 presents the required interfaces for the components considered in this text. This table also lists, in the third column, all of the required methods for each event handler type. Java requires that if even one of these

Table 9.7 **GUI Component Events Types**

Component	Required Interface Type	Required Methods	Available Adapter Class
Window	WindowListener	windowClosing(WindowEvent) windowClosed(WindowEvent) windowOpened(WindowEvent) windowActivated(WindowEvent) windowDeactivated(WindowEvent) windowIconified(WindowEvent) windowDeiconified(WindowEvent)	WindowAdapter
Mouse	MouseMotionListener	mouseDragged(MouseEvent) mouseMoved(MouseEvent)	MouseMotionAdapter
	MouseListener	mousePressed(MouseEvent) mouseReleased(MouseEvent) mouseClicked(MouseEvent)	MouseAdapter
Keyboard	KeyListener	keyPressed(KeyEvent) keyReleased(KeyEvent) keyTyped(KeyEvent)	KeyAdapter
Button	ActionListener	actionPerformed(ActionEvent)	ActionAdapter
Text Field	TextListener	textValueChanged(TextEvent)	(None)
Check Box	ItemListener	itemStateChanged(ItemEvent)	(None)
Radio Button	ItemListener	itemStateChanged(ItemEvent)	(None)
Focus Events	FocusListener	focusGained(FocusEvent) focusLost(FocusEvent)	FocusAdapter

methods is implemented in a listener class, all of the listed methods must be implemented, even if they consist of empty bodies.

Now concentrate on the listener class's internal construction. Notice that the class consists of no declared variables and seven methods, only one of which has a non-empty body. This single nonempty method is the windowClosing() method, and the single statement constituting its body is System.exit(0). This statement should be familiar because it is the same statement used to close all of the programs in Part One that used the Swing package to implement a dialog box. The other six methods are still required by any listener class that is implemented as a WindowListener, as listed in Table 9.7, even if we are not interested in using them. Because we are only concerned with the windowClosing() method, these other methods are constructed as empty methods with no internal statements.

Having taken care of constructing the event handling class (step 1), the two remaining steps must be completed. Step 2, instantiating an object of the listener class, is accomplished in Program 9.3 using the statement

```
WinHandler handler = new WinHandler();  // Phase 2 - Step 2: create an event handler
```

This statement should also look familiar because it is one of the standard ways that we have used throughout the text to instantiate (i.e., create) an object. In this particular case, the name handler is a programmer-selected reference variable that is declared to be of type WinHanlder, which is the name of the WindowListener class that we constructed for step 1. As always, this single statement can be replaced by two statements, one that first declares a reference variable and the second that instantiates an object. Using two statements, step 2 can also be realized as

```
WinHandler handler;
handler = new WinHandler();
```

The statement in Program 9.3 that performs step 3 and attaches the `WindowListener` object named `handler` created in step 2 to the desired component, which in our specific case is `mainFrame`, is

```
mainFrame.addWindowListener(handler);  // Phase 2 - Step 3: register (activate) the handler
```

We will discuss `add()` methods in detail in the next section, so for now, we simply use this statement as is. This statement activates the listener object created in step 2 and is formally referred to as a registration statement.

When Program 9.3 is compiled and run using the statements

```
javac SecondWindow.java
java SecondWindow
```

the GUI in Figure 9.8 is displayed. Except for the title bar, this is the same GUI created by Program 9.2 and previously shown in Figure 9.6. The central difference between these two GUIs is that clicking the Close (X) button on the window constructed by Program 9.3 not only closes the window but shuts down the underlying Java program and returns control appropriately to the operating system.

Adapter and Inner Classes

In Program 9.3, the listener class is constructed as a separate class. Thus, it has two minor problems that can be easily rectified. The first problem is that, even though we only need to handle one event, the listener class is required to contain the seven event handling methods in Table 9.7 for a `WindowListener`. The second problem is that the listener class code (step 1) is located after the GUI class code at the end of the program, when it would be preferable to have it closer to the code that instantiates (step 2) and registers (step 3) the listener. We will solve these problems one at a time.

First, Java provides a special set of classes, referred to as **adapter classes**, that declare empty event handling methods for a given interface type, such as the `WindowListener` class in Table 9.7. Because an adapter class provides all of the method declarations for an interface, it can be used as the parent class for a listener class. By construction, all adapter classes are constructed in Java as abstract classes. An *abstract class* is a class from which objects cannot be directly instantiated but which can be used as a parent from which other classes can be derived. For example, as listed in Table 9.7, the adapter class provided in Java that can be used as a parent class to

FIGURE 9.8 **The window displayed by Program 9.3**

create a `WindowListener` is named `WindowAdapter`. Now consider the following listener class, which extends the adapter class named `WindowAdapter`.

```
 // extend an adapter class to handle window events
class WinHandler extends WindowAdapter
{
  public void windowClosing(WindowEvent e) {System.exit(0);}
}  // end of listener class
```

Because we are extending an adapter class that provides definitions for all of the required window event methods, all we need to do is provide code for the event method that we are actually interested in. Our class's single `windowClosing()` method will override the method with the same name in the parent `WindowAdapter` class, and the six other required methods are provided for by the remaining empty methods defined in the adapter class.

Using our new `WinHandler` class in place of the longer version provided in Program 9.3 and renaming our basic GUI class as `ThirdWindow` result in Program 9.4. Here the new class is boldfaced so you can easily see where we have made the change. Also notice the boldfaced line in the basic GUI class, which is

```
mainFrame.addWindowListener(new WinHandler());
```

This line both instantiates an object of the `WinHandler` listener class and registers the class in a single statement; it is used in place of these equivalent two lines from Program 9.3.

```
WinHandler handler = new WinHandler();  // Phase 2 - Step 2: create an event handler
mainFrame.addWindowListener(handler);   // Phase 2 - Step 3: register (activate) the handler
```

Because you will see both single-line and double-line statements for creating and registering an event handler object, you should be familiar with both styles. In your own work, select one of these two styles based either on preference, policy, or instruction and be consistent in its usage throughout all of your programs.

The output displayed when Program 9.4 is run appears in Figure 9.9. Except for the window's title bar, this GUI is identical to that provided by Program 9.3. As with the prior program's operation, both the window and the underlying Java program will be correctly shutdown when the Close button is pressed.

Notice that we have significantly reduced the size of the listener class using an adapter class. The next minor problem that we would like to address is to have the event handling class placed closer to the point at which the event handler object is created and registered. Doing so centralizes all aspects of the event handling mechanism in one place for easy reference.

Notice that in both Programs 9.3 and 9.4, the listener class is coded as a separate class that is located outside the class used to construct the GUI. Whenever the code for an event handling class is significantly longer than the `WinHandler` class coded in Program 9.3, it should be created in this manner. For small listener classes, however, which our `WinHandler` class has become, the code can easily be nested inside the main GUI class without unduly breaking up the code used to create the visual display of components. This is done by nesting the listener class into the main GUI class.

When one class is nested inside another class, it is referred to as an **inner class.** As an example of such a class, consider Program 9.5. Notice that this program's `WinHandler` class is identical to that in Program 9.4, but it is now located inside the

FIGURE 9.9   **The window displayed by Program 9.4**

Program 9.4

```
import javax.swing.*;
import java.awt.event.*;
public class ThirdWindow extends JFrame
{
  private JFrame mainFrame;

  public ThirdWindow() // a constructor
  {
    mainFrame = new JFrame("Third GUI Window");

    mainFrame.setSize(300,150);
    mainFrame.show();

     // create and register the handler in one statement
    mainFrame.addWindowListener(new WinHandler());
  }
  public static void main(String[] args)
  {
    new ThirdWindow();
  }
}  // end of GUI class

  // extend an adapter class to handle window events
class WinHandler extends WindowAdapter
{
  public void windowClosing(WindowEvent e) {System.exit(0);}
}  // end of listener class
```

GUI class. This is done precisely to move the event handling class closer to where the creation and registration of the event handling object is made.

Figure 9.10 shows the window displayed by Program 9.5. Again, except for the title bar, this GUI is the same as that produced by Programs 9.3 and 9.4, and all three programs operationally shutdown in the same way.

Although we have chosen in Program 9.5 to use Program 9.4's adapter class version of the listener class as an inner class within the defining GUI class, the same could have been done with the longer listener class provided in Program 9.3. You may also see a listener class nested within a separate class that includes the main()

FIGURE 9.10   **The window displayed by Program 9.5**

Program 9.5

```java
import javax.swing.*;
import java.awt.event.*;
public class FourthWindow extends JFrame
{
  private JFrame mainFrame;

  public FourthWindow() // a constructor
  {
    mainFrame = new JFrame("Fourth GUI Window");

    mainFrame.setSize(300,150);
    mainFrame.show();

     // create and register the handler in one statement
    mainFrame.addWindowListener(new WinHandler());
  }

     // an inner class to handle window events
   class WinHandler extends WindowAdapter
   {
     public void windowClosing(WindowEvent e) {System.exit(0);}
   }  // end of inner class

  public static void main(String[] args)
  {
    new FourthWindow();
  }
}  // end of GUI class
```

method if the instantiation of the event handling object is performed within the
main() method.

We are now almost finished with the various ways listener classes are constructed
in practice. The overriding rule in all cases is that the listener class be made as short
as possible, without sacrificing clarity, and that the code be placed as close as possible
to where an object of the class is actually instantiated. For larger listener classes, this

means creating a separate class that is placed outside the class used to create the GUI, and for smaller classes, it means using an inner class. If only one or two event methods are actually needed, an adapter class should be used to shorten the code, either as an inner or a separate class.

Anonymous Classes

The last extensively used variation for creating event handling classes is provided by anonymous classes. As the term suggests, an **anonymous class** is a class without a name. The advantage of this type of class is that it permits placing the event handling class code directly into the statement that creates an instance of the event handling class. Such classes can only be used when the event instantiation and registration are accomplished using a single statement. This is because an individual instantiation statement first requires declaring an event object with the name of a specific class, which precludes using a class having no name.

As a specific example of an anonymous class, consider the following code, which would qualify as a stand-alone class if it had a standard class header line. This missing header line qualifies the class as anonymous.

```
{
  public void windowClosing(WindowEvent e) {System.exit(0);}
}
```

Carefully compare this anonymous class to Program 9.5's `WinHandler` class, which is repeated for convenience.

```
class WinHandler extends WindowAdapter
{
  public void windowClosing(WindowEvent e) {System.exit(0);}
}
```

Notice that except for the anonymous class's missing header line, these two classes are identical and that both classes have the same body and, therefore, perform the exact same function.

The question now becomes: Where is this anonymous class placed? The answer is that the class is placed wherever a listener class name would normally be used to create a new instance of the class. As a specific example of this placement, consider the creation and registration statement used in Program 9.5, which is repeated here for convenience.

```
mainFrame.addWindowListener(new WinHandler());
```

What we are now going to do is move the last parenthesis and closing semicolon from this statement down to provide space for three additional lines as follows:

```
mainFrame.addWindowListener(new WinHandler()

);
```

It is within these newly created empty lines that the anonymous class is placed, producing the following code:

```
mainFrame.addWindowListener(new WindowAdapter()
{    // anonymous class
  public void windowClosing(WindowEvent e) {System.exit(0);}
}
);
```

First, notice that the interface type, `WindowAdapter`, is specifically designated in the header line. Second, because whitespace does not count in Java, at a minimum, the last two lines of code are usually placed together as `});`. Program 9.6 uses this code in our final version of creating a window closing event handler. For convenience, we have boldfaced the statements that create and register the listener object using the anonymous class.

Program 9.6

```
import javax.swing.*;
import java.awt.event.*;
public class FifthWindow extends JFrame
{
  private JFrame mainFrame;

  public FifthWindow() // a constructor
  {
    mainFrame = new JFrame("Fifth GUI Window");

    mainFrame.setSize(300,150);
    mainFrame.show();

    // create and register the handler in one statement
    // using an anonymous inner class
    mainFrame.addWindowListener(new WindowAdapter()
    {    // anonymous class
      public void windowClosing(WindowEvent e) {System.exit(0);}
    });
  }

  public static void main(String[] args)
  {
    new FifthWindow();
  }
}  // end of GUI class
```

When Program 9.6 is compiled and run, the GUI in Figure 9.11 is produced. Operationally, this window is closed in the same manner as all of the previous programs that provided window closing event handling code.

In addition to the version of the anonymous class used to handle the window closing event that we have used in Program 9.6, be prepared to see other space-saving versions of this code, such as

```
mainFrame.addWindowListener(new WindowAdapter()
{public void windowClosing(WindowEvent e) {System.exit(0);}});
```

FIGURE 9.11   **The window displayed by Program 9.6**

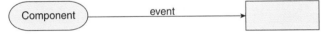

Anonymous classes should only be used when an event handler consists of a single method that is only one or two lines in length. Because our event handler class fits this description perfectly, it is an ideal candidate for implementation as an anonymous class. Also notice that an anonymous class is always used within a statement that creates an instance of the class. Because the creation statement must itself be contained within a class, the placement of an anonymous class will always force it to be an inner class.

Finally, be aware that in all of our event handling code we have constructed a single listener object for a single event source, which in our particular case has been a window. This situation is shown in Figure 9.12a. For completeness, it should be mentioned that multiple listener objects can be registered to the same event source (Figure 9.12b) and that a single listener object can be registered to multiple event sources

FIGURE 9.12   **Various registration configurations**

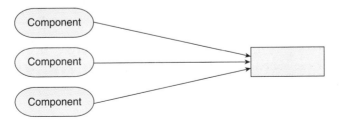

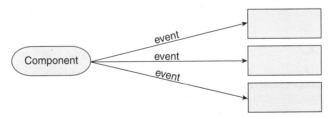

(Figure 9.12c). In the next chapter (Section 10.4), we will present a practical example of this last case where the same event handler is registered to two components. For this situation, the event handler must use its input argument to determine the component that triggered the event and then take appropriate action.

Exercises 9.3

1a. Compile, execute, and run Program 9.3 on your computer.

b. Repeat Exercise 1a but remove the registration statement

```
mainFrame.addWindowListener(handler);  // Phase 2 - Step 3: register (activate) the handler
```

With this statement removed, determine what happens when you now close down the displayed window using the window's Close (X) button.

2. Modify Program 9.3 so that it displays a Message box with the message `The Underlying Java Program will now be closed` when the Close button is clicked. Only when the user clicks the Message box's OK button should the program terminate.

3a. Compile, execute, and run Program 9.4 on your computer.

b. Make sure to first compile Program 9.3 and then change Program 9.4's single `main()` method's statement from `new FourthWindow();` to `new ThirdWindow();`. Now compile, execute, and run the modified Program 9.4. Determine what happened and why.

4. What is meant by an inner class?

5a. Describe the purpose of an adapter class.

b. Must an adapter class always be used as an inner class?

6a. Describe the difference between an anonymous class and a nonanonymous class.

b. Must an anonymous class always be used as an inner class?

7. Why do you think the `TextListener` and `ItemListener` classes have no equivalent adapter classes? (Tip: See Table 9.7.)

8. Write a Java program that constructs a window having the title `The Hello Application - Ver. 1.0`. Make sure that your program contains a window closing event object that correctly closes the window when the Close (X) button is clicked.

9.4 Adding a Button Component

Although the application presented in the previous section is a useful introduction to a JFrame container-based GUI and a window closing event handler that we will use in all of our subsequent GUIs, it is not a very useful application in itself. To make it practical, we have to add lightweight components, such as buttons and data entry and display fields with their related event classes. The process that we will always follow in adding components to a GUI is the following two-phase procedure:

Phase 1: Construct the component so that it appears visually
   Step 1: Create a specific component
   Step 2: Add the component into a container

Phase 2: Provide an event handler for the component
>***Step 1: Write the code for an event handler class (a listener class)***
>***Step 2: Create an instance of the event handler class (a listener object)***
>***Step 3: Register the listener object***

In phase 1, the component is added into a container, which in our case will always be a JFrame. This creates the actual graphical interface that the user sees on the screen. By providing each component with an event handler (phase 2), the component comes "alive" so that when it is selected something actually happens.

In this section, we illustrate this two-phase process using a button component as a specific example. Thus, we first create a GUI containing a button (phase 1) and then attach an event handler to the added component (phase 2). After constructing and activating one lightweight component into a GUI, you will have learned the method for placing and activating all other Java components, such as labels and data entry components, into a top-level container. Specific examples of each of these other components, however, are provided in the next chapter.

Adding a Button

A button component, which is also referred to as both a *push button* and a *command button*, is constructed from a JButton component. For our next GUI, we will use this component type to create the user interface shown in Figure 9.13.

Phase 1: Construct the Component So That It Appears Visually

Specifically, when adding a lightweight component, be it an intermediate container or an atomic component, into a top-level container, the two steps in this phase become

>***Step 1: Create a specific component***
>***Step 2: Add the component to the JFrame's content pane***

Numerous examples of step 1 have been provided throughout this chapter when we have used a top-level `JFrame` component to create a basic GUI window. When adding lightweight components into a top-level container, they must be added to the container's content pane. A container's content pane directly or indirectly holds all of the container's visible components. Thus, the really new step is step 2, which is used to bind a component to the underlying top-level JFrame container. Let's, however, take these steps one by one to create and add a functioning button into our basic GUI.

FIGURE 9.13   **The `ButtonGuiOne` class's GUI**

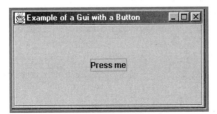

Step 1: Create a Button

Recall that an instance of a JFrame has been constructed throughout this chapter by first declaring a class variable to be of type JFrame using the statement

```
private JFrame mainFrame;
```

It is important to note that the variable name we have chosen, in this case main-Frame, can be any valid variable name that satisfies Java's identifier rules. Once a variable is declared to be of type JFrame, an actual JFrame object was created using a statement similar to

```
mainFrame = new JFrame("Example of a Gui with a Button");
```

In exactly the same manner, a button component, which is of type JButton, can be created. First, we will declare a class variable to be of type JButton using the statement

```
private JButton firstButton;
```

As with all class variable names, the specific name, which in this case is firstBut-ton, is programmer selected. Next, to create an object of the desired JButton type, we will place the following statement within the class's constructor method:

```
firstButton = new JButton("Press me");  // create a button
```

Here the string in quotes provides the text that is displayed inside the button when the component is displayed as part of the GUI. This text is referred to as the button's *caption.*

Step 2: Add the Component to the JFrame's Content Pane

Once a button object is created, it must be added to a container's content pane to be displayed. This can be accomplished using two statements: one for obtaining the content pane and the second for actually adding the component to the pane. For our specific example, in which we have a JFrame object named mainFrame, the statement

```
Container c = mainFrame.getContentPane();
```

defines a reference variable named c that has access to our mainFrame object's content pane. Although the name of the Container reference variable can be any valid Java identifier, the general syntax of this statement is standard and will be used throughout all of our remaining Swing-based programs. This syntax is

```
Container ContainerName = JFrameName.getContentPane();
```

Once the content pane is available, a component is added to it using one of the Container class's add() methods. At a minimum, all of the various add() methods require the name of the component that is to be added as an argument. An additional argument frequently can be used to fine-tune the object's placement by overriding the layout manager's default placement. As a specific example, for the button object that was created and named firstButton in step 1, the statement

```
c.add(firstButton);
```

will add this button into our JFrame's content pane.

Although we have used a two-statement procedure of first getting a content pane and then adding a component to it, these two statements can be compressed into a single statement. For our particular components, the single-statement equivalent for step 2 is

```
mainFrame.getContentPane().add(firstButton);
```

In practice, you will encounter both the one- and two-statement forms for adding a component to a JFrame's content pane (step 2).

Program 9.7 uses the four statements that we have described for creating and adding a JButton component into a basic JFrame GUI. For convenience, each of the statements we have introduced in this section has been boldfaced and annotated with a comment as to which step it specifically refers to. The rest of the code in this program should be familiar because it is the same basic code that we have used throughout this chapter to create a JFrame-based window with a window closing event handler.

Program 9.7

```
import javax.swing.*;
import java.awt.event.*;
import java.awt.Container;  // need this to add controls
public class ButtonGuiOne extends JFrame
{
  private JFrame mainFrame;
  private JButton firstButton;                     // Phase 1 - Step 1: first statement

  public ButtonGuiOne() // a constructor
  {
    mainFrame = new JFrame("Example of a Gui with a Button");

    // create a button object
    firstButton = new JButton("Press me");   // Phase 1 - Step 1: second statement

    // get the content pane
    Container c = mainFrame.getContentPane(); // Phase 1- Step 2: first statement

    // add the button to the ContentPane
    c.add(firstButton);                              // Phase 1 - Step 2: second statement

    mainFrame.setSize(300,150);

    // define and register window event handler
    mainFrame.addWindowListener(new WindowAdapter()
    {
      public void windowClosing(WindowEvent e) {System.exit(0);}
    });

    mainFrame.show();
  }

  public static void main(String[] args)
  {
```

(continued)

(continued)
```
    new ButtonGuiOne();  // instantiate a GUI object
  }

} // end of ButtonGuiOne class
```

When Program 9.7 is compiled and run, the displayed GUI will appear as in Figure 9.14. Although the GUI can be closed and the underlying Java application correctly shut down by clicking the window's Close button, clicking the JButton produces no effect. This is because we have not included and registered any button event handler. Before doing this, however, we will add both a ToolTip and an accelerator key to the button shown in Figure 9.14.

Adding ToolTips and Accelerator Keys

The current Window's look and feel includes both ToolTips and accelerator keys. A *ToolTip* is any single line of text that appears when a user positions the mouse cursor over a GUI component. Its purpose is to provide a quick single-line documentation for the selected component. An *accelerator key*, which is referred to as a *mnemonic key* in Java, is any key that initiates an action by pressing the Alt key and a designated letter.

Both ToolTips and mnemonics are created using a set() method, which is inherited from Java's JComponent Swing class. Specifically, the general syntax to create a ToolTip is

```
objectName.setToolTipText("string value");
```

As a specific example, the statement

```
firstButton.setToolTipText("This is a button");
```

uses this syntax to create the ToolTip `This is a button` for a component object named `firstButton`.

In like manner, the general syntax for creating an accelerator key is

```
objectName.setMnemonic('letter');
```

For example, assuming that we have a button named `firstButton`, the statement

```
firstButton.setMnemonic('P');
```

creates the letter `P` as the mnemonic for the button. Within a button's caption, the first occurrence of the designated letter, if it exists, is underlined to indicate its status as the mnemonic for the button. If the letter is not contained in the button's caption, it will still act as an accelerator but will not be explicitly designated as such in the cap-

FIGURE 9.14 **The GUI displayed by Program 9.7**

FIGURE 9.15   **The ToolTip and mnemonic key created by Program 9.8**

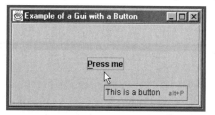

tion. In effect, the accelerator key then becomes a "hidden" hot-key sequence. Such hidden key sequences are studiously avoided by professional programmers because they generally serve to annoy users who accidentally activate the sequence or make an insecure user nervous about other unexpected features that can produce unanticipated results. Users of a program generally have all they can manage in learning how all documented features of a program work; providing hidden features that can surprise a user is almost always a sign of a very inexperienced programmer.

Program 9.8 illustrates the inclusion of both a ToolTip and mnemonic key for the button previously created in Program 9.7. The results of these two new features appear in Figure 9.15.

Program 9.8

```java
import javax.swing.*;
import java.awt.event.*;
import java.awt.Container;  // need this to add controls
public class ButtonGuiTwo extends JFrame
{
  private JFrame mainFrame;
  private JButton firstButton;                    // Phase 1 - Step 1: first statement

  public ButtonGuiTwo() // a constructor
  {
    mainFrame = new JFrame("Example of a Gui with a Button");

      // create a button object
    firstButton = new JButton("Press me");     // Phase 1 - Step 1: second statement

      // get the content pane
    Container c = mainFrame.getContentPane(); // Phase 1 - Step 2: first statement
      // add the button to the ContentPane
    c.add(firstButton);                         // Phase 1 - Step 2: second statement

    firstButton.setToolTipText("This is a button"); // create a ToolTip
    firstButton.setMnemonic('P');                      // create a Mnemonic key

    mainFrame.setSize(300,150);

      // define and register window event handler
    mainFrame.addWindowListener(new WindowAdapter()
```

(continued)

```
(continued)
  {
    public void windowClosing(WindowEvent e) {System.exit(0);}
  });

  mainFrame.show();
}

public static void main(String[] args)
{
  new ButtonGuiTwo();  // instantiate a GUI object
}

}  // end of ButtonGuiTwo class
```

Adding an Event Handler

An extremely important feature of our two-phase GUI development procedure is that it permits seeing how a GUI will appear before any event code has to be written. Thus, Program 9.8 can be executed to verify that its button component appears correctly without the necessity of first supplying it with event handling code. Once the visual aspects of a component are satisfied, the second phase in the process, which is to create and register an event handler for the component, can be completed. We now do this for the button component displayed by Program 9.8 so that an appropriate response occurs when the button is clicked.

An event handler for an atomic component, such as a button, is created and registered in the same way that the window closing method was created and registered for a JFrame container in the last section. Specifically, for the button added into the GUI in Program 9.8 we now apply phase 2 of the development process.

> *Phase 2: Provide an event handler for the component*
> *Step 1: Write the code for an event handler class (a listener class)*
> *Step 2: Create an instance of the event handler class (a listener object)*
> *Step 3: Register the listener object*

Phase 2: Provide an Event Handler for the Component

Providing the button with an event handler will make the component come alive so that something actually happens when it is selected. In our particular case, we will have the program display a message box when the button is clicked.

Step 1: Write the Code for an Event Handler Class (a Listener Class)

Using Table 9.7, we see that the required event handler interface for a button is an Ac-tionListener and that the class implementing this handler must define a single method named actionPerformed(). In addition, the same table provides the information that this method expects to receive an ActionEvent parameter type. Naming our class ButEventHandler and using the Java convention of naming the passed parameter e (both are programmer-selected names), the basic structure of our listener class is

```
class ButEventHandler implements ActionListener
{
  public void actionPerformed(ActionEvent e)
  {
      // this is currently an empty method body
  }
}
```

For purposes of illustration, we will simply have our button display the message box shown in Figure 9.16 when the button is clicked. The required statement to produce this dialog is

```
JOptionPane.showMessageDialog(null, "Button was Pressed",
    "Event Handler Message",JOptionPane.INFORMATION_MESSAGE);
```

Placing this showMessageDialog() call into the body of the actionPerformed() method of our listener class completes the class definition as follows:

```
class ButEventHandler implements ActionListener
{
    public void actionPerformed(ActionEvent e)
    {
      JOptionPane.showMessageDialog(null, "Button was Pressed",
        "Event Handler Message",JOptionPane.INFORMATION_MESSAGE);
    }
  }
```

Step 2: Create an Instance of the Event Handler Class (a Listener Object)

To create an instance of our listener class, which is named ButEventHandler (and recall this is a programmer-selected name), we can use the following statement:

```
ButEventHandler bhandler = new ButEventHandler();  // instantiate a handler
```

In this statement, the name of the reference variable, bhandler, is also a programmer-selected name. As always, this single-line declaration and instantiation statement can be constructed using a separate declaration followed by an instantiation. Thus, the statement can also be written as

```
ButEventHandler bhandler; // declare a reference variable
bhandler = new ButEventHandler();  // instantiate the event handler
```

The instantiated event handler object is formally referred to as a listener object.

Step 3: Register the Listener Object

Once a listener object has been created, it still must be attached to one or more components to be invoked. Attaching a listener object to a component is accomplished by

FIGURE 9.16 **Message box produced by Program 9.9**

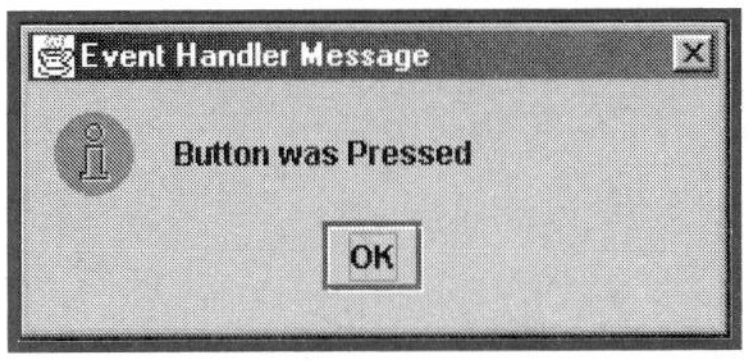

a registration statement using a variation of an add() method. For an event class that has been implemented as an ActionListener, the correct registration uses an add ActionListener() method. Specifically, because our listener object was instantiated using the reference variable name bhandler and we want to attach this listener to the component named firstButton, the following registration statement must be used:

```
firstButton.addActionListener(bhandler);   // register the handler
```

Program 9.9 includes all of the event handling code that we have presented in this section within the context of the GUI created in Program 9.8. For convenience, this code has been boldfaced. In reviewing this code, notice that the event handling class has been constructed as an inner class.

When Program 9.9 is run, the GUI in Figure 9.15 is displayed, which is the same GUI displayed by Program 9.8. However, since we have now supplied the button with event handling code, when the button is clicked, the dialog shown in Figure 9.16 is displayed.

Program 9.9

```java
import javax.swing.*;
import java.awt.event.*;
import java.awt.Container;   // need this to add controls
public class ButtonGuiThree extends JFrame
{
  private JFrame mainFrame;
  private JButton firstButton;

  public ButtonGuiThree() // a constructor
  {
    mainFrame = new JFrame("Example of a Gui with a Button");

      // create a button object
    firstButton = new JButton("Press me");

      // get the content pane
    Container c = mainFrame.getContentPane();

      // add the button to the ContentPane
    c.add(firstButton);

    firstButton.setToolTipText("This is a button");
    firstButton.setMnemonic('P');

    mainFrame.setSize(300,150);

      // define and register window event handler
    mainFrame.addWindowListener(new WindowAdapter()
    {
      public void windowClosing(WindowEvent e) {System.exit(0);}
    });
```

```
    // create and register the button event handler
   ButEventHandler bhandler = new ButEventHandler();  // instantiate a handler
   firstButton.addActionListener(bhandler);  // register the handler

   mainFrame.show();
 }


   // inner class for the button event handler
 class ButEventHandler implements ActionListener
 {
   public void actionPerformed(ActionEvent e)
   {
     JOptionPane.showMessageDialog(null, "Button was Pressed",
       "Event Handler Message",JOptionPane.INFORMATION_MESSAGE);
   }
 }  // end of inner class

 public static void main(String[] args)
 {
   new ButtonGuiThree();  // instantiate a GUI object
 }

}  // end of ButtonGuiThree class
```

Exercises 9.4

1a. To what top-level pane must all GUI components be added?

  b. What method is used to obtain the internal component referred to in Exercise 1a?

  c. What method is used to add a component to the internal frame referred to in Exercise 1a?

2. Enter, compile, and run Program 9.7 on your computer.

3. Create a Java program that has a single `JButton` object with the caption <u>M</u>essage.

4. Modify the program written for Exercise 3 to include the M key as a keyboard accelerator key. Additionally, the button should be equipped with a ToolTip that displays the string `Displays a message`.

5. Enter, compile, and run Program 9.8 on your computer.

6. Enter, compile, and run Program 9.9 on your computer.

7. Modify Program 9.9 to display the message `Hello World!` when the button is clicked.

8. Write, compile, and run a Java program that prints your name and address in a message box when the user clicks a `JButton` object. The JButton's caption should be `Name and Address`. In addition, the button should use the letter N as a keyboard accelerator key and provide a ToolTip of your choosing.

9. Modify Program 9.9 so that the button's listener class is coded as an anonymous class.

9.5 **Common Programming Errors**

The common programming errors related to creating Swing-based GUIs are

1. Forgetting to include all of the following statements when creating a full-featured Swing-based GUI:

```
import javax.swing.*; // needed for creating a Swing-based GUI
import java.awt.event.*; // needed for event handling
import java.awt.Container;  // needed for adding atomic components
```

2. Mistyping JButton as Jbutton. Both the J and B must be capitalized. In general, spelling and letter case mistakes are the most common programming errors made in Java. If your GUI does not display a component or an event handler does not seem to operate, you should first check that all component and method names are spelled correctly.

3. Creating an event handler and failing to register it. An event handler is not activated until both an object of the handler class is instantiated and the handler object is registered. If the event handler object is not registered, the expected event will not be handled, which is the same result that occurs if no handler were written for the event.

4. Incorrectly spelling the `getContentPane()` method name when adding a component, such as a JButton, into a top-level container. The only letters that must be capitalized in this method name are the C for Content and the P for Pane. This is just a variation on the spelling error listed in error 2.

5. Modifying a GUI class that has previously been compiled and changing its name but forgetting to change the name when an instance of the class is created in the `main()` method. The application runs but creates an object of the earlier GUI class. This happens because the previous compilation resulted in a `.class` file for the earlier GUI class, which is still stored and available to instantiate an object, even though the source code for the class may no longer exist in any source code file.

6. Creating a mnemonic key with a letter that is not contained as part of a button's caption. Although the designated key will act correctly as an accelerator key when it is pressed with the Alt key, a user will not know this because the letter will not be underlined in the button's caption.

9.6 **Chapter Review**

KEY TERMS

accelerator key	event-based program	listener object
adapter class	graphical user interface	mnemonic key
anonymous class	GUI	shortcut key
atomic components	heavyweight components	Swing package
button	inner class	text field
containment hierarchy	intermediate container	top-level container
event delegation model	label	
event handler	layout manager	

SUMMARY

1. Event-based programs execute program code depending on what events occur, which in turn depend on what the user does. Thus, the order of events is determined by the user's actions and not predetermined by program code.

2. GUIs are graphical user interfaces that provide the user with components that recognize user actions, such as the clicking of a mouse, and generate events when a user-generated action takes place.

3. Java handles events triggered by GUI components using an event delegation model. This model distinguishes between the code used to display a GUI component from the code used to handle events associated with the component. In effect, the component delegates event handling to a separate class. The class constructed to handle component-related events is referred to as a listener class.

4. The Swing package of classes, which was introduced in Java 2.0, provides a relatively straightforward means of constructing GUIs. This package of classes provides three generic types of graphical components: top-level containers that connect a GUI to the underlying operating system, intermediate containers that can be used to simplify component placement, and atomic components such as buttons, labels, and text areas.

5. Graphical components are structured into a Swing-based GUI following a containment hierarchy. This hierarchy requires that atomic components must be placed into containers, the most basic of which is a top-level container. The most commonly used top-level Swing container is the JFrame.

6. To be visible, a JFrame object must execute either a `show()` or `setVisible (true)` method. These two methods can be used interchangeably.

7. Functioning components are added into a JFrame container using the following two-phase process:

   Phase 1: Construct the component so that it appears visually
      Step 1: Instantiate a specific component
      Step 2: Add the component to the JFrame's content pane
   Phase 2: Provide an event handler for the component
      Step 1. Write the code for an event handler class, which is known as a listener class
      Step 2. Create an instance of the event handler class (this means instantiating an object of the class using the new operator); the created object is known as a listener object
      Step 3. Register the listener object created in step 2

8. An instantiated component is added to a JFrame's content pane (phase 1, step 2) using both a `getContentPane()` and `add()` method. For example, if a JFrame object named `mainFrame` has been instantiated, the statement

   ```
   Container c = mainFrame.getContentPane();
   ```

   defines a reference variable named `c` that has access to the `mainFrame` object's content pane. For an instantiated button object named `firstButton`, the statement

   ```
   c.add(firstButton);
   ```

   then adds this button into `mainFrame`'s content pane.

The two-statement procedure of first getting a content pane and then adding a component to it can always be combined into a single statement. Thus, the previous two statements can be replaced by the equivalent single statement

```
mainFrame.getContentPane().add(firstButton);
```

9. The size of a component can be set using a `setSize()` method. For example, if `mainFrame` is the name of a `JFrame` object, the method call `mainFrame.set-Size(300,150)` will set the size of the displayed frame to 300 pixels wide × 150 pixels high.

10. The name of the listener class for each Swing component must be a Java-specified name. For the components presented in this text, if a listener class is provided for a component, the required listener class names are

Component	Required Listener Class Name
Window	`WindowListener`
Mouse	`MouseMotionListener`
	`MouseListener`
Keyboard	`KeyListener`
Button	`ActionListener`
Text Field	`TextListener`
Check Box	`ItemListener`
Radio Button	`ItemListener`

11. Each implemented listener class requires a specific set of methods that must be included, even if this means creating empty method bodies. The required methods for the listener classes corresponding to the components presented in this text are

Listener	Required Methods
`WindowListener`	`windowClosing(WindowEvent)`
	`windowClosed(WindowEvent)`
	`windowOpened(WindowEvent)`
	`windowActivated(WindowEvent)`
	`windowDeactivated(WindowEvent)`
	`windowIconified(WindowEvent)`
	`windowDeiconified(WindowEvent)`
`MouseMotionListener`	`mouseDragged(MouseEvent)`
	`mouseMoved(MouseEvent)`
`MouseListener`	`mousePressed(MouseEvent)`
	`mouseReleased(MouseEvent)`
	`mouseClicked(MouseEvent)`
`KeyListener`	`keyPressed(KeyEvent)`
	`keyReleased(KeyEvent)`
	`keyTyped(KeyEvent)`
`ActionListener`	`actionPerformed(ActionEvent)`
`TextListener`	`textValueChanged(TextEvent)`
`ItemListener`	`itemStateChanged(ItemEvent)`

For example, the following class named `WinHandler` implements a `Win-dowListener` class in which only the window closing event is actually handled. The remaining six methods required of a `WindowListener` are given empty bodies.

```
      // A  listener class to handle window events
   class WinHandler implements WindowListener
   {
     public void windowClosing(WindowEvent e) {System.exit(0);}
     public void windowClosed(WindowEvent e) {}
     public void windowOpened(WindowEvent e) {}
     public void windowIconified(WindowEvent e) {}
     public void windowDeiconified(WindowEvent e) {}
     public void windowActivated(WindowEvent e) {}
     public void windowDeactivated(WindowEvent e) {}
   }  // end of listener class
```

12. Listener classes can be nested inside the class used to instantiate and display GUI components. Such nested classes are referred to as inner classes.

13. Certain listener classes can be constructed by extending Java-supplied adapter classes. An adapter class is a class that defines empty event handling methods for a corresponding listener class. All adapter classes are constructed in Java as abstract classes, which means that objects cannot be directly instantiated from the class but that it can be used as a parent class from which other classes can be derived. The correspondence between listener classes and the adapter classes that can be used to construct them are

Listener Name	Available Adapter Class
WindowListener	WindowAdapter
MouseMotionListener	MouseMotionAdapter
MouseListener	MouseAdapter
KeyListener	KeyAdapter
ActionListener	ActionAdapter
TextListener	(None)
ItemListener	(None)

For example, the following extended class named WinHandler uses the adapter class named WindowAdapter to create a listener class that actively handles only the window closing event

```
   // extend an adapter class to handle window events
   class WinHandler extends WindowAdapter
   {
     public void windowClosing(WindowEvent e) {System.exit(0);}
   }  // end of listener class
```

14. Once a listener class has been defined, an object of the class type must be instantiated, and this object must be registered for the event handler to be activated. For example, the following two statements

```
WinHandler handler = new WinHandler(); // instantiate an event handler object
mainFrame.addWindowListener(handler);  // register the handler
```

first instantiate an object named handler from a listener class named WinHandler and then register the object. These two statements can be combined into the single statement

```
mainFrame.addWindowListener(new WinHandler());
```

15. An anonymous class can be used to construct a listener class whenever a single-statement listener object instantiation and registration are employed. An anonymous class is a class that does not use a class header line to name the class, and should only be used when a listener class's body consists of one or two statements. When used, the class definition is placed within the statement that instantiates a listener object. For example, the statement

```
mainFrame.addWindowListener(new WindowAdapter()
{ // anonymous class
  public void windowClosing(WindowEvent e) {System.exit(0);}
});
```

uses the anonymous (unnamed) class

```
{
  public void windowClosing(WindowEvent e) {System.exit(0);}
}
```

directly within the instantiation and registration statement.

10

Additional Components and Event Handlers

In this chapter, we show how additional GUI components can be added to the basic JFrame GUI presented in Chapter 9. We illustrate the procedure presented for adding components using text fields, radio buttons, and check boxes. Providing a GUI with these components produces a rather complete graphical user interface that is more than adequate for the majority of Java programs you will write. It also provides you with the ability to add other components as you need them. In addition, we discuss layout managers that permit you to position the additional components in various configurations.

We also provide listener classes for each of the new components presented. We present a new type of listener class, referred to as a focus listener, for detecting and appropriately responding to focus events. Specifically, the focus events considered are when a component gains or loses focus. Finally, we present procedures for validating user input on a keystroke-by-keystroke basis, as each key is pressed.

10.1 Adding Multiple Components

Adding components to a container uses the same procedure that was presented in the previous chapter for adding a single button. To review, this procedure consists of the following two phases:

> ***Phase 1: Construct the component so that it appears visually***
> ***Step 1: Instantiate a specific component***
> ***Step 2: Add the component to the JFrame's content pane***
> ***Phase 2: Provide an event handler for the component***
> ***Step 1: Write the code for an event handler class (a listener class)***
> ***Step 2: Instantiate an instance of the event handler***
> ***Step 3: Register the listener object***

The additional consideration, however, when adding more than one component is the placement of each component within its container. As described in Section 9.1, each container—both top-level and intermediate—has an associated default layout manager. This default, which can be changed by explicitly indicating a different manager, determines how components are to be sized and positioned.

Layout Managers

The available **layout managers**, which were listed in Table 9.3 and are repeated in Table 10.1 for convenience, can be categorized as simple (FlowLayout and GridLayout), flexible (BoxLayout and GridBagLayout), and special purpose (BorderLayout and CardLayout). In this chapter, we show how to use FlowLayout and BorderLayout managers to position multiple components into a JFrame-based GUI. When not explicitly specified, the default manager for a JFrame container is BorderLayout.

Table 10.1   **Layout Managers**

Manager	Description	Use Type
FlowLayout	Components are added to the container from left to right and top to bottom, in a row-by-row manner, starting from the top left corner of the container.	Simple
GridLayout	All components are created equal in size and displayed in the requested number of rows and columns. Blank areas fill in unused columns	Simple
BorderLayout	Up to five components can be placed in the container. The components are placed in positions denoted as north, south, west, east, and center. These positions correspond to the top, bottom, left side, right side, and center positions of the container.	Special Purpose
CardLayout	This layout permits implementation of an area that can contain different components at different times.	Special Purpose
BoxLayout	Components are placed into either a single row or column. Column components can be center, left-edge, or right-edge aligned.	Flexible
GridBagLayout	Components are placed in a spreadsheet type grid of cells, with components permitted to span across and down multiple cells.	Flexible

For our first example, we use a FlowLayout manager to create a GUI containing three buttons. Because a FlowLayout manager is not the default for a JFrame container, we will need to use a `setLayout()` method to explicitly set it as the defining layout manager. The general syntax for this method is

```
containerName.setLayout(new managerName());
```

For example, if c is the name of a JFrame content pane container, and we want to explicitly declare the FlowLayout manager for positioning components within this container, the required statement is[1]

```
c.setLayout(new FlowLayout());
```

Once set, either by default or explicit specification, the layout manager has complete control over the sizing and positioning of components. It is the sole determiner of how components are initially shaped and then reshaped and repositioned when their holding container is resized and moved about the screen. Table 10.2 provides three methods that can be used to influence the sizing of a component, but these settings are generally only used by each manager as a guideline in its efforts to shape and position each component.

Program 10.1 explicitly sets a FlowLayout manager and then adds three buttons into a JFrame container. The statement setting the layout manager and the statements for creating and adding each button into the container are boldfaced. In reviewing this program, first notice that the statement `import java.awt.*;` is needed for our selection of layout managers. Also notice that each button component is individually created and added into the container's content pane with a three-statement sequence similar to the following used for the first button:

```
  // declare a button to be of type JButton
private JButton messageButton;
  // create the button object
messageButton = new JButton("Message");
  // add the button to the ContentPane
c.add(messageButton);
```

Using a FlowLayout manager, each component is added into its designated container in the order that its `add()` method is encountered. The first component is

Table 10.2   **Component Sizing Methods**

Method	Description
component.setPreferredSize(int pixels)	Sets the component's preferred size in pixels.
component.setMaximumSize(int pixels)	Sets the component's maximum size in pixels.
component.setMinimumSize(int pixels)	Sets the component's minimum size in pixels.

---

[1] It should be noted that this single-line specification is equivalent to the two-statement form

```
FlowLayout manager = new FlowLayout()
c.setLayout(manager);
```

where the name `manager` is any valid user-selected identifier.

FIGURE 10.1   **The GUI displayed by Program 10.1**

added beginning at the top-left side of the container, and additional components are sequentially placed on the same row, continuing until the right edge of the container is reached. A new row is started if additional space is required. The GUI displayed when Program 10.1 is run appears in Figure 10.1.

Program 10.1

```java
import javax.swing.*;
import java.awt.event.*;
import java.awt.Container;  // need this to add controls
import java.awt.*;  // need this for layout manager

public class MultiButtons extends JFrame
{
  private JFrame mainFrame;
  private JButton messageButton;
  private JButton clearButton;
  private JButton exitButton;

  public MultiButtons() // a constructor
  {
    mainFrame = new JFrame("The Hello Application - Ver. 1.0");

      // create the button objects
    messageButton = new JButton("Message");
    clearButton = new JButton("Clear");
    exitButton = new JButton("Exit");

      // get the content pane & specify layout manager
    Container c = mainFrame.getContentPane();
    c.setLayout(new FlowLayout());

      // add the button to the ContentPane
    c.add(messageButton);
    c.add(clearButton);
    c.add(exitButton);

      // create accelerator keys
    messageButton.setMnemonic('M');
    clearButton.setMnemonic('C');
    exitButton.setMnemonic('x');

    mainFrame.setSize(300,100);
```

```
        // define and register window event handler
    mainFrame.addWindowListener(new WindowAdapter()
    {
        public void windowClosing(WindowEvent e) {System.exit(0);}
    });

    mainFrame.show();
  }

  public static void main(String args[])
  {
    MultiButtons app; // declare a MultiButtons variable
    app = new MultiButtons();  // instantiate a GUI object
  }

}  // end of class
```

It is important to note that although Program 10.1 contains no event handlers for its atomic components, it can still be compiled and run to produce the GUI in Figure 10.1.

Properties Tables

Once you begin constructing GUIs with multiple components, it is very useful to create a table that contains all of the relevant data about the components that will be added to the interface. The table that performs this function is referred to as a **properties table**. This table becomes very useful for both documentation and programming purposes. As a programming tool, you should prepare the table before writing any code. Doing so provides you with all of the component names that you intend to use and initial settings that must be set. For example, the properties table for Program 10.1, at its current stage of development, is listed in Table 10.3.

Table 10.3   **Program 10.1's Initial Properties Table**

Object	Property	Setting
JFrame	Name	mainFrame
	Caption	The Hello Application - Ver. 1.0
	Layout manager	FlowLayout
JButton	Name	messageButton
	Caption	Message
	Mnemonic	M
JButton	Name	clearButton
	Caption	Clear
	Mnemonic	C
JButton	Name	exitButton
	Caption	Exit
	Mnemonic	x

Table 10.4   **Program 10.1's Expanded Properties Table**

Object	Property	Setting	Listener Class	Listener Object
JFrame	Name	mainFrame	anonymous	
	Caption	The Hello Application - Ver. 1.0		
	Layout manager	FlowLayout		
JButton	Name	messageButton	MessageButtonHandler	mhandler
	Caption	Message		
	Mnemonic	M		
JButton	Name	clearButton	ClearButtonHandler	chandler
	Caption	Clear		
	Mnemonic	C		
JButton	Name	exitButton	ExitButtonHandler	ehandler
	Caption	Exit		
	Mnemonic	x		

Adding the Event Handler

Adding **event handlers** constitutes the second phase of completing a graphical user interface. As we have repeatedly seen throughout the previous chapter, this phase consists of the following steps:

Phase 2: Provide an event handler for the component
  Step 1: Write the code for an event handler class (a listener class)
  Step 2: Instantiate an instance of the event handler class
  Step 3: Register the listener object

The GUI constructed by Program 10.1 already contains our standard window closing event handler, which we have constructed as an anonymous class. To complete the GUI, we now provide each of the three buttons with an event handler. The names that we have selected for each handler are listed in Table 10.4, which is an expanded version of the original properties table.

The first two button event handlers in Table 10.4 will display a message box indicating that the button was clicked, while the third handler will close the application. The following code, which would be placed immediately before the constructor's closing brace—that is, after the mainFrame.show(); statement—accomplishes this.

```
    // inner classes for the button event handlers
class MessageButtonHandler implements ActionListener
{
  public void actionPerformed(ActionEvent e)
  {
    JOptionPane.showMessageDialog(null, "Message Button was Clicked",
     "Event Handler Message",JOptionPane.INFORMATION_MESSAGE);
  }
} // end of inner class

class ClearButtonHandler implements ActionListener
{
```

```
    public void actionPerformed(ActionEvent e)
    {
      JOptionPane.showMessageDialog(null, "Clear Button was Clicked",
       "Event Handler Message",JOptionPane.INFORMATION_MESSAGE);
    }
}  // end of inner class

class ExitButtonHandler implements ActionListener
{
  public void actionPerformed(ActionEvent e)
  {
    System.exit(0);
  }
}  // end of inner class
```

Once this code is included in Program 10.1, all that remains is to instantiate and register each event handler (steps 2 and 3 of phase 2). The following statements, which would be placed before `mainFrame.show();` in Program 10.1, accomplish this.

```
  // create and register the button event handlers
MessageButtonHandler mhandler = new MessageButtonHandler();  // instantiate a handler
messageButton.addActionListener(mhandler);  // register the handler

ClearButtonHandler chandler = new ClearButtonHandler();  // instantiate a handler
clearButton.addActionListener(chandler);  // register the handler

ExitButtonHandler ehandler = new ExitButtonHandler();  // instantiate a handler
exitButton.addActionListener(ehandler);  // register the handler
```

In creating our three button event handlers, we have followed the current Java convention of providing each atomic component with its individual event handler. An alternative, which you will encounter in your programming work, is to use a single-button handler class for all buttons in a GUI, in which the event handler determines which button was clicked. Then, depending on the button selected, appropriate processing is performed. Using this approach, the following single-button handler class, which we have named `ButtonsHandler`, can replace the three previously presented individual classes.

```
  // inner class for the button event handler
class ButtonsHandler implements ActionListener
{
  public void actionPerformed(ActionEvent e)
  {
    if (e.getSource() == messageButton)
      JOptionPane.showMessageDialog(null, "Message Button was Clicked",
       "Event Handler Message",JOptionPane.INFORMATION_MESSAGE);
    else if (e.getSource() == clearButton)
      JOptionPane.showMessageDialog(null, "Clear Button was Clicked",
       "Event Handler Message",JOptionPane.INFORMATION_MESSAGE);
    else if (e.getSource() == exitButton)
      System.exit(0);
  }
}  // end of inner class
```

This single-listener class approach has the advantage of centralizing all button event handling. In reviewing this class, notice that a getSource() method determines which button was actually clicked. Here the argument that we have named e, which is passed into the method, provides the source of the ActionEvent that triggered the event handler. Using the getSource() method permits us to specifically identify this source as one of the three buttons. Once the button that triggered the event has been identified, the code provides the appropriate processing.

As with all event processing code, it still remains to instantiate and register an event handling object. Here we need only instantiate the single button event handler and then register the same object for each of the three buttons. The following code can be used:

```
// create and register a single button event handler
ButtonsHandler bhandler = new ButtonsHandler(); // instantiate a handler
messageButton.addActionListener(bhandler);  // register the handler
clearButton.addActionListener(bhandler);    // register the handler
exitButton.addActionListener(bhandler);   // register the handler
```

Figure 10.2 shows the message boxes that are displayed when either form of the event handlers we have presented is incorporated into Program 10.1 (which we leave for Exercises 2 and 3). Clicking the Exit button closes the application in the same manner as clicking the window's Close button.

In the next section, we will complete Program 10.1 by adding a text display area and appropriate event handler for this new component. Before doing so, however, we can use Program 10.1 to introduce two important concepts connected with any GUI: keyboard focus and tab sequence.

Keyboard Focus and Tab Control

When an application is run and a user is looking at the container, only one of the container's controls will have **keyboard focus**, or the focus for short. The control with the focus is the object that will be affected by pressing a key or clicking the mouse. For example, when a button has the focus, its caption will be surrounded by

FIGURE 10.2   **Message boxes displayed by the button event handlers**

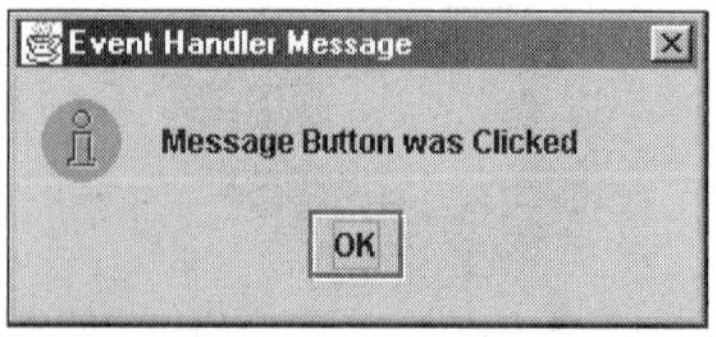

(a) The Message button display

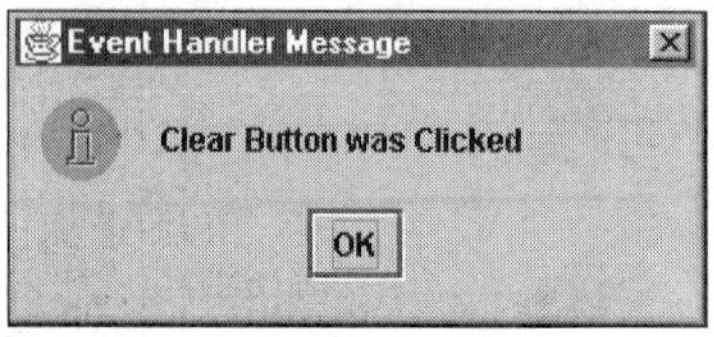

(b) The Clear button display

A BIT OF BACKGROUND

Numerosophy

The ancient Greeks attached great philosophical and religious significance to numbers. They considered the natural (counting) numbers, 1, 2, 3, . . . , to be examples of perfection, and ratios of whole numbers (fractions) were somewhat suspect. Diophantus (third century B.C.) called negative numbers "absurd."

According to tradition, Hipparchus (second century B.C.) was drowned when he discussed the scandalous irrational nature of the square root of 2 outside the Pythagorean Society. The first mention of the square root of a negative number was by Heron of Alexandria (third century A.D.). Such concepts were treated with disbelief and even considered wicked.

Today, of course, it is not unusual to use negative, irrational, "artificial," and complex numbers all at once to represent such concepts as vectors and points in a plane. The Greeks of that Golden Age would probably regard our modern mathematics as truly degenerate.

either a solid or dotted rectangle (Figure 10.3). Similarly, when a text area has the focus, a solid cursor appears, indicating that the user can type data.

An object can only receive keyboard focus if it is capable of responding to user input through either the keyboard or mouse. Thus, controls such as labels and lines can never receive the focus. To get the focus, a visible control must be enabled. By enabling a visible object, you permit it to respond to user-generated events, such as pressing a key or clicking a mouse. As the default setting for a component is that it is enabled, you do not usually have to be concerned with this setting unless you want to disable it explicitly. A component capable of receiving focus, such as a button, can get the focus in one of four ways.

1. A user clicks the mouse directly on the object.
2. A user presses the TAB key until the object gets the focus.
3. A user presses the accessor key for the object.
4. The code activates the focus.

To see how the first three methods operate, compile and run Program 10.1. Once the program is running, click any of the buttons. As you do, notice how the focus shifts. Now press the TAB key a few times and see how the focus shifts from component to component. Do the same by pressing the accelerator key for each button. The

FIGURE 10.3   **A button with and without focus**

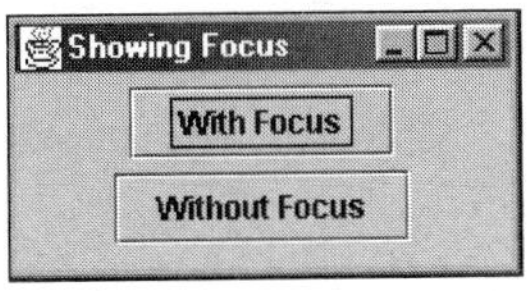

sequence in which the focus shifts from component to component as the TAB key is pressed is called the **tab sequence**. This sequence is initially determined by the order in which components are placed on the container, but it can be explicitly modified using program code. For our specific example, focus shifts from the Message button to the Clear button to the Exit button and then back again to the Message button.

The default tab order obtained as a result of placing components on the container can be altered by invoking the setNextFocusableComponent() method. For example, the sequence of statements

```
messageButton.setNextFocusableComponent(exitButton);
exitButton.setNextFocusableComponent(clearButton);
clearButton.setNextFocusableComponent(messageButton);
```

would alter the focus sequence from the Message button to the Exit button to the Clear button and then back to the Message button. To explicitly set the first component that receives focus, you must either detect when the window itself gets the focus or use a focus listener to force the focus to switch when the first component receives focus. How to do this is presented at the end of Section 10.3.

Exercises 10.1

1. Enter, compile, and run Program 10.1 on your computer.

2. Modify Program 10.1 to include the three individual listener classes presented in this section. Compile and run your program to verify that it operates correctly.

3. Modify Program 10.1 to include the single listener class presented in this section. Compile and run your program to verify that it operates correctly.

4. How is an accelerator key created for a JButton component?

5. What are the four ways that an atomic component can receive focus?

6a. Write a Java program that creates a GUI having the following properties table:

Object	Property	Setting
JFrame	Name	mainFrame
	Caption	Messages
	Layout	FlowLayout
JButton	Name	cmdGood
	Caption	Good
	Mnemonic	G
JButton	Name	cmdBad
	Caption	Bad
	Mnemonic	B

b. Add individual event handlers to the program written for Exercise 6a so that when a user clicks the Good button, the message Today is a good day! appears in a dialog box, and when the Bad button is clicked, the message I'm having a bad day today! is displayed.

7. Write a Java application having three buttons. Clicking the first button should produce the message See no evil, clicking the second button should produce the message Hear

no evil, and clicking the third button should produce the message `Speak no evil` in the text box.

8. Create a graphical interface that contains four buttons and two text fields. The names of these components should be `butOne`, `butTwo`, `butThree`, and `butFour`. These components should be added into a JFrame content pane in the order `butThree`, `butOne`, `butTwo`, and `butFour`. Using code, set the tab sequence so that tab control goes from `butThree` to `butFour` to `butTwo` to `butOne`.

10.2 Text Components for Display

The three Swing-provided text entry and display components are text fields, password fields, and text areas. Objects of these types are constructed from JTextField, JPasswordField, and JTextArea component types. We consider each of these components in this section, with particular attention on the JTextField component.

Adding a JTextField Component

A **JTextField** component can be used for both entering data and displaying results on a single line. In our current application, we will add a JTextField component for displaying a message when the messageButton in Program 10.1 is clicked. The object instantiated from a JTextField component is referred to as a *text field*.

Placing and activating a text field on a container are accomplished using the same two-phase procedure that we have used throughout this and the previous chapter — that is, by first instantiating and adding the text field object into a container and then by instantiating and registering an appropriate event handler. The statements that we will use for the first phase, which is instantiating and adding a text field to the container in Program 10.1, are

```
private JTextField tField; // declare a class variable
tField = new JTextField("Hello World!"); // instantiate an object
c.add(tField,BorderLayout.NORTH);   // add the object to the container
```

Except for the second statement

```
tField = new JTextField("Hello World!"); // instantiate an object
```

which is used to instantiate a new `JTextField` object, the first and third statements should be familiar. These statements are similar to those that were used in Section 10.1 to add the three buttons into the GUI in Figure 10.1. The second statement uses one of four possible constructors for instantiating a `JTextField` object. The four available constructors are

```
JTextField(initial displayed string)
JTextField(initial displayed string, integer text field size)
JTextField(integer text field size)
JTextField()
```

When an initial string is included in the constructor, the string is displayed when the text field is visible. Similarly, when an integer field size is provided, it specifies a scale factor for determining the width of the field. The actual size of the field is internally determined by multiplying the integer argument by the width, in pixels, of the average character for the current text field's font. If the field size is not large enough to accommodate a displayed string, only the portion of the string that can fit in the specified size is displayed. The remaining part of the string can then be seen by scrolling throughout the field.

Program 10.2 includes the three statements for adding a text field into our GUI within the context of a complete program. For convenience, these three statements have been boldfaced. Also notice that we have used the default BorderLayout manager for placement of each component. Because we have placed the text field in the north, or topmost, position, the width of the field is determined by the width of the JFrame container. In this configuration, any size provided for the text field in its constructor is ignored by the layout manager.

Program 10.2

```java
import javax.swing.*;
import java.awt.event.*;
import java.awt.Container;  // need this to add controls
import java.awt.*;  // need this for layout manager
public class TextGuiOne extends JFrame
{
  private JFrame mainFrame;
  private JButton messageButton;
  private JButton clearButton;
  private JButton exitButton;
  private JTextField tField;

  public TextGuiOne() // a constructor
  {
    mainFrame = new JFrame("The Hello Application - Ver. 2.0");

      // create all components
    messageButton = new JButton("Message");
    clearButton = new JButton("Clear");
    exitButton = new JButton("Exit");
    tField = new JTextField("Hello World!");
      // get the content pane
    Container c = mainFrame.getContentPane();

      // add the components to the ContentPane
    c.add(tField,BorderLayout.NORTH);
    c.add(messageButton,BorderLayout.WEST);
    c.add(clearButton,BorderLayout.CENTER);
    c.add(exitButton,BorderLayout.EAST);

      // create accelerator keys
    messageButton.setMnemonic('M');
    clearButton.setMnemonic('C');
    exitButton.setMnemonic('x');

    mainFrame.setSize(300,150);
```

```
        // define and register window event handler
     mainFrame.addWindowListener(new WindowAdapter()
     {
       public void windowClosing(WindowEvent e) {System.exit(0);}
     });

     mainFrame.show();
  }

  public static void main(String args[])
  {
    new TextGuiOne();  // instantiate a GUI object
  }

}  // end of class
```

In reviewing Program 10.2, notice that, in the `main()` method, we have instantiated a `TextGuiOne` object without specifically declaring a `TextGuiOne` reference variable. This can be done because we have no later need within the method to access the GUI object by name. The GUI displayed when Program 10.2 is compiled and run is shown in Figure 10.4.

At this point, we have assembled all of the components required for our application. Properties Table 10.5 provides a summary of the initial property settings for each component. Thus, within the context of complete program development, we have finished the first phase in our two-phase process for each component that we want added into our JFrame-based GUI, which is

> **Phase 1: Construct the component so that it appears visually**
>   **Step 1: Instantiate a specific component**
>   **Step 2: Add the component to the JFrame's content pane**

All that remains is to add the event handling code so that each button performs its designated task when it is clicked.

Adding Event Handlers

Now that the physical appearance of our GUI is set (The Hello Application - Ver. 2.0 in Figure 10.4), we still need to supply the three buttons with event code. Because the text field is only for display purposes in response to clicking either the Message or Clear button, this component will have no associated event code. Thus, we will initially

FIGURE 10.4   **The GUI displayed by Program 10.2**

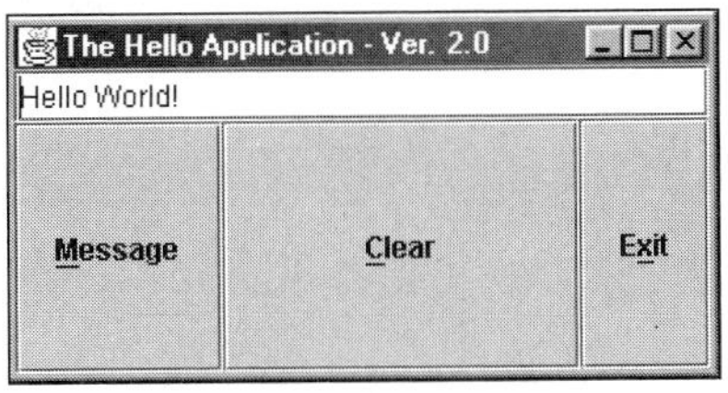

Table 10.5 **Program 10.2's Initial Property Settings**

Object	Property	Setting
JFrame	Name	mainFrame
	Caption	The Hello Application - Ver. 2.0
JButton	Name	messageButton
	Caption	Message
	Mnemonic	M
JButton	Name	clearButton
	Caption	Clear
	Mnemonic	C
JButton	Name	exitButton
	Caption	Exit
	Mnemonic	x
JTextField	Name	tField
	Text	Hello World!

create three mouse click event objects, each of which will be activated by clicking one of the three buttons. Two of these event procedures will change the text displayed in the text box, and the last will exit the program.

The listener classes for our button events are:

```
class MessageButtonHandler implements ActionListener
{
  public void actionPerformed(ActionEvent e)
  {
    tField.setText("Hello World Once Again!");
  }
}  // end of inner class


class ClearButtonHandler implements ActionListener
{
  public void actionPerformed(ActionEvent e)
  {
    tField.setText("");
  }
}  // end of inner class


class ExitButtonHandler implements ActionListener
{
  public void actionPerformed(ActionEvent e)
  {
    System.exit(0);
  }
}  // end of inner class
```

These event classes are fairly straightforward. The simplest of the three listener classes is the last one, which closes the application when the Exit button is clicked.

This last event code thus operates exactly the same as the event code that closes the application when the window's Close button is clicked.

Both the code for the <u>M</u>essage and <u>C</u>lear buttons use a `setText()` method to set the text into the text field. Specifically, the statement `tField.setText("Hello World Once Again!");` is executed when the <u>M</u>essage button is clicked. Notice that this statement changes a property of one object, the text displayed in a text field, using an event associated with another object, a button. Similarly, the statement `tField.setText("");` forces display of an empty string when the <u>C</u>lear button is activated. An *empty string* is defined as a string with no characters. Setting the text displayed in the text field to this string value has the effect of clearing the text field of all text. Note that a value such as `"    "`, which consists of one or more blank spaces, would also clear the text field. A string with one or more blank spaces, however, is not an empty string, which is defined as a string having *no* characters. Program 10.3 contains this event code, which is boldfaced for easier identification, within the context of a complete program. Also included in the program are the required statements to instantiate and register the three event handlers, which have also been boldfaced.

Program 10.3

```
import javax.swing.*;
import java.awt.event.*;
import java.awt.Container;  // need this to add controls
import java.awt.*;  // need this for layout manager
public class TextGuiTwo extends JFrame
{
  private JFrame mainFrame;
  private JButton messageButton;
  private JButton clearButton;
  private JButton exitButton;
  private JTextField tField;

  public TextGuiTwo() // a constructor
  {
    mainFrame = new JFrame("The Hello Application - Ver. 3.0");

      // create all components
    messageButton = new JButton("Message");
    clearButton = new JButton("Clear");
    exitButton = new JButton("Exit");
    tField = new JTextField("Hello World!");

      // get the content pane
    Container c = mainFrame.getContentPane();

      // add the components to the ContentPane
    c.add(tField,BorderLayout.NORTH);
    c.add(messageButton,BorderLayout.WEST);
    c.add(clearButton,BorderLayout.CENTER);
    c.add(exitButton,BorderLayout.EAST);
```

(continued)

(continued)

```java
    // create accelerator keys
  messageButton.setMnemonic('M');
  clearButton.setMnemonic('C');
  exitButton.setMnemonic('x');

  mainFrame.setSize(300,150);

    // define and register window event handler
  mainFrame.addWindowListener(new WindowAdapter()
  {
    public void windowClosing(WindowEvent e) {System.exit(0);}
  });

    // create and register the button event handlers
  MessageButtonHandler mhandler = new MessageButtonHandler(); // instantiate a handler
  messageButton.addActionListener(mhandler);   // register the handler

  ClearButtonHandler chandler = new ClearButtonHandler();  // instantiate a handler
  clearButton.addActionListener(chandler);   // register the handler

  ExitButtonHandler ehandler = new ExitButtonHandler();  // instantiate a handler
  exitButton.addActionListener(ehandler);   // register the handler

  mainFrame.show();
}

  // inner classes for the button event handlers
class MessageButtonHandler implements ActionListener
{
  public void actionPerformed(ActionEvent e)
  {
    tField.setText("Hello World Once Again!");
  }
}  // end of inner class

class ClearButtonHandler implements ActionListener
{
  public void actionPerformed(ActionEvent e)
  {
    tField.setText("");
  }
}  // end of inner class

class ExitButtonHandler implements ActionListener
{
  public void actionPerformed(ActionEvent e)
  {
    System.exit(0);
```

```
    }
    }  // end of inner class


    public static void main(String args[])
    {
       new TextGuiTwo();  // instantiate a GUI object
    }

}  // end of class
```

In reviewing Program 10.3, locate the inner listener classes, the statements that instantiate each listener object from these classes, and the listener object registration statements. When Program 10.3 is compiled and run, the GUI in Figure 10.5 is displayed.

Notice that when the program is first run, focus is on the text field, which is indicated by the cursor at the start of the field. Focus is on this component because it was the first component added to the container. The initial string in this field was placed there by the constructor that was used to instantiate the field from the JTextField class.

FIGURE 10.5   The GUI displayed by Program 10.3

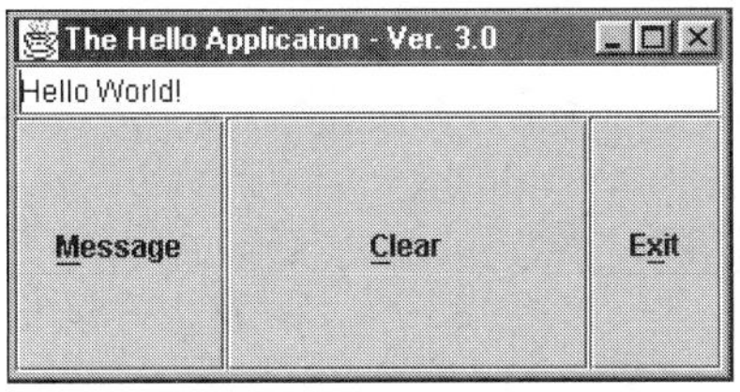

Now click the Message button. Doing so will trigger this button's button click event handler and display the message shown in Figure 10.6.

Clicking the Clear button invokes the chandler event object, which clears the text field, and clicking the Exit button invokes the ehandler() listener object. This object terminates program execution.

Before leaving Program 10.3, one additional point should be mentioned. Because we have constructed the program essentially to use the text field for output display purposes, we will explicitly alter the operation of the text field so that a user cannot enter data into the field. We do this with a setEditable() method. For example, the statement

```
tField.setEditable(false); // don't allow user input
```

FIGURE 10.6   The GUI after the Message button is clicked

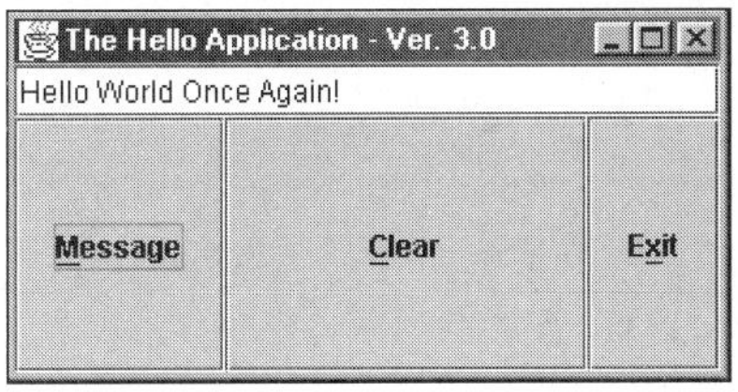

makes the tField component unavailable for user input. This statement can be placed anywhere following the instantiation of the tField reference variable and before the statement that adds tField into the content pane. If this is done, the uneditable text field will be shown with a default gray background in place of the default white background (Figure 10.6).

A JPasswordField component works in exactly the same manner as a JTextField with one exception. The exception is that each character sent to a JPasswordField, either because it is being entered at the keyboard or being sent under program control, will be displayed as a single asterisk, *. Data retrieved from a JPasswordField, however, are in a string format, exactly as if they were entered into a JTextField; it is only the display that disguises the actual data.

Setting Font and Color

In addition to the `setText()` and `setEditable()` methods presented in this section, there are a number of other very useful JComponet methods that can be used in conjunction with a text field. A number of these methods have wider applicability and can be used with other Swing-based components. Table 10.6 lists these methods, including the two we have already encountered.

Font

In setting a component's **font** for its displayed text, such as a button's caption, a label's text, or the text presented within a text field, the `setFont()` method is used. This method uses a `Font` argument that is formally specified using a typeface, style, and point size. The desired typeface must be enclosed in double quotes, such as `"Arial"`, `"TimesRoman"`, or `"Courier"`. If you select a specific typeface that is not installed on the computer running the program, a substitute default font will be used. In addition, a generic typeface, such as `"Serif"`, `"MonoSpaced"`, or `"SansSerif"` can also be specified. Here Java will substitute a default, which is usually Times Roman for the serif font, Courier for the monospaced font, and either Helvetica or Arial for the sans-serif font.

For selecting a style, one or more of three symbolic constants are typically used. These constants, which are named `Font.PLAIN`, `Font.BOLD`, and `Font.ITALIC`,

Table 10.6 Common Set Methods

Method	Description	Example
object.setText(string)	Places the string into the designated object.	tField.setText("This is a test");
object.setEditable(boolean)	Enables or disables a text component for input.	tField.setEditable(false);
object.setFont(Font);	Sets font as to typeface, style, and point size.	tField.setFont(new Font("Arial", Font.BOLD,10));
object.setEnable(boolean)	Enables or disables a component.	mButton.setEnable(false);
object.setForeground(color)	Sets a component's color.	mButton.setForeground(red);
object.setBackground(color)	Sets a component's background color.	mButton.setBackground(gray);

designate either a plain, bold, or italic presentation, respectively. In addition, the expression `Font.BOLD + Font.ITALIC` will yield a boldface and italic text style. The point size must be an integer value that sets the point size of the displayed type (there are 72 points in an inch). For example, the statement

```
tField.setFont(new Font("Courier", Font.BOLD, 12));
```

will set the text in the tField component to be displayed as 12-point Courier bold. It should be noted that the previous statement setting the font can be written in a number of other ways, including the following:

```
Font myFont = new Font("Courier", Font.BOLD, 12);
tField.setFont(myFont);
```

Regardless of the statements that set the font, a `repaint()` method must be used to apply the new font to text currently displayed in a component. For example, if we wish to have a newly set font applied to text currently displayed by a component named tField, the statement `tField.repaint()` should be used.

Color

The last two methods listed in Table 10.6 permit specification of a component's foreground and background colors. The foreground color determines the color of any displayed text or graphics, and the background color determines the color of the background. For example, the foreground color of this page is black, and its background color is white.

The vast majority of color monitors are of the RGB type, which means that they create their colors from combinations of red, green, and blue. Every color presented on the screen is defined by using three separate numbers: one for red, one for green, and one for blue. Individually, the red, green, and blue components of a color are represented by an integer number between 0 and 255. Table 10.7 lists the red, green, and blue content of a number of commonly used colors.

Table 10.7 **RGB Color Values**

Color	Red Content	Green Content	BlueContent
Black	0	0	0
Blue	0	0	255
Cyan	0	255	255
Dark Gray	64	64	64
Gray	128	128	128
Green	0	255	0
Light Gray	192	192	192
Magenta	255	0	255
Orange	255	200	0
Pink	255	175	175
Red	255	0	0
Yellow	255	255	0
White	255	255	255

Although the color values in Table 10.7 specify the relative intensity of red, green, and blue in the final color, the actual displayed color depends on the color monitor. The `Color` class, which is provided as part of the `java.awt` package, provides a number of methods for both selecting and setting desired foreground and background colors. To get a clear understanding of the color codes, you can use the `Color()` method, which permits setting the color code by individually specifying the red, blue, and green content of the desired final color. The format of this method is[2]

```
Color(red, green, blue)
```

where:

> *red* is an integer number in the range 0 to 255 that represents the color's red component.
>
> *green* is an integer number in the range 0 to 255 that represents the color's green component.
>
> *blue* is an integer number in the range 0 to 255 that represents the color's blue component.

For example, the statements

```
Color myColor;
myColor = new Color(255,255,0);
```

or the single-line equivalent statement

```
Color myColor = new Color(255,255,0);
```

specifies that the variable `myColor` designates the color yellow (see Table 10.7). Using a value less than 0 or greater that 255 for a color component results in a compiler error message.

In addition to individually specifying the red, green, and blue content of a color, the `Color` class provides the symbolic color constants listed in Table 10.8 (see Table 10.7 for the individual red, green, and blue components provided by each of these constants).

For example, using the `magenta` constant, the statement

```
Color someColor = Color.magenta;
```

can replace the statement

```
Color someColor = new Color(255, 0, 255);
```

Once you have determined your desired colors, the `setForeground()` and `setBackground()` methods (see Table 10.6) can set the foreground and background colors, respectively, of any GUI component, including the content pane itself. For example, if c is the object name of the JFrame content pane, each of the following statements

```
c.setBackground(Color.blue);
c.setBackground(new Color(0, 0, 255));
```

---

[2] Another form of this method is `Color(float red, float green, float blue)`, where each color component is represented as a floating- point value between 0.0f and 0.1f. The f suffix is required because, in its absence, the compiler will interpret the values as double-precision numbers.

Table 10.8   **Color Constants**

Class	Constant	Color
Color	static final black	black
Color	static final blue	blue
Color	static final cyan	cyan
Color	static final darkGray	dark gray
Color	static final gray	gray
Color	static final green	green
Color	static final lightGray	light gray
Color	static final magenta	magenta
Color	static final orange	orange
Color	static final pink	pink
Color	static final red	red
Color	static final white	white
Color	static final yellow	yellow

sets the background color of the content pane to blue. Similarly, either of the following statements sets the foreground color to red.

```
c.setForeground(Color.red);
c.setForeground(new Color(255, 0, 0));
```

Because the first form of each of these statements clearly designates the color, it is the preferred statement. You should only use the second form whenever you are using a color that is not listed in Table 10.8, and then you should document what the intended color is, either as a comment or in a declaration statement with an identifier name that corresponds to the selected color. In like manner, both the foreground and background colors of any component can be specified. All that is required is that the appropriate set() method is prefixed with the name of the desired component.

JTextArea Components

For GUI output that requires a single displayed line, a JTextField component is the Swing component of choice. There are times, however, where you will need to display more than one line of text. For these situations, an object constructed from the JTextArea class can be used. In addition, as we will see in the next section, JTextField, JPasswordField, and JTextArea components can also be used for input.[3]

A **JTextArea** component is constructed in almost the same manner as a JTextField, but the JTextArea constructor requires two arguments: one to indicate the number of rows for the text area and one to indicate the number of columns. For example, the expression new JTextArea(10,30) will create a text area that consists of 10 rows and 30 columns.

---

[3] However, as noted earlier, the JPasswordField component will display an asterisk for each character entered.

Once a text area is instantiated, text can be displayed in it using an `append()` method. For example, if we have already constructed a JTextArea component named `outArea`, the statement `outArea.append("This is a test");` will display the string argument in the text area. Each additional `append()` invocation adds text to the end of the string already displayed. For example, the code

```
outArea.setFont(new Font("Courier", Font.PLAIN, 10)); // set the font
for (num = 1; num < 11; num++)
  outArea.append("The number is now" + num + '\n');
```

first sets the display font to Courier and then causes the following display in the text area object named `outArea`:

```
The number is now 1
The number is now 2
The number is now 3
The number is now 4
The number is now 5
The number is now 6
The number is now 7
The number is now 8
The number is now 9
The number is now 10
```

Notice that to produce this display we have placed a newline escape sequence within the argument passed to `append()`. This escape sequence is very common and almost always necessary when using a text area for display purposes. If either the row or column size specified for a text area is too small to accommodate the displayed string, the appropriate specification is ignored and the text area is automatically expanded to accommodate the output string.

Program 10.4 uses a text area to display a table of 10 numbers, including their squares and cubes. The code for creating a table is in the class method named `createTable()`. Except for the use of an `append()` method rather than a `print()` method, this code is almost identical to Program 5-10, and it is instructive to compare these two programs. For convenience, the three statements that create the text area object have been boldfaced in Program 10.4. These boldfaced statements should be extremely familiar because they are the same types of statements that have created all of our Swing-based GUI components.

FIGURE 10.7   The GUI produced by Program 10.4

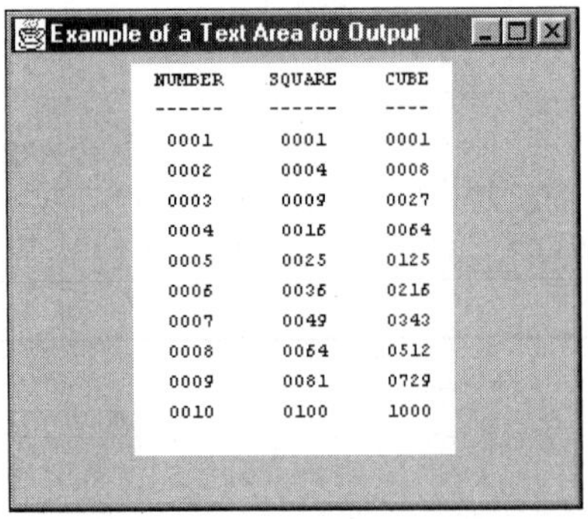

After reviewing how a text area is constructed, you should notice the use of the `append()` method for displaying text within the text area object. Finally, pay particular attention to the invocation of the `createTable()` method within the `main()` method. Because `createTable()` is a nonconstructor class method, it must be invoked with a specific class object for it to operate on. The output created when Program 10.4 is run appears in Figure 10.7.

Program 10.4

```java
import javax.swing.*;
import java.awt.event.*;
import java.awt.Container;
import java.awt.*;    // need this for layout manager
import java.text.*;   // need this for formatting
public class ShowTextArea extends JFrame
{
  private JFrame mainFrame;
  private JTextArea outArea;

  public ShowTextArea() // a constructor
  {
    mainFrame = new JFrame("Example of a Text Area for Output");

      // create all components
    outArea = new JTextArea(10, 28);

      // get the content pane
    Container c = mainFrame.getContentPane();
    c.setLayout(new FlowLayout());

      // add the components to the ContentPane
    c.add(outArea);

    mainFrame.setSize(300,250);

      // define and register window event handler
    mainFrame.addWindowListener(new WindowAdapter()
    {
      public void windowClosing(WindowEvent e) {System.exit(0);}
    });

    mainFrame.show();
  }

  public void createTable()
  {
    int num;
    DecimalFormat df = new DecimalFormat("0000");
```

(continued)

(continued)

```
        outArea.setFont(new Font("Courier", Font.BOLD, 10));
        outArea.append("  NUMBER     SQUARE     CUBE\n");
        outArea.append("  ------     ------     ----\n");

        outArea.setFont(new Font("Courier", Font.PLAIN, 10));
        for (num = 1; num < 11; num++)
        {
          outArea.append("     " + df.format(num));
          outArea.append("          " + df.format(num*num));
          outArea.append("          " + df.format(num * num * num) +'\n');
        }

        return;
    }

    public static void main(String args[])
    {

        ShowTextArea app;  // declare an object of type ShowTextArea
        app = new ShowTextArea();  // instantiate a GUI object

        app.createTable();
    }

}  // end of class
```

Exercises 10.2

1. Compile and run Program 10.3 on your computer.

2. Create a graphical interface that contains two buttons and two text fields. The names of these components should be butOne, butTwo, txtFirst, and txtSecond. These components should be added into a JFrame content pane in the order txtFirst, butOne, butTwo, and txtSecond. Using code, set the tab sequence so that tab control goes from txtFirst to txtSecond to butTwo to butOne.

3a. Write a Java program that creates a GUI having the following properties table:

Object	Property	Setting
JFrame	Name	mainFrame
	Caption	Messages
	Layout	FlowLayout
JButton	Name	cmdGood
	Caption	Good
	Mnemonic	G

Object	Property	Setting
JButton	Name	cmdBad
	Caption	Bad
	Mnemonic	B
JTextField	Name	txtMessage
	Text	(None)

b. Add individual event handlers to the program written for Exercise 3a so that when a user clicks the <u>G</u>ood button, the message `Today is a good day!` appears in the text field, and when the <u>B</u>ad button is clicked, the message `I'm having a bad day today!` is displayed in the text field.

4. Write a Java application having three buttons and a text field. Clicking the first button should produce the message `See no evil` in the text field, clicking the second button should produce the message `Hear no evil`, and clicking the third button should produce the message `Speak no evil` in the text field.

5a. Create a text field component that has a red foreground color and a blue background color. The initial text displayed in the field should be `Welcome to Java`.

b. Add a text field component to the GUI created for Exercise 5a that has a white foreground color and a red background color. The initial text displayed in the field should be `Object-oriented language`.

6. Write, compile, and run a Java program that contains a text field and three buttons. The text field should initially contain the text `This is a test`. When the first button is clicked, the text in the text field should change to Helvetica font, when the second button is clicked, the text should change to Garamond font (if your system does not have Garamond, select a font that you do have), and when the third button is clicked, the text should change to Courier font.

7a. Write a Java program that creates a GUI having the following properties table:

Object	Property	Setting
JFrame	Name	mainFrame
	Caption	TypeFace Example
	Layout	FlowLayout
JButton	Name	cmdBold
	Caption	Bold
	Mnemonic	B
JButton	Name	cmdItalic
	Caption	Italic
	Mnemonic	I
JTextField	Name	txtMessage
	Text	This is a test

By clicking the text field, the user should be able to enter any desired text in nonboldface and nonitalic font. When the user clicks the <u>B</u>old button, the text in the text field should change to boldface, and when the user clicks the <u>I</u>talic button, the text should change to italic.

b. From a user's viewpoint, what is the problem with the program as it is written?

8. Add two more buttons to the program written for Exercise 7a. One of the additional buttons, when clicked, should change the text displayed in the text field to a nonbold state. When the second button is clicked, the text should be displayed in a nonitalic state. (Tip: See Exercise 6.)

9. Compile and run Program 10.4 on your computer.

10. Modify Program 10.4's JTextArea to be 5 rows by 10 columns and verify that the program ignores both dimensions when it is run.

11. Add three command buttons to Program 10.4. Clicking the first button should produce the table shown in Figure 10.7, clicking the second button should clear the text area, and clicking the third button should cause the program to close. (Tip: Move the code in the current createTable() to the first button's event handler class.)

10.3 Text Field Components for Data Entry

Although we have only used a JTextField component for output, it is also the most versatile and common atomic component for interactive user input. This control permits the user to enter a string at the terminal, which can easily be retrieved and processed.

When used for input, a JTextField component is almost always used in conjunction with a label control, where the label provides a prompt and the text field provides the actual means for the user to input data. For example, consider the properties table for Program 10.5, which is listed in Table 10.9. The GUI corresponding to this table is shown in Figure 10.8.

In the GUI shown in the figure, the label is Enter a Fahrenheit temperature: and the corresponding text field provide an input area for the user to enter data.

Table 10.9   Program 10.5's Properties Table

Object	Property	Setting	Listener Class	Listener Object
JFrame	Name	mainFrame	anonymous	
	Caption	Temperature Conversion		
	Layout manager	FlowLayout		
JLabel	Name	fahrLabel		
	Caption	Enter a Fahrenheit temperature:		
JLabel	Name	celsLabel		
	Caption	The corresponding Celsius value is:		
JTextField	Name	fahrField		
	Size	5		
JTextField	Name	celsField		
	Size	5		
JButton	Name	convertButton	ConvertButtonHandler	chandler
	Caption	Convert		
	Mnemonic	C		
JButton	Name	exitButton	ExitButtonHandler	ehandler
	Caption	Exit		
	Mnemonic	x		

FIGURE 10.8   **The user interface corresponding to Table 10.9**

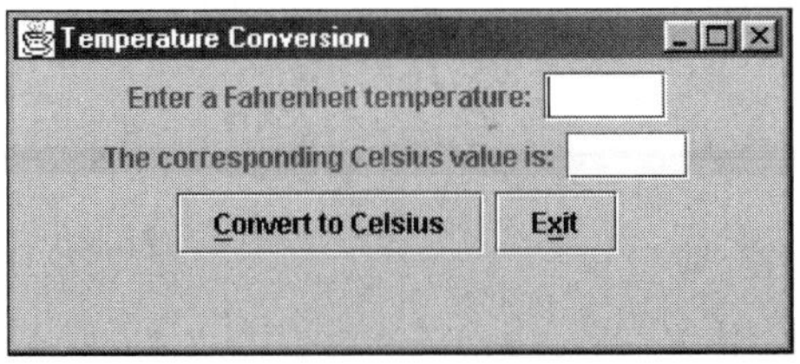

Label objects are constructed from JLabel atomic components, and a label is created in the same manner as in constructing buttons and text fields. For example, the first label in Figure 10.8 was constructed using the following statements, which are the same type of statements that have added atomic components to all of the GUIs illustrated in this and the previous chapter:

```
private JLabel fahrLabel;    // declare a class variable
fahrLabel = new JLabel("Enter a Fahrenheit temperature:"); //instantiate an object
c.add(fahrLabel); // add the object to the content pane
```

The `fahrField` text field listed in Table 10.9 will be used for data input while the program is running. All data entered into a text field are assumed by Java to be string data. This means that if numbers are to be input, the entered string must be explicitly converted to numerical data. It also means that some data validation is typically required to ensure that a user does not enter data that will cause the application to crash.

Consider again the interface in Figure 10.8 where the user is prompted to enter a temperature in degrees Fahrenheit. Once a user enters a Fahrenheit temperature, the program will compute the corresponding temperature in degrees Celsius and display the calculated value in the second text field.

Now consider Program 10.5, which implements the GUI defined by Properties Table 10.9, paying particular attention to the `ConvertButtonHandler` listener class code, which has been boldfaced for easier identification.

Program 10.5

```
import java.text.*;  // need this for formatting
import javax.swing.*;
import java.awt.event.*;
import java.awt.Container;
import java.awt.*;  // need this for layout manager


public class ConvertTempOne extends JFrame
{
  private JFrame mainFrame;
  private JButton convertButton;
  private JButton exitButton;
  private JTextField fahrField;
  private JTextField celsField;
  private JLabel fahrLabel;
  private JLabel celsLabel;
```

(continued)

(continued)

```java
public ConvertTempOne() // a constructor
{
  mainFrame = new JFrame("Temperature Conversion");

    // create all components
  convertButton = new JButton("Convert to Celsius");
  exitButton = new JButton("Exit");
  fahrLabel = new JLabel("Enter a Fahrenheit temperature:");
  celsLabel = new JLabel("The corresponding Celsius value is:");
  fahrField = new JTextField(5);
  celsField = new JTextField(5);

    // get the content pane
  Container c = mainFrame.getContentPane();
    // set the layout manager
  c.setLayout(new FlowLayout());

    // add the components to the ContentPane
  c.add(fahrLabel);
  c.add(fahrField);
  c.add(celsLabel);
  c.add(celsField);
  c.add(convertButton);
  c.add(exitButton);

    // create accelerator keys
  convertButton.setMnemonic('C');
  exitButton.setMnemonic('x');

  mainFrame.setSize(350,150);

    // define and register window event handler
  mainFrame.addWindowListener(new WindowAdapter()
  {
    public void windowClosing(WindowEvent e) {System.exit(0);}
  });

    // create and register the button event handlers
  ConvertButtonHandler chandler = new ConvertButtonHandler();  // instantiate a handler
  convertButton.addActionListener(chandler);  // register the handler

  ExitButtonHandler ehandler = new ExitButtonHandler();  // instantiate a handler
  exitButton.addActionListener(ehandler);  // register the handler

  mainFrame.show();
}
```

```
   // inner classes for the button event handlers
class ConvertButtonHandler implements ActionListener
{
  public void actionPerformed(ActionEvent e)
  {
    DecimalFormat num = new DecimalFormat(",###.##");
    String instring;
    double invalue, outvalue;

    instring = fahrField.getText();  // read the input value
    invalue = Double.parseDouble(instring);  // convert to a double
    outvalue = 5.0/9.0 * (invalue - 32.0);
    celsField.setText(num.format(outvalue));
  }
}  // end of inner class

class ExitButtonHandler implements ActionListener
{
  public void actionPerformed(ActionEvent e)
  {
    System.exit(0);
  }
}  // end of inner class

public static void main(String args[])
{
  new ConvertTempOne();  // instantiate a GUI object
}

}  // end of class
```

The actual calculation and display of a Celsius temperature are performed whenever the <u>C</u>onvert button is activated. This conversion is accomplished using the three statements

```
instring = fahrField.getText();  // read the input value
invalue = Double.parseDouble(instring);  // convert to a double
outvalue = 5.0/9.0 * (invalue - 32.0);
```

which is followed by a call to a `setText()` method to display the calculated result.

Notice that a `getText()` method retrieves the string contained in the `fahrField` text field. The `getText()` method is the input equivalent to the `setText()` method, which sends a string to a text field. Here the retrieved string is stored into the `instring` string. In the next statement, this string value is converted to a double-precision number by passing the string as an argument to the `parseDouble()` method (if necessary review Section 3.3 for an explanation of this method). Finally, the third statement converts the input value into an equivalent Celsius temperature. Figure 10.9 illustrates a sample run of Program 10.5.

FIGURE 10.9 **A sample run of Program 10.5**

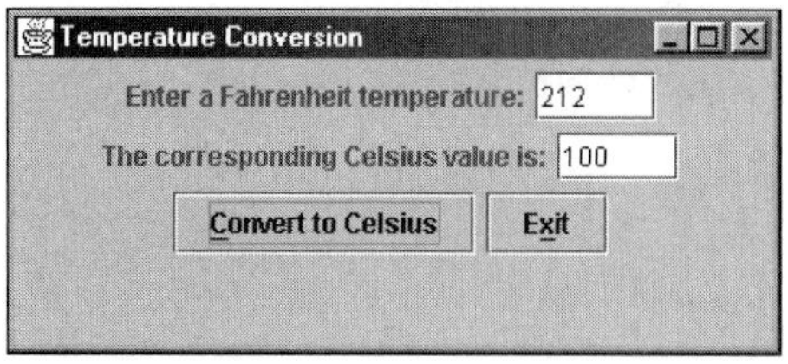

Before leaving Program 10.5, we point out a number of minor but important problems that can occur with it. These problems will be corrected at the end of this section and Section 10.5. First, reconsider the conversion statement

```
invalue = Double.parseDouble(instring);
```

This statement operates correctly when a user enters any string that can be considered as a number, such as 212 or 187.45. If a user inadvertently types a string such as 212a, however, the program will crash. This is because the parseDouble() method is not equipped to handle invalid numerical characters. In addition, parseDouble() is not equipped to convert an empty string, which is produced whenever the user clicks the Convert button without first entering any data into the input text field. To handle this latter problem, we can simply check for an empty string before performing the conversion calculation. The detection of invalid characters, however, is typically handled by inspecting each key as it is pressed. A data-input validation technique that accomplishes this using keyboard event handling is presented in Section 10.5.

A second set of problems is that, due to the event driven nature of the program, a user could inadvertently attempt to enter a Celsius rather than a Fahrenheit temperature. Similarly, after having one Fahrenheit temperature converted, the user could then enter a second such temperature, which would overwrite the first temperature that was correctly converted. At that point, the interface would show the new Fahrenheit temperature alongside the Celsius temperature that corresponded to the previously entered value. In creating GUIs, it is the programmer's responsibility to forestall this type of operation. Doing so requires constructing special event handler classes known as **focus listeners**.

Constructing Focus Listeners

In Section 10.1, we introduced the concept of keyboard focus. Whenever a component receives the focus, it automatically triggers a focus-gained event, and whenever it loses focus, it triggers a focus-lost event. The sequence is that the component that loses focus triggers a focus-lost event before the next component that receives focus triggers a focus-gained event.[4] A listener class that is constructed to handle these events must be implemented as a FocusListener class and, as listed in Table 10.10, must contain two required methods. Optionally, a FocusAdapter class may also be used as the parent class for a FocusListener.

---

[4] The terms *fires an event* and *triggers an event* are synonyms.

Table 10.10   Required `FocusListener` Event Methods

Method	Description
`public void focusGained(FocusEvent e)`	This method is triggered when a component receives keyboard focus.
`public void focusLost(FocusEvent e)`	This method is triggered when a component loses keyboard focus.

One of the first requirements of a `FocusListener` class is to determine the component that triggered the focus event. Consider the following skeleton code for a listener class that we have named `FocusHandler`. This class implements a `Focus-Listener` for detecting when two components named `fahrField` and `celsField` receive and lose focus. First notice that the class correctly includes a `focusGained()` and `focusLost()` method, and each method uses an `if-else` statement to detect which specific component triggered the focus event. This is accomplished by using the `FocusEvent` argument, which we have named `e`, and a `getSource()` method to determine the source of each event with the individual components of interest.

```
class FocusHandler implements FocusListener
{
  public void focusGained(FocusEvent e) // this detects when a component gets
  {                                      // the focus
    if(e.getSource() == fahrField)      // this detects that the fahrField component
    {                                    // got the focus
        // do something
    }
    else if(e.getSource() == celsField) // this detects that the celsField
    {                                    // component got the focus
        // do something
    }
  }
  public void focusLost(FocusEvent e)   // this detects when a component loses
  {                                      // the focus
    if(e.getSource() == fahrField)      // this detects that the fahrField component
    {                                    // lost the focus
      // do something
    }
    else if(e.getSource() == celsField) // this detects that the celsField
    {                                    // component lost the focus
      // do something
    }
  }
}  // end of FocusListener class
```

We will use this skeleton `FocusListener` class to correctly handle two of the user-related problems that were identified for Program 10.5 and make the program respond in a "reasonable" manner. To understand what reasonable means, recall that the purpose of Program 10.5 is to permit a user to enter a Fahrenheit temperature and then, by clicking the Convert button, have the program calculate and display the corresponding Celsius temperature. As it stands, however, a user can inadvertently enter a Celsius rather than a Fahrenheit temperature. Similarly, after a Fahrenheit temperature has been correctly converted, entry of a second Fahrenheit temperature would put the GUI in a state where the newly entered Fahrenheit value is displayed alongside the Celsius temperature corresponding to the previously entered value.

To forestall such program operation, the new event handlers that will be provided and a commentary on why we have chosen the specified actions for each handler follow:

Event Handler for the Fahrenheit Text Field Listener

When this box gets the focus:
Set the value in the Fahrenheit text field to a blank.
Set the value in the Celsius text field to a blank.

Commentary on this event handler:
This will set up the Fahrenheit text field to receive a new input value and prevents display of an incorrect Celsius value while the user is entering a new Fahrenheit temperature.

Event Handler for the Celsius Text Field Listener

When this box gets the focus:
Set the focus to the Fahrenheit text field.

Commentary on this event handler:
This will prevent a user from entering a value into the Celsius text field because this box can only get the focus if the user tabs to it or clicks it.

Under these conditions, our event handler will automatically set the focus on the Fahrenheit box, which is where users should be if they are trying to enter a value.

Once the focus gets shifted to the Fahrenheit box, that box's focus-gained event will clear the Celsius text field and disable it.

Event Handler for the Convert Button Listener

When this button is clicked:
Retrieve the Fahrenheit text field's data value.
If no input has been entered, set the input to "0".
Convert the Fahrenheit data to a Celsius value using the formula
  Celsius = 5 / 9 * (Fahrenheit − 32)
Enable the Celsius text field.
Display the calculated Celsius value.

Commentary on this event handler:
This is a straightforward task of converting the input value to an output value and enabling the Celsius text field so that the displayed value is not shadowed. The check for an empty string will detect the case where the user clicks the Convert button without having entered any data into the Fahrenheit text field.

Event Handler for the Exit Button Listener

When this button is clicked:
Close down the application.

Commentary on this event handler:
This is the standard closing event handler.

Table 10.11   Useful Focus Control Methods

Method	Description
grabFocus(Component)	Sets the focus on its component argument if it does not already have it. Although it will set focus on a component that has been setEnabled() to false, in this case it will not be useful because the component has been disabled. Another approach is to use an isRequestFocusEnabled(), setRequestFocusEnabled(), and requestFocus() sequence.
requestFocus(Component)	Sets the focus on its component argument only if the component's setRequestFocusEnabled() has been set to true and the component does not already have the focus.
setRequestFocusEnabled(boolean)	Sets whether the receiving component can obtain the focus when requestFocus() is called.
isRequestFocusEnabled(Component)	Returns a Boolean value of true or false, indicating whether the component can receive focus using requestFocus().
setNextFocusableComponent(Component)	Specifies the next component to receive focus but does not shift focus to this component.

Although the actions taken by our event handler methods are straightforward and typical of the types of actions that a reasonably simple Windows program must take, we will need some help from the JComponent class to perform them. Table 10.11 lists a number of extremely useful JComponent methods, the first and last of which complete our skeleton FocusListener class. The methods are used for both setting and determining the next component to receive focus under normal circumstances and for forcing focus onto a different component under program control. One of these methods, setNextFocusableComponent(), was presented and used in Section 10.1.

The required event handlers, which were previously described, can now be written using the methods listed in Table 10.11, and they are presented as ConvertTempOne's FocusListener class's code.[5]

ConvertTempOne Event Handler FocusListener Class's Event Code

```
class FocusHandler implements FocusListener
{
  public void focusGained(FocusEvent e)
  {
    if(e.getSource() == fahrField)
    {
```

---

[5] It should be noted that the statement fahrField.grabFocus(); in this code can be replaced by the two statements

```
        fahrField.setRequestFocusEnabled(true);
        fahrField.requestFocus();
```

Typically, before using these statements, a test would be made using the isRequestFocusEnabled() method. We use the grabFocus() unconditionally here because we know that the fahrField component can always accept the focus.

```
            fahrField.setText("");  // blank input textfield
            celsField.setText("");  // blank Celsius textfield
        }
        else if(e.getSource() == celsField)
        {

          celsField.setNextFocusableComponent(fahrField);
          fahrField.grabFocus();
        }
    }
    public void focusLost(FocusEvent e)
    {
        if(e.getSource() == fahrField)
        {
          fahrField.setNextFocusableComponent(convertButton);
        }
    }
}  // end of focus listener class

class ConvertButtonHandler implements ActionListener
{
  public void actionPerformed(ActionEvent e)
  {
    DecimalFormat num = new DecimalFormat(",###.##");
    String instring;
    double invalue, outvalue;

    celsField.setEnabled(true); //enable Celsius text field
    instring = fahrField.getText();  // read the input value
      // prevent entry of an empty string
    if (instring.equals(""))
    {
      instring = "0";
      fahrField.setText("0");
    }
    invalue = Double.parseDouble(instring);  // convert to a double
    outvalue = 5.0/9.0 * (invalue - 32.0);
    celsField.setText(num.format(outvalue));
  }
}

class ExitButtonHandler implements ActionListener
{
  public void actionPerformed(ActionEvent e)
  {
    System.exit(0);
  }
}
```

Having defined the required `FocusListener` class's event handlers, all that remains is to enter them as part of the application. Listener objects for the last two event classes, `ConvertButtonHandler` and `ExitButtonHandler`, can be instantiated and registered as previously listed in the code for Program 10.5. A listener object of the `FocusHandler` class can then be instantiated and registered using the following statements:

```
FocusHandler fhandler = new FocusHandler();
fahrField.addFocusListener(fhandler);
celsField.addFocusListener(fhandler);
```

Notice that the last two statements register the same listener object to both the `fahrField` and `celsField` components. We leave the insertion of these statements into Program 10.5 as Exercise 7b.

Input Validation Revisited

The event code for the `ConvertTempTwo` class retouches on the necessity of validating user input by employing one of the more common techniques associated with text field input, which is to explicitly test for an empty string. This conversion can be done either immediately after the user has entered the data, in which case it will be triggered by the component's focus-lost event, or it can be done immediately before the data are used or stored, as in our previous example. Clearly, both places ensure that invalid data will not enter the system and corrupt any results derived by it.

Another very important type of validation occurs while the user is entering data on a keystroke-by-keystroke basis. This type of front-end key-by-key validation is made using a `KeyListener` class, which detects keyboard events triggered by a keystroke. This permits action to be taken that rejects an invalid keystroke before the key's value is accepted into the input string. Keyboard events return both the Unicode value of each key as well as detecting if the Function, Arrow, and Control keys have been pressed. Using these events for data validation is based on selecting the desired characters and rejecting undesirable characters from entering the final string. The methods for performing a keystroke-by-keystroke validation using a `KeyListener` class are presented in Section 10.5.

Exercises 10.3

1. Enter and run Program 10.2 on your computer.

2. Enter and run Program 10.3 on your computer.

3. Modify Program 10.3 so that the user cannot enter any text into the text field component (Tip: Use a `setEditable(false)` method.)

4. Enter and run Program 10.4 on your computer.

5. Modify Program 10.5 to include the `ConvertTempOne` class's `FocusListener` developed in this section.

6. Rewrite the `ConvertTempOne` class's `FocusListener` developed in this section as two `FocusListeners`— one for the `fahrField` component and one for the `celsField`

component. Name these classes `FahrFocusListener` and `CelsFocusListener`, respectively.

7a. What statements are needed to instantiate listener objects for the classes written for Exercise 6 and to have these objects correctly registered. Assume the listener object for the `FahrFocusListener` class is named `fahrhandler` and the listener object for the `CelsFocusListener` class is named `celshanlder`.

b. Enter and run Program 10.5 using the focus handler classes written for Exercise 6 and the instantiation and registration statements written for Exercise 7a.

8a. Write by hand a Java program that uses a JLabel component to display the following prompt:

Enter the amount of the bill:

After accepting a value for the amount of the bill in a text field, your program, upon the click of a Calculate button, should calculate the sales tax, assuming a tax rate of 6 percent. The display of the sales tax, as a dollar amount, should appear in a text field named `taxShow` when the Calculate button is clicked. A second button should be provided to terminate the application.

b. Include the event procedure written for Exercise 8a in a working program. For testing purposes, verify your program using an initial amount of $36.00. After manually checking that the result produced by your program is correct, use your program to complete the following table:

Amount (dollars)	Sales Tax (dollars)
36.00	
40.00	
52.60	
87.95	
125.00	
182.93	

9a. Write a Java program that converts Celsius temperatures to their equivalent Fahrenheit values. Use a label to display the following prompt:

Enter the temperature in degrees Celsius:

After accepting a value entered from the keyboard into a text field, the program should convert the entered temperature to degrees Fahrenheit using the equation *Fahrenheit* = *(9.0 / 5.0) * Celsius + 32.0.* The program should then display the temperature in degrees Fahrenheit in a clearly labeled text field. A JButton button should be provided to terminate the application.

b. Verify the program written for Exercise 9a by first calculating the Fahrenheit equivalent of the following test data by hand and then using your program to see if it produces the correct results.

Test data set 1: 0 degrees Celsius
Test data set 2: 50 degrees Celsius
Test data set 3: 100 degrees Celsius

When you are sure your procedure is working correctly, use it to complete the following table:

Celsius	Fahrenheit
45	
50	
55	
60	
65	
70	

10. Write and run a Java program that displays the following prompts using two label components:

```
Enter the length of the office:
Enter the width of the office:
```

Have your program accept the user input in two text fields. When a button is clicked, your program should calculate the area of the office and display the area in a text field. This display should be cleared whenever the input text fields receive the focus. A second button should be provided to terminate the application. Verify your procedure with the following test data:

Test data set 1: length = 12.5, width = 10
Test data set 2: length = 12.4, width = 0
Test data set 3: length = 0, width = 10

11a. Write and run a Java program that displays the following prompts and uses two text fields to receive the input data:

```
Enter the miles driven:
Enter the gallons of gas used:
```

Your program should calculate and display the miles per gallon in a text field when a button is clicked. Use the equation *miles per gallon = miles / gallons used*. The display should be cleared whenever one of the text fields gets the focus. A second button should be provided to terminate the application. Verify your procedure using the following test data:

Test data set 1: miles = 276, gas = 10 gallons
Test data set 2: miles = 200, gas = 15.5 gallons

When you have completed your verification, use your procedure to complete the following table:

Miles Driven	Gallons Used	mpg
250	16.00	
275	18.00	
312	19.54	
296	17.39	

b. For the procedure written for Exercise 11a, determine how many verification runs are required to ensure the procedure is working correctly and give a reason supporting your answer.

12. Write a Java program that displays the following prompts:

```
Enter the length of the swimming pool:
Enter the width of the swimming pool:
Enter the average depth of the swimming pool:
```

Have your program accept the user input in three text fields. When a button is clicked, your program should calculate the volume of the swimming pool and display the volume in a fourth text field. This display should be cleared whenever the input text fields receive the focus. A second button should be provided to terminate the application. In calculating the volume, use the equation *volume = length * width * average depth*.

13. Write and run a Java program that provides three text fields for the input of three user-input numbers. There should be a single label prompt that tells the user to enter three numbers in the text fields. When the user clicks a button, the program should calculate the average of the numbers and then display the average in a clearly labeled fourth text field. The displayed value should be cleared whenever one of the text fields receives the focus. A second button should be provided to terminate the application. Verify your procedure with the following test data:

Test data set 1: 100, 100, 100
Test data set 2: 100, 50, 0

When you have completed your verification, use your program to complete the following table:

Numbers	Average
92, 98, 79	
86, 84, 75	
63, 85, 74	

14. Write a Java program that prompts the user to input two numbers, each accepted by a text field, and that has a button with the caption Swap. When this button is clicked, the values in the two text fields should be switched.

10.4 Check Box, Radio Button, and Group Components

Check box and radio button components are extremely useful in presenting users with a set of defined choices from which they must make a selection. The difference between the two types of components is in the nature of the selection that must be made. In a radio button group, the user can select only one choice from a mutually exclusive set of choices—for example, selecting a category of being either single, married, divorced, or widowed. Here the user is presented with a list of choices from which one and only one selection can be made. In a check box control, the user is also presented with a list of one or more choices, but each choice can be selected or not selected independently of any other selection. An example is providing a list of style choices for displaying text, such as bold and italic. The user can select one, both, or neither choice. As these two types of components are closely related, we present both in this section.

Check Boxes

The **check box** control provides a user with a simple yes or no type of option. For example, the interface in Figure 10.10 has two check boxes. The properties table for this interface is listed in Table 10.12.

As illustrated in Figure 10.10, both check boxes are unchecked. This is the default setting when a JCheckBox component is added to a container and can be altered using a `setSelected()` method. For example, the statement `boxItalic.set-`

FIGURE 10.10   **An interface with two check boxes**

Table 10.12   **Figure 10.10's Properties Table**

Object	Property	Setting
JFrame	Name	mainFrame
	Caption	Check Box Example
JLabel	Name	inLabel
	Caption	Enter Some Text:
JTextField	Name	LinField
	Text	(Blank)
	Font	SansSerif
	style	Font.PLAIN
JCheckBox	Name	boxItalic
	Caption	Italic
	Mnemonic	I
JCheckBox	Name	boxBold
	Caption	Bold
	Mnemonic	B
JButton	Name	exitButton
	Caption	Exit
	Mnemonic	x

Selected(true); would cause the Italic check box in Figure 10.10 to be checked. In addition, whether a check box is checked or not may be altered by the user at run time by either clicking the box, pressing the Space key when the box is in focus, or pressing the accelerator key specified for the box. It can also be changed at run time using the setSelected() method within running program code.

Each check box in an application is independent of any other check box. This means that the choice made in one box has no effect on, and does not depend on, the choice made in another box. Thus, check boxes are useful for providing a set of one or more options that can be in effect at the same time, provided that each option is individually of the yes-no, on-off, or true-false type. For example, in the interface shown in Figure 10.10, the check box options consist of a set of two check boxes that permit independent selection of how the text is to be displayed. Selecting or deselecting Bold has no effect on the choice for italic or nonitalic.

Because of their on-off nature, check boxes are also known as toggle selections, where a user can effectively toggle, or switch back and forth, between a check mark and no check mark. If no check mark appears in a box, clicking it changes its selected state to `true` and causes a check to appear; otherwise, if the box has a check, clicking it changes its selected state to `false` and causes the check to be cleared.

Program 10.6 provides the code for constructing the interface in Figure 10.10. The statements that create and display the check box components are boldfaced for easy reference.

Program 10.6

```java
import javax.swing.*;
import java.awt.event.*;
import java.awt.Container;  // need this to add controls
import java.awt.*;  // need this for layout manager
public class CheckBoxOne extends JFrame
{
  private JFrame mainFrame;
  private JButton exitButton;
  private JLabel inLabel;
  private JTextField tinField;
  private JCheckBox boxItalic;
  private JCheckBox boxBold;

  public CheckBoxOne() // a constructor
  {
    mainFrame = new JFrame("Check Box Example");

      // create all components

    exitButton = new JButton("Exit");
    inLabel = new JLabel("Enter Some Text:");
    tinField = new JTextField(20);
    boxItalic = new JCheckBox("Italic");
    boxBold = new JCheckBox("Bold");

      // get the content pane
    Container c = mainFrame.getContentPane();
      // set the layout manager
    c.setLayout(new FlowLayout());

      // add the components to the ContentPane
    c.add(inLabel);
    c.add(tinField);
    c.add(boxItalic);
    c.add(boxBold);
    c.add(exitButton);

      // create accelerator keys
    boxItalic.setMnemonic('I');
    boxBold.setMnemonic('B');
    exitButton.setMnemonic('x');
```

```
   mainFrame.setSize(250,150);

      // define and register window event handler
   mainFrame.addWindowListener(new WindowAdapter()
   {
     public void windowClosing(WindowEvent e) {System.exit(0);}
   });

      // create and register the exit button event handler

   ExitButtonHandler ehandler = new ExitButtonHandler();  // instantiate a handler
   exitButton.addActionListener(ehandler);  // register the handler

   mainFrame.show();
 }

     // inner class for the Exit button event handler
 private class ExitButtonHandler implements ActionListener
 {
   public void actionPerformed(ActionEvent e)
   {
     System.exit(0);
   }
 }  // end of inner class


 public static void main(String args[])
 {
   new CheckBoxOne();  // instantiate a GUI object
 }

}  // end of class
```

Adding a Check Box Listener Class

Having provided the user interface for making a selection, it still remains to provide the code to determine the selection and then to act appropriately based on the selection. The event code to do this follows:

Program 10.6's Check Box Listener Class's Event Code

```
// Check Box listener class code
class ChkBoxHandler implements ItemListener
{
  private int italicFont;
  private int boldFont;
```

(continued)

(continued)

```
  public void itemStateChanged(ItemEvent e)
  {

    if (e.getSource() == boxBold)
      if (e.getStateChange() == e.SELECTED)
        boldFont = Font.BOLD;
      else
        boldFont = Font.PLAIN;
    else
      if (e.getStateChange() == e.SELECTED)
        italicFont = Font.ITALIC;
      else
        italicFont = Font.PLAIN;

    tinField.setFont( new Font( "Courier", italicFont + boldFont, 14));
    tinField.repaint();
  }
}  // end of Check box listener class
```

Notice in this event code that the `itemStateChanged()` methods for both the Italic and Bold check boxes use an `if` statement to determine which box triggered the event. Within each `if` statement is a further `if` statement to determine whether the box has been selected or not. Based on this determination, the respective text field style property, `Font.ITALIC` and `Font.BOLD`, is either set or `Font.PLAIN` is used. If we had needed to, a statement such as `boxBold.setSelected(true);` can force the `boxBold` check box to be checked under program control.

Once the `ItemListener` class is written, the last step is to instantiate an instance of this class and register it to each individual check box in the interface. This is accomplished by the following statements:

```
ChkBoxHandler chandler = new ChkBoxHandler();
boxItalic.addItemListener(chandler);
boxBold.addItemListener(chandler);
```

To have our `ItemListener` class integrated into Program 10.6 requires placing the foregoing instantiation and registration statements either immediately before or after the similar statements used for the `exitButton` and placing the `ItemListener` class as an inner class either before or after the `exitButton`'s inner listener class. We leave this as Exercise 3. Figure 10.11 illustrates how text entered into the text area appears

FIGURE 10.11 **A sample display with both boxes checked**

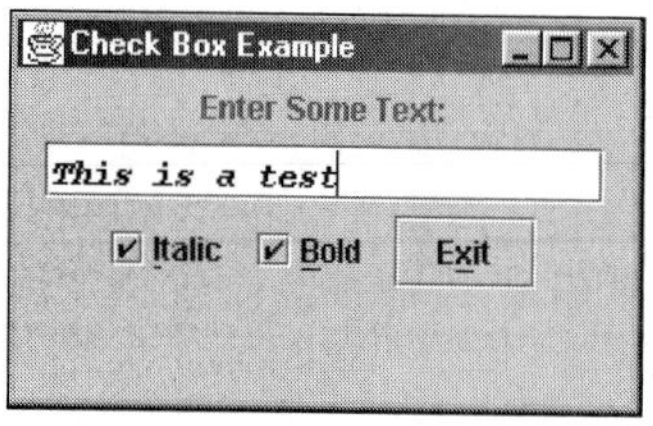

when the listener class has been implemented and both check boxes have been checked.

Radio Buttons

A group of radio button controls provides a user with a set of one or more choices, only one of which can be selected. The radio buttons in a designated group operate together, where selecting one radio button in the group immediately deselects and clears all the other buttons in the group. Thus, the choices in a radio button group are mutually exclusive. The term **radio button** was selected for these components because they operate in the same manner as the channel selector buttons on radios, where selecting one channel automatically deselects all other channels.

As an example of using radio buttons, consider a form that requires information on the marital status of an individual. As an individual can be either single, married, divorced, or widowed, selection of one category automatically means the other categories are not selected. This type of choice is ideal for a radio button group, as shown in Figure 10.12, where the group consists of four individual radio buttons.

Each radio button placed in a container, by default, forms its own group of one. To group a number of radio buttons together, you must add them into a Button-Group. The ButtonGroup is not an object that is displayed on the GUI, and it has no effect on how the radio buttons are displayed; it does, however, keep track of the internal relationship between buttons in the group. Thus, the ButtonGroup ensures only one button at a time can be selected. As an example of how a button group is created, assume that we have three radio button objects named rdbutCourier, rdbutSansSerif, and rdbutSerif. The following statements instantiate a Button-Group object named rgroup and assign each component to this group:

```
   // instantiate a ButtonGroup object
ButtonGroup rgroup = new ButtonGroup();
   // add buttons into this group
rgroup.add(rdbutCourier);
rgroup.add(rdbutSansSerif);
rgroup.add(rdbutSerif);
```

Now let's see how to create the three buttons that we have just grouped together. As an example, consider the interface shown in Figure 10.13. This interface consists of three radio buttons with the captions Courier, SansSerif, and Serif, respectively. We will use these buttons to select the style of print that is displayed in the text field.

FIGURE 10.12 **A radio button group**

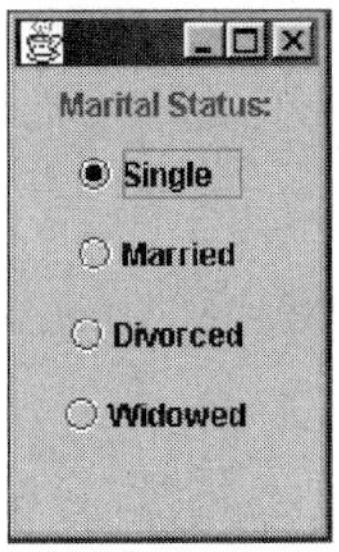

FIGURE 10.13   **An interface containing a radio button group**

Since these styles are mutually exclusive in that only one style can be operational at a given time, the choice of radio buttons for this selection is appropriate. The properties table for this interface appears in Table 10.13.

Notice in Table 10.13 that only one of the radio buttons has been selected. If an attempt is made to select more than one button in a group, only the last selection is activated. Radio buttons are constructed from JRadioButton components following the same procedure that we have used throughout this chapter for instantiating all of our Swing-based components. The specific statements that create the interface in Figure 10.13 are included in Program 10.7 and are boldfaced for easy referencing.

Table 10.13   **Figure 10.13's Interface Properties Table**

Object	Property	Setting
JFrame	Name	mainFrame
	Caption	Radio Button Example
JFrame	Name	inLabel
	Caption	Enter Some Text:
JTextField	Name	tinField
	Text	(Blank)
	Font	Courier
	Style	Font.PLAIN
	Size	12
JRadioButton	Name	rdbutCourier
	Caption	Courier
	Mnemonic	C
	Selected	true
JRadioButton	Name	rdbutSansSerif
	Caption	SansSerif
	Mnemonic	S
	Selected	false
JRadioButton	Name	rdbutSerif
	Caption	Serif
	Mnemonic	f
	Selected	false
JButton	Name	exitButton
	Caption	Exit
	Mnemonic	X

Program 10.7

```java
import javax.swing.*;
import java.awt.event.*;
import java.awt.Container;
import java.awt.*;   // need this for layout manager
public class RadioButtons extends JFrame
{
  private JFrame mainFrame;
  private JButton exitButton;
  private JLabel inLabel;
  private JTextField tinField;
  private JRadioButton rdbutCourier;
  private JRadioButton rdbutSansSerif;
  private JRadioButton rdbutSerif;

  public RadioButtons() // a constructor
  {
    mainFrame = new JFrame("Radio Button Example");

      // create all components

    exitButton = new JButton("Exit");
    inLabel = new JLabel("Enter Some Text:");
    tinField = new JTextField(20);
    rdbutCourier = new JRadioButton("Courier");
    rdbutSansSerif = new JRadioButton("SansSerif");
    rdbutSerif = new JRadioButton("Serif");

      // put the buttons into a single group
    ButtonGroup rgroup = new ButtonGroup();
    rgroup.add(rdbutCourier);
    rgroup.add(rdbutSansSerif);
    rgroup.add(rdbutSerif);

      // get the content pane
    Container c = mainFrame.getContentPane();
      // set the layout manager
    c.setLayout(new FlowLayout());

      // add the components to the ContentPane
    c.add(inLabel);
    c.add(tinField);
    c.add(rdbutCourier);
    c.add(rdbutSansSerif);
    c.add(rdbutSerif);
    c.add(exitButton);
```

(continued)

(continued)

```
      // create accelerator keys
   rdbutCourier.setMnemonic('C');
   rdbutSansSerif.setMnemonic('S');
   rdbutSerif.setMnemonic('f');
   exitButton.setMnemonic('x');

     // set the initial button and corresponding font
   rdbutCourier.setSelected(true);
   tinField.setFont(new Font("Courier", Font.PLAIN, 12));

   mainFrame.setSize(300,150);

     // define and register window event handler
   mainFrame.addWindowListener(new WindowAdapter()
   {
     public void windowClosing(WindowEvent e) {System.exit(0);}
   });

     // create and register the event handlers
   ExitButtonHandler ehandler = new ExitButtonHandler();  // instantiate a handler
   exitButton.addActionListener(ehandler);   // register the handler

   mainFrame.show();
 }

   // inner class for the Exit button event handler
 class ExitButtonHandler implements ActionListener
 {
   public void actionPerformed(ActionEvent e)
   {
     System.exit(0);
   }
 }  // end of inner class

 public static void main(String args[])
 {
   new RadioButtons();  // instantiate a GUI object
 }

}  // end of class
```

In reviewing the code within Program 10.7 that specifically relates to creating the three radio buttons, the additional steps needed for radio buttons that are not common to most other components are

■ Their inclusion into a single `ButtonGroup`

■ The use of a `setSelect()` method to initially select one of the buttons

If a `setSelect()` method were not used to initially select one of the radio buttons, none of the buttons would be selected when the GUI is first displayed. Similarly, if the buttons were not placed together into a single group, each button would individually constitute its own group and be independent of any other button. This would, of course, defeat the purpose of providing three mutually exclusive choices.

Adding a Radio Button Listener Class

As always, once a Swing-based component has been placed on a GUI, all that remains is to provide it with an appropriate listener class. The radio button listener class for Program 10.7 is listed here:

Program 10.7's Radio Button Listener Class's Event Code

```
// Listener class for the Radio button handlers
private class RButHandler implements ItemListener
{
  public void itemStateChanged(ItemEvent e)
  {

    if (e.getSource() == rdbutCourier)
        tinField.setFont(new Font("Courier", Font.PLAIN, 12));
    else if (e.getSource() == rdbutSansSerif)
        tinField.setFont(new Font("SansSerif", Font.PLAIN, 12));
    else if (e.getSource() == rdbutSerif)
        tinField.setFont(new Font("Serif", Font.PLAIN, 12));

    tinField.repaint();
  }
}  // end of inner class
```

The primary function of this listener class code is to determine which button in a group was actually selected and then to use this information appropriately. Thus, the first task handled by the listener class is to determine which button was selected. This is accomplished using a `getSource()` method and comparing the returned value to each radio button object's name. Once the selected button is identified, the code sets the font to the selected choice.

The last step in providing our GUI with a working version of the listener code is to instantiate a listener object from the class and then register it to each radio button. This can be accomplished by the following statements:

```
RButHandler rhandler = new RButHandler();
rdbutCourier.addItemListener(rhandler);
rdbutSansSerif.addItemListener(rhandler);
rdbutSerif.addItemListener(rhandler);
```

These statements should be placed either immediately before or after the `exitButton`'s registration statements. Similarly, the `ItemListener` class itself should be placed, as an inner class, either before or after the `exitButton`'s inner listener class. The integration of the listener class and activation statements into Program 10.7 is left as Exercise 6. Assuming this is done, Figure 10.14 provides an example of how user-entered text looks when the `Serif` radio button has been selected.

The text in Figure 10.14 and any subsequently entered text can now be changed by the user using the radio buttons. While the program is running, a radio button can be selected in one of the following ways:

FIGURE 10.14   **An example of user-entered text**

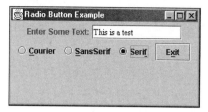

- Clicking the mouse on the desired button
- Using the accelerator keys
- Using a `setSelected()` method under program control, as for example, `butCourier.setSelected(true);`

For example, if the user clicks the <u>C</u>ourier radio button, the text will appear as in Figure 10.15.

Before leaving Program 10.7, one further comment is in order. Notice that, unlike the check box event code, no selection statement is required once the selected button has been identified. This is because a selected check box can be in one of two states, checked or unchecked, but a selected radio button, by definition, must be checked. Thus, once a radio button is selected and triggers an event, the event can be acted upon immediately, with no further processing needed to determine the button's state.

FIGURE 10.15   **The text in Courier font**

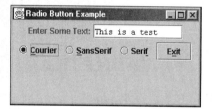

Exercises 10.4

1. Determine whether the following choices should be presented on a GUI with check boxes or with radio buttons:

   a. The choice of air conditioning or no air conditioning on a new automobile order form.

   b. The choice of automatic or manual transmission on a new automobile order form.

   c. The choice of AM/FM, AM/FM tape, or AM/FM CD radio on a new automobile order form.

   d. The choice of tape backup system or no tape backup system on a new computer order form.

   e. The choice of a 17-, 19-, or 21-inch color monitor on a new computer order form.

f.   The choice of CD-ROM drive or no CD-ROM drive on a new computer order form.

g.   The choice of a 4-, 6-, or 8-speed CD-ROM drive on a new computer order form.

h.   The choice of a 800-, 900-, or 1,000-MHz Pentium processor on a new computer order form.

2.   Enter and run Program 10.6 on your computer to verify that it correctly produces the GUI shown in Figure 10.10.

3.   Add the appropriate listener class provided in this section to Program 10.6. Compile and run your program to verify that it operates correctly.

4a. Modify the Program written for Exercise 3 so that the choices presented by the check box are replaced by two radio buttons.

b.   Based on your experience with Exercise 4a, determine what type of input choice is best presented using a check box rather than radio buttons.

5.   Enter and run Program 10.7 on your computer to verify that it correctly produces the GUI shown in Figure 10.13.

6.   Add the appropriate listener class provided in this section to Program 10.7. Compile and run your program to verify that it operates correctly.

7a. Modify Program 10.6 so that the choices presented by the check boxes are replaced by radio buttons.

b.   Based on your experience with Exercise 7a, determine what type of input choice is best presented using a check box rather than a radio button.

8a. Modify the GUI produced by Program 10.7 so that the user can additionally specify the point size for the text field. The default point size should be 10, with the user capable of choosing among 8, 10, and 12 points.

b.   Add event code to the program written for Exercise 8a to correctly handle the selection of point size.

9.   Modify Program 10.7 so that rather than selecting font type, a user can select whether to make the displayed text uppercase or lowercase using a radio button group consisting of two buttons. Make sure to include event code so that the displayed text corresponds to a user's selection. (Tip: Use the `String` class's `toUpperCase()` and `toLowerCase()` methods. For example, the expression `"abcd".toUpperCase()` creates the string `"ABCD"`.)

10.5   Keystroke Input Validation

Validating user input is an essential part of a professionally written program. For example, a professional program would not permit the input of a date such as 5/33/02, which contains an obviously invalid day. Similarly, division of any number by zero within a program, such as 14 / 0, should not be allowed. Both examples illustrate the need for **input validation** in which program code checks for improper input data before an attempt is made to process them further. We now have most of the tools to supply keystroke-by-keystroke input data validation to programs such as the temperature conversion in Program 10.5.

Table 10.14   Required KeyListener **Event Methods**

Method	Description
public void keyPressed(KeyEvent e)	This method is invoked when a key is pressed.
public void keyReleased(KeyEvent e)	This method is invoked when a key is released.
public void keyTyped(KeyEvent e)	This method is invoked when a key is typed.

Clearly, Program 10.5 expects that the user will enter a number and not a text string into the text field. If the data entered cannot be converted to numerical data, the program will crash when it attempts to convert this quantity to a Celsius temperature. In Section 10.3, an input validation technique was presented that was used just prior to using the input data within a calculation. Ideally, however, it is preferable to validate the input data either on a character-by-character basis, as each character is entered, or immediately after the input component loses focus. This latter verification is in fact one of the primary uses of the focusLost() method: to validate the data before they are passed into the system for further processing or storage. If the data do not pass their required validation, a suitable error message can be displayed, and focus immediately shifts back to the input component until valid data are entered.

In a keystroke-by-keystroke validation, each character is verified as the user enters it. Typically, this type of validation is made using either keyPressed(), keyReleased(), or keyTyped() event methods. How to perform this type of validation is presented in this section.

The three methods that can be employed in a keystroke-by-keystroke validation are listed in Table 10.14.

Each of the event methods in the table provides information about the key being activated by a user. The difference between these event methods is the amount of information provided. The keyTyped() method can only be used to supply the Unicode character of a character key, whereas the keyPressed() and keyReleased() methods can detect and process the Function, Cursor control, Enter, and Shift keys in addition to the printable character keys. Because we will need to detect when non-character keys, such as the Enter, Backspace, and Function keys, have been entered, we will need either the keyPressed() or keyReleased() methods.

As a specific example, consider the GUI shown in Figure 10.16. The properties table for this interface is listed in Table 10.15, and the class corresponding to this GUI and table is named Validation. As provided in Program 10.8, the code for this class also includes event handler objects for both the Window Closing button and the internal Exit button.

FIGURE 10.16   The GUI corresponding to Table 10.15

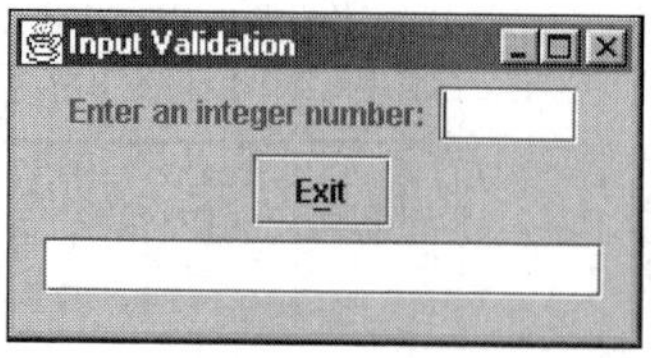

Table 10.15 The `validation` Class's Initial Properties Table

Object	Property	Setting
JFrame	Name	mainFrame
	Caption	Input Validation
JLabel	Name	inputLabel
	Caption	Enter an integer number:
JTextField	Name	inputField
	Text	(Blank)
	Size	5
JTextField	Name	messageField
	Text	(Blank)
	Size	20
JButton	Name	exitButton
	Caption	Exit
	Mnemonic	x

Program 10.8

```java
import javax.swing.*;
import java.awt.event.*;
import java.awt.Container;
import java.awt.*;  // need this for layout manager

public class Validation extends JFrame
{
  private JFrame mainFrame;
  private JButton exitButton;
  private JTextField inputField;
  private JTextField messageField;
  private JLabel inputLabel;

  public Validation() // a constructor
  {
    mainFrame = new JFrame("Input Validation");

      // create all components
    exitButton = new JButton("Exit");
    inputLabel = new JLabel("Enter an integer number:");
    inputField = new JTextField(5);
    messageField = new JTextField(20);

      // get the content pane
    Container c = mainFrame.getContentPane();
      // set the layout manager
    c.setLayout(new FlowLayout());
```

(continued)

(continued)

```
    // add the components to the ContentPane
c.add(inputLabel);
c.add(inputField);
c.add(exitButton);
c.add(messageField);

    // create accelerator keys
exitButton.setMnemonic('x');

mainFrame.setSize(250,125);

    // define and register window event handler
mainFrame.addWindowListener(new WindowAdapter()
{
    public void windowClosing(WindowEvent e) {System.exit(0);}
});

    // create and register the button event handler
ExitButtonHandler ehandler = new ExitButtonHandler();  // instantiate a handler
exitButton.addActionListener(ehandler);  // register the handler

mainFrame.show();
}

    // inner class for the exit button event handler
class ExitButtonHandler implements ActionListener
{
    public void actionPerformed(ActionEvent e)
    {
        System.exit(0);
    }
}  // end of button listener class

public static void main(String args[])
{
    new Validation();  // instantiate a GUI object
}

}  // end of class
```

For the GUI in Figure 10.16, the entered data must be an integer, which means each key pressed should either be the Enter key, the Backspace key, or correspond to a character between 0 and 9. To ensure that only numerical data are entered, we can validate each typed character and reject any keystrokes that do not result in one of the characters 0 through 9. This can be done by adding a key listener to the input-Field which monitors all key press events. Using the keyReleased() method and implementing the key listener class using an adapter class provide the following class and event header lines:

```
class InputFieldKeyHandler extends KeyAdapter
{
  public void keyReleased(KeyEvent e)
{
```

Notice that, like all listener classes, the name we have selected for our class, Input-FieldKeyHandler, is a programmer-selected name. It is now time to determine the validation code that is to be executed after each key is released.

The KeyEvent argument, which we have named e, that is passed into key-Released() provides both the character value of all printable keys as well as the codes corresponding to the nonprintable keys. The two methods needed to extract the character and code information are listed in Table 10.16.

On a very superficial plane, an invalid integer character is one that falls outside the range of 0 to 9 and can be detected by the following code:

```
keyChar = e.getChar(); // get the character
If e.getKeyChar() < '0' || e.getKeyChar() > '9' // see if an invalid key was pressed
```

Having detected an invalid key, however, we are still left with removing it from the entered string. Because our validation procedure involves directly manipulating the displayed text field string, we must also be concerned with removing a character when the user presses the Backspace key. Thus, we will have to detect the Backspace key and make adjustments to the displayed string by removing a character each time this key is released.

Finally, for completeness, there is one additional verification that we should make. Most users expect that pressing the Enter key will terminate data input. This, of course, is not the case for text fields, where the user must either press the TAB key, click another object, or use accelerator keys to move off the field. We can, however, check the value of the key just pressed to determine if it was the Enter key.

Java provides named constants for each key, both character and noncharacter, available on a keyboard. A list of the more common named constants appears in Table 10.17. It is to these constants that the key code of the last key pressed can be compared, which permits determining exactly which nonprintable key was pressed. The information in Tables 10.16 and 10.17 permits us to create a statement such as

```
if(e.getKeyCode() == VK_ENTER)
  exitButton.grabFocus();
```

This statement will cause the focus to shifted to the exitButton component whenever the last key detected was the Enter key. We will use this statement in our final validation routine.

We now have all of the pieces assembled, except for one, to create a key listener that will provide the appropriate validation that only a valid integer has been

Table 10.16   Retrieving Keystroke Character and Code Information

Method	Description	Example
getKeyChar()	Returns the character for the key typed, pressed, or released.	e.getKeyChar()
getKeyCode()	Returns a code for the key pressed or released.	e.getKeyCode()

Table 10.17 **Java Key Named Constants**

Named Constants	Key
VK_0 to VK_9	0 to 9
VK_A to VK_Z	A to Z
VK_BACK_SPACE	Backspace
VK_F1 – VK_F12	Function keys F1 to F12
VK_UP	UP ARROW key
VK_DOWN	DOWN ARROW key
VK_ENTER	Enter key
VK_TAB	TAB key
VK_SPACE	Space key
VK_PAGE_UP	PAGE UP key
VK_PAGE_DOWN	PAGE DOWN key
VK_SHIFT	Shift key
VK_ADD	+ key
VK_SUBTRACT	− key
VK_HOME	HOME key

entered into the text field box for the GUI in Figure 10.16. The algorithm for this validation is

> *Upon detection of a key release event*
>   *1. Clear any previous error messages*
>   *2. Read in the string from the text field*
>   *3. Process the last key detected as follows*
>   *If the key pressed was the Enter key*
>   *shift focus to the next component*
>   *Else If the key pressed was the Backspace key*
>   *remove the last character from the string*
>   *Else If the key is not a valid integer character*
>   *remove the last character from the string*
>   *4. Display the string in the text field*

The last remaining piece is how to correctly remove the last entered character from the input string. We do this with one of the string methods presented in Chapter 7. This is the substring() method, which has the syntax

```
stringObject.substring(starting index number, ending index number)
```

The first argument to the substring() method specifies the starting index from which characters are to be extracted (recall that the first character in a string has an index value of 0), and the ending index specifies the index that is one beyond the last character to be extracted. For example, the expression "123a".substring(0,3) yields the string value "123". This result is obtained as follows: The first argument specifies extraction is to start at index position 0, which contains the character '1'. Extraction of characters stops at one less than index position 3, which is the second argument. Thus, the extraction of characters ends at index position 2, which contains the character '3'. Hence, using the substring() method, we can remove the last entered character. This is done either because the Backspace key was pressed, indicating the user's explicit desire to erase the last entered character or because the validation code has determined that the last character is not a valid integer digit. Understanding that the class name, InputFieldKeyHandler, is a programmer-selected name and that we have chosen to construct the KeyListener using its corresponding KeyAdapter class, the completed integer validation routine is

```
// key stroke validation written as a key listener
class InputFieldKeyHandler extends KeyAdapter
{
  public void keyReleased(KeyEvent e)
  {
    int keyCode, length;
    char keyChar;
    String inputGood;

    keyCode = e.getKeyCode();    // get the integer code of the last key pressed
    keyChar = e.getKeyChar();    // get the character code of the last key pressed
                                 // when a character key is pressed

    messageField.setText("");    // clear last error message

    inputGood = inputField.getText(); // get the current string
    length = inputGood.length();
      // process the last key pressed
    if (keyCode == KeyEvent.VK_ENTER)  // shift focus
    {
      //System.out.println("Enter key was pressed");
      exitButton.grabFocus();
    }
    else if (keyCode == KeyEvent.VK_BACK_SPACE) // erase last character
    {
      //System.out.println("Backspace key was pressed");
      length = inputGood.length();
      inputGood = inputGood.substring(0, length);
      //System.out.println("length = " + length + "  input = " + inputGood);
    }
    else if (keyChar < '0' || keyChar > '9')
    {
      messageField.setText("       Invalid Character - Not Accepted");
      inputGood = inputGood.substring(0, length - 1);
      //System.out.println("length = " + length + "  input = " + inputGood);
    }

      // display the validated string
    inputField.setText(inputGood);
  }
} // end of key listener class
```

Having constructed a `KeyListener` class, the last step is to instantiate an instance of this class and register it to the `inputField` text field that we are monitoring. The following statements do this:

```
// instantiate and register the input field's key listener
InputFieldKeyHandler khandler = new InputFieldKeyHandler();
inputField.addKeyListener(khandler);
```

To integrate our `KeyListener` class into Program 10.8 requires placing the foregoing instantiation and registration statements either immediately before or after the similar statements used for the `exitButton` and placing the `KeyListener` class as an inner class either before or after the `exitButton`'s inner listener class. We leave this as Exercise 2.

Exercises 10.5

1. Enter, compile, and run Program 10.8 on your computer.

2. Add the `KeyListener` class developed in this section to Program 10.8, including the statements to instantiate a listener object, and have it registered to Program 10.8's input text field.

3a. Modify the program written for Exercise 2 so that the error message text field is disabled whenever the field is cleared of any message.

 b. Modify the program written for Exercise 3a so that the error message field has a red background and a white foreground whenever an error message is written to it.

4a. Rewrite the `KeyListener` presented in this section so that the validation routine is provided in a `public` method named `checkInteger(char keyChar, int keyCode)` that can be used by any other `KeyListener` object. Your method should be called each time a key pressed event is triggered, and the call to the method should come from the `KeyListener` code.

 b. From a practical viewpoint, why shouldn't the code for shifting focus when the Enter key is detected be included in the method written for Exercise 4a?

5. Modify the `KeyListener` class developed in this section to verify that a valid real number is being input. Such a number consists of the digits 0 through 9 and at most a single decimal point.

6a. Rewrite the `KeyListener` written for Exercise 5 so that the validation part of the listener is provided in a `public` method named `checkInteger(char keyChar, int keyCode)` that can be used by any other `KeyListener` object. Your method should be called each time a key pressed event is triggered, and the call to your method should come from the `KeyListener` code.

 b. From a practical viewpoint, why shouldn't the code for shifting focus when the Enter key is detected be included in the method written for Exercise 6a?

10.6 Common Programming Errors

The common programming errors related to the Swing-based components presented in this chapter are

1. Mistyping JTextField as JTextfield and making a similar error with both the JPassword-Field and JTextArea components. If your GUI does not display a component or an event handler does not seem to operate, you should first check that all component and method names are spelled correctly.

2. Forgetting to include a radio button into a `ButtonGroup` object. By default, each radio button forms its own group of one.

3. Creating an event handler and failing to register it. An event handler is not activated until both an object of the listener class is instantiated and the listener object is registered. If the listener object is not registered, the expected event will not be handled, which is the same result that occurs if no handler were written for the event.

10.7 **Chapter Review**

KEY TERMS

check box	input validation	layout manager
event handler	JTextArea	properties table
focus listener	JTextField	radio button
font	keyboard focus	tab sequence

SUMMARY

1. The Swing package provides a number of atomic components that can be added into a Swing-based GUI. The most common are command buttons, labels, text areas, check boxes, and radio buttons.

2. Text area components include JTextField, JPasswordField, and JTextArea controls. The first two of these components permit entry and display of a single line of text, with the JPasswordField component displaying each character as an asterisk for password protection. The JTextArea component permits entry and display of multiple lines of text.

3. In most cases, a text field has an associated label component. This is a read-only field that is created from a JLabel component.

4. A check box is a control that appears as a square box with an attached label and provides a yes-no type of selection. If multiple check boxes are used, the choice supplied by each box can be selected or not independently of any other selection. Thus, a user can select one, all, or no boxes.

5. In a radio button group, the user can select only one choice from a mutually exclusive set of choices. Here the user is presented with a list of choices from which one and only one selection can be made.

6. The placement of atomic components is determined by a container's layout managers. The default layout manager for a JFrame container is the BorderLayout. In this layout, up to five components can be placed in positions corresponding to the top, bottom, left side, right side, and middle of the container. Another layout manager can be specified using a `setLayout()` method. The other available layout managers consist of FlowLayout, GridLayout, CardLayout, BoxLayout, and GridBagLayout.

7. Once an atomic component has been placed on a GUI, it should be provided with an event handler. The steps for adding an event handler are:

> ***Step 1: Write the code for an event handler class (a listener class)***
> ***Step 2: Instantiate an instance of the listener class***
> ***Step 3: Register the listener object***

8. A properties table is a table that lists all of the components in a GUI and their associated listeners. This table is very helpful both in documenting the objects on a GUI and in providing a programmer's quick reference to the names and properties of each component.

9. When an application is run and a user is looking at the container, only one of the container's controls will have keyboard focus, or the focus for short. The control with the focus is the object that will be affected by pressing a key or clicking the mouse.

10. A focus listener is an event handling class that responds to focus-generated events. Such events are triggered whenever a component receives or loses focus.

Part Five

Additional Programming Topics

11 Additional Class Capabilities

All of the classes that we have created provide the capability to declare, initialize, assign, manipulate, and display data members. In this chapter, we add to this basic set of capabilities. First, the `this` reference, introduced in Section 2.3 is expanded upon. Specifically, we show how to use the `this` reference to permit one class method to internally call another class method. This capability will permit us to add a number of useful methods to our `Date` class. Copy constructors are then introduced that have the ability to correctly deal with reference variables. Additionally, we will also see how to extend existing classes using Java's inheritance features. Finally, we introduce abstract classes; these are classes for which objects cannot be instantiated but that can be used as the basis for other classes.

11.1 **Additional Class Features**

This section presents two additional and important features pertaining to classes. Although both are related to reference variables, they can be read independently of each other.

The `this` Reference

Except for `static` variables, which are shared by all class objects, each object, as we have seen, maintains its own set of instance variables (if necessary, review Section 2.3). This permits each object to have its own clearly defined state as determined by the values stored in its set of instance variables. For example, consider the basic `Date` class first presented in Section 5.6 and listed, for convenience, as Program 11.1.

Program 11.1

```java
import java.text.*;  // needed for formatting
public class Date
{
  // class variable declaration section
  private int month;
  private int day;
  private int year;

  // class method definition section
  public Date()   // default constructor
  {
    setDate(7, 4, 2005);
  }

  public Date(int mm, int dd, int yyyy)  // overloaded constructor
  {
    setDate(mm, dd, yyyy);
  }

  public void setDate(int mm, int dd, int yyyy) // mutator
  {
    month = mm;
    day = dd;
    year = yyyy;
  }

  public void showDate() // modified accessor
  {
    DecimalFormat df = new DecimalFormat("00");

    System.out.println(df.format(month)
              + '/' + df.format(day) + '/'
              + df.format(year % 100)); // extract the last 2 year digits
```

(continued)

(continued)

```
  }

  /* This method acts on a Date object to determine the Date's day of the week
     Parameters: none
     Return value: an integer representing a day of the week, as follows
        0 if the date is a Saturday,
        1 if the date is a Sunday,
        2 if a Monday, and so on, with a 6 being a Friday.
  */
  public int dayOfWeek()
  {
    int T, mm, dd, yy, cc;

    mm = month;
    yy = year;
    if (mm < 3)
    {
      mm = mm + 12;
      yy = yy - 1;
    }
    cc = (int)(yy/100);
    yy = yy % 100;
    T = day + (int)(26 * (mm + 1)/10) + yy;
    T = T + (int)(yy/4) + (int)(cc/4) - 2 * cc;
    dd = T % 7;
    if (dd < 0) dd = dd + 7;;
    return dd;
  }
}
```

Each time an object is created from this Date class, a distinct area of memory is set aside for its instance variables. For example, if two objects referenced by the variable names `firstDate` and `secondDate` are created from this class, the memory storage for these objects is as shown in Figure 11.1. Notice that two sets of instance variables are created, with each set having its own storage in memory.

As was noted in Section 2.3, this replication of data storage is not implemented for member methods. In fact, for each class, *only one copy of each member method is retained in memory*, and each and every object uses these same methods.

FIGURE 11.1 **The storage of two Date objects in memory**

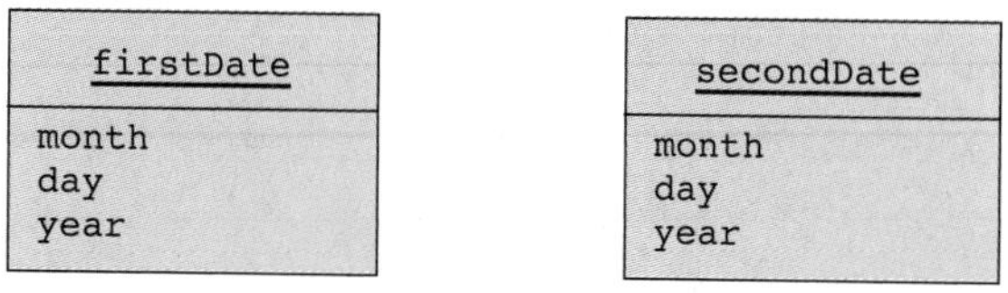

A BIT OF BACKGROUND

Artificial Intelligence

One of the major steps toward creating dynamic machines that "learn" as they work is the development of dynamic data structures.

In 1950, Alan Turing proposed a test in which an expert enters questions at an isolated terminal. Presumably, artificial intelligence (AI) is achieved when the expert cannot discern whether the answers returned to the screen have been produced by a human or by a machine. Although there are problems with the Turing test, its concepts have spawned numerous research efforts.

By the mid-1960s, many AI researchers believed the efforts to create "thinking machines" were futile. Today, however, much lively research and development focus on topics such as dynamic problem solving, computer vision, parallel processing, natural language processing, and speech and pattern recognition—all of which are encompassed within the field of artificial intelligence.

The development of techniques that allow machines to emulate humans has proliferated in recent years with the development of computers that are smaller, faster, more powerful, and less expensive. Most people agree that computers could never replace all human decision making. There is also general agreement that society must remain alert and in control of important decisions that require human compassion, ethics, and understanding.

Sharing member methods requires providing a means of identifying which specific object a member method should be operating on. This is accomplished by providing each non-`static` method with an implicit parameter, which is the object name that is used when the method is invoked. For example, using our `Date` class and assuming `firstDate` is the name of an object instantiated from this class, this object is referred to as the **implicit object,** or more formally as the *implicit parameter,* that is passed to the method. The implicit parameter tells the non-`static` method (recall that `static` methods do not use or operate on an implicit object) which object to locate and operate on.

An obvious question at this point is how this reference to the stored object is actually passed to `showDate()` and where this referencing information is stored. The answer is that the location information for the implicit object is stored in a special reference parameter named `this`, which was briefly introduced in Section 2.3. The location information passed to the **this parameter** is automatically supplied to each non-`static` member method when the method is called. That is, each member method actually receives an extra argument that permits it to locate the particular object it is to operate on. Although it is usually not necessary to do so, this extra reference argument, which can be considered a "hidden" argument, can be made explicit and used in member methods. For example, consider Program 11.2, which incorporates the `this` reference in accessing all instance variables within each member method.

Program 11.2

```java
import java.text.*;  // needed for formatting

public class Date
{
  // class variable declaration section
  private int month;
  private int day;
  private int year;

  // class method definition section
  public Date()    // default constructor
  {
    setDate(7, 4, 2005);
  }

  public Date(int mm, int dd, int yyyy)  // overloaded constructor
  {
    setDate(mm, dd, yyyy);
  }

  public void setDate(int mm, int dd, int yyyy) // mutator
  {
    this.month = mm;
    this.day = dd;
    this.year = yyyy;
  }

  public void showDate() // modified accessor
  {
    DecimalFormat df = new DecimalFormat("00");

    System.out.println(df.format(this.month)
              + '/' + df.format(this.day) + '/'
              + df.format(this.year % 100)); // extract the last 2 year digits
  }

  /* This method acts on a Date object to determine the Date's day of the week
     Parameters: none
     Return value: an integer representing a day of the week, as follows
        0 if the date is a Saturday,
        1 if the date is a Sunday,
        2 if a Monday, and so on, with a 6 being a Friday.
  */
  public int dayOfWeek()
  {
    int T, mm, dd, yy, cc;
```

```
      mm = this.month;
      yy = this.year;
      if (mm < 3)
      {
        mm = mm + 12;
        yy = yy - 1;
      }
      cc = (int)(year/100);
      yy = yy % 100;
      T = this.day + (int)(26 * (mm + 1)/10) + yy;
      T = T + (int)(yy/4) + (int)(cc/4) - 2 * cc;
      dd = T % 7;
      if (dd < 0) dd = dd + 7;
      return dd;
  }

  public static void main(String[] args)
  {
    Date firstDate = new Date();              // create two Date objects
    Date secondDate= new Date(12,18,2007);

    System.out.print("\nThe date stored in firstDate is originally ");
    firstDate.showDate();  // display the original date
    firstDate = secondDate;   // assign secondDate's value to firstDate
    System.out.print("After assignment, the date stored in firstDate is ");
    firstDate.showDate();  // display firstDate's values
    System.out.println();
  }
}
```

The output produced by Program 11.2 is

```
The date stored in firstDate is originally 07/04/05
After assignment, the date stored in firstDate is 12/18/07
```

This is the same output that would be produced by the class code in Program 11.1, which does not use the this reference to explicitly access an object's instance variables. Clearly then, using the this reference in Program 11.2 is unnecessary and simply clutters the class methods' code. There are times, however, when a method must either return a reference to the current object being processed or internally call another non-static method. In these situations, the this reference is required. In this section, we provide examples of both cases.

As an example of the first case, where one non-static method calls another non-static method, consider the Date class's dayOfWeek() method, as listed in Program 11.1. Assume that we now need to include a method that returns a boolean value of true if the day corresponds to a weekday and a boolean value of false for a day corresponding to a weekend day. Using the same algorithm as that incorporated into the dayOfWeek() method, we can easily construct this new method by using the method header line

```
public boolean isWeekDay()
```

and then use the same code as in dayOfWeek() but replace the return statement with the following if-else statement:

```
if (dd == 0 || dd == 1)
   return false; // not a week day
else
   return true; // is a week day
```

Doing so results in the following class method:

```
public boolean isWeekDay()
{
   int T, mm, dd, yy, cc;

   mm = month;
   yy = year;
   if (mm < 3)
   {
      mm = mm + 12;
      yy = yy - 1;
   }
   cc = (int)(yy/100);
   yy = yy % 100;
   T = day + (int)(26 * (mm + 1)/10) + yy;
   T = T + (int)(yy/4) + (int)(cc/4) - 2 * cc;
   dd = T % 7;
   if (dd < 0) dd = dd + 7;

   if (dd == 0 || dd == 1)
      return false; // not a week day
   else
      return true; // is a week day
}
```

In reviewing this code, notice that the complete method body, with the exception of the last if-else statement, is a repetition of the dayOfWeek()'s code. This implies that a simpler and better approach would be to call the dayOfWeek() method within the isWeekDay() method. The problem, however, is how to invoke dayOfWeek() from within isWeekDay() so that both methods operate on the same Date object. The answer is to use the this reference internally within isWeekDay().

To make this more tangible, consider a call such as firstDate.isWeekDay(). This call invokes the isWeekDay() method and tells it to operate on the Date object referenced as firstDate, which is passed to isWeekDay() as an implicit parameter. Within the method, this implicit parameter is known as the parameter named this, which can subsequently be used to call the dayOfWeek() method. Using the this reference, the isWeekDay() method can be coded as follows:

```
public boolean isWeekDay()
{
   int dd;

   dd = this.dayOfWeek(); // call dayOfWeek() with the same object that
                          // is used to call isWeekDay()
```

```
    if (dd == 0 || dd == 1)
     return false;
    else
     return true;
}
```

The key statement within this code is the call to dayOfWeek() using the expression this.dayOfWeek(). This statement both invokes the dayOfWeek() method and tells it to operate on the object referenced by the this parameter, which is the same object that was used to invoke isWeekDay(). Thus, no matter which object is used when the call to isWeekDay() is made, the same object, now referenced as this, will also be used in the call to dayOfWeek().

Program 11.3 illustrates using this new method, assuming that it has been included in Program 11.1's Date class.

Program 11.3

```
public class CheckDay
{
  public static void main(String[] args)
  {
    Date firstDate = new Date(9, 26, 2003); // a Friday
    Date secondDate = new Date(9, 27, 2003); // a Saturday

    firstDate.showDate();
    if (firstDate.isWeekDay())
      System.out.println("  is a week day.");
    else
      System.out.println("  occurs on a week end.");

    secondDate.showDate();
    if (secondDate.isWeekDay())
      System.out.println("  is a week day.");
    else
      System.out.println("  occurs on a week end.");
  }
}
```

Following is the output produced by Program 11.3:

```
09/26/03
  is a week day.
09/27/03
  occurs on a week end.
```

As this output correctly shows, the first date corresponds to a weekday (it is a Friday), and the second date occurs on a weekend (it is a Saturday).

Memberwise Assignment

In Chapter 2, we saw how Java's assignment operator, =, performs assignment between variables. Here we illustrate how assignment works when it is applied to objects. For a specific assignment example, reconsider Program 11.2's main() method.

Notice that the `Date` class's method definition section contains no assignment method. The assignment statement `firstDate = secondDate;` in `main()` causes the object referenced by firstDate to be the same as that referenced by secondDate. This is verified by the following output, which is produced whenever Program 11.2 is executed:

```
The date stored in firstDate is originally 07/04/05
After assignment the date stored in firstDate is 12/18/07
```

The type of assignment illustrated in Program 11.2 performs a shallow copy similar to that performed on section arrays (see Section 8.2). Before considering the problems that can occur with reference data members, let's see how to construct our own explicit assignment method that performs a deep copy, which is also referred to as a *memberwise assignment* copy.

An assignment method, like all class methods, must be defined in the class's method definition section. For our specific purposes, we will name our method `setEqual()` and provide it with a `Date` parameter. Using this information, a possible method definition is

```
public void setEqual(Date newdate)
{
    day = newdate.day;      // assign the day
    month = newdate.month;   // assign the month
    year = newdate.year;    // assign the year
}
```

In the header line for this method, the keyword `void` indicates that the method will not return a value, and the parameter name that we have arbitrarily given to `newdate` has been correctly declared as a `Date` object type. Within the body of the method, the `day` member of the `newdate` object is assigned to the `day` member of the object that is referenced when the method is called, which is then repeated for the `month` and `year` members. A statement such as `firstDate.setEqual(second-Date);` can then be used to call the method and assign `secondDate`'s member values to the `Date` object named `firstDate`. Program 11.4 contains our assignment method within the context of a complete program. For ease of reading, the `day-OfWeek()` method has been omitted from the `Date` class's definition.

Except for the addition of the `setEqual()` method and the omission of the `day-OfWeek()` method, Program 11.4 is identical to Program 11.2 and produces the same output. Its usefulness is in illustrating how we can explicitly construct our own assignment methods.

Two potential problems exist with the `setEqual()` method as it is currently implemented. As written, our simple assignment method returns no value, which precludes using it in making multiple assignments, such as `a.setEqual(b.setEqual(c))`. To provide for this type of method call, which is referred to as both a **cascading** and **concatenated call,** our method must declare that it will return a reference to a `Date` type and then include a `return` statement consistent with the declaration. Providing the correct return type is easily handled by returning the `this` reference, which returns a reference to the current object being processed. Program 11.5 incorporates these changes in its `setEqual()` method. Within the `main()` method, a cascading method invocation is created using the expression `a.setEqual(b.setEqual(c))`, where a, b, and c have been defined as `Date` objects.

Program 11.4

```java
import java.text.*;  // needed for formatting
public class Date
{
  // class variable declaration section
  private int month;
  private int day;
  private int year;

// class method definition section
  public Date(int mm, int dd, int yyyy) // constructor
  {
    month = mm;
    day = dd;
    year = yyyy;
  }

  public void setEqual(Date newdate)
  {
    day = newdate.day;        // assign the day
    month = newdate.month;    // assign the month
    year = newdate.year;      // assign the year
  }

  public void showDate()
  {
    DecimalFormat df = new DecimalFormat("00");

    System.out.print(df.format(month)
                    + '/' + df.format(day) + '/'
                    + df.format(year % 100));
  }

  public static void main(String[] args)
  {
    Date firstDate = new Date(04,01,2005); // create two Date objects
    Date secondDate = new Date(12,18,2007);

    System.out.print("\nThe date stored in firstDate is originally ");
    firstDate.showDate();       // display the original date
    firstDate.setEqual(secondDate);   // assign secondDate's value to firstDate
    System.out.print("\nAfter assignment the date stored in firstDate is ");
    firstDate.showDate();  // display firstDate's values
    System.out.println();
  }
}
```

Program 11.5

```java
import java.text.*;  // needed for formatting
public class Date
{
  // class variable declaration section
  private int month;
  private int day;
  private int year;

  // class method definition section
  public Date(int mm, int dd, int yyyy) // constructor
  {
    month = mm;
    day = dd;
    year = yyyy;
  }

  public Date setEqual(Date newdate)
  {
    day = newdate.day;      // assign the day
    month = newdate.month;  // assign the month
    year = newdate.year;    // assign the year

    return this;
  }

  public void showDate()
  {
    DecimalFormat df = new DecimalFormat("00");

    System.out.print(df.format(month)
                     + '/' + df.format(day) + '/'
                     + df.format(year % 100));
  }

  public static void main(String[] args)
  {
    Date a = new Date();            // create three Date objects
    Date b = new Date(12,18,2007);
    Date c = new Date(04,01,2009);

    System.out.println("\nThe initial dates are:");
    a.showDate();   system.outprintIn();
    b.showDate();   system.outprintIn();
    c.showDate();
    a.setEqual(b.setEqual(c)); // here is the cascading call
```

```
        System.out.println("\nAfter assignment, the dates are:");
        a.showDate();    system.outprintIn();
        b.showDate();    system.outprintIn();
        c.showDate();
    }
}
```

The output produced when Program 11.5 is compiled and run is

```
The initial dates are:
07/04/05
12/18/07
04/01/09

After assignment, the dates are:
04/01/09
04/01/09
04/01/09
```

As this output verifies, the setEqual() method correctly returns a Date type that can be used as an argument within a cascading call.

The remaining problem with our setEqual() method is that it provides what is called a **shallow copy.** What this means, why it is only a problem when an object contains a reference variable, and how to deal with it are presented in Section 11.4.

Exercises 11.1

1. Enter and run Program 11.1 on your computer.

2. Enter and run Program 11.2 on your computer.

3. Write a program to test Program 11.1's dayOfWeek() method. In testing this method, select at least seven different dates, where each date corresponds to a different day of the week.

4a. Include the code for the isWeekDay() method within Program 11.1's Date class.

  b. Test the modified class constructed for Exercise 4a using the following seven dates: 12/25/03 is a Thursday, 12/26/03 is a Friday, 12/27/03 is a Saturday, 12/28/03 is a Sunday, 12/29/03 is a Monday, 12/30/03 is a Tuesday, and 12/31/03 is a Wednesday.

5. Construct a Date class method named isWeekEnd() that returns a boolean value of true if the Date object corresponds to a Saturday or Sunday and a boolean value of false for all weekdays. You method should call the isWeekDay() method presented in this section.

6a. Construct a Date class method named dayName() that returns a string containing the name of the day corresponding to the day of the week returned by Program 11.1's dayOfWeek() method.

    b.   Test the method constructed for Exercise 6a using at least seven different dates, where each date corresponds to a different day of the week.

    c.   Modify Program 11.2 to use the `dayName()` method to identify the name of the days used in the program.

7.   Enter and run Program 11.3 on your computer.

8.   Enter and run Program 11.4 on your computer.

9.   Enter and run Program 11.5 on your computer.

11.2   Additional Applications

In this section, we present a complete simulation that uses two separate classes. The first class models a gas pump, and the second class models the arrival of a customer and various requests for differing amounts of gas to be pumped. The complete simulation is based on the following requirement:

> *We have been requested to write a program that simulates the operation of a gas pump. At any time during the simulation, we should be able to determine, from the pump, the price per gallon of gas and the amount remaining in the supply tank from which the gas is pumped. If the amount of gas in the supply tank is greater than or equal to the amount of gas requested, the request should be filled; otherwise, only the available amount in the supply tank should be used. Once the gas is pumped, the total price of the gallons pumped should be displayed, and the amount of gas in gallons that was pumped should be subtracted from the amount in the supply tank.*
>
> *For the simulation, assume that the pump is randomly idle for 1 to 15 minutes between customer arrivals and that a customer randomly requests between 3 and 20 gallons of gas. Although the default supply tank capacity is 500 gallons, assume that the initial amount of gas in the tank for this simulation is only 300 gallons. Initially, the program should simulate a one-half-hour time frame.*
>
> *Additionally, for each arrival and request for gas, we want to know the idle time before the customer arrived, how many gallons of gas were pumped, and the total price of the transaction. The pump itself must keep track of the price per gallon of gas and the amount of gas remaining in the supply tank. Typically, the price per gallon is $1.50, but the price for the simulation should be $1.35.*

Application 1: A Single-Class Gas Pump Simulation

In analyzing this problem, first notice that it involves two distinct object types. The first is a person who can arrive randomly between 1 and 15 minutes and can randomly request between 3 and 20 gallons of gas. The second object type is the gas pump. In this application, our goal will be to create a suitable gas pump class that can be used in the final simulation, which is completed in the next application.

The model for constructing a gas pump class that meets the requirements of the simulation is easily described in pseudocode as

Put Pump in Service
  Initialize the amount of gas in the supply tank
  Initialize the price per gallon of gas

Display Values
  Display the amount of gas in the supply tank
  Display the price per gallon

Pump an Amount of Gas
  If the amount in the supply tank is greater than or equal to the requested amount
      Set the pumped amount of gas equal to the requested amount
  Else
      Set the pumped amount equal to the amount in the supply tank
  EndIf
  Subtract the pumped amount from the amount in the supply tank
  Calculate the total price as the price per gallon times the pumped amount
  Display the gallons of gas requested
  Display the gallons of gas pumped
  Display the amount remaining in the supply tank
  Display the total price for the amount of gas pumped

From the pseudocode description, the implementation of a `Pump` class is rather straightforward. The attributes of interest for the pump are the amount of gallons in the supply tank and the price per gallon. The required operations include supplying initial values for the pump's attributes, interrogating the pump for its attribute values, and satisfying a request for gas. The UML diagram for this class is shown in Figure 11.2.

Because the two attributes—the amount in the tank and the price per gallon—can have fractional values, it is appropriate to make them double-precision values. Additionally, three services need to be provided. The first consists of initializing a pump's attributes, which consists of setting values for the amount in the supply tank and the price per gallon. The second consists of satisfying a request for gas, and the

FIGURE 11.2   The `Pump` class UML diagram

```
                          Pump

 -amtInTank: double
 -price: double
 -AMOUNT_IN_TANK: static double = 500.0;
 -DEFAULT_PRICE : static double = 1.50;

 +Pump()
 +Pump(amtInTank, price)
 +request(gallons)
 +getValues()
```

third service simply provides a reading of the pump's current attribute values. A suitable class definition that provides these services is

```java
import java.text.*;    // needed for formatting
public class Pump
{
  // class variable declaration section
  private double amtInTank;
  private double price;
  private static final double AMOUNT_IN_TANK = 500.0;
  private static final double DEFAULT_PRICE = 1.50;

  // class method definition section
  public Pump()  // this is the default constructor
  {
    amtInTank = AMOUNT_IN_TANK;
    price = DEFAULT_PRICE;
  }

  public Pump(double start, double todaysPrice)  // an overloaded constructor
  {
    amtInTank = start;
    price = todaysPrice;
  }

  public void getValues()
  {

    DecimalFormat num = new DecimalFormat("$##.00");

    System.out.println("\nThe gas tank has " + amtInTank
                       + " gallons of gas.");
    System.out.println("The price per gallon of gas is "
                       + num.format(price) + ".");
  }

  public void request(double pumpAmt)
  {
    double pumped;

    DecimalFormat num = new DecimalFormat("$##.00");

    if (amtInTank >= pumpAmt)
      pumped = pumpAmt;
    else
      pumped = amtInTank;

    amtInTank -= pumped;
    System.out.println();
```

```
System.out.println(pumpAmt + " gallons were requested.\n"
                + pumped + " gallons were pumped.\n"
                + amtInTank + " gallons remain in the tank.");
System.out.println("The total price for the pumped gas is "
                + num.format(pumped * price) + ".");
     }
}
```

We can analyze this class by individually inspecting both its data and method members. First, notice that we have declared four data members and four member methods. As `private` members, the data attributes can only be accessed through the class's member methods: `Pump()`, `getValues()`, and `request()`. It is these methods that provide the external services available to each `Pump` object.

The two `Pump()` methods, which have the same name as their class, are the constructor methods, one of which will be automatically called when an object of type `Pump` is created. For both constructors, when a `Pump` object is declared, it will be initialized to a given amount of gas in the supply tank and a given price per gallon. If no values are given, the default constructor will use the default values of 500 gallons and $1.50 per gallon.

The `getValues()` method is a modified accessor method that provides a readout of the current attribute values. The `request()` method is the most complicated because it provides the primary `Pump` service. The code follows the requirement that the pump provides all of the gas required unless the amount remaining in the supply tank is less the requested amount. Finally, it subtracts the amount pumped from the amount in the tank and calculates the total dollar value of the transaction.

To test the `Pump` class requires testing each class operation. To do this, consider Program 11.6.

Program 11.6

```
public class TestPump
{
  public static void main(String[] args)
  {
    Pump a = new Pump(300,1.35);
    Pump b = new Pump();     // use the default constructor's values
    a.getValues();
    a.request(30);
    a.request(280);
    b.getValues();
  }
}
```

Notice that in Program 11.6 we have constructed the test program as its own class, separate from the class being tested. Our program assumes that the `Pump` class has been compiled and resides in the same folder as the `TestPump` class. If this were not the case, we would have to include an `import` statement for the `Pump` class at the top of the program (see Appendix F for how this can be accomplished using packages).

Within the `main()` method, six statements are included. The first two statements create two objects of type `Pump`. The supply tank for the first `Pump` object contains 300 gallons and the price per gallon is set to $1.35, while the second `Pump` object uses the default values `AMOUNT_IN_TANK` and `DEFAULT_PRICE`, which are 500 and $1.50, respectively.

    A call is then made to `getValues()` to display the first pump's attribute values. The next statement is a request for 30 gallons of gas from the first `Pump` object. This is followed by a request for 280 gallons, which exceeds the remaining gas in the supply tank. Finally, the attribute values for the second pump are displayed. The output produced by Program 11.6 is

```
The gas tank has 300.0 gallons of gas.
The price per gallon of gas is $1.35.


30.0 gallons were requested.
30.0 gallons were pumped.
270.0 gallons remain in the tank.
The total price for the pumped gas is $40.50.


280.0 gallons were requested.
270.0 gallons were pumped.
0.0 gallons remain in the tank.
The total price for the pumped gas is $364.50.


The gas tank has 500.0 gallons of gas.
The price per gallon of gas is $1.50.
```

Application 2: A Multiclass Gas Pump Simulation

Having constructed a `Pump` class to model the operation of a gas pump in the previous application, we can now use this class within the context of a complete simulation. We do so by first providing a `Customer` class and then controlling the interaction between these two classes using a `main()` method.

    In constructing the complete simulation program, we again assume that the code for the `Pump` class is stored in the same directory as all remaining classes written for this simulation. Once this is done and the `Pump` class has been compiled, it will automatically be accessed by any program in the same directory that attempts to use it. For documentation purposes, however, the statement `import Pump;` can be included at the top of the program.

The Customer

For this simulation, there are multiple instances of customers arriving randomly between 1 and 15 minutes and requesting gas in amounts that vary randomly between 3 and 20 gallons. From an object viewpoint, however, we are not interested in storing the arrival and number of gallons requested by each customer. We simply need a `Customer` object to present us with an arrival time and a request for gas in gallons. Thus, our `Customer` object type need have no attributes but must provide two operations. The first operation, which we will name `arrival()`, provides a random arrival time between 1 and 15 minutes. The second operation, which we will call `gallons()`, provides a random request of between 3 and 20 gallons of gas. The UML class diagram for this class is presented in Figure 11.3.

FIGURE 11.3 The `Customer` class UML diagram

```
┌─────────────────────────────────────────────┐
│                 Customer                      │
├─────────────────────────────────────────────┤
│                                               │
├─────────────────────────────────────────────┤
│  +arrival()                                   │
│  +request(amtInTank, price)                   │
└─────────────────────────────────────────────┘
```

The actual class implementation can be coded as

```java
public class Customer
{
  // class variable declaration section
  // no class variables needed

  // class method definition section
  public Customer() {} // this is a default do-nothing constructor

  public int arrive()
  {
    return (1 + (int)(Math.random() * 14));
  }

  public int gallons()
  {
    return (3 + (int)(Math.random() * 17));
  }
}
```

In reviewing this code, notice that the class constructor is a do-nothing constructor that can be omitted with no effect on the class. The real purpose of the class is to provide the two member methods, `arrive()` and `gallons()`, which create a random arrival time for a new customer and a request for a random number of gallons to be dispensed (review Section 6.8 if you are unfamiliar with the `Math.random()` method). The `arrive()` method returns a random integer between 1 and 15, and the `gallons()` method returns a random integer between 3 and 20 (we leave it as Exercise 5 for you to rewrite the `gallons()` method to return a noninteger value).

Again, for later convenience in writing the complete simulation program, assume that the code for the `Customer` class is placed in the same directory as the `Pump` class.

Having analyzed and defined the two classes that we will be using, we still need to analyze and define the logic to correctly control the interaction between `Customer` and `Pump` objects for a valid simulation. In this particular case, the only interaction between a `Customer` object and a `Pump` object is that a customer's arrival, followed by a request, determines when the `Pump` is activated and how much gas is requested. Thus, each interaction between a `Customer` and a `Pump` can be expressed by the pseudocode

> *Obtain a Customer arrival time*
> *Obtain a Customer request for gas*
> *Activate the Pump with the request*

Although this repetition of events takes place continuously over the course of a day, we are only interested in a one-half-hour period. Therefore, we must place these three events in a loop that is executed until the required simulation time has elapsed.

Having developed and coded the two required classes, `Pump` and `Customer`, what remains to be developed is the control logic within the `main()` method for correctly activating class events. This will require a loop controlled by the total arrival time for all customers. A suitable control structure for `main()` is described by the algorithm

> *Create a Pump object with the required initial supply of gas*
> *Display the values in the initialized Pump*
> *Set the total time to 0*
> *Obtain a Customer arrival time // first arrival*
> *Add the arrival time to the total time*
> *While the total time does not exceed the simulation time*
>   *Display the total time*
>   *Obtain a Customer request for gas*
>   *Activate the Pump with the request*
>   *Obtain a Customer arrival time // next arrival*
>   *Add the arrival time to the total time*
> *EndWhile*
> *Display a message that the simulation is over*

Java code corresponding to this algorithm is listed as Program 11.7.

Program 11.7

```java
public class PumpSimulation
{
  private final static double SIMTIME = 0.5;   // simulation time in hours
  private final static int MINUTES = 60;       // number of minutes in an hour

  public static void main(String[] args)
  {
    Pump firstPump = new Pump(300, 1.35);   // declare 1 object of type Pump
    Customer customer = new Customer();     // declare 1 object of type Customer

    int totalTime = 0;
    int idleTime;
    int amtRequest;
    int SimMinutes;  // simulation time in minutes

    SimMinutes = (int) (SIMTIME * MINUTES);
    System.out.println("\nStarting a new simulation - simulation time is "
                  + SimMinutes + " minutes.");
    firstPump.getValues();
```

```
        // get the first arrival
     idleTime = customer.arrive();
     totalTime += idleTime;

     while (totalTime <= SimMinutes)
     {
       System.out.println("\nThe idle time is " + idleTime + " minutes,"
                     + " and we are " + totalTime
                     + " minutes into the simulation.");
       amtRequest = customer.gallons();
       firstPump.request((double)(amtRequest));

         // get the next arrival
       idleTime = customer.arrive();
       totalTime += idleTime;
     }
     System.out.println("\nThe idle time is " + idleTime + " minutes."
             + "\nAs the total time now exceeds the simulation time, "
             + "this simulation run is over.");

   }
}
```

Assuming that the `Pump` and `Customer` classes have been thoroughly tested and debugged, testing and debugging Program 11.7 are really restricted to testing and debugging the `main()` method. This specificity of testing is precisely one of the advantages of an object-oriented approach. Using previously written and tested class definitions allows us to focus on the remaining code that controls the flow of events between objects, which in Program 11.7 centers on the `main()` method.

By itself, the `main()` method in Program 11.7 is a straightforward `while` loop where the `Pump` idle time corresponds to the time between customer arrivals. The output of a sample run, shown next, verifies that the loop is operating correctly.

```
Starting a new simulation - simulation time is 30 minutes.

The gas tank has 300.0 gallons of gas.
The price per gallon of gas is $1.35.

The idle time is 2 minutes, and we are 2 minutes into the simulation.

18.0 gallons were requested.
18.0 gallons were pumped.
282.0 gallons remain in the tank.
The total price for the pumped gas is $24.30.

The idle time is 3 minutes, and we are 5 minutes into the simulation.

17.0 gallons were requested.
17.0 gallons were pumped.
265.0 gallons remain in the tank.
The total price for the pumped gas is $22.95.
```

The idle time is 11 minutes, and we are 16 minutes into the simulation.

16.0 gallons were requested.
16.0 gallons were pumped.
249.0 gallons remain in the tank.
The total price for the pumped gas is $21.60.

The idle time is 6 minutes, and we are 22 minutes into the simulation.

18.0 gallons were requested.
18.0 gallons were pumped.
231.0 gallons remain in the tank.
The total price for the pumped gas is $24.30.

The idle time is 4 minutes, and we are 26 minutes into the simulation.

10.0 gallons were requested.
10.0 gallons were pumped.
221.0 gallons remain in the tank.
The total price for the pumped gas is $13.50.

The idle time is 13 minutes.
As the total time now exceeds the simulation time, this simulation run is over.

Exercises 11.2

1. Compile the `Pump` class provided in this section.

2. Enter and run Program 11.6 on your computer.

3. Enter and run Program 11.7 on your computer.

4. In place of the `main()` method used in Program 11.7, a student proposed the following:

```
public static int main(String[] args)
{
  Pump a = new Pump(300, 1.00);   // declare 1 object of type Pump
  Customer b = new Customer();     // declare 1 object of type Customer
  int totalTime = 0;
  int idleTime;
  int amtRequest;
  int SimMinutes;   // simulation time in minutes

  SimMinutes = (int) (SIMTIME * MINUTES);
  System.out.println("\nStarting a new simulation - simulation time is "
                    + SimMinutes + " minutes.");
  firstPump.getValues();

  while (true)   // always true
```

```
{
    idleTime = customer.arrive();
    totalTime += idleTime;
    if (totalTime > (SIMTIME * MINUTES))
    {
        System.out.println("\nThe idle time is " + idleTime + " minutes."
                + "\nAs the total time now exceeds the simulation time, "
                + "this simulation run is over.");
        break;
    }
    else
    {
        System.out.println("\nThe idle time is " + idleTime + " minutes"
                            + " and we are " + totalTime
                            + " minutes into the simulation.");
        amtRequest = customer.gallons();
        firstPump.request((double)(amtRequest));
    }
}
}
```

Determine if this `main()` method produces a valid simulation. If it does not, discuss why not. If it does, discuss which version you prefer and why.

5. Modify the `Customer` class's `gallons()` method to return a floating-point number between 3.0 and 20.0. The value should be rounded to the closest tenth before being returned.

6. Using the `Elevator` class defined in Section 6.8 and defining a new class named `Person`, construct a simulation whereby a `Person` randomly arrives at any time from 1 to 10 minutes on any floor and calls the elevator. If the elevator is not on the floor that the person is on, it must move to that floor. Once inside the elevator, the person can select any floor except the current one. Run the simulation for three randomly arriving people and have the simulation display the movement of the elevator.

11.3 **Class Inheritance**

The ability to create new classes from existing ones is the underlying motivation and power behind class and object-oriented programming techniques. Doing so facilitates reusing existing code in new ways without the need for retesting and validation. It also permits the designers of a class to make the class available to others for additions and extensions without relinquishing control over the basic class's features.

Constructing one class from another is accomplished using a capability called inheritance. Related to this capability is an equally important feature named polymorphism. Polymorphism provides the ability to redefine how methods of related classes operate based on the object being referenced. In fact, for a programming language to be classified as an object-oriented language, it must provide the features of classes, inheritance, and polymorphism. In this section, we describe the inheritance and polymorphism features provided in Java.

FIGURE 11.4   **Relating object types**

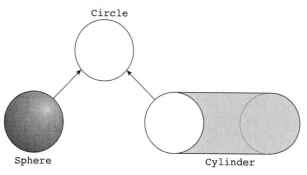

Inheritance

Inheritance is the capability of deriving one class from another class. The initial class that forms the basis for the derived class is referred to as either the **base**, *parent*, or *superclass*. The derived class is referred to as either the **derived**, *child*, or *subclass*.

A derived class is a completely new class that incorporates all of the variables and methods of its base class. It can, and usually does, however, add its own new data and method members and can override any base class method. As an example of inheritance, consider three geometric shapes consisting of a circle, cylinder, and sphere. For these shapes, we can make the circle a base type for the other two shapes (Figure 11.4). Reformulating these shapes as class types, we would make the circle the base class and derive the cylinder and sphere classes from it.

The relationships illustrated in Figure 11.4 are examples of simple inheritance. In **simple inheritance**, each derived type has only one immediate base type. The complement to simple inheritance is multiple inheritance. In **multiple inheritance**, a derived type has two or more base types. Figure 11.5 presents an example of multiple inheritance, which is not supported in Java.

FIGURE 11.5   **An example of multiple inheritance**

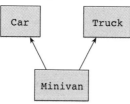

The class derivations in Figures 11.4 and 11.5 are formally referred to as **class hierarchies** because they illustrate the hierarchy, or order, in which one class is derived from another. Let's now see how to derive one class from another.

A derived class has the same form as any other class in that it consists of both variable and method members. The only difference is in the header line for the class. For a derived class, this line is extended to include a base class name and has the syntax

```
public class  derivedClassName extends baseClassName
```

For example, if `Circle` is the name of an existing class, a new class named `Cylinder` can be derived as follows:

```
public class Cylinder extends Circle
{
    // add any additional variable declarations and
    // method definitions in here
}
```

Except for the keyword `extends` and the base class name, there is nothing inherently new or complicated about the construction of the `Cylinder` class. Before providing a description of the `Circle` class and adding data and method members to the derived `Cylinder` class, we need to reexamine visibility specifications and how they relate to derived classes.

Visibility Specifications

Until now, we have only used `private` and `public` visibility specifications within a class. Giving all instance variables `private` visibility ensures that they can only be accessed by a class's methods. This restricted access prevents access by any nonclass methods, which also precludes access by any derived class's methods. This is a sensible restriction because if it did not exist, anyone could "jump around" the `private` designation simply by deriving a class.

To retain a restricted type of access across derived classes, Java provides a third visibility specification: `protected`. `protected` visibility behaves identically to `private` visibility within a class, but it permits this restriction to be inherited by any derived class. Thus, a `protected` visibility is essentially a `private` visibility that can be extended into a derived class.

An Example

To illustrate the process of deriving one class from another, we will derive a `Cylinder` class from a base `Circle` class. The definition of the `Circle` class is

```
public class Circle
{
    // class variable declaration section
    public final static double PI = 2.0 * Math.asin(1.0);
    protected double radius;

    // class method definition section
    public Circle(double r)   // constructor
    {
        radius = r;
    }

    public double calcval()    // this calculates an area
    {
        return(PI * radius * radius);
    }
}
```

Except for the substitution of the visibility specifier `protected` in place of the usual `private` specification for the class's variables, this is a standard class definition. Notice also the declaration of the constant `PI`, which is used later in the `calcval()` method. This is defined as

```
public final static double PI = 2.0 * Math.asin(1.0);
```

This is a "trick" that forces the computer to return the value of PI accurate to as many decimal places as allowed by your computer. This value is obtained by taking the arcsin of 1.0, which is $\pi / 2$, and multiplying the result by 2. The keyword static ensures that this value is calculated and stored only once per class, and the keyword final ensures that the value cannot be changed by any subsequent method. Finally, the keyword public makes this value accessible by any and all methods within or external to the class.

Having defined our base class, we can now extend it by a derived class. The definition of the derived class is

```java
public class Cylinder extends Circle  // Cylinder is derived from Circle
{

  // class variable declaration section
  protected double length;  // add an additional data member

  // class method definition section
  public Cylinder(double r, double l)
  {
    super(r);
    length = l;
  }

  public double calcval()   // this calculates a volume
  {
    return (length * super.calcval()); // note the base method call
  }
}
```

This definition encompasses several important concepts relating to derived classes. First, as a derived class, Cylinder contains all of the variable and method members of its base class, Circle, plus any additional members that it may add. In this particular case, the Cylinder class consists of a radius data member, inherited from the Circle class, plus an additional length member. Thus, each Cylinder object contains *two* data variables, as illustrated in Figure 11.6. As a public class, Cylinder must be stored in its own source file named Cylinder.java.

In addition to having two data members, the Cylinder class also inherits both Circle's symbolic constant PI and its method members. This is illustrated in the

FIGURE 11.6   **The relationship between Circle and Cylinder data members**

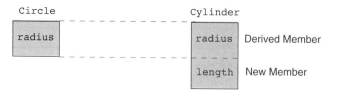

Cylinder constructor, which uses the reserved word super. When this keyword is used by itself and with zero or more arguments, it refers to a base class's constructor having the matching argument list. Notice that the Cylinder's calcval() method also makes a call to one of its base class's methods using the keyword super. Here the expression super.calcval() refers to the base class version of the calcval() method.

In both classes, the same method name, calcval(), has been specifically used to illustrate the overriding of a base method by a derived method. When a Cylinder object calls calcval(), it is a request to use the Cylinder version of the method, whereas a Circle object call to calcval() is a request to use the Circle version. In this case, the Cylinder class can still access the Circle class's version of calcval() using the keyword super. Program 11.8 uses the Cylinder class within the context of a complete program. Assuming that the Circle class source file exists in the same directory as the Cylinder class source file, and that both classes have been compiled, the output produced by Program 11.8 is[1]

```
The area of circleOne is 3.141592653589793
The area of circleTwo is 12.566370614359172
The volume of cylinderOne is 113.09733552923255
```

This output is straightforward and is produced by the first three println() calls in the program. As the output shows, a call to calcval() using a Circle object activates the Circle version of this method, and a call to calcval() using a Cylinder object activates the Cylinder version.

Program 11.8

```java
public class Cylinder extends Circle  // Cylinder is derived from Circle
{

  // class variable declaration section
  protected double length;  // add an additional data member

  // class method definition section
  public Cylinder(double r, double l)
  {
    super(r);
    length = l;
  }

  public double calcval()    // this calculates a volume
  {
    return (length * super.calcval()); // note the base method call
  }
```

(continued)

---

[1] If the Circle class source file does not exist in the same directory, an import statement, as described in Appendix F, must be included in the Cylinder source code.

```
(continued)
 public static void main(String[] args)
 {
    Circle circleOne = new Circle(1);  // create two Circle objects
    Circle circleTwo = new Circle(2);
    Cylinder cylinderOne = new Cylinder(3,4);      // create one Cylinder object

    System.out.println("The area of circleOne is " + circleOne.calcval());
    System.out.println("The area of circletwo is " + circleTwo.calcval());
    System.out.println("The volume of cylinderOne is " + cylinderOne.calcval());
 }
}
```

Abstract Classes and Interfaces

An abstract class is a class that *can only* be used as a base class for another class; that is, no objects of an **abstract class** can be instantiated. A class becomes an abstract class by including the keyword `abstract` in the class's header.

Typically, an abstract class will contain one or more **abstract methods**, which are methods that have a header line but no body. For example, the following is an example of an abstract method:

```
abstract public String message(int item);
```

Notice that this header line includes the keyword `abstract` and is terminated with a semicolon rather than containing a well-defined method body. What the method header does, as always, is to provide a name for the method, any parameters required by the method, and the type of data, if any, that must be returned. It will be up to any class that is derived from the abstract class to define the method's body in a way that is consistent with the header line in using all of the designated parameters and returning the correct data type if a non-`void` return type is specified. Thus, an abstract methods is essentially a placeholder that requires all derived classes to override and complete the method.

Any class that contains at least one abstract method *must be* declared as an abstract class. This ensures that an object cannot be instantiated from such a class, which would contain an incomplete method. However, an abstract class is not restricted to including only abstract methods, and it may include any number and combination of abstract and nonabstract (i.e., completed) methods. A class is declared as abstract by including the keyword `abstract` in the class's header line. For example, the class header line

```
abstract public class Ergy
```

declares the `Ergy` class as abstract. This has the practical effect of ensuring that no objects can be instantiated from this class and that the intention is to make this a base class that can be used in the creation of a derived class. Any nonabstract class derived from an abstract class must, however, override all of the abstract class's abstract methods. Because of this requirement, abstract methods *cannot* be declared as either `static` or `final`.

An interface consists of constants and abstract methods only and has the general syntax

```
interface interfaceName
{
    constant declarations;
    abstract method declarations;
}
```

All abstract methods declared in an interface must be `public` and `abstract`; thus, these two keyword modifiers can be omitted in the method header lines. Similarly, because constants declared in an interface must be `public` and `final`, they need not be explicitly designated as such. For example, assume that the following declaration was in an interface

```
double FACTOR = 0.23;
```

By default, this declaration is actually

```
public final double FACTOR = 0.23;
```

and can be explicitly declared as such.

A class that is derived from an interface indicates it is doing so by using the keyword `implements` followed by the interface's name. The general syntax for this derivation is

```
class className implements interfaceName
{
    override definitions of all abstract methods;
}
```

Because all constants declared in an interface are effectively numbers, they can only be stored in variables within a derived class that have been declared as the same data type as the constant. Therefore, for the constant FACTOR to be used within a derived class in a statement, such as

```
steelFactor = FACTOR;
```

the variable `steelFactor` would have to be declared, not unexpectedly, as a double-precision variable.

Polymorphism

The overriding of a base member method using an overloaded derived member method, as illustrated by the `calcval()` method in Program 11.8, is an example of polymorphism. **Polymorphism** permits the same method name to invoke one response in objects of a base class and another response in objects of a derived class. The determination of which overloaded method is actually called is made at run time, when the call statement is encountered, and is based on the object making the call. This type of selection is referred to as **run-time binding,** *late binding,* and *dynamic binding* (the terms are synonymous). By default, Java uses late binding in all method calls. This type of binding means that the object being operated on ultimately determines the appropriate method to be called and is required for a language to implement true polymorphic behavior.

In contrast to late binding is **compile-time binding**, in which the method that will actually be called is set at compile time. This type of binding, which is also referred to as both *static* and *early binding*, is the default binding technique used in languages that do not support true polymorphic behavior. Such early binding can be forced in Java by making a method `final`.

FIGURE 11.7 **Sample inheritance diagrams**

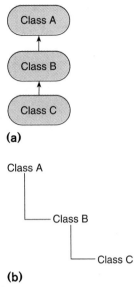

(a)

(b)

Inheritance Diagrams

The hierarchy diagrams that were introduced in Chapter 1 and that we have been using throughout the text are one type of inheritance diagrams, where an *inheritance diagram* illustrates the relationship between a base class and one or more derived classes. As shown in Figure 11.7, these diagrams can be drawn in a number of ways, but *a base class is always drawn at the top of the diagram and a derived class is drawn under its base class.* In this sense, the figure can be slightly misleading because the base class, upon which all other classes are built, is placed at the top of the figure rather than at its bottom, or base.

Figures 11.7a and 11.7b illustrate the relationship between three classes, which are named A, B, and C. In both cases, class A is the parent class to class B, which in turn is the parent class to class C. In Figure 11.7a, the relationship is indicated by level, with derived classes placed underneath base classes. In Figure 11.7b, which is the standard hierarchy diagram format we have been using throughout this text, a parent/child relationship is implied by location and indentation, with a child class always indented and placed below its parent class.

As a further example of a hierarchy diagram, Figure 11.8 illustrates the relationship of the `DecimalFormat` Java class to the `java.lang.Object` class. As indicated

FIGURE 11.8 **The `DecimalFormat` inheritance hierarchy**

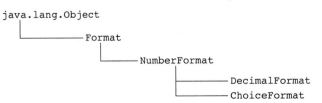

in this figure, this class's base class is the `NumberFormat` class. The figure also shows that the `ChoiceFormat` class is derived from this same base class.

Exercises 11.3

1. Define the following terms:

a. inheritance

b. base class

c. derived class

d. simple inheritance

e. multiple inheritance

f. class hierarchy

g. polymorphism

h. late binding

i. dynamic binding

j. early binding

2. What three features must a programming language provide for it to be classified as an object-oriented language?

3a. Describe the two methods Java provides for implementing polymorphism.

b. Which of the two methods in Exercise 3a qualifies a language to be a true object-oriented language and why is this the case?

4. Describe the difference between a `private` and a `protected` class member.

5a. Rewrite Program 11.8 to create a derived class named `Sphere` from the base `Circle` class. The only additional class members of `Sphere` should be a constructor and a `calcval()` method that returns the volume of the sphere. (*Note: volume = 4 / 3 π radius³*)

b. Include the class constructed for Exercise 5a in a working Java program. Have your program call all of the member methods in the `Sphere` class.

6a. Create a base class named `Point` that consists of an *x* and *y* coordinate. From this class, derive a class named `Circle` having an additional data member named `radius`. For this derived class, the *x* and *y* data members represent the center coordinates of a circle. The method members of the first class should consist of a constructor, an area method named `area` that returns zero, and a `distance()` method that returns the distance between two points, where

$$distance = \sqrt{(x2 - x1)^2 + (y2 - y1)^2}$$

In addition, the derived class should have a constructor and an override method named `area` that returns the area of a circle.

b. Include the classes constructed for Exercise 6a in a working Java program. Have your program call all of the member methods in each class. In addition, call the base class `distance()` method with two `Circle` objects and explain the result returned by the method.

7a. Using the classes constructed for Exercise 6a, derive a class named `Cylinder` from the derived `Circle` class. The `Cylinder` class should have a constructor and a member method named `area()` that determines the surface area of the `Cylinder`. For this method, use the algorithm *surface area = 2 π r (l + r)*, where *r* is the radius of the cylinder and *l* is the length.

b. Include the classes constructed for Exercise 7a in a working Java program. Have your program call all of the member methods in the `Cylinder` class.

c. What do you think might be the result if the base class `distance()` method was called using two `Cylinder` objects?

8a. Create a base class named `Rectangle` that contains `length` and `width` data members. From this class, derive a class named `Box` having an additional data member named `depth`. The method members of the base `Rectangle` class should consist of a constructor and an `area()` method. The derived `Box` class should have a constructor and an override method named `area()` that returns the surface area of the box and a `volume()` method.

b. Include the classes constructed for Exercise 8a in a working Java program. Have your program call all of the member methods in each class and explain the result when the `area()` method is called using two `Box` objects.

11.4 Reference Variables as Class Members[2]

A class's instance variables can be declared using any valid Java data type, and we have seen a number of examples that have included reference variables, the majority of which were string types. Thus, the inclusion of a reference variable should not be unfamiliar. In some cases, however, using reference data members can result in seemingly strange behavior for the unwary.

For example, assume that we need to store a list of book titles, with each stored as a string. Such an arrangement appears in Figure 11.9, which shows two objects, `book1` and `book2`, each of which consists of a single reference data member. As depicted, object `book1`'s single data member references the title `Windows Primer`, and object `book2`'s data member references `A Brief History of Western Civilization`.

A declaration for a class data member used to store a title, as illustrated in Figure 11.9, could be

```
private String title;   // a reference to a book title
```

The definition of the constructor method, `Book()`, and the display method, `showTitle()`, are defined in the method definition section as

```
// class method definition section
public Book(String booktitle)  // constructor
{
  title = booktitle;
}

public void showTitle()
{
  System.out.println("The title is " + title);
}
```

---

[2] This topic can be omitted on first reading without loss of subject continuity.

FIGURE 11.9 Two objects containing reference data members

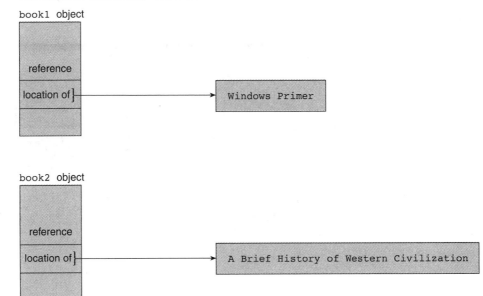

The body of the Book() constructor contains a single statement that initializes an object's title data member to the string provided when a Book object is instantiated. The showTitle() method is an accessor method that displays the string value stored in the title data member.

Program 11.9 illustrates this class within the context of a complete program. Notice that it is in the main() method that the book1 and book2 objects are instantiated.

Program 11.9

```
public class Book
{
  // class variable declaration section
  private String title;

  // class method definition section
  public Book(String booktitle)  // constructor
  {
    title = booktitle;
  }

  public void showTitle()
  {
    System.out.println("The title is " + title);
  }
```

(continued)

```
(continued)
  public static void main(String[] args)
  {
    Book book1 = new Book("Windows Primer");
    Book book2 = new Book("A Brief History of Western Civilization");

    book1.showTitle();
    book2.showTitle();
  }
}
```

The output displayed by Program 11.9 is

```
The title is Windows Primer
The title is A Brief History of Western Civilization
```

Figure 11.10a illustrates the arrangement of references and allocated memory produced by Program 11.9 just before it completes execution. Now consider Program

FIGURE 11.10a   **Before the assignment book2 = book1;**

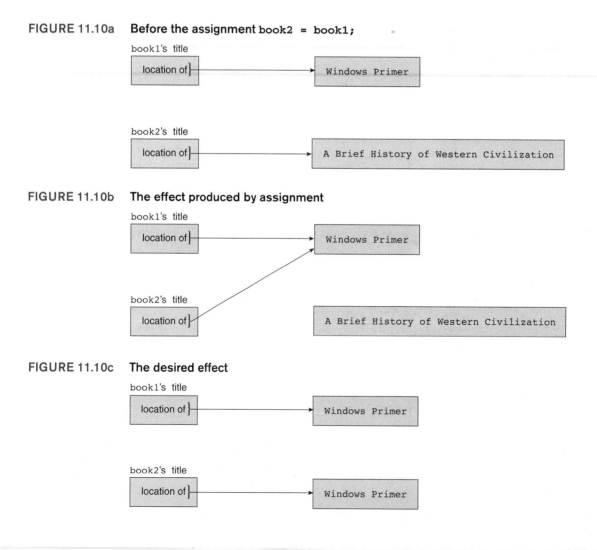

FIGURE 11.10b   **The effect produced by assignment**

FIGURE 11.10c   **The desired effect**

11.10, which is essentially the same as Program 11.9 with one major modification: We have inserted the assignment statement `book2 = book1;` into the `main()` method. As we know from Section 11.1, this assignment produces a memberwise copy that copies the value in the `book1` reference variable into the `book2` reference variable. The consequence of this shallow copy is that both reference variables now reference the `Book` object that contains the string `Windows Primer`, and the reference to the title `A Brief History of Western Civilization` has been lost.[3] This situation is illustrated in Figure 11.10b.

Program 11.10

```java
public class Book
{
  // class variable declaration section
  private String title;


  // class method definition section
  public Book(String booktitle)   // constructor
  {
    title = booktitle;
  }

  public void showTitle()
  {
    System.out.println("The title is " + title);
  }

  public static void main(String[] args)
  {
    Book book1 = new Book("Windows Primer");
    Book book2 = new Book("A Brief History of Western Civilization");

    book1.showTitle();
    book2.showTitle();

    book2 = book1;
    System.out.println("\nAfter assignment");
    book1.showTitle();
    book2.showTitle();
  }
}
```

---

[3] See Sections 8.2 and 11.1 for a review of shallow copies.

The output produced by Program 11.10 is

```
The title is Windows Primer
The title is A Brief History of Western Civilization

After assignment
The title is Windows Primer
The title is Windows Primer
```

This output is produced because both the `book1.title` and `book2.title` reference variables refer to the same `String` object (Figure 11.10b). Because the memberwise assignment illustrated in this figure results in the loss of the location of `A Brief History of Western Civilization`, the memory allocated to this string will ultimately be released by Java's automatic garbage collection system.

Unlike the effect produced by Program 11.10, what is usually desired is that the book titles themselves be copied, as shown in Figure 11.10c, and that their references be left alone. Because `String` objects cannot be copied, we have two solutions to the problem. The easiest and preferred solution is to use `StringBuffer` class objects rather than `String` objects because the `StringBuffer` class does permit copying and overwriting of existing string values. The second method uses a workaround that essentially performs a **deep copy.** This is accomplished by first creating a new `String` object and then adjusting references so that the `book2.title` reference variable correctly points to the newly created string (as in Figure 11.10c) rather than pointing to the `book1` string (as in Figure 11.10b). To achieve this desired assignment, we must explicitly write our own assignment method. A suitable definition for this method is

```
public void setEqual(final Book oldbook)
{
  Book temp = new Book(oldbook.title);  // create a new Book object
  title = temp.title;
}
```

This definition first creates a new `Book` object having the same value as the object that is passed into it. The word `final` in the parameter list ensures that the method itself cannot alter the passed object. The method first instantiates a new `Book` object and then assigns the reference to this newly instantiated object to the reference of the object used in making the call. Thus, for example, a call such as `book2.set Equal(book1)` creates the arrangement in Figure 11.11. Here, as shown in

FIGURE 11.11a Create a new object and reference

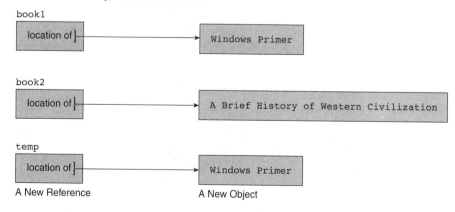

FIGURE 11.11b   **Adjust book2's reference value**

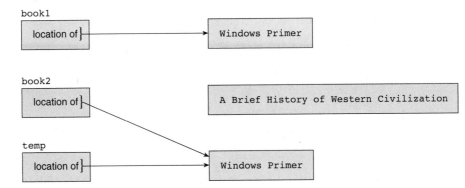

Figure 11.11a, a new object is first created that contains the string Windows Primer. This object and its reference are created by the statement temp Book = new Book(book1.title). The statement title = temp.title then produces the situation shown in Figure 11.11b. Here the book2.title reference variable now correctly points to its own distinct String object. Program 11.11 includes this setEqual() method within the Book class and uses this class within the context of a complete program.

Program 11.11

```
public class Book
{
  // class variable declaration section
  private String title;

   // class method definition section
  public Book(String booktitle)  // constructor
  {
    title = booktitle;
  }

  public void setEqual(final Book oldbook)
  {
    Book temp = new Book(oldbook.title);  // create a new Book object
    title = temp.title;
  }

  public void showTitle()
  {
    System.out.println("The title is " + title);
  }
```

(continued)

(continued)

```
public static void main(String[] args)
{
    Book book1 = new Book("Windows Primer");
    Book book2 = new Book("A Brief History of Western Civilization");

    book1.showTitle();
    book2.showTitle();

    book2.setEqual(book1);
    System.out.println("\nAfter assignment");
    book1.showTitle();
    book2.showTitle();
}
}
```

The output produced by Program 11.11 is

```
The title is Windows Primer
The title is A Brief History of Western Civilization

After assignment
The title is Windows Primer
The title is Windows Primer
```

Although this output is the same as that produced by Program 11.10, it is now produced because each reference variable, `book1.title` and `book2.title`, points to its own distinct `String` object.

Exercises 11.4

1. Compile Program 11.9 and run the program to verify its operation.

2a. Compile and run Program 11.10 on your computer.

  b. Compile and run Program 11.11 on your computer.

  c. Although Programs 11.10 and 11.11 produce the same result, identify the difference between them.

3a. Construct a class named `Car` that contains the following four data members: a double-precision variable named `engineSize`, a character variable named `bodyStyle`, an integer variable named `colorCode`, and a string named `vinNum` for a vehicle identification number. The method members should include a constructor and a display method that prints the engine size, body style, color code, and vehicle identification number.

  b. Include the class written for Exercise 3a in a working Java program that creates two `Car` objects and displays the objects' values.

4. Modify the program written for Exercise 3 to include a method that assigns the values of one `Car` object to a second `Car` object. Your method should perform the assignment so that each reference variable refers to a distinct object in memory and not the same string value.

5. Using Program 11.9 as a model, write a program that creates five `Book` objects. The program should allow the user to enter the five book titles interactively and then display the entered titles.

6. Modify the program written in Exercise 5 so that it sorts the entered book titles in alphabetical order before it displays them. (*Tip:* You will have to define a sort routine for the titles.)

11.5 Common Programming Errors

The more common programming errors associated with the class capabilities presented in this chapter are:

1. Forgetting to use the `this` reference when calling one non-`static` method from within a non-`static` method.
2. Forgetting to make instance variables `protected` if you intend to use the class as a base class.
3. Using a user-defined assignment operator in a multiple assignment expression when the operator has not been defined to return an object.
4. Performing a memberwise copy of instance variables with a variable that is a reference when a deep copy of the item being referenced is desired. A memberwise copy produces a copy of the value in the reference, not a copy of the object being referenced.

11.6 Chapter Review

KEY TERMS

abstract class	concatenated call	multiple inheritance
abstract method	deep copy	polymorphism
base class	derived class	run-time binding
cascading call	implicit object	shallow copy
class hierarchy	inheritance	simple inheritance
compile-time binding	interface	`this` parameter

SUMMARY

1. For each class, only one copy of each member method is created, and each object uses the same method. The location of the object's data members is provided to the member method by using a reference argument named `this`. The `this` reference may be used explicitly by a member method to access an object's instance variables or as an implicit parameter in calling another non-`static` class method.
2. A programmer-created assignment method may be included within a class. Such methods are typically only required when a class declares reference instance variables. This is because the default assignment operation will perform a shallow copy of reference values rather than a deep copy.
3. A shallow copy occurs when two reference variables both locate one and the same object.
4. A deep copy occurs when two reference variables locate two distinct objects, where both objects contain the same information.

5. Inheritance is the capability of deriving one class from another class. The initial class used as the basis for the derived class is referred to as either the base, parent, or superclass. The derived class is referred to as either the derived, child, or subclass.

6. A class hierarchy is a description of the order in which one class is derived from another.

7. Polymorphism permits the same method to invoke different responses based on the object making the method call.

8. In early binding, the determination of which method will be invoked is made at compile time. In late binding, the determination is made at run time.

12 Files

The data for the programs we have seen so far have either been assigned internally within the programs or entered interactively during program execution. This type of data entry works well for small amounts of data.

In this chapter, we present how to store data outside a program using Java's object-oriented capabilities. This external data storage permits a program to use the data without the user having to re-create them interactively each time the program is run. This also provides the basis for sharing data between programs so that the data output by one program can be input directly to another program.

12.1 Files and Streams

To store and retrieve data on a file in Java, two items are required:

1. A file
2. A file stream object

Files

Any collection of data that is stored together under a common name on a storage medium other than the computer's main memory is called a **data file**. Typically, data files are stored on a disk, magnetic tape, or CD-ROM. For example, the Java programs that you store on disk are examples of files. These particular files are referred to as *program files* and consist of the program code that becomes input data to the Java compiler.

A file is physically stored on an external medium, such as a disk, using a unique file name referred to as the **external file name**. The external file name is the name of the file as it is known by the operating system. It is the external name that is displayed when the operating system displays the contents of a directory or folder.

Each computer operating system has its own specification as to the maximum number of characters permitted for an external file name. Table 12.1 lists these specifications for the more common operating systems.

To ensure that the examples presented in this text are compatible with all of the operating systems in Table 12.1, we will generally, but not exclusively, adhere to the more restrictive DOS and VMX specifications. If you are using an operating system that permits longer names, you should take advantage of the increased length specification to create more descriptive file names. The selected name, however, should always be a manageable length, which is typically considered to be no more than 12 to 14 characters, with an outside maximum of 25 characters. Very long file names should be avoided. Although such names can be extremely descriptive, they take more time to type and are prone to typing errors.

Using the DOS convention, the following are all valid computer data file names:

```
prices.dat      records       info.txt
exper1.dat      scores.dat    math.mem
```

Table 12.1   **Maximum Allowable File Name Characters**

Operating System	Maximum Length
DOS	8 characters plus an optional period and 3-character extension
VMX	8 characters plus an optional period and 3-character extension
Windows 95, 98, 2000	255 characters
UNIX	
Early versions	14 characters
Current versions	255 characters

A BIT OF BACKGROUND

Privacy, Security, and Files

Data files have been around a long time, mainly on paper stored in filing cabinets. Terms such as *open*, *close*, *records*, and *lookup* that we use in handling computer files are reminders of older techniques for accessing paper files stored in drawers.

Today, most files are stored electronically, and the amount of information that is collected and stored proliferates wildly. Because it is easier to transit bits and bytes than to ship paper folders, increasingly serious problems of security have arisen with concerns over people's privacy.

Whenever an individual fills out a government form or a credit application, submits a mail order, applies for a job, writes a check, or uses a credit card, an electronic data trail is created. Each time those files are shared among government agencies or private enterprises, the individual loses more of his or her privacy.

In order to help protect U.S. citizens' constitutional rights, the Fair Credit Reporting Act was passed in 1970, followed by the Federal Privacy Act in 1974. These acts specify that it is illegal for a business to keep secret files, that you are entitled to examine and correct any data collected about you, and that government agencies and contractors must show justification for accessing your records. Efforts continue to create mechanisms that will serve to maintain an individual's security and privacy.

Computer file names should be chosen to indicate both the type of data in the file and the application for which it is used. Frequently, the first eight characters describe the data themselves, and an extension (the characters after the decimal point) describes the application. For example, the Excel® spreadsheet program automatically applies an extension of `xls` to all spreadsheet files, Microsoft's Word® and Corel's WordPerfect® word processing programs use the extensions `doc` and `wpx` (where `x` refers to the version number), respectively, and Java compilers require a program file to have the extension `java`. When creating your own file names, you should adhere to this practice. For example, using the DOS convention, the name `exper1.dat` is appropriate in describing a file of data corresponding to experiment number 1.

File Stream Objects

A **file stream** is a one-way transmission path that is used to connect a file stored on a physical device, such as a disk or CD-ROM, to a program. Each file stream has its own mode, which determines the direction of data on the transmission path—that is, whether the path will move data from a file into a program or whether the path will move data from a program to a file. A file stream that receives or reads data from a file into a program is referred to as an **input file stream**. A file stream that sends or writes

PROGRAMMING NOTE

Input and Output Streams

A *stream* is a one-way transmission path between a source and a destination. What gets sent down this transmission path is a stream of bytes. A good analogy to this "stream of bytes" is a stream of water that provides a one-way transmission path of water from a source to a destination.

Two stream objects that we have already used extensively are the input stream object named `System.in` and the output stream object named `System.out`. The `System.in` object provides a transmission path from keyboard to program, whereas the `System.out` object provides a transmission path from program to terminal screen. The `System.in` stream object is an instance of `java.io.BufferedInputStream`, which is a subclass of `java.io.InputStream`. The `System.out` object is an instance of `java.io.PrintStream`, which is a subclass of `java.io.OutputStream`. These two stream objects are automatically declared and instantiated by the Java compiler for use by the compiled program.

File stream objects provide essentially the same capabilities as the `System.in` and `System.out` objects, but they connect a program to a file rather than to the keyboard or terminal screen. In addition, file stream objects must be explicitly instantiated.

data to a file is an **output file stream**. Notice that the direction, or mode, is always defined in relation to the program and not the file; data that go into a program are considered input data, and data sent out from the program are considered output data. Figure 12.1 illustrates the data flow from and to a file using input and output file streams.

For each file that your program uses, a distinct file stream object must be created. If you are going to read and write to a file, both an input and output file stream object are required. Depending on where the file is stored and whether data in the file are stored as character-based or byte-based values, the specific stream objects will be created from different classes. Table 12.2 lists the most common file stream classes for input and output from both **character-based**, which are also known as **text files**, and **byte-based files**. A detailed description of these two file types is provided in Section 12.9. Briefly, however, the characters and numbers stored in a byte-based file use the same binary code as specified by Java for its primitive data types, whereas character-based files store each individual letter, digit, and special symbols such as the decimal point and dollar sign using an individual character code. This permits such files to be read by either a word processing program or text editor.

FIGURE 12.1   **Input and output file streams**

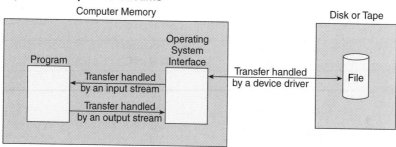

Table 12.2 **Basic I/O Stream Class Usage**

Mode	For a Character-Based File	For a Byte-Based File
Input	Use a `FileReader` class	Use a `FileInputStream` class
Output	Use a `FileWriter` class	Use a `FileOutputStream` class

For example, if you need to read data from a character-based file, the information in Table 12.2 indicates that you would use Java's `FileReader` class to create an input stream object. Similarly, for writing to a byte-stream file, the appropriate output stream object should be created from Java's `FileOutputStream` class.

Creating a file stream object is almost a cookbook procedure in which a physical communications path is established between a program and an external data file. This path defines both the direction of data transfer and the capabilities provided by the stream for data conversions and the buffering of data between a program and a file.

An input file stream object automatically attempts to open its associated file in read mode. This means that data in the file can be read by the program, and the file is referred to as an **input file**. An explicit check is usually made, using techniques presented at the end of the next section, to ensure that a file intended for reading actually exists before an input stream attempts to open it.

An output file stream can open its associated file in one of two ways: write or append. When the output stream opens a file for writing, which is the default, the file is made available for accepting data from the program, and the file is referred to as an **output file**. If a file exists with the same name as a file opened for writing, the old file is erased. For this reason, an explicit check is usually also made on output files, using techniques presented in Section 12.6, to alert the user to this possibility before a file is opened.

A file opened for appending makes an existing file available for data to be added to the end of the file. If the file opened for appending does not exist, a new file with the designated name is created and made available to receive output from the program. The only difference between a file opened in write mode and one opened in append mode is where the data are physically placed in the file. In write mode, the data are written starting at the beginning of the file, whereas in append mode, the data are written starting at the end of the file. For a new file, the two modes are identical.

As a specific example, let's take a moment to see how an object stream is created in practice. Assume that we wish to read data from an existing character-based file named `prices.txt`. Figure 12.2 illustrates the structure of the input stream necessary for reading the file. The complete stream begins at the file and ends at the program.

FIGURE 12.2 **A `FileReader` input stream**

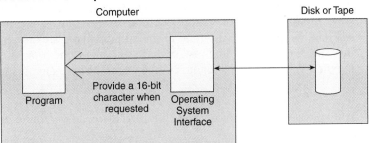

Using the information in Table 12.2, we see that to read data from a character-based file, we can construct the basic input stream object to connect the file to the program from the `FileReader` class. Arbitrarily selecting the reference variable name `fr` for our input stream object, the following code creates the necessary input file stream object:

```
// set up the basic input stream
FileReader fr = new FileReader("prices.txt");
```

Notice that this declaration statement both creates an input stream and causes the `prices.txt` file to be opened for reading. Because the specific details of establishing this physical communications link between the program and data file are handled by Java and the operating system and are transparent to the program, the programmer need not consider them, except for ensuring that the link is successfully established. In practice, you will frequently see this declaration statement written over two lines as

```
FileReader fr =
    new FileReader("prices.txt");
```

and we will use the single-line and double-line forms throughout this chapter.

Besides establishing the actual physical connection between a program and a data file, the instantiated file stream created by this declaration equates the file's external computer name to the reference variable name used internally by the program. From a programming perspective, this is of primary importance because once the `fr` stream object has been created, the program will access the file using the reference variable name `fr`, while the computer's operating system continues to know the file by the name `prices.txt`. As an object created from the `FileReader` class, the program can now use this class's methods to read data from the file. For example, the statement

```
fr.read()
```

causes the next character from the `prices.txt` file to be read.

In a similar manner, character-based output stream objects can be created from the `FileWriter` class. For example, the statement

```
FileWriter fw =
    new FileWriter("backup.txt");
```

creates a character-based output stream object to a file named `backup.txt`. When an output stream object is created, a file with the given external name is automatically created by the operating system, whether or not such a file name already exists. If a file with the given external name does exist, *it will be erased* and a new empty file with the same name is created in its stead. Thus, any data in the original file are automatically lost. It is precisely to prevent erasing an existing file that you should always check if a file exists before opening it for output. Once the new file is created, any data written by the program to the output stream are automatically placed in the new file. For the preceding instantiation statement, the program accesses this file using the reference variable name `fw`. For example, a statement such as

```
fw.write('a');
```

will cause the appropriate code for the lowercase letter `a` to be placed on the `backup.txt` file.

It should be noted that character-based streams created from the `FileReader` and `FileWriter` classes always transmit characters as 16-bit data. For the majority of current computers that use 8-bit file systems, however, which are typically based on the ASCII code, these 16-bit data are encoded and stored as 8-bit ASCII characters using the computer's default character-encoding scheme (this is explained more fully in Section 12.9).

Because the stream objects created from the basic I/O classes listed in Table 12.2 (for both character-based and byte-based files) are restricted to byte-processing capabilities, the basic input and output stream objects created from these classes are almost always enclosed into other stream objects that provide expanded capabilities. These expanded streams are referred to as *processing streams* because of the additional processing capabilities that they provide. Processing stream objects that are created from `FileReader` and `FileWriter` stream objects are presented in Section 12.2, where character-based file processing is described in detail. Similarly, processing stream objects that are created from `FileInputStream` and `FileOutputStream` stream objects are presented in Section 12.3, where byte-based file processing is described in detail. In all cases, the construction of an expanded processing stream object requires that a basic stream object is first created from one of the classes listed in Table 12.2.

Closing a Stream Object

A file stream object is closed using its class's **`close()`** method. This method closes the basic I/O stream object and all processing streams created from it. For example, the statement

```
fw.close();
```

closes the object stream named `fw`. As indicated, the `close()` method takes no argument.

Since all operating systems have a limit on the maximum number of files that can be accessed at one time, closing stream objects that are no longer needed makes good sense. Any open streams existing at the end of normal program execution are automatically closed.

Buffering

Every time a byte or sequence of bytes is written to or read from a file, a call to the underlying operating system is required. Because the number of accesses to a file storage medium, such as a disk, and the resulting operating system calls can be significantly reduced by **buffering**, this type of transfer is used for almost all file transfers. How buffering is conceptually constructed for transferring data between a program and a data file is illustrated in Figure 12.3.

As illustrated in Figure 12.3, when transferring data between a program and a file using a buffered stream, the buffered stream provides a storage area that is used by the data as they are transferred between the program and the file. In most cases, a buffered stream will provide enhanced I/O speed and performance.

From its side, the program either writes a set of data bytes to the buffered stream or reads a set of data bytes from the stream. On the file side of the stream, the transfer of data between the device storing the actual data file (usually a tape, disk, or CD-ROM drive) and the stream is handled by special operating system programs that

FIGURE 12.3   **The data transfer mechanism**

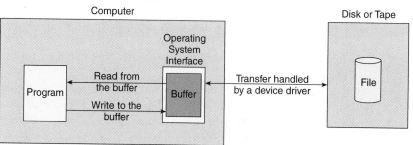

are referred to as *device drivers.*[1] Typically, a disk device driver will only transfer data between the disk and stream buffer in fixed sizes, such as 1,024 bytes at a time. Thus, the stream buffer provides a convenient means of permitting a device driver to transfer data in blocks of one size while the program can access them using a different size (typically as individual characters or as a fixed number of characters per line).

Buffered object streams are created from buffered stream classes. The creation of a buffered stream, however, always requires the prior creation of a basic I/O stream object from one of the stream classes listed in Table 12.2. That is, you cannot create a buffered stream object without first creating a basic I/0 stream object. Except for one case used to illustrate unbuffered file I/O presented at the end of Section 12.2, all of the file examples in this chapter use buffered streams. The actual construction of such streams is presented in Section 12.2 for character-based files and Section 12.3 for byte-based files.

Exercises 12.1

1. Using the reference manuals provided with your computer's operating system, determine the maximum number of characters that can be used to name a file for storage by your computer system.

2. Would it be appropriate to call a saved Java program a file? Why or why not?

3a. What are the basic input and output stream classes used for constructing input and output stream objects for use with a character-based file?

 b. What are the basic input and output stream classes used for constructing input and output stream objects for use with a byte-based file?

4. Write suitable Java statements to create individual input streams named `fr` for each of the following character-based files: `inData.txt`, `prices.txt`, `coupons.dat`, and `results.mem`.

---

[1] Device drivers are not stand-alone programs but are an integral part of the operating system. Essentially, the device driver is a section of operating system code that accesses a hardware device, such as a disk unit, and handles the data transfer between the device and the computer's memory. Thus, it must correctly synchronize the speed of the data transferred between the computer and the device sending or receiving the data. This is because the computer's internal data transfer rate is generally much faster than any device connected to it.

5. Write suitable Java statements to create individual output streams named `fw` for each of the following character-based files: `outData.txt`, `prices.txt`, `coupons.dat`, and `results.mem`.

6. Write suitable Java statements to create individual input streams named `fis` for each of the following byte-based files: `inData`, `distance`, `rates.dat`, and `coupons.dat`.

7. Write suitable Java statements to create individual output streams named `fos` for each of the following byte-based files: `outData`, `distance`, `rates.dat`, and `coupons.dat`.

8. Write individual statements to create appropriate stream objects for the following external data files:

External Name	File Type	Stream Name	Mode
`coba.mem`	text	`memo`	input
`book.let`	text	`letter`	input
`coupons.bnd`	text	`coups`	output
`yield.bnd`	byte-based	`yield`	input
`test.dat`	byte-based	`inFile`	output
`rates.dat`	byte-based	`outFile`	output

9. Write `close()` statements for each of the file stream objects created in Exercise 8.

12.2 Reading and Writing Character-Based Files

Reading and writing character-based files involve almost the identical operations used for reading input from a keyboard and writing data to a display screen. For writing to a character-based file, a `FileWriter` stream object (see Table 12.2) provides the basic stream object that connects a file to a program.

As was described in Section 12.1, however, `FileWriter` output stream objects are extremely restrictive in that they only provide the capability to write a character at a time from a file. For this reason, the additional processing stream classes listed in Table 12.3 are provided. Each of these classes provides extensions to a `FileWriter` stream object that can be used both to enhance performance and improve data transfer capabilities. It is important to realize, however, that an expanded output stream object cannot be created without first constructing a basic `FileWriter` input stream object. This is because all expanded character-based output streams are built around

Table 12.3 Character-Based Output Stream Classes

Class	Type	Comments	Common Methods
`FileWriter`	Basic Output	Basic stream used for character-based output.	`write()`, `flush()`, `close()`
`BufferedWriter`	Buffering	Provides output buffering, which typically improves performance.	`write()`, `flush()`, `close()`
`PrintWriter`	Processing	Provides a number of useful output methods.	`flush()`, `close()`, `print(char)`, `print(String)`, `print(int)`, `print(float)`, `print(double)`, `print(boolean)`, and corresponding `println()` methods

and based on a `FileWriter` stream object. So this basic stream object must always be created first. As this is the first time we will be creating an expanded set of stream objects, we will individually present and explain each required declaration. For a specific example, assume that we want to open an output stream to a text file named `prices.txt`. For this, the following code can initially be used:

```
// set up the basic output stream
FileWriter fw =
    new FileWriter("prices.txt");
```

Notice that we have selected `fw` as the reference variable name to reference a `FileWriter` object that will be connected to the external file named `prices.txt`. Once this statement is executed, we can use the `FileWriter` class's `write()` method to write individual characters to the `prices.txt` file, as was illustrated in Section 12.1.

At this point, we should mention that a basic `FileWriter` output stream can be created in a manner that opens its associated file in append mode. For example, the statement

```
// set up the basic output stream and open a file in append mode
FileWriter fw =
    new FileWriter("prices.txt", true);
```

opens the file named `prices.txt` and makes it available for data to be appended to the end of the file. It is the second argument in the preceding statement, the boolean value `true`, that causes the file to be opened in append mode.

Regardless of the way the file connected to a basic `FileWriter` output stream object is opened, the associated stream methods restrict output to a character at a time. To create an output stream object that can directly handle character representations of numerical data, such as integers and double-precision numbers, and sequences of character data stored as strings, we must expand the basic output stream object.

To accomplish this, the first enhancement is almost always to make the output stream into a buffered stream. This permits the Java program to write characters to the buffered stream without forcing a call to the underlying operating system for each character that is written. What happens with a buffered stream is that all the data are first written into an internal buffer, which is then written to the actual file only if the buffer reaches its capacity, the buffer stream is closed, or the buffer stream is flushed using a `flush()` method.

Assuming that a `FileWriter` object named `fw` has already been created using one of the previous declaration statements, a buffered output stream can now be created using the `fw` reference variable as follows:

```
// buffer the stream for faster output
BufferedWriter bw =
    new BufferedWriter(fw);
```

In this statement, the reference variable name `bw` is programmer selected, and any valid Java variable name can be used instead. Because buffering almost always provides improved performance, it is recommended that you use it for all file I/O. Unfortunately, even though buffered byte streams improve I/O performance, these streams are still restricted to the byte or string output methods provided by the `Buffered-Writer` class. For example, assuming that our `BufferedWriter` object is referenced by the variable named `bw`, the statement

```
bw.write('a');
```

causes the code for the lowercase letter to be placed into the buffer. Similarly, the sequence of statements

```
bw.write("This is a test");
bw.newLine();
```

causes the string `This is a test` followed by a newline separator to be written to the output buffer.

The output buffer can be flushed, which forces a write to the corresponding file, at any time using the statement `bw.flush()`. It should be noted that since we now have two file stream objects, we could write to the file using references to each stream. Although this is possible, good programming practice indicates that you use the methods applicable to the last object stream created. It should also be noted that the final instantiation of a `BufferedWriter` object using the two executable statements

```
FileWriter fw =
    new FileWriter("prices.txt");
BufferedWriter bw =
    new BufferedWriter(fw);
```

can be identically created using the single statement

```
BufferedWriter bw =
        new BufferedWriter(new FileWriter("prices.txt"));
```

In your programming career, you will see both single- and double-statement instantiations, with individual statements themselves placed over one or two lines, so you should become familiar with each approach.

The last enclosing stream object that we need to create is a `PrintWriter` object. The reason is that the `PrintWriter` class contains a number of extremely useful class methods that will permit us to write the character representations of strings, doubles, floats, integers, and Boolean data to a file. Although we can construct a `Print-Writer` stream from either a `FileWriter` stream or a `BufferedWriter` stream, we will always use a buffered stream. Doing so provides us with the inherent performance advantages associated with buffering. Thus, the complete set of statements for creating the output streams that we will use throughout this chapter to construct character-based files is[2]

```
   // set up the basic output stream
FileWriter fw =
    new FileWriter("prices.txt");
   // buffer it for faster output
BufferedWriter bw =
    new BufferedWriter(fw);
   // this provides a set of useful methods
PrintWriter pw =
    new PrintWriter(bw);
```

As always, this set of three statements can be implemented with a single statement. For our particular example, a single-statement equivalent that you should be prepared to encounter in your programming career (with variations on white space) is

---

[2] As you might imagine, a similar set is required for writing to a byte-based file. The byte-based equivalents are presented in Section 12.3.

```
PrintWriter pw =
      new PrintWriter(new BufferedWriter(new FileWriter("prices.txt")));
```

Once the last stream has been created, we can use the methods provided by the `PrintWriter` class (see Table 12.3) for actually writing data to the file.

No matter which methods we use, however, it is always a sequence of one or more characters that will be output to a text file. For example, if `pw` is declared as a `PrintWriter` stream object, each of the following output statements places one or more characters onto the file connected to the `pw` stream.

```
pw.print('a');
pw.print("Hello World!");
pw.print(22);     // print an integer as a string
pw.print(39.95); // print a double as a string
pw.println("Have a Good Day"); // print a string and a newline sequence
```

The file stream name `pw` in each of these statements, in place of the `System.out` you have been using, directs the output stream to a specific file instead of to the standard display device. Program 12.1 illustrates the use of the `PrintWriter` methods to write a list of descriptions and prices to a file named `prices.txt`. In examining this program, notice that the `main()` header line uses the phrase `throws java.io.IOException`. Because we are not providing `main()` with any I/O exception handling capabilities, we must instruct it to throw any such exceptions that might occur up to the next level (this is the same reasoning as described in Section 3.3 for keyboard input). If an I/O exception does occur and `main()` passes it up, the program stops running and an error message is displayed.

Program 12.1

```java
import java.io.*;
public class WriteTextPrices
{
  public static void main(String[] args)
    throws java.io.IOException
  {
      // set up the basic output stream
    FileWriter fw =
        new FileWriter("prices.txt");
      // buffer it for faster output
    BufferedWriter bw =
        new BufferedWriter(fw);
      // this provides a set of useful methods
    PrintWriter pw =
        new PrintWriter(bw);

    pw.println("Mats 39.95");
    pw.println("Bulbs 3.22");
    pw.println("Fuses 1.08");

    pw.close();
  }
}
```

FIGURE 12.4   **The `test.dat` file as stored by the computer**

```
4D 61 74 73 20 33 39 2E 39 35 0D 0A 42 75 6C 62 73 20
 M  a  t  s     3  9  .  9  5 cr lf  B  u  l  b  s

33 2E 32 32 0D 0A 46 75 73 65 73 20 31 2E 30 38 0D 0A
 3  .  2  2 cr lf  F  u  s  e  s     1  .  0  8 cr lf
```

When Program 12.1 is run, a file named `prices.txt` is created and saved by the computer. The file is a sequential file that, after it is opened, is written with the following data:

```
Mats 39.95
Bulbs 3.22
Fuses 1.08
```

The actual storage of characters in the file depends on the character codes used by the computer. Although only 30 characters appear to be stored in the file, corresponding to the descriptions, blanks, and prices written to the file, the file actually contains 36 characters. The extra characters consist of the carriage return and line feed at the end of each line that is created by the `println()`'s newline escape sequence. Assuming characters in the file are stored using the ASCII code, the `prices.txt` file is physically stored as illustrated in Figure 12.4. For convenience, the character corresponding to each hexadecimal code is listed below the code. A code of 20 represents the blank character. In addition, your particular system may append an end-of-file marker as the last byte stored in the file.

Embedded and Interactive File Names

Although Program 12.1 provides the basics of creating and storing data into a character-based file, there are three practical problems with the program as it stands.

1. The external file name is embedded within the program code.
2. There is no provision for a user to enter the desired file name while the program is running.
3. There is no checking to see that a file of the existing name does not already exist.

Techniques to correct the third problem, file checking, are presented in detail in Section 12.6. Here we present techniques that appropriately deal with the first two problems.

The first problem, embedding a file's name within the code, can be alleviated by assigning the file name to a string variable at the top of the program. As you will see, this solution also makes it easy to correct the second problem because once a string variable is used for the name, this variable can be assigned to an external name either by explicit assignment of a string value or by interactively reading in a file's name when the program is running.

To see how this is done, first consider Program 12.2, where we have assigned the string value `prices.txt` to the string variable named `fileName`. The output file produced by Program 12.2 is identical to that produced by Program 12.1.

Program 12.2

```java
import java.io.*;
public class WriteTextPrices2
{
  public static void main(String[] args)
    throws java.io.IOException
  {
    String fileName = "prices.txt";

      // set up the basic output stream
    FileWriter fw = new FileWriter(fileName);
      // buffer it for faster output
    BufferedWriter bw = new BufferedWriter(fw);
      // this provides a set of useful methods
    PrintWriter pw = new PrintWriter(bw);

    pw.println("Mats 39.95");
    pw.println("Bulbs 3.22");
    pw.println("Fuses 1.08");

    pw.close();
  }
}
```

Once a string variable is declared to store a file's name, it can be used in one of two ways. First, as in Program 12.2, it can be placed at the top of a program to clearly identify a file's external name rather than be embedded within one or more statements throughout the program, as in Program 12.1. Next, we can use the string variables to permit the user to enter the file name as the program is running. Doing so eliminates the need to recompile the program each time the file name has to be changed. For example, the code

```java
  // set up a basic keyboard input stream
InputStreamReader isr = new
    InputStreamReader(System.in);

  // buffer it so we can use a readLine()
BufferedReader br = new
    BufferedReader(isr);

String fileName;

System.out.print("\nEnter the file's name: ");
fileName =  br.readLine();
```

allows a user to enter a file's external name at run time using the keyboard input techniques presented in Section 3.3. The only restriction in this code is that the user must not enclose the entered string value in double quotation marks, which is a plus, and that the entered string value cannot contain any blanks. The reason is that the compiler will terminate the string when it encounters a blank. We leave it as Exercise 3 to include this code in Program 12.2.

Reading from a Text File

Reading data from a character-based file is almost identical to reading data from a standard keyboard, except that the System.in object is replaced by the file stream object declared in the program. The same problem that we had with keyboard input, however, still remains, which means that the basic input from a text file will be either a character or a string. This is reinforced by referring to Table 12.4, which lists the two main file stream classes available for text file input. As is seen in the table, the two methods that we will have to rely on are the character input method read() and the string input method readLine(). Thus, from the point of view of reading a text file, it is useful to consider each line in the file as a string. Using this approach, each line can first be input and then separated into constituent pieces using the StringTokenizer methods presented in Section 9.3.

Program 12.3 illustrates reading the prices.txt file that was created in Program 12.1. Each line is input one at a time using a readLine() method. In effect, the program is really a line-by-line text-copying program, reading a line of text from the file and then displaying it on the terminal.

Program 12.3

```java
import java.io.*;
public class ReadTextPrices
{
  public static void main(String[] args)
    throws java.io.IOException
  {
    String fileName = "prices.txt";
    int i;
    String inLine;

      // set up the basic input stream
    FileReader fr =
       new FileReader(fileName);
     // buffer the input stream
    BufferedReader br =
       new BufferedReader(fr);

     // read and display three lines
    for(i = 0; i < 3; i++)
    {
      inLine = br.readLine();  // read a line
      System.out.println(inLine);  // display the line
    }

    br.close();
  }
}
```

Table 12.4   Character-Based Input Stream Classes

Class	Type	Comments	Common Methods
FileReader	Basic Input	Basic stream used for character-based input. Supplies character-by-character input.	read()
BufferedReader	Processing	Provides buffering, which typically improves performance. Supplies character-by-character and line-by-line input and typically uses a FileFileReader object argument.	read() readLine()

The display produced by Program 12.3 is

```
Mats 39.95
Bulbs 3.22
Fuses 1.08
```

Although Program 12.3 uses a fixed-count for loop to read in exactly three lines, it is frequently more convenient to have the program keep reading lines until there are no more data left in the file. This is easily accomplished because the Buffered-Reader method readLine() used in the program automatically returns a null when the input stream contains no more lines. Thus, in place of the for loop in Program 12.3, the following while loop can be substituted:

```
while ( (inLine = br.readLine()) != null)
{
  System.out.println(inLine);  // display the line
}
```

It should be noted that the parentheses surrounding the expression (inLine = br.readLine()) are necessary to ensure that a line is first read and assigned to the reference variable named inLine before this reference is compared to the null reference value. In their absence, the complete expression would be inLine = br.readLine() != null. Due to the precedence of operations, the relational expression br.readLine() != null would be executed first. Because this is a relational expression, its result is either a Boolean true or false based on the data retrieved by the br.readLine() method. Attempting to assign this Boolean result to the string referenced by inLine is an invalid conversion across an assignment operator and results in a compiler error.

Finally, if it were necessary to obtain the description and price as individual variables, the string returned by readLine() in Program 12.3 can be processed further to extract the individual data items. This is typically accomplished using a String-Tokenizer object in the same manner as for multiple value keyboard input (see Section 3.3). For example, assuming that the variable st has been declared as a StingTokenizer object, desc as a String object, and price as a precision variable, the statements

```
st = new StringTokenizer(inLine);
desc = st.nextToken();
price = Double.parseDouble(st.nextToken());
```

PROGRAMMING NOTE

A Way to Clearly Identify a File's Name and Location

During program development, data files are usually placed in the same directory as the program. Therefore, an expression such as `File inFile = new File("test.dat");` causes no problem in locating the file. In production systems, however, it is not uncommon for data files to reside in one directory and program files to reside in another. In this situation, you would include the full pathname of any file you are using. When a full pathname is used, however, a double delimiter, `\\`, must separate file names. The double backslashes provide an escape sequence where the first backslash tells the compiler to correctly consider the next character as a backslash.

Another important convention is to list all file names at the top of a program instead of embedding the names deep within the code. This is easily accomplished by assigning each file name to a string variable. For example, if a declaration such as

```
String inputFile = "C:\\jdk\\test.dat";
```

is placed at the top of a program file, both the name of the file and its location are clearly visible. Then, if some other file is to be used, all that is required is a simple one-line change at the top of the program.

Using a string variable for the file's name is also useful for any subsequent file checks and display messages. For example, consider the statement

```
System.out.println("The file " + inputFile + " is not available for input.");
```

Here the name of the offending file is printed as part of the message without explicitly rewriting the full pathname a second time.

can be used to extract description and price values from the `inLine` string read within Program 12.3's `for` loop. These statements, which are boldfaced for easier recognition, are used within the context of a complete program in Program 12.4. Notice also that a single-line declaration is used in Program 12.4 to open the buffered output stream in place of the two-line declaration employed in Program 12.3. Either style of declaration is acceptable, and both are found in practice.

Although we have not used Program 12.4's values in a numerical calculation, the program does illustrate the process of converting text-based file data into numerical data types. Clearly, once string values have been converted into numerical values, these values can subsequently be used in appropriate numerical calculations. Finally, it should be noted that the stripping of individual values requires that the programmer knows how the data are placed within each line of the file.

The output produced by Program 12.4 is

```
Description: Mats      Price: 39.95
Description: Bulbs     Price: 3.22
Description: Fuses     Price: 1.08
```

Program 12.4

```
import java.io.*;
import java.util.*;   // needed for StringTokenizer
public class ReadTextPrices2
{
  public static void main(String[] args)
    throws java.io.IOException
  {
    String fileName = "prices.txt";
    int i;
    double price;
    String inLine, desc;
    StringTokenizer st;

      // set up a buffered input stream - notice the single statement used
    BufferedReader br = new BufferedReader(new FileReader(fileName));

      // read and display three lines
    for (i = 0; i < 3; i++)
    {
      inLine = br.readLine();
      st = new StringTokenizer(inLine);       // here is where the string is
      desc = st.nextToken();                  // parsed into individual values
      price = Double.parseDouble(st.nextToken());
      System.out.println("Description: " + desc + '\t'
                      + "Price: " + price);
    }

    br.close();
  }
}
```

Checking the Connection

Recall from Section 4.2 that an exception is an error that occurs while a program is running. The Java Virtual Machine (JVM) automatically checks for a number of exceptions and generates an exception object when one is detected. The generation of an exception object is referred to as throwing an exception.

Exception detection and processing are especially important in processing files because the existence of a file and the format of the data can usually be altered by a user from outside a program using operating system commands. For example, a user may be able to delete a file or manually edit one and change the data using a text editor program. Any of these modifications can easily cause a Java program to fail, as for example, if a user deletes a file that will be opened for reading.

To protect against these errors and throughout the process of opening a file, for either writing or reading, the JVM automatically checks that a proper connection has been established and that no processing errors have occurred. When an error is detected, the JVM will throw an exception. The most important exceptions are listed in Table 12.5 (review Section 4.2 if you are unfamiliar with exceptions).

Table 12.5   **File Exceptions**

Exception	Detects
`EOFException`	Thrown by certain methods when reading from an input stream and the end of the stream has been reached.
`FileNotFoundException`	Thrown by certain methods when an attempt to read from a nonexistent file occurs or an attempt is made to write to a file that is specified in a nonexistent folder.
`IOException`	Thrown when an exceptional condition has occurred that prevents continued processing using either an input or output stream.

If any of the exceptions listed in Table 12.5 occur, the JVM will handle them by displaying an error message and closing down the program. For example, the following error message is typical of that displayed for a `FileNotFoundException` and was produced by deleting the `prices.txt` file before executing Program 12.3.

```
Exception in thread "main" java.io.FileNotFoundException: prices.txt(The
System cannot find the file specified)
        at java.io.FileInputStream.open(Native Method)
        at java.io.FileInputStream.<init>(FileInputStream.java:68)
        at java.io.FileReader.<init>(FileReader.java:35)
        at ReadTextFile.main(ReadTextFile.java, Compiled Code)
```

From a user's viewpoint, this type of exception message is frustrating and confusing. As a programmer, it is your responsibility to make any exceptions that can occur clearly understandable to the user. In this case, a more useful message would be to display a message that the required file is unavailable and to please check that it exists before continuing. This is easily accomplished by overriding the exception handler provided for any exception in Java with one of our own.

As presented in Section 4.2 and repeated here for convenience, the general syntax of the code required to throw and handle an exception is

```
try
{

  // one or more statements,
  // at least one of which should
  // be capable of throwing an exception;
}
catch(exceptionName argument)
{
   // one or more statements
}
finally
{
   // one or more statements
}
```

In this code, the `try` block statements are executed. If no error occurs, the `catch` block statements are omitted and processing continues with the statement following

PROGRAMMING NOTE

Checking That the File Was Successfully Located

It is important to check that a file stream has successfully established a connection between a method and an external file. This is because establishing a file stream is really a request to the operating system that can fail for a variety of reasons. Chief among these is a request to open an existing file for reading that the operating system cannot locate, which causes a `FileNotFoundException`. If the operating system cannot locate the requested file, you need to know about it and gracefully terminate your program. Failure to do so almost always results in some abnormal program behavior or a subsequent program crash.

The most common method for checking that the operating system successfully located the designated file is the one coded in Program 12.5, the key coding points of which are repeated here for convenience.

```
try  // this block tries to open the file and create the input stream
{
  // set up the basic input streams which can throw a FileNotFoundException

  // perform all required file processing

  // close the file
}
catch (FileNotFoundException e)
{
  System.out.println("The file " + fileName
                     + " was not successfully opened."
                     + "\nPlease check that the file currently exists.");
  System.exit(0);
}
```

Although this code determines a successful file location of files for both input and output, a more rigorous check is sometimes required when an output file is opened. This is because, on output, the file is almost guaranteed to be found. If it exists, it will be found, and if it does not exist, the operating system will create it (unless append mode is specified and the file already exists). Knowing that the file has been found, however, can be insufficient for output purposes when an existing output file *must not* be overwritten. For these cases, the file can first be opened for input, and then, if the file is found, the following check can be placed within the `try` block to ensure that the user does want the existing file overwritten.

```
try
{
  // open a basic input stream simply to check if the file exist
  FileReader fr = new FileReader(fileName);
   // only get here if the file was found; otherwise the catch block takes control
  System.out.println("A file by the name " + fileName + " currently exists.\n"
                     + "Do you want to overwrite it with the new data (y or n): ");
  response = (char)System.in.read();
  if (response == 'n' || response == 'N')
  {
     fr.close();
     System.out.println("The existing file has not been overwritten.");
     System.exit(0);
```

```
        }
    }
    catch(FileNotFoundException e) {};   // a do-nothing block that permits
                                         // processing to continue
    // open the file in write mode and continue with file writes
```

Alternatively, and more efficiently, the existence of the file can first be checked using the `File` class's `exist()` method, which is presented in Section 12.6.

the `catch` block. In this case, the statements within the optional `finally` block would be run, followed by any statements that might occur after the `finally` block. However, if any statement within the `try` block causes an exception, the `catch` block whose exception matches the thrown exception is executed. If no `catch` block is defined for an exception that can be thrown, the exception will be sent to the calling method. This means that a `throws` statement must be included in the method header for any exceptions that are not handled by `catch` blocks in the method.

Most times, but not always, the `catch` block displays an error message and terminates processing with a statement such as `System.exit(0)`. Regardless of what the `catch` block does, the `finally` block, if it exists, will be executed. Thus, the code within the `finally` block is always run, with or without an exception occurring. Typically, the `finally` block is used to close all open files or complete a calculation before the program shuts down.

Program 12.5 illustrates the statements required to open a file in read mode that includes exception handling for a `FileNotFound` error.

Program 12.5

```java
import java.io.*;
public class ExceptionExample
{
  public static void main(String[] args)
    throws java.io.IOException
  {
    String fileName = "prices.txt";
    int i;
    String inLine;

    try  // this block tries to open the file and create the input stream
    {
        // set up the basic input streams
      FileReader fr = new FileReader(fileName);
        // buffer the input stream
      BufferedReader br = new BufferedReader(fr);

        // read and display three lines
      for(i = 0; i < 3; i++)
      {
```

(continued)

(continued)

```
        inLine = br.readLine();  // read a line
        System.out.println(inLine);  // display the line
      }
      br.close();  // close the file
    }
    catch (FileNotFoundException e)
    {
      System.out.println("The file " + fileName
                    + " was not successfully opened."
                    + "\nPlease check that the file currently exists.");
      System.exit(0);
    }
  }
}
```

The exception message produced by Program 12.5 when it was run after the `prices.txt` file was deleted is

```
The file prices.txt was not successfully opened.
Please check that the file currently exists.
```

This error message is certainly more user-friendly than the one produced by Program 12.3. In reviewing Program 12.5, notice that the `throws java.io.IOException` statement has been included within the method's header line. This is required because this exception is not caught and handled within the method using a `catch` block. The remaining programs presented in this text will either use the exception handler illustrated in Program 12.5 or one more appropriate to the processing being illustrated.

Unbuffered I/O[3]

The examples illustrating text file input and output in this section have all used buffered streams. There are cases, however, when it is useful to read and write individual characters in an unbuffered manner. To show how this can be done, we present an extremely simple application that performs a file copy one character at a time.

Specifically, for our example, assume that we wish to read the data from a character-based file named `info.txt` one character at a time and write these data to a file named `backup.txt`. Essentially, this application is a file copy program that reads the data from one file in a character-by-character manner and writes them to a second file. For purposes of illustration, assume that the characters stored in the input file are as shown in Figure 12.5.

Figure 12.6 illustrates the structure of the streams that are necessary for producing our file copy. In this figure, the input stream object referenced by the variable `fr` will read data from the `info.txt` file, and the output stream object referenced by the variable `fw` will write data to the `backup.txt` file.

---

[3] This topic can be omitted on first reading without loss of subject continuity.

FIGURE 12.5　**The data stored in `info.txt`**

```
Now is the time for all good people
  to come to the aid of their party.
Please call (555) 888-6666 for
  further information.
```

Because we are dealing with character-based files, we must construct our basic input and output stream objects from the stream classes `FileReader` and `FileWriter`, respectively (refer to Table 12.2). Arbitrarily using the reference variable names `fr` and `fw`, the following statements create the appropriate file stream objects:

```
    // set up the basic input stream
FileReader fr =
    new FileReader("info.txt");
    // set up the basic output stream
FileWriter fw =
    new FileFileWriter("backup.txt");
```

Streams created from either the `FileReader` and `FileWriter` classes always transmit characters as 16-bit data regardless of how the characters are actually stored in a file (and most file systems currently store characters as 8-bit ASCII data—see Section 12.9). Thus, the character read into a Java program using a `FileReader` `read()` method will return a 16-bit Unicode value rather than an 8-bit ASCII character code. In addition to its intended purpose of accommodating Unicode data, the return of a 16-bit value permits the `read()` method to alert us to the fact that the end of a stream has been reached and no more data are available. This is accomplished by `read()` returning a − 1 value whenever the end of a stream is reached. Because − 1 has no character representation, it ensures that when this value is detected, it can never be confused with any legitimate character that could be encountered as normal data in the file.

Now consider Program 12.6, which omits any stream buffering before performing its file copy. It does, however, illustrate the unbuffered reading and writing of a text file. When it has finished running, a file named `backup.txt` will be an exact duplicate of the `prices.txt` file created in Program 12.3.

FIGURE 12.6　**The file copy stream structure**

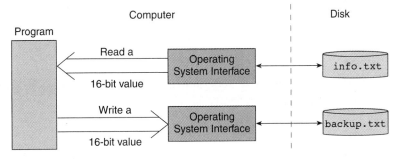

PROGRAMMING NOTE

Opening More Than One File Stream

When more than one file stream is opened, opening each file stream in its own `try` block permits exact isolation and identification of which file caused an exception, should one occur. In doing so, however, you must be sure to nest all `try` blocks. For example, consider Program 12.6, which is rewritten here so that each of its two files is opened in its own `try` block.

```java
import java.io.*;
public class CopyText
{
  static final int EOF = -1;
  public static void main(String[] args)
    throws java.io.IOException
  {
    try  //this block tries to open the input file
    {
       // open a basic input stream
      FileReader fr = new FileReader("info.txt");
      try  // this block tries to open the output file and
      {    // perform all file processing
        // open a basic output stream
        FileWriter fw = new FileWriter("backup.txt");
        int c;

        while ((c = fr.read()) != EOF)
          fw.write(c);

        fr.close();
        fw.close();
      }  // end of inner try block
      catch (FileNotFoundException e)  // catch for inner try block
      {
        System.out.println("The file backup.txt was not successfully opened.");
        System.exit(0);
      }
    }  // end of outer try block
    catch (FileNotFoundException e)  // catch for outer try block
    {
      System.out.println("The file info.txt was not successfully opened.");
      System.exit(0);
    }
  }
}
```

The important point to notice in this program is that `try` blocks are almost always nested. If the two `try` blocks in the preceding program were not nested, the file reference `fr`, which is declared and instantiated in the first block, could not be used in the second block. Similarly, although it is not needed here, the file reference `fw`, declared in the second block, would not be usable in the first block. The reason for this is that all variables declared in a block of code, which is defined by an opening and closing brace pair, are local to the block in which they are declared (see Section 3.5).

Program 12.6

```java
import java.io.*;
public class CopyText
{
  static final int EOF = -1;
  public static void main(String[] args)
    throws java.io.IOException
  {
    try //this block tries to open the files and create appropriate streams
    {
      // open a basic input stream
      FileReader fr = new FileReader("info.txt");
      // open a basic output stream
      FileWriter fw = new FileWriter("backup.txt");
      int c;

      while ((c = fr.read()) != EOF)
        fw.write(c);
      fr.close();
      fw.close();
    }
    catch (FileNotFoundException e)
    {
      System.out.println("One of the required files, \ninfo.txt or "
                        + "backup.txt, was not successfully opened.");
      System.exit(0);
    }
  }
}
```

In reviewing Program 12.6, notice that we are using unbuffered `FileReader` and `FileWriter` stream objects and their associated `read()` and `write()` methods. We are also using a named constant `EOF` that has been equated to the value −1. The reason for creating this value as a named constant is that the `read()` method returns a −1 when it locates the end of the input stream.

Within Program 12.6, the statement

```java
while( (c = fr.read()) != EOF)
```

continually reads a value from the `fr` input stream until the `EOF` value is detected. As long as the returned value does not equal the `EOF` value, the value is written out to the unbuffered `fw` object stream. It should be noted that the parentheses surrounding the expression `(c = fr.read())` are necessary to ensure that a value is first read and assigned to the variable `c` before the retrieved value is compared to the `EOF` value. In their absence, the complete expression would be `c = fr.read() != EOF`. Due to the precedence of operations, the relational expression `fr.read() != EOF` would be executed first. Because this is a relational expression, its result is either a boolean `true` or `false` value based on the data retrieved by the `read()` method.

PROGRAMMING NOTE

Using while *Loops to Read File Data*

while loops are frequently used to read data from an input file because they can be easily terminated by an end-of-data sentinel or EOFException error and do not require knowing, in advance, the exact number of lines or data in the file. There are three common types of while loops that you will encounter and use in your programming work.

For input methods that throw an EOFException notification, such as the DataInputStream's readChar(), readDouble(), readFloat(), readInt(), and similar methods, the following code is frequently used. In this code, the EOFException is caught by the catch block, which automatically breaks the while loop and terminates data input.

```
try
 {
 while (true)
 {
     // read and process file data in here
 }
 catch (EOFException e) // end-of-file transfers processing to here
 {
    // close the file and display any terminating messages
 }
 }
```

In cases where an EOFException notification is not thrown by the input method, while loops can still be used as long as the input method's return character is known when no more data are available for reading. For example, because the BufferedReader class's readLine () method returns a null when no more lines of data are available because the end-of-file has been reached, the following loop construction can be used with this method.

```
while ( (inLine = br.readLine()) != null)
{
   // processing in here
}
```

An example of this syntax is used in Program 12.5, where the variable inLine is declared as a string variable.

A similar construction can be used with both the BufferendInputStream's and the FileReader's (an unbuffered stream) read() methods. For these methods, which return a –1 when no bytes can be read because the end of the stream has been reached, the while loop takes the following form:

```
while ((c = fr.read()) != -1)
{
   // processing in here
}
```

An example of this syntax is used in Program 12.6, where the variable c is declared as a char variable.

Attempting to assign this boolean result to the variable c is an invalid conversion across an assignment operator and results in a compiler error.

Finally, for simplicity, Program 12.6 attempts to open both the input and output files within the same try block. More generally, each file would be opened in its own try block so that appropriate catch blocks could clearly identify which file could not be opened in case of a failure. When this is done, because of block scoping rules (see the Programming Note on page 626) the try blocks must be nested, and all processing must occur within the inner nested block; otherwise, the file references created in one block will not be available to code in any other block.

Exercises 12.2

1. Enter and run Program 12.1 on your computer.

2. Enter and run Program 12.2 on your computer.

3. Modify Program 12.2 to permit the user to interactively enter the name of a file.

4. Enter and run Program 12.3 on your computer.

5. Enter and run Program 12.4 on your computer.

6a. Enter and run Program 12.5 on your computer.

  b. Verify the output displayed by Program 12.5 when the prices.txt file has been deleted and is not available for input.

7a. Enter and run Program 12.6 on your computer.

  b. Verify that the catch block in Program 12.6 runs correctly when the info.txt file has been deleted and is not available for input.

8. Modify Program 12.6 by including the statement System.out.println(e) as the first statement within the catch block. Determine the display produced by this statement by deleting the info.txt file and then running the program.

9a. Write a Java program that accepts five lines of text from the keyboard and writes each line to a file named text.dat.

  b. Modify Program 12.3 to read and display the data stored in the text.dat file created in Exercise 9a.

10. Determine the operating system command or procedures provided by your computer to display the contents of a saved file. Compare its operation to the program developed for Exercise 9b.

11. Write, compile, and run a Java program that writes the four real numbers 92.65, 88.72, 77.46, and 82.93 to a text file named results.txt. After writing the data to the file, your program should read the data from the file, determine the average of the four numbers read, and display the average. Verify the output produced by your program by manually calculating the average of the four input numbers.

12a. Write, compile, and run a Java program that creates a text file named points and writes the following three lines of data to the file:

```
 6.3   8.2   18.25   24.32
 4.0   4.0   10.0    -5.0
-2.0   5.0    4.0     5.0
```

b. Using the data in the `points` file created in Exercise 12a. write, compile, and run a Java program that reads each line and interprets the first and second numbers in the line as the coordinates of one point and the third and fourth numbers as the coordinates of a second point. Have your program compute and display the slope and midpoint of each pair of entered points.

13a. Write, compile, and run a Java program that creates a text file named `grades.txt` and writes the following five lines of data to the file:

```
90.3   92.7   90.3   99.8
85.3   90.5   87.3   90.8
93.2   88.4   93.8   75.6
82.4   95.6   78.2   90.0
93.5   80.2   92.9   94.4
```

b. Using the data in the `grades.txt` file created in Exercise 13a, write, compile, and run a Java program that reads each line in the file, computes the average for each line, and displays the average.

14a. Create a file containing the following car numbers, number of miles driven, and number of gallons of gas used by each car:

Car No.	Miles Driven	Gallons Used
54	250	19
62	525	38
71	123	6
85	1,322	86
97	235	14

b. Write a Java program that reads the data in the file created in Exercise 14a and displays the car number, miles driven, gallons used, and the miles per gallon for each car. The output should also contain the total miles driven, total gallons used, and average miles per gallon for all the cars. These totals should be displayed at the end of the output report.

15a. A file named `polar.txt` contains the polar coordinates needed in a graphics program. Currently, this file contains the following data:

Distance (inches)	Angle (degrees)
--------	---------
2.0	45.0
6.0	30.0
10.0	45.0
4.0	60.0
13.0	55.0
8.0	15.0

Write a Java program to create the data in this file on your computer system (without the header lines).

b. Using the `polar.txt` file created in Exercise 15a, write a Java program that reads this file and creates a second file named `xycord.dat`. The entries in the new file should contain the rectangular coordinates corresponding to the polar coordinates in the `polar.txt` file. Polar coordinates are converted to rectangular coordinates using the equations

$x = r \cos\theta$

$y = r \sin\theta$

where r is the distance coordinate and θ is the radian equivalent of the angle coordinate in the `polar.txt` file.

16a. Store the following data in a file: 5 96 87 78 93 21 4 92 82 85 87 6 72 69 85 75 81 73.

b. Write a Java program to calculate and display the average of each group of numbers in the file created in Exercise 16a. The data are arranged in the file so that each group of numbers is preceded by the number of data items in the group. Thus, the first number in the file, 5, indicates that the next five numbers should be grouped together. The number 4 indicates that the following four numbers are a group, and the 6 indicates that the last six numbers are a group. (Tip: Use a nested loop.)

17. Enter the data shown in Figure 12.5 into a character-based file named `info.txt`.

18. Enter and run Program 12.6 on your computer. When the program has finished running, verify that a file named `backup.txt` exists and contains the data created for the `info.txt` file created in Exercise 18.

19. Rewrite Program 12.6 so that it uses buffered input and output streams in place of the unbuffered `FileReader` and `FileWriter` streams.

20. Modify Program 12.6 so that the input file is read using a `readLine()` method and the output file is written using a `println()` method. (Tip: You will have to add processing streams to the existing `FileReader` and `FileWriter` streams. See Exercise 20.)

12.3 Reading and Writing Byte-Based Files

An alternative to text files, where each character in the file is represented by a unique code, is byte-based files. The advantage of a byte-based file is that Java's primitive data types, such as `ints` and `doubles`, are written, stored, and read directly in their binary representation. This means that there is no number-to-string conversion required when writing a number and no string-to-number conversion required when a value is read back from the file. For files consisting predominantly of numerical data, this is a distinct advantage and can improve program efficiency. The disadvantage is that the ability to easily inspect the file using either a word processing or text editing program and to see the numerical values as textual information is lost. In this section, we first present the creation of a byte-based file using an output stream and then show how to read the file using a byte-based input stream.

Table 12.6 lists the common byte-based output file streams. Like their character-based counterparts, a basic byte-based output stream is typically wrapped into other streams that provide additional processing capabilities.

Table 12.6   Common Byte-Based File Output Stream Classes

Class	Mode	Comments	Typical Object Name
FileOutputStream	Output	Basic stream used for byte-based output. Supplies byte-by-byte output.	fos
BufferedOutputStream	Output	Provides buffering, which improves performance. Typically uses a FileOutputStream object argument.	bos
DataOutputStream	Output	Supplies additional output methods. Typically uses either a FileOutputStream object or a BufferedOutputStream object argument.	dos

For output, the set of stream objects typically instantiated from the classes in Table 12.6 is

```
// set up the basic output stream
FileOutputStream fos =
    new FileOutputStream(outFile);

// buffer it for faster output
BufferedOutputStream bos =
    new BufferedOutputStream(fos);

// this provides a set of useful methods
DataOutputStream dos =
    new DataOutputStream(bos);
```

In this set of instantiations, the terms fos, bos, and dos are commonly used programmer-selected names for their respective stream types. The outFile argument in the creation of the first stream can be either a string variable, string constant, or File object name, as described in Section 12.6.

The primary reasons for the first wrapping, which results in the creation of a BufferedOutputStream object, are that this stream provides for writing complete lines rather than just single bytes, as provided by a FileOutputStream, and that buffered output is generally more efficient than unbuffered byte-by-byte output.

The primary reason for the second wrapping, which results in the creation of a DataOutputStream, is that this stream provides a rich set of methods for writing both string and numerical data. Table 12.7 lists the common class methods provided by the DataOutputStream class. As is evident from this table, we now have a rather large set of methods from which to choose when writing various types of data to a byte-based file.

In a similar manner, an output stream can be created that opens its associated file in append mode. If the file opened for appending does not exist, a new file with the designated name is created and made available to the output stream to receive data from the program. Connecting an output stream to a file opened in append mode is

Table 12.7 **`DataOutputStream` Class Methods**

Method	Description
`flush()`	Flushes the stream, which forces any buffered output bytes to be written to the file.
`close()`	Closes the file output stream.
`writeByte(int b)`	Writes a `byte` to the underlying output stream as a 1-byte value.
`writeBoolean(boolean v)`	Writes a `boolean` to the underlying stream as a 1-byte value. The value `true` is written as the cast value `(byte) 1`, and the value `false` is written as the cast value `(byte) 0`.
`writeBytes(String s)`	Writes the `String` `s` to the underlying output stream as a sequence of bytes. The higher 8 bits of each character are discarded (not written).
`writeChar(int v)`	Writes a `char` to the underlying output stream as a 2-byte Unicode value, with the high byte written first.
`writeChars(String s)`	Writes the `String` `s` to the underlying output stream as a sequence of characters. Writes each character to the underlying output stream as a 2-byte Unicode value.
`writeDouble(double v)`	Converts the `double` value `v` to a `long` and then writes the `long` value to the underlying output stream using 8 bytes, with the high byte written first.
`writeFloat(float v)`	Converts the `float` value `v` to an `int` and then writes the `int` value to the underlying output stream using 4 bytes, with the high byte written first.
`writeInt(int v)`	Writes an `int` to the underlying output stream using 4 bytes, with the high byte written first.
`writeLong(long v)`	Writes a `long` to the underlying output stream using 8 bytes, with the high byte written first.
`writeShort(int v)`	Writes a `short` to the underlying output stream using 2 bytes, with the high byte written first.

accomplished by adding a boolean argument to the first stream object created. For our example, the statement

```
// set up the basic output stream and open the file in append mode
FileOutputStream fos =
    new FileOutputStream(outFile, true);
```

opens the `outFile` and makes it available for data to be appended to the end of the file.

Alternatively, the construction of a buffered `DataOutputStream` using three individual statements can be accomplished with a single statement. Thus, for writing to a new file, the previous three statements can be combined into the single statement

```
DataOutputStream dos = new DataOutputStream(
                new BufferedOutputStream(
                    new FileOutputStream(outFile)));
```

As a specific example of creating a byte-based file that checks for a `FileNot-FoundException` and asks the user whether an existing file should be overwritten if a file with the given name is found, consider Program 12.7.

Program 12.7

```java
import java.io.*;
public class WritePrices
{
  public static void main(String[] args)
  throws java.io.IOException
  {
    String fileName = "prices.dat";
    char response;

    try
    {
      // open a basic input stream to check if the file exists
      FileReader fr = new FileReader(fileName);

      System.out.println("A file by the name " + fileName + " currently exists.\n"
                  + "Do you want to overwrite it with the new data (y or n): ");
      response = (char)System.in.read();
      if (response == 'n' || response == 'N')
      {
        fr.close();
        System.out.println("The existing file has not been overwritten.");
        System.exit(0);
      }
    }
    catch(FileNotFoundException e) {}; // a do-nothing block that permits
                                       // processing to continue

    DataOutputStream dos = new DataOutputStream(
                      new BufferedOutputStream(
                        new FileOutputStream(fileName)));
    dos.writeDouble(39.95);
    dos.writeDouble(3.22);
    dos.writeDouble(1.08);

    dos.close();
    System.out.println("A new " + fileName + " has been successfully written.");
  }
}
```

In reviewing Program 12.7, first notice that a check is made for the file's existence *before* it is opened for writing. This provides the user with the opportunity to stop overwriting an existing file. Although we have used the method described in the Programming Note on page 622 for this check, a more efficient procedure is to use the File class's exists() method, which is presented in the next section.

The byte-based file created by Program 12.7 is illustrated in Figure 12.7, which uses hexadecimal values to indicate the equivalent binary values.[4] Although the

---

[4] The specific byte patterns shown are those obtained using the real number storage specification presented in Appendix I.

FIGURE 12.7   **The stored binary data in the `prices.dat` file and their decimal equivalent**

```
|40 43 F9 99 99 99 99 9A|  <-- corresponds to 39.95
|40 09 C2 8F 5C 28 F5 C3|  <-- corresponds to 3.22
|3F F1 47 AE 14 7A E1 48|  <-- corresponds to 1.08
```

figure separates the file's data into three individual lines, with bars (|) used to distinguish individual items, in actuality the file is stored as a consecutive sequence of bytes. As indicated in the figure, each value consists of 8 bytes, which is the size of a double-precision number specified in Java.

Reading a byte-based file, such as that illustrated in Figure 12.7, requires constructing an input byte-based stream and then using appropriate stream methods for data input. Table 12.8 lists the common byte-based input file streams.

As with all stream objects, the purpose of creating an initial basic stream, in this case using the `FileInputStream` class, and then wrapping this initial object into other streams is to obtain the additional features, such as buffering, and the additional methods provided by each subsequent stream. For byte-based streams, the `DataInputStream` class provides the methods listed in Table 12.9. A comparison of these methods to those of Table 12.7 reveals that the `DataInputStream` methods are the input counterparts of the output methods provided by the `DataOutputStream` class. These input methods permit reading primitive data types directly from a file into a program without the need for any intermediate conversions.

Program 12.8 illustrates the opening of a byte-based input stream object, the input of the data stored in the file created in Program 12.7, and the display of these data. Because the construction of the input stream objects should be familiar, we have used the single file declaration syntax for creating the final buffered `DataInputStream` reference, `dis`. In reviewing the actual input of the data, notice that the individual data items are read directly as double-precision values using the `readDouble()` method. Although we have chosen to display the input values directly, in a more typical application, the input values would be assigned to double-precision variables for further numerical processing.

Table 12.8   **Common Byte-Based File Input Stream Classes**

Class	Mode	Comments	Typical Object Name
`FileInputStream`	Input	Basic stream used for byte-based input. Supplies byte-by-byte input.	`fis`
`BufferedInputStream`	Input	Provides buffering, which improves performance. Supplies byte-by-byte input. Typically uses a `FileInputStream` object argument.	`bis`
`DataInputStream`	Input	Supplies additional input methods. Typically uses either a `FileInputStream` object or a `BufferedInputStream` object argument.	`dis`

Table 12.9 **DataInputStream** Class Methods

Method	Description
close()	Closes the input stream.
readBoolean()	Reads a boolean from the input stream.
readByte()	Reads a byte from the input stream.
readChar()	Reads a char (16-bits) from the input stream.
readDouble()	Reads a double (64-bits) from the input stream.
readFloat()	Reads a float (32-bits) from the input stream.
readInt()	Reads an int (32-bits) from the input stream.
readLong()	Reads a long (64-bits) from the input stream.
readShort()	Reads a short (16-bits) from the input stream.
readLine()	Replaced by BufferedReader.readLine().

Program 12.8

```java
import java.io.*;
public class ReadPrices
{
  public static void main(String[] args)
    throws java.io.IOException
  {
    String fileName = "prices.dat";

    try  // this block tries to open the file and create the input stream
    {
        // set up the input stream
      DataInputStream dis = new DataInputStream(
                        new BufferedInputStream(
                            new FileInputStream(fileName)));

      System.out.println("The values read from the " + fileName
                      + " file are:");
      System.out.println(dis.readDouble());
      System.out.println(dis.readDouble());
      System.out.println(dis.readDouble());

      dis.close();
    }
    catch (FileNotFoundException e)
    {
      System.out.println("The file " + fileName
                      + " was not successfully opened."
                      + "\nPlease check that the file currently exists.");
      System.exit(0);
    }
  }
}
```

The output produced by Program 12.8 is

```
The values read from the prices.dat file are:
39.95
3.22
1.08
```

Caution

Table 12.9 lists a `readLine()` method provided by the `DataInputStream` class. This method has been deprecated in Java 2.0, which means that it may not be supported in some future release.

The reason for deprecating the `DataInputStream`'s `readLine()` method is that it can cause programs to pause indefinitely when reading files that are either sent over a network or input via the keyboard. This occurs because this particular method uses a carriage return, line feed sequence (`\r\n`) to determine when to stop reading. For locally stored files, this pair of codes is typically created whenever a line has been written, so `readLine()` rarely causes a problem for this type of file. However, if your program uses this method and a file is sent over a network that does not specify the `\r\n` sequence as an end-of-line (the HTTP protocol does specify this pair as a required line termination), your program can go into a permanent pause state.

Before this problem became known, `readLine()` was widely and conveniently used to read byte-based files that contained string data as the last item on a line. For example, if a line consisted of a sequence of numerical data and then string data, the numerical data would have been read using the primitive data type read methods listed in Table 12.9, followed by a `readLine()`. This technique is now replaced by reading and appending individual characters to a `StringBuffer` variable (see Section 7.3) until a known end-of-line character is encountered. A typical implementation of this replacement approach would appear as follows, where `inchar` has been declared as a character variable, `dis` as a `DataInputStream` object, and `sbvar` as a `StringBuffer` variable.

```
while( (inchar = dis.inChar()) != '\r')
    sbvar.append(inchar);
```

In this example, it is assumed that each line is terminated by a single carriage return code.

Exercises 12.3

1. Enter and run Program 12.7 on your computer. Once the `prices.dat` file has been written, execute Program 12.7 a second time to verify that it does not overwrite the existing file without your permission.

2. Enter and run Program 12.8 on your computer.

3. Write, compile, and run a Java program that writes the numbers 92.65, 88.72, 77.46, and 82.93 as double-precision values to a byte-based file named `results.dat`. After writing the data to the file, your program should read the data from the file, determine the average of the four numbers read, and display the average. Verify the output produced by your program by manually calculating the average of the four input numbers.

4a. Write, compile, and run a Java program that creates a byte-based file named `points` and writes the following numbers to the file:

```
6.3     8.2    18.25  24.32
4.0     4.0    10.0   -5.0
-2.0    5.0    4.0    5.0
```

b. Using the data in the `points` file created in Exercise 4a, write, compile, and run a Java program that reads four numbers using a `for` loop and interprets the first and second numbers in each record as the coordinates of one point and the third and fourth numbers as the coordinates of a second point. Have your program compute and display the slope and midpoint of each pair of entered points.

5a. Write, compile, and run a Java program that creates a byte-based file named `grades.bin` and writes the following five lines of data to the file:

```
90.3    92.7    90.3    99.8
85.3    90.5    87.3    90.8
93.2    88.4    93.8    75.6
82.4    95.6    78.2    90.0
93.5    80.2    92.9    94.4
```

b. Using the data in the `grades.bin` file created in Exercise 5a, write, compile, and run a Java program that reads, computes, and displays the average of each group of four grades.

6a. Create a byte-based file containing the following car numbers, number of miles driven, and number of gallons of gas used by each car:

Car No.	Miles Driven	Gallons Used
54	250	19
62	525	38
71	123	6
85	1,322	86
97	235	14

b. Write a Java program that reads the data in the file created in Exercise 6a and displays the car number, miles driven, gallons used, and the miles per gallon for each car. The output should also contain the total miles driven, total gallons used, and average miles per gallon for all the cars. These totals should be displayed at the end of the output report.

7a. A byte-based file named `polar.dat` contains the polar coordinates needed in a graphics program. Currently, this file contains the following data:

DISTANCE (INCHES)	ANGLE (DEGREES)
--------	---------
2.0	45.0
6.0	30.0
10.0	45.0
4.0	60.0
13.0	55.0
8.0	15.0

Write a Java program to create the data in this file on your computer system (without the header lines).

b. Using the `polar.dat` file created in Exercise 7a, write a Java program that reads this file and creates a second byte-based file named `xycord.dat`. The entries in the new file should contain the rectangular coordinates corresponding to the polar coordinates in the `polar.dat` file. Polar coordinates can be converted to rectangular coordinates using the equations

$x = r \cos\theta$

$y = r \sin\theta$

where r is the distance coordinate and θ is the radian equivalent of the angle coordinate in the `polar.dat` file.

12.4 Application: Creating and Using a Holiday Table

A not uncommon programming requirement is the necessity of creating and maintaining a small file of constants, reading and storing these constants into a list, and then providing methods for checking data against the constants in the list. For example, a scientific program might require a set of temperatures at which various elements freeze or change state, or an engineering program might require a set of material densities (e.g., various grades of steel and iron ore). In financial and scheduling programs, this requirement takes the form of reading in a set of holiday dates and then checking a date against the data in the table. This determination is extremely important in many applications to ensure that contractual settlement dates and delivery dates are not scheduled on a holiday.

Our objective in this application is to create a `Date` class method that determines if a given date is a holiday, using concepts that are equally applicable to any program that needs to check data against a list of constants, be they temperatures, densities, or other parameters. Specifically, two methods are developed that complete the `Date` class that we have been constructing throughout the text. The fist method constructs a list of holidays, which is referred to as a holiday table, and consists of legal holiday dates that have previously been stored in a file. The second method compares any given `Date` object to the dates in the table and determines if the `Date` object matches any dates in the table.

The creation of a list of holidays is based on reading data from a file that contains the necessary dates. Because these dates change each year, a separate class is frequently created to maintain the holiday dates. Typically, starting with dates toward the latter part of December, a program would automatically either send a reminder to the user to update the holiday dates, start a holiday maintenance program that is used to update the file, or be terminated by the user. In this application, we will consider the North American holidays listed in Table 12.10 as providing the dates that our `Date` class will store in its holiday table.

Assume that only the holiday dates listed in Table 12.10 have been stored in a file named `Holidays.txt`. Such a file can easily be created using either a text editor, copying the file from the Web site provided for this text, or writing a program that accepts the dates, as strings, from a user and writing the string data to a file, one line per date. Table 12.11 illustrates the 15 holiday dates, one per line, as they are stored in the `Holidays.txt` file.

Table 12.10   **North American Government Holidays**

Holiday	Date
New Year's Day	1/1/2004
Martin Luther King Jr.'s Birthday	1/19/2004
Presidents' Day	2/18/2004
Good Friday	4/9/2004
Easter	4/11/2004
Cinco de Mayo	5/5/2004
Victoria Day	5/24/2004
Memorial Day	5/31/2004
Canada Day	7/1/2004
Independence Day	7/4/2004
Labor Day	9/6/2004
Columbus Day	10/11/2004
Canadian Thanksgiving	10/11/2004
United States Thanksgiving	11/31/2004
Christmas	12/25/2004

Our first task will be to develop a method, which we will name `getHolidays()`, that reads the dates in the `Holidays.txt` file and stores them in an array. We then develop a method, which we will name `isHoliday()`, to compare a date to each entry in the holiday array. If the date matches an entry, the method will return a boolean value of `true`, which indicates the date corresponds to a holiday; otherwise, the method will return a boolean value of `false`, which indicates that the date is not a holiday. We construct the `getHolidays()` method first.

Table 12.11   **The `Holidays.txt` File**

1/1/2004
1/19/2004
2/18/2004
4/9/2004
4/11/2004
5/5/2004
5/24/2004
5/31/2004
7/1/2004
7/4/2004
9/6/2004
10/11/2004
10/11/2004
11/31/2004
12/25/2004

The `getHolidays()` Method

The purpose of the `getHolidays()` method is to read the `Holidays.txt` file and construct an array of dates. For our purposes, we will construct the array as an `ArrayList`, which was described in detail in Section 8.5. This type of array is the list of choice because it automatically expands to fit the number of objects being stored, which can change over time as new holidays are declared, and vary for each country.[5] Thus, the fact that the United States has a different number of official holidays than Canada or Mexico does not matter. We simply let the `ArrayList` expand, if necessary, as a date is read from the holiday file, and when the last date has been stored, we trim the list to the exact number of dates, using the `trimToSize()` method.

For convenience, we will read each line in the file as a string, convert it to a `StringTokenizer` object (see Section 4.1), and then parse the `StringTokenizer` to extract its month, day, and year values. Once these individual values have been extracted, we can use them as arguments in the `Date` class's `setDate()` method to modify an existing `Date` object, which can then be added into the `ArrayList`. We will name this `ArrayList` hTable. Because only one instance of hTable is needed, which must be available to all `Date` objects, it will be declared in the `Date` class's data declaration section using the statement

```
static ArrayList hTable = new ArrayList();
```

Assuming that hTable has been declared, the pseudocode describing the algorithm for reading the holiday file is

getHolidays() Algorithm

Instantiate a Date object
Open the Holidays.txt file, throwing an exception if the file cannot be found
While there are dates in the file
  Read a line as a string value
  Convert the string value to a StringTokenizer object
  Parse the StringTokenizer object into a month, day, and year value (use the / as a delimiter)
  Assign the parsed month, day, and year values to the instantiated Date object
  Add the Date object to the hTable ArrayList
Close the file
Trim the hTable ArrayList to the exact number of dates stored

The coding of `getHolidays()` is rather straightforward once its underlying algorithm is understood. There are three points, however, worth emphasizing.

The first point is that the method has been declared using the keyword `static`. This means that the method is a general-purpose one and is not called to operate on a specific `Date` object. (Formally, this means that the method *does not* use an implied object that is passed into the `this` reference parameter and that all arguments must be explicitly passed through the parameter list, which in this case is empty.) This

---

[5] An alternative is to first read the file simply to determine the number of dates in the file. An array of `Dates` can then be declared using this number, and the file read a second time, at which point each date would be stored in the array. The advantage of this approach is that we are always dealing with `Date` objects rather than the `ArrayList`'s `Object` objects, which must always be cast back into `Date` objects. The disadvantage is that it requires two file reads.

designation is appropriate for this method because it will be called only once to establish the holiday array.

Following is the Java code that corresponds to this pseudocode:

```java
public static void getHolidays()
  throws java.io.IOException
{
  String fileName = "Holidays.txt";
  String inline;
  int mm, dd, yy;
  Date a = new Date();  // create a single Date object

  try    // this block tries to open the file and create the input streams
  {
      // set up the basic input streams
    FileReader fr = new FileReader(fileName);
      // buffer the input stream
    BufferedReader br = new BufferedReader(fr);

      // read and store each date
    //System.out.println("The parsed data read from the " + fileName + " file is:");
    while ( (inline = br.readLine()) != null)
    {
      StringTokenizer parser = new StringTokenizer(inline, "/ \t\n\r,");
      mm = Integer.parseInt(parser.nextToken());
      dd = Integer.parseInt(parser.nextToken());
      yy = Integer.parseInt(parser.nextToken());
      // System.out.println("   " + mm + "   " + dd + "   " + yy);
      a.setDate(mm, dd, yy);   //convert to a date
      hTable.add(a);   // add the holiday into the array
    }
    // System.out.println("The Holiday file was successfully read and stored.");
    br.close();
    hTable.trimToSize(); // remove any blank records
  }
  catch (FileNotFoundException e)
  {
    System.out.println("The file " + fileName + " was not successfully opened."
                  + "\nPlease check that the file currently exists.");
    System.exit(0);
  }
}
```

The second point is that dates are stored within the Holidays.txt file in the conventional manner, which uses a forward slash to delimit the month, day, and year values. Thus, when these values are parsed, we must inform the nextToken() method that the forward slash, /, should be used to separate values. This information is provided within the constructor called in the statement

```
StringTokenizer parser = new StringTokenizer(inline, "/ \t\n\r,");
```

The last argument in the constructor sets the slash, space character, tab, newline, carriage return, and comma as valid delimiters. Thus, if a date such as 12/25/2004 were stored in the file as either 12,25,2004 or 12 25 2004, the program would still correctly parse the data.

The last point, which is more subtle, is that all objects stored in the `ArrayList` are stored as `Object` types and not as `Date` types. As detailed in Section 8.5, the `Object` type is the generic type stored in an `ArrayList`, into which each object is implicitly cast before insertion into the list. At this point, the fact that `Object` objects, rather than `Date` objects, are stored does not directly affect us. However, when we retrieve an object from the `ArrayList`, we will have to be aware that an `Object` type has been retrieved because it will have to be cast into a `Date` type before any comparisons can be made.

Verifying the `getHolidays()` Method

Once the `getHolidays()` method has been included within the `Date` class, we can test its operation. To make this testing easier, notice the three lines that have been commented out, which are repeated here for convenience.

```
//System.out.println("The parsed data read from the " + fileName + " file is:");
//System.out.println("   " + mm + "   " + dd + "   " + yy);
//System.out.println("The Holiday file was successfully read and stored.");
```

If we remove the comment slashes, //, these three lines can be used to monitor the operation of the method as data are read and parsed from the `Holidays.txt` file and then stored in the `ArrayList`. Program 12.9 can be used to provide a quick verification of `getHolidays()`'s performance.

Program 12.9

```
public class TestHolidayRead
{
  public static void main(String[] args)
    throws java.io.IOException
  {
    Date.getHolidays();
  }
}
```

Assuming that the specified display lines have been uncommented in `get-Holidays()`, that this method has been included in the `Date` class code, that the `Date` class has been recompiled, and that the `Holidays.txt` file listed in Table 12.11 has been created, the output produced by Program 12.9 is

```
The parsed data read from the Holidays.txt file is:
  1   1   2004
  1   19  2004
  2   18  2004
  4   9   2004
  4   11  2004
```

```
5   5   2004
5   24  2004
5   31  2004
7   1   2004
7   4   2004
9   6   2004
10  11  2004
10  11  2004
11  31  2004
12  25  2004
The Holiday file was successfully read and stored.
```

As indicated by this output, the file's data have been successfully read, parsed, and stored by getHolidays().

The isHoliday() Method

The requirement for this method is that it accept a Date object as an implied parameter and check it against the dates stored in the class's static holiday ArrayList. If a matching date is found, the method should return a boolean value of true; otherwise, it should return a boolean value of false. Before the check is made, however, the method must first determine if the table is empty; if it is, the getHolidays() method should be called to create a valid table. The algorithm describing this process, in pseudocode, is

isHoliday() Algorithm

If the holiday table is empty,
    Call getHolidays()
For all holidays in the table
    Retrieve the holiday from the table
    Retrieve the holiday's month, day, and year
    Compare the holiday's month, day, and year to the
    implicit object's month, day, and year
    If there is a match
        Return true
EndFor
Return false

Written in Java code, this algorithm becomes

```
public boolean isHoliday()
 throws java.io.IOException
{
  int i, mm, dd, yy;
  Object holiday;

   // read the Holiday file if the Holiday table is empty
  if (hTable.isEmpty())
   getHolidays();
    // search the Holiday table for the given Date
```

```
        for(i = 0; i < hTable.size(); i++)
        {
          holiday = hTable.get(i);   // retrieve a holiday
          mm = ((Date)holiday).getMonth();
          dd = ((Date)holiday).getDay();
          yy = ((Date)holiday).getYear();
          if ( month == mm && day == dd && year == yy )
            return true;
        }
        return false;
    }
```

In reviewing this code, notice that the object retrieved from the linked list holiday table, hTable, is actually of type Object, which is the generic data type stored in an ArrayList. Thus, the first requirement is to cast this retrieved Object type into a Date type, which is accomplished by the (Date) expression. The three accessor methods, getMonth(), getDay(), and getYear(), which will have to be written, are then applied to this Date object so that the individual values can be compared to the implied object's instance variables. If there is a match, the method breaks out of the loop and returns the boolean true value. If the loop exits normally, indicating that no match was found, the boolean false value is returned. Program 12.10 includes the isHoliday() method and the three new accessor methods within the context of a complete Date class. For ease of reading, this new code has been highlighted, and the dayOfWeek() and isLeapYear() codes have been omitted.

Program 12.10

```
import java.text.*;   // needed for formatting
import java.io.*;     // needed to read in Holiday File
import java.util.*;   // needed for ArrayList
public class Date
{

  // class variable declaration section
  static ArrayList hTable = new ArrayList();

  private int month;
  private int day;
  private int year;

  // class method definition section
  public Date()    // default constructor
  {
    setDate(7, 4, 2005);
  }


  public Date(int mm, int dd, int yyyy)  // overloaded constructor
  {
```

(continued)

(continued)

```
    setDate(mm, dd, yyyy);
  }


  public void setDate(int mm, int dd, int yyyy) // mutator
  {
    month = mm;
    day = dd;
    year = yyyy;
  }


  public void showDate() // modified accessor
  {
    DecimalFormat df = new DecimalFormat("00");

    System.out.println(df.format(month)
                + '/' + df.format(day) + '/'
                + df.format(year % 100)); // extract the last 2 year digits
  }

// accessors
public int getMonth() {return month;}
public int getDay() {return day;}
public int getYear() {return year;}

public boolean isHoliday()
 throws java.io.IOException
{
  int i, mm, dd, yy;
  Object holiday;

   // read the Holiday file if the Holiday table is empty
  if (hTable.isEmpty())
   getHolidays();

   // search the Holiday table for the given Date
  for(i = 0; i < hTable.size(); i++)
  {
    holiday = hTable.get(i);  // retrieve a holiday
    mm = ((Date)holiday).getMonth();
    dd = ((Date)holiday).getDay();
    yy = ((Date)holiday).getYear();
    if ( month == mm && day == dd && year == yy )
      return true;
  }
  return false;
}
```

```java
public static void getHolidays()
  throws java.io.IOException
{
  String fileName = "Holidays.txt";
  String inline;
  int mm, dd, yy;
  Date a = new Date();  // create a single Date object

  try    // this block tries to open the file and create the input streams
  {
      // set up the basic input streams
    FileReader fr = new FileReader(fileName);
      // buffer the input stream
    BufferedReader br = new BufferedReader(fr);

      // read and store each date
    //System.out.println("The parsed data read from the " + fileName + " file is:");

    while ( (inline = br.readLine()) != null)
    {
      StringTokenizer parser = new StringTokenizer(inline, "/ \t\n\r,");
      mm = Integer.parseInt(parser.nextToken());
      dd = Integer.parseInt(parser.nextToken());
      yy = Integer.parseInt(parser.nextToken());
      //System.out.println("    " + mm + "  " + dd + "  " + yy);
      a.setDate(mm, dd, yy);  //convert to a date
      hTable.add(a);  // add the holiday into the array
    }
    //System.out.println("The Holiday file was successfully read and stored.");
    br.close();
    hTable.trimToSize(); // remove any blank records
  }
  catch (FileNotFoundException e)
  {
    System.out.println("The file " + fileName + " was not successfully opened."
                  + "\nPlease check that the file currently exists.");
    System.exit(0);
  }
}
}
```

Verifying the isHoliday() Method

Program 12.11 provides a quick verification of Program 12.10's isHoliday() method by testing one holiday and one nonholiday date.

Program 12.11

```java
public class TestDate
{
  public static void main(String[] args)
    throws java.io.IOException
  {
    Date a = new Date(1, 15, 2004);
    Date b = new Date(12, 25, 2004);

    a.showDate();
    if (a.isHoliday())
      System.out.println(" is a holiday.");
    else
      System.out.println(" is not a holiday.");

    b.showDate();
    if (b.isHoliday())
      System.out.println(" is a holiday.");
    else
      System.out.println(" is not a holiday.");

  }
}
```

The output produced by Program 12.11 is

```
01/15/04
 is not a holiday.
12/25/04
 is a holiday.
```

As indicated by this output, isHoliday() method appears to be working correctly.

Exercises 12.4

1. Explain why the class named Date is required in Program 12.9's call to getHolidays().

2. Include the getHolidays() method in the Date class and compile the new class code.

3. Enter, compile, and run Program 12.9.

4. Enter and compile the Date class presented in Program 12.10.

5. Enter and run Program 12.11 on your computer. To accomplish this successfully, you will have to complete Exercise 4.

6. Replace the following statements in Program 12.10 with a call to a method named isEqual().

   ```java
   mm = ((Date)holiday).getMonth();
   dd = ((Date)holiday).getDay();
   ```

```
yy = ((Date)holiday).getYear();
if ( month == mm && day == dd && year == yy )
    return true;
```

The method header isEqual() should be

```
public boolean isEqual(Date secDate).
```

7. Program 12.9's getHolidays() method is actually one of three methods typically used in creating, maintaining, and using a list of constants stored in a file. Thus, this method can be defined in its own class, which would contain all of the necessary file-related methods. For this exercise, place the getHolidays() method within a class named Holidays and make all of the necessary adjustments to the Date class to ensure that the isEqual() method works correctly when Program 12.11 is run.

8a. Add a method named setHolidays() to the Holidays class created in Exercise 7. This new method should read and display the current list of holidays and then let the user change, add, or delete holidays from the list. After a holiday has been either modified, deleted, or added, the method should sort the holidays and display the new list. Finally, the method should ask the user whether the new list should be saved; if the user responds positively, the method should write the new data to the existing Holidays.txt file, overwriting the contents of the existing file.

b. Add a method named createHolidays() to the Holidays class created in Exercise 7. This new method should be used to create a completely new Holidays.txt file and overwrite the existing file when the user provides positive confirmation that the file should be written.

9a. A file named Polar.dat contains the polar coordinates needed in a graphics program. Currently, this file contains the following data:

Distance (inches)	Angle (degrees)
2	45
6	30
10	45
4	60
12	55
8	15

Write a Java program to create this file on your computer system.

b. Using the Polar.dat file created in Exercise 9a, write a Java program that accepts distance and angle data from the user and adds the data to the end of the file.

c. Using the Polar.dat file created in Exercise 9a, write a Java program that reads this file and creates a second file named XYcoord.dat. The entries in the new file should contain the rectangular coordinates corresponding to the polar coordinates in the Polar.dat file. Polar coordinates are converted to rectangular coordinates using the equations

$x = r \cos(\theta)$
$y = r \sin(\theta)$

where *r* is the distance coordinate and θ is the radian equivalent of the angle coordinate in the `Polar.dat` file.

10. Pollen count readings, which are taken from August through September in the northeastern region of the United States, measure the number of ragweed pollen grains in the air. Pollen counts in the range of 10 to 200 grains per cubic meter of air are typical during this time of year. Pollen counts above 10 begin to affect a small percentage of hay fever sufferers, counts in the range of 30 to 40 will noticeably bother approximately 30 percent of hay fever sufferers, and counts between 40 and 50 adversely affect more than 60 percent of all hay fever sufferers.

Write a Java program that updates a file containing the 10 most recent pollen counts. As a new count is obtained, it is to be added to the end of the file, and the oldest count, which is the first value in the file, is to be deleted. Additionally, the averages of the old and new files' data must be calculated and displayed.

To test your program, first create a file named `Pollen.dat` that contains the following pollen count data: 30, 60, 40, 80, 90, 120, 150, 130, 160, 170. Here the first value, 30, corresponds to the oldest pollen count, and the last value, 170, corresponds to the most recent pollen count. The pseudocode for the file update program is

Display a message indicating what the program does
Request the name of the data file
Request a new pollen count reading
Open the data file
Do for ten data items
    Read a value into an array
    Add the value to a total
EndDo
Calculate and display the old ten-day average
Calculate and display the new ten-day average
Write the nine most recent pollen counts from the array to the file
Write the new pollen count to the file
Close the file

11a. Write a Java program to create a data file containing the following information:

Student ID Number	Student Name	Course Code	Course Credits	Course Grade
---------	-----------	------	-------	------
2333021	Bokow, R.	NS201	3	A
2333021	Bokow, R.	MG342	3	A
2333021	Bokow, R.	FA302	1	A
2574063	Fustil, D.	MK106	3	C
2574063	Fustil, D.	MA208	3	B
2574063	Fustil, D.	CM201	3	C
2574063	Fustil, D.	CP101	2	B
2663628	Kingsley, M.	QA140	3	A
2663628	Kingsley, M.	CM245	3	B
2663628	Kingsley, M.	EQ521	3	A
2663628	Kingsley, M.	MK341	3	A
2663628	Kingsley, M.	CP101	2	B

b. Using the file created in Exercise 11a, write a Java program that creates student grade reports. The grade report for each student should contain the student's name and identification number, a list of courses taken, the credits and grade for each course, and a semester grade point average. For example, the grade report for the first student should be:

```
Student Name: Bokow, R.
Student ID Number: 2333021

Course        Course      Course
Code          Credits     Grade
------        -------     ------

NS201            3          A
MG342            3          A
FA302            1          A

Total Semester Course Credits Completed: 7
Semester Grade Point Average: 4.0
```

The semester grade point average is computed in two steps. First, each course grade is assigned a numerical value (A = 4, B = 3, C = 2, D = 1, F = 0), and the sum of each course's grade value times the credits for each course is computed. This sum is then divided by the total number of credits taken during the semester.

12a. Write a Java program to create a data file containing the following information:

Student ID Number	Student Name	Course Credits	Cumulative Grade Point Average (GPA)
2333021	Bokow, R.	48	4.0
2574063	Fustil, D.	12	1.8
2663628	Kingsley, M.	36	3.5

b. Using the file created in Exercise 12a as a master file and the file created in Exercise 11a as a transactions file, write a file update program to create an updated master file.

12.5 Random Access Files

The manner in which data in a file are written and retrieved is called **file access**. All of the files created so far have used **sequential access**, which means that data in the file are accessed sequentially, one item after another. Thus, for example, the fourth item in a sequentially accessed file cannot be read without first reading the first three items in the file, and the last item in the file cannot be read without first reading all of the previous items. Because data within a sequential file cannot be replaced, updating a sequential access file requires a file update procedure in which a completely new file is created for each update (e.g., see the second application in the previous section). For applications in which the majority of the data in a file must be read and updated, such as updating a monthly payroll file, sequential access conforms to the way the file must be updated and is not a restriction.

In many applications, random access to data in the file, where individual data in the middle of the file can be retrieved, modified, and rewritten without reading or writing any other data, is preferable. **Random access** files, also referred to as **direct**

FIGURE 12.8   **Fixed-length records consisting of 16 bytes**

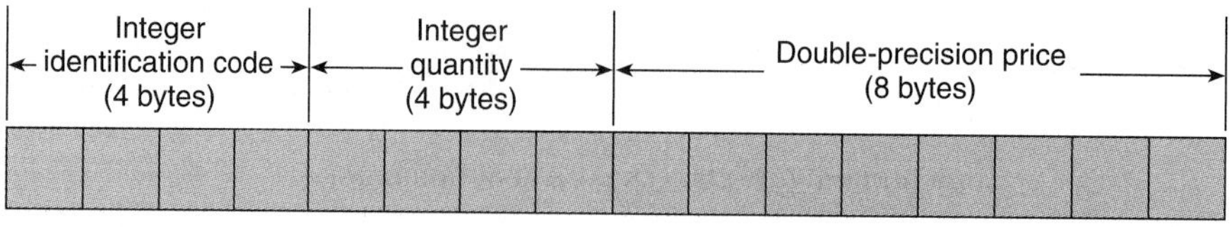

access files, provide this capability. In this section, you will see how to create and use random access files. In Java, random access files are typically created as byte-based files using methods almost identical to those provided by the `DataInputStream` and `DataOutputStream` presented in Section 12.3.

The key to creating and using random access files is imposing a structure on the file so that specific items can be located and updated in place. The most common structure consists of fixed-length records that themselves consist of a set of fixed-length items. This permits locating any specific record and any specific item in a record by skipping over a fixed number of bytes. For example, Figure 12.8 illustrates a record consisting of an integer product identification code, an integer number representing the quantity in stock, and a double-precision number representing the item's selling price. Using a byte-based file, each integer value requires 4 bytes of storage, and the double-precision value requires 8 bytes. Thus, each record in the file requires 16 bytes of storage, and the identification code, quantity, and price are stored in the same positions in every record.

A random access file is created as an object of the class `RandomAccessFile`. The basic stream object needed for creating and using a random access file requires a file name, either as a string variable, string constant, or `File` object, and a mode. The mode can be either an "`r`" for read only or "`rw`", which permits reading and writing to the same file. For example, the statement

```
RandomAccessFile raf =
    new RandomAccessFile("products.dat", "rw");
```

creates a random access file stream to the file named `products.dat`, on the current directory, that can be read from and written to. If this file exists, it will be opened; otherwise, it will be created.

Once a random access file stream has been opened in read-write mode, reading and writing the file are almost identical to reading and writing a byte-based file. That is, the `RandomAccessFile` methods are similar to those of the `DataInputStream` and `DataOutputStream` classes in that they permit primitive data values to be read from and written to the file. Table 12.12 lists the methods provided by the `RandomAccessFile` class.

The key to providing random access to a file is that each random access stream establishes an internal file position pointer. This pointer keeps track of where the next byte is to be read from, written to, or skipped over. The two member methods that are used to access and change the file position marker are the first two listed in Table 12.12, `seek()` and `getFilePointer()`.

The `seek()` method permits the programmer to move to any byte position in the file, whether for reading, writing, or skipping over. To understand this method fully, you must first understand how data are referenced in the file using the file position pointer.

Table 12.12 `RandomAccessFile` **Member Methods**

Name	Type	Description
`seek()`	Access	Moves the file pointer.
`getFilePointer()`	Access	Retrieves the current file pointer.
`length`	Information	Returns the number of bytes in the file.
`getFD()`	Information	Retrieves the file descriptor.
`close()`	Close	Closes the file.
`read()`	Input	Reads bytes.
`readBoolean()`	Input	Reads a `boolean` value.
`readByte()`	Input	Reads an 8-bit `byte`.
`readChar()`	Input	Reads a 16-bit `char`.
`readDouble()`	Input	Reads a 64-bit `double`.
`readFloat()`	Input	Reads a 16-bit `float`.
`readFully()`	Input	Reads the requested number of bytes, using blocking until read is complete.
`readInt()`	Input	Reads a 32-bit `int`.
`readLine()`	Input	Reads a line.
`readLong()`	Input	Reads a 64-bit `long`.
`readShort()`	Input	Reads a 16-bit `short`.
`readUnsignedByte()`	Input	Reads an unsigned 8-bit `byte`.
`readUnsignedShort()`	Input	Reads an unsigned 8-bit `short`.
`readUTF()`	Input	Reads using UTF code.
`skipBytes()`	Input	Skips bytes.
`writeBoolean()`	Output	Writes a `boolean` value.
`writeByte()`	Output	Writes an 8-bit `byte`.
`writeChar()`	Output	Writes a 16-bit `char`.
`writeDoouble()`	Output	Writes a 64-bit `double`.
`writeFloat()`	Output	Writes a 16-bit `float`.
`writeInt()`	Output	Writes a 32-bit `int`.
`writeLine()`	Output	Writes a line.
`writeLong()`	Output	Writes a 64-bit `long`.
`writeShort()`	Output	Writes a 16-bit `short`.
`writeUTF()`	Output	Writes using UTF code.

Each byte in a random access file can be accessed by its position in the file. The first byte in the file is located at position 0, the next byte at position 1, and so on. A byte's position is also referred to as its offset from the start of the file. The first byte has an offset of 0, the second byte has an offset of 1, and so on for each byte in the file.

The `seek()` method requires a single argument: an offset, as a long integer, into the file. The offset is always calculated from the beginning of the file. Using this argument, the `seek()` method sets the current value of the file's internal position pointer. All subsequent read, write, or skip operations then operate on the file starting at the position indicated by this file pointer. As a specific example, assume that a data file named `test.dat` consists of the data illustrated in Figure 12.9.

FIGURE 12.9   **The data in the `test.dat` file**

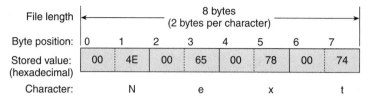

Notice that each character stored in the file in Figure 12.9 consists of 2 bytes. This is because the file was created using the `DataOutputStream`'s `writeChar()` method, which writes characters using 2 bytes per character. In practice, the file can be constructed either as a byte-based file or as a random access file because the output streams that create both of these files use the same type of output methods. (The creation of this file is left as Exercise 1.)

For the file shown in Figure 12.9, the length of the file is 8 bytes, and a statement such as `raf.seek(4)` places an internal file position pointer at the start of the 2-byte sequence that stores the letter x in the file. Now, if the expression `raf.readChar()` is executed, the next 2 bytes of storage will be read and the file's position pointer is automatically moved to byte position 6. This type of automatic adjustment to the file pointer is made whenever a read, skip, or write is encountered.

Program 12.12 illustrates the `seek()` method to read the characters in a byte-based file named `test.dat` in reverse order, from the last character to the first. As each character is read, it is also displayed.

Program 12.12

```java
import java.io.*;
public class DisplayReversed
{
  static final int SIZEOFCHAR = 2;   // there are 2 bytes per char
  public static void main(String[] args)
    throws java.io.IOException
  {
    String fileName = "test.dat";
    char ch;
    long last, position, setbytepos;
      // set up the basic random access input/output stream
    RandomAccessFile raf =
       new RandomAccessFile(fileName, "rw");
    last = raf.length();  // get length of the file
    position = last - SIZEOFCHAR; // starting position of last char
    while(position >= 0)
    {
      raf.seek(position);    // move to the character
      ch = raf.readChar();
      System.out.print(ch + " | ");
      position = position - SIZEOFCHAR;  // position of prior char
    }
    raf.close();
  }
}
```

Assuming the file `test.dat` contains the data in Figure 12.9, the output displayed by Program 12.12 is

```
t | x | e | N |
```

First, notice that Program 12.1 does not check for a `FileNotFound Exception`. Because we are opening the file in read-write mode, the program will automatically create the file if it is not found; therefore, a `catch` block based on this exception would never be executed. A more useful check is to verify the file's existence using one of the techniques presented in the Programming Note on pages 622 and 655.

In terms of actual file processing, Program 12.12 initially goes to the last character in the file. The position of this last character is obtained as the length of the file, which in our case is 8 bytes minus 2. If we had simply set the file's position pointer to 8, we would be pointing to the end of the last character, but we want to start at the beginning of the last character. The position of this last character, as seen in Figure 12.9, is at byte position 6, which is 2 bytes before the end of the file. The first invocation of the `seek()` method positions the internal file pointer value to correctly locate the start of this last character. As each character is read, the character is displayed and the position is adjusted to access the next character.

While the `seek()` method moves the file pointer's value, the `getFilePointer()` method returns the value in the file position pointer. For example, after the first `readChar()` is executed in Program 12.12, the method call

```
raf.getFilePointer()
```

would return the long integer value 8. In Program 12.12, the `getFilePointer()` method is not used. The important point illustrated by Program 12.12 is that accessing files randomly does require knowing exactly how the data in the file are stored and having some means for precisely locating the byte position of each data item in the file. In practice, this is typically accomplished by aggregating data items into fixed-length records, which is presented next.

Using Fixed-Length Records[6]

Because random access of data in a random access file is by byte position, applications that use random access files must provide a known means of locating each data item in the file. In practice, this is accomplished by ensuring that the data items are assembled into fixed-length records and providing each record with an identification number or account code that can be converted, either directly or indirectly, into a byte offset.

For example, assume that a random access file containing the data in Table 12.13 is to be created. This is accomplished by writing five records to the file. Each record in the file stores a product identification number, the quantity of the product in stock, and the product's selling price, with each data item stored in numerical form and not as strings. Specifically, the product identification number has been selected as a four-digit integer so that subtracting 1000 from the identification number yields the correct record number. Thus, the data for product identification number 1001 will be stored in record number 1, the data for product identification number 1002 will

---

[6] This topic can be omitted on first reading without loss of subject continuity.

Table 12.13   **Product Information to Be Stored in a Random Access File**

Identification Number	Quantity in Stock	Selling Price
1001	476	28.35
1002	348	32.56
1003	517	51.27
1004	284	23.75
1005	165	35.25

be stored in record number 2, and so on. (Converting an identification code to a record number is formally called *hashing*.) Program 12.13 creates the required file.

Program 12.13

```java
import java.io.*;
public class WriteRandom
{
  public static void main(String[] args)
     throws java.io.IOException
  {
    String fileName = "products.dat";
    String acctstring, amtstring, pricestring;
    int acct, amt;
    double price;

      // set up the keyboard for string input
     InputStreamReader isr =
       new InputStreamReader(System.in);
     BufferedReader br =
        new BufferedReader(isr);

      // set up the basic random access input/output stream
    RandomAccessFile raf =
       new RandomAccessFile(fileName, "rw");

      // enter and store data for five records
    for(int i = 1; i <= 5; i++)
    {
      System.out.print("Enter the identification number: ");
      acctstring = br.readLine();
      acct = Integer.parseInt(acctstring);
      raf.writeInt(acct);
      System.out.print("Enter the quantity in stock: ");
      amtstring = br.readLine();
      amt = Integer.parseInt(amtstring);
```

```
        raf.writeInt(amt);
        System.out.print("Enter the price: ");
        pricestring = br.readLine();
        price = Double.parseDouble(pricestring);
        raf.writeDouble(price);
      }

    System.out.println("The file " + fileName
                       + " has been written.");
    System.out.println("The length of the file is "
                       + raf.length() + " bytes.");
    raf.close();
  }
}
```

In reviewing Program 12.13, notice that most of the coding is concerned with inputting data from the keyboard and converting the entered data into numerical form. The actual writes of the numerical data to the random access file are handled by the following three statements within the `for` loop:

```
raf.writeInt(acct);
raf.writeInt(amt);
raf.writeDouble(price);
```

When Program 12.13 is run, and assuming that the data in Table 12.13 are entered correctly, the byte-based file created by the program is illustrated in Figure 12.10. Hexadecimal values are used in the figure to indicate the equivalent binary values. Although the figure separates the file's records into individual lines, with bars, |, used to distinguish individual items in each record, in actuality the file is stored as a consecutive sequence of bytes. The file will be exactly 80 bytes in length, which corresponds to five records of 16 bytes each. Figure 12.11 lists the data in the file converted into a decimal format. To check these values, you would first have to convert the hexadecimal values in Figure 12.10 to their binary equivalent. Then, for the first two integer values in each record, you can use the techniques presented in Section 1.9 to convert from binary to decimal. To convert the double-precision data in the last 8 bytes of each record, you will need the information presented on real number storage in Appendix I.

FIGURE 12.10 **The data in the file produced by Program 12.13**

```
|00 00 03 E9|00 00 01 DC|40 3C 59 99 99 99 99 9A| <- 1st record of 16 bytes
|00 00 03 EA|00 00 01 5C|40 40 47 AE 14 7A E1 48| <- 2nd record of 16 bytes
|00 00 03 EB|00 00 02 05|40 49 A2 8F 5C 28 F5 C3| <- 3rd record of 16 bytes
|00 00 03 EC|00 00 01 1C|40 37 C0 00 00 00 00 00| <- 4th record of 16 bytes
|00 00 03 ED|00 00 00 A5|40 41 A0 00 00 00 00 00| <- 5th record of 16 bytes
|<-4 bytes->|<-4 bytes->|<---- 8 bytes ---->|
```

FIGURE 12.11   **The decimal equivalent of the data in Figure 12.10**

```
|1001|  476|   28.35| <-- 1st record
|1002|  348|   32.56| <-- 2nd record
|1003|  517|   51.27| <-- 3rd record
|1004|  284|   23.75| <-- 4th record
|1005|  165|   35.25| <-- 5th record
```

Program 12.14 illustrates using the numerical methods readInt() and read-Double() to directly input the numerical data in the random access file created by Program 12.13. Notice that because we are sequentially reading all of the data in the file, starting with the first identification number, the program does not yet directly make use of random access features of the file.

Program 12.14

```java
import java.io.*;
public class ReadRandom
{
  public static void main(String[] args)
    throws java.io.IOException
  {
    String fileName = "products.dat";
    int acct, amt;
    double price;

      // set up the basic random access input/output stream
    RandomAccessFile raf =
       new RandomAccessFile(fileName, "rw");

      // print the headings
    System.out.println("              Quantity");
    System.out.println("ID No.   in Stock    Price");
    System.out.println("------   --------   ------");

      // read and print the data
    for(int i = 1; i <= 5; i++)
    {
      acct = raf.readInt();
      amt = raf.readInt();
      price = raf.readDouble();
      System.out.println(" " + acct
                        + "         " + amt
                        + "       $" + price);
    }

    raf.close();
  }
}
```

The output produced by Program 12.14 is

```
              Quantity
  ID No.      in Stock   Price
  ------      --------   ------
    1001         476     $28.35
    1002         348     $32.56
    1003         517     $51.27
    1004         284     $23.75
    1005         165     $35.25
```

The real advantage to random access files is that records in the file can be read and written in any order. This permits the lookup of a single record anywhere in the file and the capability to update each accessed record. To illustrate this, consider Program 12.15, which requests a user to enter an identification number. If the record corresponding to the desired identification number is located, the user is requested to enter a new quantity, and the updated data are written to the existing record; otherwise, the user is informed that no record exists for the entered identification number.

Program 12.15

```java
import java.io.*;
public class UpdateRandom
{

  static final int RECLEN = 16;      // record length in bytes
  static final int BASEREC = 1000;

  public static void main(String[] args)
    throws java.io.IOException
  {
    String fileName = "products.dat";
    String acctstring, amtstring, pricestring;
    int acct, amt;
    int recnum;
    double price;
    long filelen, position, setbytepos;

      // set up the keyboard for string input
    InputStreamReader isr =
      new InputStreamReader(System.in);
    BufferedReader br =
      new BufferedReader(isr);

      // set up the basic random access input/output stream
    RandomAccessFile raf =
      new RandomAccessFile(fileName, "rw");

    filelen = raf.length();  // get length of the file
    System.out.print("Enter the identification number (999 to stop): ");
    acctstring = br.readLine();
```

(continued)

(continued)

```
    while (!acctstring.equals("999"))
    {
       // calculate the record number for this id number
      recnum = Integer.parseInt(acctstring) - BASEREC;
       // calculate the starting byte position for this record
      position = (recnum - 1) * RECLEN;
       // make sure this is a valid byte position
      if (position < 0 || position > (filelen - 1))
      {
        System.out.println("There is no record for this id number");
        System.out.print("Please recheck and reenter the identification "
                      + "number (999 to stop): ");
        acctstring = br.readLine();
        continue;
      }
      raf.seek(position);  // move to the record
      acct = raf.readInt();
      setbytepos = raf.getFilePointer();
      amt = raf.readInt();
      System.out.println("The current quantity in stock is: " + amt);
      System.out.print("Enter the new quantity: ");
      amtstring = br.readLine();
      amt = Integer.parseInt(amtstring);
      raf.seek(setbytepos);  // reset position to the amt field
      raf.writeInt(amt);
      System.out.println("The record has been updated.");
      System.out.print("Enter a new identification number (999 to stop): ");
      acctstring = br.readLine();
    }

    raf.close();
  }
}
```

Following is a sample run of Program 12.15 in which two existing records have been successfully updated and one incorrectly entered identification number has been correctly detected.

```
Enter the identification number (999 to stop): 1003
The current quantity in stock is: 517
Enter the new quantity: 436
The record has been updated.
Enter a new identification number (999 to stop): 1008
There is no record for this id number
Please recheck and reenter the identification number (999 to stop): 1005
The current quantity in stock is: 165
Enter the new quantity: 196
The record has been updated.
```

Exercises 12.5

1. Either by copying the file from the Web site associated with this text or by writing a Java program, create a byte-based file named `test.dat` that stores the following four letters as individual characters (see Figure 12.12 on page 672):

   Next

   The file can be created in Java using either `DataOutputStream` or `RandomAccessFile` methods.

2. Enter and run Program 12.12 to read and display the data in the file created in Exercise 1 in reverse order.

3. Assume that a text editor created the file `test.dat` for Exercise 1 or the file was created as a text-based file using methods from the `PrintWriter` class. In this case,

   a. How would the stored characters differ from those shown in Figure 12.12?

   b. What modification would you have to make to Program 12.12 to read and display the characters in the file?

4. Write and run a Java program that reads and displays every second character in the `test.dat` file created for Exercise 1.

5. Write a method named `findChars()` that returns the total number of characters in a byte-based file. Assume that the file consists of character data only.

6a. Write a method named `readBytes()` that reads and displays n characters starting from any position in a byte-based file that consists of stored characters only. The method should accept three arguments: a file name, the position of the first character to be read, and the number of characters to be read. The character position argument should be in characters, not in bytes. Thus, if the letters `An unusual opportunity` are stored in the file, the first u in `unusual` would be designated as character number 4.

   b. Modify the `readBytes()` method written for Exercise 6a to store the characters read as either a `String` or `StringBuffer` object. The method should return the `String` or `StringBuffer` object that is created.

7. Enter and run Program 12.13 on your computer.

8. Enter and run Program 12.14 on your computer.

9. Enter and run Program 12.15 on your computer.

12.6 The `File` Class

Before attempting to read from or write to a file, good programming practice requires that you check the status of the desired file that will be attached to a file stream. These checks can be done using the methods of a Java class named `File`. It should be noted that the methods of this class do not let you perform any file input or output; for this, you need to establish appropriate file stream objects. What the `File` class does provide is a number of useful methods that permit you to perform relevant checks on a file's status. Table 12.14 lists the methods provided by this class.

Program 12.16 illustrates a number of the `File` class's methods within the context of a complete program.

Table 12.14 **Common `File` Class Methods**

Method	Description
canRead()	Returns a boolean `true` if the file can be read from.
canWrite()	Returns a boolean `true` if the file exists and can be written to.
delete()	Deletes the designated file and returns a boolean `true` if successful.
exists()	Returns a boolean `true` if the designated file exists.
getAbsolutePath()	Generates the full pathname of this file from system directory information.
getName()	Returns the file name of this file from the given pathname.
getParent()	Returns the pathname of the parent directory of the file from the given pathname.
isDirectory()	Returns a boolean `true` if the designated file is a directory.
isFile()	Returns `true` if the file is a regular (nondirectory) file.
length()	Returns the size of the file, in bytes, as provided by the operating system.
renameTo()	Renames the file.

Program 12.16

```java
import java.io.*;
public class CheckFile
{
  public static void main(String[] args)
    throws java.io.IOException
  {

    String fileName = "C:\\jdk\\prices.dat";  // note that a full pathname
                                              // requires two delimiters
    String nextName = "backup.dat";   // a relative pathname can also be used

    File inFile = new File(fileName);
    File newName = new File(nextName);

    if (inFile.exists())
    {
      System.out.println("The file " + fileName + " exists");

        // check the type of file
      if (inFile.isDirectory())
        System.out.println("  This is a directory");
      else if (inFile.isFile())
        System.out.println("  This is a regular file");

        // check if file is readable
      if (inFile.canRead())
        System.out.println("  The file can be read");
      else
        System.out.println("  The file is not readable");
```

```
      // check if file is writeable
    if (inFile.canWrite())
    System.out.println("  The file can be written to");
    else
      System.out.println("  The file is not writeable");

    // report the file's length
    System.out.println("The file length is " + inFile.length() + " bytes");

     // report the file's directory path
   System.out.println("The pathname of this file's parent is "
                      + inFile.getParent());

     // rename the file
  inFile.renameTo(newName);
  System.out.println("The file has been renamed " + newName);
  System.out.println("The full pathname for this file is "
                     + newName.getAbsolutePath());
  }
  else
    System.out.println("The file " + fileName + " does not exist");
  }
}
```

The output produced by Program 12.16 is

```
The file prices.dat exists
   This is a regular file
   The file can be read
   The file can be written to
The file length is 24 bytes
The pathname of this file's parent is C:\jdk
The file has been renamed backup.dat
The full pathname for this file is C:\jdk\backup.dat
```

Although the display produced by Program 12.16 is rather straightforward, a few items in this output should be mentioned. First, the pathname returned by the get-Parent() method is obtained from the pathname provided in the program. If a relative pathname is provided, getParent() will return a null value. If you want the program to generate the full pathname of a file from system information, you must use the getAbsolutePath() method, as is illustrated by the last displayed line. Additionally, the renameTo() method will only rename a file if the new name is not already in use. Once a file is renamed, however, the previous name is no longer valid. Finally, a practical notational consideration needs to be explained. In practice, as is done in Program 12.16, the expression if (inFile.exists()) is used in preference to the longer expression if(inFile.exists() == true). It is important to become familiar with the shorter notation, as it is the one preferred by most professional programmers. Similarly, an expression such as if (inFile.exists() == false) would be coded by a professional Java programmer as if (!inFile.exists()).

File Checking

One of the most important uses of the `File` class is to check that files intended for input exist and are readable. Similarly, if you intend to write to a file, you should first check that a file with the given name does not already exist. If it does, all of the data in the file will be erased at the moment that an output stream is connected to the file.

Program 12.17 illustrates two typical checks that should be used before any file is opened for reading. First, the program checks that the file exists. Next, if the file does exist, the program checks that it can be read. Such checks are especially important for UNIX-based systems, where read privileges can be easily turned off.

Program 12.17

```java
import java.io.*;
public class CheckForRead
{
  public static void main(String[] args)
    throws java.io.IOException
  {
    String fileName = "prices.dat";

    File inFile = new File(fileName);

      // check that the file exists and can be read
    if (inFile.exists() == false)
    {
      System.out.println("The file " + fileName
                         + " does not exist - please check and rerun.");
      System.exit(0);
    }
    else if(inFile.canRead() == false)
    {
      System.out.println("The file " + fileName
          + " exists but does not have read permission - please check.");
      System.exit(0);
    }

      // set up the input stream and read the file

    System.out.println("The file " + fileName + " exists and can be read.");

  }
}
```

Assuming that the `prices.dat` file does not exist on the directory where Program 12.17 is stored, the following message is displayed:

```
The file prices.dat does not exist - please check and rerun.
```

Similarly, if the file does exist but does not have read privileges, the following message is displayed:

PROGRAMMING NOTE

Determining a File's Existence

There are cases when you will need to check whether a file exists before proceeding with any processing. Such situations are typically associated with writing to a file that may already exist, and if so, you do not want the overwrite to occur.

In these situations, using the `FileNotFoundException` notification, by itself, is not useful because the operating system will create a nonexistent file for output, and a file with the requested name will always be located. There are a number of solutions to this problem. You can open the file for input to see if it exists and then use the procedure presented in the Programming Note on page 622.

Another approach is to use the `File` class's `exists()` method to determine that the file exists before any attempt is made to open a stream to the file. If the file does exist, you can then use code similar to the following to determine whether the user wishes to continue and overwrite the file.

```
String fileName = "C:\\jdk\\prices.dat";  // note that a full pathname
                                           // requires two delimiters

 File inFile = new File(fileName); // create a File reference variable
 char response;

 if (inFile.exists()) // check for the file's existence
 {
    System.out.println("A file by the name " + fileName
             + " currently exists.\n"
             + "Do you want to overwrite it with the new data (y or n): ");
    response = (char)System.in.read();
    if (response == 'n' || response == 'N')
    {
    System.exit(0);
 }
```

```
The file prices.dat exists but does not have read permission - please check.
```

In both cases, the `System.exit()` method will terminate program execution. If the file does exist and can be read, the message

```
The file prices.dat exists and can be read.
```

is displayed. In practice, this statement would be replaced by statements that read and process the data in the file as presented in the previous sections.

On the output side, whenever data are to be written to a file, you should always check if a file with the desired name already exists on the system. If it does, you can then either choose not to open an output stream to the file or give the user the choice as to whether the output stream should be opened. This is an important decision because once an output stream is opened for writing, the data in the existing file are automatically lost, unless the existing file is opened in append mode. How this type of check is accomplished in practice is illustrated in Program 12.18.

Program 12.18

```java
import java.io.*;
public class CheckForWrite
{
  public static void main(String[] args)
    throws java.io.IOException
  {
    String fileName = "prices.dat";
    char response;

    File outFile = new File(fileName);

      // check that the file does not already exist
    if (outFile.exists())
    {
      System.out.println("The file " + fileName + " currently exists.");
      System.out.print("Are you sure you want to write to it? Enter y or n:");
      response = (char) System.in.read();
      if (response == 'n')
        System.exit(0);
    }

      // set up the output stream and write to the file
    System.out.println("The file " + fileName + " can be written to.");
  }
}
```

Assuming that a file named `prices.dat` is available on the current directory, a sample run of Program 12.18 will display the following output lines:

```
The file prices.dat currently exists.
Are you sure you want to write to it? Enter y or n:
```

Depending on how the user responds, the file will either be erased and written over or the program will terminate. In practice, the severity of the message presented to the user and whether or not the user is even given a choice to delete an existing file depends on the application and the importance of the file being considered.

Exercises 12.6

1a. Describe the difference between numbers stored in a character-based file and numbers stored in a byte-based file.

b. Describe the difference between letters stored in a character-based file and letters stored in a byte-based file.

2. Enter and run Program 12.16 on your computer.

3. Modify Program 12.16 so that the file name can be interactively entered by a user.

4. Modify Program 12.1 to include the file checks provided by Program 12.16.

5. Enter and run Program 12.17 on your computer.

6. Enter and run Program 12.18 on your computer.

7. Modify Program 12.1 to include the input file check provided by Program 12.18.

12.7 Common Programming Errors

The following programming errors are common when using files:

1. Using a file's external name in place of the internal file stream object reference variable when accessing the file. The only stream method that uses the data file's external name is the first stream used to open the file.

2. Not realizing that a file opened when an output stream is instantiated is, by default, in write mode. This automatically erases all file data. If data are to be added to an existing file, the file should be opened for appending.

3. Testing for the end-of-file in an incorrect way. In general, a `null` value is returned when a read beyond the end of a character-based file is attempted, and an EOF exception is generated when reading beyond the end of a byte-based file is attempted. When an incorrect end-of-file test is made, a program will generally either terminate abnormally or go into an infinite loop.

4. Forgetting to surround the expression `c = fr.read()` in a loop such as `while ( (c = fr.read()) != EOF)`, used to read bytes from a file stream, in parentheses. The parentheses are necessary to ensure that a byte is first read and assigned to the variable c before the retrieved value is compared to the EOF value. In their absence, the complete expression would be `c = fr.read() != EOF`. Due to the precedence of operations, the relational expression `fr.read() != EOF` would be executed first. Because this is a relational expression, its result is either a boolean `true` or `false` value based on the data retrieved by the `c.read()` method. Attempting to assign this boolean result to the variable c is an invalid conversion across an assignment operator and results in a compiler error. This same error occurs when the parentheses surrounding the expression `(inLine = br.readLine())` in a loop such as `while ((inLine = br.readLine()) != null)`, used to read lines from a file, are omitted.

12.8 Chapter Review

KEY TERMS

buffering	embedded file names	output file
byte-based files	external file name	output file stream
character-based file	file access	random access
`close()`	file stream	sequential access
data file	input file	text file
direct access	input file stream	

SUMMARY

1. A data file is any collection of data stored together on an external storage medium under a common name.

2. A character-based file is one in which each data item in the file is stored using a character-based code, such as ASCII. A character-based file is also referred to as a text file. Java imposes no structure on a character-based file, which means that what data are stored is determined by the application and the placement of the character data created by the programmer.

3. A byte-based file is one in which each data item in the file is stored using the computer's internal binary code. A byte-based file is also referred to as a binary file. Java imposes no structure on a byte-based file, which means that what data are stored is determined by the application and the placement of the data created by the programmer.

4. Character-based and byte-based files can be opened for reading, writing, or appending. A file opened for writing creates a new file or erases any existing file having the same name as the opened file. A file opened for appending makes an existing file available for data to be added to the end of the file. If the file does not exist, it is created. A file opened for reading makes an existing file's data available for input.

5. The file stream classes that are used to create input and output streams for character-based files are:

Class	Type	Comments	Methods
`Reader`	Abstract	Abstract class for byte-based input.	–
`FileReader`	Basic Input	Basic stream used for byte-based input. Supplies byte-by-byte input.	`read()`
`BufferedReader`	Input	Provides buffering, which typically improves processing performance.	`read()` `readLine()`
`Writer`	Abstract	Abstract class for byte-based output.	
`FileWriter`	Basic Output	Basic stream for byte-based output.	`write(), flush(), close()` `write(int c)`
`BufferedWriter`	Output	Provides buffering, which typically improves performance.	`write(String s, int start, int end)`
`PrintWriter`	Output	Provides a number of useful output methods.	`flush(), close(), print(char),` `print(String), print(int),` `print(float), print(double),` `print(boolean),` and corresponding `println()` methods

6. For writing to a character-based file, an output stream must be instantiated. A commonly used output stream is created using the following instantiations:

```
    // set up the basic output stream
FileWriter fw =
    new FileWriter(fileName); // The fileName can be a File argument,
                              // String variable, or String constant

  // buffer it for faster output
BufferedWriter bw =
    new BufferedWriter(fw);

  // this provides a set of useful methods
PrintWriter pw =
    new PrintWriter(bw);
```

This set of individual instantiations can also be implemented using the single statement

```
PrintWriter pw =
    new PrintWriter(new BufferedWriter(new FileWriter(fileName)));
```

The first instantiation in this sequence of statements opens the associated file in write mode. To open it in append mode, this instantiation should be written as

```
FileWriter fw =
    new FileWriter(fileName, true);
```

7. The `PrintWriter` class contains the following methods for writing numerical values in character-based form:

```
print(char), println(char)
print(String), println(String)
print(int), println(int)
print(float), println(float)
print(double), println(double)
print(boolean), println(boolean)
```

8. For reading from a character-based file, an input stream must be instantiated. A commonly used input stream is created using the following instantiations:

```
  // set up the basic input stream
FileReader fr =
    new FileReader(fileName);  // The fileName can be a File argument,
                               // String variable, or String constant

  // buffer the input stream
BufferedReader br =
    new BufferedReader(fr);
```

This set of individual instantiations can also be implemented using the single statement

```
BufferedReader br =
    new BufferedReader(new FileReader(fileName));
```

9. The `BufferedReader` class permits reading character-based file data either as individual bytes using a `read()` method or complete lines using a `readLine()` method. A line is considered any sequence of bytes terminated by a carriage return (\r), line feed (\n), carriage return and line feed (\r\n), or end of stream marker. Generally, character-based files are read using `readLine()`,

and then individual data items are parsed from the line using `String-Tokenizer` methods.

10. The file stream classes that are used to create byte-based files are

Class	Mode	Comments	Typical Object Name
InputStream	Input	Abstract class for byte-based input.	–
FileInputStream	Input	Basic stream used for byte-based input. Supplies byte-by-byte input.	fis
BufferedInputStream	Input	Provides buffering, which improves performance. Typically uses a `FileInputStream` object argument.	bis
DataInputStream	Input	Supplies additional input methods. Typically uses either a `FileInputStream` object or `BufferedInputStream` object argument.	dis
OutputStream	Output	Abstract class for byte-based output.	–
FileOutputStream	Output	Basic stream used for byte-based output. Supplies byte-by-byte output.	fos
BufferedOutputStream	Output	Provides buffering, which improves performance. Typically uses a `FileOutputStream` object argument.	bos
DataOutputStream	Output	Supplies additional output methods. Typically uses either an `FileOutputStream` object or `BufferedOutputStream` object argument.	dos

11. For writing to a byte-based file, an output file stream must be instantiated. For opening the file in write mode, the following set of statements is typically used:

```
// set up the basic output stream
FileOutputStream fos =
    new FileOutputStream(outFile);


// buffer it for faster output
BufferedOutputStream bos =
    new BufferedOutputStream(fos);


// this provides a set of useful methods
DataOutputStream dos =
    new DataOutputStream(bos);
```

The first instantiation in this sequence of statements opens the associated file in write mode. To open it in append mode, this instantiation should be written as

```
FileOutputStream fos =
    new FileOutputStream(outFile, true);
```

12. For reading from a byte-based file, an input stream object must be instantiated. This is typically accomplished using the following set of statements:

```
// set up the basic input stream
FileInputStream fis =
    new FileInputStream(inFile);
```

```
        // buffer it for faster input
BufferedInputStream bis =
        new BufferedInputStream(fis);

        // this provides a set of useful methods
DataInputStream dis =
        new DataInputStream(bis);
```

13. Input and output streams and random access files are formally closed using a `close()` method. The syntax of this method is

    `streamName.close()`

    Although all streams and files are automatically closed when the program they are opened in finishes running, they may be closed as empty files.

14. The manner in which data are written to and read from a file is called the file's access method.

    a. In a sequential access file, data are accessed in a sequential manner. This means that the second data item in the file cannot be read until the first data item has been read, the third data item cannot be read until the first and second data items have been read, and so on until the last data item is read. Similarly, a data item cannot be written until all previous data items have been written.

    b. In a random access file, any data item can be read, written, or replaced without affecting any other data item in the file. Typically, data in a random access file are stored in a fixed-length record format, where each record contains a value that can be translated into a record position value.

15. The `RandomAccessFile` class is used to create random access file streams.

16. For reading and writing to a random access file, a file stream must be instantiated. This is typically accomplished using a statement of the form

    ```
    // set up the basic random access input/output stream
    RandomAccessFile raf =
            new RandomAccessFile(fileName, "rw");
    ```

    If the last argument in this instantiation is `"r"` rather than `"rw"`, the file can only be used for input and cannot be written to using the instantiated file stream.

17. The `seek()` method provides the capability to set a random access file's internal file pointer at any byte position in the file. Subsequent read, write, or skip operations all commence from the position indicated by the internal file pointer.

18. Although files created as character-based and byte-based can be read as a random access file, the class methods used for a random access file stream most closely match those methods used for byte-based streams. Thus, random access is most closely associated with byte-based files.

19. If a file is to be read, a check, using the `File` class's methods, should be made to ensure that the file exists.

20. If a file is to be written, a check, using the `File` class's methods, should be made to ensure that a file of the same name *does not* already exist.

Table 12.15   Selected ASCII Codes and Unicodes

Character	ASCII Binary Value	ASCII Hex Value	Unicode Binary Value	Unicode Hex Value
0	00110000	30	00000000 00110000	0030
1	00110001	31	00000000 00110001	0031
2	00110010	32	00000000 00110010	0032
3	00110011	33	00000000 00110011	0033
4	00110100	34	00000000 00110100	0034
5	00110101	35	00000000 00110101	0035
6	00110110	36	00000000 00110110	0036
7	00110111	37	00000000 00110111	0037
8	00111000	38	00000000 00111000	0038
9	00111001	39	00000000 00111001	0039
.	00101110	2E	00000000 00101110	002E
Tab	00001001	09	00000000 00001001	0009
Blank Space	00100000	20	00000000 00100000	0020
Carriage Ret.	00001101	0D	00000000 00001101	000D
Line Feed	00001010	0A	00000000 00001010	000A

12.9 Chapter Supplement: Character and Byte File Storage

The files in which we have stored our Java programs are referred to as text or character-based (the designations are synonymous) files. This means that each character in the files is stored using a character code, which is typically ASCII. This code assigns a specific code to each letter in the alphabet, to each of the digits 0 through 9, and to special symbols such as the period and dollar sign. Table 12.15 lists the correspondence between the characters 0 through 9 and their ASCII and Unicode representations in both binary and hexadecimal notation. Additionally, the ASCII and Unicode codes for a decimal point, blank space, carriage return, tab, and line feed characters are included in the table. In all cases, notice that the lower 8 bits in the Unicode representation are identical to the ASCII bit code and that the upper 8 bits are all 0s. This correspondence is true for the first 128 codes; thus, the Unicodes for these first 128 characters are identical to the ASCII codes (the upper bytes of these Unicodes are all 0s), except that the extra Unicode byte is a 0. Because of this correspondence, the ASCII uppercase and lowercase letter codes can be obtained from the Unicode letter codes previously provided in Table 2.3.

Using Table 12.15, we can determine how the decimal number 67432.83, for example, is stored in a data file using the ASCII code. In ASCII, this sequence of digits and decimal point require eight character storage locations and are stored using the codes in Figure 12.12.

FIGURE 12.12   The number 67432.83 represented in ASCII Code

```
36 37 34 33 32 2E 38 33
```

The advantage of using character codes for data files is that the file can be read and displayed by any word processing or editor program provided by your computer system. Such word processing and editor programs are called text editors because they are designed to process alphabetical text. The word processing program can read the character code in the data file and display the letter, symbol, or digit corresponding to the code. This permits a data file created in Java to be examined and changed by other than Java text editor programs.

An alternative to character-based files, where each character in the file is represented by a unique code, is *byte-based* or *binary files* (the terms are synonymous). Byte-based files store numerical values using the program's internal numerical code.[7] For example, assume that the program stores integer numbers internally using Java's 32-bit designation in the format described in Section 1.9. Using this format, the decimal number 8 is represented as the 32-bit binary number 00000000 00000000 00000000 00001000, the decimal number 12 as 00000000 00000000 00000000 00001100, and the decimal number 497 as 00000000 00000000 00000001 11110001. As hexadecimal numbers, these are 00 00 00 08, 00 00 00 0C, and 00 00 01 F1, respectively. Figure 12.13 shows how these three numbers are stored using byte-based codes.

FIGURE 12.13   **The numbers 8, 12, and 497 stored as bytecodes**

```
00 00 00 08 00 00 00 0C 00 00 01 F1
```

The advantages of using this format are that no intermediary conversions are required for storing or retrieving the data (since the external storage codes match the Java program's internal storage representation), and for files consisting of large double-precision numbers, the resulting file usually requires less storage space than its character-based counterpart. The primary disadvantage is that the file can no longer be visually inspected using a text editing program.

Notice that the term byte-based can be misleading because both byte-based and character-based files store data using bytes. It is the interpretation of what the byte stream represents when applied to numbers that distinguishes the two file types. In character-based files, all numbers are stored as a sequence of individual digits, each one of which is represented by the character symbols 0 through 9, including a possible decimal point. In byte-based files, numbers are stored as a fixed sequence of bytes that represents the binary equivalent of the number.

For alphabetical characters, both byte-based and character-based files use the same individual character codes, but in a text-based file, a character is typically represented using its ASCII code, stored as 8 bits, while a byte-based code stores characters as the 16-bit character data type specified in Java's Unicode format. As an example, Figures 12.14a and 12.14b show how the characters `Hello World` are stored in character- and byte-based formats, respectively, using a hexadecimal representation.

---

[7] This topic assumes that you are familiar with the computer storage concepts presented in Section 1.9.

FIGURE 12.14a   **Hello World stored as an ASCII text file**

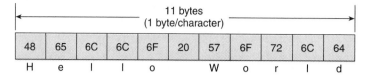

FIGURE 12.14b   **Hello World stored as a byte-based file**

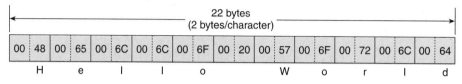

The individual character codes shown in Figures 12.14a and 12.14b can be obtained from both Table 2.3 and Table 12.15. In comparing these figures, notice that the byte-based file in Figure 12.14b uses 2 bytes for each character where the upper byte consists of zeros and the lower byte is the same as the bytecode used in the ASCII text file in Figure 12.14a.

13

Collections: List Creation and Maintenance

As we saw in Section 8.5, Java provides an `ArrayList` class for storing, ordering, and retrieving objects that permits the list to expand or contract as objects are added or removed from it. In this chapter, we present three additional types of list maintenance classes, and all are supported by the same Collection Framework set of classes and interfaces from which `ArrayLists` are derived.

All of the three new classes are based on the concept of a linked list, which is explained in Section 13.2. The first interface, named `LinkedList`, permits direct construction of a classical linked list. The remaining types, stacks and queues, are specialized forms of a linked list, which can also be constructed using the Collection Framework classes and interfaces. Because the Collection Framework forms the basis for all of these new list types, a review of the framework is provided at the end of Section 13.1.

FIGURE 13.1   **The typical components of a video game character**

```
Name:
Type:
Location in Dungeon:
Strength Factor:
Intelligence Factor:
Type of Armor:
```

13.1 The Collection Framework

Formally, a *list* is a collection of items, all of which have the same data type. All of the lists presented in the chapter store items as objects. For example, consider the individual items that might be stored for a video game character, as illustrated in Figure 13.1. In Java, these data would be created as an object from a class such as that shown in the Unified Modeling Language (UML) class diagram of Figure 13.2.

Although the individual items that are stored and accessed within Java's advanced list types must always be objects, in real-life applications they are more generally referred to as *records*. For example, a typical business might require the record structure shown in Figure 13.3.

Similarly, Figure 13.4 shows the class diagram for a telephone directory record. In this chapter, we will use the terms *record* and *object* interchangeably. The individual data items within a record are formally referred to as *data fields*. In Java, these data fields are most commonly created from instance variables. However, if there were characteristics common to all of the objects, these would be coded as `static` variables.

We have already seen two examples of lists, arrays and `ArrayLists`, in Chapter 8. Although arrays are most often used to directly store primitive numerical data types, they still retain general list characteristics common to more advanced list types. For example, a list can be empty, which means that it currently holds no items. In a more general context, a list can be considered as a container that is used to hold a collection of zero or more items, each of which is of the same type. For this reason, lists are referred to as both *containers* and *collections,* and we will use these terms interchangeably. Additionally, a list must provide a means for accessing individual elements. In an array, this ability is provided by the position of each element in the array, which is designated using an integer index value. More formally, any data type that provides this minimum set of capabilities is referred to as a *data structure*. Under this definition, a record is itself a data structure as are all of the list types presented in this chapter.

FIGURE 13.2   **The class structure for a video game character record**

```
┌─────────────────────────────┐
│       VideoCharacter        │
├─────────────────────────────┤
│ -name: String               │
│ -type: integer              │
│ -xLocation: double          │
│ -yLocation: double          │
│ -strength: double           │
│ -intelligence: double       │
│ -armor: integer             │
└─────────────────────────────┘
```

FIGURE 13.3   **A UML class diagram for a business record**

```
                EmployeeRecord

-name: String
-identificationNum: String
-regularPayRate: double
-overtimePayRate: double
```

In Java, as has been noted, records are always constructed as objects. For example, a basic class that could be used for a very simplified employee pay rate record is

```java
public class NameRate
{
  // data declaration section
  private String name;
  private double payRate;
}
```

If this class were used to construct an object, each employee record would consist of two data fields: name and payRate. More generally, a record is constructed from a class that will also includes a constructor for initializing each record and accessor methods for reporting each record's state. Thus, a more complete and useful class for defining an employee pay rate record is

```java
public class NameRate
{
  // data declaration section
  private String name;
  private double payRate;

  // method definition section
    // constructor method
  public NameRate(String nn, String rate)
  {
    name = nn;
    payRate = rate;
  }
    // accessor methods
  public String getName(){return name;}
  public double getRate(){return payRate;}
}
```

FIGURE 13.4   **A UML class diagram for a telephone directory record**

```
                TelephoneRecord

-name: String
-areaCode: integer
-phoneNumber: long
```

PROGRAMMING NOTE

Homogeneous and Heterogeneous Data Structures

Both lists and records are data structures. The difference between these two structures is the types of elements they contain. A list is a *homogeneous* data structure,
which means that each of its components must be of the same data type. A record
is a *heterogeneous* data structure, which means that its components can be of different
data types. Thus, a list of records would be a homogeneous data structure whose
elements are of the same heterogeneous type. An example is a list of employee
records where each record consists of a string name and double-precision
pay rate.

Notice that the two accessor methods have both been written on a single line. This
is typically done when a method's body consists of a single statement. Although each
of these accessors can be written more conventionally using four lines of code—as for
example in the following `getName()` implementation—doing so really adds nothing
to understanding the code.

```
public String getName()
{
  return name;
}
```

Once a record's structure has been defined, a means is still needed for collecting
all of the records into a single list. The list itself should also be appropriate for the application that will use the record. As we will shortly see, there is a variety of basic list
types, each of which differs in its capabilities and intended usage. Each of these basic
types, which include the `ArrayList` (see Section 8.5), linked lists, stacks, and
queues, can be easily constructed using Java's Collection Framework of list classes.

Before describing linked lists, stacks, and queues in detail, it is worthwhile emphasizing that each individual record, or object, is constructed from the variables declared in a class's data declaration section, and it is the object and not the methods
that is stored in the list. The methods, which apply to the class as a whole, provide a
means of initializing each object before it is placed into the list and a means of reporting what is in an object once it has been extracted from the list. Figure 13.5 illustrates
the complete process for creating a record, creating a list, initializing individual
records, and reporting a record's state, both before it is placed in a list and after it is
extracted from the list.

The Collection Framework of classes has already been described in detail in Section 8.5.[1] Briefly, this collection of classes provides a number of generic list structures,
called containers, that can be used to store, maintain, and retrieve individual records.
Each record is stored as a generic `Object` data type, which is a generalized data struc-

[1] The Collection Framework (note that the word Collection is singular) is frequently and informally referred to in the plural as the collections framework. To avoid confusion with the
`Collections` class (note the plural here), which is described later in this chapter, we will
always use the correct and formal singular designation for the Collection Framework.

FIGURE 13.5 **The list creation process**

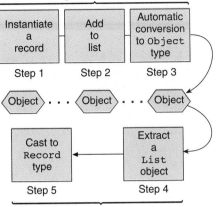

Adding a Record to a List

Instantiate a record	Add to list	Automatic conversion to `Object` type
Step 1	Step 2	Step 3

Object · · · Object · · · Object

Cast to Record type	Extract a List object
Step 5	Step 4

Extracting a Record from a List

ture that a record is automatically converted into when it is inserted into the list (step 3 in Figure 13.5). When extracted from the list, each `Object` type must be explicitly converted into its original record type (step 5 in Figure 13.5); otherwise, a run-time error can occur when individual information is extracted from the record.

Table 13.1 summarizes the three basic list types supported by the `Collection Framework`, which are named `List`, `Set`, and `Map`, and the various individual container types that can be created from these interfaces. The four containers listed as historical types refer to container types introduced in the first version of Java that are still supported by the newer framework types. Included in the table are the distinguishing features of each type and a sample application using each type.

In addition to the interfaces in Table 13.1, the framework provides a helper interface, named `Collections`, for searching, sorting, random shuffling, and reverse ordering a list as a whole. Finally, a number of additional interfaces named `Iterator`, `Comparator`, and `Comparable` are part of the `Collection Framework`. The `Iterator` interface has a method for determining if a list has additional elements and a method for returning the next element in the list, if such an element exists. The `Comparator` and `Comparable` interfaces provide methods for ordering elements and are used in sorting a list. Table 13.2 summarizes these additional support interfaces and their uses.

Table 13.1 **The Collection Framework List Structures**

	`List` Types	`Set` Types	`Map` Types
Current	`ArrayList`	`HashSet`	`HashMap`
	`LinkedList`	`TreeSet`	`TreeMap`
Historical	`Vector`	–	`Hashtable`
	`Stack`		`Properties`
Distinguishing Feature	List of records	Duplicates not permitted	Single unique name-value pairs
Examples	A list of student records	A list of card hands	A list of telephone directory records

Table 13.2 The Collection Framework Support Classes and Interfaces

Name	Support Functions
Collections	Works on a list as a whole to search, sort, fill, randomly shuffle, replace, reverse elements, etc.
Iterator	Determines if more elements exist in the list and returns the next element.
Comparator	Places a default order to elements for sorting purposes.
Comparable	Places a programmer-supplied ordering sequence to elements for sorting purposes.

Exercises 13.1

1. Define the following terms:
   a. container
   b. collection
   c. Collection Framework
   d. data field
   e. data structure
   f. list
   g. record

2. How are records constructed in Java?

3. What container types can be created from the `List` interface?

4. What container types can be created from the `Set` interface?

5. For each of the following, define a single class named `Student` that contains only a data declaration section and can be used to create the following records. Each part (a through e) should have its own `Student` class.
   a. a student record containing a student identification number, the number of credits completed, and a cumulative grade point average
   b. a student record capable of holding a student's name, date of birth, number of credits completed, and cumulative grade point average
   c. a mailing list containing a title field, last name field, first name field, two street address fields, a city field, a state field, and a zip code field
   d. a stock record containing the stock's name, the price of the stock, and the date of purchase
   e. an inventory record containing an integer part number, a string part description, an integer number of parts in inventory, and an integer reorder value

6. For each of the individual classes declared in Exercise 5, add a suitable constructor and accessor method. Test each method to initialize and display the following data:
   a. Identification Number: 4672

      Number of Credits Completed: 68

      Grade Point Average: 3.01
   b. Name: Rhona Karp

      Date of Birth: 8/4/60

Number of Credits Completed: 96

Grade Point Average: 3.89

c. Title: Dr.

Last Name: Kingsley

First Name: Kay

Street Address: 614 Freeman Street

City: Indianapolis

State: IN

Zip Code: 47030

d. Stock: IBM

Price Purchased: 134.5

Date Purchased: 10/1/86

e. Part Number: 16879

Description: Battery

Number in Stock: 10

Reorder Number: 3

7a. Write a Java program that prompts a user to input the current month, day, and year. Store the data entered in a suitably defined object and display the date in an appropriate manner.

b. Modify the program written in Exercise 7a to use a record that accepts the current time in hours, minutes, and seconds.

8. Define a class capable of creating objects that can store a business's name, description of the business's products or services, address, number of employees, and annual revenue.

9. Define a class capable of creating records for various screw types held in inventory. Each record should contain a field for an integer inventory number, double-precision screw length, double-precision diameter, kind of head (Phillips or standard slot), material (steel, brass, other), and cost.

10. Write a Java program that defines a class capable of creating records for storing the name of a stock, its estimated earnings per share, and its estimated price-to-earnings ratio. Have the program prompt the user to enter these items for five different stocks. When the data have been entered for a particular stock, have the program compute and display the anticipated stock price based on the entered earnings and price-per-earnings values. For example, if a user entered the data XYZ 1.56 12, the anticipated price for a share of XYZ stock is (1.56) * (12) = $18.72.

13.2 **Linked Lists**

A classic data-handling problem is making additions or deletions to existing records that are maintained in a specific order. This is best illustrated by considering the alphabetical telephone list shown in Figure 13.6. Starting with this initial set of names and telephone numbers, assume that we now need to add new records to the list in the proper alphabetical sequence and to delete existing records in such a way that the storage for deleted records is eliminated.

FIGURE 13.6   **A telephone list in alphabetical order**

```
Acme, Sam
(555) 898-2392
Dolan, Edith
(555) 682-3104
Lanfrank, John
(555) 718-4581
Mening, Stephen
(555) 382-7070
Zebee, Frank
(555) 219-9912
```

Although the insertion or deletion of ordered records can be accomplished using an `ArrayList` of objects, these arrays are not efficient representations for adding or deleting records internal to the list. This is because deleting a record from an `ArrayList` creates an empty slot that requires shifting up all references below the deleted record's reference to close the empty slot. Similarly, adding a record to the list requires that all references in the array below the addition be shifted down to make room for the location information of the new entry. Thus, either adding or deleting records in an `ArrayList` requires restructuring the underlying array—an inherently inefficient practice even though it is automatically handled by the `ArrayList` class.

A **linked list** provides a convenient method for maintaining a constantly changing list without the need for continually reordering and restructuring. A linked list is a set of objects for which there exists at least one reference variable per object that references the next logically ordered object in the list. Thus, rather than requiring each record to be physically stored in the proper order, each new record is physically added wherever the computer has free space in its storage area. The required linking is accomplished by adjusting reference values for the records immediately preceding and following the newly inserted record. Thus, from a programming standpoint, there is always information as to where the next record is located, no matter where this next record is actually stored.

The classical concept of a linked list is illustrated in Figure 13.7, where each record internally contains a reference to the next record in the list. Although the actual data for the Lanfrank record in the figure may be physically stored anywhere in the computer, the additional reference variable included at the end of the Dolan record maintains the proper alphabetical order. This reference variable provides the location of the Lanfrank record.

FIGURE 13.7   **Using references to link objects**

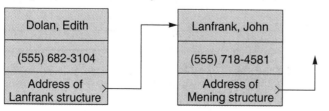

PROGRAMMING NOTE

The Object *Type*

All Collection Framework lists maintain records of type Object. Thus, any record that is added into a framework list is automatically converted to this data type regardless of the original record's structure. This can lead to possible errors unless you are careful only to add the same type of record to each list.

For example, you could, in theory, add a String object into a Collection based list followed by a record consisting of both an integer identification number and a double-precision pay rate. Both records will be converted into an Object type and stored in the list with no error reported by the compiler. You would only notice the error if, after retrieving each record, you attempted to cast them both into a single record type. This last step would be necessary if you wanted to retrieve a record's individual data fields. *Because a list is intended to store records of the same type, be careful to add only such records into a list.*

To see the usefulness of the reference in the Dolan object, let us add a telephone number for June Hagar into the alphabetical list in Figure 13.7. The data for June Hagar are stored in a data object using the same type as that used for the existing objects. To ensure that the telephone number for Hagar is correctly displayed after the Dolan telephone number, the reference variable in the Dolan object must be altered to locate the Hagar object, and the reference variable in the Hagar object must be set to the location of the Lanfrank object. This is illustrated in Figure 13.8. Notice that the reference variable in each object simply locates the next ordered object, even if that object is not physically located in the correct order.

Removal of an object from the ordered list is the reverse process of adding an object. The actual object is logically removed from the list by changing the reference variable's value in the object preceding it to the location of the object immediately following the deleted object.

Because each object in a linked list has the same format, it is clear that the last object cannot have a reference value that points to another object, since there is none. To satisfy this requirement, the last record in the list will always have a null value in

FIGURE 13.8 **Adjusting addresses to point to appropriate objects**

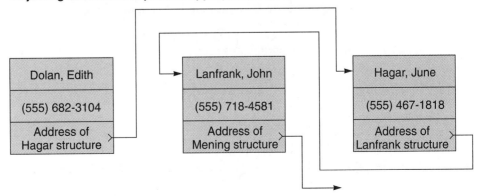

FIGURE 13.9   **The use of the initial and final reference values**

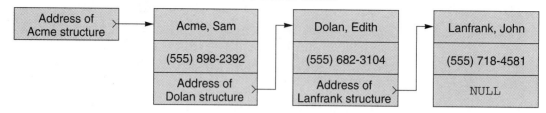

its reference variable. Similarly, a special reference must also be provided for storing the location of the first object in the list. Figure 13.9 illustrates the complete structure of references that can be used for a list consisting of three names.

There are two fundamentally different approaches to constructing a linked list. The first approach is to "make your own," in which the programmer creates the list; the second approach is to use the Java Collection Framework's LinkedList class. Except for exceedingly specialized cases, you should almost always use the Collection Framework class, which will be described shortly. However, because it is useful to understand what is actually being provided by this class and the concepts underlying it, we will also illustrate the basics of creating your own linked lists. For both approaches, we will use the same example: constructing a linked list for the simplified telephone records illustrated in Figure 13.10.

Constructing Your Own Linked List[2]

The key to constructing a linked list is to provide each record with at least one reference variable. For example, assuming we name our class NameTele, a suitable data declaration section that describes the telephone record type shown in Figure 13.10 is

```
public class NameTele
{
   // data declaration section
   private String name;
   private String phoneNum;
}
```

To provide a link from one object to the next, we will have to add an extra variable into each record. As this variable must be a reference to an object of type NameTele, a suitable declaration for the required instance variable is

FIGURE 13.10   **A UML class diagram for a telephone directory record**

TelephoneRecord
-name: String -phoneNumber: String

---

[2] This topic can be omitted on first reading without loss of subject continuity.

PROGRAMMING NOTE

When to Use an Array or LinkedList *Container*

If you have a list of primitive data types or objects that does not have to be expanded or contracted, the container of choice is an array.

If you have a list of objects that can be grouped as an array but must be expanded or contracted, the container of choice is a LinkedList.

If you have a list of primitive data types that must be expanded or contracted, you will either have to convert the primitive type to its wrapper class equivalent (Integer, Float, etc.) and use a LinkedList or use an array and recurring deep copies between arrays to create expanded and contracted array types.

```
private  NameTele link; // create a reference variable to a NameTele object
```

Including this declaration into the previous data declarations results in the following:

```
public class NameTele
{
  // data declaration section
  private String name;
  private String phoneNum;
  private NameTele link;
}
```

The inclusion of a reference variable in a data declaration section should not be surprising because an object is permitted to contain any Java data type. In this case, the variable named link will be used to reference an object of type NameTele. In addition to this new variable, we will need to supply the class with a set of constructor, mutator, and accessor methods that includes setting and retrieving the value stored in link. Program 13.1 provides a complete class definition that includes these methods.

Program 13.1

```
public class NameTele
{
  // data declaration section
  private String name;
  private String phoneNum;
  private NameTele link;

  // method definition section
   // constructor
  public NameTele(String nn, String phone)
  {
    name = nn;
    phoneNum = phone;
    link = null;
```

(continued)

```
         (continued)
          }
            // mutator method to set link value
          public void setLink(NameTele ll){link = ll;}
            // accessor methods
          public String getName(){return name;}
          public String getPhone(){return phoneNum;}
          public NameTele getLink(){return link;}


          }
```

Program 13.2 illustrates using the `NameTele` class by specifically defining four objects having this form, which have been named `head`, `r1`, `r2`, and `r3`. The name and telephone members of three of these records are initialized with actual name and telephone numbers when the records are defined, using the data listed in Figure 13.10.

Program 13.2

```
class UseNameTele
{
  public static void main(String args[])
  {
    NameTele head = new NameTele("xx", "xx");   // create an empty record

      // create three records
    NameTele r1 = new NameTele("Acme, Sam", "(555) 898-2392");
    NameTele r2 = new NameTele("Dolan, Edith", "(555) 682-3104");
    NameTele r3 = new NameTele("Lanfrank, John", "(555) 718-4581");

      // link all of the records
    head.setLink(r1);   // have the head link point to the first record
    r1.setLink(r2);
    r2.setLink(r3);

      // retrieve each record using the link from the prior record
    System.out.println( (head.getLink()).getName());
    System.out.println( (r1.getLink()).getName());
    System.out.println( (r2.getLink()).getName());
  }
}
```

The output produced by Program 13.2 is

```
Acme, Sam
Dolan, Edith
Lanfrank, John
```

The important concept illustrated by Program 13.2 is the use of a reference variable in one record to access the next record in the list, as illustrated in Figure 13.11.

The initialization of the names and telephone numbers for each of the objects defined in Program 13.2 is straightforward. Although each object consists of three vari-

FIGURE 13.11   **The relationship between objects in Program 13.2**

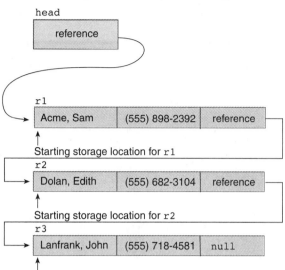

ables, only the first two variables in each are initialized when a record is instantiated. The remaining variable, which is the reference, is then assigned the location of the next object in the list.

The three assignment statements in Program 13.2 perform the correct reference assignments. The expression `head.setLink(r1);` stores the location of the first telephone record in the reference variable of the object named `head`. The expression `r1.setLink(r2);` stores the location of the `r2` object into the reference member of the `r1` object. Similarly, the expression `r2.setLink(r3);` stores the location of the `r3` object into the reference member of the `r2` object.

Once name and telephone values have been assigned to each record and correct location information has been stored in the appropriate references, the references are used to access each object's name member. For example, the expression `(head.getLink()).getName()` is used to locate the `r1` record and then extract its name value. The parentheses surrounding the expression `head.getLink()` can be omitted because the dot operator . is evaluated from left to right. Thus, the complete expression `head.getLink().getName()` is evaluated as `(head.getLink()).get-Name();` that is, the link is extracted before the `getName()` accessor is applied. For clarity, however, we have included the first set of parentheses.

More generally, the links in a linked list of records can be used to loop through the complete list. As each record is accessed, it can either be examined to select a specific value or used to print a complete list. Equally as important is that a linked list can easily expand as new objects are added and contract as objects are deleted.

For records that need to be inserted internally within a list, the new record's link would also have to be set to locate the next record in the list, and the prior record's link would also have to be adjusted to correctly locate the inserted record. Deleting a record is accomplished by removing the link to the record and adjusting the prior record's link to locate the next valid record in the list.

FIGURE 13.12 **The LinkedList class structure**

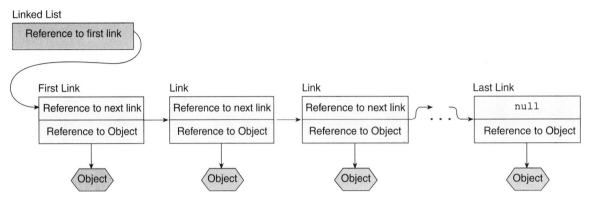

To actually program all of the required insertion and deletion methods takes time and care. Using the Collection Framework's LinkedList class obviates the need for all of this programming and provides a complete set of tested methods for performing all of the maintenance tasks associated with a linked list.

LinkedList Class Implementation

Figure 13.12 presents the internal structure used by the LinkedList class to maintain a list of linked objects. The important point to notice is that the only access through the list is via the link cells. Using this structure, a new object can be easily inserted into the list by storing it in any available memory location and adjusting the location information in at most two link cells. That is, unlike an array implementation, contiguous memory locations are not required. Similarly, an object can be removed by adjusting the link information in one link cell. The implication of this, as noted at the beginning of this section, is that expansion and contraction of the list are more efficient than the same operations using an ArrayList approach. Random access, however, is not available because the only way to reach an internal object is to traverse the links sequentially until the desired object is obtained. Figure 13.13 presents the hierarchy diagram for the LinkedList class.

Table 13.3 lists the complete set of LinkedList class methods. The highlighted methods are the additional methods provided by the LinkedList class that are not

FIGURE 13.13 **The LinkedList class hierarchy diagram**

```
java.lang.Object
   |
   +--java.util.AbstractCollection
         |
         +--java.util.AbstractList
               |
               +--java.util.AbstractSequentialList
                      |
                      +--java.util.LinkedList
```

Table 13.3   Summary of `LinkedList` Class Methods

Method	Return Value	Use
Constructors		
`LinkedList()`	N/A	Creates an empty `LinkedList`.
`LinkedList(Collection c)`	N/A	Creates a `LinkedList` containing the objects of the specified container.
Additional Class Methods		
`add(int index, Object obj)`	void	Inserts the `obj` at the specified index position.
`add(Object obj)`	boolean	Appends the `obj` to the end of the `LinkedList`.
`addAll(Collection c)`	boolean	Appends all of the objects in `c` to the end of the `LinkedList`.
`addAll(int index, Collection c)`	boolean	Inserts all of the objects `c` into the `LinkedList` starting at the specified index position.
`addFirst(Object obj)`	void	Inserts `obj` as the first object in the list.
`addLast(Object obj)`	void	Inserts `obj` as the last object in the list.
`clear()`	void	Removes all of the `LinkedList`'s objects.
`clone()`	LinkedList	Returns a shallow copy of the `LinkedList`.
`contains(Object obj)`	boolean	Determines `obj` exists.
`equals(Object obj)`	boolean	Compares `obj` with the `LinkedList` for equality.
`get(int index)`	Object	Returns the object at the specified index position.
`getFirst(Obj)`	Object	Returns the first object in the list.
`getLast(Obj)`	Object	Returns the last object in the list.
`indexOf(Obj)`	int	Returns the index value for the first occurrence of `obj` in the list or −1 if `obj` is not in the list.
`lastIndexOf(Object obj)`	int	Returns the index value for the last occurrence of `obj` in the list or −1 if `obj` is not in the list.
`listIterator(int index)`	ListIterator	Returns a list iterator for this list starting at the specified index.
`remove(int index)`	Object	Removes the object at the specified index.
`remove(Object obj)`	boolean	Removes the first occurrence of `obj` in the list.
`removeFirst()`	Object	Removes and returns the first object in the list.
`removeLast()`	Object	Removes and returns the last object in the list.
`set(int index, Object obj)`	Object	Replaces the object at the specified index with `obj`.
`size()`	int	Returns the number of objects in the `LinkedList`.
`toArray()`	Object[]	Returns an array containing all of the objects in the list.
`toArray(Object[] a)`	Object[]	Returns an array containing all of the objects in the `LinkedList` with the type of the array specified by the array argument.

in the `ArrayList` class. As can be seen, these deal with adding, removing, and locating objects from the front and rear of the list. Also noteworthy are the methods that are not in the table. These include `ensureCapacity()`, `lastElement()`, and `trim()`. As these three methods deal with the underlying array that maintains the list structure in an `ArrayList`, which is not used in a linked list structure, there is no need for them. Also missing is the isEmpty() method. Applications that use linked list generally make use of the Iterator and ListIterator interfaces. These two interfaces, which are described later in this section, provide a compact but complete set of methods for determining if a list is empty and for traversing the list forward, starting from the first list object, and backward, starting from the last list object.

Now consider QuickTest Program 13.3, which creates and displays a single linked list of names. Because the program uses String objects, it permits us to sidestep the issue of creating our own object types and converting a retrieved object from list's generic Object type to a user-specified record type. At the end of this section, we show how to store and retrieve programmer-created records. For now, however, QuickTest Program 13.3 permits us to initially concentrate on creating and displaying a linked list.

QuickTest Program 13.3

```java
import java.util.*;
class CreateLinkedList
{
  public static void main(String args[])
  {
    int j;
    LinkedList names = new LinkedList();
    // now add individual names to the end of the list
    names.add("Lanfrank-John");
    names.add("Zebee-Frank");
    names.add("Dolan-Edith");
    names.add("Acme-Sam");

    // display the list
    System.out.println("The original list size is: " +  names.size());
    System.out.println("The original list is: " + names);

    // display the list using an index value
    System.out.println("\nThe list displayed by index value is:");
    for (j = 0 ; j < names.size(); j++)
      System.out.println("   " + j + ": " + names.get(j));
  }
}
```

The first statement in QuickTest Program 13.3 that uses a LinkedList() method is

```java
    LinkedList names = new LinkedList();
```

This statement both declares the identifier named names as a LinkedList reference variable and creates an empty linked list container.[3]

The next four statements append string elements to the list. Implicit in adding a name to the list is that each String object is automatically converted to type Object. Thus, the statement

---

[3] This declaration can also be written as List names = new LinkedList():.

PROGRAMMING NOTE

Application Considerations

`ArrayLists` are the preferred list type whenever you need random access to records without the need for many insertions or deletions. The reason is that an index value can be used to go directly to the desired record. Insertions and deletions require modifying the underlying array supporting the `ArrayList` and can be costly in terms of overhead time required to perform these operations when many insertions and deletions are required.

Because the only way to get to an element in the middle of a `LinkedList` is by traversing all of the elements either before it or by traversing elements from the back of the list toward the desired element, random access tends to be costly in terms of access time. Thus, a `LinkedList` is the preferred list type whenever many record insertions and deletions need to be made and record access tends to be sequential.

Finally, if you only need to store primitive data types, such as integers or double-precision values, a simple array should be your first choice.

```
names.add("Dolan-Edith");
```

converts the string `Dolan-Edith` to an `Object` type and makes it the first object in the linked list. The next three names are also automatically converted to an `Object` type and appended, one at a time, to the list. The remaining statements are used to display the names stored in the list. The first display is produced by providing the `println()` method with the list's name, and the second display is produced by navigating through the list, item by item. Notice that this navigation uses an index value, which follows the ordering of objects within the list from first to last. That the names were correctly added to the list is verified by QuickTest Program 13.3's output.

```
The original list size is: 4
The original list is: [Lanfrank-John, Zebee-Frank, Dolàn-Edith, Acme-Sam]

The list displayed by index value is:
    0: Lanfrank-John
    1: Zebee-Frank
    2: Dolan-Edith
    3: Acme-Sam
```

The Collections Helper Class

The `Collections` class, introduced in Section 8.5, provides the same capabilities for the `LinkedList` class as it does for the `ArrayList` and `Vector` classes. Table 13.4 provides a short summary of commonly used `Collections` class methods. The hierarchy diagram for the `Collections` class is provided in Figure 13.14.

QuickTest Program 13.4 illustrates the last three methods listed in Table 13.4 applied to the same `LinkedList` that was constructed in QuickTest Program 13.3.

Table 13.4   Summary of Commonly Used `Collections` Class Methods

Method	Return Value	Use
`binarySearch(List list, Object elem)`	`int`	Returns the index value of the first occurrence of `elem` in using a binary search.
`reverse(List list)`	`void`	Reverses the current order of elements in the `list`.
`shuffleList list)`	`void`	Shuffles the order of elements in the `list`.
`sort(List list)`	`void`	Sorts the `list` into ascending order.

QuickTest Program 13.4

```java
import java.util.*;
class SortLinkedList
{
  public static void main(String args[])
  {
    int j;
    LinkedList names = new LinkedList();

    // now add individual names to the end of the list
    names.add("Lanfrank-John");
    names.add("Zebee-Frank");
    names.add("Dolan-Edith");
    names.add("Acme-Sam");

    System.out.println("\nThe linked list is \n   " + names);

    Collections.sort(names);  // sort the names
    System.out.println("\nThe linked list in sorted order is \n   " + names);

    Collections.reverse(names);  // reverse the sorted list
    System.out.println("\nThe linked list in reverse order is \n   " + names);

    Collections.shuffle(names);  // randomly shuffle the list
    System.out.println("\nThe linked list in shuffled order is \n   " + names);
  }
}
```

The list initially created in QuickTest Program 13.4 is the same list that was created in QuickTest Program 13.3. This list is first displayed by QuickTest Program 13.4

FIGURE 13.14   The `Collections` class hierarchy diagram

```
java.lang.Object
  |
  +--java.util.Collections
```

and is then sorted, reversed, and randomly shuffled using the three highlighted `Collections` class methods. The following output produced by QuickTest Program 13.4 verifies the operation of these methods.

```
The linked list is
    [Lanfrank-John, Zebee-Frank, Dolan-Edith, Acme-Sam]

The linked list in sorted order is
    [Acme-Sam, Dolan-Edith, Lanfrank-John, Zebee-Frank]

The linked list in reverse order is
    [Zebee-Frank, Lanfrank-John, Dolan-Edith, Acme-Sam]

The linked list in shuffled order is
    [Dolan-Edith, Acme-Sam, Zebee-Frank, Lanfrank-John]
```

The `Iterator` and `ListIterator` Interfaces

Figure 13.15 shows the UML diagram for the `Iterator` class, which is useful for traversing a `LinkedList` in the forward direction—that is, starting from a given element and moving toward the end of the list. In addition, the `ListIterator` class provides the corresponding ability for traversing a `LinkedList` in the reverse direction (from last element to first). Table 13.5 presents the complete set of methods provided by the `ListIterator` class. Because the `ListIterator` class is derived from the `Iterator` class (Figure 13.16), it provides the same methods listed in Figure 13.15.

A list iterator can be considered as a generalized index that keeps track of an object's position within a container. Obtaining an iterator is extremely simple. For example, if x is the name of a `LinkedList`, then a statement such as

```
ListIterator iter i = x.listIterator();
```

can be used.[4] This statement both declares a variable of `ListIterator` type (the identifier `iter` is a programmer-selected identifier) and initializes the list iterator to point to the first element in the container named x. The usefulness of an iterator resides in the fact that it can then be used with the `ListIterator` class methods listed in Table 13.5.

Program 13.5 illustrates obtaining and using a list iterator for traversing through a `LinkedList` of names in the forward and reverse directions. In both cases, the size

FIGURE 13.15 **The `Iterator` interface**

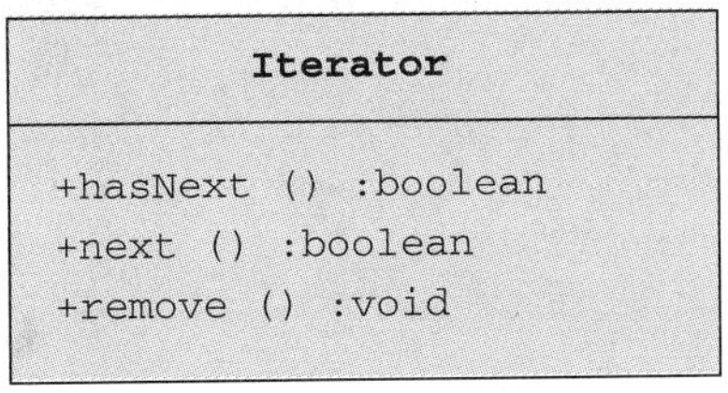

Iterator
+hasNext () :boolean +next () :boolean +remove () :void

---

[4] The `iterator()` method is found in the `Collection` interface class (not `Collections`).

Table 13.5   The `ListIterator` Class Methods

Method	Return Value	Use
add(Object obj)	void	Inserts obj into the list.
hasNext()	boolean	Returns true if the list has more elements when traversing in the forward direction.
hasPrevious()	boolean	Returns true if the list has more elements when traversing in the reverse direction.
next()	boolean	Returns the next object in the list.
nextIndex()	int	Returns the index of the object that would be returned by next().
previous()	boolean	Returns the previous object in the list.
previousIndex()	int	Returns the index of the object that would be returned by previous().
remove()	void	Removes the object that was returned by next() or previous().
set(Object obj)	void	Replaces the last object returned by next() or previous() with obj.

FIGURE 13.16   The `ListIterator` interface is derived from the `Iterator` interface

```
java.util.Iterator
    |
   +--java.util.ListIterator
```

of the list is not required because the hasNext() and hasPrevious() methods are used to determine if there are remaining objects in the list. It is the next() and previous() methods that actually extract an object from the list.

Program 13.5

```
import java.util.*;
class ShowLinkedList
{
  public static void main(String args[])
  {
    int j;
    LinkedList names = new LinkedList();

    // now add individual names to the end of the list
    names.add("Lanfrank-John");
    names.add("Dolan-Edith");
    names.add("Zebee-Frank");
    names.add("Acme-Sam");

    ListIterator i = names.listIterator();
    Collections.sort(names);   // sort the names

    System.out.println("\nThe list displayed by a forward iteration value is:");
    while (i.hasNext())
    {
```

```
        System.out.println(i.next());
    }

    System.out.println("\nThe list displayed by a reverse iteration value is:");
    while (i.hasPrevious())
    {
        System.out.println(i.previous());
    }
  }
}
```

The output produced by Program 13.5 is

```
The list displayed by a forward iteration value is:
Acme-Sam
Dolan-Edith
Lanfrank-John
Zebee-Frank

The list displayed by a reverse iteration value is:
Zebee-Frank
Lanfrank-John
Dolan-Edith
Acme-Sam
```

Linking User-Defined Records

In practice, the majority of real-life applications using linked lists require a programmer-defined record consisting of a combination of data types. For example, consider again the NameRate class previously defined on page 677 and repeated as Program 13.6 for convenience.

Program 13.6

```
public class NameRate
{
  // data declaration section
  private String name;
  private double payRate;

  // method definition section
    // constructor method
  public NameRate(String nn, double rate)
  {
    name = nn;
    payRate = rate;
  }
    // accessor methods
  public String getName(){return name;};
  public double getRate(){return payRate;};

}
```

This class permits constructing records consisting of `name` and `payRate` instance variables, an appropriate constructor, as well as accessor methods for setting and retrieving these variables. Program 13.7 instantiates records of this class and stores the records within a linked list. Notice that the first three records, for convenience, have been created as an array, which is then used within the linked list's constructor to initialize the linked list. After the list has been created, a fourth record is then inserted into the list. Finally, the complete list is displayed.

Program 13.7

```java
import java.util.*;
class EmployeeRates
{
  public static void main(String args[])
  {
     // for convenience, create an array of records
    NameRate[] nt = {
                      new NameRate("Acme, Sam", 26.58),
                      new NameRate("Mening, Stephen", 15.85),
                      new NameRate("Zebee, Frank", 17.92)
                 };

     // instantiate a list and initialize the list
     // using the records in the array
    LinkedList employee = new LinkedList(Arrays.asList(nt));

     // insert an individual record into the list
    employee.add(1,new NameRate("Bender, Jim", 18.55));
    System.out.println("The size of the list is " + employee.size());
    System.out.println("\n     Name            Pay Rate");
    System.out.println("--------------- -------------");

     // retrieve all list objects and cast each one to a NameRate record type
     // use accessor methods to extract the name and pay rate
    for(int j = 0; j < employee.size(); j++)
    {
      System.out.print( ((NameRate)(employee.get(j))).getName() );
      System.out.println("\t    " + ((NameRate)(employee.get(j))).getRate() );
    }
  }
}
```

The output produced by Program 13.7 is

```
The size of the list is 4

     Name            Pay Rate
--------------- -------------
Acme, Sam          26.58
Bender, Jim        18.55
Mening, Stephen    15.85
Zebee, Frank       17.92
```

The important point to notice in Program 13.7 is that each record retrieved from the list must be cast into a `NameRate` record type. This is accomplished by the expression `(NameRate)(employee.get(j))` within the highlighted `print()` method. This explicit casting was not required in Programs 13.3 because each record in that program consisted of a single string value, and the `print()` method will automatically attempt to convert all of its arguments into string values. This implicit casting form `Object` type to `String` type hides the fact that what is retrieved from the linked list is actually of type `Object`, and except for simple string records, an explicit cast must be used or an error will occur.

Exercises 13.2

1. Modify Program 13.4 to prompt the user for a name. Have the program search the existing list for the entered name. If the name is in the list, display the corresponding phone number; otherwise, display this message: `The name is not in the current phone directory.`

2. Write a Java program containing a linked list of 10 integer numbers. Have the program display the numbers in the list.

3. Using the linked list of objects illustrated in Figure 13.7, write the sequence of steps necessary to delete the object for Edith Dolan from the list.

4. Generalize the description obtained in Exercise 3 to describe the sequence of steps necessary to remove the `nth` object from a list of linked objects. The `nth` object is preceded by the `(n - 1)` st object and followed by the `(n + 1)` st object.

5. Determine the output of the following program:

```java
import java.util.*;  // needed for the Collection Framework classes
public class ShowIterator
{
  public static void main(String[] args)
  {
    int intValue;
    double sum = 0.0;
    double average;

    // create an array of Integer objects
    Integer nums[] = {new Integer(1), new Integer(2),
                      new Integer(3), new Integer(4),
                      new Integer(5)};

    // instantiate a LinkedList of Integer objects using a
    // constructor that initializes the LinkedList with values
    LinkedList x = new LinkedList(Arrays.asList(nums));

    System.out.println("\nThe LinkedList x initially has a size of "
                  + x.size() + "," + "\n  and contains the elements: ");
    System.out.println(x);
```

(continued)

(continued)

```
    Iterator iter = x.iterator();
    while (iter.hasNext())
    {
      intValue = ((Integer)iter.next()).intValue();
      sum = sum + intValue;
    }
    average = sum / x.size();
    System.out.println("The average of these numbers is: " + average);
  }
}
```

6. Remove the explicit cast to `NameRate` in Program 13.7 and explain the resulting compiler error message.

7a. A doubly linked list is a list in which each object contains a reference to both the following and previous objects in the list. Define an appropriate type for a doubly linked list of names and telephone numbers.

b. Using the type defined in Exercise 7a, modify Program 13.4 to list the names and phone numbers in reverse order.

13.3 **Stacks**

A **stack** is a special type of list in which objects can only be added and removed from the top of the list. Thus, it is a **last-in, first-out (LIFO)** data object—an object in which the last item added to the list is the first item that can be removed. An example of this type of operation is a stack of dishes in a cafeteria, where the last dish placed on top of the stack is the first dish removed. Another example is the in-basket on a desk, where the last paper placed in the basket is typically the first one removed. Stacks provide this simple reversal capability.

Consider Figure 13.17, which illustrates an existing list of three last names. As shown, the top name on this list is Barney. If we now restrict access to the list so that names can only be added and removed from the top of the list, then the list becomes a stack. This requires that we clearly designate which end of the list is the top and which is the bottom. Since the name Barney is physically placed above the other names in Figure 13.17, by implication, this is considered the top of the list. To explicitly signify this, however, we have used an arrow to clearly indicate the list's top.

Figure 13.18 illustrates how the stack expands and contracts as names are added and deleted. For example, in Figure 13.18b, the name Ventura has been added to the list. By Figure 13.18c, a total of two new names have been added, and the top of the

FIGURE 13.17 **A list of last names**

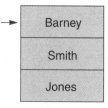

A BIT OF BACKGROUND

Dr. Lukasiewicz and RPN

Dr. Jan Lukasiewicz, born in 1878, studied and taught mathematics at the University of Lvov, in Poland, before becoming a respected professor at the University of Warsaw. He received an appointment in 1919 to the post of Minister of Education in Poland and, with Stanislaw Lesniewski, founded the Warsaw School of Logic.

After World War II, Dr. Lukasiewicz and his wife, Regina, found themselves exiled in Belgium. When he was offered a professorship at the Royal Academy in Dublin, they moved to Ireland, where they remained until his death in 1956.

In 1951, Dr. Lukasiewicz developed a new set of postfix algebraic notation, which was critical in the design of early microprocessors in the 1960s and 1970s.

The actual implementation of postfix algebra was done using stack arithmetic, in which data were pushed on a stack and popped off when an operation needed to be performed. Such stack handling instructions require no address operands and made it possible for very small computers to handle large tasks effectively.

Stack arithmetic, which is based on Dr. Lukasiewicz's work, reverses the more commonly known prefix algebra and became known as reverse Polish notation (RPN). Pocket calculators developed by the Hewlett-Packard Corporation are especially notable for their use of RPN and have made stack arithmetic the favorite of many scientists and engineers.

list has changed accordingly. By now removing the top name, Lanfrank, from the list in Figure 13.18c, the stack shrinks to that shown in Figure 13.18d, and Ventura now resides at the top of the stack. As names continue to be removed from the list (Figures 13.18e and 13.18f), the stack continues to contract.

FIGURE 13.18   An expanding and contracting stack of names

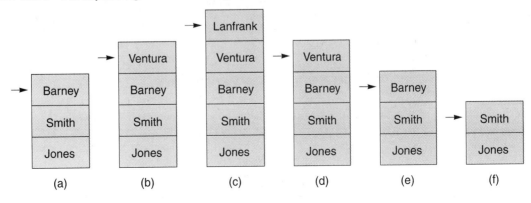

FIGURE 13.19   **The stack class hierarchy diagram**

```
java.lang.Object
   |
   +--java.util.AbstractCollection
        |
        +--java.util.AbstractList
             |
             +--java.util.Vector
                  |
                  +--java.util.Stack
```

Although Figure 13.18 is an accurate representation of a list of names, it contains additional information that is not provided by a true stack object. When adding names to a stack or removing them, no record is kept of how many names have been added or deleted or of how many items the stack actually contains at any one time.

For example, in examining each of the illustrations in Figure 13.18, you can determine how many names are on the list. In a true stack, the only item that can be seen and accessed is the top item on the list. To find out how many items the list contains would require continual removal of the top item until no more items exist.

Stack Class Implementation

Creating a stack requires that the following four components be present:

1. *An object for holding items in the list*
2. *A method of designating the current top stack item*
3. *An operation for placing a new item on the stack*
4. *An operation for removing an item from the stack*

By convention, the operation of placing a new item on the top of a stack is called a **push**, and the operation of removing an item from a stack is called a **pop**. How each of these operations is implemented depends on the object used to represent a stack. In Java, a stack can be easily created using the Collection Framework's Stack class. Figure 13.19 shows the hierarchy diagram for this class.

Table 13.6   **Summary of stack Class Methods**

Method	Return Value	Use
Constructor		
Stack()	N/A	Createss an empty ArrayList.
Additional Class Methods		
empty()	boolean	Tests if the stack is empty.
peek()	Object	Returns the next element without removing it from the stack.
pop()	Object	Returns the next element from the top of the stack and removes it from the stack.
push(object obj)	Object	Returns the next element from the top of the stack and pushes obj onto the top of the stack.
search(object)	int	Returns the position of obj within the stack.

Program 13.8 incorporates the `Stack` class within the context of a complete program. The program is straightforward in that only one stack is instantiated, and user-entered names are pushed onto the stack until the sentinel value of x is entered. Upon detection of this sentinel string value, the names are popped from the stack while the stack is not empty.

Program 13.8

```java
import java.util.*;  // needed for Collection Framework
import java.io.*;    // needed to access the keyboard
public class StackExample
{
  public static void main(String[] args)
  throws java.io.IOException
  {
    String name;
    Stack nameStack = new Stack();  // create an empty stack

    // set up the keyboard input stream
    BufferedReader br = new BufferedReader(
                        new InputStreamReader(System.in));

    System.out.println("Enter as many names as you wish, one per line");
    System.out.println(" To stop enter a single x");
      // push names onto the stack
    while(true)
    {
      System.out.print("Enter a name (or x to stop): ");
      name = br.readLine();
      if (name.equalsIgnoreCase("x")) break;
      nameStack.push(name);
    }
    System.out.println("\nThe names in the stack are:");
     // pop names from the stack
    while(!nameStack.empty())
    {
      name = (String)nameStack.pop();
      System.out.println(name);
    }
  }
}
```

Following is a sample run using Program 13.8:

```
Enter as many names as you wish, one per line
 To stop enter a single x
Enter a name (or x to stop): Jane Jones
Enter a name (or x to stop): Bill Smith
Enter a name (or x to stop): Jim Robinson
Enter a name (or x to stop): x
```

```
The names in the stack are:
Jim Robinson
Bill Smith
Jane Jones
```

Exercises 13.3

1. State whether a `Stack` object would be appropriate for each of the following tasks. Indicate why or why not.

   a. A word processor must remember a line of up to 80 characters. Pressing the Backspace key deletes the previous character, and pressing Ctrl and Backspace deletes the entire line. Users must be able to undo deletion operations.

   b. Customers must wait one to three months for delivery of their new automobiles. The dealer creates a list that will determine the "fair" order in which customers should get their cars; the list is to be prepared in the order in which customers placed their requests for a new car.

   c. You are required to search downward in a pile of magazines to locate the issue for last January. Each magazine was placed on the pile as soon as it was received.

   d. A programming team accepts jobs and prioritizes them on the basis of urgency.

   e. A line forms at a bus stop.

2. Modify Program 13.8 to implement a stack of integers rather than a stack of strings.

3. Modify Program 13.8 to instantiate three stacks of digits named `digits1`, `digits2`, and `digits3`. Initialize `digits1` to contain the digits 9, 8, 5, and 2, which is the number 2589 in reverse digit order. Similarly, the `digits2` stack should be initialized to contain the digits 3, 1, 5, and 7, which is the number 7513 in reverse digit order. Calculate and place the sum of these two numbers in the `digits3` stack. This sum should be obtained by popping respective elements from `digits1` and `digits2` and adding them together with a variable named `carry`, which is initialized to 0. If the sum of the two popped elements and `carry` does not exceed 10, the sum should be pushed onto `digits3` and the `carry` set to 0; otherwise, the `carry` should be set to 1, and the units digit of the sum pushed onto the `digits3` stack.

4. Write a Java program that permits a user to enter a maximum of 100 integers into a `Stack` object. Then have your program:

   a. Reverse the stack contents into a second stack of integers.

   b. Using two additional stacks, reverse the contents in the original stack. Thus, if the stack originally contains the integers 1, 2, 3, and 4, at the end of your program it should contain the integers 4, 3, 2, and 1.

5. Write a Java program that permits a user to enter a maximum of 50 characters into a `Stack` object. Then have your program sort the stack contents into increasing order. Thus, if the contents of the stack are initially D, E, A, and B, the final contents of the stack will be A, B, D, and E.

6. Stacks can be used to efficiently determine whether the parentheses in an expression are correctly balanced. This means that each left facing parenthesis is matched by a right facing parenthesis. For example, consider the string

```
(a + b) / ((x + y) * z)
```

Using a stack, each character in this string, starting from the left, is examined. If the character is a left facing parenthesis, it is pushed onto the stack. Whenever a right facing parenthesis is encountered, the top stack element is popped. An unbalanced expression results if a right facing parenthesis is encountered and the stack is empty or if the stack is not empty when the end of the string is encountered. Using this information, write a Java program that permits the user to type a string and determines if the string contains a balanced set of parentheses.

7. The program written for Exercise 6 can be expanded to include braces,{}, and brackets,[], as well as parentheses delimiters. For example, consider the string

```
{ (a + b) / [(x + y) * z] }
```

To determine if such strings contain balanced pairs of braces, brackets, and parentheses using a stack, each left facing delimiter is pushed onto a stack of characters starting from the leftmost character. Whenever a right facing delimiter is encountered, the top stack element is popped. An unbalanced expression results if a right facing delimiter is encountered and the popped element is not its matching left facing delimiter or if the stack is not empty when the end of the string is encountered. Using this information, write a Java program that permits the user to type a string and determines if the string contains balanced sets of braces, brackets, or parentheses.

8. A group of people have arrived at a bus stop and are lined up in the order indicated:

1. Chaplin	4. Laurel	7. Oliver	10. Garland
2. West	5. Smith	8. Hardy	11. Wayne
3. Taylor	6. Grisby	9. Burton	12. Stewart

Read the names from an input file into a stack and display the order in which they board the bus.

9. Write a single-line word processor. As characters are typed, they are to be pushed onto a stack. Some characters have special meanings:

Erase the previous character (pop it from the stack).
@ Kill the entire line (empty the stack).
?, !, ., or Enter   Terminate line entry. Move the characters to an array and write the contents of the array to the screen.

10. In recursive methods, the parameters are usually stored on a stack. For example, when the method

```
int factorial(int n)
{
   int fact;

   if (n = 0)
     fact = 1;
   else
     fact = n * factorial(n - 1);
   return (fact);
}
```

704 CHAPTER 13 ■ Collections: List Creation and Maintenance

is called, the successive values of the parameter n are stored on a stack. For example, if the initial call were `value = factorial(5)`, then 5 would be pushed onto the stack for n. The next call to factorial would push 4, then 3, and so on, until the last parameter value of 0. Then the values would be popped one at a time and multiplied by the previous product until the stack is empty.

Using this information, write a Java program that performs the same operation as the factorial procedure for a given value of n, entered by the user. After each push, the contents of the stack should be displayed. After each pop, the contents of the stack and the value of factorial should be displayed. Once the display indicates proper operation of your method, stop the display and have the method return the proper factorial value.

13.4 Queues

A **queue** (pronounced "cue") is a list in which items are added to one end of the list, called the top, and removed from the other end of the list, called the bottom. This arrangement ensures that items are removed from the list in the exact order in which they were entered. This means that the first item placed on the list is the first item to be removed, the second item placed on the list is the second item to be removed, and so on. Thus, a queue is a **first-in, first-out (FIFO)** data object—an object in which the first item added to the list is the first item that can be removed.

As an example of a queue, consider a waiting list of people who want to purchase season tickets to a professional football team. The first person on the list is to be called for the first set of tickets that become available, the second person is to be called for the second available set, and so on. For purposes of illustration, assume that the names of the people currently on the list are shown in Figure 13.20.

As illustrated in Figure 13.20, the names have been added in the same fashion as on a stack; that is, as new names are added to the list, they have been stacked on top of the existing names. The difference in a queue is in how the names are popped off the list. Clearly, the people on this list expect to be serviced in the order that they were placed on the list—that is, first in, first out. Thus, unlike a stack, the most recently added name to the list *is not* the first name removed. Rather, the oldest name still on the list is always the next name removed.

To keep the list in proper order, where new names are added to one end of the list and old names are removed from the other end, it is convenient to use two references: one that points to the front of the list for the next person to be serviced and one that points to the end of the list where new people will be added. The reference that points to the front of the list where the next name is to be removed is referred to as the tail reference. The second reference, which points to the last person in the list and indicates where the next person entering the list is to be placed, is the head reference. Thus, for the list shown in Figure 13.20, the tail points to Jane Jones and the head points to Harriet Wright. If Jane Jones were now removed from the list and Lou

FIGURE 13.20 A queue with its references

```
Harriet Wright <----- last name on the queue (head)
Jim Robinson
Bill Smith
Jane Jones <----- first name on the queue (tail)
```

> ## A BIT OF BACKGROUND
>
> ## Stacking the Deque
>
> Stacks and queues are two special forms of a more general data object called a *deque* (pronounced "deck"). Deque stands for double-ended queue.
>
> In a deque object, data can be handled in one of four ways:
>
> 1. Insert at the end and remove from the end. This is the last-in, first-out (LIFO) `Stack` object.
> 2. Insert at the end and remove from the beginning. This is the first-in, first-out (FIFO) `Queue` object.
> 3. Insert at the beginning and remove from the end, which represents a type of inverted FIFO queue.
> 4. Insert at the beginning and remove from the beginning, which is also a LIFO technique.
>
> Implementation 1 (`Stack` object) was presented in Section 13.3 and implementation 2 (`Queue` object) is presented in Section 13.4. Implementations 3 and 4 are sometimes used for keeping track of memory addresses, such as when programming is done in machine language or when objects are handled in a file. When a high-level language, such as Java, manages the data area automatically, users may not be aware of where the data are being stored or of which type of deque is being applied.

Hazlet and Teresa Filer were added, the queue and its associated position indicators would appear as in Figure 13.21.

`LinkedList` Class Implementation

Although the Collection Framework does not have a `Queue` class, one can easily be derived as a subclass of the `LinkedList` class. Creating a queue requires that the following three components be present:

1. *An object for storing items in the list*
2. *An operation for placing a new item at the back of the queue*
3. *An operation for removing an item from the front of the queue*

FIGURE 13.21   **The updated queue references**

```
Teresa Filer <----- head
Lou Hazlet
Harriet Wright
Jim Robinson
Bill Smith  <----- tail
```

The object for storing items will be a `LinkedList`. We will extend this class, however, to provide specific methods for the remaining two items.

The operation of placing a new item on the queue is formally referred to as **enqueuing** and conventionally referred to as a push operation, while removing an item from a queue is formally referred to as **serving** and conventionally as a pop operation. Operationally, enqueuing is an operation similar to pushing on one end of a stack, and serving from a queue is an operation similar to popping from the other end of a stack. How each of these of these operations is implemented depends on the object used to represent a queue.

Because we will use the `LinkedList` class as our base class, we can easily create the push and pop operations using the `LinkedList` methods `addLast()` and `removeFirst()`. The construction of the new `push()` and `pop()` methods using the `LinkedList` class as a base class is presented in Program 13.9. The only additional item to note is that a check is made that the list is not empty before a serve is performed.

Program 13.9

```
import java.util.*;   // needed for Collection Framework
public class Queue extends LinkedList
{
    // constructor for an empty queue
    // instantiates an empty linked list
  public Queue()
  {
    LinkedList queue = new LinkedList();
  }
  public void push(Object obj)
  {
     addLast(obj);
  }
  public Object pop()
  {
    return removeFirst();
  }
  public boolean isEmpty()
  {
    if (size() == 0)
     return true;
    else
     return false;
  }
}
```

Program 13.10 illustrates using the `Queue` class within the context of a complete program.

Program 13.10

```java
import java.io.*;    // needed to access the keyboard
public class QueueExample
{
  public static void main(String[] args)
  throws java.io.IOException
  {
    String name;
    Queue nameQueue = new Queue();   // create an empty queue

    // set up the keyboard input stream
    BufferedReader br = new BufferedReader(
                        new InputStreamReader(System.in));

    System.out.println("Enter as many names as you wish, one per line");
    System.out.println(" To stop enter a single x");
      // push names onto the queue
    while(true)
    {
      System.out.print("Enter a name (or x to stop): ");
      name = br.readLine();
      if (name.equalsIgnoreCase("X")) break;
      nameQueue.push(name);
    }

    System.out.println("\nThe names in the queue are:");
     // pop names from the stack
    while(!nameQueue.isEmpty())
    {
      name = (String)nameQueue.pop();
      System.out.println(name);
    }
  }
}
```

A sample run using Program 13.10 produces the following:

```
Enter as many names as you wish, one per line
 To stop enter a single x
Enter a name (or x to stop): Jane Jones
Enter a name (or x to stop): Bill Smith
Enter a name (or x to stop): Jim Robinson
Enter a name (or x to stop): x

The names in the queue are:
Jane Jones
Bill Smith
Jim Robinson
```

Exercises 13.4

1. State whether a queue, a stack, or neither object would be appropriate for each of the following tasks. Indicate why or why not.

   a. A waiting list of customers to be seated in a restaurant.

   b. A group of student tests waiting to be graded.

   c. An address book listing names and telephone numbers in alphabetical order.

   d. Patients waiting for examinations in a doctor's office.

2. Modify Program 13.10 to use a queue of integers rather than a queue of strings.

3. Write a Java program that permits a user to enter a maximum of 50 double-precision values into a queue. Then have your program sort the queue contents into increasing order. Thus, if the contents of the queue are initially D, E, A, and B, the final contents of the queue will be A, B, D, and E.

4. Write a queue program that accepts an object consisting of an integer identification number and a floating-point hourly pay rate.

5. Add a menu method to Program 13.10 that gives the user a choice of adding a name to the queue, removing a name from the queue, or listing the contents of the queue without removing any objects from it.

6. A group of people have arrived at a bus stop and are lined up in the order indicated:

1. Chaplin	4. Laurel	7. Oliver	10. Garland
2. West	5. Smith	8. Hardy	11. Wayne
3. Taylor	6. Grisby	9. Burton	12. Stewart

   Read the names from an input file into a queue and display the order in which they board the bus

7. Write a queue handling program that asks each customer for their names as they place orders at a fast-food restaurant. Each object in the queue should consist of a name field with a maximum of 20 characters and an integer field, which keeps track of the total number of customers served. The value in the integer field should be automatically provided by the program each time a name is entered. Orders are processed in the same sequence as they are placed. The order taker examines the queue and calls the names when the order is ready. When the queue is empty, print a message telling the staff to take a break.

8. Descriptions of jobs waiting in a computer for the printer are generally kept in a queue. Write a Java program that keeps track of printing jobs, objected by user name and anticipated printer time (in seconds) for the job. Add jobs to the queue as printouts are requested and remove them from the queue as they are serviced. When a user adds a job to the queue, display a message giving an estimate of how long it will be before the job is printed. The estimate is to consist of the sum of all the prior jobs in the queue. (Tip: Store the accumulated times in a separate variable.)

9a. On your electronic mail terminal, you receive notes to call people. Each message contains the name and phone number of the caller as well as a date in the form month/day/year and a 24-hour integer clock in the form hours:minutes that objects the time that the message was received. A latest attempt field is initially set to 0, indicating that no attempt has yet been made to return the call. For example, a particular object may appear as

Jan Williamson (555)666-7777   8/14/96 17:05   0

Write a Java program to store these objects in a queue as they arrive and to feed them to you, one at a time, upon request. If you cannot reach a person when you try to call, place that object at the end of the queue and fill the latest attempt field with the time you tried to return the call, in the form days later/hours:minutes. Thus, if your last unsuccessful attempt to return Jan Williamson's call was on 8/16/96 at 4:20, the new enqueued object would be

Jan Williamson (555)666-7777   8/14/96 17:05   2/16:20

b. Modify the program written for Exercise 9a so that the time and date fields are automatically filled in using system calls to time and date methods provided by your compiler.

13.5   Common Programming Errors

There are two common programming errors related to using linked lists, stacks, and queues. Both errors are related to the fact that all of these list structures store records as `Object` types, with the conversion to this type being implicitly made when an element is inserted into the list. Specifically, these two common errors are:

1. Inserting records instantiated from different classes into the same list. Because all records are automatically and implicitly converted to type `Object` when they are inserted into a list, this conversion is applied regardless of the underlying record type. That is, the conversion to type `Object` *does not* check the data type of the record being inserted. It is up to the programmer to ensure that the same types of records are added into a specific list.

2. Not casting a retrieved object from a linked list into a specific record type before attempting to use the record. Because each record type is automatically converted into an `Object` type when inserted into a list, you may forget that the inserted object *is not* of the type defined for your record and that it must be explicitly cast into the correct type upon retrieval from the list. For simple record types, such as a string or a primitive data type, no error occurs when the object is displayed. This is because the `print()` methods automatically cast the `Object` into a string type. For most applications, however, where the record consists of numerous instance variables and accessors are used to extract specific data items, a run-time error will occur if an explicit cast to the defined record type is not made.

13.6   Chapter Review

KEY TERMS

Collection Framework	linked list	serving
enqueuing	pop	stack
first in, first out (FIFO)	push	
last in, last out (LIFO)	queue	

SUMMARY

1. A record object allows individual data items under a common variable name. The simplest record is constructed as an object of a class having at least one instance variable and no methods.

2. A linked list is a list of records in which each record contains a reference variable that locates the next record in the list. Additionally, each linked list must have a reference to locate the first record in the list. The last record 's reference variable is set to `null` to indicate the end of the list.

3. Linked lists can be automatically constructed using the Collection Framework's `LinkedList` class. This class automatically and implicitly converts each stored record into an `Object` type. Except in very simple lists, such as those whose records consist of a single string, objects retrieved from a `LinkedList` must be cast into their underlying record type.

4. A stack is a list consisting of objects that can only be added and removed from the top of the list. Such an object is a last-in, first-out (LIFO) list in which the last object added to the list is the first object removed. Stacks can be implemented using the Collection Framework's `Stack` class.

5. A queue is a list consisting of objects that are added to the top of the list and removed from the bottom of the list. Such an object is a first-in, first-out (FIFO) list in which objects are removed in the order in which they were added. Queues can be implemented using a programmer-created class derived from the `LinkedList` class.

14

Additional Capabilities

14.1 **Additional Features**

14.2 **Bit Operators**

14.3 **Command-Line Arguments**

14.4 **Chapter Review**

Previous chapters have presented Java's basic structure, statements, and capabilities. This chapter presents additional capabilities that you may require or find useful as you progress in your understanding and use of Java. None of these are advanced features, but their usage is typically rather restricted. The features described in Sections 14.1 and 14.2 are almost never used to the extent of the topics presented in the prior chapters. Unlike the other topics, command-line arguments, the topic of Section 14.3, are used extensively by some programmers. The topic is included in this chapter because it can be introduced almost at any point within your study of Java.

14.1 Additional Features

This section presents a number of additional Java features and statements.

Other Number Bases

In addition to explicitly specifying integer literals as decimal numbers, such values can also be specified as either octal or hexadecimal numbers. Any integer having a leading 0 is taken to be an octal value, and any integer beginning with a leading 0x or 0X is considered a hexadecimal number. Thus, for example, the value 0347 is considered an octal integer number in Java, whereas the number 0x467adf is considered a hexadecimal value. Appending the letter L to either of these two values would make them long integer literals.

The `flush()` Method

Whenever you have used a `print()` or `println()` method, what actually happens is that the arguments placed within the parentheses are sequentially put in a temporary holding area called a **buffer.** For example, if the statement `System.out.print ("This");` is executed, the letters T, h, i, and s are placed in the buffer, as illustrated in Figure 14.1. This buffer is continually used until it is forced to send its contents to an output stream. This forced sending of the buffer's contents to an output stream is referred to as *flushing the buffer*, or **flushing** for short.

Flushing occurs whenever a line terminator character is encountered, the end of the program is reached, or an explicit `flush()` method is called.[1] For example, the following three statements cause the buffer to be filled with the characters This is a test.

```
System.out.print("This");
System.out.print(" is a");
System.out.print(" test.");
```

The contents of the buffer will automatically be flushed and sent to the screen when the program containing these statements has finished running. However, by using a `flush()` method, which has the syntax `System.out.flush();`, you can

FIGURE 14.1 Displayed characters are first stored in a buffer

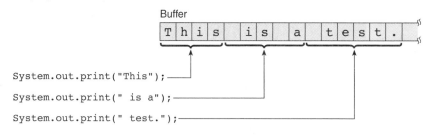

---

[1] Flushing to `System.out` is automatic when a line terminator is encountered because this stream is, by default, an autoflush stream.

force the contents of the buffer to be immediately displayed and the buffer cleared. Adding the statement after the previous three `print()` statements will force an immediate display of the buffer's contents and clear the buffer.

The following section of code produces the same single-line message `This is a test.` as the previous lines of code:

```
System.out.print("This");
System.out.flush()
System.out.print(" is a");
System.out.flush()
System.out.print(" test.");
System.out.flush()
```

This last section of code forces each set of characters to be output immediately after they have been placed in the buffer. Notice that both sets of statements leave the cursor at the end of the displayed line because clearing the buffer does not cause a new line to be started. Only a newline character, \n, will force the display to start on a new line. The appending of a newline character to the data it placed in the buffer by the `println()` method both causes the buffer to be flushed and the cursor to be moved to the start of the next line as part of displaying the current buffer contents.

Conditional Expressions

A conditional expression uses the conditional operator, `?:`, and provides an alternative way of expressing a simple `if-else` statement. The syntax of a conditional expression is

```
condition ? expression1 : expression2
```

If the value of the condition is true, *expression1* is evaluated; otherwise, *expression2* is evaluated. The value for the complete conditional expression is the value of either *expression1* or *expression2* depending on which expression was evaluated. As always, the value of the expression may be assigned to a variable.

Conditional expressions are most useful in replacing simple `if-else` statements. For example, the `if-else` statement

```
if (hours > 40)
  rate = .045;
else
  rate = .02;
```

can be replaced with the one-line statement

```
rate = (hours > 40) ? .045 : .02;
```

Here the complete conditional expression

```
(hours > 40) ? .045 : .02
```

is evaluated before any assignment is made to `rate` because the conditional operator, `?:`, has a higher precedence than the assignment operator. Within the conditional expression, the expression `hours > 40` is evaluated first. If this expression is true, the value of the complete conditional expression is set to .045; otherwise, the conditional expression has a value of .02. Finally, the value of the conditional expression, either .045 or .02, is assigned to the variable `rate`.

The conditional operator, `?:`, is unique in Java in that it is a ternary operator. This means that the operator connects three operands. The first operand is always a relational or logical expression that is evaluated first. The next two operands are other valid expressions of the same or compatible data types, which can be single constants, variables, or more general expressions. The complete conditional expression consists of all three operands connected by the conditional operator symbols, `?` and `:`.

In general, conditional expressions tend to be unclear and are best avoided. They are only useful in replacing `if-else` statements when the expressions in the equivalent `if-else` statement are not long or complicated. For example, the statement

```
maxValue = a > b ? a : b;
```

is a one-line statement that assigns the maximum value of the variables a and b to maxValue. A longer, equivalent form of this statement is

```
if (a > b)
  maxValue = a;
else
  maxValue = b;
```

Because of the length of the expressions involved, a conditional expression *would not* be useful in replacing the following `if-else` statement:

```
if (amount > 20000)
  taxes = .025(amount - 20000) + 400;
else
  taxes = .02 * amount;
```

14.2 **Bit Operators**

Java operates with data entities that are stored as one or more bytes, such as character, integer, and double-precision constants and variables. In addition, Java provides for the manipulation of individual bits of character and integer constants and variables. The operators that are used to perform bit manipulations are called **bit operators**. The bit operators presented in this section are listed in Table 14.1.

All of the operators in Table 14.1, except ~, are binary operators, which means that they require two operands. For these bit operators, each operand is considered as a binary number consisting of a series of individual 1s and 0s. The respective bits

Table 14.1   **Bit Operators**

Operator	Description
&	Bitwise AND
|	Bitwise inclusive OR
^	Bitwise exclusive OR
~	Bitwise complement
<<	Bitwise left shift with zero fill
>>	Bitwise right shift with sign fill
>>>	Bitwise right shift with zero fill

in each operand are then compared on a bit-by-bit basis, and the result is determined based on the selected operation.

The first three bit operations in Table 14.1 can also be used in related expressions. When this is done on boolean values, the & and | operators perform the same function as the && and || operators but always evaluate both operands. That is, they do not use the short-circuited evaluation performed by the boolean operators && and || (see Section 5.1). Because this is generally not desirable, you should use the short-circuit && and || operators for Boolean operations unless a specific result is required or you must logically compare two integer operands.

The AND Operator

The bitwise AND operator causes a bit-by-bit AND comparison between its two operands. The result of each bit-by-bit comparison is 1 only when both bits being compared are 1s: otherwise, the result of the AND operation is 0. For example, assume that the following two 8-bit numbers are to be ANDed:

```
1 0 1 1 0 0 1 1
1 1 0 1 0 1 0 1
---------------
```

To perform an AND operation, each bit in one operand is compared to the bit occupying the same position in the other operand. Figure 14.2 illustrates the correspondence between bits for these two operands. Bitwise AND comparisons are determined by the following rule: *The result of an AND comparison is 1 when both bits being compared are 1s; otherwise, the result is 0.* The result of each comparison is, of course, independent of any other bit comparison.

AND operations are extremely useful in masking, or eliminating, selected bits from an operand. This is a direct result of the fact that ANDing any bit (1 or 0) with a 0 forces the resulting bit to be 0, whereas ANDing any bit (1 or 0) with a 1 leaves the original bit unchanged. For example, assume that the variable op1 has the arbitrary bit pattern x x x x x x x x, where each x can be either 1 or 0, independent of any other x in the number. The result of ANDing this binary number with the binary number 0 0 0 0 1 1 1 1 is

```
op1 =    x x x x x x x x
op2 =    0 0 0 0 1 1 1 1
         ---------------
Result = 0 0 0 0 x x x x
```

As can be seen from this example, the 0s in op2 effectively mask, or eliminate, the respective bits in op1, and the 1s in op2 filter, or pass, the respective bits in op1 through with no change in their values. In this example, the variable op2 is called a

FIGURE 14.2 **A sample AND operation**

```
  1 0 1 1 0 0 1 1
& 1 1 0 1 0 1 0 1
  ---------------
  1 0 0 1 0 0 0 1
```

mask. By choosing the mask appropriately, any individual bit in an operand can be selected, or filtered, out of an operand for inspection. For example, ANDing the variable op1 with the mask 0 0 0 0 0 1 0 0 forces all the bits of the result to be 0, except for the third bit. The third bit of the result will be a copy of the third bit of op1. Thus, if the result of the AND is 0, the third bit of op1 must have been 0, and if the result of the AND is a nonzero number, the third bit must have been 1.

The Inclusive OR Operator

The inclusive bitwise OR operator, |, performs a bit-by-bit comparison of its two operands in a similar fashion to the bit-by-bit AND. The result of the bitwise OR comparison, however, is determined by the following rule: *The result of the comparison is 1 if either bit being compared is 1; otherwise, the result is 0.*

Figure 14.3 illustrates an OR operation. As shown in the figure, when either of the 2 bits being compared is 1, the result is 1; otherwise, the result is 0. As with all bit operations, the result of each comparison is, of course, independent of any other comparison.

Inclusive OR operations are extremely useful in forcing selected bits to take on a 1 value or for passing through other bit values unchanged. This is a direct result of the fact that ORing any bit (1 or 0) with a 1 forces the resulting bit to be 1, and ORing any bit (1 or 0) with a 0 leaves the original bit unchanged. For example, assume that the variable op1 has the arbitrary bit pattern x x x x x x x x, where each x can be either 1 or 0, independent of any other x in the number. The result of ORing this binary number with the binary number 1 1 1 1 0 0 0 0 is

```
   op1 =   x x x x x x x x
   op2 =   1 1 1 1 0 0 0 0
           ---------------
Result =   1 1 1 1 x x x x
```

As can be seen from this example, the 1s in op2 force the resulting bits to 1, and the 0s in op2 filter, or pass, the respective bits in op1 through with no change in their values. Thus, using an OR operation, a similar masking operation can be produced as with an AND operation, except the masked bits are set to 1s rather than cleared to 0s. Another way of looking at this is to say that ORing with a 0 has the same effect as ANDing with a 1.

The Exclusive OR Operator

The exclusive OR operator, ^, performs a bit-by-bit comparison of its two operands. The result of the comparison is determined by the following rule: *The result of the comparison is 1 if one and only one of the bits being compared is 1; otherwise, the result is 0.*

FIGURE 14.3   **A sample OR operation**

```
  1 0 1 1 0 0 1 1
| 1 1 0 1 0 1 0 1
  ---------------
  1 1 1 1 0 1 1 1
```

FIGURE 14.4   **A sample exclusive OR operation**

```
   1 0 1 1 0 0 1 1
 ^ 1 1 0 1 0 1 0 1
   ───────────────
   0 1 1 0 0 1 1 0
```

Figure 14.4 illustrates an exclusive OR operation. As shown in the figure, when both bits being compared are the same value (both 1 or both 0), the result is 0. Only when both bits have different values (one bit a 1 and the other a 0) is the result 1. Again, each pair or bit comparison is independent of any other bit comparison.

An exclusive OR operation can be used to create the opposite value, or complement, of any individual bit in a variable. This is a direct result of the fact that exclusive ORing any bit (1 or 0) with a 1 forces the resulting bit to be of the opposite value of its original state, and exclusive ORing any bit (1 or 0) with a 0 leaves the original bit unchanged. For example, assume that the variable op1 has the arbitrary bit pattern x x x x x x x x, where each x can be either 1 or 0, independent of any other x in the number. Using the notation that $\bar{x}$ is the complement (opposite) value of x, the result of exclusive ORing this binary number with the binary number 0 1 0 1 0 1 0 1 is

```
    op1 = x x x x x x x x
    op2 = 0 1 0 1 0 1 0 1
          ---------------
 Result = x x̄ x x̄ x x̄ x x̄
```

As can be seen from this example, the 1s in op2 force the resulting bits to be the complement of their original bit values, and the 0s in op2 filter, or pass, the respective bits in op1 through with no change in their values.

The Complement Operator

The bitwise Complement operator, ~, is a unary operator that changes each 1 bit in its operand to 0 and each 0 bit to 1. For example, if the variable op1 contains the binary number 11001010, ~op1 replaces this binary number with the number 00110101. The complement operator can be used to force any bit in an operand to 0, independent of the actual number of bits used to store the number. For example, the statement

```
    op1 = op1 & ~07;   // 07 is an octal number
```

or its shorter form

```
    op1 &= ~07;    // 07 is an octal number
```

both set the last three bits of op1 to 0. Either of these two statements can, of course, be replaced by ANDing the last three bits of op1 with 0s if the number of bits used to store op1 is known. If op1 is a 16-bit short integer, the appropriate AND operation is

```
    op1 = op1 & 0177770;    // in octal
```

or

```
    op1 = op1 & 0xFFF8;    // in hexadecimal
```

For a 32-bit integer value, the foregoing AND sets the leftmost or higher order 16 bits to 0 also, which is an unintended result. The correct statement for a 32-bit integer is

```
op1 = op1 & 027777777770;    // in octal
```

or

```
op1 = op1 & 0xFFFFFFF8;      // in hexadecimal
```

Using the bitwise NOT operator in this situation frees the programmer from having to consider the storage size of the operand.

The Shift Operators

The left shift operator, <<, causes the bits in an operand to be shifted to the left by a given amount. For example, the statement

```
op1 = op1 << 4;
```

causes the bits in `op1` to be shifted 4 bits to the left, filling any vacated bits with a 0. Figure 14.5 illustrates the effect of shifting the binary number 1111100010101011 to the left by 4 bit positions.

The right shift operator, >>, causes the bits in an operand to be shifted to the right by a given amount. For example, the statement

```
op2 = op1 >> 4;
```

causes the bits in `op1` to be shifted to the right by 4 bit positions. Figure 14.6a illustrates the right shift of the binary number 1111100010101011 by 4 bit positions. As illustrated, the 4 rightmost bits are shifted "off the end" and are lost, and the sign bit is reproduced in the vacated bits. Figure 14.6b illustrates the right shift of a positive binary number by 4 bit positions, where the sign bit is reproduced in the vacated bits.

The type of fill illustrated in Figures 14.6a and 14.6b, where the sign bit is reproduced in vacated bit positions, is called an arithmetic right shift. In an arithmetic right shift, each single shift to the right corresponds to a division by 2.

Instead of reproducing the sign bit in right-shifted signed numbers, the right shift operator, >>>, automatically fills the vacated bits with 0s. This type of shift is called a

FIGURE 14.5   **An example of a left shift**

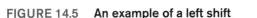
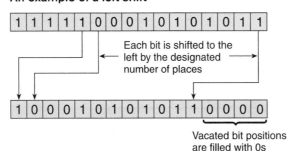

Each bit is shifted to the left by the designated number of places

Vacated bit positions are filled with 0s

FIGURE 14.6a   **The right shift of a negative binary number**

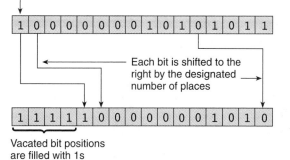

FIGURE 14.6b   **The right shift of a positive binary number**

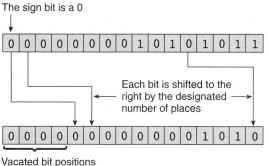

logical shift. For numbers where the leftmost bit is 0, both arithmetic and logical right shifts produce the same result. The results of these two shifts are only different when negative numbers are involved.

14.3 Command-Line Arguments

Arguments can be passed to any method in a program, including the main() method. In this section, we describe the procedures for passing arguments to main() when a program is initially invoked and having main() correctly receive and store the arguments passed to it. Both the sending and receiving sides of the transaction must be considered. Fortunately, the interface for transmitting arguments to a main() method has been standardized in Java, so both sending and receiving arguments can be done almost mechanically.

All the programs that have been run so far have been invoked by typing the words Java and a class name, which is the same as the class that contains the main() method to be executed. The line on which these two items are typed is formally referred to as the **command line.** This line always starts with the operating system prompt, which for the UNIX operating system is usually the $ symbol and for a DOS window is typically a C>.

Assuming that you are using a DOS window that uses a C> prompt, the complete command line for executing a main() method within a class named CommandLine-Args is

    C> java CommandLineArgs

As illustrated in Figure 14.7, this command line causes the CommandLineArgs byte-code program to begin execution with its main() method, but no arguments are passed to main().

Now assume that we want to pass the five separate string arguments three blind mice showed up directly into CommandLineArgs's main() function. Sending arguments into a main() method is extremely easy. It is accomplished by including the arguments on the command line used to begin program execution. Because the arguments are typed on the command line, they are, naturally, called **command-line arguments.** To pass the arguments three blind mice showed up directly into the main() method of the CommandLineArgs program, we only need to add the desired words after the program name on the command line.

    C> java CommandLineArgs three blind mice showed up

Upon encountering the command line CommandLineArgs three blind mice showed up, the operating system automatically passes the sequence of five strings after the program's name into main().

Sending command-line arguments to main() is always this simple. The arguments are typed on the command line, and the operating system passes them into main() as a sequence of separate strings. Now let's see how main() stores and accesses these arguments.

Arguments passed to main(), like all method arguments, must be declared as part of the method's definition. To standardize argument passing to a main() function, only one type of argument is allowed, which is an array of strings. This array is named args and is declared as String[] args. Notice that this declaration has been included in the header line that we have been using throughout this text for main(), which is

    public static void main(String[] args)

FIGURE 14.7 **Invoking the CommandLineArgs bytecode program**

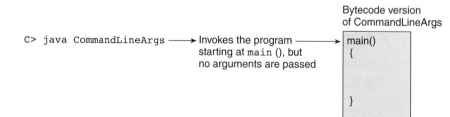

Thus, all of the programs in this text have been constructed to receive command-line arguments. The `args` array declared in the header line is actually an array of references, where each reference can be used to access one of the string arguments passed to `main()`. Thus, if any arguments are passed to `main()`, `args[0]` refers to the first argument, `args[1]` to the second argument, and so on. Figure 14.8 illustrates how the arguments `three blind mice showed up` are stored and referenced using the `args` array. Notice that the number of command-line arguments is determined using the expression `args.length`, which is the number of references stored in the `args` array. For the arrangement shown in Figure 14.8, `args.length` is five.

Once command-line arguments are passed to a Java program, they can be used like any other Java strings. Program 14.1 causes its command-line arguments to be displayed from within `main()`.

Program 14.1

```java
// A program that displays command-line arguments
public class CommandLineArgs
{
  public static void main(String[] args)
  {
    int i, numOfArgs;

    numOfArgs = args.length;
    System.out.println("The number of command-line arguments is " + numOfArgs);
    System.out.println("These are the arguments that were passed to main():");
    for (i = 0; i < numOfArgs; i++)
      System.out.println(args[i]);
    System.out.println();
  }
}
```

The output of this program for the command line

```
C> Java CommandLineArgs three blind mice showed up
```

is

```
The number of command-line arguments is 5
These are the arguments that were passed to main():
three
blind
mice
showed
up
```

As illustrated by this output, the term `args.length` correctly determines that the number of command-line arguments is five. Also notice that each command-line argument is referenced using an `args` array element.

Two final comments about command-line arguments are in order. Any argument typed on a command line is considered to be a string. If you want numerical data passed to `main()`, it is up to you to convert the passed string into its numerical

FIGURE 14.8   **Accessing command-line arguments using the `args` array**

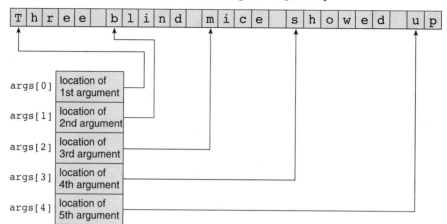

counterpart. This is seldom an issue because most command-line arguments are used as string flags to pass appropriate processing control signals to an invoked program. Second, it is interesting to note that there is nothing inherently special about the parameter name `args`. By convention, however, it is the name that is used and understood by Java programmers to refer to command-line arguments passed to `main()`.

Exercises for Chapter 14

1.   Rewrite each of the following `if-else` statements using a conditional expression:

a.   `if (a < b);`

    `minimunValue = a;`

 `else`

    `minimumValue = b;`

b.   `if (num < 0)`

    `sign = -1;`

 `else`

    `sign = 1;`

c.   `if (flag == 1)`

    `value = num;`

 `else`

    `value = num * num;`

d.   `if (credit == plus)`

    `rate = prime;`

 `else`

    `rate = prime + delta;`

   e.   `if (!bond)`

        `coupon = .075;`

      `else`

        `coupon = 1.1;`

2.   Determine the results of the following operations:

a.
```
  11001010
&10100101
----------
```

b.
```
  11001010
| 10100101
-----------
```

c.
```
  11001010
^ 10100101
----------
```

3.   Write the octal representations of the binary numbers given in Exercise 2.

4a.   Assume that the arbitrary bit pattern xxxxxxxx, where each x can represent either 1 or 0, is stored in the integer variable `flag`. Determine the octal value of a mask that can be ANDed with the bit pattern to reproduce the third and fourth bits of `flag` and set all other bits to 0. The rightmost bit in `flag` is considered bit 0.

b.   Determine the octal value of a mask that can be inclusively ORed with the bit pattern in `flag` to reproduce the third and fourth bits of `flag` and set all other bits to 1. Again, consider the rightmost bit in `flag` to be bit 0.

c.   Determine the octal value of a mask that can be used to complement the values of the third and fourth bits of `flag` and leave all other bits unchanged. Determine the bit operation that should be used with the mask value to produce the desired result.

5.   Enter and run Program 14.1 on your computer.

6.   Write a program that accepts two integer values as command-line arguments. The program should multiply the two values entered and display the result. (Tip: The command line must be accepted as string data and converted to numerical values before multiplication.)

7a.   Write a program that accepts the name of a data file as a command-line argument. Have your program open the data file and display its contents, line by line, on the screen.

b.   Would the program written for Exercise 7a work correctly for a program file?

8.   Modify the program written for Exercise 7a so that each line displayed is preceded by a line number.

14.4 **Chapter Review**

KEY TERMS

bit operators	command line	flushing
buffer	command-line arguments	mask

SUMMARY

1. The `print()` method simply places its text input into a buffer, and the buffer's contents are then displayed either when the program is finished running or a `flush()` method is invoked. The input to a `println()` method is automatically flushed from the buffer, with a terminating newline escape sequence added, as part of the `println()` method call.

2. A conditional expression provides an alternative way of expressing a simple `if-else` statement. The general form of a conditional expression is

```
condition ? expression1 : expression2
```

The equivalent `if-else` statement is

```
if (condition)
    expression1;
else
    expression2;
```

3. Individual bits of character and integer variables and constants can be manipulated using Java's bit operators. These are the AND, inclusive OR, exclusive OR, NOT, and shift operators.

4. The AND and inclusive OR operators are useful in creating masks. These masks can be used to pass or eliminate individual bits from the selected operand. The exclusive OR operator is useful in complementing an operand's bits.

5. The NOT operator changes each 1 bit in its operand to 0 and each 0 bit to 1.

6. The shift operators permit all of the bits in an operand to be shifted left or right by a specified amount.

7. Arguments passed to `main()` are termed command-line arguments. Java provides a standard argument-passing procedure in which `main()` can accept any number of arguments passed to it. Each argument passed to `main()` is considered a string and is stored using an array of references named `args`. The total number of arguments on the command line can be determined as `args.length`.

Operator
Precedence Table

Table A.1 presents the symbols, precedence, descriptions, and associativity of Java's operators. Operators toward the top of the table have a higher precedence than those toward the bottom. Operators within each section have the same precedence and associativity.

Table A.1   Summary of Java Operators

Operator	Description	Associativity
( )	Function call	Left to right
[ ]	Array element	
.	Member reference	
++	Postfix increment	Left to right
--	Postfix decrement	
++	Prefix increment	Right to left
--	Prefix decrement	
-	Unary minus	
!	Logical negation	
~	One's complement	
new	Object instantiation	
(type)	Type conversion (cast)	Right to left
*	Multiplication	Left to right
/	Division	
%	Remainder (modulus)	
+	Addition	Left to right
+	String concatenation	
-	Subtraction	
<<	Left shift	Left to right
>>	Right shift with sign	
>>	Right shift with zero fill	
<	Less than	Left to right
<=	Less than or equal to	
>	Greater than	
>=	Greater than or equal to	
==	Equal to	Left to right
!=	Not equal to	
&	Bitwise AND	Left to right
^	Bitwise exclusive OR	Left to right
|	Bitwise inclusive OR	Left to right
&&	Logical AND	Left to right
||	Logical OR	Left to right
? :	Conditional expression	Right to left
=	Assignment	Right to left
+= -= *=	Assignment	
/= %=	Assignment	
<<= >>= >>>=	Assignment	
&= ^= |=	Assignment	

Unicode
Character Set

Unicode provides 65,536 different codes, with each code using 2 bytes (16 bits). The following are the first 256 characters in the Unicode character set. The first 128 of these characters are the same as the ASCII character set, except that ASCII characters are stored using 8 bits and thus do not store the leading 8 bits of zeros in the corresponding Unicode character. Characters having decimal values of 0 through 31, except for codes 13 and 27, are referred to as control characters because they are created by pressing the Control key and a letter key at the same time.

Key(s)	Dec	Hex	Key	Dec	Hex	Key	Dec	Hex	Key	Dec	Hex
Ctrl 1	0	0000	Space	32	0020	@	64	0040	`	96	0060
Ctrl A	1	0001	!	33	0021	A	65	0041	a	97	0061
Ctrl B	2	0002	"	34	0022	B	66	0042	b	98	0062
Ctrl C	3	0003	#	35	0023	C	67	0043	c	99	0063
Ctrl D	4	0004	$	36	0024	D	68	0044	d	100	0064
Ctrl E	5	0005	%	37	0025	E	69	0045	e	101	0065
Ctrl F	6	0006	&	38	0026	F	70	0046	f	102	0066
Ctrl G	7	0007	'	39	0027	G	71	0047	g	103	0067
Ctrl H	8	0008	(	40	0028	H	72	0048	h	104	0068
Ctrl I	9	0009	)	41	0029	I	73	0049	i	105	0069
Ctrl J	10	000A	*	42	002A	J	74	004A	j	106	006A
Ctrl K	11	000B	+	43	002B	K	75	004B	k	107	006B
Ctrl L	12	000C	,	44	002C	L	76	004C	l	108	006C
Ctrl M	13	000D	-	45	002D	M	77	004D	m	109	006D
Ctrl N	14	000E	.	46	002E	N	78	004E	n	110	006E
Ctrl O	15	000F	/	47	002F	O	79	004F	o	111	006F
Ctrl P	16	0010	0	48	0030	P	80	0050	p	112	0070
Ctrl Q	17	0011	1	49	0031	Q	81	0051	q	113	0071
Ctrl R	18	0012	2	50	0032	R	82	0052	r	114	0072
Ctrl S	19	0013	3	51	0033	S	83	0053	s	115	0073
Ctrl T	20	0014	4	52	0034	T	84	0054	t	116	0074
Ctrl U	21	0015	5	53	0035	U	85	0055	u	117	0075
Ctrl V	22	0016	6	54	0036	V	86	0056	v	118	0076
Ctrl W	23	0017	7	55	0037	W	87	0057	w	119	0077
Ctrl X	24	0018	8	56	0038	X	88	0058	x	120	0078
Ctrl Y	25	0019	9	57	0039	Y	89	0059	y	121	0079
Ctrl Z	26	001A	:	58	003A	Z	90	005A	z	122	007A
Esc	27	001B	;	59	003B	[	91	005B	{	123	007B
Ctrl <	28	001C	<	60	003C	\	92	005C	|	124	007C
Ctrl /	29	001D	=	61	003D	]	93	005D	}	125	007D
Ctrl =	30	001E	>	62	003E	^	94	005E	~	126	007E
Ctrl -	31	001F	?	63	003F	_	95	005F	del	127	007F

Key	Dec	Hex	Key	Dec	Hex	Key	Dec	Hex	Key	Dec	Hex
**	128	0080	(space)	160	0100	À	192	0120	à	224	0140
**	129	0081	¡	161	0101	Á	193	0121	á	225	0141
**	130	0082	¢	162	0102	Â	194	0122	â	226	0142
**	131	0083	£	163	0103	Ã	195	0123	ã	227	0143
**	132	0084	¤	164	0104	Ä	196	0124	ä	228	0144
**	133	0085	¥	165	0105	Å	197	0125	å	229	0145
**	134	0086	¦	166	0106	Æ	198	0126	æ	230	0146
**	135	0087	§	167	0107	Ç	199	0127	ç	231	0147
**	136	0088	¨	168	0108	È	200	0128	è	232	0148
**	137	0089	©	169	0109	É	201	0129	é	233	0149
**	138	008A	ª	170	010A	Ê	202	012A	ê	234	014A
**	139	008B	«	171	010B	Ë	203	012B	ë	235	014B
**	140	008C	¬	172	010C	Ì	204	012C	ì	236	014C
**	141	008D	-	173	010D	Í	205	012D	í	237	014D
**	142	008E	®	174	010E	Î	206	012E	î	238	014E
**	143	008F	‾	175	010F	Ï	207	012F	ï	239	014F
**	144	0090	°	176	0110	Ð	208	0130	ð	240	0150
**	145	0091	±	177	0111	Ñ	209	0131	ñ	241	0151
**	146	0092	²	178	0112	Ò	210	0132	ò	242	0152
**	147	0093	³	179	0113	Ó	211	0133	ó	243	0153
**	148	0094	´	180	0114	Ô	212	0134	ô	244	0154
**	149	0095	µ	181	0115	Õ	213	0135	õ	245	0155
**	150	0096	¶	182	0116	Ö	214	0136	ö	246	0156
**	151	0097	·	183	0117	×	215	0137	÷	247	0157
**	152	0098	¸	184	0118	Ø	216	0138	ø	248	0158
**	153	0099	¹	185	0119	Ù	217	0139	ù	249	0159
**	154	009A	º	186	011A	Ú	218	013A	ú	250	015A
**	155	009B	»	187	011B	Û	219	013B	û	251	015B
**	156	009C	¼	188	011C	Ü	220	013C	ü	252	015C
**	157	009D	½	189	011D	Ý	221	013D	ý	253	015D
**	158	009E	¾	190	011E	Þ	222	013E	þ	254	015E
**	159	009F	¿	191	011F	ß	223	013F	ÿ	255	015F

**These characters have no Unicode-specified meaning.

Compiling and Running a Java Program

Using a Sun-based compiler, the simplest syntax of the command to compile a program stored as *name*.java, where *name* is the name of a specific program and .java is the required extension that the program was saved with, is:

```
javac name.java
```

The line on which this command is typed is formally referred to as the *command line*. This line always starts with the operating system prompt, which for computers that use the UNIX operating system is usually the $ symbol and for Windows-based systems is typically C>.

Assuming that you have a Windows-based computer that uses a C> prompt, this command would appear as

```
C> javac name.java
```

As a specific example of this format, the command line

```
C> javac DisplayHelloWorld.java
```

will compile the program named DisplayHelloWorld.java. The output of the compilation, assuming it was successful, is automatically named and saved in the file named DisplayHelloWorld.class. It should be noted that the javac compiler is pronounced "ja-vack" and not "ja-va-see."

In addition to performing a simple compilation, the javac compiler also provides for a number of useful output options, which appear in Table C.1. As shown in this table, the general syntax of the compilation command line is

```
C> javac <options> <source files>
```

where C> is provided by the operating system, <options> means select any or none of options listed in Table C.1, and <source files> means a list of zero or more source files (supplying no source files brings up the information in Table C.1).

As a specific example of selecting a number of options, assume you want the compiler both to tell you how it is progressing and to provide debugging information as compilation is taking place for the program named DisplayHelloWorld.java. The following command accomplishes this:

```
javac -verbose -g DisplayHelloWorld.java
```

Here the -verbose option, which is formally referred to as a command-line argument, instructs the compiler to output messages indicating what the compiler is doing, and the -g option tells the compiler to generate debugging information for any compiler-detected error.

The output of a successful compilation is automatically saved with the same name as the source file, but with a `.class` extension instead of the `.java` extension. The compiled version of the source code with the `.class` extension is an encoded set of bytes that can only be run on a Java Virtual Machine. If this code contains a `main()` method, execution of the code can be initiated using the command line

```
C> java name
```

where *name* is the class name used to save the program initially. For example, if the program named `DisplayHelloWorld.java` has been successfully compiled to yield the `DisplayHelloWorld.class`, the command line

```
C> java DisplayHelloWorld
```

will initiate execution of the compiled program.

Table C.1   javac Compiler Options

Usage: `javac <options> <source files>`

where `<options>` includes:

Option	Description
`-g`	Generates all debugging information.
`-g:`	Generates no debugging information.
`-g:{lines, vars, source}`	Generates some debugging information.
`-O`	Optimizes: May hinder debugging or enlarge class files.
`-nowarn`	Generates no warnings.
`-verbose`	Outputs messages about what the compiler is doing.
`-deprecation`	Outputs source locations where deprecated application programming interfaces (APIs) are being used.
`-classpath <path>`	Specifies where to find user class files.
`-sourcepath <path>`	Specifies where to find input source files.
`-bootclasspath <path>`	Overrides location of bootstrap class files.
`-extdirs <dirs>`	Overrides location of installed extensions.
`-d <directory>`	Specifies where to place generated class files.
`-encoding <encoding>`	Specifies character encoding used by source files.
`-target<release>`	Generates class files for a specific Virtual Machine version.

Obtaining Locales

The locales available on your computer system can be obtained using the following program:

```java
import java.util.*;   // needed for Locale
import java.text.*;   // needed for NumberFormat
public class DisplayLocales
{
  public static void main(String[] args)
  {
    int i, number;

    Locale availableLocales[] = NumberFormat.getAvailableLocales();
    System.out.println("The available locales are:");
    number = availableLocales.length;

    for (i = 0; i < number; i++)
    System.out.println(availableLocales[i].getDisplayName());
  }
}
```

The following are the first 30 lines displayed when this program was run on the author's computer:

```
The available locales are:
English
English (United States)
Arabic
Arabic (United Arab Emirates)
Arabic (Bahrain)
Arabic (Algeria)
Arabic (Egypt)
Arabic (Iraq)
Arabic (Jordan)
Arabic (Kuwait)
Arabic (Lebanon)
Arabic (Libya)
Arabic (Morocco)
Arabic (Oman)
Arabic (Qatar)
Arabic (Saudi Arabia)
Arabic (Sudan)
Arabic (Syria)
Arabic (Tunisia)
Arabic (Yemen)
Byelorussian
Byelorussian (Belarus)
Bulgarian
Bulgarian (Bulgaria)
Catalan
Catalan (Spain)
Czech
Czech (Czech Republic)
Danish (Denmark)
```

Creating Leading Spaces

As described in Section 4.4, one potentially annoying problem associated with formatting is that leading unfilled digit positions are padded with zeros (as an example of this effect, review the output produced by Program 4.9). Following is a method named addSpaces() that can create leading blank spaces. This method requires the number of desired leading spaces, which is accepted as the parameter n, and returns a string consisting of exactly n spaces. It is to this string that the desired integer number must then be concatenated.

```
// this method creates a string with n space characters
public static String addSpaces(int n)
{
  StringBuffer temp = new StringBuffer(n);
  int i;
    // modify temp to contain the desired number of spaces
  for(i = 0; i < n; i++)
  temp.append(' ');    // append a blank

  return temp.toString();   // convert to a string and return it
}
```

To use this method, first determine the number of digits in the integer part of the number being output using the String class's length() method. This value is then subtracted from the desired display field width to determine the number of required leading spaces. It is this value that is passed as an argument into addSpaces(). After addSpaces() returns a string with the designated number of spaces, the number to be displayed is then appended to this blank string. This yields a final string with the desired number of leading spaces.

To see how this is realized, consider Program E.1, which displays the number 6 in a total field width of eight. Because the value being displayed consists of one digit, we will need to add seven leading spaces to this number before displaying it.

This leading space technique also works with floating-point and double-precision numbers, with one additional step. Because the leading number of blank spaces is determined by the number of digits in the integer part of a number, if a number with a fractional part is to be displayed, the integer portion of the number must first be extracted for correct computation of the needed spaces. In all cases, however, this technique will only align multiple rows of numbers correctly when a monospaced font, such as Courier, is used.

Program E.1

```java
public class PadWithSpaces
{
  public static void main(String[] args)
  {
    final int WIDTH = 8;  // this sets the size of the output field
    int n, numlength;
    String outstr = "";
    int testNumber;

    testNumber = 6;  // this is the number we will output
    outstr += testNumber;  // convert to a string
    numlength = outstr.length();  // get the number of integer digits

    n = WIDTH - numlength;  // determine number of spaces needed
    outstr = addSpaces(n) + outstr;
    System.out.println(outstr);
  }


    // this method creates a string with n space characters
  public static String addSpaces(int n)
  {
    StringBuffer temp = new StringBuffer(n);
    int i;

    for(i = 0; i < n; i++)
    temp.append(' ');     // append a blank

    return temp.toString();
  }
}
```

Creating and Using Packages

A **package** consists of one or more individual class files that are stored in the same directory and have been assigned a package name. Using an appropriate `import` statement, this package name then provides a simple and convenient way of permitting access to all of the classes in the package to any Java program that might wish to use them.

As a specific example of a package, consider Figure F.1, which consists of two classes named `ClassOne` and `ClassTwo`. As required by Java, each of these classes has been stored in a separate file, with each file having the same name as its class followed by the `.java` extension. Thus, as shown in Figure F.1, the file containing `ClassOne` is stored as `ClassOne.java` and the file containing `ClassTwo` is stored as `ClassTwo.java`. To make each of these classes a member of the same package, which for illustration purposes we will name `foobar.utilities`, requires that the statement `package foobar.utilities;` be included as the first line in each file. Notice that this is the case for the two files shown in Figure F.1.

FIGURE F.1 Creating a Package Consisting of Two Class Files

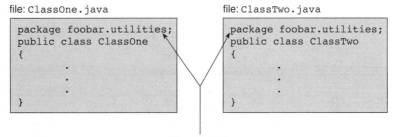

file: `ClassOne.java`

file: `ClassTwo.java`

```
package foobar.utilities;
public class ClassOne
{
    .
    .
    .
}
```

```
package foobar.utilities;
public class ClassTwo
{
    .
    .
    .
}
```

These specify
the package

Once a package has been created, an `import` statement is used to make the classes in the file available to any Java program that needs access to one or more of the classes in the package. For example, if a Java program needed to access a class in the `foobar.utilities` package, the `import` statement

```
import foobar.utilities.*;
```

would make both classes in this package available for use by the new Java program. The new Java program need not be in the same directory as the package because the package name tells the compiler where to look for the classes. Thus, the name selected for a package is not arbitrary but must be a pathname containing the directory in which all of the classes in the package are stored. An additional option with the `import` statement is that it need not make all of the classes in a package available to a new Java program. For example, if only the `ClassOne` file is needed in the new Java program, the statement

```
import foobar.utilities.ClassOne;
```

can be used. Generally, however, since an `import` statement only notifies the compiler of the location of the files, the more general syntax `import packageName.*;` is used. The compiler ultimately will include only the classes in a package that it needs.

It should also be noted that a package name always separates directories using a period rather than either a backward, \, or a forward slash, /, used by the Windows and UNIX operating systems, respectively. Finally, because package names are generally relative and not full pathnames, the root directory of the full pathname must be set in the `CLASSPATH` variable of your operating system. For example, if the full pathname of the `foobar.utilities` directory is `c:\java\programs\foobar\utilities`, then the system `CLASSPATH` variable must be set using a statement similar to

```
CLASSPATH=c:\java\programs      <-- this is for a Windows-based system
CLASSPATH /usr/java/programs    <-- this is for a UNIX-based system
```

The setting of the `CLASSPATH` variable should only be done by someone familiar with setting system-dependent variables.[1]

Fully Qualified Names

Because an `import` statement provides the compiler with enough information to locate the desired class, this statement relieves the programmer of listing the complete pathname of the desired file when a class is being accessed. However, an `import` statement is not strictly required. For example, if the `ClassOne` class shown in Figure F.1 contains a `public` method named `sample()`, this method can be accessed as `java.programs.foobar.utilites.sample()` without the program

---

[1] In a Windows-based system, the `CLASSPATH` variable is typically set in the `autoexec.bat` file, while in a UNIX-based system, the variable is set in a shell file. If an existing path is already set, append the new setting to the existing one with a preceding semicolon. Additionally, either a `SET` or `setenv` keyword may be required with the `CLASSPATH` statement.

using it having an `import` statement for the package in which `sample()` is located. This is because the statement itself provides the compiler with complete location information for `sample()`. When the package name is included in this manner, the method name is referred to as *fully qualified*. With one exception, a fully qualified name is always required whenever an `import` statement *is not included* for the named package. The one exception is when the `java.lang` package is involved. Because this package of classes is used in almost every Java program, the compiler will automatically import it with or without an explicit `import` statement for this package. This permits us to use a statement such as `System.out.println("Hello");`, for example, rather than the fully qualified name `java.lang.System.out.println("Hello");`, even though the program containing this statement does not contain the statement `import java.lang.*:`.

A Keyboard Input Class

Section 4.1 presented the Java-provided statements required to set up input streams for reading data entered at the keyboard. In place of the techniques described in that section, you can use the read methods provided in the class named KBR, which is presented in this appendix. The code for this class, whose name is derived from the term *keyboard read*, is listed at the end of this appendix and is available on this text's Web site. This appendix explains how to access and use the methods in the KBR class. This class provides the following five methods:

```
readChar()
readInt()
readLong()
readFloat()
readDouble()
```

Each of these is a general-purpose method that can read a single character, integer, long, float, or double value, respectively, that is entered at the keyboard. Each of these methods automatically sets up the necessary input streams, described in Section 4.1, for reading data entered at the keyboard, and all of the methods are used in essentially the same manner. For example, a statement such as

```
number = KBR.readInt();
```

will read data entered at the keyboard. If the data represent a valid integer value, the number is accepted and stored in the variable named number. Here number can be any programmer-selected variable that has been declared as an integer data type. If the entered data do not correspond to a valid integer value, the method will display an error message and request that the user reenter an integer value. Program G.1 illustrates all of the KBR class's read() methods within the context of a complete program.

Program G.1

```java
public class KeyBoardReadTest
{
  public static void main (String[] args)
  throws java.io.IOException
  {
    char key;
    int num1;
    long num2;
    float num3;
    double num4;

    System.out.print("Enter a character: ");
    key = KBR.readChar();
    System.out.println("The character entered is " + key);

    System.out.print("Enter an integer value: ");
    num1 = KBR.readInt();
    System.out.println("The integer entered is " + num1);

    System.out.print("Enter a long integer value: ");
    num2 = KBR.readLong();
    System.out.println("The long integer entered is " + num2);

    System.out.print("Enter a float value: ");
    num3 = KBR.readFloat();
    System.out.println("The floating point value entered is " + num3);

    System.out.print("Enter a double value: ");
    num4 = KBR.readDouble();
    System.out.println("The double value entered is " + num4);
  }
}
```

As seen in Program G.1, all of the KBR class's read() methods are called in the same manner by preceding the desired method with the class name, KBR, and a period and assigning the entered value to a variable of the appropriate data type. Also notice in Program G.1 that no input streams have been declared. The reason is that the required streams are constructed from within the KBR class.

All that is required to use the methods in this class is that this complete class code be copied from the Web site associated with this text into the directory (folder) that you use for your Java programs. Once the class code is copied into your programming directory, you must compile it using the statement

```
javac KBR.java
```

After the class has been compiled, the corresponding class file will be available for use in all of your programs, and the methods can be used as shown in Program G.1.

KBR Class Code

```
// This class can be used to enter single character and numerical
// values at the keyboard, as described in Appendix G of the text.

import java.io.*;    // needed to access input stream classes
public class KBR
{

  // This method sets up the basic keyboard input streams
  // and reads a line of characters from the keyboard.
  // It returns all characters entered as a string, with any
  // entered whitespace included.
  public static String readData()
  throws java.io.IOException
  {
      // set up the first input stream, which is
      // needed for conversion capabilities
    InputStreamReader isr = new InputStreamReader(System.in);
      // set up a buffered stream, which is
      // needed to access readLine()
    BufferedReader br = new BufferedReader(isr);

    return br.readLine();  // read and return the entered data
  }

  // This method captures and returns the first character entered
  // at the keyboard. If no characters are entered, it will return
  // the code for the Enter key.
  public static char readChar()
  throws java.io.IOException
  {
    String inString = null;
    char key;

    inString = readData();
    if (inString.length() == 0)
      key = 0x000D;    // Unicode value for the Enter key
    else
      key = inString.charAt(0);  // 1st character entered
    return key;

  }

  // This method attempts to convert the characters entered at the
  // keyboard to an integer value. If the conversion cannot
  // be done, an error message is displayed and the read is
```

```
// continued until a valid integer is entered.
public static int readInt()
throws java.io.IOException
{
  int inValue = 0;  // must initialize the variable
  boolean validNumber = false;
  String inString = null;

  while(!validNumber)
  {
    try
    {
      inString = readData();
      inValue = Integer.parseInt(inString.trim());
      validNumber = true;
    }
    catch(NumberFormatException e)
    {
      System.out.println("  The value you entered is not valid. ");
      System.out.println("  Please enter only numeric digits.");
      System.out.print("Enter an integer value: ");
    }
  }
  return inValue;
}

// This method attempts to convert the characters entered at the
// keyboard to a long integer value. If the conversion cannot
// be done, an error message is displayed and the read is
// continued until a valid long integer is entered.
public static long readLong()
throws java.io.IOException
{
  long inValue = 0L;  // must initialize the variable
  boolean validNumber = false;
  String inString = null;

  while(!validNumber)
  {
    try
    {
      inString = readData();
      inValue = Long.parseLong(inString.trim());
      validNumber = true;
    }
    catch(NumberFormatException e)
    {
      System.out.println("  The value you entered is not valid. ");
```

(continued)

(continued)

```java
            System.out.println("  Please enter only numeric digits.");
            System.out.print("Enter a long integer value: ");
        }
    }
    return inValue;
}


// This method attempts to convert the characters entered at the
// keyboard to a float value. If the conversion cannot
// be done, an error message is displayed and the read is
// continued until a valid float is entered.
public static float readFloat()
throws java.io.IOException
{
    float inValue = 0F;  // must initialize the variable
    boolean validNumber = false;
    String inString = null;

    while(!validNumber)
    {
        try
        {
            inString = readData();
            inValue = Float.parseFloat(inString.trim());
            validNumber = true;
        }
        catch(NumberFormatException e)
        {
            System.out.println("  The value you entered is not valid. ");
            System.out.println("  Please enter only numeric digits");
            System.out.println("  and, at most, a single decimal point.");
            System.out.print("Enter a float value: ");
        }
    }
    return inValue;
}

// This method attempts to convert the characters entered at the
// keyboard to a double value. If the conversion cannot
// be done, an error message is displayed and the read is
// continued until a valid double is entered.
public static double readDouble()
throws java.io.IOException
{
    double inValue = 0;  // must initialize the variable
    boolean validNumber = false;
    String inString = null;
```

```
  while(!validNumber)
{
  try
  {
    inString = readData();
    inValue = Double.parseDouble(inString.trim());
    validNumber = true;
  }
  catch(NumberFormatException e)
  {
    System.out.println("  The value you entered is not valid. ");
    System.out.println("  Please enter only numeric digits");
    System.out.println("  and, at most, a single decimal point.");
    System.out.print("Enter a double value: ");
  }
}
return inValue;
}
}
```

Applets

This appendix may be downloaded from the Course Technology Web site located at www.course.com. To obtain this appendix, go to the Web site at www. course.com and select the Disciplines category. From this category, select Computer Science and then select Java. Locate the text *Object-Oriented Program Development Using Java* and click DownLoad Appendix H.

Real Number Storage

The two's complement binary code to store integer values was presented in Section 1.9. In this appendix, the binary storage format to store single-precision and double-precision numbers is presented. Collectively, both single- and double-precision values are commonly referred to as both *real* and *floating-point* values, respectively, with the two terms considered synonymous.

Like their decimal number counterparts that separate the integer and fractional parts of a number with a decimal point, floating-point numbers are represented in a conventional binary form using a binary point for the same purpose. For example, consider the binary number 1011.11. The digits to the left of the binary point (1011) represent the integer part of the number, and the digits to the right of the binary point (11) represent the fractional part.

To store a floating-point binary number, a code similar to decimal scientific notation is used. To obtain this code, the conventional binary number format is separated into a mantissa and exponent. The following examples illustrate floating-point numbers expressed in this scientific notation:

Conventional Binary Notation	*Binary Scientific Notation*
1010.0	1.01 exp 011
−10001.0	−1.0001 exp 100
0.001101	1.101 exp −011
−0.000101	−1.01 exp −100

In binary scientific notation, exp stands for exponent. The binary number in front of exp is referred to as the mantissa, and the binary number following exp is the exponent value. Except for the number 0, the mantissa always has a single leading 1 followed immediately by a binary point. The exponent represents a power of 2 and indicates the number of places the binary point should be moved in the mantissa to obtain the conventional binary notation. If the exponent is positive, the binary point is moved to the right. If the exponent is negative, the binary point is moved to the left. For example, the exponent 011 in the number 1.01 exp 011 means move the binary point three places to the right so that the number becomes 1010. The −011 exponent in the number 1.101 exp −011 means move the binary point three places to the left so that the number becomes 0.001101.

In storing floating-point numbers, the sign, mantissa, and exponent are stored individually within separate fields. The number of bits in each field determines the precision of the number. Single-precision (32-bit) and double-precision (64-bit) data formats are defined by the Institute of Electrical and Electronics Engineers (IEEE) Standard 754-1985 to have the characteristics given in Table I.1. The format for a single-precision real number is illustrated in Figure I.1.

FIGURE I.1   **The Single-Precision Real Number Storage Format**

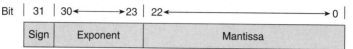

The sign bit shown in Figure I.1 refers to the sign of the mantissa. A sign bit of 1 represents a negative number, and a bit value of 0 represents a positive value. Since all mantissas, except for the number 0, have a leading 1 followed by their binary points, these two items are never stored explicitly. The binary point implicitly resides immediately to the left of mantissa bit 22, and a leading 1 is always assumed. The binary number 0 is specified by setting all mantissa and exponent bits to 0. For this case only, the implied leading mantissa bit is also 0.

The exponent field contains an exponent that is biased by 127. For example, an exponent of 5 would be stored using the binary equivalent of the number 132 (127 + 5). Using eight exponent bits, this is coded as 10000100. The addition of 127 to each exponent allows negative exponents to be coded within the exponent field without the need for an explicit sign bit. For example, the exponent −011, which corresponds to −3, would be stored using the binary equivalent of +124 (127 − 3).

Figure I.2 illustrates the encoding and storage of the decimal number 59.75 as a 32-bit single-precision binary number. The sign, exponent, and mantissa are determined as follows:

The conventional binary equivalent of

```
-59.75
```

is

```
-111011.11
```

Expressed in binary scientific notation, this becomes

```
-1.1101111 exp 101
```

The minus sign is signified by setting the sign bit to 1. The mantissa's leading 1 and binary point are omitted, and the 23-bit mantissa field is encoded as

```
11011110000000000000000
```

Table I.1   IEEE Standard 754-1985 Floating-Point Specification

Data Format	Sign Bits	Mantissa Bits	Exponent Bits
Single-precision	1	23	8
Double-precision	1	52	11

The exponent field encoding is obtained by adding the exponent value of 101 to 1111111, which is the binary equivalent of the 127_{10} bias value.

```
  1 1 1 1 1 1 1        =      127₁₀
        + 1 0 1        =       +5₁₀
  ---------------             -----
  1 0 0 0 0 1 0 0      =      132₁₀
```

FIGURE I.2   The Encoding and Storage of a Binary Number

Sign	Exponent	Mantissa
1	10000100	11011110000000000000000

Solutions and Source Code

Solutions to selected odd-numbered exercises and source code for all programs listed in the text may be downloaded from the Course Technology Web site located at www.course.com.

To Obtain Solutions

To obtain solutions to selected odd-numbered exercises, go to the Web site at www.course.com and select the Disciplines category. From this category, select Computer Science and then select Java. Locate the text *Object-Oriented Program Development Using Java* and click DownLoad Java Solutions.

To Obtain Source Code

To obtain the source code for the programs listed in the text, go to the Web site at www.course.com and select the Disciplines category. From this category, select Computer Science and then select Java. Locate the text *Object-Oriented Program Development Using Java* and click DownLoad Java Source files.

CREDITS

Page 49, Charles Babbage's Analytical Engine, Courtesy of the Charles Babbage Institute, University of Minnesota

Page 50, ENIAC, Courtesy IBM Corporation

Page 51, The Mark 1, Courtesy IBM Corporation

Page 55, An IBM 701 in 1952, Courtesy IBM Corporation

Page 55, Internal picture of a Pentium® microprocessor chip, Courtesy Intel Corporation

Page 56, Original (1980's) IBM Personal Computer, Courtesy IBM Corporation

Page 57, A current IBM Notebook Computer, AP/Wide World Photos